HISTORY OF
TENNESSEE

HISTORY OF
TENNESSEE

FAMILY AND PERSONAL HISTORY

VOLUME IV

LEWIS HISTORICAL PUBLISHING COMPANY, INC.
NEW YORK
1960

dred miles along the river. His work in making these surveys included problems of accretion, reliction, reappearance, erosion, recession and avulsion. In property suits growing out of changes in the course of the river he was often called into court as a witness. Among his important cases was one in particular, Stockley vs. Cissna, which was in litigation for a period of nineteen years, and terminated in a suit between the states of Arkansas and Tennessee. Mr. Richardson made his first survey in this connection in 1899, and was active through the final test of the case by the United States Supreme Court in March, 1918. Other significant cases were Davis vs. Anderson-Tully; Arkansas vs. Turner-Farber-Love Company, involving the land in Horseshoe Bend; C. W. Hunter Company vs. Woods Brothers Construction Company; Clements vs. Riegel; and Ethel Top vs. Hunter Company. He was also employed to make various surveys of Island 35 and several towheads near that island. In some of his work it was necessary for Mr. Richardson to do research, going back as far as the Spanish grants, and tracing the changing course of the river from 1814, to complete his assigned work. He made surveys along the Mississippi River as special state land surveyor for the state of Arkansas under commission for the commissioner of state lands. One of his outstanding pieces of work—referred to by his associates as "probably his toughest assignment and one of the toughest ever made in this area"—was a survey of Island 40, the results of which satisfactorily settled a number of property claims. He was called in on many other cases involving surveys, and many of these, in which various states were the litigants, were of national consequence.

In 1824 Mr. Richardson left Memphis for Detroit, Michigan, where he was chief construction engineer with the Blair Construction Company. He was in full charge of field layouts, heavy machinery foundations, quantity estimates, and cost records on Memphis Plant, the Rouge River Steel Mill in Michigan, and the Somerville, Massachusetts, Plant of the Ford Motor Company. For nearly two years he represented the Blair Construction Company on a board of arbitration.

After another year of construction work in Michigan, Mr. Richardson returned to his general practice in Memphis. From 1930 to 1947 this practice included drainage and sewer-system projects and surveys. One of his important professional engagements was as land expert for the Anderson-Tully Lumber Company of Memphis and Vicksburg. He made numerous detailed surveys for this company involving several thousand acres of valuable timberland.

Mr. Richardson was an active figure in the largest of engineers' national organizations, the American Society of Civil Engineers, and in his later years was vice president of its Mid-South Section. At the time of his death he was a nominee for the directorship of the Memphis Chapter of the National Society of Professional Engineers. He was a member of the Tennessee Society of Professional Engineers, and of the Memphis Engineers Club. He was a member of the Free and Accepted Masons and of the higher bodies of the order, holding the Thirty-second Degree and belonging to the Ancient Arabic Order of Nobles of the Mystic Shrine. He was fond of sports, particularly hunting and fishing, and belonged to the Horseshoe Lake Fishing Club in Crittenden County. He and his family attended Grace St. Luke's Episcopal Church.

On June 11, 1906, St. George Tucker Richardson married Ann Mussenden, in a ceremony taking place in St. Mary's Episcopal Church in Memphis. She is a daughter of Benjamin George Wolseley and Elizabeth Heliger (Cruger) Mussenden, and was born in Memphis on November 8, 1884. Like her husband, she has been active in Grace St. Luke's Episcopal Church.

Mr. Richardson's death occurred on October 18, 1952. The various organizations to which he had belonged, as well as innumerable personal friends, paid him tribute. "Throughout his life," commented a memorial prepared by colleagues for an American Society of Civil Engineers publication, "his work was characterized by ability, integrity, and untiring industry." A resolution signed by members of the Memphis Engineers Club contained these lines:

. . . His gracious demeanor and friendliness endeared him to all his acquaintances. His fairmindedness, integrity and skill based on many years' experience commanded the respect and esteem of his associates. . . . The Engineers' Club of Memphis has lost a loyal, faithful and outstanding member.

From a resolution passed by his local chapter of the National Society of Professional Engineers come these words: "So faithfully did he serve the mid-South area with skill and integrity that his name has become legend to all who knew him." A close friend, who knew him well, wrote of him:

. . . His ability as a surveyor, especially in the woods, was unsurpassed. He was recognized by even the Federal Government as being an authority upon surveys along the Mississippi River and especially at those points where a change in the river shifted state lines. In this field he will be greatly missed. St. George was a lovable character, made friends easily, had a delightful approach and was kind and considerate of those who worked under him.

THOMAS WALKER GILMER RICHARDSON

In the course of his nearly four decades in the real estate brokerage business in Memphis, Gilmer Richardson not only became widely known throughout the Southeast, but won a nationwide reputation as a dealer in farm, plantation and cattle lands. In his understanding of this sphere of property values, he had few peers anywhere. He was a constructive worker in political and public life; consistently supported all worthwhile local causes; and was a leader in realtors' groups.

Mr. Richardson was a native of Memphis, and was born on Court Street on June 13, 1894, son of Robert Brooks and Lucy Beverley (Tucker) Richardson. He could trace his ancestry back to King Alfred of England, and had

Gilmer Richardson

extensive genealogocial charts showing his descent on his mother's side. In that line he was related to the Gilbert and Tucker families, who were among the earliest settlers in Virginia. He was named for his great-grandfather, Thomas Walker Gilmer, Governor of Virginia and Secretary of the Navy under President Tyler. His father, Robert B. Richardson, followed the profession of civil engineer.

When the future real estate executive was young, the family lived on a farm, but he commuted between there and Memphis on the old Raleigh streetcar line, attending Captain Collier's School. In 1916-1917, he attended Cumberland University, taking classes at its law school. Although he did not remain to receive a degree, he credited his law training with being of great value to him in the real estate business.

This field he entered in June, 1919, joining the Interstate Realty Company when it was headed by W. W. Farris. It was th eonly organization with which he was ever identified in his business life, and he took an active part in its operations for nearly forty years, until his death. Its offices have long been located at 107 Madison Avenue in Memphis. In connection with this business, Mr. Richardson specialized in the sale of farm, plantation and cattle lands, not only in the Memphis area but throughout the Southeast. He would frequently get calls from cities as distant as New York in regard to farm properties. Commenting on his qualities as a businessman, a journalist wrote of him in the editorial columns of the Press-Scimitar:

His first love in business was selling land. He loved the land itself, and it made him wealthy, because he understood its capabilities and demonstrated its resources to others in the market for it.

Not even his heart condition could restrain him from making long trips into the country to look at land a hundred miles or more from Memphis.

He remained active as president and treasurer of his company until the last day of his life.

Mr. Richardson was perhaps better known to the general public in the Memphis area for his activities in the political sphere. In 1938, he was named chairman of a committee to re-elect Governor Gordon Browning, who had broken with the Memphis machine. He remained a Browning supporter, and his work was ultimately effective when Mr. Brown was elected in 1948. He also supported the candidacy of Estes Kefauver for United States Senator. The only public office he himself held was the chairmanship of the Shelby County Election Commission, which he filed from 1950 to 1952. In that capacity he proved himself an effective worker for clean elections. He was active in Civic Research and a member of its board of directors. On occasion he had been candidate for the state legislature, and although he proved himself a strong contender, was never elected. He once qualified to run against Representative Cliff Davis, but withdrew. In the mid-1950s, he supported Edmund Orgill in his successful race for mayor.

Another contribution which Mr. Richardson made to his city and its people was his role in establishing the Heart Fund in Memphis. He joined two heart specialists, Drs. Otis Warr and Newton Stern, in instituting the first such campaign, which was thereafter continued on an annual basis. He was chairman of the first drive, and made available his office at 107 Madison for use as its headquarters.

Mr. Richardson was an earnest student of history, and a member of the West Tennessee Historical Society. He also belonged to The Egyptians, a writing group meeting monthly at Southwestern. Youth work claimed its share of his attention, and he was a member of the Chickasaw Council of the Boy Scouts of America, and active on behalf of the campaigns of the Young Men's Christian Association.

As a real estate executive, he was active in the Real Estate Board of Memphis, which he had served as president. He was also a past president of the Tennessee Association of Real Estate Boards, and a director of the National Association of Real Estate Boards. His nonprofessional memberships included the Memphis Agricultural Club, the Kiwanis Club, Rivermont Club, University Club, and the lodge of the Free and Accepted Masons. In Masonry, he was a member of the higher bodies of the Scottish Rite, held the Thirty-second Degree, and belonged to the Ancient Arabic Order of Nobles of the Mystic Shrine.

Another outstanding aspect of Mr. Richardson's career was his service to the Idlewild Presbyterian Church. For many years he served as an elder, and while in that capacity, attended every meeting. A memorial resolution passed by church officials at the time of his death referred to his work in these words:

. . . Except for illness or absence from the city, he never missed a regular church service, a Session meeting or the monthly dinner and program of the Men of Idlewild. A profoundly great churchman, he was in every sense of the word a so-called "pillar" of his church and it can be said that he yielded to no one his record of love, duty and devotion to it.

At the Raleigh Baptist Church in Raleigh, on April 30, 1919, Gilmer Richardson married Lillian Alpine Wesson, daughter of John W. and Kate (Massey) Wesson. The couple were the parents of three children: 1. Thomas Walker Gilmer, Jr., who was born on February 22, 1921. 2. Kathryn Madelyn, born June 4, 1924. 3. Lillian Wesson, born on October 29, 1927. She married Rogers Hall, and they have two children: i. James Rogers Hall. ii. Richard Gilmer Hall.

Memphis lost a valued leader in its business affairs, its civic, cultural and organizational life, when Gilmer Richardson died suddenly of a heart attack on May 27, 1959. He had known of the threat to his life implicit in his physical condition, but had accepted it with a most constructive philosophy: "There was nothing for me to do but deliver myself into the hands of God.

I wasn't even frightened." Something of the character of the man emerges in descriptive lines from the memorial statement from his church, already quoted: . . . Although he stood out as a specialist in his business, and even though local, state and national organizations of his calling honored him, he never lost the common touch. He was an independent thinker and had the courage of his convictions at all times and vocally expressed that independence regardless of whether his position was popular or unpopular with his hearers.

In an editorial in a local newspaper, this appraisal of his character appeared:

Gilmer Richardson will be missed for the time he put into character-building organizations, service clubs and cultural groups, but most of all he will be remembered as a man who stood by himself and guided his own course.

A fellow townsman paid him final tribute in these words:

Gilmer Richardson found happiness in public service, enthusiasm for living in his business, peace . . . Gilmer Richardson will live in the hearts of Memphis and Mid-South people as a courageous man who fought for justice and found peace.

From the resolutions passed by the session of the Idlewild Presbyterian Church, we quote the following poem:

A friend has passed across the bay
So wide and vast, and put away
The mortal form that held his breath.
But through the storm that men call death,
Erect and straight, unstained by years.
At Heaven's gate—a man appears.

HUGH TODD SHELTON, JR.

Hugh Todd Shelton, Jr., like his father, selected the practice of law for his life's work. Admitted to the bar in 1946, he has been in practice since that time.

He was born in Columbia, on August 10, 1915, the son of Hugh T. and Katherine (Towler) Shelton. His father, born July 22, 1891, in Atlanta, Georgia, received his Bachelor of Laws degree from Cumberland University in 1912 and has practiced law in Columbia since 1912. During these years, he has served as Maury County attorney for one term, and as Columbia City Attorney for three terms. During World War II, he was chairman of the ration board. He is a stockholder in the First Farmers and Merchants Bank of Columbia and is a member of the Elks Lodge. Mr. Shelton is also a member of the American Bar Association, a former vice president of the State Bar Association, former president of the Maury County Bar Association, and a member of the Columbia Chamber of Commerce. His wife, whom he married on June 3, 1914, was born January 8, 1896, in Columbia, and is a member of a long established Tennessee family. She is active in the Presbyterian Church and community affairs. She graduated from Caldwell College, now known as Center College, at Danville, Kentucky.

Hugh Todd Shelton, Jr., attended public schools in Columbia and Columbia Military Academy, from which he graduated before attending the University of the South at Sewanee, where he graduated with a Bachelor of Arts degree in 1937. He received his Bachelor of Laws degree from George Washington University in 1941 and then entered the Air Force during World War II. In his college days, Mr. Shelton was prominent in athletics, winning nine letters while playing football, basketball and tennis. He was Tennessee State Inter-Collegiate Tennis champion for one year and was ranked fourteenth in the Southern Tennis Championships. He was a member of Phi Gamma Mu, Omicron Delta Kappa and The Blue Key, honorary societies, and Sigma Alpha Epsilon fraternity. He entered service as a private and was discharged in 1946 with the rank of lieutenant colonel. He became a flying cadet, received his wings and second lieutenant's commission at Albany Air Base, Albany, Georgia, where he was later an instructor of advanced training. He was assigned to multiple engine aircraft and participated in bombing missions over Japan as a B-29 pilot and holds the Air Medal, Bronze Star and Pacific Theater ribbons, as well as two Presidential Citations. He is a stockholder of the First Farmers and Merchants Bank of Columbia, and one of the organizers and a director of the First Federal Savings and Loan Association. He is a member of the Elks, and of the Columbia Chamber of Commerce.

He is married to the former Ann Anderson Roess, of Jacksonville, Florida. Mrs. Shelton, born April 14, 1922, is a graduate of Duke University, where she received her Bachelor of Arts degree and is a member of Phi Beta Kappa and Pi Gamma Mu, honorary societies, and Pi Beta Phi sorority. The Sheltons have four children: 1. Ann Pattillo, born January 23, 1947 at Lake Wales, Florida; 2. Hugh Todd, III, born July 30, 1948 at Columbia; 3. Mary Kathrine, born July 7, 1951 in Columbia; and 4. Leslie Towler, born November 3, 1957, also at Columbia.

Mr. Shelton's sister, Suzie Bell, born November 2, 1922, attended Stevens College in Missouri and the University of Mississippi at Oxford, Mississippi. She is married to Brooke Shreaves, a chemical engineer of New Church, Virginia, and now a resident of Saint Louis, Missouri. They have five children: Katherine, born June 8, 1946 at Columbia; Brooke, born on March 12, 1951; Sidney, born July 21, 1952 at Nashville; Jane Daniel, born in February, 1957, in Saint Louis, Missouri, and Valerie, born in October, 1958.

WILLIAM REID SMITH-VANIZ

Founder of the Royal Feed and Milling Company, William Reid Smith-Vaniz brought the organization to Memphis early in its existence, and continued there as its executive head until its merger with Nutrena Mills. One of the leading manufacturers of poultry feeds in the South in his day, he held a prominent place in the business community, and also took a constructive part in civic affairs in Memphis, and in the city's organizational life.

He was born on the family plantation near Canton, in Madison County, Mississippi, on January 23, 1876, and was a son of Dr. George W. and Elizabeth (Reid) Smith-Vaniz. Both of his parents were likewise natives of Madison County, Mississippi, where they lived their entire lives. The Smith-Vaniz family were prominent planters whose forebears were among the early settlers in that county. Dr. George W. Smith-Vaniz was a brother of Thomas J. Smith-Vaniz, a veteran of service in the Confederate States Army; and he himself also participated in that conflict, serving in the Medical Corps. During the remaining years of his life he conducted a general practice as physician, and he was also a planter. He took his medical studies in Philadelphia, and made the trips from there to Mississippi on horseback. Miss Reid, whom he married, came of a family of early settlers in Madison County, Mississippi, who had originally come from South Carolina.

William R. Smith-Vaniz received his early education under the private tutelage of his uncle, Thomas J. Smith-Vaniz, and later attended the University of Mississippi. After early experience in the oil mill business, he founded his own organization, the Royal Feed and Milling Company, at Jackson, Mississippi, in 1912. In 1917 he moved its headquarters to Memphis. Shortly after coming to that city, he closed out the Jackson, Mississippi, branch. He later opened a branch at Meridian, Mississippi, which is still operating under the present firm name. He maintained his own headquarters at Memphis, where he continued as president of the firm until about four years before his death. In the early 1950s it merged with Nutrena Mills, by which it is still operated. He was respected in the industry as one of the pioneer producers of stock and poultry feed in his region. Following his retirement for executive duties at the head of his firm, Mr. Smith-Vaniz continued active in business affairs, turning his attention to investments.

He was fond of travel, and had toured in all parts of the United States, Mexico, and Canada. His local memberships included the Memphis Merchants Exchange and the Memphis Country Club. Affiliated with the Free and Accepted Masons, he was a member of the higher bodies in Masonry, and of the Ancient Arabic Order of Nobles of the Mystic Shrine. His fraternity was Delta Psi. Active in the circles of his industry, he was a member of the National Feed Manufacturers Association, as well as other business organizations.

Mr. Smith-Vaniz was a public-spirited man and a firm supporter of all civic causes pertaining to the progress of Memphis. He was of a most charitable nature and a generous contributor to all philanthropic causes and helped many who were in need. He was a communicant of the Episcopal Church.

In Natchez, Mississippi, on April 27, 1918, William Reid Smith-Vaniz married Louise McDowell, a native of that city and daughter of Seaborn and Mary (Fore) McDowell. Her father was a native of Wilkinson County, Mississippi, and became a wholesale and retail hardware merchant in Natchez. Her mother came from Shelbyville, Kentucky, but was of an old Natchez family, and was reared in that city by her maternal grandmother, Anna Willis McComas, who was the wife of General Josiah H. McComas. The Willis family was a Colonial family of Virginia. Mr. and Mrs. Smith-Vaniz became the parents of two children: 1. William Reid, who was born in Memphis on February 16, 1925. He married Joan Pollard of Marion, Massachusetts, and they are the parents of a daughter, Alison Smith-Vaniz, born on February 14, 1957. 2. Elizabeth, who was born on February 5, 1927, in Memphis. She is the wife of James Blades of New Bern, North Carolina. She has two children by a previous marriage: Lisa Goncharov and Andrew Goncharov. To her marriage to Mr. Blades one daughter, Molly Blades, has been born.

The death of William R. Smith-Vaniz, in Memphis, on May 5, 1955, brought to a close a most useful career in the industrial and commercial life of his city and the Mid-South.

ALF E. CLAGETT

Alf E. Clagett, judge of the Giles County Court and a former mine manager by profession, devotes much of his time to his herd and dairy cattle and hog farm, and to the enjoyment of his long-standing hobby—hunting, and the raising and training of bird dogs and fox hounds.

He was born in Centerville in 1890. His father, Robert Montgomery Clagett, born in Centerville in 1863, was chancery court clerk and teller in the First National Bank of Centerville which his father founded. His wife, Tommie (Easley) Clagett, was born in Centerville in 1863. Her father was Captain Thomas Easley of the Confederate Army, in whose honor the Centerville Daughters of the Confederacy post is named, and who was postmaster in Centerville. The union of the Easley and Clagett families merged two of the old established Hickman County lines which go back to the early days of Tennessee settlement.

Alf Clagett graduated from Columbia Military Academy in Columbia and, immediately after graduation, entered the phosphate mining business in Hickman County. During World War I, he served as first sergeant of the 105th Mobile Ordnance Repair Shop of the 30th Division, serving overseas with the American Expeditionary Forces and in action at Saint-Mihiel, the Argonne and Woeve Woods. He was discharged in 1919 and immediately returned to phosphate mining for the International Minerals and Chemical Corporation as manager of the Wales Plant. He had previously been assistant manager of the Old Volunteer Mine in Centerville from 1912 until he entered the army in 1917. Upon his retirement from his firm in 1955, he was elected County Judge of Giles County and holds this post to the present time. Judge Clagett is a Mason, an Elk, a member of the American Legion and the Veterans of Foreign Wars, and belongs to the Pulaski Chamber of Commerce. Like his father before him, he is active in church affairs and serves as a trustee of the Methodist Church in Pulaski.

He married the former Linda Tom Primm in Centerville in 1919. Born in Centerville in 1899, Mrs. Clagett is the daughter of the late Tom Primm of Centerville and Lizzie (Nixon) Primm. She attended Old Belmont College in Nashville and was a teacher of piano and music in Georgia for a number of years. Alf and Linda Clagett have no children.

TOM WHITE MOORE

Tom White Moore has devote his life to the practice of law in his native city. Because of his strong civic interest and work, he was elected city attorney by the people of Pulaski, a post he holds to this day.

Tom Moore was born in Pulaski on June 20, 1911, the son of the late banker Tom Williams Moore, born at Elkton on May 3, 1882 and who died in Pulaski in 1913. His widow, Lucile Gallaway (White), born in Pulaski on June 6, 1887, makes her home in Pulaski.

Mr. Moore attended Branham and Hughes Military Academy in Springhill and later Washington and Lee University in Lexington, Virginia. He studied law at Cumberland University, graduating from this institution in 1937 with a Bachelor of Laws degree.

After graduation, he returned to Pulaski where he began his private practice in 1937 and where he has continued since, with the exception of his World War II service. After his discharge, he resumed his practice and in 1954 was elected to the post of city attorney and has been in this office since. He is a director of the Union Bank and is its general counsel.

As a member of the Tennessee National Guard, he was called into Federal service on January 21, 1941. He served throughout the war in the Pacific Theater, seeing action in many areas including the Philippines. He entered active duty as a first lieutenant and retired from active duty as a major. Since the end of the war, he has continued his military service and is currently in the Tennessee National Guard with the rank of lieutenant colonel.

In addition to the American Bar Association, he belongs to the Tennessee and the Giles County bar associations. He is a Past Exalted Ruler of the Elks. He is a member of the Exchange Club, having served as state president of this organization in 1955-1956, is a past president of the Pulaski Chamber of Commerce, and past president of the Giles County Young Democratic Club.

He married the former Barbara Jeanice Byrne at DuQuoin, Illinois, on June 17, 1941. Mrs. Moore, born in DuQuoin on November 17, 1917, is the daughter of the late Dr. John D. Byrne of Indiana, a physician and surgeon in DuQuoin until his death in 1941. His widow, Dorothy (Deuser) Byrne, born in Charlestown, Indiana, in 1890, makes her home in DuQuoin. Mrs. Moore attended Western College in Missouri and graduated from Michigan University with a Master of Arts degree. She taught music and the piano at Martin College in Pulaski and later at Bradley College in Peoria, Illinois. She continues to teach the piano and has a group of private students in Pulaski. Tom and Jeanice Moore have three children: 1. Jeanice Byrne, born July 5, 1942 in Oklahoma City, Oklahoma, and now attending Giles County High School; 2. Tom White, Jr., born July 19, 1943 at Nevada City, California; and 3. James Byrne, born January 3, 1952, in Pulaski.

John William Berry

Prior to settling in Pulaski in 1926, John William Berry travelled extensively throughout the South while a student and while working for the Federal Government. For the past thirty-one years he has been head of the animal clinic he established in 1926 and is an active member of the community in business, banking and social activities.

He was born in Weatherford, Texas, on July 20, 1894, son of James Jesse and Emma Marilda (Burleson) Berry, retired farmers. He attended Hamilton, Alabama, High School and then graduated from Alabama Polytechnic Institute at Auburn, Alabama, where he received his degree in veterinary medicine in 1923. In college, he was a pitcher on the baseball team and a member of Alpha Psi fraternity.

Upon graduation from college, he went to work for the Federal Government, testing cattle for tuberculosis, with headquarters in Asheville, North Carolina. In 1926, he left government service and moved to Pulaski where he established the Berry Animal Clinic and has operated this very successful business since. He is a member of the American Veterinarian and the Southern Tennessee Veterinarian Associations. As a result of his World War I overseas service, as a private in the Thirty-first Division, he is a member of the American Legion and the Veterans of Foreign Wars. He is also a Mason, an Elk, a member of the Rotary Club and the Hill Crest Country Club.

He married the former Mary Christine Black in Pulaski on December 25, 1935. Mrs. Berry, born in Minor Hill, Tennessee, on April 12, 1908, is the daughter of John Petty Black, born in Minor Hill in 1887, where he still makes his home. His wife, Rosalee (Booth) Black, born in 1887, attended Martin College in Pulaski and later Florence State Teachers College in Florence, Alabama. She is very active in the Methodist Church. The Booth and Black families trace their lineage to early Tennessee stock and were among the first to settle in Giles County. Mary Christine Berry attended Minor Hill High School before attending the University of Tennessee where she graduated in 1928. A Home Economics major in college, she taught this subject in Lynchburg and later Pulaski for six years but retired from teaching after her marriage. She is active in the American Legion Auxiliary and in the Twentieth Century Literary Club.

John and Mary Christine Berry have two children: 1. Beverly Reeder, born November 9, 1937 in Pulaski and now a student at Alabama Polytechnic Institute, majoring in Physical Education; and 2. Constance Booth, born June 26, 1948 in Pulaski where she attends elementary school.

A. B. Williams, M. D.

ANDREW LEE TODD, JR.

Son of an attorney, Andrew Lee Todd, Jr., selected law for his business career and, in 1928, opened his office for the private practice of law in Murfreesboro where he is well known for his civic and community interest.

Born in Murfreesboro in 1904, Mr. Todd is the son of the late Andrew Lee Todd, Sr., and Minnie Ola (Wilson) Todd who makes her home in this city. Andrew L. Todd, Sr. was an eminent and respected attorney in the city of Rutherford where he was born, and as the publisher of the Murfreesboro News Journal. During his long legal service, Mr. Todd was Speaker of the State House of Representatives in 1919, and later Speaker of the Senate in 1921. He was also a banker with the Murfreesboro Bank and Trust Company and served for many years on the State Board of Education. Mr. Todd died in 1945.

Andrew Todd, Jr., was educated in the public schools of Murfreesboro, later attending Sewanee Military Academy, and the University of the South at Sewanee, and graduated from Cumberland University in 1928 with a Doctor of Laws degree. A Democrat, Mr. Todd has served as Mayor of Murfreesboro, having been elected in 1953 and prior to that had served as General Sessions Judge. He is a member of the Chamber of Commerce, a director of the Murfreesboro Bank and Trust Company, and is deacon of the Baptist Church he and his family attend.

He married the former Martha Fox of Murfreesboro in 1929. Mrs. Todd is the daughter of H. L. Fox of Murfreesboro and the late Betty (Gumn) Fox also of that city. The Todds are the parents of two sons. They are: 1. Andrew Lee, III, born in 1930. A graduate of Vanderbilt University, he now works for the State Farm Mutual Insurance Company. He is married to Marjorie Patterson of Toledo, Ohio, and they have four children: Andy, born in 1951; twins David and Katherine, born in 1953; and Ann, born in 1955. 2. Aaron, born in 1937, and currently studying at Georgia Tech where he is majoring in chemistry.

ARTHUR BOUTILLIER WILLIAMS, M.D.

A distinguished record of more than a half century of service in medical practice in Memphis was that of the late Dr. Arthur Boutillier Williams. He held responsible staff positions with several hospitals; gave evidence of a deep interest in civic affairs; and also proved his versatility as a writer and composer.

Born in Halifax, Nova Scotia, on October 20, 1869, he was a son of Arthur, Sr., and Robertina Eleanor (Thompson) Boutillier. His father, a musician and composer, died when he was very young, his mother remarried, and the future physician was adopted by his step-father, whose name was Williams. He attended the public schools of Yarmouth, Nova Scotia, and St. Johns, New Brunswick, and came to western Tennessee when he was twenty-two years old. There he enrolled at the Medical School of the University of Tennessee, received his degree of Doctor of Medicine there in 1897, and took postgraduate courses in New York before beginning his career in general medical practice at Memphis in 1897.

Over the fifty-two years which followed, Dr. Williams proved himself an exceptionally skilled and conscientious practitioner, winning the confidence of his patients and the respect of colleagues alike. He was at various times a member of the staffs of the John Gaston Hospital and St. Joseph's Hospital, and he was an honorary staff member at St. Joseph's at the time of his death. He kept up an active practice until a short time before the end of his life. His memberships in medical groups included: Shelby County, Tennessee State, and American Medical Association.

Dr. Williams was deeply interested in civic affairs and found time in his busy schedule for a constructive role in such activities. He had served as president of the Greenwood Civic Club, and as chairman of the music committee of the Memphis Chamber of Commerce. Tribute was paid to his civic efforts when in 1925 he was nominated for the trophy awarded annually to the person making the most noteworthy contribution to the community. He was particularly fond of music, and had played contrabass in orchestras in both Atlanta and Memphis. He composed a number of pieces of music, including several marches.

As a writer, Dr. Williams was the author of books of verse, but his major interest was in historical writing. He was a gifted and deeply interested research student in history, and had prepared a number of papers for the United Daughters of the Confederacy and the Daughters of the American Revolution. In the later years of his life he was at work on a history dealing with the Natchez Trace from Nashville to Memphis, and it was near completion when his death occurred. He was a talented musician, playing cello, piano and bass. He composed, and set his poems to music.

Dr. Williams was a loyal citizen of the region he had chosen to make his home. In a tribute written at the time of his death, this quality was emphasized:

A man of dynamic personality and intense feeling, Dr. Williams was loyal to his adopted county and city, and truly Southern in his viewpoint regarding States Rights and all questions pertaining to the South. While tolerant and considerate of others in all discussions, he was ever ready to defend the South, and the principles for which the South stands, in which he believed. A long life, well spent, leaves behind an inspiration and an example worthy of emulation.

Active in the lodge of Free and Accepted Masons, Dr. Williams was a member of the higher bodies of the order, and held the Thirty-second Degree. He attended St. Mary's Episcopal Church.

In Memphis, on April 20, 1898, Dr. Arthur Boutillier Williams married

Emma Irene Arnold. A native of that city, she is a daughter of Herman Frank and Victoria Regina (Luciani) Arnold. Her father had come to this country from Germany, where he was born on October 6, 1837. Her mother was a native of Philadelphia, Pennsylvania.

Dr. and Mrs. Williams became the parents of two children: 1. Arthur Arnold, who was born on March 23, 1899, at St. Francis, Arkansas. He married Katherine Young of Paris, Tennessee, and they have one daughter, Martha E. Williams. 2. Victoria Eleanor, born January 23, 1901, in Memphis. She married Richard Green Clarke, and they have two children: i. Rosalind Rogers, who married Harry Reed. ii. William Mercer Clarke.

A career most useful in the service of his fellows came to an end with the death of Dr. Williams on April 11, 1950.

WILLIAM PRENTICE COOPER

A farmer all his adult life—a lawyer from the last decade of the last century—a bank executive for the past thirty years, William Prentice Cooper has taken an unusually full part in the life of the Shelbyville area. His experience has also included public office, for he has served as mayor and as a member of the Tennessee House of Representatives.

He is a native of Smith Mills, in Henderson County, Kentucky, and was born on September 27, 1870, the son of Dr. James William and Eliza (Royster) Cooper. His father was a physician and surgeon. William P. Cooper completed his preparatory education at Webb School in Bell Buckle, Tennessee. He then entered Vanderbilt University, where he completed his studies in 1890.

From the beginning of his career, Mr. Cooper owned and operated farms, and still remains active in the management of farm acreage. Admitted to the bar on the completion of his studies, he began practice at Henderson, Kentucky, in 1891, and after ten years of practice there, moved to Shelbyville, Tennessee, where he has since had law offices. He has been president of the Peoples National Bank of Shelbyville for about thirty years, and is now chairman of its board of directors.

Within a few years of his arrival in Shelbyville, Mr. Cooper was elected mayor of the city, for the 1905-1906 term. He served the people of his district in the Tennessee House of Representatives in 1915-1916, and was speaker of the house during this biennium. Mr. Cooper served as trustee of the University of Tennessee for forty-three years.

He is a Rotarian, and served as district governor of Rotary International in 1934. His fraternity is Sigma Alpha Epsilon, and he is a communicant of the Methodist Episcopal Church, South.

At Shelbyville, on October 25, 1894, William Prentice Cooper married Argentine Shofner, daughter of Jacob Morton and Melissa (Landis) Shofner.

The couple are the parents of one son, William Prentice, Jr., who was born on September 28, 1895.

RICHARD EDWARD DAVIS

Richard Edward Davis came to Trenton, Tennessee, in the early 1940s to assume duties as editor and publisher of The Herald-Register. Since he has been there, he has rendered valuable service to the community in other capacities. Outstanding among the contributions was his part in founding the Gibson County Stock Yards, Inc. He has held office in a number of local organizations, and is a constructive worker in his political party.

Born at Rutherford, Tennessee, on February 24, 1895, he is a son of Nathaniel Lee and Lula Dale (Rigsbee) Davis. His father was a blacksmith early in life, but later became an undertaker and embalmer. At one time he served as mayor of Rutherford. Richard E. Davis attended the public schools of that town, completing the tenth grade in Rutherford High School. He then transferred to the Fitzgerald-Clarke School, Trenton and Tullahoma, Tennessee, where he took his eleventh- and twelfth-grade studies. At that school, he received the mathematics medal and the general scholarship medal. For his advanced studies, he entered Southwestern Presbyterian University at Clarksville, Tennessee (now Southwestern at Memphis). There he graduated with the highest honors, being valedictorian of his class, and receiving his degree of Bachelor of Arts in 1917. One summer he did graduate work at the University of Arkansas, where he averaged straight A's in scholarship.

Mr. Davis began his career as high school teacher at Hamburg, Arkansas, teaching there during the 1913-1914 academic year. In 1917-1918, he taught at the Fitzgerald-Clarke School in Tullahoma. He then entered wartime military service, enlisting in the Field Artillery. He served as second lieutenant in Battery B, Seventieth Field Artillery, at Camp Knox, Kentucky, and was regimental radio officer. He was never in combat.

In 1919, shortly after his return to civilian life, Richard E. Davis began his career in the newspaper field as editor and publisher of The Dyer Reporter (later The Dyer Progressive) at Dyer, Tennessee, and The Kenton Observer at Kenton. He became editor of The Ashley County Leader, at Hamburg, in 1920. Also during the 1920-1921 school year, he was mathematics teacher at Helena High School. In 1921 he was named principal of the school, and served until 1923. Assuming duties as superintendent of schools at Helena in that year, he served until 1926.

Mr. Davis returned to the newspaper publishing field in 1926, becoming editor and publisher of The Bolivar Commercial at Cleveland, Mississippi. He returned to Tennessee in 1941 to begin his duties as editor and publisher of The Herald-Register, the position he has held throughout the seventeen years since.

He is an author as well as a newspaperman, having written a genealogy

STEPHEN KENT JONES

of his family titled "Some Migratory Davises and Their Relations," which was published at Cleveland, Mississippi, in 1936.

It was Mr. Davis who first proposed, before a meeting of the Trenton, Tennessee, Rotary Club, the organization of a livestock auction in his city. He was appointed to an organizing committee which took steps leading to the formation of Gibson County Stock Yards, Inc., and he has served as its secretary since that time. This facility furnishes to farmers in this and adjoining counties a market for an average of three million dollars' worth of livestock per year. It has been in existence since 1946.

Mr. Davis was chairman of the Municipal Democratic Committee of Cleveland, Mississippi, an elective office, while he lived in that city. He has retained an interest in Democratic politics, although he holds no office at the present time. He was also secretary and president of the Exchange Club at Cleveland, and held office as district governor. He is a past president of the Rotary Club at Trenton, and he organized a Rotary Club at Humboldt, Tennessee. Since the Gibson County Historical Society was organized, he has been its president. He and its other members are engaged in preparing a history of their county.

Mr. Davis' fraternity is Pi Kappa Alpha, and he has served its Theta Chapter as secretary and president. A Methodist, he has served as steward of the churches at Cleveland, Mississippi, and Trenton, and also as choir director at both places, his record of service going back for over thirty years. For five years he was superintendent of the Sunday school at Cleveland.

On September 28, 1918, at Hamburg, Arkansas, Richard Edward Davis married Nellie Lee Dunn, daughter of Thomas Judson and Nellie Lee (Dyson) Dunn. The couple are the parents of the following children: 1. Richard Edward, who was born on December 14, 1919; he is paymaster at the Henry J. Siegel Corporation at Dickson, Tennessee; he married Martha Grant and they have a daughter Janet Marie. 2. Nathaniel Raymond, born October 15, 1921; he is with the National Weather Records Center in Asheville, North Carolina; he married Katie Crider. 3. Donald Frederick, born July 28, 1923; he is an electrical engineer with Flinn and Humphries Company in Memphis; he married Sarah Davis and they have a son Stephen Frederick. 4. Dorothy Nell, born June 6, 1926. 5. Kenneth Robert, born March 31, 1934; he is associated with the Southern Bell Telephone Company at Nashville; he married Sunshine Hollar.

STEPHEN KENT JONES

As a contracting executive, Stephen Kent Jones of Memphis performed services of outstanding value to his region through his work in the construction of highways, levees and dams. He headed the S. K. Jones Construction Company for nearly four decades, and was a leader in the Mississippi Valley Flood Control Branch of Associated General Contractors.

Born near Jackson, at Van Winkle, Mississippi, on June 20, 1872, he was a son of Lewis and Sarah Jane (Williams) Jones. The public schools of Jackson provided his entire formal education, and at the beginning of his career, he entered the construction field. For a number of years he was engaged in a variety of projects in Louisiana and Mississippi.

The last forty years of Mr. Jones' productive career were spent in Memphis, and there he headed his own organization, the S. K. Jones Construction Company. This firm specialized in heavy construction work on the Mississippi River, completing contracts at points from Cape Girardeau, Missouri, on the north to New Orleans on the south. Before a federal control plan of levee construction was undertaken, he contracted with local boards for work on these projects. He continued as active head of his firm until a short time before his death at the age of eighty-six. When he was seventy-five, he headed a group of Memphis contractors who undertook to build a large part of the huge Garrison Dam on the Missouri River in North Dakota. Two years before his death he supervised earth-moving on a multi-million-dollar federal project to control the Mississippi above Baton Rouge, Louisiana. He also contracted for many highway projects, and at the time of his death his company was responsible for the construction of a segment of the federal interstate highway system on Highway 51 near Senatobia, Mississippi. He built his organization into one of the Mid-South's leaders in its field. He was greatly devoted to his work, and it was his hobby as well as his profession.

About 1930, Mr. Jones helped organize the Mississippi Valley Flood Control Branch of Associated General Contractors. He had served as trustee and as president of this branch, and at the time of his death was its secretary and treasurer. In January, 1952, he received a testimonial appreciation in recognition of his effective and unselfish service to the program.

Mr. Jones was a Kiwanian, and a member of the lodge of Free and Accepted Masons. In Masonry he belonged to the higher bodies, held the Thirty-second Degree, and was a member of the Ancient Arabic Order of Nobles of the Mystic Shrine. An Episcopalian, he was a communicant of St. Mary's Cathedral in Memphis.

At Crystal Springs, Mississippi, on December 31, 1907, Stephen Kent Jones married Eleanor Johnston. Born at Dry Grove, near Jackson, Mississippi, she is a daughter of Edgar and Augusta (Rogers) Johnston. Her father, a native of Raymond, Mississippi, had served as judge. Her mother was born at Carrollton, Mississippi. Mr. and Mrs. Jones became the parents of one son, Edgar Kent Jones, who was born at Tallulah, Louisiana, on November 22, 1915. He is a graduate of the University of Tennessee. During World War II he served with the U.S. Navy as a lieutenant, junior grade. He took part in the invasion of Normandy on "D" Day. He has been associated with his father's construction firm. He married Miriam Knox of Pine Bluff, Arkansas, and they have one daughter, Judith Eleanor, who was born on December 20, 1947.

Mr. Jones' death occurred in his eighty-seventh year, on August 25, 1958.

BURGIN ESTEL DOSSETT

In the course of his career, Burgin Estel Dossett has been an educator, corporation executive, and public official. He has been Commissioner of Education for the State of Tennessee and for the past decade has been president of East Tennessee State College. He makes his home in Johnson City.

Dr. Dossett is a native of Campbell County, born near Jacksboro on February 2, 1898, and is a son of Thomas David and Mary Talitha (Hunter) Dossett. After completing his courses through the secondary years in the public schools, Dr. Dossett entered the University of Tennessee, where he took his degree of Bachelor of Arts in 1922. For his graduate courses he went to Harvard University, where he received his Master of Arts degree in 1924.

He began his teaching career in 1921, as instructor at the summer school of the University of Tennessee. He continued teaching there summers until 1927. When he had received his master's degree in 1924, he began four years of service as principal of Jacksboro High School in his home state, and in 1928 became county superintendent of schools of Campbell County—a position he held until 1935. During 1934-1935, he also held a state post as secretary to United States Senator Bachman.

He entered government service on a full-time basis in 1935, when he was named East Tennessee Administrator of the Works Progress Administration. Serving in this capacity through 1936, he was named manager of the Social Security Board at Knoxville in 1937. When he resigned from that post in 1945, he became Commissioner of Education for the State of Tennessee. Dr. Dossett capably filled that state post until 1949. That year he had been appointed president of East Tennessee State College at Johnson City. Since 1930, he has been active in his state's program to provide education for the orphans of veterans. He was candidate for Governor in 1936, and had managed the Tennessee gubernatorial and senatorial campaigns in 1934. Among the state offices which Dr. Dossett has held in recent years are chairmanship of the Tennessee State Board of Education and the Tennessee State Board for Vocational Education, and he has also served as chairman of the board of trustees of the Tennessee Teachers Retirement System. He is a former chairman of the education committee of the Southern Governors Conference, and chairman of the Southern Regional Committee on Veterans Education. He is chairman of the veterans committee, National Council of Chief State School Officers, and a member of its executive committee. Dr. Dossett also served as a trustee of the University of Tennessee from 1945 to 1949.

Among his business connections, Dr. Dossett is vice president and was a member of the board of directors of Jellico Mountain Coal and Land Company, and he is a past director of the Campbell County Bank and Trust Company.

A veteran of World War I service in the United States Army, he served with the 38th Division and the First Flying Cadet Company from 1917 to 1919; and following the war was a cadet in the Reserve Officers Training Corps at the University of Tennessee, 1919-1920. In 1922 he was commissioned a second lieutenant in the 405th Area Squadron, and served as a reserve officer until 1935. Dr. Dossett has served as a member of the Defense Council, and as chairman of the Selective Service Board of Campbell County. Active in the American Legion, he has held a number of offices, including alternate national committee, member of the national legislative committee, in 1936, and Tennessee representative of the Director of Education of Orphans of Veterans, Department of Tennessee. This last-named post he has filled continuously since 1939. He was commander of the Department of Tennessee in 1935-1936.

As an educational administrator, Dr. Dossett is active in the Tennessee Education Association, and was chairman of its legislative joint committee from 1934 to 1936. He was treasurer of the East Tennessee Education Association from 1926 to 1936. Work for welfare causes has claimed its share of his time and energies, and he was a member of the board of directors of the Middlesboro Division, American Red Cross, from 1929 to 1943. He is deeply interested in the program of the American Cancer Society, and has served on the board of directors of its Tennessee Division, and as chairman of its education committee in that state. His fraternities include Tau Kappa Alpha, Alpha Phi Epsilon, Sigma Delta Kappa, Sigma Delta Psi, and Acacia. He is a member of the Junior Order of United American Mechanics, the Exchange Club of Knoxville, the Lions Club of Jacksboro, and the lodge of Free and Accepted Masons. He is a member of the higher bodies of the Scottish Rite in Freemasonry, and of the Ancient Arabic Order of Nobles of the Mystic Shrine. Dr. Dossett is a Democrat and a Methodist.

On June 4, 1925, Burgin Estel Dossett married Nell Jennings, and they are the parents of the following children: 1. Mary Julia, who was born on September 6, 1927. She graduated from University of Tennessee and received her master's degree from Northwestern University; she is married to W. R. Webb; they have two children: Julia and Susan. 2. Dr. Burgin Estel, born on September 15, 1931; graduated from Vanderbilt University and received an M.D. degree from the University of Tennessee; he served as captain in the Army Medical Corps; he is married to Harriett Kane. They have two children: Harriett Kane and Hunter Leigh. 3. Thomas D., born on January 16, 1933; he graduated from East Tennessee State College, then received his law degree from University of Tennessee. He served in the army, highest commission a captain in the Judge Advocate Division. He is married to Veda Rose Hensley. 4. Eugenia, born on October 28, 1934; graduated from East Tennessee State

College and received her master's degree. She is married to James Payson Matthews. 5. Ann, born on January 16, 1942; a student in Johnson City.

BOB GUINN

Bob Guinn has found a rewarding career in the petroleum industry and the contracting business. He has been active in political and public affairs, and has served as mayor of Savannah, where he resides in the historic Cherry Mansion. A breeder of Tennessee walking horses, in 1958 one of his mares and a colt were national champions.

He is a native of Savannah, and was born on September 5, 1899, son of A. K. and Cora (Bruce) Guinn. His father was a postal employee. Bob Guinn completed his formal education with his graduation from Savannah Institute, a private school. Throughout most of the years since he has been active in the oil business, and as a contractor for highway construction.

An influential figure in the Democratic party, Mr. Guinn was for twelve years state committeeman from the Eighth Congressional District. He has been a member of the Hardin County Court for twenty-five years, and he served as mayor of the City of Savannah for twelve years, and in 1957 he was elected vice mayor, having been off the commission about ten years. His program has been acquiring industries for Savanah. His success in this program put him back on the commission. For nine years, he was West Tennessee director of the Tennessee Bureau of Aeronautics. He served as chairman of Hardin County Selective Service Board, also of the OPA Board. He is chairman of the board of directors of Citizens Bank of Savannah.

Deeply interestd in Tennessee history, Mr. Guinn is familar with the background of his region. The Cherry Mansion, in which he lives, is one of the historical landmarks of the region. He is a member of The American Road Builders Association, the Lions Club and the lodge of Free and Accepted Masons; and in Masonry he is a member of the higher bodies and has held several offices. He has served as patron of the Order of the Eastern Star. He attends the First Methodist Church of Savannah.

At Corinth, Mississippi on February 24, 1953, Bob Guinn married Martha Shaw, daughter of Charles Wright and Blanche (Paulk) Shaw. The couple have one daughter, Mary Ann Guinn, born on April 12, 1955.

DR. HENRY HARRINGTON HILL

In the course of his varied career as educator, Henry Harrington Hill has been identified with many colleges and school systems in various parts of the South. For over a decade he has been president of George Peabody College for Teachers at Nashville.

Dr. Hill is a native of Statesville, North Carolina, and was born on September 20, 1894, son of James Henry and Anne (Harrington) Hill. From 1910 to 1913, he attended Davidson College in North Carolina, and he was later a student at the University of Virginia, where he graduated in 1921 and took the degrees of Bachelor of Arts and Master of Arts. He took graduate courses at Columbia University, 1927-1928, and completed requirements for his degree of Doctor of Philosophy there in 1930. He has since received honorary degrees of Doctor of Laws from the University of Pittsburgh (1943), Davidson College (1948), and Union University (1949) and the University of Kentucky (1950); the honorary degree of Doctor of Humane Letters from Columbia University in 1954, and the Doctor of Laws degree from Harvard University in 1955.

He began his teaching career in 1916, as high school teacher and school superintendent at Walnut Ridge, Arkansas. He remained there until 1920, and returned in 1922, after a year as instructor in Spanish at the University of Virginia, and another year as high school principal at North Little Rock, Arkansas. Dr. Hill left Walnut Ridge in 1927, and during 1928-1929, was supervisor of high schools for the state of Arkansas.

In 1929 he joined the faculty of the University of Kentucky as professor of school administration. He remained at the university as lecturer on education, 1930-1940, while concurrently serving, throughout that decade, as superintendent of Lexington's public schools. For some months in 1941, Dr. Hill was assistant superintendent of schools in charge of general administration, at St. Louis, Missouri. He returned to the University of Kentucky in July, 1941, to serve as dean, a position he held through August, 1942. Then, until 1945, he was superintendent of schools at Pittsburgh, Pennsylvania.

Dr. Hill came to Nashville in 1945 to accept the presidency of George Peabody College for Teachers, a post for which his own varied experience in educational posts admirably qualified him.

In addition to the above continuous record in teaching and administration, Dr. Hill has held a number of temporary posts with institutions in various parts of the country. He was lecturer in education at the University of Virginia during the summers of 1928 and 1929, at the University of Utah in 1932, at the University of Alabama in 1936, at Duke University in 1937 and 1939, and at Harvard University in 1939. From 1935 to 1939, he was a member of the executive committee on Curricular Problems and Research of the Southern Association of Colleges and Secondary Schools. He served as president of the association in 1949. Dr. Hill was chairman of the Safety Education Commission of the American Association of School Administrators from 1938 to 1940. Within this same organization, he served as chairman of the Summarization Committee, 1941-1942; as a member of the Executive Committee from 1942 to 1947; and as president during the 1946-1947 term. He was trustee of the Educational Testing Service, for ten years, serving as chairman of the board of trustees for three years. His work in safety education led to his ap-

Thos. H. Allen.

pointment as trustee and vice president of the American Automobile Association's Foundation for Traffic Safety. Dr. Hill was a member of the White House Conference on Education, 1954-1955. A member of the Educational Policies Commission from 1948 to 1952, he was its chairman in the final year of this connection. He served on the executive committee, American Council on Education, from 1945 to 1948. In 1946, he traveled to Germany on the United States Education Mission. He is a member of the National Education Association and the Horace Mann League.

Authorship is among Dr. Hill's achievements. He has written one full-length work, "State High School Standardization," which was published in 1930. He has also contributed articles to educational journals. In the various cities in which he has lived, he has found time for much worth-while community work, particularly in the field of welfare. While in Pittsburgh, he was a director of that city's chapter of the American Red Cross, and was also a director of the Pittsburgh Community Fund. He was at one time president of the Lexington, Kentucky, Community Chest and served as the first president of United Givers Fund in Nashville.

Dr. Hill is a Rotarian, and a member of Phi Delta Kappa and Kappa Delta Pi fraternities. He belongs to Rotary, the Belle Meade Country Club, and the Round Table in his home city of Nashville.

On August 16, 1922, Dr. Henry Harrington Hill married Elizabeth Eloise Wilkes. They have one daughter, Adrienne Wilkes, who is now the wife of Dr. K. W. Todd, a plastic surgeon of Nashville, Tennessee. They are parents of four children. Kirkland Wiley, Lyman Harrington, and twins Henry Harrington and Katherine Elizabeth Todd.

MAJOR THOMAS H. ALLEN

An unusually full role in the life of his city of Memphis was played by Major Thomas H. Allen. An engineer by profession, he headed a consulting firm in the city for many years, and served as president of the Memphis Light, Gas and Water Division. As city commissioner and in other offices of public trust, he had contributed to the growth and modernization of the municipality. He was a forceful proponent of public control of utilities. He was a dedicated man in his political actions and in his religious faith, and in his service to the many organizations to which he belonged.

Although born at St. Louis, Missouri, on October 27, 1881, he came of an old Memphis family. His parents, Richard H. and Lizzie Conner (Walker) Allen, had moved to St. Louis to escape the epidemic of yellow fever then raging in their home city. Richard's father, Thomas H. Allen (for whom the Major was named) had played an important part in the development of the city. He was a cotton broker, maintaining offices there and in New Orleans, and having large plantation holdings in Mississippi and Arkansas. He conducted his business under the name of Thomas H. Allen and Company. His son Richard continued in the cotton business, in which he prospered. Richard's death occurred March 2, 1928. Lizzie Conner Walker, whom he married in Memphis was a daughter of Samuel Walker, who was also a successful business man in Memphis. Mrs. Allen died in 1905, leaving three children: Thomas H.; James Seddon, who became an attorney in Memphis; and Mrs. Warwick Aiken, who also made her home there.

Major Allen attended the public schools, then entered the University of Tennessee, where he took his degree of Bachelor of Science in Mechanical Engineering in 1903. Long before he had completed his studies there, he had determined the direction his career was to take. He knew he would be an engineer and in all likelihood a utility engineer. To gain experience, he took a summertime job, between college sessions, in the engine room which supplied power and light to the city of Memphis. Its total capacity at that time, he recalled, was 2750 kilowatts. "I was just an untrained helper, but I was in the utility business."

He did not enter the industry immediately on graduation, however, but joined the Allis-Chalmers Manufacturing Company of Milwaukee, Wisconsin, beginning as apprentice machinist, advancing to district engineer in 1906, and serving the company's interests in Philadelphia in 1907-1908 as sales engineer. In the course of his five years with the organization, he worked in New York and Chicago as well. This experience, with the opportunity for travel, amply proved to him that Memphis was the place where he must make his home. After a brief connection as sales engineer with the firm of Robert Weatherall and Company of Chester, Pennsylvania, in 1908, he returned to Memphis to live for the rest of his life. His first position there was as manager with the Livermore Foundry Company, but a year later, in 1910, he entered business for himself, founding the Allen Engineering Company, a consulting organization. This firm is still in existence today, but is known as Allen and Hoshall. Major Allen's son, Lorin, and his lifelong friend, Robert Hoshall, are partners and owners. In the course of his years as consultant, Major Allen had a hand in planning some of the important structures of the South, including the Peabody Hotel, the Shrine Building, the Cotton Exchange Building, the Elks Building, and several of the largest water works in the state of Tennessee.

When this country became involved in World War I, he was exempt from the draft by reason of age, but he promptly volunteered his services, enlisting as a private in May, 1917. He was sent to officers' training camp at Fort Oglethorpe, Georgia, and on June 23 was commissioned a captain, commanding Company F of the 306th United States Engineers. This unit was attached to the 81st Division, which shipped overseas and landed in England on August 11, 1917. In March, 1918, while stationed in France, Thomas H. Allen was promoted to major and placed in command of the Second Battalion. He spent a total of thirty-six days in the front lines, and once was slightly gassed while deactivating a bomb. He received his honorable discharge at Fort Oglethorpe on July 9, 1919.

Major Allen resumed his consulting engineering business when he returned to Memphis, but to an increasing degree, from that time, public affairs claimed his attention. He was elected a city commissioner on November 10, 1919, having been candidate on a ticket of "politically inexperienced business and professional men, dedicated to clean, efficient and businesslike operation of the city's affairs." The words in this political platform were descriptive of his attitude throughout the remainder of his public career. He served as commissioner of streets, bridges and sewers, 1920-1921, and was then transferred to the office of commissioner of fire and police. While serving in that office, until 1927, he was concurrently vice mayor of the city. During his tenure, Memphis' first city plan was developed. He himself was the author of many decisions involving public works. He was active in rallying support of business and civic leaders for the Bartholomew Plan. When in 1927 Mayor Paine sought re-election, Major Allen declined to join him on the ticket, but served as his campaign manager. Their efforts were defeated by the Crump machine. The following year both Major Allen and Mr. Crump were allied in efforts to elect Hill McAlister governor. It has been said of the two that they were "never intimates and often foes, had deep respect for one another's abilities."

Major Allen became water commissioner in 1934, and was appointed to the Board of Light and Water Commissioners in 1935, serving until 1939. Also, in 1934, he was named to a responsible state post as engineer for the Public Works Administration in Tennessee. In 1939, he was named to the public office which he filled so capably for the remaining years of his life— membership on the Board of Light, Gas and Water Commissioners. He was vice president and chief engineer of the board, 1939-1940, and its president from 1940. He devoted himself over the years to securing his city a dependable water supply, building new pumping stations and treatment plants. He earned a reputation as a water conservationist, and was instrumental in getting the United States Geological Survey to keep check on the city's underground water supply. He fostered federal legislation for water studies. Commented a local journalist regarding his record: "Building big, building sturdily, with care for the future and an eye for beauty were part of Allen's thinking as a utility man." It was he who planned Memphis' present electric generating station, the world's largest city-owned steam plant—although it had not been completed at the time of his death. He survived every challenge to his power as one of the city's most influential officials. Once, in 1947, when opposition developed, the public rallied to his support. Later, the Shelby legislative delegation enacted a law which would have permitted packing the board with men hostile to him, but the action was never carried out.

In the course of his career, Major Allen was recipient of many honors.

Southwestern University conferred on him the honorary degree of Doctor of Science in 1950. In 1953 he received the Distinguished Service Award of the American Public Power Association, and the same year, Post No. 684 of the Veterans of Foreign Wars granted him its Annual Citizenship Award. He received a citation for meritorious service from the Tennessee Valley Public Power Association in 1954; was named Engineer of the Year by the Tennessee Society of Professional Engineers in 1955; and received the Dougherty Award of the University of Tennessee in 1957. The Civitan Club of his city conferred on him its Outstanding Citizen Award in 1956; and in 1958 he received the Citation for Meritorious Service and Loyal Cooperation of American Legion Post No. 1. He received the Gideon Bible Award in the same year.

During the World War II years, Major Allen served on the War Production Board, Natural Gas Division. A registered engineer in the states of Tennessee, Arkansas, and Mississippi, he served from 1926 to 1951 as a member of the State Board of Architectural and Engineering Examiners. A member of the American Public Power Association, he served as its president in 1948. He was a fellow of the American Institute of Electrical Engineers, and was chairman of its Memphis Section during 1944-1945. He was also a member of the Tennessee Valley Public Power Association, the Tennessee Society of Professional Engineers, the National Society of Professional Engineers, and the American Society of Mechanical Engineers. A charter member of the Engineers Club of Memphis when it was founded in 1914, he served as its president in 1924. Major Allen was a member of the board of trustees of the University of Tennessee from 1923 to 1953. He was also a member of the board of regents of the Dallas Theological Seminary, a director of the Mid-South Bible Institute, and served on the board of trustees of Young Life Institute. He was a director of the National Board of the Young Life Campaign. A director of the Memphis Union Mission, he had served as its president in 1955. Religion played a large part in his life, and he was an active and devoted communicant of the First Evangelical Church. He had been reared in the Episcopal faith, being confirmed at Calvary Protestant Episcopal Church in 1897. He was a member of Gideons International. His other memberships included The Egyptians, a literary club, and the lodge of Free and Accepted Masons. In Masonry, he held the Thirty-second degree and belonged to the Ancient Arabic Order of Nobles of the Mystic Shrine. His fraternities were Sigma Alpha Epsilon, Phi Kappa Phi, Phi Beta Phi, and Tau Beta Pi.

On February 24, 1909, Thomas H. Allen married Phyllis Blanchard, daughter of Frank Danford and Gracia Phylinda (Bond) Blanchard. She was born in Milwaukee, Wisconsin, on May 6, 1887. Her father worked for the St. Paul Railroad in that city, and died in 1894. Major and Mrs. Allen became the parents of the following children: 1. Thomas Hampton, 4th, who was born on April 20, 1910, and died on July 12th, 1956. He was an educator and was studying for the ministry at the time of his death in Port Arthur,

Gene Carroll Daves

Texas. He married Mary Frances Ooten, and they had two children: i. Linda Keith. ii. Thomas Hampton 5th. 2. Lorin Blanchard, born on November 22, 1913. He married Martha McKean, and their children are: i. Lorin Blanchard, Jr. ii. Harry McKean. iii. Martha Woodis. 3. Gracia Elizabeth, born on July 11, 1915.

Major Allen's death, on December 27, 1958, deprived the city of Memphis of one of its most capable and respected leaders. In a full-length editorial column ln a local paper the following comment was made on his career and its significance:

Major Allen came to retirement age in impaired health seven years ago, but he carried on the responsibilities of a multi-million-dollar business owned by the municipal government . . . in part because he was so intensely interested in the outcome of things he had started, and in part because it was so extremely difficult to find a replacement for him. . . . Tom Allen was known far and wide as a believer in the ability of the public to control their own utilities and as a bright light of successful demonstrations of that belief. . . .

In religion he was a Christian who worked at it, devoting uncounted hours and unsparing effort to his personal religious life and to helping others through the religious approach.

The esteem in which he was held by the public which knew him only at a distance, the men who worked with him daily, people who disagreed with him on some subjects, and the experts in his specialties was a rare thing to experience.

Few men are privileged to go out on the crest. Few have so richly deserved it.

Recently, the Thomas H. Allen Pumping Station and the Thomas H. Allen Electric Generating Station, newly completed structures in the city's utility system, were named in his honor, and the Board of Commissioners paid him the following tribute at that time: "He has given unselfishly of his knowledge, energy and wisdom, with the result that the City of Memphis, with all of its people organizations and enterprises, have benefited therefrom with dependable service at low cost."

Major Allen's reaction to the words of tribute heaped upon him in his lifetime was a modest disclaimer, couched in words which unmistakably revealed the depth of his religious faith: "Whatsoever of merit there is in me or good in anything that I have done, it is because of belief and faith in Jesus Christ, my Lord and my God."

GENE CARROLL DAVES

As a mechanical supervisor and capable executive, Gene Carroll Daves played a considerable part in the growth of the Buckeye Cellulose Corporation at Memphis, in which he remained active to the end of his career.

Born at Leicester, North Carolina, which is located in Buncombe County, on May 26, 1892, he was a son of William Sidney and Lillie Lou (Brooks)

Daves. Both of his parents were likewise natives of Leicester. The public schools of that community provided the entire education of Gene C. Daves. Reared on a farm, he was very ambitious and industrious, he entered business life at the age of sixteen years and was "on his own" from that time on; his success was due entirely to his own efforts. He left home to begin his career in industry in a position with the Champion Fiber Company at Canton, North Carolina. He worked for that firm until 1915, leaving to take a position with E. I. duPont de Nemours and Company at Hopewell, Virginia, where he remained until 1918. His next move took him to Akron, Ohio, where he was employed by Goodyear Rubber Company for a short time. Then returning to Canton, North Carolina, he rejoined Champion Fiber Company, and remained there until he was offered a position by the Buckeye Cotton Oil Company in Memphis in 1920.

This firm was the predecessor of the present Buckeye Cellulose Corporation, and Mr. Daves was continuously employed by the organization from that time until his death in 1957. When he first joined the company, it was an entirely new enterprise, and he was given responsibility for the renovation of buildings purchased from the old nitrating plant of World War I previously located at Old Hickory, Tennessee, also being placed in charge of equipping the company's plant. He also played an important part in the development of equipment to improve the quality and production rate of cotton linters cellulose. When in 1930 the firm invested heavily in equipment to sheet the cellulose for customers, he was again called upon for duties in connection with the construction and setting up of mechanical equipment for this process. From that time until the end of his life, he was in charge of maintenance of the machinery, although he was released for a number of special assignments. His wide experience brought him appointment as construction superintendent at the time of the erection of three cottonseed and soya bean solvent extraction plants, located at Greenwood, Mississippi, Little Rock, Arkansas, and Augusta, Georgia.

Commenting on the talents and attitudes which he brought to the service of his company, a journalist reviewing his career in the pages of the Memphis Press-Scimitar wrote:

Associates say he was always interested in the human relations of men working for him and never lost an opportunity to pass on to younger men the knowledge and know-how of his mechanical experience. He was one of the pioneer developers of safety in the organization. He just didn't like to see any of his men get hurt, and thru careful training, planning and observance, his crews always had a perfect safety record. His ability as a mechanical supervisor could not be overrated . . .

He possessed a great sense of humor and always seemed to have a joke to share with his associates. He was called the "Will Rogers" of the corporation.

Mr. Daves was a member of the Engineers Club of Memphis. As an avocation he enjoyed farming, and spent many hours cultivating the soil on his farm on James Road near Raleigh. He owned a fine stable of horses, and enjoyed horseback riding. He was a communicant of the Raleigh Methodist Church. He had few other civic or organizational interests.

At Waynesville, in his native state of North Carolina, on July 25, 1914, Gene Carroll Daves married Blanche Lelia Hipps. Born at Webster, in Jackson County, North Carolina, in 1897, she is a daughter of William A. and Hattie Elizabeth (Mann) Hipps. Both of her parents were likewise native North Carolinians, her father having been born in Jackson County on August 12, 1869, and her mother on December 18, 1873, in Haywood County.

Mr. and Mrs. Daves became the parents of the following children: 1. Howard Winfred, who was born at City Point in Prince George County, Virginia, on April 18, 1916. He graduated from the University of Tennessee in 1939 with a degree in engineering, and is now chief engineer at the plant of Alcoa Aluminum Company in Alcoa, Tennessee. On March 18, 1939, Howard Winfred Daves married Margaret Elizabeth Bean, and they are the parents of two sons: i. Harry Gene, born on November 26, 1940. ii. Stephen Carroll, born July 10, 1945. 2. Margaret Elizabeth, who was born on May 28, 1918, also at City Point, Prince George County, Virginia. She is the wife of Kenneth S. McCann. 3. Carroll Edward, born in Memphis on March 16, 1921. In 1947 he graduated from the University of Tennessee, taking his degree of Bachelor of Science, and he now has a Plymouth and Chrysler dealership at Columbus, Georgia. He married Ann Crumby.

Mr. Daves' death occurred at the Methodist Hospital in Memphis on January 27, 1957.

JAMES EDWARD WOODARD, D.D.S.

One of Columbia's prominent professional men, Dr. James Edward Woodard, D.D.S., has been in practice in Columbia since the end of the war. He was born on January 14, 1918 at Ardmore in Giles County. His father, Dr. Bernard Hatcher Woodard, Doctor of Medicine, born in 1881 in Lincoln County, Tennessee, has a general practice in Spring Hill. He received his Doctor of Medicine degree from Old South Campus, University of Tennessee. He has been closely associated with the Methodist Church all his life, as has his wife, Bessie (Carter) Woodard, who was born in Giles County in 1888.

James E. Woodard received a Bachelor of Arts degree from Vanderbilt University in 1940 and his Doctor of Dental Surgery degree from the University of Tennessee in 1943. He entered service in the Dental Corps in 1943 and served in New Mexico, Central Africa and India. It was upon his discharge in 1946 that Dr. Woodard opened his office in Columbia. He is a member of the Kiwanis Club and has been both president and secretary. He serves on the Maury County Board of Education and Maury County Board of Health. His other memberships are all in the professional field, the American Dental Association, the Tennessee State Dental Association and the local District Dental Association. He is also a member of the Tennessee Board of Dental Examiners.

He married Dorothy Carter on September 21, 1946 in Atlanta, Georgia, where Mrs. Woodard was born on October 21, 1920. She attended the Brenau College in Gainesville, Georgia, and the Music Seminary in Atlanta where she studied the piano and the organ. Her father, Dr. Henry Grady Carter, M.D., was born in north Georgia, served in the Army in World War I and died at Atlanta in 1927. His widow, Mrs. Lillian Mann Carter, is living in Honolulu; she was born in 1897.

Dr. and Mrs. Woodard are both active in the Methodist Church where Mrs. Woodard heads the children's division, and Dr. Woodard has served in several capacities including superintendent of the church school and chairman of the official board. They have three children: 1. Joseph Anderson, born October 23, 1949 in Nashville. 2 and 3. Twins, Dorothy Louise and Daniel Carter, born December 12, 1951 in Nashville.

DAVID FRANKLIN FULTON

David Franklin Fulton was born on November 13, 1902, in Zion Community. His father, David Franklin Fulton, Sr., was born on November 24, 1857, in Laurel Hill, Lawrence County, and died in 1926 in Maury County. He was a farmer all his life, a devoted churchman in the Zion Presbyterian Church, singing in the choir and serving as an Elder. His wife, Louisa Goode (Watkins) was born in Zion Community on November 12, 1869 and now makes her home in Columbia.

David Franklin Fulton, the younger, attended public school, the Zion School and Central High School in Columbia before entering Vanderbilt University in Nashville. After graduation, he worked for a surveying crew for a time and then turned to farming. He was appointed deputy county clerk of Maury County in 1932 and held this post until 1942, when he entered the Navy as an instructor in airplane mechanics at Millington, Tennessee. He was discharged in 1945 and returned to farming until he was appointed clerk and master of Chancery Court of Maury County in 1949, the position he still holds. He is a member of the Elks and the Junior Order of United American Mechanics. His hobbies include genealogy and the study of history.

Like his father, David Franklin Fulton is an Elder in the Zion Presbyterian Church in Zion Community near Columbia. The church, built in 1807, before the settlers built their own homes, has recently celebrated its one hundred and fiftieth birthday. Franklin Fulton serves as treasurer of Zion Cemetery Association, Inc., Clerk of the Congregation, and for more than thirty years as treasurer of the church as well as a Bible teacher, while Mrs. Fulton is the organist for the church.

He married Ruth Cornelia Hill at Augusta, Georgia, where she was born on February 8, 1913. Her father, Wylie Thomas Hill, born March 2, 1872, in Taliaferro County, Georgia, died August 2, 1958, in Augusta, where his widow, Jessie Gertrude (Eubanks) Hill, continues to live; she was born December 1, 1890, in Aiken, South Carolina. Ruth Fulton attended Georgia State College and Peabody College in Nashville, where she received a degree in Library Science. She taught at Central High School in Columbia and in schools in Augusta, Georgia.

The Fultons have three children all attending school: 1. Louisa Eubanks, born April 6, 1943 in Memphis. 2. Ruth Hill, born September 23, 1946 in Columbia. 3. Dixie Watkins, born July 26, 1948, in Columbia.

CHARLES PHILLIPS HATCHER

At an early age Charles P. Hatcher, son of a judge and attorney, chose the legal profession as his career. He established his office, first in Columbia and later in Nashville where he was active in Democratic Party politics and civic affairs. His was a life of quiet and resultful service to his time, fully consonant with high family tradition.

Mr. Hatcher was born in Columbia, October 27, 1881, attended Wallace Preparatory School in Nashville and then graduated from the University of Virginia. He received his Bachelor of Laws degree from Columbia University in New York and then returned to practice law in his native Tennessee. He was a member of Sigma Mu fraternity at the University of Virginia.

He served as a director of the Commerce Union Bank and on the Board of the National Life and Accident Company. He belonged to the Belle Meade Country Club and the Hermitage Club. He spent his leisure hours on his farm where he raised horses and Jersey cattle as a hobby.

He married Olivia ("Olive") Hill Dobbins in Columbia on April 18, 1911. Mrs. Hatcher, born November 26, 1888 in Columbia, is a graduate of schools in her native city and of Wards Seminary School in Nashville, since renamed the Ward Belmont School. She is a member of the American Red Cross, president of the non-profit Rose Hill Endowment Association; member of the Nashville Garden Club, the Garden Club of America, and she is first vice president of the Polk Memorial Auxiliary and chairman of the Polk Garden Association. Her father, Wilson Bills Dobbins, born in Columbia in 1847, served in the Confederate Army in 1864-1865. He was a farmer and business man all his life, and died in 1914. His wife, Catherine Innes (Adams) Dobbins, born in Texas, attended Columbia Athenaeum in Columbia. She graduated from the old French school, Le Fevre, in Montgomery, Alabama, and later from Columbia Athenaeum. She taught music and piano at Athenaeum and Ashwood Hall school. A Daughter of the Confederacy, she has held offices at both national and local levels.

Mrs. Hatcher is the youngest of five children: 1. Innes, a vice president of Belknap Hardware in Louisville, was born in Columbia in 1878. He married Mignone Murphy and they had three children—Innes, Jane and John. He died in 1945. 2. Louise, married to Dr. Joseph T. Meadors, D.D.S., and the mother of John Allen and Lilly Minge. 3. Jean Ruffin, who died at Chattanooga in 1951, married to James Preston Hoskins. 4. Lily Evelyn, married to Jackson Chadwick Minge of Demopolis, Alabama. 5. Olivia ("Olive"), Mrs. Charles P. Hatcher.

Charles P. Hatcher died in Nashville on January 1, 1939.

JAMES R. STOLTZ

Within a few years after graduation, James R. Stoltz returned to the business school where he was trained, this time as its owner, and he has operated this school ever since.

James R. Stoltz was born in Hickman County on May 11, 1927. His father, Charlie Monroe Stoltz, born in 1906, is a farmer in Hickman County. His mother, Emma (Qualls) Stoltz was also born in Hickman County in 1907. He attended public schools in Pleasantville and after graduating from Hickman County High School, attended Columbia Business College and Steed College of Technology in Johnson City, graduating in 1949. He also attended Middle Tennessee State College, Murfreesboro, Tennessee. His education was interrupted during 1945-1946 when he served in the Army Quartermaster Corps as a technical sergeant.

After graduation, he worked for the Cullom and Gertner Printing Company in Nashville and then moved to Columbia where he was employed first with the Columbia Power System and then with the Blue Plate Foods in 1952. In April of that year, he bought the Columbia Business College and has operated it since, with an average annual enrollment of one hundred students. The standing of the institution continues high, and its graduates are in steady demand by business and industry.

The school is a member of the National Association and Council of Business Schools and the Tennessee Council of Business Schools. It is also approved by the Tennessee Department of Education and approved by the Veterans Administration for the training of veterans.

Mr. Stoltz is a member of the Church of Christ, the Masons, the American Legion and the Rod and Gun Club in Columbia. He is Secretary of the Columbia Investment Club and is a member of the Board of Directors of Columbia Civitan Club. A Democrat, he has never sought political office.

He married, on June 4, 1950, in Columbia, Virginia Claire Moore, born in Culleoka on March 3, 1922. She attended public schools there and then graduated from Columbia Business College and Steed College of Technology, returning to Columbia Business College as an instructor in 1944. She is a member of the Order of the Eastern Star and the Columbia Civinettes. Her parents, William and Lillian (Bailey) Moore, live in Culleoka, where Mr. Moore is a

salesman. James and Virginia Stoltz have two children, both born in Columbia: 1. James Ralph, Jr., born February 8, 1954. 2. David Moore, born June 25, 1956.

SPENCER DE WOOTEN, JR.

A pioneer in bringing radio broadcasting to the Memphis area, Spencer De Wooten, Jr., was a co-founder of Station W R E C, and after remaining active in its operation for some years, left to establish his own electronic supply house. He was also an inventor.

Born at Coldwater, Mississippi, on January 22, 1905, he was a son of Spencer De Wooten, Sr., and his wife, the former Betty Mayfield. The elder Spencer De Wooten was a theater owner and had other business interests at Coldwater, and was also prominent in its public life, serving as mayor and as justice of the peace. Miss Mayfield, whom he married, was a native of Mayfield, Kentucky. After attending the public schools of his city, the younger Spencer De Wooten entered Mississippi State College, where he studied engineering. Even before this, he had shown an exceptional interest in technical subjects. At the age of fifteen, before radio receiving sets were on the market, he built a set of his own and became an amateur radio operator. As soon as he could save up one hundred and fifty dollars, he spent it on transmitting equipment.

Mr. Wooten shaped his own career in the broadcasting industry, and the enterprising spirit of his youth carried over into maturity to make him one of the influential figures in that industry in his region. He came to Memphis in 1925 and joined his brother, Hoyt Wooten, in founding Radio Station W R E C. Later, when television was beginning to make headway, Station W R E C-TV was established. Spencer De Wooten served as engineer until the early 1950s, then terminated his regular connection, although he continued to serve in advisory capacities. When he left his full-time position there, he established the W. and W. Distributing Company, which in less than a decade came to be widely known in the Mid-South as an electronic and television parts supply house, dealing at wholesale. He remained active as its president until the end of his life.

Mr. Wooten had other broadcasting interests in addition to his connection with W R E C. He had an interest in Radio Station W H B Q in Memphis, and was a vice president of this broadcasting company for a time. He had also helped to establish radio stations in Murfreesboro and Dyersburg. His hobby was amateur radio broadcasting, and he maintained his own "ham" station with the call letters W 4 E U P.

Mr. Wooten's inventions included an override circuit and a fire alarm feature, used in conjunction with the "Musi-kom," a home music and communications system also of his own invention. This he patented, and it is now distributed nationwide. He also invented and patented the "Cruis-o-matic" for automobiles, which sets a constant desired cruising speed for long trips.

His most recent invention, on which he filed a patent in 1956, was a "Cophaser," designed to solve the problem of scrambled television pictures in areas between two stations on the same channel. He was widely known as an authority on radio and electronics, and he helped train a number of students in this field. For several years during World War II, he taught radio communication at Whitehaven.

His memberships included the Mid-South Amateur Radio Association and the Tennessee Club. He gave generous support to all charitable causes, and served on the board of trustees of the Memphis Mission. He was a communicant of the Idlewild Presbyterian Church.

In his native city of Coldwater, Mississippi, on December 25, 1937, Spencer De Wooten, Jr., married Cora Belle Sides, daughter of Joshua Lee and Elizabeth (Thompson) Sides. Her father was a farmer at Ackerman, Mississippi, and both of her parents were natives of that place, where Mrs. Wooten was also born. To Mr. and Mrs. Wooten two children were born: 1. Charlotte Elizabeth, on May 30, 1943. 2. Deborah Lee, born on January 20, 1955. By an earlier marriage to Hazel West, Mr. Wooten was the father of one son, Spencer De Wooten, 3rd, born on November 10, 1929. He married Arlene Cook, and they have three children: i. Stephen Spencer. ii. Lawrence. iii. Shelley.

The death of Mr. Wooten, in Memphis on August 25, 1958, terminated a useful career in the course of which he had made a lasting contribution to the development of the radio and television industry in his area. A capable technician and a man of inventive abilities, he also possessed rare qualities in business management, and his varied talents had won him wide respect.

Edward M. Lindsey

Edward M. Lindsey of Lawrenceburg has combined a business career, political office, a command in the National Guard, and raising a family in the past twelve years. Despite this active schedule, he has included club memberships and church activities in his regular program.

Born in Sapulpa, Creek County, Oklahoma, on November 16, 1915, he is the son of Oscar Horace Lindsey, who was born in Wayne County, Tennessee December 18, 1888 and who died in Lawrenceburg in 1918. His wife, Maude (Morrow), born July 15, 1893 in Wayne County, lives in Lawrence. After the death of her husband in 1918, she married William Holoman Lindsey, who was born in Wayne County on May 22, 1876. Mr. William H. Lindsey, a lawyer, served as chairman of the Republican Executive Committee during the Hoover administration. He was first assistant United States district attorney in 1928-1929 and prior to that had served as a United States commissioner.

Edward Lindsey received his education in the public schools and after graduation from the Lawrence County High School in 1934, he worked in the furniture and decorating business until 1939. That year, in partnership with a brother, he established the firm of Lindsey's Company, manufacturing institutional as well as household furniture. He is also a partner in other business ventures in Lawrenceburg. In 1942, he joined the Army Air Corps, serving as a fighter pilot instructor at the Eastern Flying Training Command, based in Alabama. Discharged in 1945 as a first lieutenant, he returned home and resumed his business. In 1947, he took command of the local National Guard unit and served with this unit as a captain until 1952. He is now a major on the staff of the 30th Division, Tennessee National Guard. He is a member of the American Legion. He was elected mayor of Lawrenceburg in 1951 and served four years. He has also served on the board of directors of the Tennessee Municipal League. He is a member of the Lions Club, serving as president in 1949-1950. In July, 1958 he became district governor of the Lions Club, comprising twenty-three counties of middle Tennessee. He is a member of the Chamber of Commerce, the Lawrenceburg Golf and Country Club, and the Lawrence Country Historical Society, which he helped organize and which he has headed as president for the past five years. A member of the Coleman Memorial Methodist Church, he has acted as chairman of its official board and has taught in the Sunday School for the past ten years.

He married in Lawrenceburg on June 12, 1941, Virginia Freemon, born in Lawrenceburg in 1915, daughter of Charles O. Freemon, born in Lawrence County in 1881, who died in Lawrenceburg in 1956, and Lelia (Williamson) Freemon, born in Lawrence County in 1888, now lives in Lawrenceburg. Mrs. Lindsey attended Martin College in Pulaski, Tennessee.

Edward and Virginia Lindsey have a daughter, Anne Judith, who was born in Montgomery, Alabama, on May 30, 1945.

PAUL E. ROLLER

Paul Roller has spent most of his business life with the Murray Company, first in Ohio and recently in Lawrenceburg as general foreman of the plant, a post he has held with the company since 1945.

He was born in Buffalo, New York, on June 25, 1908, the son of Gustave Christian Roller, who was born in Wildburg, Germany, in 1875 and who died in Buffalo in 1932. His mother, Christine (Steimle) Roller was born in Liebelsburg, Germany, in 1876, died in Buffalo in 1941. Gustave Roller came to America in 1898 and soon after settled in Buffalo, where he engaged in the meat business all his life.

Paul Roller was educated in the public schools of Buffalo. After graduation from high school, he went to work for the Pierce Arrow Motor Company as a bookkeeper, later joining the Zero Brass and Valve Company, and Ford Motors in Buffalo. He then moved to Warren, Ohio, where he was associated with the Taylor Winfield Company and Federal Welders. He joined the Murray Company in Ohio in 1931 and has been with them since, except for a four-month period in 1933, when he served with a C.C.C. unit in Bovill, Idaho. Like his father before him, Paul Roller has devoted much time to the Lutheran Church. He is treasurer of his church as well as treasurer, chairman and super-intendent of the Lawrence Lutheran Mission.

He married Nettie Kociencki in Buffalo on February 22, 1935. Mrs. Roller's father, John Kociencki was born in Poland in 1891. He came to America as a youth and has since lived in Buffalo, where he is engaged in cabinet making. His wife, Wanda, also lived in Buffalo. She died in 1934. Nettie Roller is a handicraft hobbyist, working in leather, ceramics and sewing and is also a civic worker. The Rollers have three children: 1. David, born March 26, 1936 and a graduate of William and Mary College in Williamsburg, Virginia. 2. Christine, born July 4, 1940 in Euclid, Ohio, now a student at Roanoke College. 3. Nancy, born January 11, 1945; attending high school.

JAMES BUCHANAN WALKER, 3RD

Since he joined the staff of the First National Bank of Centerville in the early 1950s, James Buchanan Walker, 3rd, has advanced to the position of president. He is also a leader in the Democratic party in his state, and served a term as treasurer of its state organization in recent years.

Born December 15, 1926, at Centerville, he is a son of James Buchanan and Norma (Bragg) Walker. His father, also a native of Centerville, was born in 1900, and died September 8, 1956. He was for thirty-four years president of the First National Bank of Centerville, and for several years was State Treasurer, holding that office at the time of his death. He had formerly served as mayor of Centerville, and was for twenty years city alderman there. A Methodist, he served on the board of stewards of his church. He was a veteran of both World War I and World War II, serving in the Marine Corps in both conflicts, and attaining the rank of major during the second war. His father, James Buchanan Walker, Sr., had been president of the First National Bank of Centerville before him, and was the first mayor of Centerville. He married Hewry Russell. Norma Bragg, who became the wife of James B. Walker, Jr., was born in 1904 at Dresden, Tennessee. She survives her husband and lives in Centerville.

Attending the public schools of that city, James B. Walker, 3rd, completed his secondary studies at Georgia Military Academy in Atlanta and at The Citadel in South Carolina. He then entered Vanderbilt University, where he graduated in 1951, receiving both his Bachelor of Arts and his Bachelor of Laws degrees in that year.

He did not, however, seek a career at the bar, but joined the First National Bank of Centerville, of which his father was the president. He began his connection in the capacity of teller. When his father died in 1956, the son succeeded him in the presidency of the bank. He is a member of the American Bankers Association, the Tennessee Bankers Association and the Middle Ten-

Brown Harvey

nessee Bankers Association. Also, as a lawyer, he belongs to the Tennessee Bar Association and the Hickman County Bar Association.

His other memberships include Alpha Tau Omega and Phi Delta Phi fraternities. A member of the Lions Club of his home city, he is currently serving as a director, and he attends the Methodist Church.

Mr. Walker is a veteran of World War II, having served stateside in the Marine Corps. He enlisted in the Corps in 1945, and received his honorable discharge in 1946. He was state treasurer of the Democratic party in 1952.

Mr. Walker is unmarried.

ABNER BROWN HARVEY

Over the past decade, Abner Brown Harvey has been in the real estate and insurance business at Clarksville. Since 1958 he has been an independent or contract appraiser for lands to be flooded by Barkley Dam. Prior to his entering the real estate field his varied career had comprised activity as teacher and school administrator, bank official, and appraiser for government bureaus. He has taken a useful part in community affairs.

Born at Indian Creek, in Montgomery County, on September 9, 1900, he is a son of Abner Brown Sr., and Golden (McCurdy) Harvey. His sister Elizabeth is now Mrs. Senseney of Jordan Springs, Tennessee, and his brother Aubrey Eulon Harvey lost his life while serving in the navy during World War I. Attending the public schools of his native county through the elementary years, he graduated from Normandy High School, Bedford County, after which he was a student at Southwestern Presbyterian University at Clarksville. However, his teaching career had begun some time before he completed his education. He taught in a school in McDuffie County, Georgia, in 1917-1918, and while still seventeen years old, began teaching at Clarksville. During this time he registered for service in World War I, but had not been called up at the time the war ended. For one year, Mr. Harvey was principal of the Jordan Springs, Tennessee, school. This is now the Fort Campbell area.

He first began work as a credit man when in 1920 he joined the staff of the First National Bank of Southern Trust Company, as an employee in its appraisal and loan department. He left the teaching profession in 1920 to devote himself full-time to this work, and continued with the same bank until 1939, when he was appointed land appraiser for the Federal Land Bank. From 1940 to 1943 he was appraiser for the Tennessee Valley Authority and the War Department.

In 1946, Mr. Harvey entered the real estate business at Clarksville in association with L. Newton Byers, and Mr. Harvey's sons have since been admitted to the firm. They are owners of business properties, and have also played a useful part in the growth and progress of the city of Clarksville, through their work in developing subdivisions. In addition, their agency sells insurance, representing the following firms: Insurance Company of North

America, The Home Insurance Company, Two America Fore Groups and others. For twelve years, Mr. Harvey served as vice president of the Southern Trust Company. In May, 1958, Mr. Harvey became an independent or contract appraiser for lands to be flooded by Barkley Dam. To date he has had the responsibility of making the independent property appraisals for that area and the towns of Eddyville and Kuttawa, Kentucky, have just been completed. The areas up the river to Cadiz, Kentucky are now being appraised.

He is a member of the Tennessee Historical Society, and history and genealogy are among his hobbies. He has done considerable research work on the background of his own family. He is a member of the local post of the American Legion, and attends the Methodist Church. In politics he is a Democrat.

In Clarksville, on December 24, 1921, Abner Brown Harvey married Elizabeth Senseney. She was born on October 22, 1903, at Rose Hill, in the Fort Campbell area of Tennessee, daughter of Cyrus Allensworth and Cordelia (Hewell) Senseney. Her father, who was born in Henleytown, Kentucky, on January 1, 1879, was a farmer who raised tobacco on a large scale. He died February 3, 1958, surviving his wife by a half-century. She died at Rose Hill, on October 24, 1908. She was a native of that place, born January 10, 1881.

Mr. and Mrs. Harvey are the parents of three children: 1. Cathryn Elizabeth, born August 22, 1923. She married Richard M. Mehigan, and they live in Clarksville. They have two children: i. Richard Maurice, born November 17, 1947. ii. Marilyn Elizabeth, born August 17, 1953. 2. Aubrey Burns, born March 24, 1926, in Clarksville. During World War II he served in the United States Navy, was assigned to the V-5 program, and trained at Columbus, Ohio, Louisville, Kentucky, Memphis, and Athens, Georgia. He attended the University of Ohio, the University of Louisville, Kentucky, and the University of Tennessee. He is now in the real estate business with his father. Aubrey Burns Harvey married Charlyne Davenport, and they have three children: i. Stephen Burns, born June 3, 1955. ii. Alyce Elizabeth, born December 19, 1956. iii. Mary Vaughn, born March 6, 1959. 3. Abner Brown, 3rd, born December 12, 1931, in Clarksville. He graduated from Austin Peay College with the degree of Bachelor of Science in 1954, and during 1955-1956, served in the United States Army, being assigned to the Army Security Agency in Germany. He had trained at Fort Knox, Kentucky, and Fort Devens, Massachusetts. Abner B. Harvey, 3rd, married Bettie Balthrop, and they have two children: i. John Michael, born August 26, 1955. ii. Deborah Louise, born September 27, 1957.

WILLIAM OLIVER INMAN

William O. Inman, whose entire career has been devoted to teaching and educational administration, is now superintendent of schools at Paris.

He is a native of Hardin, Kentucky, and was born on January 18, 1895, son of William Alexander and Mary (Henderson) Inman. His parents were farming people. Superintendent Inman received his early education in the elementary schools of Marshall County, Kentucky, where he completed his courses in 1912; and he took his secondary studies at Marvin Preparatory School at Clinton, Kentucky, where he graduated in 1916. He then began his teaching career, but later resumed his studies enrolling at George Peabody State College. There he received his degree of Bachelor of Science in 1925; and graduate studies led to the degree of Master of Arts in 1948.

Mr. Inman began his teaching career at McKenzie, and he also taught in the schools of the following communities: Boonshill, 1921-1925 and Tiptonville, 1925-1933, before coming to Paris in the latter year. He has been superintendent of schools there since 1933.

He is a veteran of World War I, who spent his entire enlistment period at Camp Taylor, Kentucky. He held a commission as second lieutenant, and was assigned to Battery F, Seventh Regiment, Field Artillery Replacement Depot. He received his honorable discharge on December 1, 1918.

Since 1932, Mr. Inman has been a member of Lions International. He is affiliated with the Free and Accepted Masons, and is a Master Mason. He attends the Methodist Church.

At Clinton, Kentucky, on June 8, 1921, William Oliver Inman married Elizabeth Griffey, daughter of Samuel D. and Elizabeth (Samuel) Griffey. Mr. and Mrs. Inman have two children: 1. William Oliver, Jr., who was born on July 19, 1924. 2. Walter G., born on November 29, 1926.

SEALE JOHNSON

As head of the McCowat-Mercer Press, Inc., Seale Johnson, of Jackson, is playing a useful and much-appreciated role in the preservation of the annals of his region. His company is a printing and lithographing firm, but it has also published many volumes on the Civil War and Tennessee, numerous county histories, and other works. Mr. Johnson is himself a collector of rare books and documents dealing with the history of his area.

Born at Denmark, in Madison County, Tennessee, on October 31, 1893, he is a son of James Milton and Mildred (Bond) Johnson. Both parents were born in Madison County, Tennessee, and both are of pioneer ancestry in Tennessee. His father was associated with the Mobile and Ohio Railroad for many years, and died in 1935. Mildred Bond Johnson died in 1927.

After completing his elementary and secondary studies in local schools, Seale Johnson entered Union University at Jackson, where he graduated in 1914, receiving his degree of Bachelor of Arts. He took his Master of Arts degree at the University of Michigan in 1916. He became a member of Sigma Alpha Epsilon fraternity while at Union.

Mr. Johnson began his career with the Long Johnson Printing Company in 1922. He has been with McCowat-Mercer Press, Inc., at Jackson since 1937, and has held office as president and general manager since 1938. He is the publisher of eight Civil War titles, and was active in the publication of "Historic Madison," the story of the town of Jackson and of Madison County, published in 1945. Mr. Johnson is a member of the Tennessee Historical Commission, a member of the Tennessee State Library and Archives Commission, and also of the Civil War Centennial Celebration Commission.

His noteworthy collection of books and manuscripts contains valuable materials dealing with early Tennessee and the Confederacy. He is also a collector of ancient Bibles.

A veteran of World War I, Mr. Johnson served with the rank of captain in the office of the Quartermaster General. He was later assigned to the American Red Cross in France.

He is a member and president of the Jackson Rotary Club, a member of the American Legion, the Chamber of Commerce, and the lodges of the Benevolent and Protective Order of Elks and the Free and Accepted Masons. He has twice been president of the Western Tennessee Executives Club. He is a member of St. Luke's Episcopal Church and vestryman.

On October 21, 1930, at Jackson, Seale Johnson married Marian Charlton Sullivan, daughter of Belton O'Neal and Jenny (Walsh) Sullivan. The couple are the parents of two children: 1. Jane, who was born on September 29, 1931. She is the wife of Ronald Flucker of Pittsburgh, Pennsylvania. They have two children. 2. Marian Charlton, born on May 21, 1935.

John Henry Weatherly

A banker and business leader in eastern Arkansas and western Tennessee, John Henry Weatherly lived in Memphis during the later years of his career. He had banking interests in several cities of the Mid-South, and in addition had a record of achievement in the insurance field.

Born at Selmer, on March 7, 1883, he was the seventh of nine children born to John Abe and Martha Jane (Steadman) Weatherly. His father was born on February 14, 1842, and his mother on March 24, 1851. The couple moved from Rockingham County, North Carolina, to a farm near Selmer. John H. Weatherly spent his boyhood years in that community, attended its public schools, and graduated from high school there. He began his business career working in a store at Earl, Arkansas, and he later was employed in banks in Birmingham, Alabama, Amory, Mississippi, and Crawfordsville, Arkansas, where he held positions as cashier. For a number of years he was active in both banking and the insurance business at Lepanto, Arkansas.

Coming to Memphis in 1944, and retiring from active business, he made his home on North Evergreen Street. He was a communicant of the First Methodist Church, and had no fraternal or club connections.

John Henry Weatherly married Dalton Greenwood, a native of Lepanto, Arkansas, and daughter of Charles B. and Mary Ellen (Chambers) Green-

wood. Her father was one of the early settlers of his community, and laid out the streets there. The main street of the town bears his name, as does Greenwood Township, in which Lepanto is located. Mary Ellen Chambers, whom he married, was born in Missouri.

Mr. and Mrs. Weatherly were married in Memphis on June 5, 1922. She is a member of the Lunch Forum, the King's Daughters, the In His Name Circle, and the Nineteenth Century Club. The couple became the parents of one son, Jack, who was born in Memphis on August 20, 1923. Taking his premedical courses at Memphis State University, he went to the University of Arkansas for his professional training, and took his degree of Doctor of Medicine there in 1946. He received further training at Veterans' Administration Hospital in North Little Rock, at Gulfport, Mississippi, and at the Marine Hospital in New Orleans, and he is now assigned to the Psychiatric Service and Mental Hygiene Clinic at the Veterans Administration Hospital, Roosevelt Road, Little Rock. Dr. Weatherly is a member of the American Medical Association, and he joined Phi Chi medical fraternity while at the University of Arkansas. At Gulfport, Mississippi, Dr. Jack Weatherly married Miss Betty Trammell.

Rayford, the brother of John H. Weatherly, resides on the old Weatherly home place a few miles from Selmer. It was there that John A. Weatherly raised a large log house, which still stands and is well preserved and improved.

The death of the business leader and banker occurred at Baptist Hospital in Memphis on August 19, 1956.

JOHN AUGUST RIECHMAN

A Memphis industrialist and businessman, Mr. Riechman was a cofounder of the Riechman-Crosby Company, and served as its president from its founding, until his death. The late John A. Riechman was also a colorful figure and a dynamic force in the political life of his area. He was universally known and respected in his part of the state, where he had many organizational and civic connections.

Born at Cincinnati, Ohio, on October 7, 1872, he was a son of John G. and Lillie (Fieber) Riechman. He received his education in his native state, attending the schools of Wyoming, Ohio. He began his industrial career in the saw business in Cincinnati, but in 1897, when he was only twenty-five years old, he came to Memphis and joined Harry H. Crosby in forming the Riechman-Crosby Company. This machinery and industrial supply firm was built into a successful organization which served manufacturing interests throughout the South. The two original partners remained at its head for well over a half-century with Mr. Riechman serving as its president; Mr. Crosby died only one week before Mr. Riechman's death. The company's plant and offices are at 223 South Front Street. Mr. Riechman was also one of the original directors and later served as president of the Southern Industrial Distributor Association.

Mr. Riechman made his entry into Memphis' political life in 1911, when he was elected city commissioner. He became a close associate of E. H. Crump, and while Mr. Crump was mayor, it was his intention to become candidate for a second office, sheriff of the county. It was impossible for him, under the law, to enter a second candidacy while serving as mayor, and he selected Mr. Riechman as his choice to run for sheriff. However, by the time this decision had been reached, it was too late to get Mr. Reichman's name on the ballot. This fact provided the background for one of the colorful campaigns of Tennessee's political history. Mr. Riechman entered the campaign anyway, as a write-in candidate, and Beale Street was daily flooded with posters asking voters to enter his name and to "Write it Riech"—a reminder that his name was not spelled as might be expected, but with the i before the e. The campaign was successful, and the heavy Negro vote, at whom it was primarily directed, was a conspicuous factor in securing his election. It later developed that these were not the only people who could benefit from a reminder about the spelling of his name. In later years there appeared a book on politics in the South, and this example was chosen—only his name was misspelled and the episode related was that voters were instructed to place the e before the i.

Mr. Riechman performed most creditably in his office. He was, in the phrase of an editorial appearing at the time of his death, "an excellent choice for sheriff." In this connection as in his other public duties he proved that he had a mind of his own. In 1925 he proposed the erection of a new county hospital, for which there was a great need. He did not receive the support he had expected from the Crump organization in this project; and this and other differences led him to bluntly announce that he had "quit the county machine cold." It was the same commission, under his chairmanship, which later planned and supervised the erection of the Shelby County Criminal Court Building. The political break between him and E. H. Crump did not affect their personal friendship. They frequently got together socially, and regularly spent leisure time at the Five Lakes Club at Horseshoe Lake in Arkansas, until Mr. Crump's death in 1954.

In addition to his duties in managing the electrical equipment and supply firm, Mr. Riechman established the first radio station in Memphis. He was a leader in charitable work. He took a significant part in establishing the Community Fund and served as its first president. He was elected to a second and a third term in that office, but declined a fourth, despite earnest protests from his co-workers, on the ground that it was not advisable to build an organization upon an individual rather than upon a plan. Instead, he advised that a new president be elected each year, and that ex-presidents comprise an advisory committee. At the time of his death, he was honorary president of the Community Fund. He was also a past president of Associated Charities, which he had likewise helped to found. Long active in the program of the Tennessee Children's Home Society, he had held office as its treasurer. Mr. Riechman was one of the first recipients of the Memphis Press Scimitar newspaper award for having rendered the most valuable service of any citizen to the city of Memphis during 1923. The award was a large engraved loving cup.

Affiliated with the Free and Accepted Masons and a member of the higher bodies of the order, he belonged to Al Chymia Temple, Ancient Arabic Order of Nobles of the Mystic Shrine. His other memberships included the Memphis Country Club, the Hunt and Polo Club, the Tennessee Club, and the Five Lakes Club. His favorite sport was hunting, and he enjoyed working on projects designed to benefit children. He was a Lutheran in religious faith.

Mr. and Mrs. Riechman were married at Wyoming, Ohio, on April 28, 1905. She is the former Miss Gladys Fox, and was born at Walnut Hill, Cincinnati, Ohio, the daughter of Charles A. and Mary Susan (Childe) Fox. Mr. and Mrs. Riechman became the parents of two daughters: 1. Mary Louise, who married Robert B. Driver. They have the following children: i. Lucy Baylor Driver, who married Earl King. ii. Mary Louise Driver, who is the wife of Roland D. Carlson. iii. Ann Riechman Driver. iv. Robert B. Driver, Jr. 2. Gladys Augusta, who married Lawson M. Wilhoite. They have a son, John Riechman Wilhoite.

A career of great usefulness in commercial affairs, public life, and welfare came to an end with the death of John A. Riechman on December 17, 1956.

Lois Dilliard Bejach

A veteran Memphis attorney, Lois Dilliard Bejach has capably filled a variety of public offices. He was for ten years a member of the Tennessee House of Representatives. He has been county attorney, and chancellor of the Chancery Court; and since 1954 has been judge of the Court of Appeals, State of Tennessee, Western Division, at Jackson. He makes his home in Memphis, where he has long taken a prominent part in business and organizational affairs.

Born at Moscow, in Fayette County, Mr. Bejach is a son of Samuel and Lumbia (Dilliard) Bejach. His father was a merchant. The future lawyer and jurist completed his secondary studies at Memphis University School, where he graduated in 1904. Entering Vanderbilt University, he graduated there with the degree of Bachelor of Science in 1908; and he took his law courses at Harvard University, receiving his Bachelor of Laws degree there in 1911.

Admitted to the bar of his state, he commenced practice in Memphis in July, 1911, and remained in active practice until September, 1933, when he was named to the bench as chancellor of the Chancery Court of Shelby County. He was also absent during the World War I period, serving in the

Field Artillery. Attending the Central Officers Training School at Camp Zachary Taylor, Kentucky, from August to December, 1918, he was commissioned a first lieutenant. Later promoted to captain in the Field Artillery Reserve, he retired as a major in the Reserve.

In 1913 and 1923, Mr. Bejach served his district in the Tennessee House of Representatives, having in the meantime, in 1921, served in the State Senate. In the year he took his seat, he authored a bill granting property rights to married women, known as the Bejach Law. He served as county attorney of Shelby County from 1924 to 1933. Becoming chancellor in the latter year, he served until 1954, when he was named to the bench of the State Court of Appeals at Jackson. He has occupied the bench as one of its three judges since that time, and his long experience in the law, and marked judicial talents, have made his service most valuable to the state. He was first appointed to the Court of Appeals to fill a vacancy, but has since been elected to the bench to fill an eight-year term beginning September 1, 1958.

Judge Bejach has been a member of the Tennessee Historical Commission since 1950. He was formerly a director of the Commercial and Industrial Bank and of the Security Bank and Trust Company (now defunct), both of Memphis.

As a lawyer he is a member of the following bar associations: Memphis and Shelby County, Tennessee State and American Bar Associations. He is a charter member of Memphis Post No. 1 of the American Legion, and also a charter member of the Memphis Chapter of the Military Order of the World Wars. In this latter veterans' group, he has held office in past years as chapter commander and state commander. He is affiliated with the Free and Accepted Masons, being past master of his lodge and a member of the higher bodies. He is past commander of the Council in the Scottish Rite of Masonry and he holds the rare Thirty-third Degree. He is a member and past potentate of the Ancient Arabic Order of Nobes of the Mystic Shrine. His other memberships include the Army-Navy Club of Memphis, and the Horseshoe Lake Hunting and Fishing Club of Hughes, Arkansas.

A communicant of the First Methodist Church of Memphis, Judge Bejach was formerly a member of its board of stewards. Mrs. Bejach is a member of the First Congregational Church of Memphis.

Judge Lois Dilliard Bejach has been twice married. His first wife was Ailene Oliver, whom he married at Lebanon, on December 28, 1922. She was the daughter of Andrew and Frances (Boulton) Oliver. The conuple were the parents of one daughter: Ailene Oliver, who was born on June 25, 1926. She is now the wife of Charles A. Speight of Dallas, Texas, and they have two children: Lois Patricia and Judith Lynn Speight. Ailene (Oliver) Bejach died on February 18, 1933, and on February 26, 1934, Judge Bejach married, second, Wilena (Roberts) Lanning, the ceremony taking place at Norman, Oklahoma. She is the daughter of William Hilliard and Lura (Kronmiller)

Roberts. One daughter has been born to this second marriage of Judge Bejach, a daughter, Lois Patricia, on March 3, 1935. The family's residence is at 43 Belleair Drive, Memphis.

ROBERT LEE KINCAID

Following early experience in the publishing industry, Dr. Robert Lee Kincaid joined the administrative staff of Lincoln Memorial University at Harrogate, Tennessee, and after a decade as its president, is now president-emeritus. He is an author as well as an educator, with three books to his credit.

A native of Blairsville, Georgia, he was born on May 17, 1893, son of James R. and Virginia A. (Wild) Kincaid. After completing his studies in local public schools, he entered Lincoln Memorial University, where he graduated with the degree of Bachelor of Arts in 1915. For a year he studied at the School of Journalism of the University of Missouri.

When he had completed his studies there, he returned to Lincoln Memorial University to serve as secretary. This position he held continuously until 1922, with the exception of the war years 1917-1918, when he was in the United States Army. He served as sergeant-major in a Coast Artillery outfit. After leaving the secretaryship of Lincoln Memorial University, Dr. Kincaid became managing editor of the Middlesboro Daily News at Middlesboro, Kentucky, in 1923. The following year he became business manager of the Grafton Sentinel, at Grafton, West Virginia; but he resumed his duties as managing editor of the Middlesboro Daily News in 1926, and continued in his connection with that paper until 1937.

In the latter year, Dr. Kincaid returned once again to Lincoln Memorial University as vice president. He had retained membership on its board of directors, and had also held the position of chairman of the executive committee, since 1927. He continued to serve in the vice presidency until 1947, when he assumed duties as president. On June 1, 1958, Dr. Kincaid retired as president and was elected as president-emeritus. Dr. Kincaid received the honorary degree of Doctor of Laws from his Alma Mater, Lincoln Memorial University, in 1937. In 1957 the honorary degree of Doctor of Literature was conferred upon him by the University of Chattanooga. He is active in the Alumni Association of Lincoln Memorial University, and has held office as president of that association.

From 1943 to 1946, Dr. Kincaid served as vice chairman of the Kentucky National Park Commission. For the past five years he has served as a member of the Tennessee Historical Commission, resigning recently when he moved from the state. Continuing his connection with the news publishing field, he is president of the Citizens News Company of Middlesboro, Kentucky. As a veteran of World War I, he belongs to the American Legion, and his fraternity is Kappa Alpha. A Kiwanian, he is past president of the club in his city, and he is also a member of the Filson Club. He is a Baptist and a Republican.

Dr. Kincaid's books are titled "Jinny and Jim" (1941), "Joshua Fry Speed" (1943), and "The Wilderness Road" (1947).

On May 24, 1917, Dr. Robert Lee Kincaid married Beulah C. Chance, and they became the parents of two children: 1. Helen, who is the wife of M. K. Henry. 2. Robert Hugh, who is deceased.

Since becoming president-emeritus of Lincoln Memorial University, Dr. Kincaid has moved to Middlesboro, Kentucky, six miles from the college.

GARNETT ANDREWS, SR.

An industrial leader in Chattanooga over many years, Garnett Andrews, Sr., arrived at a position of enviable prominence and influence, not only through his commercial activities, but through his participation in civic affairs as well.

Born in Washington, Wilkes County, Georgia, September 15, 1870, Garnett Andrews was a son of Colonel Garnett and Rosalie Champe (Bierne) Andrews. His grandfather was judge of the superior court of Georgia for twenty-seven years, and was at one time unsuccessful candidate for governor. His father, in turn, John Andrews of Virginia, was a soldier of the Revolution. A still earlier ancestor was Major William Andrews who was a member of the Virginia House of Burgesses, and one of the signers of the act by which the Commonwealth of Virginia submitted to Cromwell during the protectorate.

Colonel Andrews, father of the industrialist, was born at Washington, Georgia, in 1837. After making an enviable record for himself as a Southern officer during the Civil War, he settled in Chattanooga, where he gained increasing prominence and prosperity as a member of the bar. Miss Rosalie Champe Bierne, whom he married, was a granddaughter of Andrew Bierne, who was a congressman from Virginia. Their children were: Garnett, considered in the present sketch; Champe Seabury; Andrew Beirne; and Oliver Burnside.

Garnett Andrews' early education took place in Yazoo City, from which the family had come, and in Chattanooga. He later became a cadet in the Virginia Military Institute at Lexington, where he was a member of the class of 1890. There followed study at Worcester Polytechnic Institute, in Massachusetts, where the young man prepared himself for a career in business and industry.

Subsequent to his return to Chattanooga he was for a brief time teller in the old City Savings Bank, in that city. Then forming a partnership with W. R. Crabtree (who was later to be a candidate for governor in the Democratic primaries), he engaged in the real estate and farm land business. This partnership was dissolved in 1895, and Mr. Andrews established the Andrews warehouse. It was after this diversified experience that he permanently turned his attention to manufacturing. With a capital of four thousand five hundred

dollars, he organized the Chattanooga Knitting Mills, first located on lower Market Street, between First and Second. Subsequently the business was moved to Rossville, Georgia, where a new charter was taken out under the laws of Georgia, and the mill incorporated as the Richmond Hosiery Mills, a Mr. Edward G. Richmond being associated with Mr. Andrews in building up the enterprise. From 1900 until the time of his death, Mr. Andrews was president of the Richmond Hosiery Mills. He was also vice president of the Rockwood Mills in Tennessee, and was affiliated with the Magnet Mills, Incorporated, of Clinton, having served this company for many years as its president. He founded the Harriman Hosiery Mills, and until a short time before his death was vice president of that organization.

The prominence which came to him in these numerous capacities was recognized by his being chosen twice as president of the National Association of Hosiery and Underwear Manufacturers. In this capacity, he was instrumental in the drawing up of the Aldrich-Payne Tariff Act.

A further recognition of his significance in the founding of Tennessee industries, and in their long and successful leadership, came when, together with John L. Hutcheson, he was tendered a testimonial dinner on July 8, 1943. The two men were honored as having contributed more than any others to the development of Rossville, Georgia, which was the scene of this event. On this occasion, Governor Ellis Arnall delivered the principal address.

Carrying many other responsibilities besides those of his business, Garnett Andrews, Sr., was a member, during the war years, of the War Industries Board, and Employment Service, under the Department of Labor. He was an associate member of the N. B. Forrest Camp of Confederate Veterans, of which his father had been the first president; and he was a member of the Sons of Confederate Veterans. He also belonged to the Tennessee National Guard, in which he held the rank of captain.

He held membership in the Mountain City Club, the Fairyland Club, the Calumet Club of New York, and the Manufacturers Club of Philadelphia. He was a prominent member of the Chattanooga Manufacturers Association, and belonged to the Chamber of Commerce of that city. His religious affiliation was with St. Paul's Church.

Garnett Andrews, Sr., married, October 30, 1895, Elizabeth Lenoir Key, daughter of Judge and Mrs. D. M. Key. They were the parents of six children: Betty Beirne (Mrs. Joseph Berens Waters); Katharine Lenoir (Mrs. Samuel Carter Hutcheson); Garnett, Jr.; Margaret Avery (deceased); David Key; and Garnett III (deceased).

The death of Garnett Andrews, Sr., occurred November 11, 1946. He will long live vividly in the memories of those who knew him as a vigorous member of the community, a leader in its affairs, as he was in the chosen industry in which he gained such prominence.

JOE ANDERSON PINKERTON

Born in Williamson County on October 29, 1910, Joe Anderson Pinkerton is the son of the late Joe Anderson, Sr., and Elizabeth (Hyde) Pinkerton. The elder Pinkerton was born in 1859 in Williamson County and spent his lifetime as a representative for the Wrought Iron Range Company of Saint Louis, Missouri, and as a farmer for ten years prior to his death in 1921. His wife, born in 1885, died in 1947 at Franklin where she was an active member of the Primitive Baptist Church.

Joe Anderson Pinkerton, Jr., attended Franklin public schools and later Battle Ground Academy.

While still attending school, Mr. Pinkerton worked for the Pinkerton and Kinnard Drug Company but left their employ in 1930 to accept a job as teller of the Harpeth National Bank in Franklin. He served in this capacity until 1947 when he was made director and executive vice president of the Williamson County Bank at Franklin. He was later promoted to the post of president, the position he now holds. He is also a partner in the Hall and Pinkerton Insurance Company at Franklin.

Mr. Pinkerton has served for over twenty years as Franklin City treasurer, and is past treasurer of Williamson County Chapter, American Red Cross. He is a past member of the Junior Order of American Mechanics, a director and member of the Chamber of Commerce, and is also director, secretary and treasurer of the Franklin Industrial Corporation. He is a charter member of the Lions Club. Mr. Pinkerton is on the executive council of the Boy Scouts of America, being vice president of Middle Tennessee Council and past chairman of Williamson County District. He received the Silver Beaver Award for his service. He is a director and treasurer of Williamson County Center. He is also chairman of the board of trustees of Battle Ground Academy. He and his family are members of the First Presbyterian Church of Franklin in which he is an elder and trustee.

He married the former Estelle McCombs on November 15, 1933. Mrs. Pinkerton, born on August 9, 1909, in Boston, Massauchsetts, is the daughter of the late Henry W. McCombs. Mrs. Pinkerton attended Peabody College and taught school in Franklin for some years. Mr. and Mrs. Pinkerton are the parents of three children. They are: 1. Joe Anderson, Jr., born March 21, 1938 at Franklin. He attended schools in Franklin and graduated from Battle Ground Academy where he played on the basketball and football teams. He is now a pre-medical student at Vanderbilt University in Nashville. 2. Betty Sue, born July 8, 1940, and now attending Vanderbilt University. 3. Frank Henry, born September 4, 1945.

DAVID ALMON ALEXANDER

Admitted to the bar in 1942, Mr. Alexander did not practice law until his return to civilan life after World War II. Since that time he has conducted a highly successful private practice in Franklin and Nashville. He has served the people of his city and county in various political offices.

Mr. Alexander was born in Decatur, Alabama, on December 27, 1915. His father, the late Truman Hudson Alexander, born in October, 1890, in Birmingham, Alabama, was a well-known newspaperman who worked for the Nashville Tennessean and later the Memphis Commercial Appeal. He died September 1, 1941 at Franklin. His mother, the late Helen (Almon) Alexander, was born on February 13, 1892, at Decatur and died at Franklin on August 31, 1942.

Mr. Alexander was educated in the public schools of Nashville, later attending Battle Ground Academy. He received his Bachelor of Science degree from Peabody College and his Bachelor of Laws degree from Vanderbilt University. In World War II, he served as a lieutenant and later lieutenant commander in Atlantic, Pacific and Asiatic waters. Participating in invasions in the Pacific and in Southern France, he received shrapnel wounds and holds the Purple Heart. He was on Okinawa at the war's end and then served as flag lieutenant during the surrender ceremonies in Tokyo Bay on the U.S.S. Missouri.

Opening his law office at Franklin in 1946, Mr. Alexander was elected to the General Assembly in 1949 and acted as Administration Floor Leader for Governor Gordon Browning. He organized and served in the Department of Financial Responsibility in connection with insurance. In 1958 he opened a law office in Nashville where he spends most of his time. He is a former alderman in the town of Franklin. He is a past president of the Lions Club and is a member of the National Rifle Association. A Methodist, he is a past member of the Board of Stewards.

He is the father of two children by a former marriage. They are: 1. Julia Clayton, born in 1947; and 2. William Hudson, born in 1949. He is presently married to the former Jane Bagley of Nashville.

Rosalie Carter, D.D.S.

Dr. Rosalie Carter has gained an enviable record of achievement in her chosen field of dentistry, having been actively engaged in practice since receiving her degree from Vanderbilt University School of Dentistry at Nashville, in 1924. She has served as national president of the Association of American Women Dentists, and vice president of the Tennessee Dental Association. She is a person of broad interests as shown by her many activities and attainments in other fields. She is president of the Nashville Branch of the National League of American Pen Women, having gained professional status as a poet. She is listed in "International Who's Who In Poetry" published in London and in "Who's Who Among American Women." Her beloved poem, "Friends," has gone to every English-speaking country in the world. Currently she is collaborating with Helen Westbrook, well-known organist and composer of Chi-

cago, in the writing of hymns, anthems, and other songs. From 1935 to 1937
she served as state president of the Tennessee Federation of Business and Professional Women's Clubs. From its founding she has served on the Board of
the Williamson County Memorial Library. She is a past president of Franklin's
oldest literary club, The Allied Arts Club. Her interest in history and genealogy
are shown by her membership in the Tennessee Historical Society, National
Society of the Dames of the Magna Charta, Huguenot Society of the Founders
of Manakin, Société Vaudoise D'Histoire et D'Archéologie of Moudon,
Switzerland, (native town of her Huguenot ancestor), Daughters of the American Revolution, and National Genealogical Society. Currently she is engaged
in the writing of a book dealing with the history of her famous ancestral home,
"The Old Carter House," at Franklin, Tennessee, now preserved as a Shrine
of the War Between the States by the State of Tennessee, where three generations of her Carter family have lived, the builder being Fountain Branch Carter, her great-grand father, lineal descendent of Giles Carter of Virginia. To
the historical sketches written for this book by her father will be added numerous original photographs and poems and historical documents discovered in
the National Archives and elsewhere, and a complete genealogical record of
the descendents of the builder.

For twenty-five years it was her privilege to practice in the same office
with her father, Dr. Moscow Branch Carter (1875-1951), also an alumnus of
Vanderbilt University Dental School, life member of the American Dental Association, author of numerous contributions to dental journals, inventor of
numerous aids to dentistry and a trustee of the Franklin Presbyterian Church.
Graduating in 1896, he practiced fifty-four years in his native town of Franklin, Tennessee, assisted by his other daughter, Mrs. Corinne Carter Ward for
many years. His father was Colonel Moscow Branch Carter of the Confederate
States Army (1825-1913) who also saw service in the Mexican War, brother
of famous Captain "Tod" (Theodrick) Carter, Confederate States Army, who
is known wherever the story of the Battle of Franklin is told. Dr. Rosalie
Carter's mother was the lovely Lucy Flora Goss of Hartwell, Georgia (1879-
1957), daughter of Judge Horatio James Goss and Emily Rosalie (Lewis)
Goss, descendant of Major William Lewis who fought with Washington at
Valley Forge. Her mother was a charter member of Franklin's first Garden
Club, having over one hundred and fifty varieties of iris in her garden; char-
ter member of the Magazine Club of Franklin; member of the Daughters of
the American Revolution and Allied Arts Club; compiler of a history of the
First Presbyterian Church of Franklin; and state superintendent of Junior
Christian Endeavor.

JUDD BROOKS

Judd Brooks of Jackson brought sound knowledge, a sympathetic spirit,
and devoted effort to the promotion of scientific agriculture in his home county.

Judd Brooks

For over twenty years he was district agricultural agent under the University of Tennessee Agricultural Extension Service, and after his retirement from that post, was agricultural representative for the National Bank of Commerce at Jackson. When, toward the end of his life, "Judd Brooks Day" was observed in his community, he was paid tribute as "one who has worked long and hard to help transform this part of the country into a better place to live through sound-farming."

Born on November 28, 1885, on a farm near Hampshire in Maury County, he was a son of William Alonzo and Mary Alice (Galloway) Brooks. He was descended from John Brooks, who with his wife Susan came from England in the eighteenth century, and settled in Chatham County, North Carolina. They had a son, Mark Brooks, who married Fannie Harris. Their son, Thomas Jefferson Brooks, was born in 1782 and died in 1841. On December 29, 1803, he married Nancy Jones, and they moved to Maury County, Tennessee, about 1806. They had a son Abner, who was born in 1808 and died in 1885. Abner married Matilda (Warfield) Pinkard, and they had a son, Thomas Brantley Brooks, who was born in 1835 and died in 1921. He was married, on October 17, 1854, to Mary Brown Worley. Their son was William Alonzo Brooks, Judd Brooks' father. William A. Brooks was born in Hampshire, Tennessee, on April 1, 1861. Mary Alice Galloway, whom he married, was also a native of Hampshire, born March 10, 1863, daughter of Enoch and Hannah (Judd) Galloway.

Spending his boyhood years in Maury County, Judd Brooks began his education in a two-room school and in 1903 attended the Ford and Williams Training School for Boys in Columbia. He received his eleventh-grade certificate from the county school in Hampshire. From 1905 to 1907 he worked as a clerk in Lawson's Grocery Store in Nashville. Determined to prepare himself for a career in agricultural service at the University of Tennessee, he saved his money and enrolled there on September 15, 1907. However, by that time, illness had depleted his savings and he arrived in Knoxville with only twenty-eight dollars. Despite the fact of having to work his way, he excelled in scholarship each year, took a full part in campus activities and joined many organizations. He graduated from the university's College of Agriculture in June, 1912. On graduation day, with the most outstanding scholastic record over the four-year course to his credit, he was designated Agriculture Class Representative.

Mr. Brooks began his career by gaining practical experience in farming. From 1912 through 1915 (following a brief period at the Tennessee Experiment Station in Knoxville), he was partner and manager of Beechlawn Stock Farm at Fayetteville. He joined the staff of the University of Tennessee Agricultural Extension Service in February, 1916, as agricultural agent of Madison County, the second man to fill that post. One of the first programs he instituted was the boys' corn clubs, predecessors of the present 4-H Clubs. Overall production of corn in the county was increased so greatly that a considerable quantity of the crop was shipped out in 1917, for the first time in history, bringing in a total income of eleven thousand dollars. As pointed out in a review of his career in the local press:

Judd Brooks' zeal for organization and guidance was linked hand-in-hand with the promotion of improved agricultural practices, and he engaged the support of business and civic groups to help.

He devoted attention to better livestock and crop varieties; markedly improved the cotton yield per acre; organized demonstrations in nearly twoscore projects; introduced crimson clover and encouraged the growing of alfalfa and small grains. The stimulus he gave to the production of Duroc hogs in 1917 led the following year to the cooperative marketing of livestock in the county. He helped establish the Federation of County Organizations (which became the County Agricultural Bureau), and finally the Madison County Farm Bureau, the first such local organization in the state. His efforts were invaluable in increasing crop production for World War I. So successful were the efforts of the 4-H Club boys whom he trained that they won nearly all honors at the Tri-State Fair (now the Mid-South Fair) at Memphis, and were later subjected to a handicap to give encouragement to other such groups. In 1925 the fair board refused to let Madison County enter competitive events, and they then turned successfully to national competition.

Judd Brooks remained in the county agent's post until June 30, 1934. Concurrently, during the month of May, 1934, he served as representative to the United States Department of Agriculture on Landlord-Tenant Relationship, being on leave of absence with the Agricultural Adjustment Administration at Oklahoma Agricultural and Mechanical College in Stillwater.

Mr. Brooks assumed duties as district agricultural agent with the University of Tennessee Agricultural Extension Service on July 1, 1934. In that capacity he worked most effectively on behalf of farmers and farm youth in each of the twenty-one counties of western Tennessee. Commented an editorial writer at the time of his death:

. . . Mr. Brooks . . . really lived through and aided in accomplishing a practical revolution in West Tennessee agriculture. He was ever abreast of the times and alert to learn and adapt new developments to his field. To our mind he was particularly helpful to young people . . . The things Judd Brooks did to improve farming and help farmers to financial security were notable in themselves, but his modesty and charm of manner, his understanding heart and warm sympathy enhanced it all.

In recognition of his achievements, Mr. Brooks was accorded a number of state and national honors. In 1951 he went to Washington, D. C., to receive the Superior Service Award of the United States Department of Agriculture. This was presented in acknowledgement of the fact that he had contributed more to the economic development, progress and well-being of the farmers in his twenty-one-county area than any other individual. He received a medal, and certificate which enumerated the high points of his then thirty-five years of service as a professional agricultural worker. The citation was drafted by a board of seven experts from the agencies within the Department of Agriculture. In 1955, Mr. Brooks was recipient of another honor—the "Man of the Year" Award of Progressive Farmer magazine, in recognition of his having done the most for Tennessee agriculture of any man in that year. His citation commented that "few individuals in an administrative position have gone so far outside their regular duties to assist boys and girls. He lives by his philosophy which is, 'The greatest progress in rural living comes from the greatest development of leadership.' "

When Mr. Brooks resigned from his position with the Agricultural Extension Service on June 30, 1956, he was accorded yet another honor, by the people of his community. The Jackson-Madison County Chamber of Commerce announced a Judd Brooks Day in Jackson. More than twelve hundred friends gathered to show appreciation for his valuable services to them over a period of twoscore years in agricultural extension work.

His retirement from the state post did not mark the end of his service to the advancement of agriculture, for on July 1, 1956, he assumed new duties as agricultural representative for the National Bank of Commerce of Jackson, and in this position he was active until February 3, 1959.

Working closely with the 4-H groups, Mr. Brooks had been effective in building up a membership of forty thousand in his district. He was a charter member of the Tennessee 4-H All-Stars, and its Big Chief from 1948 to 1956. He was called a "tower of strength" to the Commercial Appeal's Plant to Prosper Competition, with which he worked from its inception, and he served for many years as chairman of its executive committee. From 1928 to 1934, he was secretary of the National Association of County Agricultural Agents. He became a charter member of Epsilon Sigma Phi, agricultural extension workers' honor society, joining its Omega Chapter when it was organized in 1927. He was also a charter member of Alpha Zeta agricultural fraternity, joining when it was formed at the University of Tennessee in 1912. Also at the university, he became a member of Phi Kappa Phi. His other memberships included the Free and Accepted Masons, of which he joined Lodge No. 45 at Jackson in 1918. A member of the higher bodies of the Scottish Rite, he had held the Thirty-second Degree from 1925. From 1920 he was a member of the Jackson Rotary Club. He was a communicant of the First Presbyterian Church in Jackson, and held office as deacon and as elder.

His work for the Agricultural Extension Service precluded the possibility of his entering party politics. However, in 1937, when Governor Browning was making up his cabinet, he earnestly and repeatedly endeavored to persuade Mr. Brooks to accept appointment as State Commissioner of Agriculture. But the veteran extension worker's complete devotion to his vocation compelled him to refuse.

At the Second Presbyterian Church in Knoxville, on December 17, 1913, Judd Brooks married Rena May Schweikerd, whom he had met while a student at the university. Her father, William Leonard Schweikerd, was born in New York City in 1860, and her mother, the former Miss Julia Anna Cable, in Jefferson City, Tennessee, in 1870. Mr. and Mrs. Brooks became the parents of two children, both of whom were born in Jackson: 1. Julia Alice, born on December 4, 1922. She married Truman Gregory Glasscock of Clovis, New Mexico, and they have a daughter, Cherie Lynn. 2. William Judd, born on June 24, 1928. Now a lieutenant in the United States Navy, he is stationed aboard the U. S. Destroyer "Eaton," and his home base is Norfolk, Virginia. Mr. and Mrs. Brooks made their home at 401 Westwood Avenue, Jackson.

The death of Mr. Brooks in February, 1959, marked the close of a career of the utmost usefulness to the cause of agriculture in the South. A tribute to his character as well as to his accomplishments appeared in this form in the editorial columns of a local newspaper:

Judd Brooks had a deep interest in agriculture.

More, he had an abiding love for people, especially farm people.

In this combination of interests, he was able to lead West Tennessee farmers into more profitable production of crops and a more abundant economic life. Judd Brooks, however, displayed his true genius in helping the people with whom he came in contact see the beauties in nature, the loveable qualities of their fellow beings.

His personal love for people inspired true affection for him, and led to closer cooperation in communities as he showed farmers and homemakers the spiritual values of life.

His gentle but firm manner served well in his guidance of youth groups such as the 4-H Clubs and Young Farmers and Homemakers.

He inspired them to an early realization that their adult lives could be happy and fruitful on the farm, and that they could be economically independent by following good farm practices.

Lessons he taught about agriculture will continue to bear fruit in the greater prosperity of our West Tennessee.

Judd Brooks will be best remembered, however, for those qualities of mind and spirit which so closely resembled the Master he served daily.

May that Master comfort those Judd Brooks loved.

MARION GRIFFIN EVANS

Veteran Memphis attorney Marion Griffin Evans had a distinguished career of legal practice in that city dating from the early years of the century. He had served on the bench of the Supreme Court of Tennessee; and in the later years of his life held office as president of the Tennessee Bar Association. As a capable lawyer, he was known and respected throughout the state, and was acknowledged to be a leading figure of the Memphis bar.

Born in Jackson County, Mississippi, on March 19, 1877, he was a son of Marion McKay and Emma Kate (Airey) Evans. His father, a merchant by

Marion G. Evans

occupation, later became lieutenant governor of Mississippi, an office he held in the late 1870s. After completing his elementary and preparatory education in the schools of his native county, Marion G. Evans entered the University of Mississippi, where he took his degree of Bachelor of Arts in 1897. The following year he studied at the University of Chicago, but he returned to the University of Mississippi to take his professional studies. There he received his degree of Bachelor of Laws in 1902.

As soon as he had completed his legal training, Mr. Evans came to Memphis and was admitted to the Tennessee bar. He began his private practice of law there, a practice he was to continue for over fifty-five years, making his a career with few parallels among his contemporaries in the state. In his later years he had his offices in the Commerce Title Building.

In his early years in the city, his proven abilities won him positions of public trust. In 1910 he was named counsel for the Memphis Board of Education, and held that post continuously for forty-three years. In 1917 he was named to the Tennessee Supreme Court as associate justice to fill out an unexpired term. It was, however, his long-term professional activities as a practicing attorney which more than anything else earned him his reputation. Year after year, he participated in major cases before the local courts.

In 1942, Mr. Evans served as president of the Memphis and Shelby County Bar Association, and he was elected president of the Tennessee Bar Association in 1948, serving through 1949. His choice to fill this office was indicative of the high regard in which he was held in professional circles throughout the state.

Apart from his professional connections, he was a member of the Memphis Country Club for over a quarter-century. His fraternity was Sigma Chi, and he attended the Methodist Church.

On April 30, 1919, in Memphis, Marion Griffin Evans married Phoebe Olivia Grosvenor, daughter of Charles Niles and Olivia (Hill) Grosvenor. She is a member of an old Memphis family. Her father was born in that city on November 23, 1850, son of Hosea Merrill and Martha (Niles) Grosvenor. When he was very young, Charles N. Grosvenor was associated with Colonel John Overton, Jr., in the real estate business in Memphis. In 1880, the two formed a partnership. Mr. Grosvenor retired in 1897 and went west, spending two years in Texas and Arizona, after which he returned to Memphis. He was a director of the Union Planters Bank, and was one of the owners of the Chickasaw Land Company, which owned three thousand acres of land in South Memphis. He was also active in establishing the suburban street-car line there. On December 30, 1885, Charles Niles Grosvenor married Olivia Polk Hill, daughter of Napoleon and Mary (Wood) Hill. Napoleon Hill was born in Marshall County on October 25, 1830, son of Dr. Duncan and Olivia L. (Bills) Hill. Early in his life the family moved to Marshall County, Mississippi, where Dr. Hill practiced. The physician was also a planter. He died in

1844, but his wife survived him by many years, and died at an advanced age in 1883, at St. Louis, Missouri. Napoleon Hill attended local schools and at the age of sixteen began his career as a clerk in a dry-goods store operated by his uncle, Major J. H. Bills of Bolivar, Tennessee. In 1850 he went to California, and remained until 1856, engaging in mining and trading. He then returned to Bolivar, Tennessee, and in 1857 moved to Memphis, where he opened a whole-sale grocery and cotton commission house under the name of Hill and Dorisen. His enterprise was successful until war broke out, and he then returned to his farm near Bolivar. After the war he re-entered business as a partner in the firm of Williamson, Hill and Company. After the death of Mr. Williamson, the firm continued as Hill, Fontaine and Company, and a branch was established at St. Louis in 1878. The rest of Mr. Hill's career was devoted exclusively to dealing in cotton. He was president of the Cotton Exchange in Memphis, president of the Union and Planters Bank, the Memphis Cotton Press and Storage Company, the City Fire and General Insurance Company, the Citizens Street Railway Company and the Chickasaw Land Company, and was vice president of the Pioneer Cotton Mill and the Bluff City Stove Works. He was a director of the Memphis and Charleston Railroad, and the Pratt Coal Mine Company. Mary W. Wood, whom he married, was a daughter of William W. Wood, a banker and planter. The family was related to President James K. Polk.

Mr. and Mrs. Evans became the parents of two children: 1. Olivia Polk, who was born on March 17, 1920. She is the wife of Mr. Joseph Crosby Jefferds of Charleston, West Virginia. 2. Phoebe Airey, who was born on March 13, 1923. She married Jack Petree of Birmingham, Alabama. They now make their home in Memphis. At the time of Mr. Evans' death there were nine grandchildren.

His death, occurring on November 30, 1957, in the Baptist Hospital, Memphis, closed a most distinguished career in the practice of law, and in the service of his fellow citizens.

Tony Black Maxey

Tony Black Maxey's four decades in the practice of law has made him a well-known figure at the Tennessee bar. He practiced at Celina for many years before coming to Livingston. There he conducts a general practice. He has served as mayor of both cities, and also has a most creditable record of service in the Tennessee State Legislature.

A native of Celina, Tennessee, he was born on June 30, 1897, son of Oglesby and Louisiana (Hampton) Maxey. His father was born in Monroe County, Kentucky, in 1863. An attorney, he practiced at Celina for forty years. He also taught school for a number of years in Clay County, and served as Clay County clerk for twelve years. He took an active role in community affairs, his leadership being particularly valuable in the programs to secure good roads and good schools. His wife, the former Louisiana Hampton, was born in 1865 in Clay County, Tennessee, and died at Celina in 1928. She was a gifted musician, playing the piano. Mr. Maxey survived her until 1933, when he died at Celina.

Attending the public schools there, Tony Black Maxey went on to Tennessee Polytechnic School at Cookeville, and for his professional studies, entered Cumberland Law School. Here he took his degree of Bachelor of Laws in 1919.

Admitted to the state bar in that year, he began practice in his native city of Celina, and continued there for twenty-seven years. In 1946 he moved to Livingston, where he has since practiced. Most of Mr. Maxey's record of public service to date had been completed before he left Celina. His fellow citizens sent him to represent them in the Tennessee State Legislature in 1923, his being the Twelfth District, Clay County. Later elected mayor of Celina, he took office in 1925 and served through 1929. In 1957, he was elected mayor of Livingston.

As a lawyer, Mr. Maxey is a member of the Tennessee Bar Association and the American Bar Association. He is affiliated with the lodge of Free and Accepted Masons and the higher bodies of the Masonic order, and he and Mrs. Maxey attended the Church of Christ.

She is the former Miss Mary Kate Stone, and was born on June 7, 1902, at Celina, daughter of William L. and Evelyn (Williams) Stone. Her father, who was born in 1859 in Clay County, was a farmer. He served his county as trustee for six years. His death occurred in Celina in 1928. Mrs. Stone died there in 1935. She too was a native of Clay County.

Miss Stone became the wife of Tony B. Maxey in a ceremony at Celina on September 20, 1920. The couple are the parents of two children: 1. Tony Evelyn, who was born on February 23, 1923. She is married to John Coward; and she has a son, Tony Maxie Ketchersid, by a previous marriage. They live in Oak Ridge. 2. Carey Lou, born April 30, 1925, in Celina. She attended school there, and graduated from Tennessee Polytechnic Institute at Cookeville, where she majored in business administration. For about two years she was instructor in the business department of the Institute. She married Walter Steele, Jr., and they live at Donaldson, Tennessee. They have two children: i. Walter, 3rd, born in 1952. ii. Wayne Hampton, born in 1954.

JESSE WALKER BEASLEY

For more than two and a half decades, Jesse Walker Beasley has been a partner in Dickson's popular pharmacy, the Jackson Drug Store. He has other interests as well, which include banking, the construction industry, and farming.

Born at Centerville in Hickman County, on July 30, 1911, he is a son of Rufus Perry Beasley, M.D., a physician who is still active professionally after having practiced for about fifty years. Dr. Beasley was born March 17, 1886, in Macon County, graduated from the Medical School of the University of

Louisville, Kentucky, and began his practice in Hickman County. After thirteen years there, he moved to Dickson, December 19, 1921, where he has been for the thirty-eight years since. For two terms, he held office as mayor of Dickson. He is past president of the Kiwanis Club there, and also past president of the Chamber of Commerce. Dr. Beasley has a general practice. He makes his home at Dickson as well as practicing there. His wife is the former Miss Willymat Walker. Born July 25, 1888, in Hickman County, she was active in the United Daughters of the Confederacy in her earlier years. Both she and Dr. Beasley are members of the Church of Christ.

Attending the public schools of Dickson, Jesse W. Beasley graduated from high school there, and then attended the University of Tennessee at Knoxville. He first turned his attention to drug store management in 1932, joining Mr. James H. Nicks at that time in the operation of the pharmacy at Dickson which they still own. To prepare himself for his calling, he began taking courses at Crows School of Pharmacy in Atlanta shortly after he had entered partnership with Mr. Nicks, and there he graduated as a pharmacist in 1937. The operation of the Jackson Drug Store has been his major interest but he also owns a farm, where he does general farming and stock raising, producing mostly beef cattle and hogs. He owns an interest in a contracting firm, the Mid-Tennessee Paving Company. Also, for the past fourteen years, he has served on the board of directors of the First Federal Savings and Loan Association of Dickson.

Mr. Beasley holds professional membership in the Tennessee Pharmacy Association and the Chamber of Commerce of his own city. He is a member of the Church of Christ.

In Dickson, on March 5, 1937, Jesse W. Beasley married Katherine Halliburton. She was born at Vanleer, in Dickson County, on March 31, 1916, and is a daughter of John P. and Bessie (Taylor) Halliburton. Her father, now deceased, was in the life insurance and casualty business, with an office at Murfreesboro. Mrs. Beasley is a member of the Garden Club and the Bridge Club in her home city.

The couple are the parents of two children: 1. Wanda Lynn, born July 12, 1940, in Dickson. A graduate of Dickson High School, she is now attending the University of Tennessee at Knoxville. 2. Margaret Ann, born February 12, 1947, in Dickson; attends elementary school.

CARNEY B. NICKS

In recent years, Carney B. Nicks has assumed a prominent role in the business affairs of Dickson. When the Bank of Dickson opened its doors, he assumed duties as its cashier and vice president, and has capably filled both offices since. He is a veteran of naval service in World War II, during which he attained the rank of lieutenant commander.

Born at White Oak Flat, in Dickson County, on April 27, 1915, he is a son of Buckner Clay and Katherine (Lyle) Nicks. His father, born at Bartons Creek, Dickson County, in 1882, entered the merchantile business and became a wholesale grocer, conducting his business at White Oaks Flat. He later conducted a similar enterprise at Dickson, where he also dealt in furniture. He was for a number of years a member of the Dickson Chamber of Commerce and was active in the Church of Christ. He died in 1941. Katherine Lyle, whom he married, was born at Southside in Montgomery County. Surviving her husband, she makes her home at Clarksville, where she teaches piano.

As a boy, Carney B. Nicks attended public school in Dickson, and completed his studies at the David Lipscomb School in Nashville. He then enrolled at the University of Tennessee, where he took his degree of Bachelor of Arts with a major in business administration.

For three years while attending the university, he taught school at Dickson. He was Dickson County Clerk from 1946 to 1954. At the time he entered naval service in 1941, he was engaged as a representative of the E. R. Squibb Pharmaceutical Company. Assigned to an amphibious unit, he saw action in both the European and Pacific Theaters, and took part in the initial landings of our troops in Morocco, the first scene of our conflict against Nazi forces. He went on through the naval supporting actions which accompanied the African, Sicilian and French campaigns, and after being transferred to the Pacific, was in on the assault on Okinawa. He attained the rank of lieutenant commander, and received a Bronze Star and a Silver Star.

In the years which followed World War II, Mr. Nicks was engaged as Dickson County court clerk. When in 1954 the Bank of Dickson was opened, he became vice president and cashier.

He is a member and past president of the Kiwanis Club in his home city, is a member and past commander of the local post of the American Legion, and also belongs to the Veterans of Foreign Wars. Attending the Church of Christ, he has been superintendent of its Sunday school for the past six years. He has consistently taken a constructive interest in civic affairs. He finds sufficient time for outdoor life to indulge in his favorite sport of fishing.

At Dickson, on March 22, 1946, Carney B. Nicks married Jane Reeves, who was born in that city on April 15, 1924. Her father, Hugh Reeves, was also a native of Dickson. He served that community as postmaster for some time, and was also a livestock dealer. His wife was the former Miss Lina Donega, who was born and reared in Dickson County.

Mrs. Nicks attended Dickson schools, graduated from high school there, and attended Stephens College in Missouri. The couple are the parents of two children: 1. Thomas Neil, born June 28, 1948. 2. William Lyle, born September 23, 1952. Both of the children were born in Dickson.

James E. Blount, Sr.

A railroadman throughout his career, James E. Blount, Sr., made his home in Memphis, where he was long identified with the Southern Railway. Members of his family have continued to contribute much to the city.

Born at Holly Springs, Mississippi, on April 11, 1868, he was a son of Wiley E. and Sarah Stewart (Spillers) Blount. The Blount family is descended from forbears who settled in this country prior to the Revolution. William Blount was the first territorial governor of Tennessee, a post to which he was appointed by George Washington. Wiley E. Blount father of James E. Blount, was born on September 3, 1825, in Carroll County, Tennessee, and was married to Sarah Stewart. Spillers at Holly Springs, Mississippi, on March 20, 1864. In his boyhood years, James E. Blount received his education from a private tutor, and he later attended Mississippi Heights Academy, a private school for boys conducted by Professor J. E. Brown and located at Blue Mountain, Mississippi.

Mr. Blount began his career in the railway industry as an engineer with the Illinois Central Railroad in 1897. He worked for that line until 1907, then transferred to the Southern Railway, with which he remained until his retirement in 1943.

He was a member of the lodge of the Free and Accepted Masons, and attended the Methodist Church.

In his native city of Holly Springs, on November 3, 1887, James E. Blount, Sr., married Margaret Eugenia Spillers. Daughter of Wiley Calhoun and Margaret Ann (Stone) Spillers, she was born in Marshall County, Mississippi, on December 8, 1869. Her mother too was a native of that county, but her father was born in Greenfield, South Carolina.

Mr. and Mrs. Blount became the parents of the following children: 1. Wiley Edney, who died in childhood. 2. Joe Thomas, who died in childhood. 3. Laura Alice (Lottie). She graduated from Memphis Law School, and is a member of Phi Delta Delta legal fraternity. She is also a member of the United Daughters of the Confederacy, the National Society of the Dames of the Court of Arms, and the Altrusa Club. 4. Beulah Irwin, who married Walter Garvey, Sr. 5. Wallace Eugene, who was born at Holly Springs on April 16, 1897. After attending schools in Tuscumbia, Alabama, and Corinth, Mississippi, where he graduated from high school, he entered Piedmont College in Lynchburg, Virginia and graduated there, having studied business administration. For a time he was associated with Carter Glass in that city. Entering the United States Army at the time of World War I, he was sent to officers' training camp at Fort Oglethorpe, Georgia, and commissioned a second lieutenant, but the war ended before he saw service. After his discharge he returned to Memphis, where he entered the office of the Standard Oil Company. Deciding to take up sales work, he joined the Grennan Bakery Company for a short time, and later, the Libby, McNeill and Libby Company,

J. C. Blount

W. F. Blount

where he became district manager at Norfolk and at Richmond, and finally at Albany, New York. He traveled throughout the United States and Canada for the firm. In 1937 he returned to Memphis and founded his own company, Blount Brothers, merchandise brokers. He continued to manage this business successfully until 1952, when he left it to devote all his time to private interests. Possessing a keen analytical mind and an exceptional knowledge of the market, he became an expert in stocks and bonds, and continued in his investment work until his death in 1957. He was an ardent sportsman, and fond of hunting and fishing, baseball and aquatics. He was a member of various national food brokerage organizations, and of the Tennessee Club, and was a charter member of the Rivermont Club. He attended the Methodist Church. He was married in Memphis to Jessie Parkin. 6. William R., who was born in October, 1900. He is president and owner of the Blount Barber and Beauty Supply Company in Memphis. He married Thelma Cross, and they are the parents of William R. Blount, Jr., a practicing attorney of Memphis. 7. Eva May, who married A. F. Edwards, Sr. They have one son, A. F. Edwards, Jr. 8. James Edward, born in Water Valley, Mississippi, on October 21, 1905. He graduated from Central High School in Memphis in 1925, then entered Furman University, where he finished the regular four-year course in three years, graduating in 1928. He was a football star at both institutions. Choosing a career in the law, he studied at Harvard Law School, after which he practiced in Memphis. During World War II, he served in the United States Navy. Commissioned a lieutenant, he was in charge of the V-12 training program at the University of South Carolina, in Columbia. He was vice commander for West Tennessee American Veterans of World War II in 1949-1950, and was judge advocate of the Memphis post of the Amvets. He was a member of the Memphis and Shelby County Bar Association. In 1925, while attending Central High School, James E. Blount, Jr., became the first youth elected to the office of boy mayor of the city. His death occurred on September 28, 1959. He was married to the former Miss Sara Armistead, and they had two children: Sandra Lynn, and James E., 3rd, ("Jeb"). 9. Henrietta. She was born in Tuscumbia, Alabama, and makes her home in Memphis, where she was educated.

The death of James E. Blount, Sr., occurred on April 15, 1950, in Memphis, and Mrs. Margaret Eugenia Spillers Blount died in Memphis July 1st, 1951.

ELMER THOMAS BUCKNER

After a number of years' experience operating a furniture business and a funeral parlor at Dickson, Elmer Thomas Buckner chose to concentrate his attention on the mortuary profession. He manages the Dickson Funeral Home at the present time. He has rendered valuable service in municipal office.

Born October 8, 1902, near Ruskin in Dickson County, he is a son of

James Adolphus and Will Ella (Williams) Buckner. Both of his parents were also natives of Dickson County, and his father has spent most of his life as a farmer at Yellow Creek. The Williamsville Inn was operated by Mr. Buckner's maternal ancestors for years before and during the Civil War near Ruskin in Dickson County. It was a stage coach stop. He has been active in the Methodist Church at Union, and Mrs. Buckner, who died in 1945, was also a devoted worker in that congregation.

Attending local public schools, Elmer T. Buckner attended Edgewood High School on Yellow Creek. Early in life he chose funeral directing as his profession, and trained for his calling at the Gupton Jones Mortuary School in Nashville, where he completed his courses in 1926. By that time he had already begun his business and professional activities, having opened a furniture store and funeral home at Dickson in 1924. He continued in both occupations—which in earlier days were closely allied—until 1952. He then disposed of the furniture store, but still continues to operate the Dickson Funeral Home.

A Democrat, Mr. Buckner was formerly a member of the Dickson city council for three years; he also served as mayor pro-tem for the three years. For four years he was chairman of the city gas board.

He has been honored by colleagues in his profession, who elected him president of the Tennessee Funeral and Embalmers Association for the 1950-1951 term. On December 7, 1955, Governor Clement appointed him to a five-year term on the Tennessee Funeral Directors and Embalmers Board, being secretary of the board for one year; he is now president of the board. He has been active in community groups as well. A member of the Lions Club at Dickson, he served as its president in 1950-1951, and is now a director. Affiliated with the Free and Accepted Masons, he is a member of the higher bodies of the order, holds the Thirty-second Degree, and belongs to the Ancient Arabic Order of Nobles of the Mystic Shrine. He is past master of his Blue Lodge, and past patron of the local chapter of the Order of the Eastern Star.

Attending the Methodist Church on Main Street in Dickson, Mr. Buckner is currently serving as a steward. His hobby is floriculture, and he is fond of hunting.

In Dickson County on October 5, 1922, Elmer T. Buckner married Bernice Reed. She was born near Kingston Springs in Cheatham County on March 14, 1903, and is a daughter of Masha Loyd and Martha Elizabeth (Stevens) Reed. Her father too was a native of that county, and was born on June 30, 1879. A carpenter and contractor, he built many of the houses now standing in Dickson. He is deceased, and is survived by his wife, the former Martha Elizabeth Stevens, who was born in Davidson County on October 7, 1876. Mrs. Buckner is active in local organizations, being a past matron of the Order of the Eastern Star, past president of the Parent-Teacher Association, and also past president of the parents' and teachers' group drawing its membership from the entire Twelfth District. She is fond of art, and enjoys painting, in which she possesses considerable skill.

The couple are the parents of two children: 1. Ruthelma, born April 6, 1936, in Nashville. She graduated from Dickson High School and attended Belmont College in Nashville, later taking her degree of Bachelor of Science, in 1957, from Austin Peay College in Clarksville. She concentrated on the study of business and secondary education, and was salutatorian of her class. While at Austin Peay College, she was listed in "Who's Who in American Colleges." She now teaches at Dickson elementary school. 2. Joe Daniel, born September 16, 1938, in Nashville; graduated from Dickson High School, and is now attending Austin Peay College. He graduated from the Southern Academy of Clinical Technology in 1958, being valedictorian of his class.

William Gideon Duffey

In the more than three decades during which he was active in the furniture sales business in Memphis, William Gideon Duffey established and successfully managed a number of stores, building a chain of outlets which attracted many faithful customers through the sale of quality products, and fair dealings. He was a man of many interests, widely traveled, and an earnest and effective worker for community causes.

A native of Humboldt, Mr. Duffey was born on March 13, 1890. He was a son of William A., a large landowner and stock raiser, and Martha (DeLoach) Duffey, both of whom were born and reared in Humboldt. The future furniture dealer attended the public schools of that city and of Bells, Tennessee, and completed his advanced courses at Vanderbilt University. Early in his business career he chose the furniture sales field, and operated a store at Humboldt, dealing in home furnishings at both wholesale and retail, before moving to Memphis about 1920.

There he again entered the furniture business, and the original store which he opened in that city grew under his capable management into a chain which included one on Main Street at Pontotoc, several others on Main, and one on Summer in Highland Heights. These he successfully operated until his retirement, three years before his death.

Those acquainted with Mr. Duffey and with his record as a merchant and a citizen have commented on his qualities of extreme generosity and sympathy; and although his many deeds of charity and kindness were unobtrusive and unpublicized, the value of these traits became generally known throughout the community. He was fond of organizational activities, and was a member of the Chickasaw Country Club, and a former member of the Tennessee Club and the lodge of the Benevolent and Protective Order of Elks. Affiliated with the Free and Accepted Masons, he was a member of the higher bodies of Masonry, holding the Thirty-second Degree, and belonged to the Ancient Arabic Order of Nobles of the Mystic Shrine. He was a communicant of the Baptist Church.

In Memphis, on December 27, 1921, William Gideon Duffey married Mary Mockbee. Born at Bells, she is a daughter of Richard Henry and Anne

(Brigham) Mockbee. Her father was born at Dover, Tennessee, son of Thomas Dye and Elizabeth (Tayloe) Mockbee. He spent his boyhood years at Dover, and was educated at Lebanon. Mrs. Duffey was reared at Bells, and attended schools there.

Mr. and Mrs. Duffey had no children. His death occurred at his home on Cadraca Drive in Memphis on December 7, 1958.

FRANK FREEMAN SOWELL

Frank Freeman Sowell turned an after school job into a full-time business career. While attending school in Columbia, he worked for the Oaks and Nichols Funeral Home. His industry and aptitude were rewarded when he was made a partner in this firm in 1948. A friendly, enthusiastic man, he belongs to numerous clubs and organizations in Columbia.

He was born on July 6, 1923, in Columbia, son of Frank Chaffin Sowell, born in Maury County in 1889, who died in Columbia in 1941, and Leatha (Freeman) Sowell, born in Robertson County in 1891 and died in 1952 in Columbia.

The senior Mr. Sowell was a member of the Odd Fellows, holding offices at state and local levels. He served on the Orphans' Home Board and was a deacon at West 7th Street Church of Christ in Columbia. His wife was a charter member of the Andrews Parent-Teacher Association in Columbia.

Frank Sowell attended Central High School in Columbia, where he was president of the student body. He entered service in 1943 in the Army Air Force and served overseas with the Eighth Air Force. A corporal, he participated in five campaigns in the European Theater. On his return from service in 1945, he attended the Gupton Jones Mortuary School in Nashville, graduating in 1947. He returned to the Oaks and Nichols Funeral Home and has been with them since.

He is a member of the American Legion, the Council of the Junior Order, Odd Fellows, is a past president of the Lions Club, belongs to the Columbia Chamber of Commerce and the Maury County Horsemen's Association.

He married Dorothy Gray at Columbia on May 11, 1943, prior to entering ing service. Mrs. Sowell was born on October 30, 1922, at Santa Fe, Tennessee, where she graduated from Santa Fe High School. Her parents live in Santa Fe where Mr. Sam Gray, born in 1890, is a farmer and carpenter. His wife, Gertrude, was born in 1891.

Frank and Dorothy Sowell have three children: 1. Jane Gray, born May 24, 1947. 2. Charles Anthony, born August 13, 1949. "Tony," at the age of eight, rescued his father from a swimming pool at a motel in Texas in June, 1958. 3. Edna Beth, born October 25, 1953.

Marshall Ledbetter

Marshall Ledbetter was born in Marshall County on October 29, 1914. His father, Ernest Ledbetter, born July 18, 1893, was a farmer and groceryman to the time of his death in 1951. His mother, Lily (Powell) Ledbetter lives in Columbia.

Marshall Ledbetter was educated in the public schools of Marshall County. He started the Victory Van Lines, local and long distance movers, in 1940 in Columbia. Owner and manager of this business, Marshall Ledbetter has also become a moving agent for North American Van Lines. He is a member of the Masons, the Shrine, the Elks and a Woodsman of the World. He also belongs to the Rotary Club, and is its president, the Columbia Chamber of Commerce, the Junior Order of American Mechanics, is a vice president of the Columbia Merchants Association and has been chairman of the Cancer Research Drive for two years.

He married Mary Alma Greer in Springfield, Tennessee in 1951. She was born in Hickman County on November 15, 1925, is a graduate of Hickman County High School and Columbia College, and is employed by the Tennessee Farm Bureau in Columbia. Her parents, George Rucker and Elsie (Anderson) Greer, live on a farm in Hickman County.

Mr. Ledbetter has two children by a former marriage: Marshall Powell, Jr., born March 21, 1936, attending Vanderbilt University, where he majors in business administration; 2. Betty Ann, born March 6, 1939, and now majoring in Education at the University of Tennessee.

Marshall and Mary Alma (Greer) Ledbetter have a son, Gary Clement, born December 15, 1954, in Columbia.

Edward Hull Crump

In any history of the city of Memphis, the name and personality of Edward Hull Crump stands out as a decisive influence in municipal and state affairs. A business man whose interests in his early years were many and varied, he became head of one of the largest insurance, mortgage and real estate firms in the South. Over a period of a half-century, he was a dominant figure in political affairs, serving as mayor of his city, as United States congressman, and in other offices. There are few phases of life in his beloved home region in which his constructive efforts were absent.

Mr. Crump was born near Holly Springs, Mississippi, on October 2, 1874, and was a son of Edward Hull, Sr., and Mollie (Nelms) Crump. His father was a farmer, who served in the Confederate States Army, holding a commission as captain in General John Morgan's Cavalry. The younger E. H. Crump's formal education was received entirely in the public schools of Holly Springs. In his early years he worked in a printer's office there, and he later engaged in general farm work on his uncle's plantation near Lula, Mississippi. He gained business experience working as clerk in a general store there.

When he first moved to Memphis in 1893, he took a position as clerk in a cotton office. He left to join the staff of a real estate office as accountant in 1895, and he later became treasurer of a firm manufacturing buggies, wagons, and harness, and selling them at wholesale and retail. Mr. Crump acquired ownership of that concern in 1903, and changed its name to E. H. Crump Buggy and Harness Manufacturing Company. He disposed of the company about 1910. After that, he devoted his full time to political activities and to public office until 1921, as detailed in subsequent paragraphs. In the latter year, he organized the firm of Crump and Trezevant, Inc., dealing in mortgage loans, real estate and insurance. He acquired Mr. Trezevant's interest in 1936, and at that time the corporation name was changed to E. H. Crump and Company. The veteran business and political leader continued as its president until his death, and his efforts and prestige built it into the largest insurance agency in the South, and one of the region's largest mortgage and real estate firms.

In addition to these varied activities, over a period of fifty years, Mr. Crump operated two Mississippi cotton plantations. Also for a number of years, through ownership vested in E. H. Crump and Company, he operated a number of Coca-Cola bottling plants in New York State. These holdings were very profitably sold to the New York Coca-Cola Bottling Company. While Mr. Crump was stockholder in a number of banks, he declined numerous requests to serve as director.

Mr. Crump's interest in politics began early in his career. He attended the Democratic state conventions of 1902 and 1904, and in 1905, was elected to the Memphis Board of Public Works. He served as fire and police commissioner in 1907. First elected mayor of Memphis in 1909, he served for three terms to 1916, and was returned to office in 1939, providing one of the most dynamic periods of leadership in the city's history. He was county trustee—a post with the duties of treasurer—four terms, which covered the years from 1916 to 1924. Mr. Crump attended his first Democratic National Convention at Baltimore in 1912. He was the party's delegate-at-large, at New York in 1924, and at Houston, Texas, in 1928. He attended the Democratic National Convention at Chicago in 1932, when Franklin D. Roosevelt was first nominated for the Presidency. Meantime, in 1931, he had taken his seat in the Congress of the United States, and he served with distinction in the Seventy-second and Seventy-third Congresses from the Tenth Congressional District of Tennessee, his tenure continuing through 1935. Once again in 1936, he attended the Democratic National Convention in Philadelphia; and he attended the party's Chicago convention in 1940. Mr. Crump became a member of the Democratic State Committee of Tennessee in 1926, and he was for some time National Committeeman for Tennessee.

He served as a member of the Sesquicentennial Committee at Philadelphia in 1925, and as national advisory committeeman for Tennessee at the New

York World's Fair of 1939-1940. He was chairman of the Mississippi River Bridge Commission at the time the new bridge linking Memphis with the state of Arkansas was constructed.

Mr. Crump was a member of the Memphis Country Club, the Tennessee Club, and Five Lakes Hunting Club. He and his family were communicants of the Episcopal Church.

On January 13, 1902, in Memphis, Edward Hull Crump, Jr., married Bessie Byrd McLean, daughter of Robert Moore and Carrie (Bruce) McLean. The couple became the parents of the following children: 1. Edward Hull, Jr., who was born on May 8, 1903. 2. Robert McLean, born December 29, 1905. 3. John, born November 5, 1910.

Mr. Crump's death, on October 16, 1954, deprived his state of one of the most eminent and capable leaders in its history. To his fellow Memphians, a phrase engraved on the large memorial, which was dedicated in 1957, will be remembered as expressive of the man and his accomplishments: "His was a life of dedicated public service, wise counsel, human understanding, designed to make Memphis the city of good abode."

FREDERICK ISAAC WOMACK

Probably the youngest man ever to have served in the Tennessee State Legislature, Frederick Isaac Womack filled his first term there while attending Cumberland University, and he served a second term after graduation from law school. Establishing his law practice in Fayetteville, he is now mayor of that city.

He was born there on January 13, 1931, and is a son of Charles Isaac and Maida M. (Foster) Womack. His father, born in Bedford County, Tennessee, in 1893, now makes his home at Fayetteville, in retirement following an active career as grocer and merchant. For thirty-five years he owned and operated Womack's Grocery in Fayetteville, and was also in the real estate business. He served in the United States Army during World War I, remaining stateside. He is now minister and elder at the Washington Street Church of Christ in Fayetteville. One of his ancestors, Jacob Womack, was one of the original thirteen commissioners of the Wautauga Settlement. Charles I. Womack attended the old Winchester Military Academy, at Winchester, Tennessee. His wife, the former Maida M. Foster, was born in Giles County, Tennessee, in 1893.

As a boy, Frederick I. Womack attended the Robert E. Lee Grammar School in Lincoln County, and he completed his secondary studies at Central High School in Fayetteville, where he graduated in 1949. He then enrolled at Cumberland University, attending its colleges of arts, science and law. He took his degree of Bachelor of Laws there in 1954.

While still attending Cumberland University, he was elected to serve in the Tennessee State Legislature in 1952-1953. Being twenty-one years old at the time, he probably established a new record for youthfulness among the state's legislators. After graduation from law school in 1954, he again served in the legislature for the 1954-1955 term.

Also in 1954, he commenced his law practice at Fayetteville. He had served as chief journal clerk of the Limited Constitutional Convention of Tennessee in 1953, and was Fayetteville's city attorney in 1955-1956. On October 1, 1956, he was elected mayor of Fayetteville, and that position he still holds. While still in his late twenties, he already has to his credit a record in public office, and in the capable service of his fellow citizens, which few men can duplicate in a long lifetime.

As a lawyer, Mr. Womack belongs to the American Bar Association, the Tennessee State Bar Association and the Fayetteville Bar Association, as well as Delta Theta Phi legal fraternity. While at Cumberland University, he was president of the Blue Key Honor Society, and he was listed in "Who's Who Among American College and University Students" for the years 1953-1954.

His memberships include the Lions Club, the Rod and Gun Club, the United Sons of Confederate Veterans and the Benevolent and Protective Order of Elks. He serves on the executive committee of the Tennessee State Young Democrats Club. He and his family attend the Church of Christ. One of Mr. Womack's interests is banking, and he is a stockholder in the Lincoln County Bank and the Union National Bank, both in Fayetteville.

In that city, on June 12, 1955, Frederick Isaac Womack married Marian Catherine Talley. Born in Fayetteville on May 25, 1935, she is a daughter of Charles A. and Lyndall (Carter) Talley. Her father is city engineer there. Mrs. Womack attended its public schools, and graduated from Middle Tennessee State College. The couple are the parents of one daughter, Valerie Lee, who was born on June 25, 1956.

FRANK L. GOODLETT

Following many years of varied business experience, which included trust company, cashiership and newspaper publishing, Frank L. Goodlett established his own real estate and insurance business at Clarksville. A resident of that city for three decades, he has played a constructive part in its civic and organizational affairs.

Born west of New Providence, in Montgomery County, on December 18, 1898, he is a son of Adam Gold and Lucy (Garrott) Goodlett. His grandfather, Adam Gibb Goodlett, was a soldier in the Confederate States Army. His great-grandfather named Adam Goodlett, established the town of Goodlettsville, Tennessee. He was a physician and also a Presbyterian minister. The family is of Scottish and Irish descent. Adam Gold Goodlett was born October 31, 1870, at Charlotte, Tennessee. He became a farmer, and also sold life insurance for the Northwestern Mutual Life Insurance Company. Previous to that business connection he had been with the Carsey Tobacco Company in

Clarksville for about ten years. He had a reputation in his area as a fine pen-man, and always got the assignment of preparing wedding invitations and similar forms. He was fond of race horses, and raised Jersey cattle. His death occurred at Clarksville on October 30, 1913. Lucy Garrott, whom he married, was born in South Christian County, Kentucky, on November 4, 1872, the daughter of Marcellus Aurelius Garrott. After rearing her children, she be-came a school teacher, teaching for fifteen years in the Clarksville public schools, where she was also for two years school librarian. Mrs. Goodlett died February 3, 1955.

This couple were the parents of the following children: 1. Collier White-field, born September 27, 1896, in New Providence, Tennessee. An attorney at Clarksville, he married Elizabeth Tandy Trabue, they had two children: i. Col-lier Whitefield, Jr., born April 17, 1920, attorney and Clarksville city judge, married Hazel Edwards; they have three children: Jean Tandy, born August 18, 1945, Collier Whitefield, III, born August 25, 1946, and May Miller, born July 8, 1953; ii. Joy Gold, born April 3, 1929, married William H. Shelton, two children: Beth Trabue, born September 30, 1951, and William Scott, born February 22, 1954. 2. Frank L., subject of this sketch, whose wife and children are listed later herein. 3. Baxter Gold, born October 14, 1902, in New Provi-dence. An attorney at West Palm Beach, Florida, he was married to Margaret Siebert. They have one daughter: Margaret Gold. 4. Clifton Vera, born June 12, 1905, at Kenwood, near Clarksville, Tennessee. He works for the Tennessee Valley Authority as soil erosion adviser, and lives at Dickson, Tennessee. He married Lora Mooney of Birmingham, Alabama. They have two children: a daughter Mary Lu, born February 18, 1933, who is married to Marshall Swift of Dickson; and a son Clifton Goodlett, Jr., born September 18, 1939, a stu-dent at the University of Tennessee. 5. Florence Clark, born June 18, 1907, in Kenwood. She was married to Walter C. Strassheim of Park Ridge, Illinois. They have two children: i. Walter C. Strassheim, Jr., born March 16, 1935, married Betty Bartee, and they have one child, Hope born March 10, 1958; and ii. Betty Lu, student, born November 29, 1943. 6. Martha Manning, born March 8, 1913, married Joseph W. Pennock, of New York, New York and they have a son Joseph W. Jr., born September 15, 1947.

Attending local public schools, Frank L. Goodlett graduated from Clarks-ville High School, and then attended Vanderbilt University, for a short time. In 1917 he commenced his business career with the Security Trust Company of Clarksville. The following year he left for military service, and took officer's training at Camp Taylor, Louisville, Kentucky. However, the war ended before he was assigned to a combat outfit or sent overseas, and he returned to his con-nection with Security Trust Company. Within a short time—before he had reached his majority—he had been promoted to cashier with this trust company and held that position until resigning to enter newspaper work in 1927.

Meantime, in 1918, he had undertaken a second business venture, joining

George Fort as a partner in the real estate and insurance business. In 1927 he and J. Ray King purchased Mr. Fort's interest.

In 1927 he became general manager of the Leaf-Chronicle, the daily newspaper published at Clarksville, a position he held until 1940. During this period the Century and a Quarter and the Clarksville Sesqui-Centennial historical editions were published. He left the newspaper field to return to the real estate and insurance business, establishing his own agency in February 1940. In 1956 Mr. Goodlett and his sons erected the Goodlett Building at 324 Franklin Street, Clarksville, their offices being on its first floor.

He is active in the Chamber of Commerce of that city, and belongs to the post of the American Legion and the Lodge of Free and Accepted Masons. In Masonry he is a member of the higher bodies, belonging to the Ancient Arabic Order of Nobles of the Mystic Shrine. Mr. Goodlett's favorite outdoor sport is golf. He has been a member of the First Baptist Church, Clarksville, since 1912 and is now chairman of its official board.

At Clarksville, on July 12, 1928, Frank L. Goodlett married Sue Neblett Ely. Born in Clarksville on June 11, 1901, she is a daughter of Edward Lawrence and Fannie (Neblett) Ely. Her father too was a native of Clarksville, born March 5, 1870, and died there in 1937. For some years he was identified with a candy company in Cincinnati, Ohio. He was a member of the Methodist Church. Mrs. Ely was a native of Clarksville, born October 20, 1870 and died there. Their only other child was Lawrence S. Ely, of Dayton, Ohio, now deceased. Mrs. Goodlett attended the public schools of Cincinnati, graduated from the University of Cincinnati, and studied music at the Cincinnati Conservatory. She plays the piano. She is a member of the Methodist Church and of its Missionary Society, and is also identified with the American Legion Auxiliary.

The couple are the parents of two children: 1. Frank Gold, who was born on August 19, 1930, at Clarksville. He graduated from the high school there, and from Vanderbilt University, in 1952, with the degree of Bachelor of Science in Civil Engineering. He took advanced courses at Massachusetts Institute of Technology, where he received a Master's degree in construction engineering. He is now in partnership with his father and brother in the real estate, insurance and construction business. From May, 1953 to July, 1956, he served in the United States Navy. He is now a lieutenant in the Navy Engineers Reserve Corps. He is a member of the Chamber of Commerce and the Junior Chamber of Commerce in his home city. He is also a Kiwanian. 2. Edward Lawrence, born on March 26, 1934, in Clarksville. He graduated from high school there, and from Austin Peay State College with the degree of Bachelor of Science. He entered the army in 1956, and was stationed at Fort Eustis, Virginia, and served six months at Thule Air Force Base in Greenland. He is a partner with his father and brother in the real estate, insurance, and

Murrel F Acroyd

W.H. Acroyd

construction business. He is a member of Civitan, the Chamber of Commerce, and Junior Chamber of Commerce.

WALTER LESLIE ACROYD

Joining Sears, Roebuck and Company as a packer in its Chicago plant, Walter Leslie Acroyd spent the remaining years of his career with this great nationwide merchandising organization, and in his later years filld the position of head of its Memphis branch. In that city he was very active in civic affairs—the Chamber of Commerce, Community Fund and the Cotton Carnival.

Born in Chicago, Illinois, on July 30, 1891, he was a son of James William and Elizabeth Jane (Warnock) Acroyd. His father was a native of Doncaster, England, born on October 12, 1857, and he died on January 30, 1913. Mrs. Acroyd, born at Douglass, Michigan, on August 25, 1863, died on September 29, 1937. Walter L. Acroyd attended the public schools of his native city, and was eighteen years old when, on October 14, 1909, he entered the employment office of Sears, Roebuck and Company in Chicago. This was four years after the large West Side store had been completed. He was given a position as a packer, and after a time his abilities led to a transfer to another department where he assumed various duties in the operating field, advancing to the position of floor manager. He was later made a buyer in the same department, and remained in that capacity until 1920. Transferred to Philadelphia when the company's plant was opened there in that year, he managed four successive departments over the next several years. In the last of these four posts, he was manager of Department 12 when the big boom came in the phonograph industry, and he successfully managed that department as well. He was next named assistant to the merchandise superintendent of Department 133, also in Philadelphia.

Mr. Acroyd thus possessed a well-rounded knowledge of merchandising and operating procedures when he was sent to Memphis in 1927, to assume duties as the first general manager of Sears, Roebuck and Company's branch in that city. He continued his duties in the same capacity for a full quarter-century, retiring in 1952. Through years marked by a depression, floods and crop failures, he brought dependable and effective leadership to the organization.

Mr. Acroyd found time for a variety of other activities as well. Until 1952 he was a member of the board of Le Bonheur Children's Hospital, and he also served on the board of the Oakville Sanatorium. He was an active backer of the Young Men's Christian Association, and gave valuable support to campaigns supporting Southwestern University. In 1932 he was chairman of the Community Fund, and continued his support of its campaign in succeeding years. He also took a full part in the program of the Memphis Cotton Carnival, which he helped to reactivate in the early 1930s. He had held office as vice president of the Chamber of Commerce, and as vice president of the

Rotary Club. He served on the board of the Tri-State Fair, and on the local board of the Salvation Army. His memberships included the Tennessee Club, Memphis Country Club, and the Newcomen Society of North America. He and his family attended Idlewild Presbyterian Church.

At Chicago, Illinois, on October 7, 1914, Walter Leslie Acroyd married Winifred Murrel Franklin. Born at Michigan City, Indiana, on February 28, 1891, she was a daughter of Robert G. and Anna Bell (Smith) Franklin. Her father was born at Boromanville, Canada, on September 5, 1857, and her mother on September 11, 1862. Mr. and Mrs. Acroyd became the parents of two children: 1. Helen Ruth, who was born on July 8, 1916. She married Robert A. Fleck, and they have two sons: i. Robert A., Jr., born on November 5, 1943. ii. John Acroyd, born September 15, 1947. 2. John Franklin, born May 9, 1926. He is a navy veteran of World War II and is associated with Union Planters National Bank of Memphis. He married Dorris June Blake, and they have two children: i. John Franklin, Jr., born on May 15, 1957. ii. Elizabeth June, born August 2, 1958.

Mr. Acroyd's useful career in business leadership and civic service ended with his death on October 6, 1954. Mrs. Acroyd died on July 4, 1959.

SIDNEY GERALD ALLEN

Since the beginning of his career, Sidney Gerald Allen has been in the concrete business at Memphis, where he is now president of Allen's Ready Mix Concrete Company.

A native Memphian, he was born on July 23, 1903, son of Harry Bertrand and Sara D. (Glass) Allen. Both of his parents were born in Nashville. Harry B. Allen became a contractor in Memphis, and was active in the business in that city for forty years before his retirement. The public elementary schools of Memphis provided Sidney G. Allen with his early education, and he completed his high school studies at Greenville, Mississippi and Florence, Alabama.

At the beginning of his career, he turned his attention to the mixing and distribution of concrete for construction projects, and was in business for himself for about a decade before he organized his present firm, Allen's Ready Mix Concrete Company, which has its headquarters at 1572 Chelsea Avenue in Memphis. He has been its sole owner since it was organized.

He is a member of the Colonial Country Club and the lodge of Free and Accepted Masons; and as a member of the higher bodies of Masonry, belongs to the Ancient Arabic Order of Nobles of the Mystic Shrine. He is fond of fishing and golfing. He attends the Christian Church, while Mrs. Allen is a communicant of the Union Avenue Baptist Church.

She is the former Miss Purnie Ann Poole, and was born in Shobonier, Illinois, daughter of James Marion and Rosetta (Galyean) Poole. Her father, a builder and contractor in Illinois, was a native of Kentucky and her mother of Illinois. When Mrs. Allen was young her family moved to Memphis, and she passed the years of her girlhood there. She became the wife of Sidney Gerald Allen in a ceremony in Memphis on August 21, 1924. Mrs. Allen is a member of the Celeste Allen Circle of the Kings Daughters, and also of the Minerva Club of Southwestern University in Memphis. The couple are the parents of one son, William Blair Allen, who was born in Memphis on December 29, 1930. He graduated from Central High School in Memphis, and received his degree of Bachelor of Science at Southwestern University in that city. During 1953-1954, he served in the United States Marine Corps, in which he held a lieutenant's commission while in active service, and he retains the rank of captain in the Marine Corps Reserve. William Blair Allen married Dorothy Julia Santos, a native of Boston, Massachusetts. The couple are the parents of two children: i. William Blair, Jr., born on February 17, 1956. ii. Richard Sidney, born June 13, 1958.

CLARENCE DUDLEY DEATON, JR.

Following his return from military service in World War II, Clarence Dudley Deaton, Jr., joined his father in founding what later became one of Memphis' prosperous transportation firms, B. and M. Express, Inc. He served in the office of vice president of this concern until its recent sale to Transcon Lines.

A native of Dennis, Mississippi, Mr. Deaton was born on July 14, 1922, and is a son of Clarence Dudley and Alta Mae (Parsons) Deaton. Both of his parents were likewise born in Mississippi. However, in Clarence D. Deaton, Jr.'s early years the family moved to Alabama, and he attended public schools in Cullman and Birmingham. After graduation from high school, he entered the University of Alabama, where he was a student until he entered the United States Army in 1942. Assigned to the Ordnance Corps, he served as a master sergeant with the Third Army in Europe for two years, and received his honorable discharge in 1945.

When he returned to civilian life, Mr. Deaton became vice president of B. & M. Express, Inc., which he and his father founded. Father and son continued to manage this firm until it was recently sold to Transcon Lines in 1959. He is now regional manager of Transcon Lines.

Mr. Deaton is a member of the Chickasaw Country Club and the Rivermont Club. His fraternity is Pi Kappa Phi, and he is a member of St. Luke's Methodist Church. His favorite sport is fishing.

At San Luis Obispo, California, on October 23, 1942, Clarence Dudley Deaton, Jr., married Elouise Thomson. A native of Danville, Arkansas, she is a daughter of William Hatton and Clyde Olive (Sellars) Thomson. Her father too was born in Danville, while her mother is a native of New Blaine, Arkansas. Mr. and Mrs. Deaton are the parents of two children: 1. Rebecca, who was born on October 27, 1947. 2. Clarence Dudley, 3rd, born on July 13, 1950.

EDMUND GREEN HARDER

From the early years of his career, Edmund, known as Edward, Green Harder has been engaged in civil service work in connection with the postal system. For more than a decade, he has capably filled the position of postmaster at Linden.

He is a native of Perry County, and was born on December 11, 1894, son of Frank W. and Mary (Bates) Harder. His parents were also born in that county, his father in 1872 and his mother the following year. Both are deceased. Frank W. Harder taught school for about forty years in Perry County. At the same time he engaged in farming, raising corn and peanuts as well as general crops. A communicant of the Primitive Baptist Church, he served as clerk of his congregation for about forty years. His father, William H. Harder, had served as a captain in the Confederate States Army, and was wounded at the Battle of Shiloh. His wife was Sarah Anderson.

Edward G. Harder received his entire formal education in the public schools of Perry County. Immediately after completing his studies, he entered civil service work in 1920, starting as a rural mail carrier and served for twenty-seven years in his home county. He became postmaster at Linden in 1946, and has held the position since.

He is a veteran of military service in World War I, having entered the army on May 27, 1918, and served until June 19, 1919. He was overseas for ten months. After returning home he taught in the public school at Lego, Perry County, for one year. He is a member of the American Legion, and is a Democrat in politics. While he is not interested in organizations of a purely civic or social nature, he is active in the Primitive Baptist Church, as his father was before him. Since 1940 he has served as home service chairman of Perry County Chapter of the American Red Cross. Since 1951, he has been a minister of the church in Perry County, and he has served his congregation as deacon for about six years.

On December 3, 1919, Edward Green Harder married Bonnie B. Kirk. Also a native of Perry County, she was born on May 25, 1901, and is a daughter of John N. and Emma (Coleman) Kirk. Both of her parents were born in Perry County. Her father, who was a veterinarian, a stockman and a farmer, is deceased, but her mother, who was born in 1880, survives. Mr. and Mrs. Harder are the parents of the following children: 1. Mary E., who was born on January 24, 1921, in Perry County. She attended the public elementary and high schools of Linden and graduated from Murray State College at Murray, Kentucky, where she majored in public school music. She also has a Master's degree from Austin Peay College. She plays the piano and is a vocalist. She is married to Thomas K. Savage of Linden, and they live in Clarksville. He is dean of students at Austin Peay College, and holds a degree of Doctor of Education from the University of Tennessee. Dr. and Mrs. Savage have five children: i. Kathy Lynne, born on January 4, 1947. ii. Susan Elaine, born on

December 13, 1948. iii. Marsha Kent, born on January 12, 1952. iv. Bonnie Alice, born on September 15, 1953. v. Rosemary Anne, born on April 7, 1956. 2. Flora Mavis, who was born on October 25, 1924, in Linden. She attended Western College at Bowling Green, Kentucky, and a business school at Jackson, Tennessee. She married Weldon W. Ragan, who comes from Dyersburg, and is now a merchant at Brownsville. They have two children: i. William Ronald, born on September 15, 1945. ii. Gwendolyn, born on February 18, 1950. 3. Eddye Mildred, born October 4, 1927, in Linden. She attended the elementary and high schools there, and graduated from Lambuth College, Jackson, Tennessee, with a degree of Bachelor of Science. She later took her Master of Arts degree at Austin Peay College, and she now teaches school at New Providence, Tennessee. She is active in the Methodist Church. 4. Martha Brown, born December 31, 1933, in Linden. She attended schools there, and for two years was a student at Martin College, Pulaski, Tennessee. She then transferred to Peabody College in Nashville, where she took her Bachelor of Science degree. She also has a Master's degree from Austin Peay College. She is former secretary at the high school in Clarksville, she is now teaching at Cumberland University, Lebanon, Tennessee. She too is active in the Methodist Church, being a soloist in its choir.

COLONEL ROANE WARING

The late Colonel Roane Waring made invaluable and lasting contributions to Memphis and his fellow citizens. He was a constructive worker in every community activity for over fifty years, and will be remembered as one who was "big of body, big of voice and very big of heart."

Born in Memphis, on July 20, 1881, he was the son of Thomas Roane and Elizabeth (Ashe) Waring.

Colonel Waring attended Christian Brothers College, where he graduated in 1899 with the degree of Bachelor of Arts. He then went to the University of Virginia, where he received his degree of Bachelor of Laws in 1902. He began his practice of law in Memphis in 1903, and in 1906 became associated with the law firm of Wright, Peters and Wright. General Luke E. Wright, senior member of this firm, was Governor-General of the Philippines, Ambassador to Japan and, later, Secretary of War under Theodore Roosevelt. In 1913 Colonel Waring became a member of the firm of Wright, Miles, Waring and Walker, which later became Waring, Walker, Cox & Lewis, of which he was senior partner at the time of his death, and which is the oldest law firm in Memphis.

In the course of his practice he represented The Memphis Street Railway Company, and in 1934 became its president and general counsel. He retired as president on January 1, 1958, but remained active as a director and member of the executive committee until his death. He served as a member of the board of directors of the American Transit Association and became its president in 1944.

Colonel Waring's distinguished military career began in 1903, when he enlisted as a private in Company E of the Tennessee National Guard. He remained in the Tennessee National Guard until 1916, when he resigned with the rank of lieutenant colonel. In 1917, at the request of the Governor, he organized a regiment of infantry, and was assigned to the 2nd Tennessee Infantry, later a part of the 119th Infantry. He was later transferred to the 33rd Division as Assistant Chief of Staff, G-3. He was awarded the Silver Star for valor on the battlefield. At the close of World War I, he entered the Reserve Corps as a colonel of infantry, and commanded the 324th Infantry Reserve for eight years. He was placed on the inactive list in 1942, and was retired in 1948 with the rank of colonel.

During World War II, Colonel Waring served as Civilian Consultant to the Secretary of War, and Special Consultant to General Brehon Somerville, Commander of the Army Service Forces. He was later appointed Civilian Aide to the Secretary of Army, which appointment he held at the time of his death.

Upon his return to civilian life in 1919 he took a leading part in forming the American Legion, and attended the St. Louis Caucus that year as head of the Tennessee Delegation, and was named in the Act of Congress as one of its founders. He organized and became the first commander of the Department of Tennessee, and was again commander some years later, thereby becoming the only person to serve two terms in this office. He also served twice as commander of his post in Memphis. He served on the National Executive Committee of The American Legion for nine consecutive years, and in 1942, was elected national commander. It was in that capacity that he so forcefully voiced the Legion's appeal to go all-out in the prosecution of World War II. At the invitation of the War Department he visited North Africa to observe and report upon the Army in its first conflict with the Nazi forces. He was later instrumental in broadening the Legion's charter to admit to membership veterans of World War II. Commenting on his role in Legion leadership over the years, an editorial writer in the Commercial Appeal said of him:

His interest in The American Legion stemmed from that organization's inception at Paris, and it never flagged from that time forward. His contribution of effort and his devotion to it on all levels-local, state and national— were such as to earn for him the National Commandership.

It was fortunate for the nation that he held that high office during the critical 1942-43 period, when survival depended on an all-out effort in every phase of national activity. Commander Waring mobilized the Legion and all of its influence behind the war effort and the Armed Forces. He undertook innumerable missions at the behest of the Government either for morale or logistical purposes. He failed in none.

Active in the Chamber of Commerce in Memphis, Colonel Waring held the office of president for three successive terms.

As a lawyer, he was a member of the Memphis and Shelby County Bar Association, the Tennessee Bar Association, and the American Bar Association. His other memberships included the Army-Navy Club of Memphis, the Rotary Club, Tennessee Club, Executives Club, and Memphis Yacht Club.

He was a Roman Catholic, a communicant of Blessed Sacrament Church in Memphis.

On October 17, 1906, Colonel Waring married Grace Titus Ford, daughter of Dr. Peter Richardson and Molly (Strange) Ford. They had three children, Mary Elizabeth, deceased, who was the wife of Coe Stone, Grace Ann Waring and Roane Waring, Jr., who is married to the former Elizabeth Fauntleroy.

Colonel Waring's sudden death on September 9, 1958, represented the loss of one of Memphis' most respected citizens. A lengthy editorial in "The Commercial Appeal" treated his career rather fully, and from it the following passages are excerpted, as representing his community's regard for an honored soldier, a tireless and effective organizational leader, a brilliant attorney, and a devoted citizen:

Colonel Roane Waring's seventy-seven years were so full, so robust and so achieving that those who would do eulogistic justice to his memory will find that an all-encompassing tribute would violate all rule of brevity.

He was learned in the law, particularly corporation law. He was the successful operating head of The Memphis Street Railway Company. He was a vocal and indefatigable champion of private industry and what is broadly termed free enterprise. He was a busy, hard working man all of the time. . . . He never dodged a fight but he held no grudges and he forgave and forgot quickly. . . . Roane Waring was a good man to have around in time of trouble, whether the source be war, flood or pestilence. . . . He was an early and implacable foe of communism and its American sympathizers and fellow travelers.

His was a pure and unselfish love of country and for this was the most marked. . . .

Roane Waring never left anybody in doubt as to where he stood on any issue and there was never indirection in his doing. . . . Memphis will miss him.

James Henry Nicks

Trained as a pharmacist, James Henry Nicks has been active in the management of the Jackson Drug Company at Dickson from the early years of his career, being co-owner. His community service has included tenure on his county's school board.

Born at Charlotte, Tennessee, on April 9, 1909, he is the eldest of four sons of Buckner Clay and Katherine (Lyle) Nicks. His father, born in Dickson County in 1882, was a merchant and also a traveling representative for the Dickson Wholesale Grocery Company. He at one time held public office as Dickson County trustee, and he was a member of the Chamber of Commerce of his home city. Both he and Mrs. Nicks were members of the Church of

Christ. Buckner C. Nicks died in 1941, but she survives him and makes her home in Dickson. She was born in Montgomery County on January 23, 1886.

James H. Nicks attended the public elementary and high schools of Dickson, then entered the University of Tennessee. He completed his courses there in 1930 as a graduate in Pharmacy. In the same year, he entered the retail drug business, in partnership with Jesse W. Beasley. They have been active in the business ever since, operating the Jackson Drug Company at Main and College streets in Dickson.

Mr. Nicks became a member of the Dickson County school board, on which he served for eleven years. He is a Democrat in his politics, and a charter member and past president of the Lions Club. He is also a past president of the Chamber of Commerce. A communicant of the Church of Christ, he serves his congregation as an elder.

In Dickson, on May 30, 1937, James Henry Nicks married Maxine Beard. Born at Hohenwald, Tennessee, on March 5, 1917, she is a daughter of William Britton and Early May (Harlan) Beard. Her father, a native of Perry County, was a merchant and a traveling salesman. He is now deceased. Mrs. Beard survives him and lives in Dickson.

Mr. and Mrs. Nicks are the parents of two children: 1. Judith Abigail, who was born on February 27, 1940, at Dickson. She is valedictorian of her graduating class at Dickson High School, and plans to attend the University of Tennessee and to major in education. She plays the piano. 2. Nancy Jane, born at Dickson on May 7, 1946. She too is musical, studying piano.

CLARENCE E. LARKINS

Clarence E. Larkins of White Bluff has had a varied career which has included school teaching, banking, and the management of an insurance agency. At the present time, he carries on the two latter activities concurrently. He is vice president of the Farmers and Merchants Bank at White Bluff, and senior partner in the White Bluff Insurance Agency.

Born in Dickson County, near White Bluff, on December 3, 1912, Mr. Larkins is a son of Leslie Dobson and Maude O. (Graham) Larkins. His father was born in the same area, on December 15, 1892, and has been a farmer all his life. He has taken an active part in farm improvement programs, and also in the campaign to secure electricity for the rural areas. For some time he served as Dickson County magistrate, and he has long been an elder in the Church of Christ. His favorite sport is bird-hunting. The grandfather of Leslie D. Larkins, James Alexander Larkins, was an early settler at Acorn Hill, or the Jones Creek Community, near White Bluff, and he served as state representative for one term. Maude O. Graham, whom Leslie D. Larkins married, was born in September, 1893, at White Bluff.

Clarence E. Larkins began his education in the public schools of that place, and later attended school at Dickson. For his advanced courses he entered Austin Peay College at Clarksville, but transferred from there to George Peabody State College in Nashville. There he trained for a career in teaching, and it was in that profession that he commenced his career. From 1932 to 1937 he taught in the schools of Dickson County.

In 1937, Mr. Larkins moved to Nashville, and in that city gained his first experience in banking, as clerk of the First American National Bank. He remained on its staff until August, 1944, then moved to White Bluff, where he assumed duties as vice president and manager of the Farmers and Merchants Bank, the position he still holds. He formed the White Bluff Insurance Agency in 1948, and has been a senior partner in the organization since that time. The agency sells all types of insurance.

One of Mr. Larkins' favorite community activities over the years has been the Boy Scouts of America. He was assistant scoutmaster for several years, and has also served on the Scouts' governing committee. He is a director of the local chapter of the American Red Cross, and is a charter member of the White Bluff Ruritan Club. This was the first such club organized in the state of Tennessee.

He is also affiliated with the Free and Accepted Masons, and serves as senior warden of his lodge. He and Mrs. Larkins are members of the Order of the Eastern Star. They attend the Church of Christ, where Mr. Larkins has been deacon and treasurer. In the course of the last decade, he has been on the board of directors of the church most of the time.

In Nashville, on December 23, 1941, Clarence E. Larkins married Marjorie Parks. Born at Mount Pleasant in Maury County, on April 7, 1918, she is a daughter of Frank and Blanche (Irwin) Parks. Her father too was born in Maury County, in 1884, and is now retired from his profession of bookkeeping. He and Mrs. Parks make their home in Nashville. She was born at Mount Pleasant in 1888.

Mrs. Larkins attended the public elementary and high schools of Nashville, and was a member of the first class to graduate from East Nashville High School, in 1934. She and Mr. Larkins are the parents of the following children: 1. Ralph Michael, who was born in Nashville on August 3, 1943. 2. Sandra V., born there on May 8, 1945. Both Ralph and Sandra are studying music. 3. Kathy, born June 20, 1952, in Dickson County. 4. Samuel Graham, who was born in that county on September 29, 1954. 5. Lockie, born there on November 14, 1956.

GILBERT D. FREEMAN

Co-owner and operator of the Dickson Hardware Store of Dickson, Tennessee, and one of the leading merchants in the area, Mr. Freeman has been active in community organizations, is a member of the Chamber of Commerce and is a former lieutenant governor of Kiwanis International of Kentucky and Tennessee.

He was born in Dickson County, Tennessee, on December 12, 1895, the son of George Thore Freeman and of Sally (Harvey) Freeman. His father was born in the Eighth District of Dickson County, Tennessee, in 1865. A stockman and farmer, he was also a stock dealer for cattle, hogs and sheep, and was a stock breeder for sheep and cattle, as well as busying himself with general farming. He received the fifty-year Masonic pin and he was a steward in the Methodist Church for more than fifty years. He died in Dickson County on February 27, 1941. Mr. Freeman's mother was born in 1868 and died in Dickson County on March 28, 1941.

Mr. Freeman attended the public schools in Dickson County, Tennessee, and then studied at Ruskin Cave College in Dickson County. During World War I, he served in the United States Army and saw action in the Argonne Forest in France. In service from 1917 to 1919, he enlisted as a private, received an individual citation, and was honorably discharged as a first sergeant.

Mr. Freeman has been active in community life and he is a member of the Masons and the Shrine, and is a past commander of Archie Wood Post No. 7 of the American Legion, at Clarksville, Tennessee; now a member of the Lucian Berry Post 115, at Dickson. He is a member of the Methodist Church, and he served for twenty-five years as a steward in Clarksville and Dickson, Tennessee. He is a Democrat in politics.

He was married in Clarksville, Tennessee, on June 17, 1922 to Nelle Brake, born in the 9th District, Dickson County, Tennessee, on April 10, 1898, the daughter of Dr. J. W. Brake and of Beatrice (Gerrin) Brake. Her father was born in Goodlettsville, Davidson County, Tennessee, on August 2, 1865, and died on April 1, 1958. He was a prominent physician in general practice for sixty years. Mrs. Freeman's mother was born in Dickson County, Tennessee.

Mr. and Mrs. Freeman have two children: 1. George Wesley, born in Clarksville, Tennessee, on December 14, 1923, attended Austin Peay College in Clarksville and then the University of Tennessee. During World War II, he served in the United States Army as a private, first class, and saw action in the European Theater. Wounded in the leg and hand, he received the Purple Heart, the Bronze Star and the Silver Star. Now a foreman at the Ford Motor Company in Nashville, Tennessee, he is married to Elizabeth Luther of Dickson, Tennessee, and they have two children, George Wesley, born in 1951, and Victoria Elizabeth, born in 1953. 2. Charles Gilbert, born in Clarksville in 1931, is now a Federal Government electrical inspector with the Civil Aeronautics Division, with headquarters in Washington, D. C. He served in the United States Air Force from 1948 to 1952, and saw action in Korea, where he was attached to the Fifth Marines, Landing Equipment and Maintenance. Wounded in the arm, he received the Purple Heart. He was honorably discharged with the rank of technical sergeant. He is now married to Jane Kanetza of Benton, Kentucky.

J.F.Crutcher

JOHN FLOWERS CRUTCHER

A professional soldier for many years of his life, John Flowers Crutcher returned in the years of his retirement to his native town of Henning. There he devoted himself to farming and stock raising, and proved himself an earnest and effective worker for his community.

Born at Henning on December 15, 1890, he was a son of Dr. James Ruben and Scrap (Flowers) Crutcher. Dr. James Ruben Crutcher was a native of Alabama, and following his graduation from Vanderbilt University at Nashville with his degree of Doctor of Medicine, he came to Henning, where he began his practice of medicine. He continued to follow his profession there until 1904, when he moved to Memphis. Miss Flowers, whom he married, was the daughter of John Henry Flowers, an extensive land owner and planter of Lauderdale County, Tennessee, and owner of the Flowers Steamship Line on the Hatchie River

John Flowers Crutcher attended the schools of Henning and Trenton, and completed his secondary studies at Central High School in Memphis. An army buddy, recalling the military leader's early years, provides a detail of his life which indicates his determination to become a professional soldier: "Without his parents' knowledge, 'Dixie' one day rode his horse into Memphis, tied it to a telegraph pole, and persuaded his Congressman on that very day to appoint him to West Point."

Throughout his period of military training—and to many who knew him, throughout his life, Major Crutcher was known as "Dixie." At West Point, he found himself in his element. The observer quoted above tells us: "He loved West Point; he lived the Code and talked of his great honor and special privilege in being a Cadet... His reverence for West Point was never diminished as the years went by. It continued to be the motivating force of his life, for the ideals of West Point were deeply embodied in this officer and gentleman of the South."

On his graduation from the United States Military Academy in 1913, he joined the 24th Infantry in Texas City, but his real preference among the services was the cavalry, and he soon managed to be transferred to the 11th Cavalry of the Regular Army at Fort Oglethorpe, Georgia. This outfit was sent to Trinidad, Colorado, to quell the miners' strike in 1914-1915. He later served under General Pershing on the expedition to the Mexican border in 1916. In May, 1917, he was promoted to the rank of captain.

In August of that year he became an aide on the staff of General J. Franklin Bell, then in command of the 77th Division of the National Army at Camp Upton, Long Island. He accompanied General Bell to France in December of that year. There he was transferred to observation service, in which he remained until March, 1918. He remained on General Bell's staff until June of that year, when he won his promotion to major. Detailed to the Tank Corps, he was ordered to England, and was later sent back to France in command of the 306th Battalion of the Tank Corps, with which he was serving at the time the armistice was signed.

After the war, Major Crutcher served in Washington, D. C., for a time, and was transferred from there to The Presidio in Monterey. He was later on recruiting duty at Dayton, Ohio; on duty with troops at Fort Benjamin Harrison and at Columbus Barracks; and was next sent to Cavalry School at Fort Riley, Kansas. His subsequent assignment took him to Governor's Island in New York Harbor, but he was soon afterwards transferred to the Adjutant General's Department and sent to Honolulu for duty.

While serving in the territory, Major Crutcher met with an accident which caused a permanent physical disability. Stationed at Fort Bliss, Texas, on his return from Hawaii, he developed a heart condition, and was sent to Walter Reed Army Hospital, where he was given his medical discharge from the army in September, 1934.

Returning to his native Henning, Tennessee, Major Crutcher made his home at the old Dr. B. G. Henning residence. It was in rather rundown condition at the time, but he and Mrs. Crutcher (whom he married early in 1920) restored it and made it one of the showplaces of the area. Both had an interest in collecting antiques, and they gathered around them an interesting collection, to which they added in the course of world travels.

Near Henning, Major Crutcher acquired farm holdings of over a thousand acres, and he also became the owner of an equally large area of land near Forrest City, Arkansas. Devoting his attention to stock raising, he pioneered in introducing registered Polled Hereford cattle in his part of the South. He was always a progressive farmer, informing himself of modern techniques and establishing a high standard of efficiency on his acreage. He took the lead in the soil conservation movement in his area.

Major Crutcher never lost his interest in military life, and he encouraged many young men to follow an army career, assisting some in securing West Point appointments. Neither did he lose an opportunity to get himself reinstated into service. At the time of World War II, he volunteered for the Army, and also for the Navy—"interservice rivalry" playing a secondary role to his desire to serve his country. However, his age was against him. He continued his farming and livestock operations to the end of his life.

He was also an effective community worker. He worked for the local chapter of the American Red Cross, taught Sunday school, and participated fully in the programs of such service groups as Rotary. He was a man of deeply religious nature, a communicant of the Methodist Church. His men's class there was donated a memorial window in the new church building in his honor.

At Clarksdale, Mississippi, on February 26, 1920, John Flowers Crutcher married Minna Watson Smith, daughter of Claud Percy and Sally (Martin) Smith. Her parents both died when Mrs. Crutcher was very young, and she and her four sisters, Sarah, Claudia, Evelyn and Martha were reared by an uncle and aunt, John Dabney and Minna Gaines Smith of Hillhouse, Mississippi.

John F. and Minna Watson (Smith) Crutcher became the parents of two children: 1. John F., who lives at Henning and manages the farms which his father owned in Tennessee and Arkansas. He was a captain in the paratroops during World War II. He married Margaret Marshall, and they have four children: Sally, Margie, Nancy, and Ginny. 2. Minna Virginia, who married Thomas P. Nash, 3rd, M.D., who is practicing medicine at Elizabeth City, North Carolina. They too have four children: Dixie, Thomas, John and Patrick.

Major Crutcher's career of loyal service to his country and his home community ended with his death at Henning on August 2, 1951.

JAMES C. CUNNINGHAM

With over two decades' experience in law practice in Clarksville, Tennessee, James C. Cunningham has become one of the city's better known professional men, a fact which has led in past years to his election to the State Legislature.

He is a native of Clarksville, and was born on February 1, 1917, son of John T. and Sarah (White) Cunningham. His father, born in Dickson County on August 12, 1877, was also an attorney, a graduate of Vanderbilt University Law School, where he took his degree of Bachelor of Laws in 1899. In the same year he commenced practice at Clarksville, where he remained throughout his professional career. He served as representative in the Tennessee Legislature, 1907-1909, and was Speaker of the House. Elected county and criminal judge in Montgomery County in 1918, he served until the time of his death, a period of twenty-seven years. The John T. Cunningham Memorial Bridge, just outside of Clarksville over the Cumberland River, was named in his honor. An organizer of the Eastern Dark Fired Tobacco Association in 1931, Judge Cunningham was president of the organization until the time of his death. He had been reared on a farm near Clarksville, where he continued to live all his life, taking an active interest in the cultivation of the acreage. He had served on the Clarksville City Council and both he and his wife, the former Sarah White, were communicants of the Methodist Church. She was a native of Nashville, and was born February 9, 1877.

Attending public school in the Ringgold Community near Clarksville in his early student years, James C. Cunningham graduated from Clarksville High School. He went on to Cumberland University, where he received his degree of Bachelor of Laws.

Admitted to the bar of his state in 1936, Mr. Cunningham started practice at Clarksville, where he has had his offices to the present time. He was absent for a time, however, in 1945-1946, serving in the United States Navy. A seaman first class, he remained stateside.

Mr. Cunningham was first elected representative from Montgomery and Houston counties in the Tennessee State Legislature for the 72nd Session, beginning in 1941, and he served through the 73rd Session of the General Asembly in 1943. He later served one term as representative of Montgomery County in the 75th Legislature.

He is a member of the Tennessee and Montgomery County bar associations. In 1935 he won an award conferred by the Blue Key National Honorary Fraternity at Cumberland University. He is a member of the Civitan Club at Clarksville, the Clarksville Golf and Country Club, and the lodge of the Free and Accepted Masons. In the Masonic order he belongs to the chapter of the Royal Arch Masons, the Knights Templar Commandery, and the Ancient Arabic Order of Nobles of the Mystic Shrine. He is a communicant of the Methodist Church, where he is currently serving as chairman of the board of stewards.

In his native city of Clarksville, on June 18, 1938, James C. Cunningham married Anne Rudolph, daughter of Paul and Cornelia (Watts) Rudolph. Her father, a lifelong resident of that city, was general manager of the Eastern Dark Fired Tobacco Growers Association, and a partner in the Paul Rudolph Tobacco Company. He died in 1952. Her mother, who survives him and lives in Clarksville, is a niece of governor Austin Peay. Mr. and Mrs. Cunningham are the parents of two children: 1. Cornelia, born May 3, 1941, in Clarksville; attending high school there. 2. Anne Chapman, born in that city on July 12, 1946, attending junior high school there.

Edgar Jones Graham

After distinguished service as state senator in his native state of Tennessee, the late Edgar Jones Graham became state comptroller, an office he held during the administrations of Governors Peay and Horton. He later became a land appraiser under the Tennessee Valley Authority. In the service of his state and in a number of other offices of public trust, he proved himself a man of rare intellectual talents, and of steady devotion to purpose.

Born at Pinewood, on August 5, 1879, he was a son of John Meredith and Ellen (Cheatham) Graham. His family can claim a long and distinguished record of public service in high office, in successive generations. His father was state senator; his grandfather, Edward S. Cheatham was speaker of the Senate, and Cheatham County was named for him. Edgar J. Graham's great-grandfather, Ephraim H. Foster, was United States Senator from Tennessee. The village of Pinewood grew up about a factory established by Samuel L. Graham, the paternal grandfather of Edgar J. Graham. Samuel L. Graham was a prosperous land owner, farmer and industrialist. His factory had been founded for the manufacture of domestic and cotton cloth rope, and was one of the first of its type in the South. The village thrived as an independent community from

Edgar J. Graham

1838 to 1894, and Edgar J. Graham was the last of the family to own it. Between 1900 and 1910, Edgar Graham managed the Council Bend Farm, owned by the Graham family. Corn, raised on this land, was exhibited at the St. Louis World's Fair in 1904 and was awarded a first prize bronze medal. By the time Mr. Graham sold Pinewood in 1923, the village was deserted. After the railroads were built, the small local factories no longer prospered, and Pinewood dwindled steadily from its maximum of eight hundred population. The large brick house occupied by the Grahams, and the store, still stand, and the home is owned by a former overseer of the farm but is unoccupied.

Edgar J. Graham attended Battle Ground Academy at Franklin, and on completing his preparatory studies there, enrolled at Auburn Polytechnic Institute in Alabama. He began his career as a farmer at Pinewood, and continued farming until he became state comptroller in 1923. In the meantime, the qualities of leadership for which citizens of this region had long looked to the Graham family had brought him other posts of responsibility, in peace and wartime. He was commissioned a captain in the National Guard in 1904, and held that rank until 1908. He organized the National Guard in Hickman County, and he also organized a volunteer regiment of infantry in World War I. From 1915 to 1919 he was a member of Governor Tom C. Rye's staff; and in 1919 he became United States Commissioner, serving until 1921.

He first took his seat as state senator in 1917, serving until 1919; and in 1921 he was returned to office, serving until 1923. In the latter year he assumed duties as state comptroller, and served with devotion and ability throughout the administrations of the Honorable Austin Peay and Honorable Henry Horton, his last term ending in 1931. When the Tennessee Valley Authority was organized, he became land appraiser under this federal organization in 1934, and served until 1937.

Mr. Graham held a number of other offices of public trust. He was chairman of the Highway Commission of Hickman County for some years; was trustee of the Tennessee State Fair from 1917 to 1923; and was president of the Farmers Institute at Columbia.

In his college days at Auburn, he had played on the football team, and he had also joined Kappa Alpha fraternity, in which he retained membership thereafter. He was also a member of the Free and Accepted Masons and the higher bodies of Masonry. Holding the Thirty-second Degree, he was a member of the Ancient Arabic Order of Nobles of the Mystic Shrine. He was a member of the Exchange Club at Nashville, and was an active member of the Vine Street Christian Church.

On April 26, 1905, Edgar J. Graham married Kate Nunnelly of Vernon, daughter of Mr. and Mrs. Walter S. Nunnelly. The couple became the parents of two daughters: 1. Eleanor, who is a curriculum assistant in the Nashville city schools. 2. Mary, who became the wife of Tom Fuqua of Nashville. They have three children: i. Eleanor Graham. ii. Tom Allen. iii. Edgar Graham. In addition, Mr. Graham was survived by a brother, Colonel Ephraim F. Graham of San Antonio, Texas, and two sisters: Mrs. Charles Caldwell of Birmingham, Alabama, and Mrs. Edmund Ivens of New Orleans.

The death of the distinguished public official occurred at Nashville on December 28, 1954.

DAVIS SCOTT PORCH, JR.

One of Waverly's younger generation of professional leaders, Davis Scott Porch, Jr., has practiced law there since he completed his training at Cumberland University. He has already distinguished himself in public office as county attorney and city attorney.

Born February 6, 1927, in Waverly, he is a son of Davis Scott, Sr., and Katherine (Harris) Porch. His father, born December 10, 1897, in Bakerville, Humphreys County, was a civil engineer until his retirement. He is a veteran of World War I, during which he attended officers' training school in Tennessee and later served in the Far East, South and Central America, and Alaska. He and Mrs. Porch now live in Waverly. The Porch family were early settlers in that area, and the attorney's grandfather, John F. Porch is still living.

Attending the public schools of Waverly and McEwen, Davis Scott Porch, Jr., graduated from Waverly High School. He then entered Cumberland University, where he graduated in 1950 with the degree of Bachelor of Laws. While at Cumberland University he became a member of Delta Theta Phi fraternity. Admitted to the practice of law in his state immediately afterwards, he has been practicing in Waverly since that time. In 1957 he became county attorney of Humphreys County, and assumed duties in addition to the offices of city attorney of the cities of Waverly and New Johnsonville. Mr. Porch is a trustee of the G. H. Weems Educational Fund which was established in 1939. He was elected to the Tennessee Constitutional Convention in 1958.

He also has business interests, and is attorney for the Citizens Bank at Waverly.

Mr. Porch is a veteran of World War II. He served in the army in the European Theater of Operations and held the rank of technician fourth grade. He is a member of both the American Legion and the Veterans of Foreign Wars.

He is a member of the American Bar Association, the Tennessee Bar Association and the Waverly Bar Association, and apart from his professional connections, belongs to the Lions Club and the lodge of the Free and Accepted Masons. He also belongs to the Scottish Rite of Nashville Consistory. He is a member of the Church of Christ.

At Corinth, Mississippi, on October 4, 1945, D. Scott Porch, Jr., married Marie Stone. She was born at Tremont, in that state, on October 15, 1927, and is a daughter of H. C. and Ruby (Coefield) Stone. Her father is now county agent for Humphreys County at Waverly, where her parents make their home at the present time. Mrs. Porch attended Cumberland University. Mr. and Mrs. Porch are the parents of three children, all of whom were born in Nashville: 1. Pamela, who was born on December 21, 1947. 2. Davis Scott, 3rd, born on December 5, 1953. 3. Amy Elizabeth, born October 13, 1958.

WILLIAM JAMES PEELER

Since graduating from the Cumberland University School of Law at Lebanon, William J. Peeler has engaged in the general practice of law at Waverly, where he has been active in the political and public life of the area. He has held office as an alderman of the City of McEwen and as Floterial Representative of the 20th Floterial District of Tennessee.

Born November 27, 1927, at Highland Park, Michigan, Peeler is the son of Aaron Herbert and Beulah (Wells) Peeler. His father, born on January 7, 1888, at Bold Springs, in Humphreys County, was reared on a farm, but has spent most of his career in business. A veteran of military service in World War I, the senior Mr. Peeler was overseas with the 2nd Combat Engineers and participated in the Battle of Chateau-Thierry, where he was wounded in action on June 13, 1918. Both he and Mrs. Peeler are members of the McEwen Church of Christ, in which community they have resided for the past thirty years. Peeler's mother, the former Beulah Wells, was born in Dickson County, Tennessee, on the 11th day of April 1899.

William J. Peeler attended the public schools of McEwen, graduating from high school there in 1945, and attended the College of Arts and Science at Cumberland University after having served in the United States Army. His military assignment was to the Corps of Engineers, and he was stationed both at Fort Lewis, Washington, and at Fort Belvoir, Virginia. Discharged at Fort Lewis, Washington, in July of 1947 in the rank of corporal, he was in uniform during 1946-1947.

Mr. Peeler graduated from Cumberland University School of Law, where he served as Student Body President, on June 12, 1952, with the degree of Bachelor of Laws, and was admitted to the bar of Tennessee on August 2, 1952. He immediately formed a partnership with Mr. Bill T. Murray and he and Mr. Murray have since engaged in the general practice of law with offices in the Turner Building in Waverly.

In 1948, Mr. Peeler was elected to office as City Alderman of McEwen, in which office he served one term. In 1958, he was elected Floterial Representative to the Tennessee General Assembly, from the 20th Floterial District of Tennessee, where he distinguished himself by introducing and passing a bill creating a uniform system of Courts of General Session in eighty-nine of Tennessee's ninety-five counties, and where he also earned the enviable record of passing every piece of legislation which he sponsored. Although a freshman legislator, he was chosen by the newspaper reporters covering the Legislative Session as one of the three most outstanding members of the 81st General Assembly. A Democrat, he has taken a lively interest in the affairs of his party on a county, state and national level. He is past president of the Young Democratic Clubs of Tennessee and past General Counsel of the Young Democratic Clubs of America. He is a charter sustaining member of the Democratic Party of the United States.

As a lawyer, Mr. Peeler, who enjoys a wide and extensive practice, and who serves as County Attorney for Humphreys County, is a member of the American Bar Association, the Tennessee Bar Association, and the Waverly Bar Association. He is a former member of the Junior Chamber of Commerce of Waverly and formerly served as vice president of the Middle Tennessee Junior Chamber of Commerce. He is at present serving as Chairman of the Humphreys County Library Board. His memberships include the Exchange Club, the Lodge of Free and Accepted Masons, the Humphreys County Great Books Discussion Club, Lambda Chi Alpha, Delta Theta Phi and Alpha Pi Omega fraternities. Like his parents, he is a member of the Church of Christ, having joined this church when he was thirteen years of age.

Mrs. Peeler, the former Miss Nancy Bradley, a communicant of St. Patrick's Catholic Church in McEwen, was born in Humphreys County on September 19, 1932, the daughter of John Lawrence, Sr., and Winnie (Burns) Bradley, both of whom are natives of Humphreys County. Mr. Bradley is engaged in varied business enterprises and has held office in recent years as Sheriff of Humphreys County and Mayor of the City of Waverly.

Mrs. Peeler, who shares her husband's interest in civic and political affairs is a part owner of B & R Ford Sales in Waverly. She received her early education at St. Patrick's Elementary School in McEwen and St. Cecilia's Academy in Nashville, where she later also attended Vanderbilt University. She is a member of the Waverly Study Club and the Waverly Garden Club, having served in the past as president of the Waverly Study Club.

Mr. and Mrs. Peeler were married at McEwen, Tennessee, on December 26, 1949, and they are the parents of two children: Nanette Peeler, born at Lebanon, Tennessee, on June 3, 1951, and Jeana Bradley Peeler, who was born April 4, 1955 in Nashville, Tennessee.

George Earl Paullus, Sr., M.D.

The elder Dr. George Earl Paullus, who was head of the prominent Memphis professional family, was born on April 23, 1882, in Coldwater, Wayne County, Missouri, son of James Cawthorn and Sally (Black) Paullus. He had two brothers and two sisters who survived him: Charles B. Paullus, of Columbia, Missouri; Robert Paullus of Greenville, Missouri; Mrs. Minnie Trontla, of Pullman, Washington; and Mrs. Daisy Edmonds, of St. Louis, Missouri.

Wayne S. Saulters

Geo. F. Saulters Jr.

After Dr. George E. Paullus, Sr., had completed his preliminary education, he entered Marvin College at Fredericktown, Missouri, then studied medicine at Washington University and Barnes University, in St. Louis. In 1908 he received his degree of Doctor of Medicine. Thereafter he devoted his entire life to the practice of his chosen profession. During World War I, he served in the Army Medical Corps, afterwards becoming active in the American Legion. He practiced at Marked Tree, Arkansas, before moving to Memphis in 1923.

Dr. Paullus was a member of the Memphis Medical Society, the Shelby County Medical Society, the Tennessee State Medical Society, the Southern Medical Society and the American Medical Association, and he also belonged to Theta Kappa Psi medical fraternity.

Aside from his medical practice, Dr. Paullus was primarily interested in people and in human relationships. Others readily responded to this interest, with the result that he was highly popular. Fond of the out-of-doors, he had his own farm in Crittenden County, Arkansas, and it constituted his major hobby and spare-time activity. Intensely interested and well informed in agriculture, he was also a widely read man generally. He liked horseback riding as a sport. Formerly he had played golf as a member of the Colonial Country Club in Memphis. He also belonged to Stonewall Lodge of the Free and Accepted Masons, and as a member of the higher bodies of the Masonic order, belonged to the Knights Templar commandery and the Ancient Arabic Order of Nobles of the Mystic Shrine. A devout Christian, he was a deacon of the Bellevue Baptist Church for twelve years. An indication of his great popularity appeared in the endless train of blood donors who came to St. Joseph's Hospital during Dr. Paullus' last illness when it became known that transfusions might save his life.

At Greenville, Missouri, on May 22, 1908, Dr. George E. Paullus, Sr., married Bessie M. Settle. She was born there, the daughter of John Henry and Belle (Harris) Settle. Dr. and Mrs. Paullus became the parents of two sons: 1. George Earl, Jr. 2. Wayne Settle. Both are subjects of accompanying sketches.

Dr. Paullus died July 29, 1944, in Memphis. Dr. Paullus was selected for inclusion in Who's Important in Medicine just before his death.

GEORGE EARL PAULLUS, JR., M.D.

The Paullus family has contributed more than its share of leadership in the medical profession at Memphis, where the Paullus Clinic has become widely known. Since the death of its founder, Dr. George E. Paullus, Sr., his sons have continued active in its management. Of these, the elder, Dr. George E., Jr., is a physician and surgeon, with a professional record of more than twenty years in the city. He was a medical officer during World War II, and he takes an interested part in community affairs, particularly in work with youth.

Born at Marked Tree, Arkansas, on August 27, 1911, he is a son of Dr. George Earl, Sr., and Bessie M. (Settle) Paullus. His father is the subject of a separate sketch accompanying. Bessie M. (Settle) Paullus was born at Greenville, Missouri. The family moved to Memphis when the younger Dr. George E. Paullus was twelve years old, and he completed his public school education there, graduating from Central High School. He then entered Southwestern University, where he began his advanced academic courses, but transferred from there to the University of Tennessee at Knoxville, graduating with the degree of Bachelor of Science in 1932. He continued with his professional training at the University of Tennessee Medical School in Memphis, and in 1936 received his degree of Doctor of Medicine.

At the outset of his career he joined his father in the Paullus Clinic. He left at the time of World War II to serve in the United States Army Medical Corps, in which he attained the rank of major. In 1944, before the war ended, the elder Dr. George E. Paullus died; and when Dr. George E., Jr., concluded his military service and returned to Memphis, he took charge of the operation of the clinic. His practice as physician and surgeon has been centered there since that time, and he is likewise of course closely involved in its administration. The clinic is located at 654 Chelsea in Memphis.

Dr. Paullus is a member of the American Medical Association and the state and local medical associations. He is a staff member of the Memphis Academy of General Practitioners and a former president of this group. He belongs to Theta Kappa Phi medical fraternity, and to Sigma Nu social fraternity. His local memberships include the Tennessee Club, Rivermont Club and Chickasaw Country Club.

Vitally interested in programs benefitting youth, Dr. Paullus was one of the organizers of Boys' Town in Memphis; he was a charter member and is a life member and serves on its board of directors. He was formerly president of the board of the Lausanne School. He is a Mason and a Shriner. An Episcopalian, he is a communicant of St. Mary's Church in Memphis.

At Hattiesburg, Mississippi, on October 27, 1944, Dr. George Earl Paullus, Jr., married Mary Elizabeth McDavid, daughter of the late Dr. Robert and Clyde McDavid. Born in 1894, Dr. McDavid died in 1940. To their marriage two children have been born: 1. Sharri Leah, who was born on November 24, 1945. 2. Tina Melissa, born January 24, 1950.

WAYNE SETTLE PAULLUS, D.D.S.

Member of a well-known professional family in Memphis, Dr. Wayne Settle Paullus has devoted his career to dentistry. He operates a clinic located at 3429 Highway 51 North. He has already held office in a nationwide dental group, and he is a veteran of naval service in World War II.

Dr. Paullus is a native of Marked Tree, Arkansas, and was born on May 29, 1916, younger son of Dr. George Earl, Sr., and Bessie M. (Settle) Paullus. His father, of whom a brief sketch accompanies, was founder of the Paullus Clinic at Memphis. The family moved to that city when Dr. Wayne S. Paullus was seven years old, and consequently he received all of his early education in its public schools. He graduated from Central High School, then entered Southwestern University. Later attending the University of Alabama, he went to the University of Tennessee Dental School for his professional training, and received his degree of Doctor of Dental Surgery there in 1943.

At the time of World War II, he entered the United States Navy with a commission as lieutenant, and served in both the Pacific and the Atlantic Theaters of Operations. For some time he was dental surgeon aboard the U.S.S. "Quincy," the ship which carried President Roosevelt to the inter-allied conference at Yalta.

Dr. Paullus took an internship in dentistry at Knoxville General Hospital before beginning his private practice. He first practiced with the Paullus Clinic and later was associated with the Gordon Hospital in Lewisburg. He then went to Miami, Florida, where for five years he practiced with offices in the Huntington Building. In 1957 he returned to Memphis, where he established his clinic on Highway 51 North. This he has operated since.

Dr. Paullus formerly served as president of the American Academy of Implant Dentures, and he holds memberships in the Southern Academy Oral Surgeons and the usual national and regional dentists' groups. His fraternities are Psi Omega and Sigma Nu. He is a past president of the American Legion at Lewisburg as well as past president of the Junior Chamber of Commerce there.

Locally, he is a member of the Fox Meadows Club, and was formerly a member of the Tennessee Club. He holds membership in the Free and Accepted Masons. He and his family attend the Presbyterian Church. While in Key Biscayne, Florida, Dr. and Mrs. Paullus were instrumental in organizing a Presbyterian Church there. The little group first met for prayer meetings at the Paullus home, but when the number became too many for their home they moved to a larger building and the church was organized with Dr. and Mrs. Paullus among the charter members. Dr. Paullus was one of the first deacons.

At West Memphis, Arkansas, September 20, 1943, Dr. Wayne Settle Paullus married Margaret Pickens of Lewisburg, daughter of the late William Ernest and Lounora (Bond) Pickens. Her father was born July 22, 1887 and died April 23, 1949. Dr. and Mrs. Paullus have three children: 1. Wayne Settle, Jr., who was born on November 26, 1944 in Memphis. 2. Lady Margaret, born September 5, 1947 at Memphis. 3. Pattijo, who was born on May 24, 1950 at Lewisburg.

J. Thomas Traughber

A lawyer who has practiced at Clarksville since the beginning of his career, J. Thomas Traughber has a distinguished record in public office to his credit. Some years ago he served in the Tennessee State House of Representatives, and more recently has held office as Attorney General.

Born in Montgomery County on October 14, 1906, he is a son of Thomas Martin and Dorothy (McDonnell) Traughber. His father, a native of the same county, was born in 1864, and was a miller by occupation. He died at Clarksville. Dorothy McDonnell, whom he married, was born in that place in 1870, and passed away on June 1, 1958. Thomas Traughber's great-grandfather, John Dillon Byrne, came to this country from Dublin, Ireland, and married Elizabeth White. Assisted by another great-grandfather, Levi Traughber, he built St. Michael's Church in Robertson County, the edifice being completed in May, 1842.

J. Thomas Traughber attended the public schools of his native Montgomery County, and for his advanced academic studies, entered the University of Notre Dame. There he graduated with the degree of Bachelor of Arts, in 1928; and in 1930 took his Bachelor of Laws degree at the same university.

Admitted to the bar, he commenced practice at Clarksville in the same year, and has been professionally active there ever since, with the exception of the four years he spent in military service at the time of World War II. Entering the United States Army Air Corps, he served in Europe with the Eighth Air Force. He was in uniform from 1942 through 1945, and advanced in rank from private to captain.

A Democrat in his politics, J. Thomas Traughber served in the state's House of Representatives in 1935. He has held office as Montgomery County attorney, and was elected attorney general of the state in 1950. He also served as investigator for the United States Department of the Treasury, in Washington, D. C.

As a lawyer, he belongs to the American Bar Association, the Tennessee Bar Association and the Montgomery County Bar Association. In his home city he helds membership in the posts of the American Legion and the Veterans of Foreign Wars, and the lodges of the Benevolent and Protective Order of Elks, the Loyal Order of Moose and the Knights of Columbus. He is a Fourth-degree member of the Knights of Columbus, and a Roman Catholic in religious faith.

At Faribault, Minnesota, on November 29, 1945, J. Thomas Traughber married Helen Gallagher. Born on March 29, 1912, she is a daughter of Patrick J. and Helene (McCall) Gallagher. Mrs. Traughber graduated from the University of Minnesota School of Music, and from the University of California with a degree in psychology. She is a pianist, and is active in the work of the Catholic Church. The couple are the parents of one son: Thomas Patrick, who was born at Clarksville on December 4, 1946.

Ralph D. Whitesell

In his profession of photography, Ralph D. Whitesell has had nearly thirty years' experience with the Boyd Studio in Lewisburg. He has a variety of other interests which include Tennessee history, genealogy, and antiques.

Born at Lillard Mills, on May 23, 1910, he is a son of George Ollie and Etta Mai (Davis) Whitesell, and a grandson of John M. S. and Mary Alice (Bradley) Whitesell and of Henry J. and Natalia Jane (Cundiff) Davis. In the paternal line, his forebears were among the early settlers of the state. His paternal grandfather was a native of Tennessee from Bedford County, and was a miller. Mary Alice Bradley, whom he married, was born in Marshall County, and her family was one of the first to settle in that county. This couple's son, George Ollie Whitesell, was born January 9, 1880, near Verona, in Marshall County. He followed his father's occupation as a miller, and was also a merchant and a dairyman. His death occurred on March 15, 1932. On February 9, 1908, he was married to Etta Mai Davis. She was born at Lillard's Mills, in Marshall County on October 1, 1877, and died May 25, 1946. Her father, Henry J. Davis, was born in Wilson County, Tennessee, and was brought to Marshall County, Tennessee, by his parents when he was six years old. There he lived the remainder of his life. His parents had come from North Carolina and Virginia. Henry J. Davis married Natalia Jane Cundiff, who was born in Marshall County of an early pioneer family. She was a direct descendant of two Revolutionary soldiers: Isaac Rainey of North Carolina (1763-1836) and Isaac Cundiff of Virginia (1757-1843). George Ollie Whitesell served in the Spanish-American War. He and his wife, the former Etta Mai Davis, became the parents of four sons: 1. John Jackson, who died in infancy. 2. Ralph Davis, of whom further. 3. William Clifft, born December 14, 1914. 4. George Ollie, Jr., born February 18, 1917.

Ralph D. Whitesell attended public schools in Eufaula, Alabama, and graduated from high school in Marshall County, Tennessee. He later attended Middle Tennessee College before entering the profession of photography in 1930.

He began his career as a photographer in the Boyd Studio in Lewisburg, and has been associated with this firm since, except for the years 1944-1945, when he was in military service in World War II. In the course of his professional pursuits, he has developed a particular interest in building up a permanent file of photographs of persons who have contributed to the life of the region, as well as of points of interest and antiquities of the area.

Mr. Whitesell has made a special study of the history of Marshall County, and particularly of the role which his family has played in that county and in the state. He is an active member of the Tennessee Historical Society, and as a veteran of World War II, belongs to the American Legion. He is a communicant of the Methodist Church. A lifelong Democrat, Mr. Whitesell has not concerned himself with politics. He is unmarried.

JUDGE MAC FARRAR

Mr. Farrar has combined a lifetime in farming with county service since 1942. Like his father before him, he has served the citizens of Bedford County as magistrate and, since 1950, as county judge.

Born in Flat Creek on September 14, 1911, he is the son of the late Clayton Farrar who was born in Bedford County on July 24, 1881. Mr. Farrar was a farmer and served as magistrate of Bedford County for twelve years prior to his death in Flat Creek. His widow, Annie Elizabeth (Thompson) Farrar, was born in the north end of Bedford County on November 27, 1883 and now makes her home in Flat Creek where she is a music teacher, and has been pianist at the Methodist Church for the past fifty years.

Mr. Farrar received his education in the public schools and graduated from Flat Creek High School before studying at Draughon's Business College in Nashville.

Upon completing his education, Mr. Farrar turned to farming and has been so associated for the past twenty years. In 1942, he was named magistrate of Bedford County and held this post until 1950 when he was elected Bedford County Judge, the post he currently holds. He was reelected in 1958 for another eight year term. He has continued to manage his extensive farm holdings while fulfilling his county duties and in addition has served as field manager for the Production Credit Association. He is a member of the Tennessee County Judges Association and is a Mason and an Elk, and a member of the Shelbyville Lions Club. He and his family are Methodists and Mr. Farrar is a trustee and steward of his church.

He was married to the former Mabel Frances Phillips on December 23, 1942. Mrs. Farrar is the daughter of the late D. B. Phillips of Bedford County, and Fannie (Dixon) Phillips, a school teacher in Shelbyville where she was born on June 4, 1887. Mabel Frances Farrar was born in Bedford County on March 24, 1920 and has lived in the county all her life. Mrs. Farrar attended Trevaco College in Nashville. She has taught in public schools for fourteen years. The Farrars are the parents of two daughters, Rheaetta, born June 24, 1947, and Lauralyn, born February 23, 1950. Both of the girls were born in Flat Creek.

FRANK FONTAINE HILL

One of Memphis' most influential figures in finance of the past generation Frank Fontaine Hill was a member of one of the city's oldest families. From his early years he took a prominent part in the management of Union and Planters Bank, of which he later became president. He organized the Hill State Bank and Trust Company, and was also founder and manager of the Hill, Fontaine Grocery and Cotton Company, and the real estate and insurance firm of Hill and Lawrence. He was an official of many other cor-

porations, and took an equally constructive part in his city's civic and organizational life.

A native of Memphis, he was born at Madison and Third Streets, where the Sterick building now stands, on June 3, 1874, and was a son of Napoleon and Mary M. Hill. The family has been established in Memphis for many generations, and Napoleon Hill was a leader in business and finance, active in the management of the Union and Planters Bank, of which he became the president. In addition to their son Frank F., their children were Olivia Hill Grosvenor, Napoleon Hill, II and Mrs. Mary Hill Overton, who was the mother of Mayor Watkins Overton.

Receiving his elementary education in local schools, Frank F. Hill later attended the University of the South at Sewanee. He was a member of the football team there when it played its first game against the Vanderbilt Commodores. Mr. Hill took his first position as a clerk with the cotton firm of Hill, Fontaine and Company, which in the course of his connection was reorganized as the Hill, Fontaine Grocery and Cotton Company. He left to enter the real estate and insurance business, organizing the Hill and Lawrence agency.

Also, from his early youth, he took an interest in banking, and at the age of twenty-one became a director of the Union and Planters Bank. Later promoted to the vice presidency of the bank, he filled that post for eight years, and was then elected to succeed his father as its president. He remained executive head of the bank for nine years, resigning at the end of that time to devote his entire time to private business interests. A resolution passed by the board of directors at the time of his retirement indicates the extent of his valuable services to the institution:

... When Mr. Frank F. Hill became president of this bank on March 11, 1915, the deposits were $5,654,000; its total resources were $7,313,000. Today, when he voluntarily servers connection with it, its deposits are $29,237,000, and its total resources are $36,103,000. These figures, more than any words that can be employed, pay eloquent and deserved tribute to his leadership.

In the course of his executive connection with Union and Planters Bank, Mr. Hill made it the first state bank in Tennessee to join the Federal Reserve System, and he also started the movement to establish a branch of the Federal Reserve Bank in Memphis.

Retirement, even to an active schedule of management of private interests, is seldom a satisfying state to a man of Frank F. Hill's wide interests and vision. In September, 1929, he organized the Hill State Bank and Trust Company, in the management of which his son, Napoleon Hill, 3rd, was associated with him. Also, at one time or another, he held office in the following organizations: Bluff City Abstract Company, Hill and Lawrence, Inc., Mammoth Spring Milling Company, Mammoth Spring Electric Light Company, and Memphis Lumber Corporation.

As a banker, he was an active member of the Memphis Clearing House

Association and the Bankers Club of Memphis, and he also belonged to the Bankers Club of New York. He took a full part in the program of the local Chamber of Commerce, and was a member of the Tennessee Club, Memphis Country Club, and the Tri-State Fair Association. He was at one time a member of the Memphis Board of Public Works. He was a member of the Old Chickasaw Guards Club, and of the Benevolent and Protective Order of Elks, and DeSoto Lodge of the Free and Accepted Masons, which he had served as treasurer. In Masonry, he was a member of the higher bodies, holding the Thirty-second Degree, and was a member of Al Chymia Temple of the Shrine. His fraternity was Sigma Alpha Epsilon.

Outside of his home city, Mr. Hill held membership in the Congressional Club of Washington, D. C., the New York Yacht Club, Chicago's Exmoor Country Club, and the Woods Hole Golf Club on Cape Cod, Massachusetts. He was a communicant of the Episcopal Church.

On April 29, 1896, in Memphis, Frank Fontaine Hill married Lizzie Willins, daughter of John Turner and Lizzie Owen (Nelson) Willins. Mr. and Mrs. Hill became the parents of the following children: 1. Napoleon Hill, Third, who was born on March 17, 1897, who joined his father in the management of the Hill State Bank and Trust Company. He was married to the former Marie Cordes, and he died in 1957. 2. Elizabeth Willins, born on August 26, 1899. She married Joseph Phillips Evans, and they have two children: i. Joseph Hill Evans. ii. Elizabeth Willins Evans. 3. Frank Fontaine, Jr., born August 30, 1901. He married Lucylle Plyler, and they have a daughter, Mary Lou Hill. 4. Marywood, born on December 10, 1907. She married Lee Saunders, and they have two children: i. Barry Hill, who is married and the father of two children: Barry Hill Saunders, Jr., and Lee Saunders. ii. Linda Lee.

Mr. Hill continued until the end of his life his interest in sports. He was also fond of travel, and in the course of his journeys in this country and abroad, collected many art objects. He remained vitally active, a force in the affairs of his city, until his death on March 13, 1935.

C. B. JAMISON, D.D.S.

Following his return from wartime service in the Army Air Corps, Dr. C. B. Jamison completed his training for a career in dentistry. He has since served in the Korean War, but now has his own practice in Waverly.

A native of Humphreys County, Tennessee, he was born on April 8, 1919, son of George Berry and Effie (Smith) Jamison. His father, who was born in Humphreys County in June, 1883, is now retired from his occupation of farming, and lives in McEwen, Tennessee. The public schools of Humphreys County provided Dr. Jamison with his early education, and he graduated from Yellow Creek High School. He later attended Marshall College in Huntington, West Virginia, but in 1941 left for service in the United States Army Air

Corps. Continuing in the air service until 1945, he served in the European Theater of Operations as a navigator with the Eighth Air Force, and flew on a number of missions over enemy-held territory. He held the rank of first lieutenant.

Following his return from service, Dr. Jamison resumed his education. He received his degree of Doctor of Dental Surgery from the University of Tennessee at Memphis in 1951. He then established an independent practice at Waverly, but a short time later, still in 1951, he was recalled to service in the United States Air Force (redesignated at the time the services had been given independent status following World War II). This time he served in his professional capacity of dentist, being stationed in Alaska, and held the rank of captain. He remained in uniform until 1953. In recognition of his Air Force service, Dr. Jamison has received the Air Medal with three clusters, the Distinguished Flying Cross, the Presidential Unit Citation, and the European-African-Middle Eastern Theater Ribbon with three campaign stars. On his second return to civilian life in 1953, Dr. Jamison resumed his practice at Waverly. He now owns the building in which he has his offices.

He is a member of the American Dental Association, the Tennessee State Dental Association, and his local dental association, the American Radio Relay League of Amateur Operators, the Exchange Club in Waverly, the lodge of Free and Accepted Masons, and the posts of the American Legion and the Veterans of Foreign Wars. He and his family attend the Methodist Church. Fond of the out-of-doors, Dr. Jamison particularly enjoys hunting and fishing.

At Huntington, West Virginia, on April 12, 1941, Dr. C. B. Jamison married Angelee Cochran. She was born in 1918 in Greenup, Kentucky, daughter of Alva J. Cochran. Her father, a native of West Virginia, was a real estate broker, and is now deceased. Dr. and Mrs. Jamison have two children: 1. Diane, who was born at Monroe, Louisiana, on July 21, 1945. 2. Cheryl, born May 11, 1955, in Dickson, Tennessee.

THURMAN THOMPSON

A practicing lawyer since 1930, Mr. Thompson has earned the respect of his fellow townsmen and as a result has been called upon to serve the people of Marshall County as a judge and more recently as a member of the State Legislature.

Born on November 17, 1902, in Dickson County, Thurman Thompson is the son of the late Allen Lee and Sarah Jane (Rogers) Thompson. Allen Lee Thompson, born July 14, 1864, in Dickson County, died near Charlotte, where he owned a farm, in 1919. His wife, Sarah Jane, born in Montgomery County, was a school teacher to the time of her death in 1915.

Mr. Thompson received his education in the public schools of Dickson County before studying at Cumberland University where he received his Bachelor of Laws degree. A lifelong Democrat, Mr. Thompson is a past General

Sessions judge of Marshall County and served in the Seventy-ninth and Eightieth Tennessee General Assembly as a Direct Representative of Marshall County in 1955, 1956, and 1957. His hobbies are hunting and guns, and he is a member of the National Rifle Association.

He married the former Christine Burt of Cornerville in 1937. Mrs. Thompson, born on June 23, 1907 at Cornerville, is the daughter of Floyd Burt, born in Marshall County and died in Nashville on December 25, 1941, and of Tina (Moore) Burt, born in Giles County and died in Lewisburg in December, 1957. Mrs. Thompson attended schools in Lewisburg and attended Vanderbilt College at Nashville. She is active in Methodist Church activities. Mr. and Mrs. Thompson are the parents of two sons. They are: 1. Burt Lee, born November 5, 1940 at Lewisburg where he graduated from high school and is now attending the University of Tennessee. 2. Bill Thompson, born August 23, 1950 also in Lewisburg.

CLARENCE COOPER OGILVIE

Throughout four decades, Clarence Cooper Ogilvie rendered service of great value to his home city of Memphis as director of the Goodwyn Institute. It was he who was instrumental in organizing its free public reference library, and he also instituted the series of free lectures there. In these ways alone, he immeasurably enriched the cultural life of the region. But these were not the extent of his achievements. He was also a lawyer and banker, corporation official and devoted organizational worker.

Born at Bell Buckle, on March 20, 1874, he was a son of Jasper and Josephine (Smith) Ogilvie. He received his early education in his home city, attending Webb School, now even more widely known than it was then. As a student there he led his class in Latin, and in recognition of his scholastic achievements, his classmates nicknamed him Solomon. Throughout life some of his old friends continued to call him "Sol." Going on from there to Vanderbilt University, he later transferred to the University of Chicago, and at both institutions, majored in English and economics. He was also a member of Delta Kappa Epsilon fraternity at both. He graduated in the depression year 1896, and being unable to secure a position in a bank—even then a major interest of his—he turned his attention to teaching and became the principal of the school at Hollow Rock. The following year he was appointed professor of Greek and English at the high school in Pine Bluff, Arkansas, where he also served as assistant principal.

Meantime, he decided upon a career in the law, and in 1899 came to Memphis where he accepted a position as bookkeeper in a cotton factor's office, while studying law in the offices of James H. Watson and G. T. Fitzhugh. In 1901 he was admitted to the bar. For the next several years, Mr. Ogilvie was claim agent for the Illinois Central and the Y. and M. V. Railroads in Memphis. He resigned from these posts in 1905 to begin private prac-

C C Ogilvie

tice as an attorney, and he continued to follow the profession of the law until 1938.

He had never lost his interest in the cause of education, and in 1904 was elected to membership on the city's board of education. At the same time another young man, a buggy and harness salesman, began his political career on the same ticket—E. H. Crump, who was candidate for alderman. The entire ticket, headed by James H. Malone as candidate for mayor, carried the election. In 1907, Mr. Ogilvie was named president of the board of education.

When in 1906 William A. Goodwyn, Memphis cotton executive and philanthropist, died and bequeathed the city funds for free lectures and educational facilities, Mr. Ogilvie was immediately considered to head the program for bringing the Goodwyn Institute into existence. Following the completion of the first building, its program was formally inaugurated with a parade on the evening of October 7, 1907. The first lecturer was the famed "Poet of the Ozarks," Opie Read. But the Institute was to have a still more famed lecturer that same year. Woodrow Wilson was at that time known only as president of Princeton University. It was five years later that he became President of the United States. He lectured on "The Ideals of Citizenship."

Mr. Ogilvie was superintendent of Goodwyn Institute from the time of its founding, his title later being changed to director. In the course of his fruitful years in the post, he was able to collect many anecdotes through his contacts with the celebrated men who came to lecture. A particularly ironic touch was his helping to nurse Roald Amundsen, discoverer of the South Pole, through a cold which confined the doughty explorer to the Hotel Peabody. On another occasion, his qualities of diplomacy were called forth when peppery Colonel "Marse Henry" Watterson refused to be presented to an audience by ex-Secretary of War Luke E. Wright, with the assertion that "no damned Republican will ever introduce me to an audience!" It was largely Mr. Ogilvie's qualities of affability, efficiency and dependability which made the series of lectures a success in the formative years. His efforts were also vital in establishing the Institute's public reference library in 1907.

Meantime, busy as he was with his duties at the Institute, Mr. Ogilvie found time to carry on his law practice. He also took a prominent part in the city's banking affairs, being one of the organizers of the Memphis Bank and Trust Company, which he thereafter served as attorney and vice president. He was also attorney for the Odd Fellows Hall and Library Association, and drew up the contract between that organization and the Columbian Mutual Life Insurance Company for the construction of Columbian Mutual Tower.

Mr. Ogilvie was a member of the Independent Order of Odd Fellows, and also of the Free and Accepted Masons. One of his major organizational interests throughout the years was Rotary, which he had joined in 1916. He was governor of the 104th District of Rotary International in 1931-1932, and president of the club at Memphis in 1932-1933. He attended a number of its international conventions as delegate. He was a communicant of Idlewild Presbyterian Church.

Finding time in his varied and productive life for several avocations, he successfully managed two farms of several hundred acres in Tallahatchie County, Mississippi, for more than a quarter of a century. He was fond of floriculture, fishing, and toy Pomeranian dogs, gardening, reading and mental games. He won a number of prizes in puzzle contests.

Twice married, Clarence Cooper Ogilvie chose as his first wife Miss Jessie Clay Wright, daughter of Dr. John M. and Georgia A. (Herron) Wright. They were married in Memphis on July 26, 1899. She lived past the observance of their golden wedding anniversary, and died in November, 1956. To this marriage, Mr. Ogilvie's daughter, Fay, was born. She is the wife of Alston Boyd Wade of Memphis, and they have three children: i. Fay Ogilvie, who married Robert Milner. Their children are: Fay Wade Milner and Robert Milner, Jr. ii. Elizabeth Boyd, who married Robert E. Larkin. They have two children: Kim Larkin and Elizabeth Larkin. iii. Alston Boyd, Jr., who married Linda Lloyd. In 1957, in Memphis, Mr. Ogilvie married as his second wife Myrtice Goff, who survives him.

The death of the distinguished community and educational leader occurred at the Baptist Hospital on May 19, 1959, at the age of eighty-five.

Dempsey Hunter Marks

At the present time, Dempsey Hunter Marks has a record of two decades of experience in the practice of law in the same city, Clarksville. He was absent from the city only at the time of his wartime military service. He has been active in local affairs, and in political life.

Born September 11, 1917, in Montgomery County, he is a son of Albert S. and Louise (Hunter) Marks. His father too was a native Tennessean, born at Winchester on October 6, 1891, son of Arthur Marks, who built Hundred Oaks. Another Albert S. Marks, Dempsey Marks' great-grandfather, was at one time governor of Tennessee. The lawyer's father was engaged in general farming. He died at Clarksville on February 13, 1943. His wife, the former Louise Hunter, survives him and makes her home at Clarksville. She was born at Southside, Tennessee, in July, 1892.

Completing his public school education at Clarksville, Dempsey H. Marks graduated from high school there, and from Cumberland Law School in 1938 with the degree of Bachelor of Laws. Admitted to the bar, he commenced practice at Clarksville, where he has continued his professional career ever since. He is a member of the firm of Marks and Fleming, with offices in the First National Bank Building. As a lawyer he belongs to the Montgomery County Bar Association, the Tennessee Bar Association and the American Bar Association.

Mr. Marks entered army service in April, 1942, four months after Pearl

Harbor, and after his basic training, was assigned to the Eighth Armored Division, with which he served in the European Theater of Operations. He became a technical sergeant. His separation from the service came in October, 1945.

In 1951, Mr. Marks became a member of the Montgomery County Board of Education, and he still serves on that board. A Democrat in his politics, he became a member of the Constitutional Convention of Montgomery County in 1953. He is a Rotarian, and a member of the Knights of Pythias. He and his family attend the Episcopal Church.

On August 25, 1948, Dempsey H. Marks married Julia Wilcox. A native of Clarksville, she was born on October 6, 1928, daughter of Robert C. and Julia (Van Cleve) Wilcox. They live in Clarksville, where Mr. Wilcox is now retired. Mrs. Marks attended the public schools of that city and Depauw, Indiana.

She and Mr. Marks are the parents of three children, all of whom were born at Clarksville: 1. Connie Louise, born on July 7, 1949. 2. Julia Van Cleve, born December 27, 1950. 3. Robert Clive, born June 15, 1956.

JOE W(ALTER) HENRY, SR.

Following experience in farming, to which he devoted the early years of his career, Joe W(alter) Henry, Sr., turned his attention to law-enforcement work. For over a decade he has been chief of police and fire chief at Pulaski.

He is a native of Lynnville, in Giles County, and was born on April 25, 1892, son of Joe Weir and Emma (Hollowell) Henry. His father was also a native Tennessean, born December 16, 1852, at Cornersville; and Emma Hollowell, whom he married, was born in Alabama in April, 1861. They were farming people. Joe Walter Henry was reared on a farm near Lynnville, and attended the public schools of Giles County, that being the extent of his formal education. He continued farming in the Lynnville area for twenty years.

His first position in public office, and also his first law-enforcement post, was that of sheriff of Giles County, an office to which he was elected in 1934, taking office in August of that year. He served for six years. His next position was as supervisor for the Red Stone Arsenal, on whose staff he served for four years. Mr. Henry became chief of police of Pulaski, Tennessee, in 1946. He has capably filled the duties of that office ever since, and concurrently throughout the same period of years, he has been the city's fire chief. As police chief, he has achieved a distinguished record in traffic safety, and in recognition of this has received the award conferred by the Tennessee State Safety Council.

Chief Henry is a Democrat in his politics. He attends the Methodist Church, of which he is an active member.

In Pulaski, on December 7, 1915, Joe W(alter) Henry, Sr., married Louise Ward. Born in Maury County on July 20, 1894, she is a daughter of Curtis J. and Maggie (Scott) Ward. The couple are the parents of six children: 1. Joe W(ard) Jr., who was born on September 20, 1916, at Lynnville,

Tennessee. He served in the army during World War II, being in action in the Mediterranean Theater and Italy. A major in the infantry, he received a bronze star and combat infantry badge. He now holds the rank of major general in the Tennessee National Guard. Receiving his degree of Bachelor of Laws from Cumberland University, he is now practicing with his brother Jack as a member of the firm of Henry and Henry at Pulaski. Joe W(ard) Henry, Jr., married Marjorie Clark of Uniontown, Kentucky. Their children: i. Joe W(ard), 3rd, born in 1948. ii. Robert Clark, born in 1951. 2. Amy, born June 30, 1920. She married Everett Chapman of Lynchburg, a farmer and livestock raiser. They have four children: i. Leonard, born in 1940. ii. James, born in 1944. iii. William, born in 1948. iv. Jack Henry, born in 1952. 3. James H., born on June 12, 1921. He served four years with the United States Marine Corps, 1941-1945, most of that time being spent in the Pacific, where the Corps carried out some of the most heroic, and costliest, campaigns in their history. At that time he held the rank of corporal. He is now a captain in the National Guard. A lawyer, he received his degree of Bachelor of Laws from Cumberland University in 1950. He practices at Tullahoma. Married to the former Mary D. Miller of Lewisburg, he is the father of three children: i. Mareese, born in 1951. ii. James H., born in 1954. iii. Patricia, born in 1958. 4. Jack Brown, born on August 4, 1926, at Lynnville. He attended school in Giles County, and Martin College at Pulaski, Tennessee Polytechnic Institute at Cookeville, and Cumberland Law School, where he took the degree of Bachelor of Laws in 1949. From 1954 to 1956 he served in the army at Fort Benning, Georgia. He was a first lieutenant in the Judge Advocate General's Corps. He is now a captain in the National Guard. Since 1950, he has practiced law at Pulaski with his oldest brother, Joe W. Henry. He is a member of the American, the Tennessee, and the Giles County Bar Associations, and in 1953 he was a member of the Constitutional Convention. He is deeply interested in Boy Scout work, and is currently chairman of the Advancement Committee of the David Crockett District. He is exalted ruler of the Elks lodge and a member of the Country Club, Exchange Club and American Legion. He is a Democrat. Jack B. Henry married Martha Fletcher of Tullahoma; she attended Cumberland University. 5. William C., born June 3, 1928, in Lynnville. He lives in Springfield, and is a highway patrolman. He served in the National Guard for twelve years. William C. Henry married Rose Ann Holland. 6. Martha, born December 23, 1938, in Lynnville. She married Joe Williams of Pulaski.

SAMUEL CHESTER MAJOR

Coming to Memphis with ample experience in the lumber industry, Samuel Chester Major played a considerable role in building up that industry in the region. First establishing his own firm as a dealer in hardwood, he later became president of the Major and Cromwell Lumber Company, the DeSoto

Samuel C. Major

Hardwood Flooring Company, and the L. D. Murrelle Lumber Company, and was an official of other concerns and of lumbermen's organizations.

A native of Clinton County, Indiana, he was born on February 10, 1865, son of William Carrick and Margaret (Barr) Major. He received his education in the rural schools of his county, and in his early years, worked on his father's farm. His first venture in the commercial world was as a partner in a furniture business at Kirklin, Indiana. He entered the lumber industry in 1887 with W. H. Guire and Brother at Kirklin, Indiana, and continued in that connection for three years. He then went to Indianapolis, where he spent five years with H. C. Long. His next connection, of equal duration, was with the firm of Hall and Frisbee at Jamestown, in western New York State. These were both lumber firms. In 1900, Mr. Major acquired an interest in the Steele and Hilliard Lumber Company of St. Louis, Missouri. He was active in the operation of that firm for four years.

At the end of that time, he came to Memphis, where he first formed an organization of his own, S. C. Major and Company, which dealt in hardwood grown in this section of the country. He was sole owner of that company as long as the firm continued in existence. Mr. Major then became president of Major and Cromwell Lumber Company. He was also secretary and treasurer of the McGraw Curran Lumber Company, as well as director and president of the DeSoto Hardwood Flooring Company and the L. D. Murrelle Lumber Company. He was a member and past president of the Memphis Lumber Club and of the National Wholesale Lumber Dealers Association.

In his own city, Mr. Major held membership in the Memphis Chamber of Commerce and the Colonial Country Club. Both he and Mrs. Major held membership in the Memphis Country Club. They were both fond of horseback riding and golf. Mr. and Mrs. Major were active in the Second Presbyterian Church. Both were fond of travel, and had taken trips to England, France, Italy, and Egypt.

She is the former Miss Georgia Bell Tidwell, daughter of Joseph Deberry and Eliza (Harris) Tidwell. Prior to her marriage, at Memphis on October 27, 1916, she had lived at Jackson, Tennessee. Mrs. Major has been very active in her church circle at Second Presbyterian Church, and is also a member of the Arts and Garden Club. She has retained her interest in travel, and recently took a trip to Honolulu in company with her sister.

Mrs. Major had a daughter by a previous marriage: Sarah Shelby Taylor. She died in infancy.

The death of the lumber executive and organizational leader occurred on May 16, 1948 at Memphis.

John Franklin Morrison, Jr.

John Franklin Morrison, Jr., has been prominent in the professional life and public affairs of Lawrenceburg, where he has practiced law since 1921. He is currently serving as city attorney, and he has rendered valuable service to the federal government as an official of the Office of Price Administration and the Office of Price Stabilization.

A native of Waynesboro, he was born on May 30, 1897, son of John Franklin, Sr., and Eulalie Agnes (Keeling) Morrison. His father, who was born in Wayne County on July 14, 1864, was a lawyer with a distinguished record in public life. He was chairman of the draft board of Lawrence County from July, 1917, to November, 1919. From 1918 to 1927, he served on the bench as county judge. He served the people of the Twenty-second Senatorial District of Tennessee in the Tennessee State Senate, in the General Assembly of 1907. Eulalie Agnes Keeling, whom he married, was born on January 16, 1865, in Giles County. They were married in that county on May 24, 1896. She died June 11, 1921, at Lawrenceburg, and he survived her until August 16, 1948, when he died at a hospital in Nashville.

The younger John Franklin Morrison attended local public schools and Lawrence County High School, where he graduated in June, 1913. For one year, 1914-1915, he was a student at Vanderbilt University, taking academic courses. He later entered the United States Army, enlisting at Camp Wadsworth, South Carolina, on September 6, 1918. He served until March 25, 1919, and was discharged as battalion sergeant major, Camp Headquarters Detachment. He then resumed his studies, and in June, 1921, received his degree of Bachelor of Laws at Cumberland University in Lebanon.

Admitted to the bar, Mr. Morrison commenced his general practice of law at Lawrenceburg in September, 1921. His practice has constituted his major activity continuously to the present time, with the exception of the years from 1943 to 1947, and again from 1951 to 1953, which were spent with the legal department of the Office of Price Administration and Office of Price Stabilization, at their Nashville District office.

Mr. Morrison assumed duties in his first local public post in May, 1931, when he became city attorney of Lawrenceburg. He served until May, 1935. Two decades later, in July, 1955, he again became city attorney, and has held office since that time. He was unsuccessful candidate for judge of the General Sessions Court of Lawrence County in the August, 1958, election.

In Mr. Morrison's record of practice is included the important case of Smith vs. City of Lawrenceburg, the original bill in which was filed in the Chancery Court at Lawrenceburg on May 15, 1934, and decided, on appeal, by the Supreme Court of Tennessee on May 19, 1934.

Mr. Morrison has taken an active interest in local politics. He was a delegate from the Sixth Congressional District of Tennessee to the Democratic National Convention at Chicago in 1944.

As a lawyer he is a member of several bar associations. He joined Sigma Nu fraternity, Vanderbilt University Sigma Chapter, while a student there, and he has a long record of membership in Lawrenceburg Lodge of the Independent Order of Odd Fellows, although now inactive. As a veteran of service in World War I, he belongs to L. O. Crane Post No. 63 of the American Legion at Lawrenceburg, which for many years has been considered "the largest country post in the world."

One of Mr. Morrison's major avocational interests is genealogy and local history. He has done considerable work on the genealogical lines of his own family and that of his wife, and has prepared a short biography of Colonel David Crockett, for use in connection with the state's new David Crockett State Park in Lawrenceburg. He took an active part in bringing about the establishment of this park. He is a charter member of the Lawrence County Historical Society at Lawrenceburg, and a member of the Tennessee Historical Society, the East Tennessee Historical Society, and the Memphis Genealogical Society. He and Mrs. Morrison are communicants of the First Methodist Church at Lawrenceburg.

She is the former Miss Janie May Guthrie, daughter of Robert Johnson and Lillian Douglas (Lacy) Guthrie. Her father was born in Williamson County, Tennessee, on September 12, 1855, and died April 1, 1937, at Lawrenceburg. He was married to Miss Lacy in Madison County on December 19, 1888. She was born in that county on February 14, 1859, and died in Lawrenceburg on November 23, 1934. Mr. and Mrs. Morrison were married at Lawrenceburg on August 28, 1918, the Rev. S. L. Fain officiating. They are the parents of three children, all of whom were born in Lawrenceburg: 1. John Franklin, 3rd, born on October 23, 1922. 2. William Guthrie, born March 8, 1924. 3. Margaret Lillian, born March 3, 1926. Mr. and Mrs. Morrison make their home at 302 South Military Avenue in Lawrenceburg.

SAM NEAL

With experience in journalism dating back to the beginning of his career, Sam Neal has for nearly two decades been the co-owner and publisher of the "Carthage Courier," which reaches a wide readership in the Carthage area. He is a veteran of World War II, and active in local organizations.

Born at Cookeville, on February 21, 1908, he is a son of Samuel Swepson and Amy (Salter) Neal. His father, born in Williamson County, in 1853, was a pharmacist at Cookeville for many years, and also operated a drug store in Nashville for some time, conducting both a wholesale and a retail business. His forebears had come to this country from Ireland. Amy Salter, whom he married, was born in 1876 in Washington, D. C., where her parents had settled on arriving in this country from Scotland. Her father, Dr. Francis Salter, was a regimental surgeon. Amy (Salter) Neal was a talented musician, playing the piano. She was active in the Methodist Church and in civic affairs.

Beginning his education in the public elementary school at Cookeville, Sam Neal graduated from high school there, and for his advanced courses, entered Tennessee Polytechnic Institute, which is also located at Cookeville.

His experience in the newspaper publishing field began when he was sixteen years of age. For seven years he worked on the staff of the Putnam County Herald, which was published at Cookeville, and he was next connected with the Nashville Banner. After this he spent some time with the Chattanooga News Free Press. He was with that paper until he purchased the Carthage Courier in 1939, and he has remained its co-owner and publisher to the present time.

In January, 1945, he left for World War II service in the United States Navy, being assigned to public relations work, in which he continued until his release from service in November, 1945. For a time prior to his entering the navy, Mr. Neal held a responsible position with the Office of War Information in New York.

He is a member of the American Legion post, and the lodge of the Benevolent and Protective Order of Elks, and is also a member of the Methodist Church. In politics he is a Democrat.

Sam Neal returned to his native city of Cookeville to be joined in marriage, on August 21, 1933, to Roberta Conditt. A native of Elmwood, she is a daughter of R. H. and Electa (Allgier) Conditt. Her father, who has been a farmer most of his life, lives at Elmwood. He was born in 1871. Mrs. Conditt died in 1931. Mrs. Neal attended school at Lebanon and Carthage, Tennessee. She is active in church work.

The couple are the parents of two children: 1. Roberta Salter, who was born at Cookeville on February 26, 1935. She attended the schools of Carthage and is a graduate of Vanderbilt University, where she majored in English and received her degree of Bachelor of Science in 1957. She is married to William Rackley of Pulaski, Tennessee, a civil engineer. 2. Kenyon Conditt, born on April 26, 1943, in Lebanon. He is attending high school and plays on the football team.

ROBERT FRANCIS SHEAHAN

In the years before his untimely death, Robert Francis Sheahan contributed much to the city of Memphis, both as industrialist and as civic worker. Coming to the city with valuable experience in commercial and industrial connections, he formed his own organization, the Robert F. Sheahan Company, which engaged in the sale and distribution of paint materials, vitamins, and processing equipment for the finishes, feed and textile industries. He was a well-known and respected figure in the field of industrial chemistry. His fellow Memphians knew him as an inspiring leader in programs for city beautification.

A native of Brookfield, Missouri, he was born on December 28, 1904, son of John Thomas and Margaret (McNamara) Sheahan. His father was a railway maintenance engineer. Attending local public schools, the Memphis executive graduated from Moberly High School in Moberly, Missouri, and commenced his advanced studies at St. Mary's College in Kansas. He transferred

Robert F. Sheahan

from there to Georgetown University in the nation's capital, where he took his degree of Bachelor of Science in 1927. He later took postgraduate work in chemistry at the University of Minnesota.

On graduating from Georgetown, he began his career in the capacity of trainee with the United Hotel Company. He left two years later to join the Thompson-Hayward Chemical Company at Kansas City, Missouri, and this firm named him manager of its Northwestern Division with headquarters at Minneapolis, Minnesota—a position he held until 1942. He left the company to take a position as manager of the Chemical Division of the Minnesota Mining and Manufacturing Company. From 1950 to 1953 he was with the Southern Shellac Manafacuring Company at Memphis, holding the position of vice president and general manager. With this varied background of experience, he formed the firm of Robert F. Sheahan Company in 1953, as a distribution and consulting firm in the paint and chemical raw material field. It grew rapidly during the few years under his capable and aggressive leadership, and now has subsidiaries at New Orleans and Minneapolis, while retaining headquarters in Memphis.

Mr. Sheahan had another business interest in association with Joe N. Pless. They formed the firm of Pless and Sheahan, dealing in feed, antibiotics, and supplements.

While living in Minnesota, Mr. Sheahan was a member of the Minnesota Industrial Chemists Forum, and at one time held office as its president. He served two terms as president of the Memphis Paint, Varnish and Lacquer Association in the later years of his life. He was a member of the Memphis Agricultural Club, and of the Chemists' Club in New York City. His other memberships included the Memphis Rotary Club, the Serra Club, and the Memphis Country Club, the Tennessee Club, and the Memphis Cotton Carnival Society. A communicant of St. Anne's Roman Catholic Church, he served on the boards of the Sons of St. Peter, and St. Jude's Hospital.

In 1954, Mr. Sheahan served as an executive of the Memphis Community Chest, and he was active in support of the Shelby United Neighbors. Probably the community work for which he will best be remembered, however, was his concentrated effort on behalf of city beautification. In the month before his death, he was named for the second year to post of general manager of the city's annual Clean-up, Paint-up, Fix-up Campaign. On other occasions throughout his life, he had been active in comparable civic campaigns.

At St. Paul's Church in Burlington, Iowa, on September 10, 1930, Robert Francis Sheahan married Frances Catherine Riling, daughter of Francis Joseph and Alice Jane (Bauch) Riling. The couple became the parents of the following children: 1. Robert R., who was born on July 30, 1931. A graduate of the United States Naval Academy at Annapolis, Maryland, he is now serving in the United States Marine Corps as a captain in its Air Division. He is married to the former Miss Anne Lilly of Memphis, and is the father of a daughter,

Marianne, and two sons, Daniel S. and David J. Sheahan. 2. John P., born on on May 28, 1935. He graduated from Georgetown University in 1957, taking the degree of Bachelor of Science, and was associated with his father in business. 3. Margaret Jane, born October 7, 1939. 4. Michael F., born October 20, 1942. 5. Mary Frances, born March 19, 1947. The family resided at 68 East Galloway Drive, Memphis, Tennessee.

A useful career in industry and in civic service came to an end with the death of Robert F. Sheahan on February 15, 1959.

WILLIAM HUBERT TURNER

In his many years of law practice at Carthage, William Hubert Turner has earned a reputation as one of the city's outstanding lawyers. He was once mayor of the city, has since been a member of the city council, and also had a seat on the Public Service Commission for six years.

Born at Temperance Hall, on August 15, 1890, he is a son of William Addison and Martha Jane (Fisher) Turner. His father, a native of Virginia, was a merchant in DeKalb County, and served in the Forest Cavalry, Confederate States Army. He died in 1896 at Temperance Hall, when his son was only six years old. Martha Jane (Fisher) Turner was born in Smith County, and died at Carthage.

After commencing his education in local public schools, William H. Turner entered Branham and Hughes Prepartory School at Spring Hill, Tennessee, to complete his secondary studies. When he had graduated there, he enrolled at Vanderbilt University in Nashville, which he attended for four years. In 1916 he graduated from Cumberland Law School. During his student years, he was active in athletics, playing football and baseball. While taking his law degree he was coach of the Cumberland University football and basketball teams.

As soon as he had completed his professional courses and was admitted to the Tennessee bar, Mr. Turner began practice at Carthage, in 1917, and has been there ever since. He served as mayor of the city from 1921 to 1924, then became a member of the city council, on which he has since served. He has also been on the school board. He was appointed to the Railroad and Public Utilities Commission of Tennessee, and served for six years on that body, which is now known simply as the Public Service Commission. He also served as judge of the criminal court in his district.

Mr. Turner is a veteran of military service in World War I. Entering the United States Army in 1917, he was assigned to the Field Artillery, and was commissioned a second lieutenant. He was in action at St. Mihiel and Verdun.

His memberships include several bar associations, and as a veteran, he belongs to the posts of the American Legion and the Veterans of Foreign Wars. Affiliated with the Free and Accepted Masons, he is a member of the higher bodies and has held all offices. He was formerly a Rotarian. A communicant of the Baptist Church, he formerly served as a deacon.

The owner of some productive farm land, Mr. Turner finds a profitable avocation in agriculture. He enjoys hunting, and always keeps some bird dogs.

In his home city of Carthage, on September 18, 1919, William Hubert Turner married Anna Lee Myer. Born in that city on September 9, 1889, she is a daughter of William E. and Virginia (Flippin) Myer. Her father, a native of Smith County, was a merchant. An amateur archeologist, he assembled one of the largest collections of Indian artifacts in the county, and formed a connection with the Smithsonian Institution. During World War I, he served with the Federal Fuel Administration. During that same period, Mrs. Turner served overseas with the Young Women's Christian Association. She is currently active in the program of the Parent-Teacher Association. The couple are the parents of two children: 1. William Hubert, Jr., who was born on July 30, 1920, in Carthage. He attended its public schools and Vanderbilt University. From 1942 until the end of World War II, he served in the United States Navy and attained the rank of commander. He was in action in the South Pacific and was at Okinawa, was wounded and received the Purple Heart. Married to the former Miss Barbara Kindt of California, he is the father of four children: i. Michael, born in 1944. ii. William, born in 1950. iii. Carl, born in 1955. iv. James Nelson, born in 1958. 2. Edward Myer, born on August 9, 1925, in Carthage. He attended schools there, and went on to Tennessee Polytechnic Institute at Cookeville, after returning from service in the United States Navy, 1943-1945. At the Institute, he majored in business administration, and he thereafter attended Cumberland Law School, graduating with the degree of Bachelor of Laws. Edward M. Turner married Jane Coward of Livingston, Tennessee, and they have five children: i. Virginia, born in 1949. ii. Kathryn, born in 1951. iii. Teresa, born in 1953. iv. Barbara Jane, born in 1956. v. Elizabeth, born in 1958.

JOHN BARNETT GORE

The profession of teaching and education has occupied the attention of John Barnett Gore for most of his adult life. His education includes Bachelor of Science, Bachelor of Laws, and Master's degrees in education. For over twenty years, he has been connected with the Smith County educational system. He has also served in the army, and has held public office.

Born in Smith County, on November 13, 1908, Mr. Gore is a son of James S. and Catherine (Gann) Gore. Both of his parents were likewise natives of Smith County, where his father was born in 1865, and his mother in 1870. James S. Gore, who died at Carthage in 1945, was a farmer, and served as a member of the Smith County Court. Catherine Gann, whom he married, was the daughter of Tom Gann, a soldier in the Confederate States Army, and for bravery in battle, was written up in a volume entitled "The Blue and the

Gray." He was for two terms trustee of Smith County. Mrs. Gore died at Carthage in 1949.

Receiving his early education in the public schools of that city, John Barnett Gore later attended Middle Tennessee State College, where he graduated in 1940 with the degree of Bachelor of Science. In 1941 he received his degree of Bachelor of Laws from the YMCA. After completing his law courses, however, he did not immediately commence practice, but began teaching school in Smith County. He followed the teaching profession for eight years, and became superintendent of schools for this county. In 1948 he began his practice of law in Carthage, where he has engaged in a general practice ever since.

Mr. Gore began a tenure with the Tennessee State Department of Taxation and Finance in 1952, and served that state department in the capacity of Supervisor in the Automobile Title Division for two and a half years. He is a Democrat in politics. He is a veteran of wartime service in the United States Army, which he entered in 1942.

Mr. Gore has long been active in the work of the Methodist Church, formerly serving as Sunday school superintendent.

In his home city of Carthage, on June 19, 1941, John Barnett Gore married Kathryn McGinness, daughter of Roscoe and Sydney (Bilbrey) McGinness. A Carthage banker, Roscoe McGinness was born in Putnam County, Tennessee, in 1880, and was for some years assistant cashier of the Smith County Bank. Both he and Mrs. McGinness are active in the Christian Church at Carthage. She was born in Overton County, Tennessee, in 1884. Mrs. Gore herself was born in Overton County, Tennessee, on April 20, 1915. She attends Cumberland University and Virginia Intermountain College, studying English and foreign languages, and taking her degree of Bachelor of Science at Cumberland University in 1936. For a decade she taught school in Smith County. She is very active on behalf of the Girl Scout Program in Carthage, and in the work of the Christian Church.

Mr. and Mrs. Gore have two children, both of whom were born in Carthage: 1. Jane, born on August 2, 1946. 2. John, who was born on September 22, 1951.

JULIAN FULENWIDER

The late Julian Fulenwider's career as an industrialist contributed much to the economic and commercial life of Memphis. He headed several important enterprises in that city, took a constructive part in organizational and civic life, and proved himself a most valuable citizen.

His family has a record of achievement in the area going back well over a century and a half, and in fact one of Mr. Fulenwider's major business interests traces its origin to his early ancestors' efforts. More than one hundred and seventy years ago, or sixty-two years before Arkansas became a state, ancestors

Georgia C. Feulenwider—

Julion Finlenvider

of Julian Fulenwider established in Lincoln County, North Carolina, one of the first furnaces for manufacturing iron into roofing and farming implements.

John Fulenwider, for fifteen years entry taker of Lincoln County, developed a knowledge of the mineral and agricultural lands of the district. He operated the High Shoal Forge in Lincoln County, and won the designation of ironmaster. He supplied the United States Government with cannon balls for use in the War of 1812. Part of his success is to be credited to a family tradition in the industry, for within a decade of the passage of the Act of 1788, four families were engaged in the manufacture of iron, all of them interrelated and destined to control the industry of the North Carolina Piedmont area for three generations. These families were the Peter Forneys, the Major Davidsons, the Alexander Brevards and the Fulenwiders. The Forneys, the Fulenwiders and the Brevards were related by marriage. It was a feeling of great pride which prompted John Fulenwider to begin his will: "I, John Fulenwider, Iron Master of Lincoln, State of North Carolina," and this great pride was communicated to his sons and to his grandsons who continued some of the works even after the Civil War.

By 1830, the resources of North Carolina were nearing the point of exhaustion. The Fulenwider forges were having difficulty operating because of the shortage of wood to provide the necessary charcoal. So the families broke up and migrated from North Carolina seeking coal fields where their iron- and steel-making activities might continue. This migration led Julian Fulenwider's grandfather to Alabama, where he purchased large agricultural lands near Alpine, Talledega, and Vincent. It was not until the generation of Julian Fulenwider that the family resumed activity in their traditional iron-making industry.

The intervening generation was represented by Henry Fulenwider, who was a plantation owner and merchant, and was also licensed to practice law. He once served as census supervisor for three states, and he held office as magistrate and later as judge of the county court. He married Margie Gorman, and their son, whom they named Julian, was born at Alpine, Alabama, on April 27, 1887. He was one of four brothers, and all were educated by private tutors on their plantation in Shelby County. Their education was under the supervision of their mother, Margie (Gorman) Fulenwider, who was one of the leading educators and musicians of her day. The boys received liberal educations with special emphasis on music and foreign languages, as well as basic subjects.

Julian Fulenwider began his business career by operating the commissary on the plantation of his father, Henry Fulenwider, in Shelby County, Alabama. In 1907 he passed the civil service examination and was employed by the federal government in the postal service.

In 1909 Julian Fulenwider joined his three brothers Jesse, Harry and Robert, in Birmingham, Alabama, where the foundation for their present business activities was laid, under the direction of Daniel Fulenwider and his son, A. L. Fulenwider. The four brothers became owners and operators of mining interests in Oneonta, Alabama. In 1914, they opened the first office of the Southern States Iron Roofing Company in Savannah, Georgia. This ultimately became the home office of a chain of businesses operated in southern cities by three of the brothers, Julian, Harry and Jesse.

Julian came to Memphis, Tennessee, in 1919, and opened an office and factory to serve the Mid-South. Later, with his wife Georgia as a partner, he established The Memphis Fence and Roofing Company and the American Steel Garage Company. In 1936, following the death of Jesse Fulenewider, these enterprises were sold to the Tennessee Coal, Iron and Railroad Company, and Julian Fulenwider operated the Memphis units for the new corporation. In 1938 he resigned and with his wife, his daughter, Joan (Fulenwider) Strong, and his son-in-law, Raymond Bunn Strong, established the partnership in existence today and known as National Pressed Steel Company.

This family also has extensive holdings in Arkansas, where they operate a fifteen-hundred-acre farm; in Hardeman County, Tennessee, where they have title to large expanses of timberlands; and in Sarasota County, Florida, where they own large orange-grove properties, bay properties, and commercial holdings. In Shelby County, Tennessee, in addition to owning a large amount of urban property, they also own the historic Raleigh Springs.

Mr. Fulenwider retired about five years before his death so that he and Mrs. Fulenwider might complete their travels to foreign countries. They made several European trips, and finally a round-the-world cruise. They also made a number of South American trips, the last of these taking them throughout the entire continent, and to all of its separate countries. Mrs. Fulenwider retains interests and connections in businesses which her late husband developed in Puerto Rico, Mexico and the Virgin Islands.

Although he was ineligible for active service in the armed forces at the time of World War I, Julian Fulenwider took a leave of absence from his business in 1917 to devote himself full-time to defense efforts. He served in the Fairfield Plant for the duration of the war. This plant produced much material for war needs. Mr. Fulenwider was cited by President Wilson for his contribution to the defense effort.

A member of Stonewall Lodge No. 723, Free and Accepted Masons, he also belonged to the higher bodies of Masonry, including Tennessee Consistory of the Ancient and Accepted Scottish Rite; he held the Thirty-second Degree. He was also a member of Al Chymia Temple, Ancient Arabic Order of Nobles of the Mystic Shrine, and of the Masonic Veterans Association. He was a member of the Sons of Confederate Veterans, and served on the staff of General Harry Rene Lee, commander-in-chief of the Confederate Veterans. He held an honorary commission as brigadier-general—a commission conferred on him for special services to the Confederate Veterans.

His memberships also included the International High Noon Club, the Tennessee Club, the Executives Club of Sarasota, Florida, the Kiwanis Club of Memphis, Sarasota Country Club, and the Chambers of Commerce of Memphis and Sarasota. He and Mrs. Fulenwider maintained a winter home at Osprey, Florida.

Episcopalians, they attended St. Mary's Cathedral, and Mr. Fulenwider served as bishop's warden there. He had served in earlier years as senior warden and junior warden of St. James Episcopal Church.

At Vincent, Alabama, on October 6, 1906, Julian Fulenwider married Georgia Deborah Crowson, daughter of Zachariah Cross and Martha Rebecca (Holmes) Crowson. Mr. and Mrs. Fulenwider became the parents of two children: 1. Joan, who was born on August 15, 1907. She married Raymond Bunn Strong, and they have two children: i. Georgianna, born June 14, 1927. She was married on November 16, 1946, to Dr. Howard Fulenwider. Their children: Jan, born December 22, 1947; Joan, born August 4, 1949; and Leslie, born August 27, 1950. ii. Raymond Julian Strong, born March 14, 1942. 2. Julian Lamar, born September 5, 1909. He is retired and lives in Winter Haven, Florida. He married January 1, 1953, Isabel (Tillie) Maltby of Corning, New York.

Mr. Fulenwider's distinguished career in industry and civic leadership came to an end with his death on February 4, 1958.

DAVID WILLIAM SHIELDS, JR.

Beginning his career as a farmer and teacher, David William Shields, Jr., has devoted most of his time to the practice of law, and has his office in Manchester. He has distinguished himself in a number of public offices, including two terms in the Tennessee State Legislature, and a number of years on the bench of the Coffee County Court.

A native of Rensselaer, Indiana, Mr. Shields was born on January 12, 1899, son of David William and Emma (Gay) Shields. Both of his parents were natives of Jasper County, Indiana, where his father was born in 1859 and his mother in 1878. The family moved to Tennessee shortly after the younger David W. Shield's birth, in 1899, and settled in Coffee County. There his father became a farmer, he having been a school teacher, newspaper man and lawyer in Indiana. Mrs. Shields taught school as she had done previously in Indiana. They were members of the Baptist Church. Both died in Coffee County. The family is of Scottish and Irish extraction.

Attending the public schools in Coffee County, David W. Shields, Jr. graduated from the local high school and attended Vanderbilt University Law School. He later attended Middle Tennessee State Teachers College at Murfreesboro. Mr. Shields was reared on a farm and for several years he farmed in Coffee County. From 1922 to 1925, he taught school there. Admitted to the State Bar in 1921, he has practiced at Manchester since 1932.

Since the beginning of his professional career, Mr. Shields has distinguished himself in a series of public posts. These posts and the years of his tenure, are as follows: Superintendent of Schools of Coffee County, 1927-1932; Member of School Board, 1938-1940; Member of the Tennessee State Legislature two terms, 1941 and 1943; Chairman of Coffee County Highway Commission, 1946-1950. At the time this is written, he has occupied the bench as Coffee County judge for nine years.

Mr. Shields served in the Student Army Training Corps during World War I.

As a lawyer, he belongs to the American Bar Association, the Tennessee State Bar Association, and local bar groups. His nonprofessional memberships include the lodges of Free and Accepted Masons, Independent Order of Odd Fellows and Knights of Pythias. He and his family attend the Methodist Church.

David William Shields, Jr. married Miss Arlie Cox on May 8, 1930, in Coffee County. She is a daughter of Sam J. and Della (Layne) Cox. Both of her parents were natives of Grundy County, Tennessee. Her father, born there on June 11, 1886, is a farmer. He and Mrs. Cox now live at Manchester. She was born in 1891. Also a native of Grundy County, Mrs. Shields was born on April 12, 1907. She and her husband are the parents of the following children: 1. David William, 3rd, who was born on April 11, 1931, in Manchester. He attended Middle Tennessee State College and graduated from Vanderbilt University, taking the degrees of Bachelor of Science and Bachelor of Laws. He now practices law in Manchester. He married Helen Rogers of Coffee County, and they now have one son, David William, 4th. 2. John Alfred, born August 17, 1932, in Coffee County. He attended the public schools there, and Middle Tennessee State College. Later transferring to the University of Tennessee at Memphis, he took his Doctor of Medicine degree there, and interned at St. Thomas Hospital in Nashville. At present, he is serving in the United States Air Force as a captain. He married Argie Haggard of Alabama, and they have two children, Johnenne and John, Jr. 3. James Edward, born May 14, 1938, in Coffee County. He is now a student at Middle Tennessee State College in engineering, and during summer vacations he gains practical experience working on construction. James E. Shields married Ada Kaye Chambers of Manchester. 4. Sam Jarrett, born September 13, 1939, in Manchester. He attended public schools there, and is now a student at Middle Tennessee State College, where he is taking a premedical course.

HORACE JAMES GARRETT

After gaining experience in the practice of law at Manchester, Horace James Garrett assumed his present duties as chancellor, part II, 12th Chancery Division of Tennessee. He has also been alderman and a member of city boards, and his performance in all these public posts has been of consistently high calibre. He is a veteran of military service in World War II and takes a constructive interest in local organizational affairs.

He was born at Antelope, Texas, on May 12, 1918, and is the fourth son of Jasper Lucius and Evelyn Harriet (Prescott) Garrett. His great-great-grandfather was Benjamin Rush Montgomery, an early-day resident of Chattanooga, who began the practice of law in that city in 1836. He was in turn the maternal grandson of Dr. Benjamin Rush, one of the signers of the Declaration of Independence, and one of America's pioneers in medical science. Jasper L. Garrett was born at Dallas, Texas, and died at Fort Worth, in the Lone Star State, in 1920. Evelyn Harriet Prescott, whom he married, was born in Grimes County, Texas, and survives her husband, making her home at Antelope in that state.

H. J. Garrett attended the public schools, and graduated from Bellevue High School, Bellevue, Texas. He then enrolled at John Tarlton Agricultural College, but later transferred to George Washington University in Washington, D. C.

In 1942 he enlisted in the service of the United States Army, and was assigned to the Signal Corps. Going overseas, he was a first sergeant with units serving in the North African and Mediterranean theaters. He participated in the assault on Italy, in the effective but costly military move to neutralize this Axis partner, and thereafter took part in the Naples-Foggia, Rome-Arno, Apennine, and Po Valley campaigns. He received the theater ribbon with four battle stars, and was recommended for the Bronze Star.

After the war, Mr. Garrett resumed his studies in the law, and enrolled at Cumberland University in 1945, where he took his degree of Bachelor of Laws in 1947. Admitted to the bar of Tennessee in that year, he established practice at Manchester, and there he continued in private practice until 1955. In that year, he was appointed to the office of chancellor by Governor Frank G. Clement and later elected for the full term.

Mr. Garrett served as alderman on the Manchester City Board, and was for three years chairman of the local Selective Service board. He was formerly executive director of the Manchester Housing Authority, and member of the Municipal Planning Commission.

As a lawyer he belongs to the American Bar Association, the Tennessee State Bar Association, the Judicial Conference of Tennessee and the Barrister Club, as well as his local bar group. His fraternities are Lambda Chi Alpha and the Blue Key. In his own city he belongs to the Chamber of Commerce, of which he is a past director. He and his family attend the Methodist Church.

On February 21, 1947, Horace James Garrett married Dorothy Roddy. She was born in Birmingham, Alabama, on April 17, 1922, daughter of Andrew Jackson and Margaret (Williams) Roddy. Her father, a native of Tracy City, Tennessee, was auditor for the Tennessee Coal and Iron Company. Margaret Williams, whom he married is a native of Missouri. Mr. and Mrs.

Garrett have six children: 1. Cynthia Anne, born July 29, 1948, in Jacksboro, Texas. 2. Jane Price, born March 31, 1950, in Sewanee. 3. John Roddy, born January 7, 1953, in Manchester. 4. Mary Evelyn, born March 9, 1954. 5. James Prescott, born January 30, 1956. 6. Mark Montgomery, born January 7, 1959. All of the younger children were born in Manchester, where the family resides.

CLARENCE HAMILTON FARRAR, M.D.

When he had completed his professional training, Dr. Clarence Hamilton Farrar commenced his medical practice at Manchester, where he is associated with his father, Dr. J. Horace Farrar. He is a veteran of the Korean War. Active in business affairs and public life as well as in the practice of medicine, he is currently serving as mayor of his city.

A native of Hillsboro, Tennessee, he was born on June 21, 1915, and is a son of Dr. J. Horace and Cornelia (Hamilton) Farrar. His father too was born in Hillsboro, on May 22, 1883. In 1908 Dr. J. H. Farrar took his degree of Doctor of Medicine from the University of Tennessee Medical School, and he has practiced in the state since. From May, 1909, to 1924, he maintained his office at Hillsboro, and he has since practiced at Manchester. While there, he has served patients in all parts of Coffee County. Until four years ago, Dr. J. Horace Farrar operated the only hospital in Manchester. A general practitioner and surgeon, he has delivered about ten thousand babies, and he has held office as president of the Coffee County Medical Society several times, being also a member of the Tennessee Medical Association and the American Medical Association. Like his son, he has taken an active and useful part in public life, having served as mayor of Manchester, and as a member of the school board. During the World War I period he was public health officer in North Carolina, this comprising the difficult period of the influenza epidemic. Dr. J. Horace Farrar was the son of another physician, Dr. C. M. H. Farrar, who also served Coffee County as a magistrate for thirty-three years. Mrs. Farrar, the former Cornelia Hamilton, is deceased.

Attending the public schools of Manchester, Dr. Clarence Hamilton Farrar graduated from high school there, then entered the University of Tennessee. There he received his degree of Bachelor of Arts in 1937. In 1949 he graduated from Emory Medical School in Atlanta, Georgia with the degree of Doctor of Medicine, and passed the following year in internship at Hillcrest Memorial Hospital at Tulsa, Oklahoma.

In 1951, he entered the service of the Army Medical Corps, and was sent to the Korean Theater, where the war between the forces of communism and democracy had broken out the preceding year. He served until 1953, and attained the rank of captain.

Since his return to civilian life, Dr. Farrar has practiced at Manchester, where he is a professional partner of his father. With an interest in business affairs, he is a director of the Timeplan Finance Corporation, an investment

firm. He was elected mayor of Manchester in 1957, and has held office since, acquitting himself well in his city's top executive post, in keeping with the long tradition of public service in his family. He is a Democrat in politics.

As a physician, Dr. Farrar belongs to the American Medical Association, the Tennessee Medical Association and the local medical society. He is a member of the Manchester Chamber of Commerce and the Rotary Club, and attends the Methodist Church.

At Fountain City, Tennessee, on December 25, 1940, Dr. Clarence Hamilton Farrar married Frances Vance, born in Chattanooga, on May 11, 1915, a daughter of Daniel Brevard and Myrtice (Matthews) Vance. Her father is a native of Woodbury, Tennessee, and her mother of Fairburn, Georgia. Mrs. Vance is a pianist. Dr. and Mrs. Farrar are the parents of two children: 1. Stephanie, born January 10, 1952. 2. Scot, born February 19, 1955. Both of the children were born in Manchester.

DWIGHT MITCHELL ARMSTRONG

During the first decades of the century, a considerable influence in the financial and commercial life of Memphis was exerted by Dwight Mitchell Armstrong. A founder of the Commercial Trust and Savings Bank, he remained one of its executives, and was also active in the management of the Greenville Stone and Gravel Company. He was a dependable and effective worker for civic and charitable causes.

Although a resident of Memphis from the time he was six years old, Mr. Armstrong was born at Zion, a Presbyterian community in Maury County, near Columbia, Tennessee, on May 4, 1868. He was a son of Dr. and Mrs. William J. Armstrong. Dr. Armstrong worked valiantly in combatting the epidemic which swept Memphis in 1878, and heroically sacrificed his own life to the disease. His son Dwight attended the public schools of Memphis for two years, then terminated his formal education to begin his career as an office boy in the law firm of Metcalf and Walker. He later became an accountant with the firm of O. K. Houck and Company. He acquired his first experience in banking as an employee of the First National Bank.

Still in his early thirties, he joined Abe Goodman and others in organizing a small bank at Main Street and Beale Street, early in 1901. This bank changed hands four years later, but suspended operations a few weeks after the sale had been consummated, the new owners having become overextended in other operations. A short time afterwards, Mr. Armstrong and others became joint stockholders in organizing the Commercial Trust and Savings Bank, and this new financial institution assumed the liabilities of the suspended concern, securing the release of its affairs from litigation. Through this action, the founders of the new bank earned considerable prestige and confidence for themselves and their institution. Mr. Armstrong was vice president of the Commercial Trust and Savings Bank from its founding in December, 1905, until the end of his life, and he was also treasurer of the Greenville Stone and Gravel Company. As a banker he had a considerable hand in the operation of the Memphis Clearing House, in which he was elected at various times to practically every office. He served on the executive council of the American Banking Association.

He gave generously of his time and energies to every worth-while project in his city. He held office as treasurer of the Chamber of Commerce for several terms, and was also treasurer of the local chapter of the American Red Cross and of Associated Charities of Memphis. At the time of World War I he was a member of the War Finance Board, and he was director for Tennessee in several war savings drives. From the time the Tri-State Fair Association was organized, Mr. Armstrong served as treasurer and a director. He was also chairman of a commission which directed the construction of the central police station in Memphis. One of his business interests was the Clover Farm Dairy, and he was a member of its original board of directors.

A universally respected member of his community, he gave unflagging support to every important civic, charitable and patriotic movement, and formed his personal friendships in all ranks of Memphis society, from laborers to the city's commercial and political leaders. Greatly interested in lodge affairs, he held membership in the Benevolent and Protective Order of Elks, the Independent Order of Odd Fellows and the Woodmen of the World. He was a communicant of the First Presbyterian Church.

On November 9, 1892, Dwight Mitchell Armstrong married Ellen Barton, daughter of Mr. and Mrs. Clark P. Barton. She was a native of Memphis, born on August 13, 1872, and survived her husband by five years, dying on December 28, 1927. She received her education at Mary Baldwin Seminary in Staunton, Virginia, and shortly afterwards came to Memphis. There she shared with her husband an intense interest in the activities of the city. At the time of her death she was president and a director of the Leath Orphanage, now Porter Leath Home, and she was also a director of the Young Women's Christian Association. She was a member of the Memphis Country Club and a communicant of the First Presbyterian Church.

The couple became the parents of a daughter, Elizabeth Barton Armstrong, who married Guy Stollenwerck. Mrs. Stollenwerck was born in Memphis on March 21, 1898. She completed her preparatory education at Miss Emma Cook's Private School in her native city and is a graduate of Ogontz College at Elkins Park, Pennsylvania, where she took her degree of Master of Arts in 1918. She was married to Mr. Stollenwerck on March 6, 1919, in Memphis, and they are the parents of two children: 1. Elizabeth A., born on November 3, 1921. She is the wife of Dr. F. P. Allen, Jr., and the mother of two children: i. Franklin Pearson Allen, 3rd, born on August 23, 1944. ii. Dian Elizabeth, born January 10, 1946. 2. Ellen, who was born on March 31, 1927. She married Marshall Clark. Deeply interested in welfare work, Mrs. Stollenwerck serves on the board of the Porter Leath Home. She is a member of the

Junior League of Memphis, the Little Garden Club, the Kings Daughters In His Name Junior Circle. Her sorority is Omega Delta. She is a communicant of the Church of the Holy Communion, Episcopal.

The death of Dwight Mitchell Armstrong occurred in Memphis on December 28, 1922—the same date on which his wife was to die five years later. A contemporary appraisal of his character is found in a resolution prepared by his colleagues at Commercial Trust and Savings Bank:

Dwight Mitchell Armstrong left behind him a name and impress that will remain as an everlasting monument to a life of beautiful and unselfish service. [He] was the builder of a noble character, a man of sterling worth, upright and honorable in all his dealings with his fellow men.

His home life was ideal. Devotion to his loved ones was sublimely beautiful and was returned in kind. He was a most charitable and benevolent man and no worthy appeal from less fortunate was ever unheeded. Many a poor boy can attribute his success to the guiding hand of this good man.

James H. Henry

Since the beginning of his professional career, James H. Henry has practiced law at Tullahoma, and he is now serving the people of his district in the Tennessee State House of Representatives. Mr. Henry is a veteran of wartime service with the United States Marine Corps.

Born June 12, 1912, in Giles County, Tennessee, he is a son of Joseph Walter and Ann Louise (Ward) Henry. His father, who was born in Marshall County in 1890, has been a law-enforcement officer for thirty years, although he has also engaged in farming. He has served as chief of police of Pulaski, Tennessee, and as sheriff of Giles County for six years. Ann Louise Ward, whom he married, was born in Maury County in 1894. For many years she has been a Sunday school teacher in the Methodist Church.

James H. Henry attended the public schools, and graduated from Giles County High School in 1939. Before he had had the opportunity of completing his advanced studies, this country had become involved in World War II, and he enlisted in the United States Marines in 1942, serving throughout the war and receiving his honorable discharge in 1945. He was in action in the combat areas of the South Pacific, where the Marines took part in some of the most sanguinary actions of the war.

After his return to civilian life, James H. Henry enrolled for his professional studies at Cumberland Law School, where he graduated in 1950 with the degree of Bachelor of Laws. Admitted to the bar in that year, he began practice at Tullahoma, where he has been since. His offices are at 205 Coop Building. He was admitted to practice before the Supreme Court of the United States on November 12, 1954. Besides practicing law, he serves on the board of directors of the First Federal Savings and Loan Association of Tullahoma.

Mr. Henry was first elected State Representative to serve in the Tennessee Legislature for the term beginning in 1957. His term ran through 1958.

As a lawyer he is a member of the following bar associations: Coffee County Bar Association, Tennessee Bar Association, American Bar Association and American Judicature Society. He is also a member of the Rotary Club, and of the Chamber of Commerce which he is currently serving as president. Affiliated with the Free and Accepted Masons, he belongs to the higher bodies of the Scottish Rite, and the Ancient Arabic Order of Nobles of the Mystic Shrine. He is also a member of the Knights of Pythias. A Methodist in religious faith, he teaches an adult class, and is a member of the official board of his church.

At Lewisburg, Tennessee, on June 30, 1949, James H. Henry married Mary D. Miller. A native of Lewisburg, she was born on August 4, 1926, and is a daughter of Virgil Graydon and Iva Pearl (Rees) Miller of Lewisburg. Her father is a veteran of World War I. Mrs. Henry attended Marshall County High School, and graduated from Brennan College, Gainesville, Georgia. For one year she taught school at Tullahoma. She is a pianist. The couple have three children: 1. Mary Rees, who was born in Lewisburg on April 15, 1952. 2. James Hollwell, born at Tullahoma on August 4, 1954. 3. Patricia Weir, born at Tullahoma on October 15, 1958.

JAMES MORRIS POWERS, D.D.S.

Since the beginning of his professional career, Dr. James Morris Powers has practiced dentistry at Waverly. He has also entered public life, serving his city as alderman; and he is a veteran of military service in the Dental Corps.

Born July 30, 1927, at Denver, Tennessee, he is a son of Reverend Mastin C. and Althea (Greene) Powers. Both of his parents were born at Palmyra, in Montgomery County, Tennessee. His father, who was born on July 18, 1884, is a Presbyterian clergyman, currently the pastor of the church of that denomination at Plant, Tennessee. He is a graduate of Bethel College. He and his wife, the former Althea Greene, became the parents of ten children. She died at Waverly on June 28, 1950.

Dr. Powers attended public schools in Humphreys County, and began his advanced courses at Austin Peay State College at Clarksville. He transferred from there to Southwestern at Memphis, and then to the University of Tennessee and in 1951 received his degree of Doctor of Dental Surgery from this institution. He then established practice at Waverly. He is owner of the building at 101 South Church Street in which his offices are located.

From 1953 to 1955, Dr. Powers was absent serving in the Army Dental Corps. Commissioned a lieutenant, he advanced to the rank of captain in the course of his duties, which took him to Germany with the occupation forces. He was attached to the Fourth Infantry Division.

Professionally, Dr. Powers is identified with the American Dental Association, the Tennessee State Dental Association and the Nashville Dental Society. As a veteran of military service, he belongs to the posts of the American Legion and the Veteran of Foreign Wars. From early manhood, he has been active in Masonry, and is a member of Caldwell Lodge No. 273, at Hustburg, of the Free and Accepted Masons, and the higher bodies of the Ancient and Accepted Scottish Rite. He holds the Thirty-second Degree, and is a member of the Ancient Arabic Order of Nobles of the Mystic Shrine and the Order of the Eastern Star. He is also a member of the Lions Club, and he attends the Cumberland Presbyterian Church.

A Democrat, Dr. Powers was elected city alderman in 1957 and continues to serve to date. His favorite outdoor sports are fishing and hunting.

At Franklin, Tennessee, on June 21, 1950, Dr. James Morris Powers married Helen Hill. Born at Franklin on January 18, 1926, she is the daughter of Howard and Lily (Anglin) Hill. Her father, a native of Lawrenceburg, is a farmer, and they live at Franklin, of which town Mrs. Hill is a native. Mrs. Powers attended Austin Peay College in Clarksville, and transferred from there to George Peabody College in Nashville, where she graduated with the degree of Bachelor of Science. She majored in home economics. For three years she taught school at Hartsville in Trousdale County, and she has also taught in the city schools of Waverly.

Dr. and Mrs. Powers are the parents of two children: 1. Jarene, who was born on December 5, 1952. 2. James Morris, born September 20, 1955.

B. Francis Nesbitt, O.D.

Dr. B. Francis Nesbitt is one of the veteran practitioners of optometry in his home area, with offices at 125 North Main Street, Dickson. He is well known professionally, having held office in his state's optometrists' association, and served as editor of the Tennessee Optometrists Journal. He has also been active in business connections, and in public affairs, having served on the Dickson County Court for several years past.

Born at Yellow Creek, in the 13th District of Dickson County, on January 19, 1897, Dr. Nesbitt is a son of Alonzo Newton and Emma Elizabeth (Gilmore) Nesbitt. His father was born October 17, 1860, at Cedar Creek in Dickson County's 11th District. Emma Elizabeth Gilmore, whom he married, was born in the same district on February 18, 1865. Both are now deceased. Alonzo N. Nesbitt was a farmer and livestock dealer.

Beginning his education in the public schools of Dickson County, Dr. Nesbitt planned on a career in business before settling on a professional goal, and attended Draughon's Business College at Nashville. This famous school is the subject of a sketch in this work. He later studied at North Illinois School of Optometry in Chicago, but transferred from there to Pennsylvania State College of Optometry, where he took his degree of Doctor of Optometry in 1922. He was awarded membership in the Omega Delta Fraternity in April 1934 for outstanding achievement.

Immediately upon obtaining his degree, Dr. Nesbitt returned to Dickson where he established his professional practice. He has practiced there continuously ever since. He won a unique honor in 1944, when he became the first optometrist from the South to win a Fellowship in the Distinguished Service Foundation of Optometry, entitling him to studies with the Foundation of Optometry. For fifteen years he was editor of the Tennessee Optometrists Journal. As a member of the Tennessee Optometrists Association, he has held office as secretary and treasurer, and he is also a member of the American Optometry Association and the Middle Tennessee Optometry Association.

He is a director of the First National Bank of Dickson, and is currently serving as chairman of the Dickson Public Utility Board, which operates in five counties. A Democrat, he has served as district magistrate in Dickson, and since 1952 has been a member of the Dickson County Court. During the World War II years, Dr. Nesbitt served in the Tennessee State Guard.

His memberships include the Dickson County Chamber of Commerce, the Farm Bureau, the Farm Club and the Kiwanis Club. Affiliated with the Free and Accepted Masons, he is a member and past master of Dickson Lodge No. 468, and a member of the higher bodies of Masonry up to and including Al Menah Temple, Ancient Arabic Order of Nobles of the Mystic Shrine at Nashville. He is past ambassador of the Shrine at Dickson. The optometrist is also active in the First Baptist Church, where he served in past years as deacon and is now chairman of the board.

Dr. Nesbitt finds a profitable and interesting avocation in farming. He owns a nine-hundred-and-fifty-acre farm near Dickson, where he raises registered polled Hereford cattle and breeding stock, and also produces hay and grain.

On September 6, 1926, in Dickson, Dr. B. Francis Nesbitt married Fay Bishop. She was born at Yellow Creek in the 13th District of Dickson County on December 9, 1901, and is a daughter of Anthony Cannon and Nanny Virginia (Coleman) Bishop. Her father is a native of Cumberland Furnace, Tennessee, and is a farmer. Mrs. Bishop was born at Yellow Creek. Attending local public schools, Mrs. Nesbitt graduated from Dickson Central High School. The couple have no children. Dr. Nesbitt had an older brother, Athy H. Nesbitt, who lost his life in the Battle of Soissons, France, on July 18, 1918.

LAWRENCE K. THOMPSON

In his home city of Memphis and far beyond its confines, Lawrence K. Thompson had a reputation as "one of the greatest financial brains of the Mid-South." Heading an investment firm, L. K. Thompson and Company, he played an outstanding individual part, both as business man and as loyal citizen, in building his city and assuring its progress. He will long be remembered for his charitable activities.

A native of Prides Station, Alabama, he was born on November 14, 1871, son of Joseph N. and Lucie (Malone) Thompson. Receiving his education in local schools, he came to Tennessee to begin his banking career with the First

National Bank of Nashville, serving on its staff for several years before moving to Memphis in 1905. In that city he first worked as an accountant for the Memphis Street Railway Company, and after a short time in that connection, joined the old National Bank of Commerce.

At about this period, Mr. Thompson began his record in individual financing operations, an activity in which he had few peers. He was in charge of financing the Memphis Courthouse, erected at a cost of one and a half million dollars. This was his first large-scale venture of the kind, and it was followed at the time of World War I by his promotion of another million-and-a-half bond issue to finance the work of the St. Francis County Levee Board in Arkansas. In 1925 he assisted in underwriting the five-million-dollar bond issue of the Federal Compress and Warehouse Company, which was the largest issue which had ever been floated in Memphis up to that time. He was also in charge of the two-million-dollar Peabody Hotel issue, and also programs for financing the Memphis Steam Laundry and the National Cottonseed Products Company. He was later a leader in war bond campaigns, and in raising money for Christian Brothers College, St. Agnes Academy, and the Little Sisters of the Poor.

During his connection with the Bank of Commerce and Trust Company, later the National Bank of Commerce, Mr. Thompson organized the first stock and bond department ever to be established in a Memphis bank. He headed the department until 1926, when he and others joined in forming the Commerce Securities Company, which was operated in connection with the bank and directed by Mr. Thompson. Following the liquidation of Commerce Securities Company, he formed his own organization in 1933, the securities and investment firm known as L. K. Thompson and Company. This he headed until he retired two years before his death.

Mr. Thompson was one of those who played a large part in organizing the National Bank of Commerce to succeed the Bank of Commerce and Trust Company. In a dramatic all-night session, he and others took actions which were successful in maintaining full value for every depositor and stockholder, while launching the new bank. During the 1930s he was president of two joint stock land banks, and in these capacities, did everything possible to aid distressed farmers. Also during that period, he was a member of the board of directors of the Tennessee Taxpayers Association and president of the Property Owners Association of West Tennessee.

Writing of his financial talents, in the editorial columns of the Memphis Press-Scimitar, a fellow townsman and journalist commented:

We recall that when Governor Peay was about to impose the tobacco tax he summoned Mr. Thompson to the capitol to tell him how much money a certain tax levy would bring in for the state's school system.

Mr. Thompson was more than an expert. He was a genius at anything dealing with finance.

He planned the financing of many business enterprises and they are as much a monument to his memory as they are to others who had a more public part in building them.

An editorial in the Commercial Appeal said of him: "He was a prime mover in obtaining financing for a number of the more substantial structures of Memphis, and a pioneer in establishing the securities and investment business."

Remembered no less for his philanthropic and public welfare activities, Mr. Thompson was active on behalf of the program of the U.S.O. during World War II. He publicly assisted a number of charities, but his private philanthropies were on a still larger scale. In April, 1946, he was made an affiliate member of the Institute of Brothers of the Christian School, a worldwide association of Catholic teachers, and an honor accorded those who have contributed to the cause of Christian brotherhood. Mr. Thompson was a member of the Knights of Columbus and of the "C" Club of C.B.C. He was a communicant of Immaculate Conception Roman Catholic Church.

His memberships included the Chamber of Commerce, the Executives Club, Oak Donic Hunting and Fishing Club, the Fishing Club, and the Memphis Country Club.

In Memphis, on January 7, 1915, Lawrence K. Thompson married Nelse Caldwell Rockwood, whose biographical sketch accompanies. To their marriage three children were born: 1. Lucia Malone, who was born on May 21, 1916. She married Gilbert C. Greenway. They are the parents of four children: Gilbert C., IV, Nelse Lawrence, George Lauder and Sarah Helen Greenway. 2. Lawrence K., Jr., born October 24, 1917. He married Ellen Griffin Shea. Their children are: Lawrence K., III, Nelse Rockwood, II, Lucien Malone, John Shea, Martin Flanagan, Ellen Griffin, William Robert and Thomas J. Thompson. 3. Helen Rockwood, born December 15, 1919. She married Livio Napolitini of Los Angeles, California.

Mr. Thompson's death occurred on January 16, 1948.

MRS. LAWRENCE K. THOMPSON

Mrs. Lawrence K. Thompson—Nelse Caldwell (Rockwood) Thompson —is one of the distinguished women of Memphis' organizational and social life. She has been a leader in welfare causes, a loyal and constructive worker in each cause which has enlisted her support, and holds many memberships.

Born Nelse Caldwell Rockwood, at Crookston, Minnesota, on August 24, 1886, she is a daughter of Charles Brigham and Sallie Tyler (Caldwell) Rockwood. Her father, who had attended Columbia University and graduated from Yale University, followed various occupations, and was talented as an inventor. In the maternal line, Mrs. Thompson is descended from John Marshall Caldwell, who was born in Shawneetown, Illinois about 1825, worked in the Post Office Department in Washington prior to the Civil War, and was later a

Nelse R. Thompson

wholesale grocer in Indianapolis. He married Augusta Tyler. Their oldest child was a son, Albert Sloo, distinguished lawyer and business leader who is the subject of an accompanying sketch. Sallie Tyler Caldwell was the third of their six children.

Mrs. Thompson received her education at Pelham Manor School in New York State, and after leaving school, spent the next ten years traveling in all parts of the world with her uncle, Albert S. Caldwell, who was a noted world traveler. On January 7, 1915, in Memphis, she became the wife of Lawrence K. Thompson, whose career is the subject of a preceding sketch. His death occurred in January, 1948. The couple were the parents of three children presented more fully in their father's record. At the outbreak of World War I when the Fatherless Children of France Incorporated was first organized, Mrs. Thompson headed an agency in Memphis through which about 2,000 French war orphans were given support.

Mrs. Thompson's outstanding record of community work goes back many years. At the time of the depression she took the lead in establishing soup kitchens in her city, to feed the needy; and her inspiring example was effective in securing the cooperation of packing houses and dairies, who gave in generous quantity the requisites for operating these kitchens. Business firms and private citizens contributed funds and later the R.F.C. assisted. The organization under her direction went on from there to help hard-pressed citizens in other ways, occasionally making the last installment payment on a home, or other major purchase, without which it would have been forfeited to the mortgagor.

In more recent years, Mrs. Thompson has been deeply interested in the cause of education. In particular, a project which has retained her loyal support is the Lausanne School for Girls. She was associated with Mrs. Emma Desaussure Jett in founding the school in 1926, and she contributed generously toward the construction of new school buildings. Mrs. Thompson was the organizer of the Mid-South Opera Guild, an affiliated branch of the Metropolitan Opera Guild of New York City, and is vice president of the Mid-South Guild as well as vice president of the Memphis Opera Theatre, Inc. She is a member of the Memphis Garden Club, Garden Club of America, Colonial Dames of America, The Contemporaries, and the Memphis Country Club, and gives useful support to the programs of each of these organizations. She is communicant of Calvary Episcopal Church.

Mrs. Thompson's home, one of the attractive residences of Memphis, is located at 1785 Harbert Avenue. Its design is based on that of the Hancock House in Boston, and it was built about fifty years ago. It is surrounded by beautiful and well-kept grounds, and is a popular center of the city's social life.

Albert Sloo Caldwell

Prominent Memphis lawyer and financier Albert Sloo Caldwell was not only influential in the business affairs of his home city, but contributed much to the rebuilding of the South during the difficult decades following the Civil War. He possessed the boldness, imagination and resources required to bring in the capital which resuscitated its commerce; and he also took the lead in programs of construction for public benefit, such as the levees. Throughout his career he gave selflessly of his abilities for the benefit of his home region.

He was born in Washington, D. C., on September 3, 1853, son of John Marshall and Charlotte Augusta (Tyler) Caldwell, and grandson of James Caldwell and of Henry Ball and Elizabeth (Brown) Tyler. John M. Caldwell's father died when he was very young, and he was reared by the family of Colonel Albert Sloo, of Vincennes, Indiana, later naming his own son for this foster-father. Prior to the Civil War, he was head of one of the departments of the post office in Washington, D. C. He later moved to Indianapolis, where he entered the wholesale grocery business.

Their son Albert Sloo Caldwell completed his institutional education at Racine College in Wisconsin, where he graduated in 1872. He began acquiring his experience in the law in the offices of Porter and Fishback in Indianapolis, Indiana, both of whose members were distinguished lawyers. Admitted to the bar in 1876, he entered a partnership with John M. Judah, their firm being known as Judah and Caldwell. In January, 1882, he became associated with Francis Smith, in the firm of Francis Smith and Company. In 1885, the F. Smith, Caldwell and Company was organized, a concern engaged primarily in attracting the investment of foreign money in the promotion of the South's commercial development. Offices were opened at Montgomery, Alabama, Vicksburg, Mississippi, and San Antonio, Texas; and Mr. Caldwell had his offices in Vicksburg until 1886 when he moved from there to Memphis.

There he continued his work in attracting financing for the development of cotton crops, these resources coming primarily from English and Scottish insurance companies. He made a number of trips abroad to arrange such loans. The firm of Smith, Caldwell and Company was dissolved in 1890, the partners dividing up their previous territory. By this arrangement, Mr. Caldwell took over the southern interests outside of Texas, while his senior partner, Mr. Smith concentrated his activities in the Lone Star State. A junior member of the firm, Bolton Smith, son of Francis Smith, retired from the business to practice law in Memphis.

Mr. Caldwell next joined in a partnership with John M. Judah, his former law partner in Indianapolis, to form the firm of Caldwell and Judah. Several years later Mr. Judah again went his own way, and Bolton Smith then became associated with Mr. Caldwell, to form the firm of Caldwell and Smith.

In 1917, when this country became involved in World War I, Albert S. Caldwell retired from law practice and offered his services to the American

ALBERT S. CALDWELL

Red Cross. However, the authorities delayed accepting his offer until March, 1918, because of his age. However, his valuable experience and his eagerness to be of assistance to the country at war finally won out and his services were accepted. In March, 1918, he went to France, and served the Red Cross cause there until October, 1918, paying his own expenses throughout that period.

One of Mr. Caldwell's lasting interests, and one through which he contributed much to the development of his region, was flood control programs. Becoming president of the Mississippi River Levee Association, he worked for a number of years securing flood protection, devoting more time to the cause than to private business interests. He was largely instrumental in securing the passage of an important flood control act appropriating forty-five million dollars for construction programs in the Mississippi Delta area. The bill was passed by the United States Congress and signed by President Woodrow Wilson in 1917. Agitation for securing such protection dated back to the disastrous floods of 1912 and 1913, which so greatly impoverished the Mississippi's lower regions. The inadequate action taken at that time by local and regional boards proved the necessity of higher-level organization, and it was this which Mr. Caldwell's efforts were effective in securing. Meantime local levee boards organized to form the Mississippi River Levee Association, of which he was the first president. As a token of his victory in securing the best possible aid for his cause, Mr. Caldwell was presented with the pen used by President Wilson in signing the appropriation bill. In March, 1917, the city of Memphis presented him with a silver loving cup as a further token of recognition of his invaluable work.

His role in civic leadership was broadly based. He served on the board of directors of the Memphis Chamber of Commerce, and was a member of the U.S. Chamber of Commerce, and was active in the Memphis Club and the Tennessee Club. An Episcopalian, he was a communicant of St. Mary's Cathedral. As a financier he was interested in numerous business enterprises, and helped assure his city of a sound commercial growth.

A world traveler from the time he first went abroad to attract English and Scottish capital for the benefit of the South, Mr. Caldwell crossed the Atlantic over sixty times, and the Pacific three times, and he made one complete trip around the world, visiting all major portions of the globe with the exception of Australia, New Zealand and South Africa. In the course of his full and active career in influential roles, he made the acquaintance of many persons of distinction. Among his friends were the poet James Whitcomb Riley, vocalist Eugene Cowles, William Mackenzie, the Dundee financier, and Julia Marlowe, Shakespearean actress. M. Paul Claudel, French ambassador, once paid Mr. Caldwell a visit to inspect his art treasures. He had a vast and valuable collection of art objects which he assembled in the course of his journeys to many countries.

In Indianapolis, Indiana, on September 6, 1882, Albert Sloo Caldwell married Cordelia Jameson, daughter of Dr. Henry Jameson. She died January 3, 1887. They had two children who died in infancy. Albert S. Caldwell's death occurred in Memphis on November 19, 1928.

Lucy White Blackwell

A distinguished record in public posts, dating from the early years of her career, is that of Miss Lucy White Blackwell of Jackson. She is currently manager of that city's office of the Tennessee Department of Employment Security. She was the first woman ever appointed to the board of the Jackson Free Library, and has served as chairman of that body.

Miss Blackwell's native city is Jackson. She was born on April 22, 1912, and is a daughter of William Francis and Mary Ethel (White) Blackwell. Her father was born at Water Valley, Mississippi, on July 23, 1878, and died in 1912; he was a linotype operator on an early labor paper. Her mother, a native of Jackson, was born on February 8, 1879. Miss Blackwell attended Jackson city schools and graduated from Jackson High School in 1929. She then enrolled at Lambeth College, which is also located in Jackson, and there she took her degree of Bachelor of Arts in 1933. She took graduate courses at West Tennessee Business College in Jackson in 1934-1935.

In March, 1935, she took a position as stenographer with the Tennessee Emergency Relief Administration, and she was employed by the Farm Security Administration in Jackson and Brownsville, Tennessee, from 1936 to 1939. In the latter year she joined the staff of the Tennessee Department of Public Welfare, but continued in that connection for only about a year. On March 1, 1940, she entered the service of the Tennessee Department of Employment Security as a clerk. She was promoted to interviewer in 1942; and on the basis of her proven aptitudes and her varied experience in public work, was named manager of the Department's local office in Jackson in 1947.

The first woman to be appointed by the Jackson City Commission to membership on the board of trustees of the Jackson Free Library, Miss Blackwell served for eight years, 1948 until 1957. She was treasurer of the board for seven of these years, and chairman for one year. For a long time she has been identified with the International Association of Personnel in Employment Security. She has served as president of the Jackson Subchapter; won first place in the statewide essay contest sponsored by the Tennessee Chapter in 1953; chaired a statewide training institute for chapter members at Lambeth College in 1956; and has also chaired the state chapter's Award of Merit Committee.

Through the years, Miss Blackwell has participated continuously and actively in numerous community health, welfare and educational projects, such as the programs of the American Red Cross, the National Association for Infantile Paralysis, the League of Women Voters, and others. Since 1943 she has been active in the work of the American Cancer Society. She served ten years as Madison County commander; two years as West Tennessee District commander; two terms as recording secretary of the society's Tennessee Division; and since 1945, member of the division's state board of directors. She organized the Madison County Unit of the American Cancer Society, served as its first president, and led the movement for the establishment of the Cancer Clinic, which has operated at Jackson-Madison County General Hospital since 1954. She was also a member of the board of directors of the Jackson Community Chest. Miss Blackwell is active in the Lambeth College Alumni Association. In 1956 she received the coveted R. E. Womack Achievement Award, presented annually by the association to one of its members "in recognition of . . . outstanding contribution to society and dedication to the ideals embodied in Lambeth's motto: 'Whatsoever things are true'." In 1955, Miss Blackwell was named Jackson's Woman of the Year, for her contributions to community welfare and betterment.

She is a former member of the Pilot Club, an international classified civic-service club for business and professional women. Active in the group for fifteen years, she served the Jackson Pilot Club as president, District Seven (State of Tennessee) as district governor, and Pilot International as international program coordinator. She has been chairman of several international committees, and a member of the international executive committee for three years. Since 1956, she has held membership in the Altrusa Club of Jackson.

Miss Blackwell was a charter member of the Johnson Memorial Presbyterian Church in Jackson, having worked and worshipped there as a child when the church was a mission Sunday school. She took a leading part in the successful movement for organization of the church in 1934. In the current year, 1959, she is a member of the First Cumberland Presbyterian Church of Jackson. She has been soprano soloist in church choirs for a number of years.

Miss Blackwell's residence is at 166 Russell Road, Jackson, and her office address is 416 East Chester Street.

HARRY EDWARD HENRY

Harry Edward Henry of Jackson has to his credit a quarter-century of experience in the food brokerage field. He is now president and principal stockholder of the Allen-Henry Company, and chief executive of the Central Warehouse Company. In the course of his active business life at Jackson, he has come to take an influential part in its civic and organizational affairs as well.

He is a native of Henderson, Tennessee, and was born on September 15, 1909. His parents are Harry Emery Henry, who was born on January 23, 1885, at Glasgow, Missouri, and Mae Crockett (Robins) Henry, born at Henderson on November 2 of that year. His father was connected with the Decker Manufacturing Company for fifty years. A resident of Jackson from his early years, Harry Edward Henry attended its public schools and graduated from Jackson High School in 1927. For two years he was a student at Union University, which is located in Jackson.

He left the classroom in 1929 to commence his commercial career, becoming part owner of a local theater in that year, and assuming duties as its manager. He entered the food brokerage business with M. O. Reams as a partner on July 1, 1933. Their partnership, under the firm name of Reams and Henry Company, continued until 1937, when Mr. Henry bought Mr. Reams' interest. The organization then continued as the Henry Brokerage Company until the tenth anniversary of its founding, July 1, 1943. At that time a consolidation was effected with the A. M. Allen Company, and the present firm of Allen-Henry Company is the result of this merger. However, Mr. Allen died several years later, and Mr. Henry acquired his interest. The firm was incorporated in 1954 under the old name, and since that time, Mr. Henry has been principal stockholder, as well as president of the corporation. He also owns and operates the Central Warehouse Company. Offices of the Allen-Henry Company are at 221 Bellevue Street, Jackson.

Mr. Henry is a member of the board of directors of the First National Bank of his city. He has also served on the boards of the Chamber of Commerce, the local Tuberculosis Association, the United Fund, and the Young Men's Christian Association, and he is a member of the board of trustees of the Jackson Little Leaguers. For four years he served on the recreation board of the city. In recognition of his useful role in civic affairs, he was elected Jackson's Man of the Year in 1953.

A twenty-year member of the Lions Club, Mr. Henry was formerly president of the organization, and serves on its board. He is a former director of the Jackson Country Club. Belonging to Lodge No. 192 of the Benevolent and Protective Order of Elks, he has held office as exalted ruler. He is also a member of the Free and Accepted Masons and the higher bodies of the order, holding the Thirty-second degree; he holds membership in the Ancient Arabic Order of Nobles of the Mystic Shrine. He is a communicant of the First Baptist Church.

At the time of World War II, Mr. Henry spent two years in the army, being assigned to Headquarters Detachment of the Fourth Service Command.

In his home city of Jackson, on April 4, 1936, Harry Edward Henry married Elizabeth Jones. She is the daughter of James Leroy Jones, who was born at Trezevant, Tennessee, on March 28, 1881, and his wife the former Leila Broome, born at Magnolia, Arkansas, on September 16, 1884. Mr. Jones is a retired railroad conductor. Mr. and Mrs. Henry have one son, Harry Lee Henry, who was born on July 15, 1947, in Nashville. The family resides at 103 Morningside Drive, Jackson.

FRANK MARSHALL GILLILAND

Following the practice of law in Memphis, Frank Marshall Gilliland distinguished himself not only in this profession but also in business and in civic leadership.

He was born June 29, 1889, in Colliersville, son of Fletcher McClure and Carolyn (Farabee) Gilliland. He was descended from early settlers in this country, of Scottish and English ancestry. One of his ancestors was Amos Richardson, Deputy Governor of Massachusetts, who was born in 1620 and died in 1683, and served under Governor Winthrop. Jonathan Richardson, grandson of Amos, married Anne Edwards, who was born in Hartford, Connecticut, in 1678, and died at Coventry in that state in 1764. She was the daughter of Richard Edwards, first Queen's Attorney in America. Other ancestors were of the Marshall, Harrison, and Berry families of Virginia. John Berry McFerrin became a bishop of the Methodist Church about 1865. Mr. Gilliland had Revolutionary descent in both family lines. Both of his grandfathers served the cause of the Confederacy during the Civil War. His paternal grandfather was Fletcher McClure Gilliland, Sr. His maternal grandfather, Captain John R. Farabee, was captured at the Battle of Fort Donelson and was held prisoner at Johnson's Island on Lake Erie during much of the war period.

Frank M. Gilliland's family moved to Memphis when he was very young. He completed preparatory studies at Webb School, in Bellbuckle, in 1908, and he then entered Vanderbilt University, where he received his degree of Bachelor of Arts in 1912. He was a member of Kappa Alpha fraternity. He went on to law school at Washington and Lee University in Virginia. He has practiced law in Memphis since becoming a member of the bar in 1913. In recent years his sons, Frank Marshall Gilliland, Jr., and James Sevier Gilliland, joined him in his law office.

A colleague, president of the Memphis and Shelby County Bar Association, said of Mr. Gilliland, "He was not only an outstanding attorney and citizen, but he was also a highly dedicated member and officer of this bar, and he did a memorable work for the association." He was also a member of the Tennessee State Bar Association and the American Bar Association. He served for twenty years as general counsel of the Memphis Cotton Carnival Association. In his private practice he specialized in general business, corporation, and tax law.

Another of Mr. Gilliland's colleagues of the bar referred to him as "a fine citizen, an excellent lawyer and one of the finest businessmen I have ever known." He served as legal counsel for Governor Sterling of Texas when he erected the Sterick Building in Memphis—the largest office building in the South at the time it was erected in 1926. Mr. Gilliland owned twenty per cent of the stock thereafter until 1950, when he became sole owner of the Sterick Building. He sold his interests in 1956. Mr. Gilliland was also president of DeSoto Properties, Inc., owning and operating realty, oil and gas interests in Louisiana.

He was a veteran of World War I, having volunteered for service in April, 1917, the month we became involved in that conflict. Commissioned a lieutenant and later promoted to captain, he served in the 120th Infantry Regiment, 30th Division, a unit which was attached to the British troops in France, and which "broke the Hindenburg Line." The 30th Division also defended the Ypres Salient, known by the British as "The Bloody Salient," and participated in the Ypres-Lys engagement in connection with the Second British Army. They were used as shock troops, together with the Fifth Australian Division and the 27th American Division, by the British Fourth Army in the great Somme offensive, so that Mr. Gilliland participated in many of the most decisive engagements of the war. He received his discharge at Camp Jackson, South Carolina, on April 29, 1919.

Mr. Gilliland was an early member of the Shelby County Post No. 1 of the American Legion, and in December, 1922, was elected its commander. He was also a member of the Legion's national legislative committee for one term of office. He took a vital interest in history, particularly that pertaining to the Civil War period. He had a diary, kept by his grandfather, John Randolph Farabee, who was a captain in the Confederate States Army. Entries in this diary cover the period when Captain Farabee was a federal prisoner at Sandusky Bay, Ohio. A latter-day advocate of the Southern cause, Mr. Gilliland would admit only under pressure that the South had been defeated, and always contended that "its principles triumphed."

Deeply interested in the cause of education, Mr. Gilliland was chairman of the board of trustees of Webb School at Bellbuckle, and was former president of the Vanderbilt Alumni Association in Memphis. He was an active leader in the local chapter of the American Red Cross for many years. He was a past king, or Ouro, of Memphi, oldest of the Cotton Carnival secret societies.

A founder of the University Club, he was its president from 1922 to 1924. During his term of office the club was moved from the old Napoleon Hill home at Madison and Third, where the Sterick Building now stands, to Central Avenue, the club's present site. Mr. Gilliland's other memberships included the Memphis Country Club, the Tennessee Club, and Wappanoca Hunting and Fishing Club near Turrell, Arkansas. He was the owner of two farms, totaling fifteen hundred acres, in that area. He won the Conservation Award for East Arkansas when he became one of the first farmers to grow rice. Cotton continued to be his main crop, but he also raised large crops of soybeans and alfalfa.

His fraternity was Kappa Alpha, and he was a communicant of St. John's Methodist Church.

In that church, on October 8, 1924, Frank Marshall Gilliland married Miss Elizabeth Irwin Jordan, daughter of Robert Lee and Louise (Hardin) Jordan. Both of her parents were natives of Tennessee, her father having been born at Milan and her mother at Savannah. Her mother was the daughter of Dr and Mrs. Robert Alexander Hardin of that city. Mr. and Mrs. Jordan were residents of Memphis from 1905, when Mr. Jordan founded the Central Cigar and Tobacco Company there. He had long represented the American Tobacco Company in the South. In 1913 he organized the Memphis Motor Car Company, and he had large investments in Delta timberlands. He devoted much attention to civic affairs, and from 1915 to 1919 was president of the Business Men's Club, predecessor of the Memphis Chamber of Commerce. He helped in the building of the Hospital School for Crippled Children; and took part in financing and planning the Red Acres subdivision. With an associate, he gave the land for the Galloway Golf Course to the city, having named the course for the chairman of the Park Commission, Colonel Robert Galloway.

Mrs. Gilliland was born at Savannah, Tennessee. She attended Miss Hutchison's School for Girls in Memphis, and graduated from National Cathedral School in Washington, D. C., in June, 1918. She continued her education in New York City, at Finch College, at the School of Fine Arts, and at the Art Students League. She spent six months in Europe completing her art studies, and on a Mediterranean cruise. In Memphis, she was one of the eight founders of Le Bonheur Club which built the Le Bonheur Children's Hospital. She was a charter member of the Little Garden Club and the Memphis Book Club, and she served as president of each of these organizations and also of the Brooks Art Gallery League. Serving as project chairman when the grounds of the Art Gallery were laid out, she was instrumental in having the work of sculpture, "Three Diving Girls," placed at the fountain. She is a member of the Colonial Dames of America, the Daughters of the American Revolution, and the Garden Club of America.

Mr. and Mrs. Gilliland became the parents of three sons: 1. Robert Jordan, who was born on May 1, 1926. He is a graduate of Webb School and holds the degree of Bachelor of Science from the United States Naval Academy, where he graduated in June, 1949. On December 4, 1954, at Winston-Salem, North Carolina, he married Cassandra Penn Wright. 2. Frank Marshall, Jr., born on November 27, 1927. Also a graduate of Webb School, he holds degrees of Bachelor of Arts (1949) and Bachelor of Laws (1951) from Vanderbilt University. He was his father's partner in law practice. At Idelwild Presbyterian Church in Memphis, on December 27, 1958, he married Miss Tandy Alice Jones. 3. James Sevier, born October 3, 1933. After graduation from Webb School, he entered Vanderbilt University, where he received his degree of Bachelor of Arts in 1955 and his Bachelor of Laws degree in 1957. He too became a law partner of his father. All three sons have served as officers in the United States Navy, and the oldest, Robert, has been an Air Force jet pilot in Germany and Korea.

The death of Frank M. Gilliland, Sr., occurred on September 25, 1959, in a Memphis hospital. Commenting on the character of the man and the significance of his achievements, a fellow member of the bar said of him:

"He was a man whom I consider always a splendid citizen of his community, a man of courage, a man of enthusiasm and a credit to anything in which he participated."

FORREST LADD

From the beginning of his career, Forrest Ladd had been identified with the John A. Denie Sons Company. At his death he was executive vice president and vice chairman of its board, and was also senior vice president of the Security American Life Insurance Company. This Memphis business leader also served in the Tennessee State Senate, and he was a veteran of wartime naval service.

Born in Ballard County, Kentucky, on July 23, 1916, Mr. Ladd was a son of Earl Rudy and Lally Helen (Abernathy) Ladd. His father is a minister of the Woodlawn Cumberland Presbyterian Church, and served as a chaplain in the United States Army during World War II. Forrest Ladd attended the public schools of his native state, graduating from Tilghman High School at Paducah. He was later a student at Western State College of Kentucky at Bowling Green, where he graduated in 1937 with the degree of Bachelor of Arts.

From the time he completed his college courses, Mr. Ladd was with John A. Denie Sons Company, at its Memphis headquarters at 373 Adams Street. He began his connection in the capacity of salesman, and became an executive vice president, and vice chairman of the board, in 1951. In 1957, he became vice president of the Security American Life Insurance Company, and also served on its board of directors.

Absent from Memphis business circles at the time of World War II, Mr. Ladd served in the United States Navy. He was in the Pacific Theater of Operations and held the rank of Lieutenant. In 1951, he was first elected to serve the people of his district in the State Senate, and he was elected to a second term in 1953. In 1951, Mr. Ladd was selected as Tennessee's outstanding young man by the Memphis Junior Chamber of Commerce. He was vice president of the Tennessee Road Builders' Association, a member of the board of the National Concrete Masonry Association and of the Southern Brick and Tile Association and chairman of the board for Licensing Contractors, State of Tennessee.

A member of Post No. 1 of the American Legion at Memphis, Mr. Ladd held office as its vice commander and commander. He was affiliated with the Free and Accepted Masons, and was a member of the higher bodies of Masonry, including Al Chymia Temple of the Ancient Arabic Order of Nobles of the Mystic Shrine. His other memberships included the Colonial Country Club, Kiwanis, the Army-Navy Club, Veterans of Foreign Wars, the 40 and 8, the Military Order of World Wars, and the Fifty Club, as well as the Memphis Chamber of Commerce, of which he was vice president in 1957 and 1958. He was a member of Calvary Episcopal Church in Memphis. Mr. Ladd died

on August 5, 1959 in San Juan, Puerto Rico. As a member of Governor Buford Ellington's official party he was attending the National Governors' Conference.

Harriet Virginia Worshum, the daughter of Harry and Mary Alice (Bennett) Worshum, became the wife of Forrest Ladd in a ceremony at Fulton, Kentucky, on February 16, 1941. The couple became the parents of two children: Courtney Ann, who was born in 1955, and Forrest, Jr., born in 1958.

John Francis Blend

John Francis Blend has been one of Tennessee's younger hospital administrators, having been in charge of the management of the Jackson—Madison County General Hospital. He has headed the West Tennessee Hospital Council and the Jackson Junior Chamber of Commerce, and has served on a number of boards of directors. He is a veteran of wartime service in the Army Air Corps.

Born February 2, 1924, at Brooklyn, New York, he is a son of Nicholas J. and Emma (Kurzyna) Blend. His father too was born in Brooklyn, on June 25, 1898, the year that city became a borough of New York City. Mrs. Blend was born August 30, 1900, and she is now deceased.

Completing his public school education in Brooklyn, John F. Blend graduated from James Madison High School in that borough in 1942. The same year he enlisted in the United States Army Air Corps, and was in service for three years, eighteen months of that time being spent in the European Theater of Operations. He was stationed in Italy, France and Germany. He was commissioned in the United States Air Force Reserve Corps in April, 1950, and discharged in 1957.

Following his return from wartime service, Mr. Blend resumed his education, entering Tulane University in New Orleans where he graduated in 1950 with a degree of Bachelor of Business Administration. He began his career with Jackson-Madison County General Hospital at Jackson, Tennessee in the capacity of business manager. It was in 1955 that Mr. Blend accepted the responsible post as administrator of the Jackson-Madison County General Hospital. As Administrator of the Jackson-Madison County Hospital, Mr. Blend led the hospital through a building program totaling 2½ million dollars and increased the capacity from 174 to 300 beds and more than doubled the square footage of the hospital with more efficient service in all areas of the hospital.

He is currently carrying on a building program at the Mobile General Hospital, Mobile, Alabama, which is anticipated to be finished in 1963. He assumed duties as administrator here in April, 1959.

Mr. Blend has served as president of the West Tennessee Hospital Council and also as president of the Tennessee Chapter, American Association of Hospital Accountants. He is past president of the Jackson Junior Chamber of Commerce. He has served on the boards of directors of the Jackson—Madison County United Fund, Family Emergency Aid, Red Cross Home Service Committee, Jackson Junior Chamber of Commerce, the Young Men's Christian Association, Madison County Tuberculosis Association, and the Madison County Chapter of the National Foundation for Infantile Paralysis. He is a member of the American College of Hospital Administrators.

As a veteran of World War II, he belonged to the local posts of the American Legion and the Veterans of Foreign Wars. His lodge affiliations are the Benevolent and Protective Order of Elks and the Knights of Columbus, and he served as judge advocate of the latter organization. He was a member of the Elks' State Nursing Scholarship Committee. He is a Roman Catholic.

In New Orleans, Louisiana, on December 23, 1948, John F. Blend married Patsy Joyce McClaugherty, daughter of James Edgar and Ella (Bramme) McClaugherty. Both of her parents are natives of Texas, her father born at Sabine and her mother at New Brunfels. Mr. and Mrs. Blend have three children: 1. Teresa Joyce, born September 23, 1953. 2. James Patrick, born November 11, 1954. 3. Margaret Ann, born August 4, 1957. All of the children were born in Jackson.

Dr. John Robert Thompson, Jr.

Active in the practice of medicine in Jackson since 1925, and county physician of Madison County since 1930, Dr. Thompson has been a member of the Public Health Council of the State of Tennessee since 1936, having been re-appointed by each governor from Governor Hill McAllister to the present Governor Buford Ellington. He is a member of the American Medical Association, the Tennessee State Medical Association and of the Consolidated Medical Assembly of West Tennessee. President of the Tennessee State Medical Society in 1954, he was a member of the Society's House of Delegates many times and was a councillor from the Eighth District from 1936 to 1940.

Dr. Thompson was born in Union City, Tennessee, on March 1, 1900, the son of John Robert Thompson, Sr., and of Mary Magdalene (Neftzger) Thompson. His father was a pharmacist at Jackson, born in Obion County, Tennessee, on January 23, 1872, and his mother in Hamlettsburg, Massac County, Illinois, on October 27, 1875. Dr. Thompson attended the Jackson City schools, graduated from Jackson High School in 1918, and studied at Vanderbilt University School of Arts and Sciences from 1919 to 1921. He obtained his medical degree at Vanderbilt University School of Medicine in 1924, and began the practice of medicine in Jackson, Tennessee, in 1925.

Active in the Officers' Training Corps in 1918 during World War I, Dr. Thompson was commissioned a first lieutenant in the Medical Corps Reserve in 1925. He became a major in the Army Medical Corps on February 19, 1940, and was assigned to the One-Hundred and Seventeenth Infantry, Thirtieth Division of the Tennessee National Guard. On active duty with the One-Hundred and Seventeenth Infantry, Thirtieth Division, on September 16, 1940, he was assigned to the Station Hospital, Fort Jackson, South Carolina. He

Jack M Burton

was promoted to the rank of lieutenant colonel in the Army Medical Corps on September 4, 1942 while at the Induction Station, Fort Jackson, South Carolina, and was made chief of the X-Ray Service on October 1, 1942. Assistant post surgeon from October, 1943 to September 1, 1944, Dr. Thompson was then administrative assistant and chief of the Hospital Section, Hospital and Domestic Affairs, Division of the Surgeon General's Office, United States Army, from September 1, 1944 to August, 1946. He became a colonel in the Army Medical Corps in April, 1946, and he now holds the rank of colonel in the United States Army Medical Corps Reserve.

A member of Alpha Tau Omega fraternity since 1919, and head of the chapter while in college, Dr. Thompson was Province Chief, supervising chapters in Kentucky and Tennessee, from 1933 to 1940. He is a member of Elks Lodge No. 192, and he also enjoys social connections as a member of the Jackson Golf and Country Club and of the Jackson, Madison County, Chamber of Commerce. He attends religious services at the First Methodist Church of Jackson; he served as chairman of the Official Board from 1953 to 1955, and was formerly superintendent of the Adult Division of the Sunday School from 1948 to 1953.

Dr. Thompson was married in Jackson, Tennessee, on June 1, 1927, to Lena Frances Wilde, the daughter of Charles Frederick Wilde and of Hattie (Manley) Wilde. Her father was born in Jackson on September 26, 1866, and her mother in Medon, Tennessee, on June 4, 1872.

Dr. and Mrs. Thompson had two children, both of whom were born in Jackson: 1. John Robert, III, born on May 27, 1931, died in infancy. 2. Jacqueline Wilde, born on January 7, 1933, is now Mrs. Richard O'Keeffe.

JACK MEREDITH BRUTON

Following varied and valuable business experience, Jack Meredith Bruton formed his own organization, the J. M. Bruton Company, Inc., manufacturers' representatives and food brokers, with headquarters on South Main Street in Memphis. He has been president of this firm for the past twenty-five years. He is also an official of Sales Producers Associates of Kansas City, Kansas, and he holds membership in several Memphis organizations.

Born at Ruston, Louisiana, on November 2, 1900, he is a son of John Walter and Alice Mae Bruton. His father had come from Virginia, and his mother from Meridian, Mississippi. Spending his boyhood years in Texas, Jack M. Bruton received his education at Texas Military Institute at Terrell in that state, and at St. Michael's College in Santa Fe, New Mexico.

He began his business career with the land department of the Humble Oil Company in Texas, working in the procurement of leases in that state, in Oklahoma, and in Louisiana. He next owned and operated an agency for the Ford Motor Company at Wells Point, Texas, while continuing in oil promotion work. He also organized the Roma Coal and Oil Company, which he operated until it was liquidated, and at that time he was offered a position as sales manager with the E. R. Durkee Company of New York City.

Resigning from this connection in 1934, Mr. Bruton organized the J. M. Bruton Company in Memphis, of which he has continued as owner and manager throughout the intervening period of more than a quarter-century. He now holds office as its president. The firm is the broker for a number of nationally known firms, among them Durkee's Famous Foods, Ralston-Purina, Continental Cans, Monarch Finer Foods, and Jack Sprat products. Commenting on his organization in the columns of Memphis Market News, a local writer observed: "His sales and office staff is comprised of loyal, aggressive, sales-minded personnel, who believe 'service can master competition.'" In addition to his major business connection, Mr. Bruton is chairman of the board of Sales Producers Associates, Inc., of Kansas City, Kansas.

Mr. Bruton is a veteran of World War I, having served for three and a half years in the United States Army under General Pershing. Regarding his civic activities, the Memphis Market News writer remarked: "He takes a vital interest in any activity that is purposed for the self-betterment of mankind." He is an active member of the Rivermont Club and the Petroleum Club. Affiliated with the Free and Accepted Masons, he is a member of the higher Masonic bodies and of Al Chymia Temple, Ancient Arabic Order of Nobles of the Mystic Shrine. He and Mrs. Bruton attend the Episcopal Church.

She is the former Miss Blanche Weakley, daughter of the late Mr. and Mrs. John L. Weakley of Sedalia, Missouri. She became the wife of Jack Meredith Bruton in a ceremony at Dallas, Texas, on June 10, 1924. The couple are the parents of a daughter, Betty Lou, who was born on February 26, 1928. She is now the wife of Edward P. Lyons, Jr., of Clearwater, Florida, and the mother of two children: i. Edward P., 3rd. ii. Marcia.

MORGAN KEITH SHORT

As a lawyer with more than three decades' experience in practice at the Tennessee bar, Morgan Keith Short has his offices in the Pythian Building in Jackson. He serves on various boards of directors, and has taken a very full part in local civic organizations, in alumni groups, and in church work.

He is a native of Jackson, and was born on September 27, 1903, son of Walter Morgan and Lotta (Keith) Short. Both of his parents were born in Tennessee. His father, a native of Franklin, died in 1928. Mrs. Short survives her husband. She was born at Jackson in 1878.

Mr. Keith Short received his early education in the public schools and Union University in Jackson. He received his Bachelor of Arts degree from the University of the South at Sewanee, in 1924. He attended Harvard Law School at Cambridge, Massachusetts, from 1925 to 1927, and was admitted to the Bar of Tennessee in 1927. He established offices in his native city and practiced before all Federal and State courts. In 1932 he was engaged by the members of the Tennessee Coca-Cola Bottlers Association as their public relations counsel, and he continues to represent that organization at the present time. He serves on the board of directors of the Jackson Coca-Cola Bottling Company, Budde & Weis Manufacturing Company, Crook Sanatorium and Jackson Wearing Apparel Company.

As a lawyer, Mr. Short is a member of the Jackson-Madison County Bar Association and has served as president of that organization on two occasions. He also belongs to the Tennessee Bar Association and American Bar Association. He has taken an interested part in the activities of his political party, and has served as chairman of the Madison County Democratic Executive Committee. Other offices which he has held in past years include: president of the Jackson Chamber of Commerce; president of the Jackson Young Men's Christian Association; president of the Jackson Exchange Club and also of the Exchange Clubs of Tennessee; president of the Tennessee Golf Association; president of the Jackson Golf and Country Club; and president of the Conversation Club. He has been president of the Jackson Sewanee Alumni Association, and of the Sigma Alpha Epsilon Alumni Association of Jackson; also of the Hundred Club, a group sponsoring athletics at Union University, and of the Quarterback Club, which sponsors athletics at Jackson High School. He is also a member of the lodges of the Benevolent and Protective Order of Elks and the Knights of Pythias, and of the Harvard Club of Tennessee.

As a communicant of St. Luke's Episcopal Church in Jackson, Keith Short has served on the vestry and as senior warden of the church.

In Jackson, on November 20, 1932, Keith Short married Rosita Scheyer, daughter of L. E. and Lillian (Hedman) Scheyer of New Orleans, Louisiana. The couple have resided for many years at 7 Northwood, in Jackson.

WALTER JOHN BAENZIGER

With ample experience in the chemical engineering phase of industry both in this country and abroad, Walter John Baenziger has advanced to a prominent place among Tennessee manufacturers as executive vice president of Aluminum Foils, Inc., at Jackson.

He is a native of Milan, Italy, and was born on February 9, 1913, son of a Swiss father and Italian mother. His father, Charles A. Baenziger, an importer and exporter, was born at St. Gall, Switzerland, on August 8, 1881; and Margaret Mozzati, whom he married, was born on January 19 of that year at Gallarate, Italy. Walter J. Baenziger received most of his education in his native city, and was a student at the University of Milan from 1931 to 1933. In 1935, he completed studies at the University of Pavia, Italy, leading to the degree of Doctor of Philosophy in Chemistry.

He began his industrial career as chemical engineer at the Martinswerk Alumina Plant at Bergheim, Germany, where he was employed during 1936-

1937. He left to return to Italy, and until 1941, was superintendent of the SAVA Alumina Plant at Marghera.

Mr. Baenziger first came to this country in 1941, to accept a position as chemical engineer with the Mining Equipment Corporation in New York City. He remained through 1942; and during 1943-1944 was employed as adviser to the government of India, at Burdwan, Bengal, a position he secured through the Board of Economic Warfare.

The year of the war's end, 1945, he resumed his residence in New York City, where he was representative of Aluminum Industrie A. G. of Lausanne, Switzerland. He continued in this capacity through 1948, and in 1949 came to Jackson to assume his present duties as executive vice president of Aluminum Foils, Inc. His extensive training and experience both here and abroad, almost entirely within the aluminum industry, have made his services most valuable, both to his own organization and to the progress of the industry as a whole. In his own company, he serves on the board of directors, as well as in executive capacity.

Mr. Baenziger is a member of the Jackson Rotary Club and the Jackson Golf and Country Club. His professional and industrial memberships include the following: American Institute of Management, and the Aluminum Association.

On June 24, 1944, Walter J. Baenziger married Mary Kuser, daughter of Peter Doelger and Lulu (Mitchell) Kuser. The couple make their home at 527 Westmoreland Place, Jackson, and they are the parents of four children: 1. John Walter, born January 30, 1946 in New York City; he died May 18, 1958 in Jackson, Tennessee. 2. Peter Charles, who was born in New York City on June 25, 1948. 3. Thomas Gerard, born April 18, 1950, in Jackson. 4. Edward Vincent, also born in Jackson, on July 27, 1951.

GEORGE COTROS

A business leader who became prominent in Memphis as partner in a wholesale grocery firm, George Cotros won recognition far beyond the confines of his city as an effective worker for welfare causes, particularly that of Greek relief. An immigrant boy who had found his opportunity in America, he never lost either his feeling of gratitude toward his adopted homeland, nor his deep concern for those living in the land of his birth. In the affairs of the Greek community in Memphis he came to be regarded as "the hub of the wheel"; and he was held in equally high regard among residents of the city generally.

Born in the village of Elatou, Greece, on March 6, 1896, he was a son of Eleftheria and Constantine (Maelaras) Cotros. Both of his parents were likewise natives of Elatou, and his father was a farmer. Receiving his education in the schools of his native place, George Cotros left his home village for the United States at the age of fifteen, and arrived here able to speak only a few

GEORGE COTROS

words of English. However, he completed his high school studies in Memphis. Beyond that point he was self-educated, but in later life he received many compliments on his mastery of the English language, and became an effective speaker, who was frequently on the roster at public meetings. One of a large family, he proved himself disciplined and resourceful at an early age, and had in fact come to this country to increase his earning power so that he might better assist in rearing and educating his five brothers and a sister. Two of the brothers, Harry and Nick Cotros, later came to this country as well, and are still living here.

It was in 1912 that he arrived in Memphis, and he soon entered the grocery business. His drive, ambition, and application to his duties assured him steady advancement, and conserving his resources, he was able to establish himself as a partner in his own wholesale grocery firm, the T. C. Collas Company, in 1918. He was senior partner in this well-known Memphis organization for many years before his death.

At the time of World War II, when the people of Greece were suffering greatly, the extent of Mr. Cotros' sympathy with them was proved in an unmistakable way. Late in 1942 he was chosen chairman of a volunteer Greek Relief Committee which set a quota of fifteen thousand dollars for the city of Memphis; and his indefatigable efforts were effective in putting the program over. In addition he served as treasurer of the building fund committee which raised money to erect the Hellenic Greek Orthodox Church. After the war he conducted a dynamic and effective campaign to have certain islands in the Mediterranean, near Greece, placed under the government of that republic, when postwar national claims were being resolved. He served as president of the local chapter of the American Hellenic Educational and Protective Association, and in this capacity, presented a Greek flag to the Governor of Tennessee. Commenting on his place in community life as a Greek-American, a local newspaper carried these paragraphs in a review of his career at the time of his death:

. . . His aid and advice were sought not only by hundreds who originally came from Greece, but by many other Memphians in need or trouble and, associates say, he never turned down a plea, whether it be from an organized charity or an individual.

He became an American citizen but he never forgot the poor of his native land and regularly sent boxes of food and money and letters of encouragement to various communities there where he knew the need was great.

A deeply religious man, Mr. Cotros had as one of his most treasured possessions throughout life a small Greek Bible which he had brought with him when he came to this country. He always accounted it a great source of strength and encouragement. He served on the board of directors of the Hellenic Greek Church. He was fond of outdoor activities, but preferred walking and swimming to competitive sports. He also enjoyed climbing mountains.

George Cotros returned to his native Greece following World War II, to pick his bride in the village of Patras. She is the former Miss Catherine Stamati, a native of that place and a daughter of Thomas and Polyxenia (Thantilis) Stamati. Both of her parents were born in Naupaktos, Greece. Mr. and Mrs. Cotros became the parents of a daughter, Eleftheria, who was born on February 25, 1948.

The death of the business leader and welfare worker occurred at Baptist Hospital in Memphis on March 19, 1957.

GUY E. YELTON

Senior partner in the law firm of Yelton and Chamberlain of Lafayette, Tennessee, and a practicing lawyer since 1947, Mr. Yelton is active in community and social organizations and is a member of the Rotary Club and of the American Legion. He also holds membership in the Tennessee Bar Association and the American Bar Association.

Mr. Yelton was born in Mount Juliet, Wilson County, Tennessee, on February 4, 1925, the son of Clarence Grey Yelton and of Irene (Hays) Yelton. His father was born in Wilson County, Tennessee, in April 1900, and he is active in the real estate and insurance business in Mount Juliet. Mr. Yelton's mother was born in Wilson County, Tennessee, in 1903, and both she and her husband are members of the Cumberland Presbyterian Church.

Mr. Yelton attended the public schools in Mount Juliet and then obtained his Bachelor of Laws degree from Cumberland University in 1947. During World War II, he served in the United States Army Infantry from June, 1943 to February, 1946, and he saw action in the European Theater of Operations. Attached to the 65th Infantry Division, Third Army, he received the Combat Infantryman's Badge. He practiced law in Nashville, Tennessee, for two years, and then moved to Lafayette in 1949 where he established his office. It was in February, 1958, that he entered into partnership with James W. Chamberlain in the firm of Yelton and Chamberlain, in Lafayette. He is a Democrat in politics. Mr. Yelton attends religious services as a member of the Methodist Church.

He was married on April 19, 1946, to Catherine Haile, born in Sumner County, Tennessee, on December 17, 1924, the daughter of Hubert H. Haile and of Norma (Hutcherson) Haile. Her father was born in Jackson County, Tennessee, in 1898, and her mother was also born in 1898. Mrs. Yelton attended David Lipscomb College in Nashville, Tennessee.

Mr. and Mrs. Yelton have two children: 1. Dianna Gay, born in Wilson County, Tennessee, on January 12, 1947. 2. Dabney Jean, born in Macon County, Tennessee, on July 3, 1953.

JAMES W. CHAMBERLAIN

A partner in the law firm of Yelton and Chamberlain of Lafayette, Tennessee, and active in the practice of law since 1954, Mr. Chamberlain is active

in professional organizations and is a member of the Tennessee Bar Association and of the American Bar Association.

He was born in Lafayette, Tennessee, on May 27, 1930, the son of James M. Chamberlain and of Lois (West) Chamberlain. His father was born in Lafayette on March 11, 1893, and died September 26, 1958; he was a retired attorney, having practiced in Lafayette for thirty-eight years. Clerk and master of the courts for thirty-five years, he was one of the founders of the city charter. He served in the Army during World War I and was stationed in the United States. Formerly active in Masonry, he also played an important role in the Red Cross. Mr. Chamberlain's mother was born in Lafayette, on January 15, 1901, and she is prominent in the Order of the Eastern Star.

Mr. Chamberlain attended the Lafayette public schools and graduated from Castle Heights Military Academy. He obtained the degree of Bachelor of Laws at Cumberland University in 1954. He then began the practice of law in Nashville, Tennessee, but after three and a half years, he moved to Lafayette, where he became a partner in the law firm of Yelton and Chamberlain in February, 1958. He is a Democrat in politics, and attends religious services as a member of the Church of Christ.

He was married at Lebanon, Tennessee, on June 24, 1955, to Gay McFarland, born at Lebanon, Tennessee, on April 9, 1936, the daughter of Sam B. McFarland and of Gwendolyn (Moss) McFarland. Her father was born in Lebanon in 1907, and her mother in Tuscumbia, Alabama, in 1907. Mrs. Chamberlain attended David Lipscomb College in Nashville, Tennessee, where she majored in home economics.

Mr. and Mrs. Chamberlain have one daughter, Kathryn, born in Lebanon, Tennessee, on November 29, 1956.

RALPH WALTON LIPSEY

After gaining valuable business experience with a variety of other business concerns, Ralph Walton Lipsey of Memphis formed his own organization, the Lipsey Fish Company, of which he has since been owner and general manager. He is active in Christian work, and as a Kiwanian.

Born at Sardis, Mississippi, on March 13, 1908, he is a son of farmer, merchant and insurance agent, William Clay and Sarah (Young) Lipsey. Both of his parents were also natives of Sardis, where his father was born on March 16, 1860 and his mother on October 14, 1870.

R. Walton Lipsey graduated from Whitehaven High School in 1927. He then completed courses in sales, accounting and business administration. In the early years of his career he held successive positions as bookkeeper and office manager with the J. O. Goshorn Lumber Company, which he left to accept a position as accountant and auditor with the nationally known accounting firm of Ernst and Ernst, later holding the same position with W. D.

Marshall and Company. Mr. Lipsey next joined the Firestone Tire and Rubber Company.

He remained with this large industrial organization until 1936, when he left to organize the Lipsey Fish Company, which has its headquarters at 176 South Front Street in Memphis. He has been its sole owner and manager of its operation since that time.

Mr. Lipsey is a member of the Harding Academy Council. He is a member of the Church of Christ and the Kiwanis Club.

At Memphis, on June 1, 1938, R. Walton Lipsey married Margaret Storey, daughter of Walter Ross and Annie Myrtle (Allen) Storey. Her father, a native of Moro, Arkansas, was born on July 9, 1891, while her mother was born at Independence, Mississippi, on May 29, 1895. Mr. and Mrs. Lipsey are the parents of the following children, all of whom were born in Memphis: 1. Ralph Walton, Jr., born on March 25, 1939. 2. Linda Margaret, born February 15, 1941. 3. Susan Ann, born March 10, 1947. 4. Jennifer Lynn, born August 16, 1953.

Mr. Lipsey's hobbies are hunting, deep sea fishing and color photography. He has many fine bird dogs and mounted trophies of game birds and fish.

CHESTER LAWRENCE FULTS

A native Grundy Countian, he was born September 26, 1918, son of Lewis F. Fults and Frances Elizabeth Walker, at Harrican, Grundy County, Tennessee (near Altamont). He was the fourth son of this family, his brothers being Malcolm Alonzo, Stanley Burr (deceased 1913), and Kermit Rye. He also has two sisters, Mildred Marie Fults McGinnis and Frances Juanita Fults Lockhart, all of Altamont.

His father, Lewis F. Fults, son of Hyrum Fults and Mary Smartt, was born at Harrican, Tennessee, September 15, 1886. He has been a merchant all his life, with stores in his native place and at Altamont. He was registrar of Deeds for Grundy County for twenty-four consecutive years and for the past fifteen years has been Mayor of Altamont. At the present time his merchandising activity is in the building materials field. He has been particularly active in the Church of Jesus Christ of Latter-Day Saints. He was branch president of the Altamont Branch for six years and he built the major portion of the Chapel there, laying the stone and doing most of the interior work. Frances Elizabeth Walker, whom he married December 25, 1907, was born October 18, 1885 at Beersheba Springs, Tennessee, a daughter of Martin Jackson Walker and Loucinda Fults. Martin Jackson Walker was a surveyor and made the first survey of Grundy County.

Chester attended public schools at Altamont, Tennessee, and graduated with honors from Grundy County High School at Tracy City, Tennessee. He entered Brigham Young University at Provo, Utah, famed institution founded by the Mormons, and graduated in 1943 with a Bachelor of Science degree, majoring in Social Science and minoring in Secondary Education. He now holds a permanent Tennessee High School Teaching Certificate.

He enlisted in the Naval Reserve in 1942 and was called to active duty along with thirty other young reservists from the Brigham Young University just two months before graduation. He attended Midshipman School at Northwestern University, Chicago, and was commissioned an ensign. He then went to Ohio State University to Recognition School before being assigned to the Gunnery School at the Navy Yard, Washington, D. C., as instructor in plane and ship recognition in November of 1943. In April of 1945 he was transferred to Great Lakes Naval Training Station as staff member of the Anti-Aircraft Training Center. He was released from active duty at this establishment as lieutenant, j.g., after thirty-seven months in uniform.

After returning from Naval service he took postgraduate courses in business at Brigham Young University in 1946-47. Mr. Fults then entered the grocery and general merchandise business at Altamont. He has continued in the same field throughout the years since. He owns and operates the Cumberland Super Market at Altamont. He is a member of Post 131 of the American Legion, Beersheba Springs, Tennessee, and is Civil Defense Director for Grundy County.

Active in the Church of Jesus Christ of Latter-Day Saints, he was branch president of the Altamont Branch, Tennessee Central District, East Central States Mission of the Church from 1954-59. He is now serving as second councilor in the Tennessee Central District Presidency.

In Washington, D. C., on April 5, 1944, Chester Lawrence Fults married Marjorie Gardner. This marriage was solemnized in the Salt Lake Temple on April 17, 1946. Marjorie Gardner was born at Provo, Utah, on February 26, 1923, the second child of Frank Trelfall and Ada Emely Hickman Gardner. Both of her parents were natives of Utah, her father having been born in American Fork, Utah, February 7, 1896, a son of James Trelfall and Sarah Jane Hill Gardner, whose parents were both among the early Mormon pioneers; her mother, daughter of George Henry and Emma Homer Hickman, was born at Provo, Utah, October 6, 1896. Mrs. Gardner died February 11, 1954 but Frank T. Gardner is still living and resides in Utah. He was for many years manager of the Tri-State Lumber Company and is now in the insurance business. He served as Provo City Commissioner from 1950-54 and Bishop of the Provo Sixth Ward of the Church of Jesus Christ of Latter-Day Saints for five years.

Mrs. Fults has two brothers—Frank Homer Gardner of Provo and Richard Merrill Gardner, now serving a three year mission for the Church in the Southern Far East Mission with headquarters at Hong Kong, China; two sisters—Helen Gardner Goold of Greeley, Colorado, and Adene Ruth Gardner Houtz of Bountiful, Utah.

The Chester Fults are parents of five children, four boys and one girl:

1. Michael Lawrence, born June 4, 1945 at Provo, Utah. 2. Gregory Merrill, born May 26, 1947 at Provo, Utah. 3. Brent Gardner, born March 22, 1950 at McMinnville, Tennessee. 4. Rickey Albert, born at McMinnville, Tennessee, December 21, 1953. 5. Pamela, born September 20, 1955, also at McMinnville.

FRANK ROLLAND BOYD

In addition to his long connection with the Coca-Cola Bottling Plant at Lewisburg, of which he has become co-manager, Frank Rolland Boyd has become active in the management of other business enterprises: a theater and a photographic studio. He has banking interests, and takes a full part in civic and church work.

Mr. Boyd is a native of Lewisburg, and was born on December 26, 1915, son of Maud P. and Bessie (Stephens) Boyd. His father, born at Rally Hill in Maury County, in May, 1877, was reared on a farm in that county. He was a son of Thomas M. Boyd, M.D., who practiced medicine at Rally Hill most of his life. His wife was the former Myra Marzee Crutcher. This couple were active in the Methodist Church, and Dr. Boyd took a constructive interest in civic and public affairs. Their son, M. P. Boyd left the farm at an early age and became a photographer, moving to Lewisburg in 1902. There he opened Boyd's Photo Studio. He spent considerable time traveling in Tennessee and Kentucky, taking pictures. He was owner of the Dixie Theater in Lewisburg, and also of considerable real estate. Bessie Stephens, whom he married, was born on February 14, 1886, at Noah, near Beech Grove in Coffee County. She attended Draughan's Business College in Nashville, and was active in the Cumberland Presbyterian Church throughout her life. Mr. Boyd died in 1948.

Attending local public schools, Frank R. Boyd completed his secondary studies at Marshall County High School, where he graduated. In 1936 he joined the staff of the Coca-Cola Bottling Plant, and became co-manager there in 1940. With his brothers and a sister, he is co-owner of two enterprises which their father previously owned and managed: the Dixie Theater, and Boyd's Photo Studio. He is a stockholder in the First National Bank of Lewisburg and the People's Union Bank there.

Mr. Boyd is a member of the Chamber of Commerce, and attends the Methodist Church. He is active in church work, serving on the board of stewards. In politics he is a Democrat.

In his native town on July 15, 1936, Frank Rolland Boyd married Angelena Moore. She was born at Cornersville, Tennessee, on November 21, 1917, daughter of James Thomas and Mae (London) Moore. Her father, a native of Marshall County, was a farmer and stock dealer, the owner of several farms. He is deceased, as is his wife, the former Mae London, a native of Marshall County, who died in 1953. Mrs. Boyd attended Cornersville High School and studied music. The couple are the parents of three children: 1. Emmaline, who was born on July 2, 1937. She attended the schools of Lewisburg and Nashville

Business College. She is now the wife of Allan Carlton Bless of Lewisburg, Tennessee, and the mother of two children: i. Frank Thomas Bless, born on April 23, 1957. ii. Mary Ann Bless, born March 29, 1958. 2. Mary Marzee, born January 3, 1940 in Lewisburg. She graduated from Marshall County High School, and is now attending Old Miss School (University of Mississippi). Like other members of her family, she is musical, and plays in the school band. 3. Michael Moore, born January 9, 1948. All of the children were born in Lewisburg.

Joseph F. Canepari

After several years' experience in automobile retailing at Memphis, Joseph F. Canepari became owner and president of Southern Motors, Inc., which has its offices, showrooms and service facilities at 341 Union Avenue. He holds membership in a number of trade and local organizations, and is vitally interested in community affairs.

A native Memphian, he was born on September 20, 1910, and is the son of Alex and Teresa (Ricossa) Canepari. His father, who was born in Italy, came to this country at the age of seventeen and settled in Memphis. He became a farmer in the Memphis area, and followed that occupation for the duration of his lifetime. He was married in Memphis to Miss Ricossa, who arrived in this country in the company of her parents when she was three years of age.

After attending elementary schools through the eighth grade in Memphis, Joseph F. Canepari graduated from Christian Brothers High School in 1928. His first position after graduation was as salesman with the Otto Schwill Seed Company in Memphis. He next entered the restaurant business in his own right, establishing a restaurant on Main Street in that city. This enterprise he sold after four years. For the next two years he was in the retail liquor business.

In 1941, Mr. Canepari joined his uncle, Lawrence Canepari, and R. R. Price in founding the Southern Truck Company as a sales agency for White trucks and equipment. This firm held the franchise for distributorship in ninety-seven counties of Tennessee, Arkansas, and Mississippi. Joseph F. Canepari was vice president and sales manager of the Southern Truck Company from the time of its founding until it was sold in 1950.

He then joined his uncle, Lawrence Canepari, in business at Southern Motors, Inc., a Cadillac and Oldsmobile agency in Memphis. Following the death of his uncle in October, 1952, Joseph F. Canepari bought all outstanding stock in the corporation, and on January 1, 1953, assumed duties as president, as well as sole owner. He has remained active in the management of the sales and service agency ever since that time.

Mr. Canepari is a member of the National Automobile Dealers Association and the Memphis Automobile Dealers Association. He is a former member and director of the Tennessee Transport Association, and a member of the Transportation Club of Memphis, the Sales Managers Club of Memphis, and the Memphis Chamber of Commerce. He also belongs to the Tennessee Club and Colonial Country Club.

A Roman Catholic and a communicant of St. Michael's Church, he is a member of the Memphis Council of the Knights of Columbus. As a spectator, he enjoys football, baseball and other sports, and his favorite outdoor pastimes are hunting and fishing.

At Sacred Heart Church in Memphis, on October 11, 1944, Joseph F. Canepari married Della Robilio, daughter of John S. and Jennie (Gaia) Robilio. Her father came to this country from Italy, but her mother was born in Memphis. John S. Robilio was co-founder of Robilio and Cuneo, manufacturers of *Ronco* products. His death occurred in 1929. Mrs. Canepari was born in Memphis on June 13, 1914. The couple are the parents of three children: 1. Diane Marie, who was born on November 18, 1945. 2. Joseph F., Jr., born October 30, 1947. 3. John Alex, born on January 29, 1950.

Donald Drinkard

One of Tennessee's younger leaders in the dry goods industry, Donald Drinkard of Memphis is now president and chairman of the board of the William R. Moore Dry Goods Company. Serving his country as an army officer during World War II, he now has a creditable record of civic service as well, being a member of a number of local organizations.

Born at Trenton, Missouri, on March 29, 1919, he is a son of Harry and Carrie A. (Kirk) Drinkard. His father, who was a farmer, is now deceased, and his mother survives, making her home in Kansas City, Missouri. It was there that Donald Drinkard received his entire education, thru the public schools and Kansas City Junior College.

He began his business career with the Fitts Dry Goods Company of Kansas City, Missouri, in 1937, and continued with that organization until 1953, when he came to Memphis. He was on leave of absence from 1943 to 1946, serving in the United States Army as a first lieutenant in the Medical Administrative Corps. He was in the American theater of operations.

Mr. Drinkard came to Memphis to begin his duties as vice president and general manager of the William R. Moore Dry Goods Company, a post to which he was appointed in 1953. This firm's well-known store is located at 183 Monroe Street, and has long held the confidence of the people of the Memphis area because of its quality merchandise and fair standards of business practice. After serving as vice president and general manager of the company for less than a year, Mr. Drinkard was promoted to the presidency in 1954, and he became chairman of the board in 1958, while retaining his duties as president.

He has become widely known throughout his industry, and was recently elected president of the National Wholesale Dry Goods Association for the 1959 term.

In his own city he has taken a constructive part in civic affairs, currently serving as president of the Children's Bureau, a Community Chest agency. He is active in the Chamber of Commerce, and is a member of the Memphis Country Club, the Tennessee Club, the Executives Club, and the lodge of Free and Accepted Masons. A member of the higher bodies of Masonry, he belongs to the Ancient Arabic Order of Nobles of the Mystic Shrine.

Mr. Drinkard is a communicant of Woodland Presbyterian Church, and is chairman of its board of deacons at the present time.

In Kansas City, Missouri, on September 29, 1939, Donald Drinkard married Helen C. Polson, daughter of James A. and Minnie (Trautwein) Polson. Mrs. Drinkard is a member of the King's Daughters and is active in church work, singing in the choir. The couple are the parents of two children: 1. Judith Christine, who was born on October 5, 1943. 2. Donald Dwight, born March 15, 1948.

S. WALTER JONES

Few men in the history of Tennessee have had as great an influence upon the profession of law in the state as the late S. Walter Jones, founder of the University of Memphis Law School. The school was established in 1909, and Mr. Jones himself assumed the duties of teacher, later becoming dean. He was an author as well, with a number of widely known legal textbooks to his credit.

Born on a farm near Independence, Mississippi, on April 9, 1874, he was a son of Zacharia Cornelius and Amanda (Wallace) Jones. His father was a planter there. Beginning his education in local public schools, Dean Jones later worked his way through National Normal University at Lebanon, Ohio, waiting on tables. He taught for one year in the public schools of Hernando, Mississippi, then enrolled at the University of Mississippi Law School, where he graduated in 1900 with the degree of Bachelor of Laws. Admitted to the Mississippi bar, he began practice at Senatobia, and shortly afterwards was elected to his first and only public office, as representative from Tate County in the Mississippi State Legislature. He served from 1900 to 1904. The youngest member of the House of Representatives at the time, he nonetheless compiled an excellent record as a legislator. He voted for appropriations for the present Capitol Building, and was an effective worker for the enforcement of poll tax collections, which went to the support of public schools. He served as secretary of a committee investigating the leasing of state convicts to plantation owners. On that committees' recommendation, the state of Mississippi purchased the fifteen-thousand-acre plantation now known as Parchman Prison Farm.

In 1909, S. Walter Jones moved to Memphis and opened law offices in the old Southern Express Building on Court Street. There a group of young men gathered who interested Mr. Jones in teaching them the principles of the law. Facilities for such professional instruction were inadequate in the Memphis area at that time, and Mr. Jones was more than willing to undertake the assignment. As he remarked in later years, "practicing law didn't appeal to me too much but I liked the science of law and loved teaching it." He began conducting small classes in his own offices, and as enrollment grew it became necessary to move to larger quarters in the First National Bank Building and later in the Young Men's Christian Association Building, now the site of the Hotel Peabody. Ultimately the much enlarged law school moved to the Goodwyn Institute Building. The Law School later became a department of the University of Memphis. Mr. Jones taught for forty-five years, and served as dean of the Law School from 1909 until 1954, when he was named dean emeritus. Concerning the importance of his role as an educator, a colleague well acquainted with his record, David Hanover, has pointed out that a large number of the more successful lawyers of the South were among the eight hundred students who received their professional preparation under him: "He was a pioneer in the field of legal education in this area and not only in Memphis, but also in Arkansas, Mississippi, West Tennessee and elsewhere." Another member of the local bar, Herbert J. Moriarty, said of him:

Certainly, I know of no man who was more conscientious and devoted to his work than Mr. Jones ... As I look back I can hardly recollect any one man or any one member of the Bar who alone has contributed so much to the advancement of the legal profession in this state and county.

In May, 1954, a testimonial dinner was scheduled at the Hotel Peabody to coincide with the announcement of his retirement. On that occasion, as reported by the Memphis Press-Scimitar, "the alertness and youthful attitude of the tall, erect, broad shouldered attorney-educator astounded many of his early students who had not seen him for some time. His 'boys and girls,' as he liked to call them, came from many miles around to pay tribute to him."

As an author, Dean Jones had written legal textbooks published under the titles "Telephone, Telegraph and Electric Law," and "Insolvent and Failing Corporations." He was a member of Phi Delta Phi legal fraternity and also held membership in the following bar groups: Shelby County, Tennessee and American Bar Associations. Mr. Jones was a wise investor in Shelby County real estate and at the time of his death he owned the most valuable undeveloped tract in the area. He was a member of the Colonial Country Club, and a communicant of the Methodist Church. Mrs. Jones attends Trinity Lutheran Church.

She is the former Miss Catherine L. Sommer. The daughter of J. A. W. and Louise (Glindkamp) Sommer, and the granddaughter of German immigrants, she became the wife of S. Walter Jones in a ceremony at Memphis on November 7, 1929. Dean Jones and Mrs. Jones adopted three children: 1. Peggy Jones, who was born on December 2, 1925. She married Sidney Davis,

and they have three children: 1. Peggy Jones, who was born on December 2, 1925. She married Sidney Davis, and they have three children: Preston, Ronnie and Suzanne Davis. 2. William Wallace, born March 30, 1927. He married Miss Mary Ann Vernor and their children are Linda, Barbara Jean, William Wallace, Jr., and Lois Diane. 3. Sidney Walter, Jr., born on July 30, 1929. He is the father of: Carol Marie, Ruth Eleanor, James Michael, and Sidney Walter, 3rd.

Dean Jones' distinguished career as lawyer and teacher came to an end with his death at Baptist Hospital in Memphis on April 20, 1958. He had been admitted to the hospital on his eighty-fourth birthday. Anyone acquainted with his career, his achievements and his character would agree with the remark of one of his friends, that his life reminded her of the proverb, "He who walks in integrity, walks in security."

GEORGE BAKER HUBBARD, M.D.

Coming to Jackson following wartime service as a lieutenant colonel in the Army Medical Corps, Dr. George Baker Hubbard has practiced in that city since. In addition to his general practice as a surgeon, he has made an important contribution to the progress of his city and the welfare of its people as a founder of the Jackson Clinic.

Born at Princeton, Kentucky, on September 3, 1912, he is the son of Allan Gid and Grace (Baker) Hubbard. Both of his parents are natives of Dixon, Kentucky, where his father was born on February 10, 1890, and his mother on April 8, 1892. Dr. Hubbard began his education locally, and graduated from Butler High School in Princeton in 1930. He commenced his advanced studies at Western Kentucky State Teachers College in Bowling Green, and completed his academic courses there in three years, receiving his degree of Bachelor of Science in 1933. In 1937 he took his degree of Doctor of Medicine at Vanderbilt University Medical School in Nashville.

For a year after receiving his degree, Dr. Hubbard took an internship in pediatrics at Vanderbilt University Hospital in Nashville. During 1938-1939 he was intern in surgery at the Nashville General Hospital; and in 1939-1940, assistant resident in surgery at that hospital. He became resident in surgery there in 1940, and remained on its staff in that capacity until he entered military service in 1941.

From that time until 1944 he served at Camp Forrest, Tennessee, where he was chief of orthopedics at the Tullahoma Station Hospital. Going overseas in 1944, he was first stationed in Bath, England, as orthopedic consultant at the 802nd Hospital Center, which consisted of nineteen station or general hospitals. In June, 1945, he was transferred to Stuttgart, Germany, and assigned to a two-thousand-bed institution operated by the 216th General Hospital. There he served as assistant chief of surgery and chief of orthopedics. Dr. Hubbard returned to the United States in 1946 and was separated from the armed services. At that time he held the rank of lieutenant colonel.

Choosing Jackson as the scene of his future professional career, he began private practice there in the specialty of general surgery. He remained in practice independently until 1950, when he joined four other physicians in organizing the Jackson Clinic. He has remained professionally active in that organization to the present time. The clinic now has eighteen physicians on its staff, representing all phases of medical practice. At the present time, Dr. Hubbard is general surgeon, and he is also president of the clinic's board of governors. In addition, he is chief of surgery at the Madison County-Jackson General Hospital.

Active in the American College of Surgeons, Dr. Hubbard is now secretary and treasurer of its Tennessee Chapter. He is a member of the American Board of General Surgery, the Tennessee Medical Association, the American Medical Association, and the Witherspoon Club, which is a Vanderbilt University Medical School organization.

His nonprofessional memberships include the Chamber of Commerce, the Rotary Club, and the lodge of the Benevolent and Protective Order of Elks, all at Jackson. He attends the Methodist Church.

At Nashville, on September 5, 1939, Dr. George Baker Hubbard married Elizabeth Beesley. Her father, William Alfred Beesley, was born at Murfreesboro on May 19, 1883, and her mother, the former Bessie Cornelius Marsh, at Petersburg on April 28, 1881. Dr. and Mrs. Hubbard make their home at 1681 Humboldt Highway. They are the parents of four children: 1. George Baker, Jr., who was born at Nashville, on October 5, 1942. 2. William Beesley, born October 17, 1946, at Jackson. 3. Allan Brooks, born September 8, 1947. 4. Elizabeth Marsh, born December 6, 1949. The younger children were also born at Jackson.

Eric Alan Catmur

Familiar with the cotton industry from the early years of his career, Eric Alan Catmur now has his headquarters in the great cotton center of Memphis, as a partner in the firm of George H. McFadden and Brothers, Inc. He has had experience in the industry in Europe and Asia as well as here.

Born in London, England, on June 11, 1913, he is a son of Harold William and Florence Helen (Kellett) Catmur. Both of his parents were born in London, and Harold W. Catmur became a cotton merchant in Amsterdam, Holland, and Bremen, Germany, representing George H. McFadden and Brothers, Inc. He is now deceased, but Mrs. Catmur survives him and makes her home at Rustington, Sussex, England.

Eric A. Catmur received his early education in that country, attending Brentwood School, and later schools in Holland and Germany. Early in life he became acquainted with the cotton industry through his father's connection with it, and became apprentice in the firm which the elder man represented, George H. McFadden and Brothers, Inc., at the age of eighteen. He came to this country at that time to receive training in the business, and in the course of that training, was sent all over the South. He later went to Brazil where he spent four years.

When he returned to the United States he worked briefly for his father-in-law's firm in Montgomery, Alabama, but terminated that connection to rejoin George H. McFadden and Brothers, Inc., which transferred him to Texas. He worked in Waco and Houston before joining the United States Navy at the time of World War II.

Going into the service early in 1944, he was assigned to the destroyer U.S.S. "Douglass H. Fox" following his training. He remained with the crew of this ship until the end of the war and received his honorable discharge in 1945.

When he returned to his peacetime pursuits and to the cotton industry, George H. McFadden and Brothers, Inc. named him its agent in Shanghai, and he remained there for a period of four years. In 1950 he became special agent in Europe, residing at Lucerne, Switzerland. After a year there, he was called back to this country and offered a partnership in the firm, at which time he established his permanent residence in Memphis.

The residence in which the Catmurs live is the one-hundred-year-old Cedar Hall Farm, originally known as the Orgill Home. It was bought and restored in 1938 by John H. McFadden, Jr. Surrounding the house are about twenty acres of ground, part of which is allocated to the cultivation of boxwood and formal gardens.

Mr. Catmur is a member of the Memphis Country Club and the Memphis Hunt and Polo Club. A communicant of St. George's Episcopal Church at Germantown, he is currently serving as senior warden in the vestry. Mrs. Catmur is active in the church's Guild.

She is the former Miss Margaret Croft Owen of Montgomery, Alabama, daughter of Charles Miller and Maggie (Croft) Owen. Her father was born and reared in Cuthburt, Georgia, and her mother at West Point, Georgia. Both are now deceased. Mrs. Catmur is a trustee of the Memphis Art Academy. Mr. and Mrs. Catmur were married in Montgomery, Alabama, on January 31, 1936. They are the parents of the following children: 1. Susan Owen, who was born May 23, 1938. 2. Eric Alan, Jr., born December 27, 1944. He attends Memphis University School. Both of these children were born in Montgomery, Alabama. 3. John Charles, born in Houston, Texas, on October 27, 1952.

KENNETH HORACE HILL

Except for a period spent in the mercantile service as captain with a steamship line, Kenneth Horace Hill of Memphis has devoted his career to the profession of electrical engineering, and is proprietor of the Hill Electric Company, with headquarters at 166 Monroe.

Born at Little Rock, Arkansas, on February 20, 1902, he is a son of Frank and Edna Hill. His father, also a native of Little Rock, is now deceased; but his mother is still living and has remarried, being now Mrs. George Peters Lee. When Kenneth Horace Hill was young the family came to Memphis, and he attended schools there and graduated from Technical High School. For his advanced studies he attended Bliss Electrical Engineering School near Washington, D. C., where he graduated.

Beginning his career as an electrical engineer in Memphis, Mr. Hill's major business interest has always been the management of the Hill Electric Company at 166 Monroe, with the exception of a period of three years as president of Valley Line Steamers Inc. He holds a captain's commission for the operation of ships on any of the bodies of water flowing into the Gulf of Mexico. Mr. Hill was in the United States Navy during World War I. In World War II he was in the maritime service and held a commission as lieutenant, junior grade.

He belongs to the lodges of the Benevolent and Protective Order of Elks and the Free and Accepted Masons, and in Masonry is a member of the higher bodies and of the Ancient Arabic Order of Nobles of the Mystic Shrine. His other memberships include the Memphis Colonial Club and the Sultan Club. He enjoys hunting and fishing, particularly in the company of his son, Donnelley Hill.

In Memphis, on December 30, 1933, Kenneth Horace Hill married Mary Louise Karsch. She is a daughter of Dr. Joseph Herman and Blanche (Hamilton) Karsch. Her father was a native of Nashville, while her mother was born in New York. The Magevaney Home on Adams Street, the oldest residence in Memphis, open to the public free of admission charge, has been identified with Mrs. Hill's family. It was given to the city by her mother, Mrs. Blanche Hamilton Karsch. She was the granddaughter of its one-time owner, Eugene Magevaney. It was he who taught the first school in Memphis. Young men attending this school brought rifles along with them on their journeys to and from home, to protect themselves from the Indians.

Mr. and Mrs. Hill's son, Donnelley Joseph, was born on December 12, 1938. He is a student at Christian Brothers College.

DAVID BARTON DEMENT, JR.

The Honorable David B. Dement, Jr., who is now serving in the Tennessee State Senate representing Rutherford, Cannon, and DeKalb counties, is by profession an attorney whose practice is in Murfreesboro. He has had a varied career, having spent several years as a cowboy in Montana, Wyoming, and other western states prior to studying for his law degree.

Born in Christiana, on September 5, 1910, he is a son of the late David

Barton Warren

Barton, Sr., and Willie Bell (Allen) Dement. His father, born at Twelve Corner, Rutherford County, on March 14, 1885, was a salesman for the Keim Simmons Company. He died in April, 1950. His widow, born in Lascassas in 1890, makes her home in Murfreesboro.

The younger David Barton Dement received his education in the public schools of Murfreesboro, and was awarded a Bachelor of Laws degree from Cumberland University at Lebanon. Since that time, on April 3, 1950, he has been admitted to practice before the Supreme Court of the United States.

During his years of practice in Murfreesboro, Mr. Dement has been elected to a number of civic posts. He served on the city council for two four-year terms. First elected to the Tennessee State Legislature to serve in the Seventy-eighth Session, he was later re-elected for two more terms, the Seventy-ninth and Eightieth sessions, as a representative from Rutherford County. In the course of his tenure in the lower house, he was chairman of the Conservation Committee, and a member of the Education, Finance, Ways and Means, Highways, and Safety and Judiciary committees.

In 1958, Mr. Dement was elected to the Tennessee State Senate, representing Rutherford, Cannon, and DeKalb counties. In the Senate he is chairman of the Committee on Correctional Institutions, and a member of the Education, Finance, Ways and Means, Insurance and Banking, Judiciary, and Local Government committees. He is a member of the Legislative Council.

Mr. Dement was chairman of an investigating committee on subversive activities, at Highland Folk School. He is a trustee of the Sam Davis Home in Murfreesboro.

He has a creditable record of military service in World War II, when he was a staff sergeant in the Fourth Air Force, United States Army Air Corps, from 1942 to 1945. He is a member of the American Legion and the Veterans of Foreign Wars. His fraternity is Alpha Delta Kappa, a national law society; and he is affiliated with the Free and Accepted Masons, being a member of both the Scottish and the York Rites, and the Ancient Arabic Order of Nobles of the Mystic Shrine. He belongs to the Murfreesboro Chamber of Commerce, the Hunting and Fishing Club, and the Stone River Country Club.

On December 28, 1952, David Barton Dement, Jr., married Marie Reed, daughter of William Taft and Lurlie (Pruitt) Reed of Brooksville, Florida. The Dements have four children; all born in Smyrna. They are: 1. Andrew Jackson, born in 1953. 2. Samuel Houston, born in 1954. 3. Debra Dianne, born in 1955. 4. Patricia Annette, born in 1958.

THOMAS DAVID MOORE, M.D.

A Memphis physician, Dr. Thomas David Moore had a nationwide reputation as a urologist, whose contribution as practitioner and as teacher were equally distinctive. For more than a decade he taught at the University of Tennessee College of Medicine, where he headed the department of urology.

Within his own professional circles, a colleague has said of him: "Dr. Moore's interest in organized medicine and knowledge of medical values gained for him membership and honors in all the urological organizations in this country and recognition throughout the world. . . . He was endowed with great human understanding and set a fine lifelong example as a practitioner of urology."

Born at Hopkinsville, Kentucky, on August 27, 1894, he was a son of the Reverend Thomas David and Mary Frances (Orsburn) Moore. His education began at the age of seven when he enrolled as a pupil at the Callis Academy at Hopkinsville, a private school which he attended for two years. He then entered the preparatory department of South Kentucky College, which he attended regularly until his graduation from this institution with a degree of Bachelor of Arts in June, 1912, at the age of seventeen years. Two years prior to his graduation the name of South Kentucky College was officially changed to McLean College.

In September, 1912, he began his medical education at Vanderbilt University, where he received the degree of Doctor of Medicine in June, 1916, at the age of twenty-one. He was considered a student of extraordinary intelligence and unusual technical skill. He was a member of Theta Kappa Psi fraternity.

The determination to obtain an internship in a large metropolitan hospital prompted him to go to New York City, where he obtained one of the coveted appointments as intern in the Willard Parker Hospital, one of the Department of Health hospitals of that city. At this time he was considering pediatrics as a medical specialty. While serving this internship he was favorably considered for a two-and-a-half-year appointment at Bellevue Hospital for a general rotating internship. Unfortunately he was unable to accept this appointment, which carried no stipend at that time other than board, room and laundry. In obtaining his medical education he had worked his way through to a large extent and not wishing to incur further indebtedness the appointment to Bellevue was reluctantly declined and he decided to accept employment temporarily and complete his specialty training later. He hoped to liquidate some indebtedness and accumulate sufficient funds to continue further training in the medical profession.

He therefore accepted a position with the Anglo-Newfoundland Development Company, Grand Falls, Newfoundland, where he became associated in an industrial practice with the late Dr. Harry B. Chamberlain. This practice began in January, 1917, upon completion of his internship at the Willard Parker Hospital in New York City. This corporation was a large pulp and paper project owned by Lord Northcliffe and Lord Rothermere and the timber limits covered some thirty-eight hundred square miles. In this area were three large lumber camps, in each of which was a practicing physician. All serious accidents, however, and patients who were severely ill, were referred to the center of operations at Grand Falls, where they were admitted to the Lady

Northcliffe Hospital under the care of Drs. Chamberlain and Moore. After five months of this association, Dr. Chamberlain died, and Dr. Moore was asked to take full charge of the medical affairs of the company, which he agreed to do on a temporary basis, and he employed one of his Vanderbilt classmates as an assistant. This was indeed an honor for such a young physician to assume this responsible position. Dr. Moore felt in later years that the general medical and surgical experience which he obtained in Newfoundland was of inestimable value in his professional life.

When the United States became involved in World War I, Dr. Moore resigned the position of company surgeon with the corporation to become effective as soon as he could be replaced. This was not possible until July, 1918, when he returned to the United States and was commissioned a first lieutenant in the Medical Corps of the United States Army, with assignment to the Base Hospital at Camp Devens, Massachusetts. Afer six months he was transferred to General Hospital No. 30, Plattsburg, New York, where he continued to serve until his honorable discharge from the army in September, 1919.

During this period of military service he applied for an appointment to a fellowship in surgery at the Mayo Foundation, Rochester, Minnesota. His application received favorable consideration, concerning which he was notified by telegram directed to his home address in Hopkinsville, Kentucky. This message was missent and delivered to another party, and in consequence the appointment was lost. While waiting for reconsideration and another appointment he served an additional period of six months, during 1919-1920, as an intern at the Madison General Hospital, Madison, Wisconsin. In March, 1920, he began a fellowship in medicine at the Mayo Foundation. After one year his desire to become a urologist was firmly established and he succeeded in transferring his fellowship from medicine to urology. After three more years of training he received the degree of Master of Science in Urology from the Mayo Foundation, University of Minnesota.

In 1923 he located in Memphis, Tennessee, and became associated with the Sanders-Warr Clinic, where he organized and became head of the Department of Urology. After an association of nine years this medical group dissolved at the worst of the depression in 1932. Dr. Moore then established his own office for the practice of urology and urological surgery at 899 Madison Avenue, Memphis, where he remained in active practice until his death.

In January, 1946, he was asked to reorganize the Department of Urology of the School of Medicine, University of Tennessee, where he was appointed full professor and head of the department. He served in this capacity until he resigned from the administrative duties in 1954. He was retained as professor of urology in this institution and continued to teach until his death.

In 1935 he was numbered among the charter diplomates and founders of the American Board of Urology. In 1949 he was elected a member of the governing body of the board representing the Section on Urology of the American Medical Association and served in this capacity until his death. Elected to membership in the American Urological Association in 1923, he served as its secretary from 1942 to 1949, and was elected president in 1951. He also served on the executive committee as representative of the Southeastern Section of the American Urological Association from 1935 to 1940 and from 1955 to 1958. At his suggestion and through his efforts the American Urological Research Foundation was organized in 1952. He served as secretary of this organization from 1952 to 1954 and as president in 1955. In 1935, he served as chairman of the Section of Urology of the Southern Medical Association. He was president of the staff of Baptist Memorial Hospital in 1949 and continued as attending urologist there until his death. He served as president of the Clinical Society of Genito-Urinary Surgeons in 1958. In 1957 he was elected a member of the board of governors of the American College of Surgeons, representing the American Urological Association, and served in this capacity until his death.

In addition to membership in the Memphis-Shelby County Medical Society and the Tennessee State Medical Society, he was a member of the American Medical Association, a fellow of the American College of Surgeons, a member of the Southeastern Sugrical Congress, the American Association of Genito-Urinary Surgeons, the Société Internationale d'Urologie, an honorary member of the Puerto Rico Urological Association, and an honorary member of the South Central Section of the American Urological Association.

Dr. Moore was the author of about one hundred and twenty-five medical articles which appeared in various medical journals throughout the years. As a writer his subjects included all phases of urology with special emphasis on visualization of the upper urinary tract with various media, serial x-rays of the kidney, pelvis and ureters, carcinoma of the bladder treated with radium, transurethral and retropubic prostatectomy, calculous disease of the urinary tract, conservation of renal tissue and reconstruction of the bladder neck. One of his colleagues commented concerning his traits as a practicing physician: Dr. Moore's thoroughness of purpose, his keen sense of proportion, his superior technical ability, his knowledge of human values, his winning smile, his fund of anecdotes—all his personal attributes—were attributes which attracted patients to him from close and distant places. His unselfish approach to the patient-doctor relationship led him on the road to success.

For a number of years Dr. Moore was interested in cattle raising. He was the first president of the Mid-South Hereford Breeders Association, which was organized in 1940, and he was widely known throughout the Mid-South among cattlemen, having formerly owned the Graceland Farm herd of polled Herefords, which he sold in 1950.

In the later years of his life, his hobbies were hunting, fishing and photography. His photographic talent was great and he had a fine library on medical subjects as well as personal and travel studies, including pictures from a three-month European tour. Dr. Moore was a member of the Memphis

Harlan Thomas

Country Club, Memphi and Five Lakes Outing Club. He was a communicant of the Lindenwood Christian Church, and was an independent in his politics.

At the Fifth Avenue Presbyterian Church in New York on July 28, 1952, Dr. Thomas D. Moore married Dorothye Adaline Nyquist, daughter of Charles Phinis and Inez Esther (Kratt) Nyquist. The couple had one son, Thomas David, Jr., born on May 11, 1954. Dr. Moore also had a daughter by a previous marriage: Ruth Marie, who was born on May 24, 1926, and is now the wife of Charles Pittman Cobb. They have four children: Thomas Oliver, Elizabeth Toff, Oliver Perry, Charles Pittman.

Dr. Moore's death occurred suddenly on April 16, 1958. In the days which followed, many tributes were paid him in the press, and in medical groups. "Memphis and the Mid-South were deeply indebted to Dr. Thomas D. Moore," commented an editorial in the Memphis Commercial Appeal. "He had been active and successful in a variety of ways that contributed to the welfare and progress of this city and section." A memoir of the Memphis-Shelby County Medical Society read in part: "He has led a full and useful life and has contributed much to the advancement of medicine, and the city of Memphis has profited by his contributions to its civic progress." Dr. Clyde L. Deming, well acquainted with Dr. Moore and his record, made the comment: "Those of us who were fortunate to have had a close association with Tom Moore realize that his life was complete and filled with devotion and loyalty to mankind."

HARLAN WHITNEY THOMAS

As a result of many years of public service, at national, state and local levels, Harlan Thomas recently served as State Representative for Hardeman County in the Tennessee Legislature. In May, 1959, he was elected mayor of Bolivar for a two year term. An ardent Democrat all his life, he was a delegate to the Democratic National Convention from the Seventh Congressional District of Tennessee in 1956. Despite an active political and business life, Harlan Thomas still finds time to devote to charitable work, notably the Heart Fund Drives, of which he was county chairman in 1955-1956 and director of the Tennessee Heart Association in 1956. He is currently a member of the County Board of Directors of the Tennessee Cancer Society and director of the Hardeman County Chapter of the American Red Cross.

He was born in the town of Michie in McNairy County on August 5, 1908. His father, the late James Edgar Thomas of McNairy County, spent most of his life in the lumber and building supply trade in the town of Selmer. His wife, Dora (Dickerson) Thomas was born in Wayne County and both sides of the family are of old Tennessee stock.

Harlan Thomas received his early education in Michie schools and then attended Freed-Hardiman College at Henderson. He studied law at the Jackson, Tennessee, Law College and Southern University Law School in Memphis.

After leaving college, he worked for the Standard Lumber Company in Selmer, leaving this connection in 1933 to join the Bureau of Internal Revenue in Memphis and remaining there until 1939. In that year he was appointed Business Manager of Western State Hospital in Bolivar. Except for service in the army from June, 1944 to December, 1945, he remained in his post at Western State Hospital until 1949 when he left to open the Thomas Hotel Courts in Bolivar which he still operates. In November, 1958 he was elected as a delegate from Hardeman County to the Tennessee Constitutional Convention which convened in July, 1959. Mr. Thomas is a Thirty-second Degree Mason, member of the Scottish Rite bodies and a Shriner. He is also a member of the American Legion, the Rotary Club, and is a past president and now director of the Bolivar Chamber of Commerce. He is also a member and a director of the Bolivar Development Corporation, and secretary of the Hardeman County Industrial Council. He is also currently chairman of the Bolivar Housing Authority.

He has been married twice. His second marriage took place in Hernando, Mississippi, on July 12, 1944, to Vergie (Bryant) who was born in Hickory Valley on December 6, 1910. Her parents, Elbert Franklin and Mary Verdna (Vaughn) Bryant are both natives of Hardeman County where they live. There are no children of this marriage but Mr. Thomas has two sons by his first marriage. They are: 1. James Harlan, born October 7, 1931, married Gwyndelon Eubanks and they have a son Michael. 2. William Ryals, born November 7, 1932. Both sons were born in Selmer.

James Roy Carter, Jr.

James Roy Carter Jr., entered the beverage industry following brief experience in teaching, and at the time of his death was vice president of the Royal Crown Bottling Company at Jackson. In this business, he was the partner of his father, J. Roy Carter, Sr., who is president of the firm. The elder Mr. Carter is a native of Clifton Forge, Virginia, and was born on November 24, 1890. Harriett Maud Pike, whom he married, was born at Bluefield, West Virginia, on April 1, 1893. Their son, James Roy, Jr., was born October 5, 1918, at Roanoke, Virginia.

He received his public school education there, and graduated from Jefferson High School in 1936. For his advanced training, he entered Virginia Military Institute at Lexington, Virginia, and there he graduated and received his degree of Bachelor of Arts in 1940.

He began his teaching career as instructor at Baylor School for Boys in Chattanooga, Tennessee, conducting courses in mathematics and English, and serving as assistant in military training. From there he went to Hargrave Military Academy at Chatham, Virginia, as instructor in mathematics and English.

Mr. Carter entered the beverage industry in 1943 as a laboratory technician with The Coca-Cola Company, at its national headquarters in Atlanta,

Georgia. The firm later transferred him to Yakima, Washington, as superintendent of the Coca-Cola Bottling Works there. His next position was as production supervisor at the Coca-Cola Bottling Company in Harrisburg, Pennsylvania.

With this valuable experience, Mr. Carter left the Coca-Cola organization in 1944, and on July 1 of that year, entered partnership with his father in purchasing the Royal Crown Bottling Company at Jackson. The plant there is a production unit of the nationally popular Royal Crown beverage. The company was incorporated January 1, 1958, with J. Roy Carter, Sr., as its president and J. Roy Carter, Jr., as vice president and general manager. He was also a member of its board of directors.

Of recent years, Mr. Carter was a leading figure in the statewide trade organization known as Tennessee Bottlers of Carbonated Beverages. He was its vice president in 1955-1956, its president during the 1957-1958 term and chairman of the board at the time of his death. He was a former vice president and former president of the Jackson Junior Chamber of Commerce; former vice president of the Tennessee Junior Chamber of Commerce; and served as director, as vice president and as president of the Jackson-Madison County Chamber of Commerce. He was a member of the Jackson Casey Jones Museum Committee and served as general chairman of "Casey Jones Day," which occasioned a first-day issue of a special stamp. In 1950, Mr. Carter received a Distinguished Service Award as Outstanding Young Man of the Year for Jackson-Madison County.

At the time of World War II, he was absent serving in the army as a second lieutenant in the Field Artillery, being assigned to the Thirteenth Brigade. He rendered capable service in public office as magistrate in the Madison County Court for the city of Jackson, an office he was holding at the time of his death.

He was a member of the Jackson-Madison County Airport Authority and member and director of the Humboldt Golf and Country Club, as well as a member of the Jackson Rotary Club and the American Legion. He was also affiliated with the Free and Accepted Masons, being a member of Lodge No. 45 at Jackson. He was a member of the First Methodist Church of Jackson.

Mrs. Carter is the former Virginia Eloise Fraley, daughter of Albert Lee and Lydia Viola (Johnson) Fraley. Her father was born at Winchester, Tennessee, on December 23, 1889, and her mother on February 5, 1894, at Chickamauga, Georgia. Mr. and Mrs. Carter were married at Middlesburg, Kentucky, on April 19, 1941. They made their home at 10 Laurel Lane, Jackson.

Mr. Carter passed away on November 24, 1958. An editorial in the local newspaper at the time said in part:

This area has suffered a definite loss in the death of J. Roy Carter, Jr. . . . he was an important member of our industrial community.

A greater measure of his worth, however, is found in his contributions to the civic, religious and charitable needs of Jackson and Madison County. . . .

JOHN LOMAR WILLIAMS

For three generations, members of the Williams family have been leaders in the engineering and construction field at Jackson. John Lomar Williams, representing the present generation, is well known in the steel industry and founder of the John Williams Steel Works, Inc., which he has successfully headed for over three decades.

In the early years of the development of Madison County and western Tennessee there came to Jackson a young civil engineer by the name of John Jay Williams. He was born at Oxford, Massachusetts, in 1818. Prior to his arrival in Tennessee, he had been employed as a civil engineer on the construction of the railroad across the Isthmus of Panama. A monument to commemorate his work there has been erected at the Pacific entrance to the Panama Canal. He came to Jackson in 1853, and was placed in charge of the construction of the Mississippi Central Railroad, which afterwards became a part of the Illinois Central Railroad, and was the first rail line to enter Jackson. He was later appointed chief engineer on the construction of the Mobile and Ohio Railroad, the second line to arrive in Jackson, in 1858. On the completion of these railroads, John Jay Williams became interested in canal construction, in which he came to be recognized as a leading authority. In 1870 he was appointed by Congress to head a commission of engineers to make a study of the artificial waterways of the European continent, and to make further studies of the Nicaragua and the Tehuantepec canal routes for connecting the Atlantic and Pacific oceans. His report on this subject was of international importance, and was published in several languages.

His son, John L. Williams, graduated from the University of Kentucky in civil engineering, after which he became prominent in railroad construction throughout the South. The last twelve years of his life were spent as city engineer of Jackson, Tennessee. John L. Williams was born in New York City, and he married Rose Hendrickson, who was born at Lenoir, California.

Their son, John Lomar Williams, born in Jackson on March 17, 1890, has followed in the professional footsteps of his father and his grandfather. He completed his education at Jackson, Tennessee. Early in his career he became interested in the structural steel industry. He founded the John Williams Steel Works, Inc., at Jackson in 1925, and it has operated successfully under his management since that time.

He is a member of the following professional and trade organization: American Institute of Steel Construction; and in his own city, he belongs to the Jackson and Madison County Chamber of Commerce. He has taken a constructive part in the fund-raising campaigns of the American Red Cross and the Community Chest, programs which are now carried on under the United

Carl W. Shorter

Fund. He is a member of the lodge of Benevolent and Protective Order of Elks. He is a communicant of St. Luke's Episcopal Church, where he serves on the Vestry.

On November 30, 1944, in Jackson, John Lomar Williams married Mary Lake. They have no children. Their home is on J. Williams Road, Jackson.

CARL WILLIAM SHORTER

One of Memphis' younger business leaders, Carl William Shorter is today executive head of two prosperous organizations, a food brokerage firm and a printing plant. He is a veteran of World War II, and is an active member of a number of local organizations. He also has a reputation as a public speaker.

Born May 5, 1921, at Davis Station in Clarendon County, South Carolina, he is a son of Thomas Porter and Camilla (Ward) Shorter. His father is deceased, and is survived by his mother, who makes her home in Sumter, South Carolina.

Carl W. Shorter received his grammar school education at Davis Station, South Carolina, and attended Manning High School.

In October, 1942, Mr. Shorter enlisted for war-time service in the United States Navy, with the rank of Petty Officer, Second Class, Carpenter's Mate. Two years of his service were spent in Bermuda, and the last year of his service, he was stationed at Millington Naval Air Station, Memphis, Tennessee, receiving his honorable discharge in October, 1945. After his discharge, he remained in Memphis.

He entered the food business as salesman for a national concern, but less than a year later left them to form his own food brokerage business, the Carl Shorter Company, in 1946. He has since headed this organization, which has its present headquarters at 1192 Airways Boulevard, and it has been successful to an extent which has made possible the establishment of a branch operation at Jackson, Mississippi, in April, 1956.

In 1954, Mr. Shorter turned his attention to a second venture, founding the Carl Shorter Printing Company, at the same address as the food brokerage firm. He has remained its owner since that time.

An effective public speaker, Mr. Shorter has addressed a number of groups on sales techniques and sales psychology.

He is a member of the National Food Brokers Association, and has served on several national committees; is past president of the Memphis Food Brokers Association; has served on the board of directors of the Memphis Sales Executives Club, Tennessee Wholesale Grocers Association, Variety Club, and Optimist Club; and is a member of the Memphis Grocery Manufacturers Association, Memphis Chamber of Commerce, Memphis Athletic Club, Rivermont Club, and Tennessee Club. He is an associate member of the Mississippi Wholesale Grocers Association, and the Memphis Retail Grocers

Association. He has served for many years on the Disaster Committee of the American Red Cross.

Mrs. Shorter is the former Miss Jo Ann Franklin of Memphis, and is the daughter of James C. Franklin, retired executive of Hirsch Brothers & Company, of Louisville, Kentucky, and Edna Franklin, of Memphis. She was married to Carl W. Shorter on May 3, 1946, and they have three children. 1. Susan Jane, born August 10, 1950. 2. Karen Ann, born September 21, 1952. 3. Carl William, Jr., born April 3, 1957.

William Russell Rice, Sr.

A lawyer who began his professional career in Jackson, William Russell Rice, Sr., is now serving as city attorney there, and has served as state senator from the Twenty-fifth Senatorial District.

He is a native of Tuscaloosa, Alabama, and was born on August 20, 1917, son of David Files, Sr., and Elizabeth (Brown) Rice. His father was associated with Gulf, Mobile and Ohio Railroad Company for 57 years. He died July 12, 1957. Both of his parents were native southerners, his father having been born at Northport, Alabama, in 1874, and his mother in 1878 at Lockhart, Mississippi. The family moved to Jackson, Tennessee, in Russell Rice's early years, and he attended public schools there. He began his advanced education at Georgia Institute of Technology, completed his studies there in 1937, and received his degree of Bachelor of Laws at Cumberland University in 1939.

Admitted to the State Bar of Tennessee, Mr. Rice commenced his practice at Jackson. In 1942 he left to enlist as a private in the United States Marine Corps, and served throughout the war, receiving his honorable discharge in 1946, by which time he held the rank of captain. He had served in the Central Pacific, commanding Dog Battery of the Eighteenth Antiaircraft Battalion, an artillery unit under the command of the Fifth Corps. He was later assistant division ordnance officer in the 30th Armored Division.

Mr. Rice had accepted a position as claims attorney with the Gulf, Mobile and Ohio Railroad Company in 1940, and he resumed this connection after the war, continuing with the railroad until 1955. Meantime, from 1947 to 1951, he had also served as city attorney at Jackson, and he was returned to that office in 1955. He still fills that city post. He was elected to the Upper House of the Legislature from the 25th Senatorial District of Tennessee in 1951. He is presently chairman of the Jackson-Madison County Airport Authority, and he is licensed to practice before the Supreme Court of the United States.

Besides his legal and public activities, Mr. Rice is a business executive, holding office as secretary of the Ideal Oil Company, Inc. He is a member of his County, State and American bar associations. Mr. Rice was given the Young Man of the Year Award in 1949 for the City of Jackson by the United States Junior Chamber of Commerce. As a veteran of World War II, he belongs to the posts of the American Legion and the Veterans of Foreign Wars.

His fraternity is Alpha Tau Omega. He and Mrs. Rice attend the First Methodist Church.

The couple were married at Jackson on November 17, 1943. She is the former Miss Edna Earle Curdts, daughter of George T. and Elizabeth (Butts) Curdts. Both of her parents were born in Norfolk, Virginia, her father in 1882 and her mother in 1889. Mr. and Mrs. Russell Rice make their home at 44 Laurel Lane in Jackson, and they are the parents of four children, all of whom were born in that city: 1. William Russell, Jr., born on September 17, 1944. 2. Janet Craig, born November 7, 1947. 3. George David, born on October 31, 1949. 4. Paul Foster, born April 8, 1957.

FRANK SCOTT PROCTOR

Manager of radio stations WTJS and WTJS-FM in Jackson since 1946, and formerly associated with the Standard Oil Company, Mr. Proctor is a director of the Sun Publishing Company, publishers of *The Jackson Sun* and licensee of stations WTJS and WTJS-FM, and he is director, secretary and treasurer of Kelly Foods, Incorporated, of Jackson.

Mr. Proctor was born in Nashville, on May 30, 1910, the son of Robert Lee Proctor and of Martha Van Meter (Scott) Proctor. His parents were born in Drakes Branch, Charlotte County, Virginia, his father on December 9, 1873, and his mother on May 12, 1875. Mr. Proctor attended Clemons Elementary School in Nashville, Tennessee, graduated from Hume-Fogg High School in Nashville, and obtained the degree of Bachelor of Engineering at the Vanderbilt University School of Engineering in 1932, and is a member of Tau Beta Pi Honorary Engineering fraternity.

Mr. Proctor entered the employ of the Standard Oil Company of Louisiana in the Tennessee Sales Division in 1932, and in 1936 was transferred to the Standard Oil Development Company of Elizabeth, New Jersey, where he was engaged in refinery engineering work in the United States, Canada and South America. In 1942, during World War II, he was granted a leave of absence from the Standard Oil Company, in order to accept a special assignment with the Petroleum Administration for War, Facilities Security Division, and he was engaged in security work in oil refineries, terminals and pipe lines throughout the eastern part of the United States. At the end of the war, he returned to the Standard Oil Company, and it was in August, 1946, that he resigned from this post to become manager of radio stations WTJS and WTJS-FM of Jackson, Tennessee.

Mr. Proctor has been active in community life and he is past president of the Jackson-Madison County Chamber of Commerce, the Jackson Rotary Club and the Jackson Civic Music Association; he has also held the presidency of the West Tennessee Community Improvement Program, the Madison County Tuberculosis Association and the Tennessee Association of Broadcasters. He is a former director of the Madison County Red Cross, the United Fund and the Young Men's Christian Association, and he is a member of the West Tennessee Area Council of the Boy Scouts, the Jackson-Madison County Council of the Girl Scouts, the Governor's Advisory Committee for Civil Defense and the Tennessee 4-H Citizens Committee. His social connections include membership in Beta Theta Pi fraternity, the Elks and the Jackson Golf and Country Club. Mr. Proctor is an elder in the First Presbyterian Church of Jackson, Tennessee.

He was married in Jackson on December 2, 1936, to Patty Brown Harvey, the daughter of George Harvey and of Patty (Person) Harvey. Her father was born in Canton, Mississippi, on February 25, 1884, and her mother in Jackson, Tennessee, on December 31, 1889.

Mr. and Mrs. Proctor have one daughter, Patty Harvey, born in Plainfield, New Jersey, on November 21, 1943.

NOLAND WILSON EZELL

Before he had attained his majority, Noland Wilson Ezell had found his true vocation in the lumber industry. During the last two decades of his life he was executive head of the firm which is now known as the Ezell-Flanagan Lumber Company in Memphis.

A native of that city, Mr. Ezell was born on January 18, 1901, and was a son of Timothy and Nannie (Havens) Ezell. His father was born at Pulaski, and his mother at Forrest City, Arkansas. Attending local public schools, Noland W. Ezell graduated from Central High School. At the age of nineteen, he began his career in the lumber business, joining the J. P. Jordan Lumber Company. Acquiring ample experience in the industry over the next decade and a half, becoming familiar with all aspects of operations, and with confidence in his ability to head his own organization, he resigned from his connection with that firm in 1936, and joined a partner in forming the Chambers-Ezell Lumber Company. This was the predecessor of the present Ezell-Flanagan Lumber Company, which has its headquarters at 760 Vance Street in Memphis. Mr. Ezell remained at the head of the firm until his death in 1957.

Mr. Ezell held no organizational memberships, and his avocational interests were chiefly home-centered. He was, however, a dependable supporter of every worth-while program for the benefit of the community and the service of its people. He was a communicant of the Lindenwood Christian Church.

In his home city of Memphis on February 8, 1931, Noland Wilson Ezell married Mary Belle Thomason. Born at Osceola, Arkansas, she is a daughter of Jasper Newton and Willie (Russell) Thomason. Both of her parents were natives of Paris, Tennessee, and J. N. Thomason was a lawyer, who practiced at Osceola, Arkansas, and later in Memphis. Mrs. Willie Thomason died on July 28, 1957. Mrs. Ezell attended Randolph Macon College and Southwestern College, and was a member of Kappa Delta sorority. The couple became the

John H DeWitt Jr

parents of three children: 1. Eleanor, who was born on November 22, 1932. She graduated from the University of Tennessee in 1954, and was a member of Delta Delta sorority while there. She is now married to John T. McAskill of Paris, Tennessee. 2. Elizabeth, born December 18, 1936. She attended Memphis State University, and belonged to Alpha Delta Pi sorority. She married David Lee Berry of Memphis. 3. Nancy, born on November 30, 1941; now a student at the University of Tennessee and a member of Alpha Omicron Pi sorority.

The city of Memphis lost one of its capable business leaders in the death of Noland W. Ezell, which occurred on July 2, 1957.

JOHN HIBBETT DEWITT, JR.

When John Hibbett DeWitt, Jr., was very young and the radio industry likewise, the two formed a lifelong alliance. Mr. DeWitt worked on the construction of one of the first stations in the region when he was only sixteen years old. Leaving for engineering training and experience in New York, he returned to join the staff of WSM, and is now president of the corporation. He has been one of the men whose technical training and personality have won for the station a nationally recognized role of leadership.

A native of Nashville, Mr. DeWitt was born on February 20, 1906, and is a son of John Hibbett, Sr., and Rebekah (Ward) DeWitt. His father, a lawyer by training, was for some years judge of the Court of Appeals in that city. The younger John H. DeWitt completed his secondary studies at Duncan Preparatory School College, where he graduated in 1924. In 1922, he worked on the construction of the first broadcasting station in Nashville, at Ward-Belmont School, and in 1925, assisted in the installation of the original equipment for WSM. This early experience determined the course of his career, and for advanced technical training, he entered Vanderbilt University Engineering School. He became a member of the technical staff of Bell Telephone Laboratories in New York City in 1929.

In 1932 he returned to Nashville, and became chief engineer of WSM, a position he held until 1942. During that decade he also carried on a consulting practice through which he served between forty and fifty other stations. It was during these years that WSM made its history-making broadcast covering the news of the disastrous flood of 1937.

By 1942, this country had become involved in World War II, and Mr. DeWitt left his normal broadcasting activities to place his abilities and training at the disposal of the government. Rejoining the staff of Bell Telephone Laboratories, he worked exclusively on the design of radar equipment for the armed forces. He was commissioned a major and later promoted to lieutenant colonel in the Signal Corps. For two years he was director of Evans Signal Laboratory, Belmar, New Jersey. He was awarded the Legion of Merit for the development of a radar mortar locator; and in 1946, as officer in charge of

Project Diana of the Army Signal Corps, made the historic first radar contact with the moon.

Since his period of wartime service, Mr. DeWitt has remained an expert consultant to the Office of the Chief Signal Officer in the field of electronics. He became consultant to the Clear Channel Broadcasting Service in 1946. Returning to WSM after the war, he was elected president of the corporation, WSM, Inc., in 1947, and has filled that position ever since.

Mr. DeWitt is a fellow of the Institute of Radio Engineers, and a member of the American Physical Society, the American Astronomical Society, and the Society of Sigma Xi. His fraternity is Phi Delta Theta.

In Nashville, on August 4, 1950, John Hibbett DeWitt, Jr., married Sykes Hewett, daughter of Strafford Reeves and Carolyn (Barbour) Hewett. The couple are the parents of one child, Cary Claiborne, born January 23, 1953; and Mr. DeWitt has a son by a previous marriage: John Hibbett, 3rd, who was born on March 1, 1934.

CECIL FREDERIC WILLIAMS

After varied experience in the news and broadcasting fields elsewhere, Cecil Frederic Williams came to Nashville in 1952 to assume editorial duties with WSM. He is now news director of both the radio and the television station which the corporation manages.

Born January 9, 1924, in Omaha, Nebraska, he is a son of Cecil Frederic and Ann Boniface (Anheuser) Williams. His father died in 1934 and his mother in 1951. The elder Cecil F. Williams was a radio continuity writer. He had served in the Kit Carson Regiment, U. S. Cavalry, during World War I. Cecil, Jr., received a parochial school education, attending St. Cecilia's Grade School and Cathedral High School, both in his native city of Omaha. He also attended the University of Omaha, being a student there for one year before transferring to Creighton University. He was enrolled there for a year, and spent another year at the University of Arizona, one year at the University of Nebraska, and one year at the University of Tennessee. He took his degree of Bachelor of Arts at Nebraska in 1951. Also, while in the United States Navy, Mr. Williams attended radio school at Great Lakes, Illinois, and sonar school at Boston, Massachusetts.

He began his working career as a laborer in the plant of the Armour Packing Company in his native city of Omaha, in 1939. His next position was as a mixer with the Stryker Soft Water Company in that city. He entered the news field when he joined the United Press Association in 1946; and from 1947 to 1952, he was editor with radio station WOW in Omaha.

Mr. Williams left his native city for Nashville in 1952, to join the staff of WSM as editor in its radio and television operations. This pioneer Mid-South station is the subject of an accompanying historical sketch. Bill Williams —as he is better known—was appointed to his present post as news director of

WSM and WSM-TV in 1957. He was formerly president of the credit union of an Omaha corporation, and still serves on its board of directors.

Mr. Williams began his naval career in 1941, and served on the submarines "O-10," "Hawkbill," and "Pilotfish." He made six successful war patrols, and participated in the Battle of the Philippines Sea, the campaigns for Saipan and Guam, and other important actions in the Pacific. He received the Silver Star from Secretary of Defense Forrestal, and was also awarded the Submarine Combat Pin with four gold stars, the Commendation Ribbon, Navy Unit Commendation, Philippines Liberation Ribbon with bronze star, Asiatic Pacific Ribbon, Defense Service Ribbon, and Good Conduct Medal. In addition to the six years which he spent in active naval service, Mr. Williams was for two years a member of a Nebraska National Guard unit.

He was once a baseball coach at Lincoln, Nebraska, and also while in that state, he had political experience managing the campaign of a friend for the office of sheriff of Douglas County. He was formerly a member of the Omaha Junior Chamber of Commerce, the Kiwanis Club, and the American Legion. At the present time, Mr. Williams holds a life membership in the Junior Foresters, and is a member of the Donelson Park Club, which he is currently serving as president. He is of Roman Catholic faith.

At Evanston, Illinois, on January 10, 1942, Cecil Frederic Williams married Eunice Margaret Cardwell, daughter of Ellsworth Morris and Ruth (Griffiths) Cardwell. Mr. and Mrs. Williams have five children: 1. Ruth Ann, who was born on December 16, 1942. 2. Mary Patricia, born August 15, 1946. 3. Thomas Patrick, born November 11, 1949. 4. John Frederic, born September 19, 1955. 5. Bryan Cardwell, born November 7, 1958.

History of WSM

In 1925 radio was in its swaddling clothes. Few people took it seriously. Thus, on October 6th of that year, when WSM opened a small one-room studio in the building that housed the National Life and Accident Insurance Company, most people looked upon the experiment as a passing fad.

In those days the WSM transmitter was located on Fifteenth Avenue near Ward-Belmont College. The station carried no commercial advertising, and it maintained a small but regular program schedule. Typical of the informality of this period was the organization of the Grand Ole Opry. This leader of all folk music programs came into being largely because an old-time fiddler, Uncle Jimmy Thompson, stopped by the station one day and announced that he would like to go on the air. George Dewey Hay, known to millions as the Opry's Solemn Old Judge, gave Uncle Jimmy a chair under a microphone and turned him loose. The mail and telephone response was terrific, and his brand of homespun music was the embryo from which grew the present Grand Ole Opry and its cast of one hundred and fifty.

By 1927, people were beginning to say that this radio fad might amount to something after all. The Federal Communications System granted WSM a power increase to five thousand watts, and a year later this station began to broadcast its first commercial programs. Advertising, which is the life breath of free American radio, had stepped in to aid a fast-growing industry.

In the beginning, WSM's only announcer was Harry Stone. By 1932, Mr. Stone had advanced to the position of general manager of the station. That same year, John H. DeWitt, Jr., who as an eighteen-year-old engineering student at Vanderbilt University, had helped construct WSM's first transmitter, returned to the station as chief engineer. Mr. DeWitt, internationally famous for his feat of "shooting the moon" with radar during the World War II period, is now president of WSM. He is the subject of a separate sketch.

The history of the station during the last two decades is a story of work and programming in the public interest. Typical of this desire to serve the people was WSM's complete devotion to its large Southern community during the disastrous 1937 flood. Until that time no radio station in this country had been given a real test during a national emergency. Then one rainy spring day the opportunity for service was presented. Following is a brief account of that historic episode.

The station had just concluded a special-event broadcast from the flooded area around Clarksville when word was received that waters were rising rapidly in the downtown section of Louisville, Kentucky. A teletype message went out from WSM volunteering help, and the following day, Sunday, January 24, 1937, Lee Coulson, at that time manager of WHAS in Louisville, wired back stating that his power might be turned off, forcing his station off the air. WSM was faced with a task without precedent in radio history. It was apparent that the station's transmitter was needed to carry on vital rescue work, and this entailed cancellation of all commercial and sustaining programs and the volunteer help of the station's personnel on a full round-the-clock basis. With threads of life hanging in the balance, WSM operated without interruption for eighty-two consecutive hours. During this entire period, only vital flood messages were broadcast. Throughout the United States, more than two hundred stations picked up the WSM signal and rebroadcast its dramatic life-saving bulletins. WSM had met the challenge and had proved radio's ability to serve America in time of emergency.

As the station has reached maturity more and more emphasis has been put on programming to meet the listening needs and desires of the people served over the several states this station covers. In its programming facilities, WSM ranks among the leaders in American radio. No other station in the South can rival the roster of two hundred entertainers who are heard broadcasting from this station's studios each week. This staff is seldom matched even by New York, Chicago, and Hollywood stations. But WSM does more than this. The station uses this great array of talent to promote a long-range program of service to our community.

Fred T. Thayer, Jr.

An example of this is WSM's public-service farm show, "Noontime Neighbors." This program, under the supervision of Farm Director John McDonald, has been called one of the finest half-hour programs in the country by many farm leaders. The best of WSM's entertainers appear on the program at a time a special survey showed that most farm listeners can conveniently be tuned in to the station. Designed especially to serve the needs of farmers in the WSM community, "Noontime Neighbors" not only presents entertainers, but is also packed with agricultural information and interviews planned to help farmers do a better agricultural job. Service to the farm community has always been considered of the utmost importance. For ten years WSM has maintained telephone lines over the two hundred and twenty-five miles between Nashville and Knoxville, from which a regular broadcast is made during the college year. The farm market report, of vital interest to farm people, has been heard over WSM for more than two decades.

On U. S. Highway 31 near Franklin, WSM operates one of the finest transmitters, and maintains one of the best physical plants, in existence. The ground system there covers more than thirty acres. The station's eight-hundred-and-eight-foot tower is one of the tallest in the United States—255 feet taller than the Washington Monument.

The field of ultra-high-frequency broadcasting is not new at WSM. In 1939 it began experimenting with W4XA, an ultra-high-frequency station. It represented an experiment in both engineering and programming, giving listeners a distinctively different kind of program service. The experiments resulted in setting up W47NV, first commercial frequency-modulation station in the United States.

WSM has originated many network programs on a regular weekly basis. Every year more than a quarter of a million people visit WSM and its Grand Ole Opry program. Some of course come merely to attend the great folk-music show, which has made the station best known to audiences throughout the nation. But many others stop by the station to visit the point of origin of their daily radio listening.

COLONEL FREDERICK THOMAS THAYER, JR.

After almost two decades of service with the United States Army and Army Air Corps, Colonel Frederick Thomas ("Pat") Thayer returned to civilian life and entered private industry at Memphis, as owner of the F. T. Thayer Construction Company. He has become active in the organizational life of his city.

He is a native of Memphis, and was born on July 24, 1910, son of Frederick Thomas, Sr., and Archie (King) Thayer. His father too was an engineer, who spent most of his career with the firm of Layne and Bowler, Inc. Attending the public schools of his home city, Colonel Thayer attended Central High School there in 1923, and he completed his secondary studies at

Nicholas Senior High School in Chicago, Illinois, and at Des Moines High School, Des Moines, Iowa, where he graduated in 1929. He then went on to advanced studies at Syracuse University, in Syracuse, New York, where he graduated with the degree of Bachelor of Science in Civil Engineering in 1932. At the same time he received a second lieutenant's commission in the Reserve Officers Training Corps.

Colonel Thayer's career in the army began in 1940, when he enlisted at Fort Bragg, North Carolina. He advanced through the grades to the rank of colonel, receiving his commission in that rank in 1948. At the time of World War II, he served with the staff of Army Services and Headquarters, Army Air Force, Washington, D. C., with the Division Engineer, Dallas, Texas. His entire military career was in an engineering capacity.

In 1946, Colonel Thayer was released from active duty. On May 1, 1950, he founded the firm of F. T. Thayer, Jr., General Contractor, in Memphis, which has its headquarters at 189 Scott Street, and specializes in the building of commercial and industrial structures. His company built the two-and-three-quarter-million-dollar plant of the DeSoto Paint and Varnish Company at Garland, Texas, and the new three-million-dollar Sears, Roebuck and Company retail store on Poplar Avenue in Memphis. High schools, gymnasiums and churches are among the other buildings completed. Colonel Thayer's long experience in the construction projects of the Corps of Engineers has proved an excellent background for further achievements in civilian life, and his qualities of leadership and executive abilities have helped shape an efficient organization which is a credit to the city. Colonel Thayer is its sole owner.

In 1952, Frederick T. Thayer, Jr., was appointed to serve in the mayor's rehabilitation program, and he is still filling this public post. He is a member of the Engineers Club of Memphis, the Serra Club, which is a business men's group, the Rivermont Club, Chickasaw Country Club, and the Catholic Club. Fraternal organizations in which he holds membership are the Scabbard and Blade, a national military engineers' group, and Sigma Chi and Theta Tau, honorary engineering societies. He is a full member of the American Society of Civil Engineers. As a Roman Catholic and a member of St. Louis' Church, he is also a Fourth-degree member of the Knights of Columbus. Active on behalf of the program of the Boy Scouts of America, he is president of the Chickasaw Council, and he holds the Silver Beaver and the St. George Awards.

At Sacred Heart Church in Memphis, on December 26, 1935, Frederick Thomas Thayer, Jr., married Katherine Chiles, daughter of Dr. Benjamin Franklin and Teresa (Finch) Chiles. Colonel and Mrs. Thayer are the parents of the following children: 1. Frederick Thomas, 3rd, born on January 15, 1938. 2. Patricia Ann, born August 23, 1940. 3. Sylvia Irene, born August 21, 1943. The Thayer home address is 4900 Briarcliff Road, Memphis.

AMERICAN INVESTORS CORPORATION

American Investors Corporation is the parent organization of a closely inter-connected group of life insurance operations and related enterprises.

American Investment Life Insurance Company of Nashville, is the initial life insurance subsidiary of American Investors Corporation. It is licensed to transact business in the District of Columbia, Florida, Georgia, Maryland, Kentucky, Louisiana, South Carolina, Tennessee, Indiana and Virginia.

Since the time American Investors Corporation established the American Investment Life Insurance Company as its first life insurance subsidiary, it has considerably expanded its operations in the life insurance field, currently operating, among others, American Investment Life Insurance Company of Maryland, Baltimore, Maryland, and American Investment Life Insurance Company of South Carolina, at Columbia. Other subsidiaries founded and acquired by the parent corporation are Southeastern Fund, The GWG Corporation, Stylecraft Homes Corporation, Investors Fire Insurance Company, Financial Life & Casualty Insurance Company— all of Columbia, South Carolina—and American Investors Life Insurance Company of Texas, Houston, Texas. These now comprise the American Investors Corporation life insurance group and closely allied fields of endeavor. In fifteen months of operation the group was licensed and operating in fifteen states and the District of Columbia, with offices in forty-four cities, and the original agency force of fifty men had been enlarged to 250. As of June 30, 1959, there was a total of $72,380,368 of life insurance in force.

President and chief executive officer of American Investors Corporation is Donald L. Connett of Atlanta, Georgia. The board of directors of American Investors and its subsidiaries consists of Charles H. Alberding, Chicago, Illinois; Eddy Arnold, Nashville, Tennessee; Roy H. Brown, Jr., Knoxville, Tennessee; John Brown Cook, New Haven, Connecticut; Jimmie Davis, Shreveport, Louisiana; Overton C. Elkins, Nashville, Tennessee; Madison Farnsworth, Houston, Texas; Warren Fleming, Houston, Texas; T. Fontell Flock, Atlanta, Georgia; Frank Gary, Columbia, South Carolina; Louis J. Grasmick, Baltimore, Maryland; Dr. Gilbert Harold, Nashville, Tennessee; Ralph C. Hewitt, Orlando, Florida; Joseph R. Ives, Washington, D. C.; Hubert Long, Nashville, Tennessee; W. J. McAnnelly, Houston, Texas; Harry A. McDonald, Washington, D. C.; Jack Musslewhite, Houston, Texas; Dr. E. C. Lunsford, Miami, Florida; Allen J. Lefferdink, Denver, Colorado; Webb Pierce, Nashville, Tennessee; Frank Smith, Jr. and Frank Smith, Sr., Columbia, South Carolina; Victor P. Tabaka, Atlanta, Georgia; Charles C. Vance, Chicago, Illinois; W. L. Vanadore, Nashville, Tennessee; Faron Young, Nashville, Tennessee; George P. Wenck, Fountain Inn, South Carolina; George Preston Marshall, Washington, D. C.; and Frank Poole, Nashville, Tennessee.

CAIN-SLOAN COMPANY

When, late in 1957, the Cain-Sloan Company opened, in Nashville, Tennessee, the largest department store ever built at one time in the South, it brought to fruition the result of more than a half-century of efficient merchandising and community service. This well-known firm began its existence on November 14, 1903, when it was founded by three young businessmen, Pat Cain, John E. Cain, and Paul Sloan. The owners had purchased the stock of a store called Comback's "Bee Hive" at fifty cents on the dollar, after acquiring merchandising experience as employees of another store known as Timothy's. They began their own operations at an address in the Strand Theater block on Fifth Avenue. The store at that location had a floor space of three thousand square feet; and its earliest records indicate a total of forty dollars in sales during the first day's operations.

Within four years, their venture had prospered so well that larger quarters were required. In 1907 the firm moved to a six-story building at 209 Fifth Avenue North. By 1915, the first enlargement at this location had been made, extending it to the corner of Fifth and Church streets. In 1930, extensive remodeling was carried out. In 1937, the Cain-Sloan Company took over the entire corner and made further improvements. Despite these expansion programs, the building then occupied had its limitations, and the quarters were getting too old and confining to be satisfactory. In the 1940s, the company began assembling properties along the entire frontage facing on Church Street across from the site of the old store. Construction of the new store was begun in 1950, but it was interrupted by a steel shortage resulting from the Korean War. It was thus not until the fall of 1957 that the present impressive department store building was completed.

The original trio of founders remained active in management during the first twenty-five years of the firm's existence. Pat Cain, who had had previous office experience, was the bookkeeper and office manager of the original store. He was secretary and treasurer at the time of his death, while Paul Sloan served as president, and John E. Cain as general manager. The partners took a personal interest in purchasing operations. John Cain bought hosiery and notions, and Paul Sloan purchased all piece goods.

By 1907, the personnel had been enlarged with the election of B. W. Landstreet, J. J. Bevington, and M. J. Cain to membership in the firm. That was a year of panic, and Cain-Sloan Company felt the slump. The firm had a practice of discounting all bills by paying them promptly. Pat Cain felt it might be necessary for the store to go to the banks for the first time, for a loan to permit continuance of this sound method. He conferred with a local banker who at once agreed to extend a line of credit, despite the general practice of refusing all loans during the panic. However, by stringent economy and personal sacrifice, the young managers were able to meet obligations promptly without using any bank money.

In 1932, Paul Sloan died and was succeeded as president by John E. Cain, who served until his own death late in 1936. At that time Paul's son, John Sloan, became president, a position he still holds.

In 1955, Cain-Sloan Company joined Allied Stores Corporation, giving it access to great buying economies and other aids. Management of the store remains in the hands of Nashvillians, with John Sloan as president, John E. Cain, Jr., as vice president, R. P. Cain, Sr., as secretary-treasurer, and Paul Sloan as vice president. John H. Dubuisson is vice president and general merchandise manager.

The recently completed store was one of but four completed within a decade in the downtown area of any major city. Its more than five hundred and forty thousand square feet are allocated to six floors of store space and eight floors of connected garage area, enabling customers to park their cars in the store itself. By the time they return to their vehicles after shopping, all purchases that they wish to take home have been delivered by the store to the garage area. The buff-colored brick structure, erected in a near-record one year and three days under the supervision of Allied Stores Corporation, has the capacity for a first-year business of twenty-million dollars. This contrasts with the eight million dollars in annual business which was transacted in the fifty-four thousand square feet of the old store—a figure which made it one of the nation's leaders in sales per square foot. The company is now considering plans to construct an additional selling floor.

Commenting on the store at the time of its completion, Mr. Sloan remarked, "It has been our objective to really have the greatest store ever placed in the Central South ... We are particularly proud that our opening comes at this time as a further evidence of the confidence we have in the future of Nashville downtown and in the economic strength of this general area." Dr. James L. Sullivan, Chamber of Commerce official, remarked, "The new Cain-Sloan store is a dramatic demonstration of faith in Nashville and the central city."

The management is, as ever, keeping its eye on the future. It is significant that the building is so designed that elevators run one floor higher than needed, and utility towers are placed an extra floor in height. All is in readiness for the day when business will make necessary even further expansion of Nashville's and the Mid-South's greatest department store.

RICHARD DUKE FULLER

For the past two decades, Richard Duke Fuller has been one of Memphis' business leaders. Throughout that period, he has headed the Fuller Alignment Service, and he is also owner of the Fuller Automotive Air Conditioning Company. He has been very active in civic and organizational affairs, in youth work, and on behalf of education.

A native of Nashville, he was born on January 10, 1904, and is a son of Richard Duke, Sr., and Birdie (Smith) Fuller. His father, an accountant, was born in Bernice, Louisiana, where the family had lived for generations, and he lived and worked in Nashville and in Chicago, Illinois. The younger Richard D. Fuller received his early education in the former city, attending Duncan Preparatory School. He later attended the Price Webb School at Lewisburg, Tennessee and went to Tennessee Technical College for his advanced studies.

In 1937, Mr. Fuller founded the Fuller Alignment Service, which he has since headed, and which is located at 853 Linden Avenue, Memphis. He established his second firm, the Fuller Automotive Air Conditioning Company, in 1955. It has its headquarters at the same address.

The program of the Boy Scouts of America has long been a major interest of Mr. Fuller. He was formerly president of its Chickasaw Council, and is now a member of the National Council. He has also held office as vice chairman of its regional executive committee. In recognition of his service, he has been given both the Silver Antelope and the Silver Beaver awards by the Boy Scouts of America. He is a director of Memphis Boys Town, and he serves on the board of trustees of Harding College at Searcy, Arkansas, and also serves as secretary of the Board. He was awarded Boys Best Friend Citation in 1954 by the Veterans of Foreign Wars, Post No. 1965.

Mr. Fuller is vice president of the Memphis Chamber of Commerce, on whose board of directors he has served for some years. He was chairman of the Welcome Committee. He was also chairman of the Chambers' Skyline Club, a membership building group which awarded him an honorary life membership in the Memphis Chamber of Commerce. A Kiwanian, he served as president of the club at Memphis in 1953; and he was president of the Memphis Executive Club in 1956. He is also past president of the Gavel Club, and has served as chief Goodfellow of the Memphis Press-Scimitar. He has taken a constructive interest in the program of the Mid South Fair, serving on its board of directors. He and Mrs. Fuller attend the White Station Church of Christ, where Mr. Fuller serves as an Elder.

Mrs. Fuller is the former Miss Jeanne Gordon, the daughter of Eugene and Minnie (Dickson) Gordon, and she became the wife of Richard Duke Fuller in a ceremony in Memphis on April 12, 1924. The couple are the parents of two daughters: 1. Jeanne Guerlayne, who was born on October 13, 1925. She is the wife of Reagan Yarbrough. They have four sons: Reagan, Jr., Richard Fuller, James Landon and Jon Walton. 2. Sara Margaret, born on April 9, 1929. She married Berryl C. Brewer and they have two children: Charles Richard and Rebecca Lynn Brewer.

HOTEL PEABODY

Hotel Peabody, long a famous Memphis and Mid-South landmark, possesses a heritage symbolic of southern tradition and progress.

For over fourscore years there has been a Hotel Peabody playing a prominent role in Memphis social and business affairs. Shortly after the Civil War the original Peabody Hotel was built, being located on the principal street of the bustling river community. This hotel was opened with a big dance on February 6, 1869, at its Main and Monroe location, the present site of one of Memphis' most prominent department stores, Lowenstein's. Credit for constructing the old Peabody goes to Colonel R. C. Brinkley, who was also instrumental in giving the hotel the name it bears today.

During the Reconstruction days following the Civil War, Colonel Brinkley was sent on a special financial assistance mission to England. He was seeking financial backing for a railroad line into Memphis, proposed by the old Memphis and Charleston Railroad, now a part of the Southern System. It was during the ocean voyage that Colonel Brinkley met George Peabody, a New England and New York philanthropist. Mr. Peabody was so interested and deeply impressed by Colonel Brinkley's zeal and sincerity that he offered his own personal assistance in obtaining the necessary financial credit for building the railroad. Out of gratitude and from the deep personal bond of friendship which had sprung up between the two men, Colonel Brinkley named his new establishment Peabody Hotel.

The first manager was D. Cockrell, a veteran hotel man who had professionally survived both the magnificence of the antebellum days and the tumultuous postwar period. Following Mr. Cockrell's death, the management of the Peabody changed several times over the years until, in 1907, the Memphis Hotel Company was formed to purchase it. It was shortly after this purchase that a new two-hundred-room addition was constructed. For a number of years this annex remained the only steel structure in Memphis.

Fifteen years later, when W. G. Poole was manager, the building, addition, and entire site were purchased as the site of Lowenstein's Department Store. It was at this time that the present Union Avenue site of Hotel Peabody was purchased, and construction work on the new hotel got under way in 1923.

The present six-hundred-and-twenty-five-room Hotel Peabody was first opened on September 2, 1925. With five and three-quarters million cubic feet under its roof, the twelve-story structure was erected at a cost of about five million dollars. The leading figure in erecting the present Hotel Peabody was A. L. Parker of the Memphis Hotel Company, who at that time had been directing head of leading hotels of Memphis for over twenty-five years. It was Mr. Parkers' dream to have the best possible hotel in plan, construction and equipment. He traveled far and wide to observe the best features in hotels both in this country and abroad. It was under his guidance and supervision that the present Hotel Peabody was erected.

Its plans were the work of architect Walter S. Alschlager of Chicago, one of the country's best-known hotel planners and designers of that time. Mr. Alschlager prepared as many as forty sketches for the exterior before he succeeded in producing the symmetrical structure which has become a Memphis landmark.

The decorative scheme of the lobby is in Eighteenth-century Southern Italian style, with the lobby floor made of marble. In the center of the lobby is a fountain carved out of a single block of Travertine marble brought from Italy.

Named manager of the new Hotel Peabody in 1925 was the late Frank R. Schutt, who eventually became vice president and general manager, following the death in 1934 of the late H. T. Bunn. It was under Mr. Schutt's guidance that the institution prospered and grew, became a center of Memphis and Mid-South social and cultural life, while gaining a reputation among travelers from all parts of the world. It was also under Mr. Schutt's management that the Plantation Roof and Skyway were added, where patrons may dine and dance the year round to music of nationally famous orchestras. Mr. Schutt also introduced the famous live ducks in the hotel's lobby fountain. Since that time they have become a veritable trademark of the Peabody.

Since its opening in 1925, a number of rooms have been remodeled, refurnished and widely publicized, such as the spacious Continental Ballroom, the Venetian Room, the Louis XVI Room, the Georgian Room and the Creel Room. Mr. Schutt became president of the Peabody in 1945. The Alsonett chain acquired the hotel in 1953 at a price of $7,431,300, with Mr. Schutt remaining as executive vice president and general manager until his retirement in 1956. He died on March 22, 1958, at the age of sixty-nine, after thirty-one years at the helm of the Peabody.

Tom J. McGinn, present manager of the Peabody, has had a long and active career in the hotel business, being assistant manager under Mr. Schutt when the new hotel was opened in 1925.

Since acquisition by the Alsonett chain, the Peabody has continued to make improvements and changes in keeping with efficient hotel management and public acceptability and comfort. New additions include the Colonial Room, the Coffee Shop with its new addition, and the recently opened Peabody Grill. Besides this, all display rooms, suites and individual rooms have been completely refinished and refurbished.

The Peabody has long been a favorite convention and meeting headquarters for Memphis as well as for national groups, with the hotel's fine cuisine and efficient catering service playing a very important role in such activities.

For thirty-three years the present Hotel Peabody has been a favorite Memphis institution, justifying its slogan: "The South's Finest—One of America's Best."

WILLIAM CONRAD HANAFEE

Identified with the Jackson Saw Mill Company of Jackson, for nearly three decades, William Conrad Hanafee is now its sole owner. This industrial concern has received several awards for its production record, and Mr. Hanafee

W C Hanafee.

himself has been deeply interested in civic affairs, and in organizational activities in his home city and in Memphis.

A native of New Albany, in Floyd County, Indiana, he was born on August 15, 1893, and is a son of John Hanafee and Amelia Mary (Broecker) Hanafee. His mother too was born at New Albany, on November 8, 1867, while his father came from Washington County, Ohio, having been born there on July 16, 1858. William C. Hanafee received a parochial school education, attending Holy Trinity Catholic School at New Albany, Indiana, and St. Xavier School in Louisville, Kentucky.

He began his business career in his native city of New Albany, taking a position at the Wood Mosaic Flooring Plant in 1909, and working there through 1910. In 1912 he joined the Wood-Mosaic Company, which in 1919 transferred him to Jackson, Tennessee. He remained with the same firm there until 1931.

In that year, Mr. Hanafee acquired an interest in the Jackson Saw Mill Company, and began his full-time connection with that firm in a managerial capacity. He acquired all remaining stock in the company in 1945, and has been sole owner since.

His company established a record of valuable service to the nation's defense at the time of World War II. On June 15, 1944, the Jackson Saw Mill Company was awarded the Army-Navy "E" for "meritorious service," having been nominated by the Navy. Top-ranking Army and Navy personnel attended the presentation ceremony held at the plant before a large assemblage of lumbermen, businessmen, and personal friends. Five months later, on November 16, 1944, the company received another honor—a renewal of the Army-Navy "E" Award with a new flag with one star affixed. On October 1, 1947, the plant and its workers were further honored when the company was asked to fly its award flag during the week preceding Navy Day, October 21.

Mr. Hanafee remains general manager of the plant, as well as president of the corporation.

In his home city of Jackson, he is a member of the lodges of the Knights of Columbus and the Benevolent and Protective Order of Elks, a former member of the Rotary Club, and a member of the Jackson Golf and Country Club. He retains membership in the Calumet Club of New Albany, Indiana, and is also a member of the Tennessee Club, the Navy Club and the Lumbermen's Club, all of Memphis. A Roman Catholic, he is a communicant of St. Mary's Church at Jackson.

At Jeffersonville, Indiana, on November 17, 1915, William Conrad Hanafee married, as his first wife, Miss Anna Mildred Tracy, who died in October, 1932. To this marriage all of his children were born: 1. Jane Mildred, born on October 27, 1916, at Jeffersonville, Indiana. She married Joseph Mooney. 2. Ann Tracy, born at Jackson on December 13, 1919. She married Robert Walt. 3. William Conrad, Jr., born in Jackson on November 25, 1921. 4. Donald

Norbert, born there on July 26, 1923; married Jeanne (Cashon). 5. Betty, born on May 7, 1926, also at Jackson. 6. David Robert, born in that city on May 7, 1926; married Rosemary Williamson. On August 11, 1934, at Jackson, Mr. Hanafee married, second, Miss Alice Taylor, daughter of Abner Utley and Ozzie Belle (Pope) Taylor. Both of her parents were natives of Denmark, Tennessee, where her father was born on July 14, 1871, and her mother on May 18, 1873. Mr. and Mrs. Hanafee make their home on Trenton Road in Jackson.

John Parry Sheftall

Over the past decade, John Parry Sheftall has been the effective force behind the operation of Clarksville's popular Station WJZM, and growth and development of Davidson County where he has developed subdivisions. He acquired his interest as a partner in 1947, shortly after his return from wartime service in the United States Navy; and his qualities of leadership have been prime factors in its dramatic growth, and increase in the scope of its services.

Mr. Sheftall is a native of Savannah, Georgia, and was born on June 29, 1902, son of Salmon and Harriet (Parry) Sheftall. His father was engaged in the brokerage business. After beginning his education in local public schools, John P. Sheftall went to Blair Academy where he completed his preparatory studies and graduated in 1921. Attending Dartmouth College in New Hampshire, he received his degree of Bachelor of Science there in 1925.

Two years later, Mr. Sheftall became vice president of the Belmont Fabric Company at Belmont, North Carolina. His next position too was in connection with the textile industry. It was at Nashville, where he was vice president of the Se-Ling Hosiery Mills from 1929 to 1933. Resigning from that executive office, he became vice president and treasurer of the Nashville Water Company in 1934, and served in those capacities until he left for naval service at the time of World War II.

With a commission in the United States Naval Reserve, Mr. Sheftall entered active service early in 1942. In the course of the war he served as personal aide to Vice Admiral Marc Mitschner and to Vice Admiral Sidney McCain. Remaining in uniform until 1946, he held the rank of lieutenant commander, and was awarded the Bronze Star.

In 1947, shortly after his separation from the service, he joined E. T. Campbell of Washington, D. C., as a partner in acquiring Station WJZM in Clarksville. Founded in 1941, this station had previously been owned by Mayor W. D. Hudson, Roland Hughes of Arkansas, and Mayor William Kleeman. Mr. Sheftall and Mr. Campbell brought it new and dynamic leadership, until the latter's death. Since that time Mr. Sheftall has been sole proprietor and manager. Under his capable direction, new meaning has been given to the station's slogan, "Your Mutual Friend." It is, incidentally, a Mutual Broadcasting System station, with a full lease wire of the Associated Press. The station,

A. D. Creighton

which has its headquarters at 411 Madison Street, Clarksville, is the subject of an accompanying sketch. Soon after acquiring WJZM Radio Station, Mr. Sheftall opened an office in Nashville and has engaged in subdivision development, dividing his time between the two enterprises.

Mr. Sheftall is a member of Chi Phi fraternity, and in his home city of Nashville, belongs to the Exchange Club, the Cumberland Club, Belle Meade Country Club, and the lodge of the Benevolent and Protective Order of Elks. He and his family attend the Presbyterian Church.

In Nashville, on March 12, 1932, John Parry Sheftall married Lillian Warner, daughter of Joseph and Lillian (Black) Warner. The couple have no children.

STATION WJZM

Clarksville's Station WJZM has won the loyalty and confidence of a large listening audience throughout Tennessee and in adjacent states as well. This station has now been in existence for nearly seventeen years. It began broadcasting on October 9, 1941, being then under the ownership of W. D. Hudson, former mayor of Clarksville. Its staff at that time consisted of five members.

In June, 1942, the station was purchased by Roland Hughes of Arkansas, who sold it to Mayor William Kleeman in August, 1942. Until April, 1947, it operated under his stewardship, with a staff consisting of six employees.

Station WJZM was purchased in 1947 by a partnership whose members were E. T. Campbell of Washington, D. C., now deceased, and J. P. Sheftall of Nashville. Mr. Sheftall is the subject of an accompanying biographical sketch. Under their management, the station showed tremendous growth, and became an indispensable factor in the economic and public service life of Clarksville and the surrounding region. With improved programming, adequate and experienced personnel, and dedication to the public interest, it grew in terms of staff membership from six to seventeen persons, its sales increased by more than five hundred per cent, and its payroll by more than nine hundred per cent. During this period of expansion, Station WJZM earned for itself the confidence and public support of Montgomery County residents, and integrated itself and its staff members into a continuing productive and respected force in the community.

The station's studios and offices are at 411 Madison Street, Clarksville.

ANDREW DONELSON CREIGHTON

Andrew D. Creighton's career has been identified with the stone industry from the outset. Formerly an official of the Foster and Creighton Company of Nashville, and is now president of the Nashville Stone Setting Company. He is a veteran of service in the air arm during World War I.

He is a native of Nashville, and was born on June 30, 1892, son of Robert Thomas and Jeannette (McKeand) Creighton. Both of his parents were natives of Nashville, and both died there. Robert T. Creighton, a contractor, organized the firm of Foster and Creighton Company, and was chairman of its board of directors at the time of his death. He was also chief engineer for the Tennessee State Centennial, and he was for many years chairman of Nashville's Board of Park Commissioners. He was a member of the Nashville Porter Rifles military organization, in which he held a commission as captain. He attended the Presbyterian Church.

Andrew D. Creighton attended the public schools of Nashville, Columbia Military Academy and Wallace University School, where he graduated in 1911. He entered Vanderbilt University, completing his engineering training in 1914. In 1912 he worked as a laborer in the Foster and Creighton Construction Company at Nashville, and when he completed his university training, he rejoined the organization on a full-time basis.

For many years Mr. Creighton served as an executive of the Foster and Creighton Company, the last three years as executive vice president. He resigned from the executive post in 1958 to assume active management of the Nashville Stone Setting Company. He became its president when the company was organized over thirty-five years ago.

Serving in the National Guard on the Mexican border at the time this country became involved in World War I, Mr. Creighton later became an aviation instructor with a commission as lieutenant. He was stationed at Eberts Field at Lone Oak, Arkansas. During World War II Mr. Creighton was a project engineer on large construction at Oak Ridge, for which he received a citation.

He is a member of the Cumberland Club and Belle Meade Country Club of Nashville. He is a member of the First Presbyterian Church, and is a Master Mason. His hobby is game cocks.

At Clarksville, on June 26, 1917, Andrew D. Creighton married Emma Joe Stout. Born at Dover, on July 22, 1897, she is a daughter of Josiah Wilkins and Emma (Brandon) Stout. Her father was a lawyer practicing at Dover. He held the office of chancellor for the Middle Tennessee District. Mrs. Creighton attended school at Clarksville.

The couple are the parents of one daughter, Mary Pope, who was born on January 13, 1920, in Nashville. She attended preparatory school at Ward Belmont School, and graduated from Vanderbilt University with the degree of Bachelor of Arts. She married Robert Masters Crichton of Johnstown, Pennsylvania. They now live in Nashville, where Mr. Crichton is president of the Super Service Motor Transport Company. The couple have four children: i. Andrew Donelson, born in 1945. ii. Robert Masters, born in 1948. iii. Richard Stout, born in 1950. iv. John Pope, born in 1952.

METHODIST HOSPITAL

The Methodist Hospital at Memphis is the result of a dream of Mr. John H. Sherard, of Sherard, Mississippi. He worked for several years to interest the annual conference in a Methodist hospital, and finally, on November 15, 1909, the Conference voted to work with a joint commission from two other conferences to consider building such a hospital.

The first meeting of the trustees was held February 7, 1911, and Mr. Sherard was named chairman. He was subsequently elected president of the board of trustees and served continuously in that capacity until his death in 1941. With Mr. Sherard was L. M. Stratton, Sr., who was also actively and vitally interested in the founding and development of the hospital. Mr. Stratton served as secretary of the board of trustees and chairman of the board of managers for many years. He succeeded Mr. Sherard as president of the board of trustees and continued as chairman of the board of managers, serving in both capacities until his death in 1949.

The trustees acquired, by gift, on June 23, 1918, the property of the Lucy Brinkley Hospital, a sixty-five-bed institution at 855 Union Avenue. By November 2, 1921, a new plant had been built on Lamar Avenue. Dr. Battle Malone, as chief of staff, headed a splendid group of physicians and surgeons. On Armistice Day, November 11, 1921, the hospital was visited by the executive officer of the Veterans Administration, and shortly afterward negotiations were entered into with the government which led to the sale of the entire hospital property on Lamar Avenue. This property was vacated June 30, 1922, and the hospital work carried on at the Lucy Brinkley Hospital for the next two years.

The present hospital site, consisting of seven acres, was bought, and plans were begun for a new hospital, which was completed September 17, 1924. At that time the patients were transferred from the Lucy Brinkley Hospital to the present building at 1265 Union Avenue. The original capacity of the first unit was one hundred and twenty-five beds. Later the Lucy Brinkley Hospital was sold, and the proceeds were invested in the Lucy Brinkley Pavilion, which added accommodations for sixty patients.

In December, 1939, construction was begun on a one-hundred-and-fifteen-bed addition to the hospital, with a one-hundred-bed addition to the Nurses' Home. Also at this time, a Doctors' Office Building was constructed in conjunction with the hospital. The idea of having a doctors' office building in conjunction with the hospital has proved to be a very wise move. Both the patients and the physicians themselves approve of having medical men at hand for consultation whenever necessary.

On January 1, 1943, the Methodist Hospital acquired a sixty-five-bed institution on Madison Avenue, the Memphis Eye, Ear, Nose and Throat Hospital.

Another extensive construction program was begun on April 1, 1949. A new and modern warehouse and laundry, new X-ray and clinical pathological laboratories, as well as administrative and accounting offices, were begun.

Along with these changes, a forty-percent increase in floor space of the Doctors' Office Building was made.

A School of Nursing has been conducted by the Methodist Hospital since 1918. It has proved very successful and has trained many young women for a professional career in nursing. Since its beginning, there have been approximately twelve hundred graduates.

The Methodist Hospital in Memphis serves not only a city, but a large agricultural district as well. Since the opening of the hospital, three hundred and forty-seven thousand patients have been admitted. More than fifty percent of the patients are from outside the city limits, for the hospital serves an area with a radius of about one hundred and fifty miles. The location of the Medical College of the University of Tennessee in Memphis has encouraged the practice of a very high type of medicine and surgery in the hospitals located in the city. The hospitals are very fortunate in having the medical school located here, inasmuch as research and consultation may be obtained through affiliation with the university.

The largest expansion program of the Methodist Hospital was planned in the early part of 1953. A campaign for funds from the public as well as from the Methodist Church was successfully completed in 1955 and approximately $2,225,000 was raised. This was supplemented with borrowing in the amount of three million dollars, and with this sum a construction program was undertaken which gives the hospital two hundred and fifty additional beds, a new cafeteria and kitchen, a new surgical unit, and labor and delivery rooms. Upon completion in 1958, the building had a total capacity of approximately five hundred adult beds and fifty bassinets.

The history of the Methodist Hospital comprises the records of several father-son combinations, such as J. H. Sherard, Sr., and J. Holmes Sherard, the son, and Jack H. Sherard, grandson; also L. M. Stratton, Sr., Leslie M. Stratton, Jr., and Leslie M. Stratton, 3rd. In addition to these was the father-son combination of G. T. Fitzhugh and his son, Mr. Millsaps Fitzhugh, the present president of the trustees. The only surviving member of the original board of trustees is the Reverend Lud H. Estes, who is now secretary of the board, a capacity in which he has served since July 22, 1921.

HISTORY OF COLLIERVILLE

The area now occupied by the Town of Collierville was opened for settlement in 1819 with removal of the Chickasaw Indians to Indian territory. Collierville was possibly a settlement as early as 1820 and was a known stage coach stop. The original town was named for an early pioneer settler, Jessie Collier, who had the first store.

Court was held in Collierville as early as 1837 and the community was a growing business center. The town was a stage coach junction for north-south and east-west travel and it is certain a tavern and inn were in operation in Collierville as early as 1840.

The Memphis and LaGrange Railroad—first train in Tennessee—passed through Collierville. In 1848 there were enough male residents to organize the Collierville Masonic Lodge Number 152. Also in 1848 Collierville had two stores, no churches and one small log schoolhouse.

According to a railroad guide book published in 1850, Collierville was a town of 250 inhabitants with stores and three schools.

The Wigfall Grays was organized in Collierville in 1861 to take part in the War Between the States. In 1863 an engagement took place in Collierville between the Federal troops and the Confederates, referred to on General. W. T. Sherman's memorial as the "Battle of Collierville."

Collierville was incorporated by an act passed February 17, 1870. In the 1870s, Bellevue Female College was in operation as was the Collierville Male Academy. The park in the center of the town square was developed in 1872 and used as a game refuge.

In 1874 the Collierville Athletics baseball team was organized and toured the South. The Collierville Herald, oldest weekly newspaper in the county, was published as early as January 11, 1879. In 1880 a State Guard unit was formed.

By 1886 Collierville had 1,200 inhabitants with a number of business houses, churches and schools.

The turn of the century saw many changes—telephones, automobiles, a public school, new businesses and residences. World War I brought other changes. The familiar commuter train which was a part of community life for many years was displaced in 1929 by use of cars.

A new sewage system was installed in 1936 and natural gas also became available. A new high school building also was completed.

Collierville today has an estimated population of 2,200 people and is the center of a progressive farming, dairying and industrial section. Some eight manufacturing firms are located in Collierville, and the town is considered an excellent example of a blending of the best elements of the Old South with the New South.

The Fayette County Free Library

Established on July 7, 1931, the Fayette County Free Library was the first such library to be founded in the state after passage of a special law by the Tennessee Legislature authorizing the establishment of free county libraries.

One of the sponsors of the county library plan was the Craddock Book Club in Fayette County and, after the establishment of the Fayette County Free Library, one of its most enthusiastic and active members, Mrs. G. W. Locke, was named to the first board of directors by the County Court. Others on this first board included: J. B. Summers, Anne Moorman, Mrs. A. P. Winfrey, Mrs. P. R. Beasley, W. M. Mayo, and P. W. Welch.

Starting out with a single volume in 1931, the Fayette County Free Library now has over 8,000 books on its shelves and, during the twenty-eight years of its existence, circulation has reached 233,833. The Library outgrew its physical capacities by 1940, and the County Court assigned two rooms in the Court House for its use as Library and Reading Room.

Mrs. G. W. Locke, in addition to serving on the first board, also was first librarian and has been succeeded by four salaried librarians. They are: Miss L. Dortch Burton, from 1931 to 1945; Mrs. Mary L. Rhea, from 1945 to 1948; Mrs. S. A. Wetzler, from 1948 to 1959, and Mrs. W. A. Rhea, Sr., who was elected in 1959 to succeed Mrs. S. A. Wetzler.

CHURCH OF THE IMMACULATE CONCEPTION

The Church of the Immaculate Conception is the oldest Catholic church in the city of Knoxville. Father Henry Vincent Brown, the first resident pastor, purchased the property at the corner of Vine and Walnut Streets in 1852. The original stone church was erected in that year. When this building became too small for the growing congregation, it was replaced in 1886 by the present beautiful edifice.

One of the early pastors of the Church of the Immaculate Conception was Father Abram J. Ryan, the former Confederate Army chaplain, whose moving tributes to the Southern cause earned for him the title "Poet-Priest of the South."

The church's present pastor is the Reverend Francis R. Shea, who has also served as instructor in the Father Ryan High School in Nashville. He is a native of Knoxville. It was he who preached the sermon when the church observed its one hundredth anniversary. Father Shea is well-known and popular among his fellow citizens of every faith.

ARTIODE SELLARI

A native of Italy, Artiode Sellari has found in this country an opportunity for the full development and use of his abilities as an industrial technologist and executive. He has built a sizable business, the Sellari Natural Wax Company, which has become an important unit in the economic and industrial life of Brownsville. For more than three and a half decades, he has devoted his attention to perfecting and manufacturing nonheating stitching waxes for use in shoe manufacturing and repairing, and in the harness-making trades.

He is a ative of Ostra, in the Province of Ancona, Italy, and was born on August 21, 1885, son of Daniele and Marietta (Ventura) Sellari. His father was a shoemaker in his native Italy, and prepared his own wax for hand work. He served for a time in the Italian Army.

Artiode Sellari received his entire formal education in the local school at

Artiode Sellari

Ostra, and at an early age began work in his father's shop. By the time he was twelve years old, he was making wax for his father, and had also gained considerable experience in hand-made custom shoes. He continued in this work with his father until he reached the age of twenty-one. In that same year, 1906, he set out for the United States.

He arrived unable to speak English, and with a knowledge of his trade and a willingness to work as his own resources. He first secured a position in a shoe rebuilding shop in Memphis, which was owned and operated by L. Barrasso and Son. There he worked for sixteen months, and by the end of that time, was proficient enough in his English to open a shop of his own. He opened his first shop in Memphis, and remained there for about a year. Then, in March, 1909, he moved to Brownsville, and opened a shoe rebuilding shop on the principal business block of the town. He arrived in the city with only his tools and a dollar and a quarter in his pocket; but he knew his trade thoroughly and quickly attracted business. The shoe rebuilding shop became successful. Its management was later turned over to his son.

Throughout his years in the shoe repair business, Mr. Sellari had made his own wax for hand use, as he had learned to do in his father's shop in Italy. A review of his career in The Shoe Repairer and Dealer, appearing some years ago, provides the details about his change in emphasis from working with shoes to the production of wax:

During all these years Mr. Sellari made his own wax for hand use. In 1912 he purchased his first stitching machine, a Landis No. 10, which was equipped with a gasoline tank to heat the wax. This, according to Mr. Sellari's ideas, was unsatisfactory and dangerous, but about this time Mr. Sellari got the idea that a wax could be made to work satisfactorily without heat in the machine the same as by hand.

In 1914 he purchased a Champion curved needle stitcher equipped with an electric heater. This was more satisfactory than the gasoline heater but he was not entirely satisfied because of heavy expenses for current and the loss of time while waiting for the wax to heat.

It was at this time that he began in dead earnest to produce a wax that would spread in this machine without heat. In 1916 he perfected a wax for his own shop which worked fairly well but he continued to experiment in the endeavor to improve his wax still more.

It was not long before friends in the shoe repair trade in neighboring towns and in the city of Memphis heard of Mr. Sellari's success in the use of what he then termed his liquid wax and he soon began furnishing them with their needs. This resulted finally in the placing of his wax on the market, which he manufactured in the back of his shoe shop.

Mr. Sellari commenced the general sale of his product in 1921, and among his first Memphis customers were the Hart Saddlery Company and the Scheibler Company. In a short time, he was selling to jobbers in the major cities throughout the country. As his business continued to grow, it became necessary to erect a factory, and establish his business on a corporate basis as Sellari Natural Wax

Company, the organization being formed in 1921. By 1953, this factory in turn had been outgrown, and he erected the present plant, also at Brownsville. Continued growth since that time led to the construction of a large addition to the plant in 1957.

The products now manufactured by the firm consist of the original Sellari's Non-heating Natural Stitching Wax, Sellari's Special A-1 McKay Wax, Sellari's Machine Cleaner and Wax Thinner, and Sellari's No. 85 Thread Lubricator; also, Sellari's No. 33 Thread Lubricator, Sellari's Peg-Set No. 55 Inseam Wax, Sellari's Wax Burnishing Ink Concentrate and Sellari's Double Wax Pot.

In 1928, Mr. Sellari became an associate member of the National Leather and Shoe Finders' Association, now known as the Shoe Service Institute of America. In the following year he attended the annual convention of that organization, in which he has since held membership. In his home city he is a member of the lodge of the Knights of Columbus, and attends St. John's Roman Catholic Church.

Twice married, Artiode Sellari chose as his first wife Anita Pellonari. They were married on November 21, 1908, in Memphis, and she died on February 21, 1931. He returned to his native Ostra, Ancona, Italy, to choose his second wife, Ernesta Giancarli. They were married in that city on August 14, 1932. Mr. Sellari is the father of eleven children: 1. Marie, born on June 10, 1910. She is the wife of Leo Nello Andreoli. 2. Carlo, born on January 9, 1912. 3. Italo, who was born on October 22, 1913, and died July July 21, 1956. 4. Lilly, born on April 22, 1915. She married Vincent A. Alfonso. 5. Harry, born on September 29, 1917. 6. Daniel, born September 22, 1919. 7. Ben Louis, born on February 26, 1924. 8. Ike L., born on August 8, 1927. 9. William S., who was born on October 14, 1929. 10 Artiode A., born on July 5, 1934. 11. Hilda Anita, who was born on February 21, 1937. She is the wife of Paul S. Poole. The two youngest children were born of Mr. Sellari's second marriage.

The following are the grandchildren of Artiode Sellari: Peggy Jean (Andreoli) Meyer and Leo Anthony Andreoli; Anita Louise (Alfonso) Newton, Fred Vincent Alfonso (deceased), Catherine Theresa Alfonso, Vincent Anthony Alfonso, Jr., Peter Michael Alfonso, William Fred Alfonso, Mary Jo Alfonso and Mario Eugene Alfonso; Anita Carol (Sellari) Smith; Terry Sellari and Jerry Sellari, twins, and Carlotta Sellari; Barbara (Sellari) Perkins and Anita Sellari; Daniel Sellari, Jr., Linda Lee Sellari, James Michael Sellari, William Arthur Sellari, and Rebecca Anne Sellari; Ben Louis Sellari, Jr.; and Patrick Smith Sellari, James Hunter Sellari, Ike L. Sellari, Jr., and William Thomas Sellari.

The following are great-grandchildren of Artiode Sellari: Mary Darlene Newton, Michael Joseph Newton and William Andrew Newton; Nickolus Anthony Meyer; and Harry E. Smith.

John Pietro Robilio

Vice president of an independent grocery warehouse which he helped organize in 1930, and owner of his own grocery firm and cafeteria, John P. Robilio is an ardent association man and business leader in Memphis.

Mr. Robilio was born in Alluvioni Cambio in the Piedmonte region of Italy on September 26, 1886. His parents, Marcello and Maria Robilio, operated a small store, wine tavern and bakery in town. Lack of money forced John Robilio to interrupt his education and to start work at an early age. During this time he learned the sausage and salami trade from his uncle. In 1907, John Robilio emigrated to the United States where he felt he would be able to make more money than in his native Italy. He arrived in Memphis and took his first job working in a grocery store. A year and a half later, he was able to buy a store in partnership with a friend. In three years, Mr. Robilio paid off his debts and in 1911 returned to Italy for a visit and to marry his childhood sweetheart. Upon his return to Memphis in 1912, he opened a store of his own under the name of John P. Robilio and Company. The store prospered and in 1922, he opened a larger store where he also sold sandwiches and later home-made spaghetti which Mrs. Robilio prepared. This led to the opening of the John P. Robilio Cafeteria to the rear of the store. In the years of 1928 and 1929, the small independent grocery stores came into contact with the newly formed supermarkets. Buying in tremendous volume enabled these stores to buy food and produce at lower cost and they passed these savings on to the customer. In 1930, Mr. Robilio and a group of nine other independent store owners formed an association called The WeOna Warehouse, purchasing food in bulk for all members and enabling them to compete with the supermarkets. This association proved its success and since 1930 has grown into a vast enterprise with over three hundred members currently purchasing through the warehouse.

Mr. Robilio is a member of the Memphis Retail Grocer Association, National Restaurant Association, Tennessee Restaurant and Memphis Restaurant Associations and the National Retail Grocer Association.

Mr. Robilio married the former Angelina (Ponzano) in Valanza DelPo, Italy, on July 24, 1911. Mrs. Robilio, daughter of Louis and Mary Ponzano of Italy, worked hard to assist her husband develop the customer relations which have paid off so handsomely for them over the years. The Robilios have two sons and two daughters. They are: 1. Stella Robilio (Bursi), born September 26, 1912; she married Eugene J. Bursi. 2. John Pietro, Jr., born November 21, 1913; married Rena Aviotti; their children are: John P. III and Charles J. Robilio. 3. Louise (Robilio) LaFont, born August 8, 1922; she married Allen A. LaFont. Their children are: John Allen and Stephen LaFont. 4. Marshall Joseph, born May 3, 1928; married Roberta Bolton. They have three children: Marsha Ann, and twins Christopher Allen and William Michael Robilio.

LEROY CLYDE TRUMBO

It has been a decade since Leroy Clyde Trumbo established one of Memphis' progressive small industries: the Trumbo Welding and Fabricating Company, which has its plant at 1106 Kansas. He is active in industrialists' groups and in local organizations, but especially in the work of his church.

A native of Joppa, Illinois, Mr. Trumbo was born on March 24, 1915, son of Ernest Elzie and Ruth Mae (Clayton) Trumbo. His father was a farmer until his retirement, and now lives in Tullos, Louisiana. The family lived in the Illinois community, however, throughout the years of Leroy C. Trumbo's boyhood, and he received his entire education in the public schools there. Coming to Memphis in 1932, he joined the Golf Shaft and Block Company. This was the predecessor of the present C. F. Work and Son Company, and Mr. Trumbo held the position of machine operator there from 1932 to 1936. He then left to join the Southern Boiler Company as a welder's helper in 1936, learning the welding trade. He remained only a year, however, and in 1938 went with the Firestone Tire and Rubber Company, with which he remained until 1939. During 1940-1941 he was a welder at the Dan Shea Boiler Works, and from 1941 until 1944, was engaged in defense work at various plants in the Memphis area and mid-south.

In 1944 he accepted a position as foreman with the firm of Brewer and Morris, fabricators, with which he remained until 1949. At that time he left to found the Trumbo Welding and Fabricating Company, putting his thorough and varied experience to good use in the management of an enterprise which he has headed to the present time. Mr. Trumbo's career has exhibited his capacity to advance on his own merits from humble positions to a place of leadership in industry. His firm has occupied an increasingly important place in the city's industrial picture.

Mr. Trumbo is a member of the National Association of Practical Refrigerating Engineers, Inc. He also belongs to the National Rifle Association of America, and the Tennessee and the Mississippi Sheriffs' and Peace Officers' Associations. In his home city he holds membership in the Chamber of Commerce. Affiliated with the Free and Accepted Masons, he is a member of the higher bodies of the Ancient and Accepted Scottish Rite. Holding the Thirty-second Degree, he belongs to the Ancient Arabic Order of Nobles of the Mystic Shrine.

His church is the First Assembly of God, located at 1084 East McLemore Avenue in Memphis. Active in its Men's Fellowship Group, he became president of that organization in 1958. Mr. Trumbo is a member of the National Association of Evangelicals. On March 9, 1959, he was appointed a member of the advisory council of Evangel College at Springfield, Missouri. A deeply religious man, he earnestly endeavors to apply Christian principles in his business life and to conduct his enterprise according to the Golden Rule.

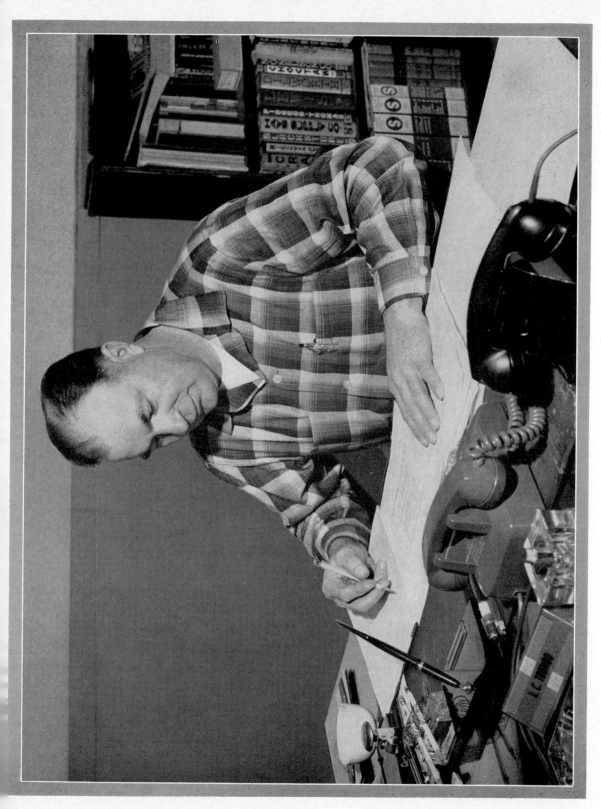

J. C. Trumbo

Mr. Trumbo is fond of the out-of-doors, and deer and fox hunting is his hobby.

On January 4, 1936, in Memphis, Leroy Clyde Trumbo married Dorothy Mae Tedder, daughter of Alvin and Waldine (Yancey) Tedder. The couple are the parents of four children: 1. Tommy Gene, who was born on October 17, 1936. He married Mary Ewing of Springfield, Missouri, and they have one son, Charles Galen, born March 22, 1958. 2. William Lester, born on January 13, 1938. 3. Ernest Alvin, born August 11, 1939. 4. Gloria Jean, born November 14, 1941.

Mr. Trumbo feels that all success and good that have come to him in his life have resulted from his faith in and his contribution to the service of the Lord Jesus Christ.

JOSEPH HENRY SCHAEFFER, JR.

As owner of the Bluff City Buick Company, Joseph Henry Schaeffer, Jr., heads one of the major automobile retailing agencies of the South, located at Memphis. For Mr. Schaeffer, the enterprise represents a rapid step forward in a career in automotive sales which began following his return from wartime service in the paratroopers.

A native of Capleville, Tennessee, Mr. Schaeffer was born on October 24, 1920, son of Joseph Henry, Sr., and Mattie Sue (Randolph) Schaeffer. His father, who is now deceased, was formerly a merchant at Capleville. The younger Joseph H. Schaeffer attended public schools and completed his secondary studies at Whitehaven High School in June, 1937.

He began his business career in 1939 with the B&W Cafeteria, and left before this country had become involved in World War II to begin a six-year stint in the United States Army. Assigned to the 467th Parachute Field Artillery Battalion, he attained the rank of captain. He received his honorable discharge, in 1946.

A review of his business record in the columns of the Memphis Press-Scimitar, appearing at the time he acquired the Buick agency, points out that Mr. Schaeffer was selling hot dogs at the time he entered the automobile sales field in 1947. His first sale was that of his own vehicle, a 1940 Ford, and impressed by the possibilities in the used-car market, he determined to devote his full attention to the business. The success with which he did so was dramatically emphasized over the next eight years, and his enterprise grew in proportion to the progress of Memphis as a used-car center. He operated under the style of J. and S. Motors, which derived its name from the fact that he was a partner of his father-in-law, Lynn Jack, who had had long experience with Bluff City Buick Company.

Mr. Schaeffer made the decision to acquire this Buick agency after eight years in the management of J. and S. Motors, which his efforts were effective in building into a large and successful organization. The agency which he now heads has been in existence since May, 1922, and was founded by Hugh J. Jetton and Wallace H. Claypool. Its first location was at Third and Gayoso, and it has occupied the present premises at 739 Union since 1933. Charles J. Creath joined the organization the year it was founded and ultimately became vice president and general manager, and a partner of Mr. Jetton and Mr. Claypool. It was he who turned the organization over to Mr. Schaeffer in June, 1955. This represented the first transfer of a major Memphis automobile dealership in many years. Mr. Schaeffer purchased the real estate as well as the cars, parts and equipment shown on the inventory.

He is a member and past president of the Memphis Automobile Dealers Association, and has taken a consistent interest in community affairs, belonging to the Chamber of Commerce, the Civitan Club, Chickasaw Country Club, Sphinx Secret Society of the Cotton Carnival Association, and the Germantown Civic Club, which he has served as president and as director. As a veteran of World War II, he holds membership in the American Legion and the Reserve Officers Association. He is affiliated with the Free and Accepted Masons, being a member of Park Avenue Lodge; Tennessee Consistory of the Ancient and Accepted Scottish Rite; and Al Chymia Temple, Ancient Arabic Order of Nobles of the Mystic Shrine. He is a member and past president of Al Chymia Oriental Band.

Church work is among Mr. Schaeffer's interests, and he is currently serving as chairman of the board of Kingsway Christian Church. He was formerly a deacon of Central Christian Church. He has also proved himself an effective public speaker, and has appeared before various groups in many parts of the country over the past several years.

In Memphis, on December 21, 1941, Joseph Henry Schaeffer, Jr., married Opal Jack, daughter of James Lynn and Tennessee (Pratter) Jack. They make their home at Germantown, Tennessee, and they are the parents of four children: 1. Elizabeth Gail, born March 20, 1943. 2. Jo Ellen, born April 4, 1949. 3. Linda Sue, born December 22, 1951. 4. Opal Ruth, born February 27, 1956.

BRUNELLE JENNINGS EVANS

A Memphis business leader whose role in the city's industrial life has been increasingly important since his return from wartime military service, Brunelle Jennings Evans is now manager of American Bakeries Company, which has its headquarters at 1553 Madison Avenue.

Mr. Evans is a native Tennessean, born at Newbern on April 7, 1917, and is a son of Robert Taylor and Flora Mai (Lomax) Evans. His father is a farmer near Newbern. Receiving his education in the public elementary and high schools of his native community, Brunelle J. Evans came to Memphis in 1940. He left again in 1942, to enter the service of the United States Army. Assigned to the 100th Division, he went to the European theater, where his

outfit joined the forces of the Seventh Army. Mr. Evans served as a platoon sergeant.

Resuming his business career in Memphis following the war, he again became identified with the American Bakeries Company in the capacity of route salesman and won promotions to the position of manager of the plant at 1553 Madison. That position he has held since 1953.

A member of the Memphis Industrial Council, Mr. Evans has served on committees of that organization. He is a member of the Variety Club and as a Master Mason, belongs to Lodge No. 285 of the Free and Accepted Masons in Newbern. His religious affiliation is with the Church of Christ.

In his native city of Newbern on May 23, 1937, Brunelle Jennings Evans married Elmer Sue Ross, daughter of James Elmer and Emma (Dyer) Ross. The couple are the parents of one daughter, Suzanne, born on February 28th, 1947.

L. W. LOYD

The varied career of L. W. Loyd of South Pittsburg has included merchandising, the sale of feeds and seed, and one of the country's largest importers of fireworks, many being manufactured from designs and specifications of the L. W. Loyd Company. The company is also a large exporter of fireworks. In addition to these activities, he has found time for a full role in public life, and is now serving as mayor of South Pittsburg.

He is a native of Bridgeport, Alabama, and was born on December 28, 1912, son of John R. and Lula (Williams) Loyd. His father was also born in Bridgeport, in June, 1880, and he still lives in that city, where he remains active as a merchant. His family have been engaged in mercantile pursuits since 1865. Like his son, John R. Loyd has taken part in the public affairs of his own city. He has served as mayor of Bridgeport, and as a member of its city council. Lula Williams, whom he married, was born in that city in 1883.

After attending the public schools of Bridgeport, L. W. Loyd completed his studies at the Freed Hardeman College at Henderson, Tennessee. He began his business career with his father at Bridgeport in 1932. Almost as early in his career, he turned his attention to the importation and distribution of fireworks. He founded and has managed the L. W. Loyd Company, Inc., a wholesale firm, for the past twenty-five years, concurrently with his other activities. The company has three branch locations, one at St. Louis, one at Springfield, Missouri, and the third at West Memphis, Arkansas. These are operated under the firm name of Atomic Fireworks, and they specialize in the import and distribution of Atomic Brand Fireworks. The main office for all operations is located at South Pittsburg, at Second and Railroad Avenue. L. W. Loyd has two brothers, John R. Loyd, Jr. and A. C. Loyd associated with him and taking an active part in the operation and management of the fireworks company.

From 1938 to 1947, Mr. Loyd operated a cotton gin in the same city, under the trade name of the Marion County Gin Company. Also, for seven years, he operated a feed mill and a wholesale feed and seed company, under the name of Farm Supply Company.

In 1954, Mr. Loyd was elected mayor of South Pittsburg, and prior to that time he had served his city most capably as vice mayor and finance commissioner.

He is a veteran of World War II, having served in the Field Artillery, and was stationed at San Luis Obispo, in California. In his home city, he is a member of the Chamber of Commerce, a member of the Sequatchie Country Club, and a member and past president of the Lions Club. He serves as first vice president and a director of the American Pyrotechnic Association. He and his family attend the Church of Christ.

In his native city of Bridgeport, Alabama, in 1942, L. W. Loyd married Avaline Miller. She was born at South Pittsburg on May 15, 1918, daughter of Leslie Harrison and Edith (Henry) Miller. Her father, who was born in South Pittsburg in 1885, was a moulder by trade, and a veteran of World War I. He died in 1953. His wife, the former Edith Henry, survives him and makes her home in South Pittsburg. Mr. and Mrs. Loyd are the parents of four children: 1. Carol Evelyn, born in 1947. 2. Lew Wilson, Jr., born in 1949. 3. John Leslie, born in 1953. 4. Lucy Elizabeth, who was born in 1955. All of the children were born in South Pittsburg.

John V. Egle

The organizer and the head of the Eagle Electric and Supply Company, Inc., of Memphis, and a leading businessman in Memphis, Mr. Egle is active in fraternal, civic and community organizations.

He was born in Providence, Webster County, Kentucky, on April 1, 1900, the son of Joe Egle and of Irene (Sights) Egle. His father was born in New Albany, Indiana, and was a cooper by trade in Kentucky. Mr. Egle's mother was born in Henderson County, Kentucky. Mr. Egle received a high school education, and he is now active in the electrical industry as the organizer and head of the Eagle Electric and Supply Company, Incorporated. Previously he had organized the Industrial Electric Company which was subsequently sold, he then formed a partnership, the firm being known as Egle and Crobaugh Electric Company; this partnership was dissolved in February, 1957, each section then becoming incorporated, our subject becoming president of the Eagle Electric and Supply Company. In February, 1959 the firm moved to its new quarters at 983 Jackson, in Memphis.

During World War I, Mr. Egle served on the Mexican Border with Company A of the First Florida National Guard in 1917, and he was later sergeant in Company A, 113th MG Battalion of the Thirtieth Division. He spent nineteen months overseas with this division. He is a charter member and past post commander of Post 1965, Veterans of Foreign Wars. He is also a member of the American Legion.

A Thirty-second Degree Mason and a Shriner, he is also a member of the Chamber of Commerce and a member and past president of the National Electrical Contractors Association. He holds membership in the Wattou Club, which was organized in Wattou, Belgium, on Septemebr 29, 1918. He attends religious services as a member of the Speedway Baptist Church. Mr. Egle's hobbies are hunting and fishing. In politics he is a registered Democratic but is not active in his party.

Mr. Egle was married at Memphis, Tennessee, on October 17, 1938, to Irene Sights, the daughter of Floyd E. Sights and of Mary Ellen (Liles) Sights of Henderson County, Kentucky. Her father is a farmer.

Lon Glenard Gentry

Lon Glenard Gentry is well established in the profession of funeral directing, having come to Fountain City after ample experience in Knoxville. He maintains high standards of practice, and has a reputation for his friendly and sympathetic dealings. He also has a completely modern and impressive establishment, which is operated with the greatest efficiency.

Mr. Gentry is a native of Fountain City, where he was born on July 9, 1904, son of Mack Hayes and Oddie Jane (Graves) Gentry. His father was engaged in the furniture business. For forty-seven years, he has lived in Fountain City, which is a suburb of Knoxville. He acquired early experience in the workaday world. At the age of eight years, he began work for the Knoxville Journal, delivering the morning paper. He continued in this work until he entered high school, meeting the Fountain City street car every morning at 4:30 to receive his papers. He remarks that through this contact he made many lifelong friends who have contributed to his present success in business. He was never without a job from the time he started his paper route until his graduation from high school.

He graduated from Central High School in Fountain City, and despite his working schedule, and maintaining high scholastic averages, found time to play on the football team. After graduating there, he chose funeral directing as his profession, and worked his way through Cincinnati College of Embalming, where he graduated in 1929.

Licensed as an embalmer, Mr. Gentry began his career with the Knoxville funeral directing firm in 1930, and remained with that organization for fifteen years, gaining valuable experience. He was employed by another Knoxville firm until 1948, when he organized his own funeral home, Gentry Mortuary, in Fountain City. This was in December, 1948. He holds office as president and treasurer of the corporation, as well as manager of the funeral home.

In addition to professional organizations, Mr. Gentry is a charter member of the Fountain City Lions Club, and a member of Bright Hope Lodge No.

557, Free and Accepted Masons. He is a member of higher bodies of Masonry: Spurgeon Bowling Chapter No. 207, Royal Arch Masons; Knoxville Council No. 75, Royal and Select Masters; Coeur de Lion Commandery No. 9, Knights Templar; Kerbela Temple, Ancient Arabic Order of Nobles of the Mystic Shrine; and Fountain City Chapter No. 160, Order of the Eastern Star of Tennessee.

Mr. Gentry is now serving his second three-year term on the board of directors of his local chapter of the American Red Cross. A communicant of the Fountain City Methodist Church, he is a member of its finance committee, its board of stewards, and has served on several building program committees.

In his home town, Fountain City, on January 27, 1940, Lon Glenard Gentry married Myrtle Ruth Daniel, daughter of Robert Jefferson and Florence B. (Adams) Daniel.

THE McCAMMON-AMMONS FUNERAL HOME

The McCammon-Ammons Funeral Home has been serving the community of Maryville for half a century. The two partners in this firm, Roy Ammons and Sam Harrison McCammon, represent fifty-four years' and forty-six years' experience respectively in their profession.

Sam Harrison McCammon was born in Maryville on September 27, 1889, the son of Samuel A. and Belle McCammon of this city.

He received his education in the schools of Maryville, entered his profession as a funeral director in 1913 and has been associated with it since. He and his family are members of the New Providence Presbyterian Church in Maryville where he married the former Effa McCulley on May 26, 1912. Mrs. McCammon is the daughter of John and Molly McCulley and both the McCammon and McCulley families stem from old Tennessee settler stock. Mr. and Mrs. Sam McCammon have a son, Dr. Charles S. McCammon, born on November 6, 1919, and now a Lieutenant Colonel in the Medical Corps stationed at Billings, Montana.

Roy Edgar Ammons was born in Maryville on July 12, 1889, the son of Thomas J. and Modenia (McCampbell) Ammons of that city where Thomas Ammons was a carpenter.

He received his education in the schools of this community and, upon completion, immediately entered his profession as a funeral director in 1905, at the age of sixteen.

Roy Ammons and his family are members of the First Baptist Church of Maryville. He is a member of the New Providence Masonic Lodge and the Maryville Rotary Club.

He married Verna May Lawrence on November 6, 1910 in Maryville. She is the daughter of John S. and Katherine (George) Lawrence of Maryville. Mr. and Mrs. Ammons have a daughter, born February 19, 1914, who

(Carpenter) McGaughran was born May 7, 1883, at Macon, Tennessee, and her family came to Memphis when she was four years old. She attended Van Horn Private School and Graham School, and graduated from Central High School, where she showed great talent for music and painting. In the early years of the century, she was organist and choir director of the Springdale Methodist Church. However, her own membership was in the Evergreen Presbyterian Church during most of the years of her life. She was an excellent oil painter, whose canvases are preserved and treasured by members of her family and many friends. She was also an ardent equestrienne, and shared with her husband an interest in working with the horses at the Collierville farm. She survived her husband by less than six months, and her death occurred at her home on Normandy Road in Memphis on February 2, 1959.

The couple became the parents of nine children: 1. Whitcomb Riley, born on August 31, 1911. He received his degree of Bachelor of Science at Southwestern University in Memphis, and a Master of Science degree from the University of New Mexico in Albuquerque. He was a track star in long-distance running at Southwestern, holding a two-mile championship. He served for a time on the faculties of Southern Methodist University in Dallas, and the University of New Mexico. Later in charge of the medical research department of Plough, Inc., in Memphis, he is now a research chemist with Merck, Sharpe and Dohme in Lansdale, Pennsylvania. On May 7, 1948, in Dallas, Riley McGaughran married Marian Lee Christy, who was born on December 12, 1917. She took a degree of Bachelor of Arts at the University of Pennsylvania, and holds a Master of Science degree in physical therapy from the Mayo Clinic. She was a captain in the Nurses Corps, United States Army, in World War II. The couple have five children: i. Donald Christy, born August 25, 1949. ii. Gerald Patrick, born October 14, 1951. iii. Sarah Irene, born June 13, 1953. iv. Alice Diane, born May 9, 1955. v. Alan, born February 18, 1959. 2. Kathleen, born in Raton, New Mexico, on May 2, 1913. She attended Memphis State University where she took her Bachelor of Science degree, and is a member of Sigma Kappa National Sorority and the Memphis Athletic Country Club. She is an airways operations specialist in communications with the Federal Aviation Agency at the Memphis Municipal Airport. She lives in Memphis. 3. Miss Emmett Aileen, born in Memphis on May 13, 1915. She attended Southwestern University in Memphis, and after working for the United States Weather Bureau in Washington, returned to Memphis, where she now works as a legal secretary. 4. Margaret Pleas, born at Raton, New Mexico, on April 4, 1917. She attended Southwestern University, and on June 26, 1943, married Roy Franklin Wenzler. The couple have three children: i. Gail Patricia, born December 28, 1946. ii. Roy Franklin, Jr., born July 3, 1949. iii. William Rex, born July 20, 1951. 5. John Patrick, born in Memphis on August 29, 1919. He attended the University of Tennessee, where he took his degree of Bachelor of Science in Electrical

Engineering, and in 1940 entered the Royal Canadian Air Force, later becoming a wing commander in the Royal Air Force and serving in England, Africa and Ceylon. He is now an electrical engineer with Wagner Electric Corporation in New Orleans. 6. Quentin, born March 19, 1921. He studied architectural engineering at the University of Tennessee, and was a first lieutenant in the United States Army Air Corps in World War II, serving in Africa, Italy, and Corsica. On November 11, 1950, he married Gwendolyn Cole Lounsbury. Her son by a previous marriage, Richard Lounsbury, is attending Purdue University. Quentin McGaughran is an architect with J. H. Hedrick Company in San Gabriel, California, and lives in South Pasadena. 7. Virginia Maude, born June 18, 1922. After attending Southwestern University and Vanderbilt, she took her Bachelor of Arts degree at the University of Tennessee. In June, 1955, she married John Max Lemmons, who is serving in the United States Navy. They have a child, John Mark, born March 10, 1957. Mrs. Lemmons is a claims agent with the Social Security Administration. 8. Lucius Timothy, born September 22, 1924; attended Memphis State University where he took his Bachelor of Science and Master of Arts degrees. He is now sales and methods engineer with International Harvester Company in Memphis. He married Thelma Louise Berry on July 2, 1949, and they have four children: i. Timothy Lee, born August 20, 1951. ii. Deborah Jane, born May 4, 1953. iii. Dennis, born June 18, 1956. iv. Carol Margaret, born February 5, 1958. 9. Seth Burnell, born December 2, 1925; attended the University of Tennessee and Vanderbilt University, where he took his Bachelor of Laws degree. He is a lawyer with offices in the Columbian Mutual Tower Building in Memphis. He married Mary Ann Seabrook, daughter Mr. and Mrs. J. H. Seabrook of Memphis. She holds a Bachelor of Arts degree from the University of Tennessee.

The death of Emmett P. McGaughran occurred at Baptist Hospital in Memphis on September 2, 1958.

LAWRENCE MILLARD RUSSELL

A tobacco warehouseman since the beginning of his career, Lawrence Millard Russell is now the proprietor of warehouses in Georgia as well as Tennessee. A resident of New Tazewell, he is a prominent civic leader of the eastern part of the state, and has interests in banking, public service, and political affairs.

Born at New Tazewell on January 31, 1906, he is a son of Garfield and Jane (Bolinger) Russell. Both of his parents were likewise natives of Tennessee, his father having been born at Goin on January 31, 1882, and his mother at Speedwell on December 9, 1884.

Lawrence M. Russell attended local public schools and graduated from Claiborne County High School in 1926. For a year he attended Knoxville Business College. Then, in 1927, he began his work in the tobacco warehousing

Lawrence M. Russell

field, joining a local warehouse as a calculator. In 1932 he organized the firm of Russell Brothers, a partnership operating tobacco warehouses—two at New Tazewell and two at Tifton, Georgia. During the war years, the partners owned and operated two warehouses in Smithfield, North Carolina, selling at auction as much as thirteen million pounds of tobacco annually. In addition to the warehouse operations, the brothers operate farms comprising about twenty-five hundred acres in Claiborne and Union Counties, on which they raise beef cattle as well as tobacco.

Mr. Russell is chairman of the board of directors of the Citizens Bank of his city. He serves on the board of education in Claiborne County, and is president of the Claiborne County Chamber of Commerce. He is a trustee and a member of the executive board of Lincoln Memorial University at Harrogate. A Republican in his politics, he went to Chicago in 1952 as delegate to the party's National Convention, at which Dwight D. Eisenhower was nominated for the presidency. In 1956 he was chosen Republican elector-at-large for Tennessee. He is now congressional chairman for Claiborne County in the First Congressional District.

Affiliated with the Free and Accepted Masons, Mr. Russell is a member of Evening Star Lodge No. 180. He attends the New Tazewell Methodist Church, and teaches a men's Bible class there.

In his native city, on June 4, 1931, Lawrence Millard Russell married Ruth Breeding, daughter of T. G. and Jo Ann (Montgomery) Breeding, both of whom were former residents of Hancock County. Mr. and Mrs. Russell are the parents of the following children: 1. Joyce Russell, born April 13, 1933. She is a graduate of the University of Tennessee. Now married to Charles Franklin Payne, she is the mother of a son, Wesley Payne, born on February 6, 1959. 2. Janice Russell, who was born on December 1, 1937, attended Florida State University, and is now married to Dr. Evan James Kurts. They have a daughter, Lisa Kurts, born on October 23, 1958. Both of the children of Lawrence M. and Ruth (Breeding) Russell were born in New Tazewell.

Dr. James Wilson Hall

In private practice in Trenton since 1948, Dr. James Wilson Hall is associated with Dr. Edward Barker in the Barker and Hall Clinic in Trenton.

Dr. Hall was born in Trenton on June 2, 1921, the only child of James Henry Hall and Zona Belle (Dowland) Hall, both of Gibson County. His father, at one time Sheriff of Gibson County and also City Marshal of Trenton, is deceased.

He attended schools in Gibson County, graduating from Peabody High School at Trenton, and then attended pre-med school at the University of Tennessee in Martin and also Memphis State University at Memphis during the years 1938, 1939 and 1940. After completing his pre-medical studies, he entered the University of Tennessee Medical College in Memphis and received his Doctor of Medicine degree there in 1945. He served his internship at John Gaston Hospital in Memphis and upon completion, entered the United States Army, serving for two years. He was discharged in 1948 with the rank of Major and has since continued his military service in the Tennessee National Guard. Upon his discharge from service in 1948, he returned to Trenton to begin his private practice. In 1949, he joined Dr. Edward Barker in the operation of the Barker and Hall Clinic.

In addition to the various medical associations to which he belongs, he is a member of Masonic Lodge 86 in Trenton, Phi Chi fraternity, the Lions Club, the Trenton Chamber of Commerce and the American Legion; and he is on the Board of Directors of the Citizens State Bank of Trenton. He and his family are members of the First Baptist Church. Dr. Hall is an ardent fisherman and hunter and enjoys recreation in these sports.

He married the former Jo Young in Memphis on July 8, 1944. Mrs. Hall, born on January 1, 1921 in Tigret, is the daughter of Warner Eugene and Eudora (Baker) Young. The Halls have four children: 1. Sandra Jo. 2. James Wilson, Jr. 3. Richard Eugene. 4. Robert Barker.

Both the Hall and the Young families can be traced through many generations of native Tennesseans who have contributed much to the progress of the state.

RAYMOND MARSHALL BRIGGS

For more than a decade, Raymond Marshall Briggs has practiced law in Memphis, being a partner in the firm of Briggs and Nixon, which recently moved to offices at 1114 Columbian Mutual Tower Building. He is interested in music and in flying, as well as in the business and civic life of his city.

A native of Memphis, Mr. Briggs was born on September 16, 1918, and is a son of Harry Raymond and Nellie Gray (Richardson) Briggs. Both of his parents were also born in Memphis. His father was a farmer and dairyman in Shelby County, the son of Thomas Jefferson Briggs, who was a large plantation owner of DeWitt, Arkansas. Harry R. Briggs is deceased, but Mrs. Briggs survives him and makes her home in Memphis. Raymond M. Briggs completed his public school education at Bartlett, graduating from Bartlett High School in 1937. He began his advanced studies at Memphis State University, and went from there to Washington and Lee University School of Law at Lexington, Virginia. However, he later transferred from there to Vanderbilt University Law School, where he graduated in 1943 with the degree of Bachelor of Laws. He was the only graduate of the Law School in the class of 1943.

By that time, Mr. Briggs had already begun acquiring his experience in law practice, having joined the firm of Goodpasture and Carpenter in Nashville in 1942. After receiving his law degree, he joined Welcome Wagon, Inc., as vice president and southern regional manager. His uncle, Thomas Winston Briggs, was the founder of this firm, and remains its president. Raymond M.

Briggs left the organization in 1948 to return to Memphis and begin his law practice there. He has since been a partner in the firm of Briggs and Nixon. He is also chairman of the board of the Federated Reserve Life Insurance Company of West Memphis, Arkansas, and chairman of the board of the Carriage Trade Foundation. Mr. Briggs has been a Public Relations Counsel for the past four years and is a member of the Memphis and Shelby County Bar Association, American Bar Association, Tennessee State Bar Association, American Judicature Society and National Association of Claimant Compensation Attorneys.

He serves as chairman of legislation of the Tennessee Federation of Music, and is legal officer of Group I of the Tennessee Wing of the Civil Air Patrol. Formerly a member of the local Junior Chamber of Commerce in Memphis, he held office as its vice president, and he is also a past member of the Memphis Rotary Club and the Memphis Yacht Club. His present memberships include the King's Club and Colonial Country Club, and the lodge of Free and Accepted Masons. In Masonry he is a member of the higher bodies of the York Rite, and the Ancient Arabic Order of Nobles of the Mystic Shrine. As a lawyer he belongs to Phi Alpha Delta fraternity, and is also a member of Kappa Alpha. For some years, Mr. Briggs followed yachting as a hobby. He attends the Baptist Church.

In Memphis, on June 22, 1942, Raymond Marshall Briggs married Muriel Lea Moore. Born in that city, she is a daughter of Bernie D. and Nettye (Miller) Moore. Mr. and Mrs. Briggs have four children: 1. Katherine D'Almaine, who was born on June 15, 1943. 2. Muriel Lea, born January 2, 1945. 3. Thomas Winston, 2nd, born December 6, 1947. 4. Raymond Marshall, Jr., born October 6, 1957.

BILLY HOLT TAYLOR

After a distinguished war career, Billy Holt Taylor returned home and in eleven years rose from employee to majority stockholder in the Eveready Auto Parts and Equipment Company, with stores in twelve communities.

His father, George Lewis Taylor, was a livestock dealer for about twenty-five years and is now with the Tennessee Department of Finance and Taxation. His mother, the former Euna Bell Holt, was born in Greenfield. George Lewis and Euna Bell (Holt) Taylor now live in Gleason.

Billy Holt Taylor was born in Greenfield, Weakley County, September 15, 1923, and was educated in the Weakley County Elementary Schools; he graduated from the Greenfield City High School in 1942, and then entered the armed services.

From 1942 to 1946, Billy Holt Taylor served in the army—three years and eight days of this time in the European Theater. Though the organization with which he served received a Unit Citation for Meritorious and Distinctive Service, he came through the War without being wounded.

Upon his discharge as a technical sergeant at Atterbury, Indiana, in 1946, Mr. Taylor went to work as an employee of the Eveready Auto Parts and Equipment Company of Trenton. In one year he owned a one-fourth interest in the business. In 1950 he increased his holdings to forty-five percent and in 1957, he secured control of the business through the purchase of an additional fifteen percent, which gave him a total ownership of sixty percent of the stock.

As recreation, Mr. Taylor is an ardent duck hunter and a great football fan, but his favorite hobby is his home workshop. He also is active in many organizations—a member of local Masonic Lodge #86, of the Rotary Club, where for the past four years he has served on the Board of Directors and as president in 1954-1955. He is a member of the Trenton School Board and is vice president of the Trenton Industrial Group Committee as well as a member of the First Presbyterian Church of Trenton.

Mrs. Taylor, the former Joann Margrove, was born March 22, 1926, in Gleason, where her father, Jess L. Margrove, was mayor. He died in 1956 at the age of sixty-six, but her mother, Pauline (Poyner) Margrove is still living.

Mr. and Mrs. Taylor were married in Gleason, Tennessee, on August 1, 1947, and are the parents of three children, all born in Humboldt. 1. Paulette, born August 27, 1949. 2. Lewis Lee, born January 1, 1955. 3. Angela, born July 5, 1957.

Edward Lindsey Rucks

One of Memphis' younger members of the legal profession, Edward Lindsey Rucks became a partner in the firm of Cole, Ruleman and Rucks in 1958. Since October 1959, he has been associated with E. W. Hale, Jr. and Rives A. Manker in private practice. He has served as assistant city attorney, deputy county divorce proctor, and is now Assistant County Attorney.

A native Memphian, he was born on November 17, 1930, and is a son of Walker Lee Rucks, M.D., and his wife, the former Clifford Lindsey. Dr. Rucks, who was born at Greenville, Mississippi, in June, 1890, has been a practicing pediatrician in Memphis for many years. He received his medical degree at the University of Tennessee. He is a fellow of the American Academy of Pediatrics, and a fellow and past president of the American College of Allergists. Miss Clifford Lindsey, whom he married, was born at Nashville in September, 1892.

Edward L. Rucks completed his preparatory studies at Castle Heights Military Academy, then entered Southwestern University in Memphis, where he took his pre-law courses and graduated with the degree of Bachelor of Arts. He began his law studies at Vanderbilt University, but transferred to the University of Mississippi, receiving his degree of Bachelor of Laws there.

Admitted to the bar of the state of Tennessee, Mr. Rucks began his general practice of law in Memphis in association with E. W. Hale, Jr., in

1957. In October, 1958, he became a partner in the firm of Cole, Ruleman, and Rucks. Since October 1959, he has been associated with E. W. Hale, Jr. and Rives A. Manker. Prior to his private practice, he served as assistant city attorney of Memphis from 1955 to 1957. He also served as deputy Shelby County divorce proctor, and is now assistant county attorney. He is a member of the Memphis and Shelby County Bar Association, the Tennessee Bar Association, the Mississippi Bar Association, the American Bar Association, and the American Judicature Society, in which membership is by invitation only.

In 1955, Mr. Rucks entered active service in the United States Army, and was commissioned a first lieutenant in the infantry, being assigned to the Ninth Division. He spent some time in Germany, and received his honorable discharge in 1957.

Mr. Rucks' local memberships include The Phoenix, a young men's service organization similar to Rotary in its aims, the Royal Club and the University Club. He is a member of the lodge of Free and Accepted Masons and of the higher bodies of that order, and his fraternities are Phi Alpha Delta (legal) and Sigma Alpha Epsilon (social). In both of these fraternities he has held office as secretary and treasurer. An Episcopalian, he is a member of Holy Communion Church.

In his home city of Memphis, on August 29, 1953, Edward Lindsey Rucks married Elizabeth Ann Ross. She is the daughter of George Cairncross and Mary Elizabeth Virginia (Grueser) Ross, both of whom are deceased. Mr. and Mrs. Rucks are the parents of three children: 1. Evelyn Lindsey, who was born on February 9, 1955. 2. Edward Lindsey, Jr., born on December 13, 1956. 3. Virginia Cairncross, born on October 15, 1958.

JOHN CRUMP KLINCK

The entire career of former Fire Chief John Crump Klinck was with the Memphis Fire Department, and he held the position as head of the organization from 1950 until his recent retirement. Under his leadership, the department had won many awards for efficiency. Mr. Klinck has himself been active in firemen's groups, and he has written two works on various phases of fire-fighting.

A native of Memphis, he was born on March 9, 1911, and is a son of Irby Monroe and Ella (Cushing) Klinck. His father before him was chief of the Memphis Fire Department. Receiving a parochial school education, John C. Klinck completed his secondary studies at the Catholic high school conducted by Christian Brothers College. He has studied fire administration at the University of Chicago, and has also attended the University of Memphis Law School.

Chief Klinck first joined the department on June 3, 1930. He was promoted to lieutenant on February 14, 1940, and to captain on September 1, 1941. On March 16, 1943, he won his promotion to district chief, a post in which he served until he entered the United States Army on June 15, 1944. Sent to Fort McClellan, Alabama, he was assigned to headquarters division of the Infantry Replacement Training Center there, and remained in uniform until May 1, 1946.

On his return from military service, he was reinstated in the Memphis Fire Department as district chief of the Personnel Division. He was named acting deputy chief on October 22, 1948, and on the first of November of that same year, was promoted to deputy chief. His promotion to chief of the department came on June 6, 1950.

Since that year, the department has won the following awards: National Fire Protection Association Grand National Award for Fire Prevention Week activity: Grand Award in 1952 and in 1956; third-place tie with Fort Wayne, Indiana, in 1950; third place, 1953; fourth place, 1954; National Fire Protection Association state rating: first place in 1950, 1951, 1952, 1953, 1954, 1955 and 1956; National Fire Protection Association population class rating, which started in 1951: second place, 1951; first place, 1952; first place, 1953; second place, 1954; third place, 1955; first place, 1956; United States Chamber of Commerce Fire Safety Award: Grand Award in 1952; honorable mention in 1951, 1953, 1954, 1955 and 1956. Chief Klinck personally received a plaque from the Southeastern Association of Fire Chiefs, as Outstanding Fire Chief of Tennessee, 1954-1955. He received a plaque presented by the International Association of Fire Chiefs for conducting an outstanding Fire Prevention Week campaign and winning the United States Grand Award in the National Fire Protection Association Fire Prevention Week in 1956.

Mr. Klinck is a member and former president of the Tennessee Firemen's Association. He has been very active in the leadership of the International Association of Fire Chiefs, in which he has held office as state vice president, chairman of the Fire Prevention Committee, member of the Firemen's Training Committee, and member of the Committee on Memberships. He is a member of the Southeastern Association of Fire Chiefs. He has served as co-chairman of the Fire Department Instructors Conference, and is chairman of the advisory board of Tennessee State Fire College. He is a member of the Committee on Indirect Application of Water in Fire Fighting.

Chief Klinck has designed various tools and appliances for use in fire departments. He is the author of two major works: "Organization and Training of Industrial Fire Brigades," published by S. C. Toof Company in Memphis in 1942, and "Standard Operating Procedures (Rules and Regulations)" published by the Memphis Fire Department in 1953.

A dependable supporter of welfare causes and civic programs, John C. Klinck has served as vice president and chairman of the Shelby County Chapter of the Muscular Dystrophy Association of America. He is a member of the advisory committee of the Cotton Carnival Association, and he was named Honorary Citizen of Arkansas by the Arkansas Traveler. A member of the American Legion, he serves on the membership committee of his local

William C. Sullivan

post, and he also belongs to the post of the Forty and Eight. He is a member of the Agricultural Club in Memphis, and is of the Roman Catholic faith.

John C. Klinck is unmarried. His address is 65 South Front Street, Memphis.

WILLIAM CHARLES TALLENT

Following useful experience in private industry as an automobile dealer, William Charles Tallent assumed responsible public duties as commissioner of finance for Knox County, and as secretary to the Board of County Commissioners. In these posts, and also as a private citizen interested in civic and organizational affairs, he has rendered useful service to his city and county.

Born November 29, 1923, in Knoxville, he is a son of Frank Nelson and Frankie Lucille (Grantham) Tallent. His father is now retired after serving many years on the Knoxville police force. William C. Tallent attended the Knoxville city schools, graduated from high school there, then entered the University of Tennessee, where he was a student from 1945 to 1947. He has since continued his education attending night classes at the university and through extension courses.

He began his career in the automobile retailing field, being associated with Rodgers and Company in the capacity of sales manager until 1950, when he became chief deputy trustee under C. Edwin Graves. He assumed his present offices as commissioner of finance for Knox County, and secretary of the Board of County Commissioners, in 1953 having been appointed by the Knox County Board of Commissioners. On September 1, 1954 he began his four year elective term and in 1958 he was reelected for his second four year term. He is a member of Knox County Planning Commission, its Beer Board and Board of Zoning Appeals.

Mr. Tallent is a veteran of World War II, having served as an infantryman with the 28th Division in Europe. He was captured by the Nazis and spent about six months in a prisoner of war camp in Germany. He was wounded and received two Purple Hearts.

He has been active in veterans' organizations since his return from the war. He is past vice commander of Post No. 2 of the American Legion; past commander of Chapter 256 of the Military Order of the Purple Heart; past commander of Post No. 4, Disabled American Veterans, of Knoxville; past commander of the Second District of the Disabled American Veterans of Tennessee; and a member of the Veterans of Foreign Wars. He is a member of the Knoxville Junior Chamber of Commerce, the North Knoxville Business Men's Club, the Knoxville Lions Club, and the Free and Accepted Masons. He holds the Thirty-second Degree in Masonry, and is a member of the York Rite bodies and also of the Ancient Arabic Order of Nobles of the Mystic Shrine.

Another of Mr. Tallent's interests is politics, and he is a devoted and effective supporter of the Republican party's program. He formerly served as vice president of the Knox County Young Republicans Club, and was treasurer of the Federation of Young Republican Clubs of the State of Tennessee in 1950. In 1956, he was his state's co-manager of the Eisenhower-for-President campaign. He and the members of his family attend Arlington Baptist Church in Knoxville. He is on the Board of Directors of the Travelers Aid Society. Fond of the out-of-doors, Mr. Tallent lists golf, fishing and boating as his favorite pastimes.

In his home city of Knoxville, on March 26, 1949, William Charles Tallent married Juanita Norris, daughter of Raymond B. and Iva (Warwick) Norris. The couple are the parents of two children: 1. William Charles, Jr., who was born on January 10, 1953. 2. Nelson Raymond, born August 16, 1954. The family resides at 2308 Tecoma Drive.

JOHN TROY DUNLAP, JR.

One of Memphis' younger members of the bar, John Troy Dunlap, Jr., has been engaged in general practice in that city since his return from the Korean War. He is also a veteran of World War II. In his home city he has become active in lodge affairs and in church work.

A native of Memphis, he was born on February 2, 1926, and is a son of John Troy, Sr., and Annie Jean (McClintock) Dunlap. His father was born at Duckhill, Mississippi, in 1889, and became a conductor on the Illinois Central Railroad. Now retired, he lived in Memphis. His wife, the former Annie Jean McClintock, is a native of Hornsby, Tennessee. Reared in Memphis and attending its public schools, the younger John T. Dunlap went from Lauderdale Grammar School to South Side High School, where he graduated. He began his advanced studies at Milligan College in Johnson City, but transferred from there to Murray State College, Murray, Kentucky. He received his professional training at the University of Tennessee in Knoxville, where he graduated with the degree of Bachelor of Laws in 1949.

Meantime, however, his education had been interrupted by service in the United States Army. Going in as an enlisted man in 1944, he was assigned to the army of occupation in Japan in 1945, and was separated from the service in 1946. Again in 1952, when our troops were at war in Korea, he was called back into the army. Assigned to the Judge Advocate General's Department, he studied at the University of Virginia, and was commissioned a first lieutenant.

Admitted to the bar following the completion of his law courses in 1949, Mr. Dunlap began his independent practice as an attorney, from which he was called for his second tour of duty in the army. When, following his return from the Korean War, he resumed his practice, he became a partner in the firm of Irwin and Dunlap, with offices in the Columbian Mutual Insurance Building in Memphis. This firm conducts a general practice and handles trial work.

John J. Shea

Mr. Dunlap is a member of the local, state, and national bar associations. Affiliated with the Free and Accepted Masons, he is a member of the higher bodies of the Ancient and Accepted Scottish Rite. He holds the Thirty-second Degree, and belongs to the Ancient Arabic Order of Nobles of the Mystic Shrine. His fraternity is Sigma Chi. A communicant of Trinity Methodist Church, he teaches Sunday school there, having a young people's class. His favorite outdoor sports are fishing and hunting.

In his home city of Memphis, on April 19, 1952, John T. Dunlap married Martha Eleanor Boyd, who was born in Corinth, Mississippi. Her father is deceased, Mr. and Mrs. Dunlap are the parents of the following children: 1. Barbara Lee, who was born on February 17, 1953. 2. John Boyd, born in December 1954. 3. Charlene, born in September 1957. 4. Keith Ellis, born in November 1958. Mrs. Dunlap is active in local affairs, and is a member of the Nineteenth Century Club. The family resides at 2751 Natchez Lane, Memphis.

JOHN JOSEPH SHEA, M.D.

Choosing Memphis as the scene of his practice as surgeon specializing in treatment of diseases of the ear, nose, and throat, Dr. John Joseph Shea won a reputation which extended beyond the confines of his own state. At the time of his death, he was president-elect of both the American Board of Otolaryngology, and the American Academy of Ophthalmology and Oto-laryngology.

A native of Memphis, he was born on January 17, 1889, son of John Joseph, Sr., an attorney and editor and publisher of the Catholic Journal, and Mary (Coyle) Shea. Beginning his education in schools there, he attended high school and college at Christian Brothers College from which he received his Bachelor of Arts degree in 1906. He received his degree of Doctor of Medicine from New York University and Bellevue Medical College in 1911. He served his internship at St. John's Seaside Hospital, Staten Island, New York, Manhattan Maternity Hospital, and Bellevue Hospital, both of New York, between 1911 and 1913. His postgraduate training was obtained at the New York Post-Graduate School and Hospital in 1914-1915, and at the University of Paris, 1918-1919.

In 1917, Dr. Shea was commissioned a first lieutenant in the United States Army Medical Corps, in which he saw service at Camp Meade, Maryland, Red Cross Hospital No. 7, Juilly Seine et Marne, and U.S.A. Base Hospital No. 57 at Paris. He was honorably discharged in 1919 with the rank of major. He later held the position of examiner for the Department of Aeronautics, 1925-1932.

After his discharge, Dr. Shea returned to Memphis, where he engaged in the practice of otorhinolaryngology and maxillo-facial surgery in the offices of Dr. Ellett and Farrington. In 1926 he established the Dr. John J. Shea Clinic, where he practiced until the time of his last illness. He was a member of the staffs of the Baptist Memorial Hospital, St. Joseph Hospital and the Memphis Eye, Ear, Nose and Throat Hospital, and was consultant with the Campbell Clinic and the Kennedy Hospital.

A fellow of the American Medical Association, Dr. Shea held office as secretary of its Section on Otolaryngology from 1931 to 1933, and was chairman of that section during the 1934-1935 term. In the Southern Medical Association, he was secretary of the Section on O. and O. from 1920 to 1922, vice chairman of the section in 1923, and its chairman in 1924. He was elected to the American College of Surgeons in 1922. As a member of the American Academy of Ophthalmology and Otolaryngology, he held office as vice president in 1924, was a member of the council from 1929 through 1932, and had been elected president for the 1953 term at the time of his death. He had served on the council of the American Laryngological, Rhinological and Otological Society from 1937 until 1939, and was its president in 1948-1949. From 1943 to 1945, he was a member of the council of the American Otological Society. He was first vice president of the American Laryngological Association in 1944-1945 and again in 1947. Dr. Shea was also active on the American Board of Otolaryngology, and had been elected its president for the ensuing term shortly before his death. A colleague familiar with the man and his record through his connection with that group wrote of him: "Those of us who had the privilege of being associated with him on the American Board of Otolaryngology appreciated his honesty, his sagacity, his straightforwardness and his unswerving sense of duty towards his fellow members and the candidates alike. His disposition was always cordial and ebullient, his sense of humor unfailing at all times. He was the exemplary 'southern gentleman.' "

A prolific writer, Dr. Shea had published ninety-four papers on all phases of otorhinolaryngology, maxillofacial surgery, and allergy, and several on diseases of the hematopoetic system. He invented the "Shea tube" for use in the postoperative treatment of nasoantral surgery in children.

In his home city, Dr. Shea was a member of the Memphis Country Club and the Catholic Club. A devout Roman Catholic, he was a communicant of St. Peter's Church, and it was said of him that his "religion meant everything that it should mean to a man and to a physician. He was a man of the highest principles, of great charity to his fellow men, a man of tolerance and understanding of the shortcomings of others, as well as his own ineptitudes."

He was a great reader. His family, friends, deep sea fishing, golf, and an occasional game of cards were his relaxations.

At St. Peter's Roman Catholic Church in Memphis, on July 5, 1917, Dr. John Joseph Shea married Catharine Flanagan, daughter of Martin and Ellen (Griffin) Flanagan. Her father, a business man of Memphis, had come to this country for Castle Park, Liscannon, County Clare, Ireland, while her

mother was a native of Memphis. Mrs. Shea has been described as "his constant and delightful companion at the meetings of the American Board of Otolaryngology and of the national otolaryngological societies, with an attendance record second only to his own." The couple became the parents of the following children: 1. Jeanne, who is the wife of William A. Leatherman. They had four children: i. Jeanne Irwin. ii. William Abbay. iii. Catharine Compton, who is deceased. iv. John Shea. 2. Catharine Marie, who married William Leslie Roberts. Their children: i. Catharine Shea. ii. Laura Leslie. 3. John Joseph Shea, Jr., M.D., the subject of an accompanying record. 4. Ellen Griffin, who is now Mrs. L. K. Thompson, Jr. They have eight children: i. Laurence K., 3rd. ii. Nelse Rockwood. iii. Lucian Malone. iv. John Shea. v. Martin Flanagan. vi. Ellen Griffin. vii. William Leslie. viii. Thomas Joseph. 5. Mary Coyle. She married David F. Dixon, and they have three children: i. David Frank, Jr. ii. John Shea. iii. Martin Stuart. 6. Martin Flanagan, whose record also follows in these pages.

A distinguished career in surgery, and one devoted to the service of his fellows and the advancement of the highest standards of his profession, came to an end with the death of Dr. John Joseph Shea, on November 28, 1952.

JOHN JOSEPH SHEA, JR., M.D.

In choosing the practice of medicine and the specialty of otology for his profession, Dr. John Joseph Shea, Jr., is following in the footsteps of his distinguished father, who was well known in the area for his pre-eminence in this sphere of the healing sciences. The younger Dr. John J. Shea has already made a distinctive personal contribution, having perfected an operative procedure to alleviate deafness.

He is a native of Memphis, and was born on September 4, 1924, son of John Joseph, Sr., and Catharine (Flanagan) Shea. Both of his parents were likewise born in Memphis, his father in 1889 and his mother in 1898. The elder Dr. Shea has a biographical record accompanying, as has the couple's other son, Martin F. Shea.

After attending schools in Memphis, Dr. Shea entered Harvard University, and graduated from its Medical School in 1947 with the degree of Doctor of Medicine. Choosing his father's specialty, he commenced practice as an otologist in Memphis in 1953, after the death of his father. In 1958 he established the Memphis Foundation of Otology, a nonprofit foundation for research into diseases of the ear. It provides fellowships for foreign graduate students. In 1956, Dr. Shea perfected a new ear operation, which has achieved dramatic results in restoring hearing in deafness due to otosclerosis (middle-ear calcification). The technique, known as fenestration of the oval window, has been widely adopted by other surgeons. At the present time it is being used in at least twenty cities in the United States, and in major cities in most of the civilized countries of the world. Dr. Shea himself toured the globe in 1959, performing operations in Hawaii, Japan, Hongkong, India, Zurich, London, and elsewhere.

Dr. Shea has written a number of articles in the field of his specialization. "Symposium-Mobilization of the Stapes," which he wrote in collaboration, appeared in The Laryngoscope in 1956; and he has since written "Tympanoplasty',' published in the Memphis Medical Journal; "Fenestration of the Oval Window," (Journal of the Tennessee State Medical Association); an article under the same title appearing in Acta-Oto-Laryngologica, in Sweden; other articles on the same subject for the Memphis Medical Journal and for Annals of Otology, Rhinology, and Laryngology; "Dihydrostreptomycin Deafness," written in collaboration and appearing in the Journal of the American Medical Association; "Fenestration of the Oval Window," (Transactions of American Academy of Ophthalmology and Otolaryngology); and "Vein Graft Closure of Eardrum Perforations." Dr. Shea is a member of the American Academy of Ophthalmology and Otolaryngology and of the Otosclerosis Study Group.

He was in active service in the United States Navy during the war years 1943-1945, and again from 1950 to 1952.

Dr. Shea's nonprofessional memberships include the Memphis Country Club, and he is a communicant of the Roman Catholic Church.

On March 12, 1949, in Boston, Massachusetts, Dr. John Joseph Shea, Jr., married Gwyn Rainer. They are the parents of two children: 1. John Joseph, 3rd, who was born in Boston on July 11, 1950. 2. Gwyn Rainer, born August 16, 1952, in Memphis.

Martin Flanagan Shea

Joining the Welsh Plywood Corporation of Memphis, following the completion of his tour of duty in the Marine Corps, Martin F. Shea is now assigned to its New York City office as the firm's eastern sales representative.

He is a native Memphian, and was born in May 20, 1930, son of Dr. John Joseph, Sr., and Catharine (Flanagan) Shea, and grandson of John Joseph and Mary (Coyle) Shea, and of Martin and Ellen (Griffin) Flanagan. His father, a distinguished ear, nose and throat specialist practicing in Memphis, is the subject of an accompanying sketch, as is another son, Dr. John Joseph, Jr. Mrs. Shea was born in Memphis on August 14, 1898.

Martin F. Shea went to famed Phillips Exeter Academy in New Hampshire to begin his preparatory studies, but later returned to Memphis, where he was a student at Christian Brothers High School in 1948. He graduated from Portsmouth Priory School at Portsmouth, Rhode Island, in 1949. Entering Yale University, he took his degree of Bachelor of Arts there in 1953. In July of that year he began his record of service in the United States Marine Corps, being sent to its Officers Candidate School at Quantico. In September, he was commissioned a second lieutenant, and he continued his

Martin F Shea

studies at Quantico until 1954. He left in April of that year on assignment to the First Marine Aircraft Wing, with which he served in Korea until June, 1955. He was commissioned a first lieutenant on March 19, and received his honorable discharge in that grade the following July.

In January, 1956, he began his connection with Welsh Plywood Corporation of Memphis, entering its training program. In August of that year, the company sent him to Japan as representative in the Far East, assigned to duties in the purchase of lumber and plywood. In the course of the ensuing year, he travelled throughout the Orient. Returning to Memphis in July, 1957, he was assigned to the sales department of his company, and after acquiring experience in this work, was transferred to New York City in April, 1958, as eastern sales representative. He is still serving the company there in that capacity.

Mr. Shea joined Chi Psi fraternity at Yale University, and while in Memphis he became a member of the Memphis Country Club. A Roman Catholic, he is a communicant of St. Peter's Church in Memphis.

ALLEN E(STES) COX, JR.

Residents of Memphis, know Allen E(stes) Cox, Jr., as a prominent attorney of their city, a partner in the firm of Waring, Walker, Cox and Lewis. He is also a farmer, his agricultural interests being centered in the state of Arkansas. He has a large number of organizational and civic connections in Memphis, where he makes his home.

Born at Milan, Tennessee, on November 4, 1902, he is a son of Dr. Allen Ennis and Lucile (Folk) Cox of Helena, Arkansas. His father, a physician and surgeon, graduated from Vanderbilt Medical School in 1896, and practiced at Milan, Tennessee, and Helena, Arkansas. In all, he was a general practitioner for over sixty years, and his death occurred in August, 1954.

Attending the public schools of Helena, Arkansas, Allen Estes Cox graduated from Helena High School in 1919, then entered Vanderbilt University, Nashville, where he took his degree of Bachelor of Arts in 1923. For his professional training, he entered Yale Law School in New Haven, Connecticut, and took his degree of Bachelor of Laws there in 1926.

Admitted to the Tennessee bar in that year, he began his professional career as an associate in the firm of Miles, Waring and Walker, in Memphis. He became a partner in the firm of Waring, Walker and Cox in 1932, and in 1958, a partner in the firm of Waring, Walker, Cox and Lewis, which has its offices in the Sterick Building, Memphis. His firm handles civil cases, corporate and probate practice, and trials.

Mr. Cox is owner of Wyanoke Plantation at Hulbert, Arkansas, where he engages in his secondary occupation of farming, associated with his elder son Allen Cox III.

As a lawyer, he is a member of the Memphis and Shelby County Bar

Association, the Tennessee State Bar Association, and the American Bar Association. In the national group, he is a member of the Insurance Section. He also belongs to Corbey Court of Phi Delta Phi legal fraternity; and his social fraternity is Kappa Alpha (Southern). He is a member and past president of the Travelers Aid Society in his home city; a member and past president of the Yale Alumni Association; and a member and past president of Vanderbilt Alumni Association.

Mr. Cox's other memberships include the Memphis Cotton Carnival Association, Memphi, Memphis Country Club, Hatchie Coon Hunting and Fishing Club and Grand Junction (Tennessee) Bird Hunting Club. He is a communicant of the Baptist Church.

At Jackson, Tennessee, on February 10, 1931, Allen E(stes) Cox, Jr., married Hortense Beare, daughter of Colonel Robert Lee and Mary (Reiney) Beare of Jackson, Mrs. Cox died October 23, 1954. The couple were the parents of three children: 1. Allen, 3rd, who was born on December 26, 1932. 2. Robert Lee, born December 20, 1935. 3. Mary Reiney, born November 12, 1937. Mr. Cox's residence is at 4315 Walnut Grove Road, Memphis.

EDWARD MARTIN LOWRANCE

Since the early 1940s, Edward Martin Lowrance has been practicing law in Memphis, and he is now associated with the firm of Waring, Walker, Cox and Lewis. A veteran of wartime service in the Army Air Corps, he attained the rank of major.

Mr. Lowrance is a native of Memphis, who was born on June 28, 1918, son of Edward Martin and Lucy (Davidson) Lowrance. His father, for many years a levee contractor at Memphis, is now deceased. The younger Edward M. Lowrance completed his preparatory studies at Sewanee Military Academy, where he was a student from 1932 to 1935. He then entered the University of Virginia, where he was a student until 1940. He transferred to Southern Law School in Memphis to complete his professional training, graduating there in 1941 with the degree of Bachelor of Laws.

Admitted to the bar of his native state, Mr. Lowrance began his practice in Memphis, but shortly afterwards, enlisted as a private in the United States Army Air Corps. He advanced steadily through the ranks in the course of his service, and held a major's commission at the time of his separation from the service in 1946. He served in the European Theater of Operations.

Resuming his law practice in Memphis following his return from the war, Mr. Lowrance became associated with the firm of Waring, Walker, Cox and Lewis in 1957. Its offices are in the Sterick Building. The firm conducts a practice of civil and corporation law, and trial work. His nonprofessional memberships include the University Club.

In his native city of Memphis on February 10, 1941, Edward M. Lowrance married Patricia McPhillips, daughter of Patrick Avila and Viola

(O'Donnell) McPhillips. The couple are the parents of three children: 1. Patricia Avila, who was born on January 10, 1943. 2. Edward Martin, 3rd, born on February 9, 1946. 3. Reed Davidson, born on April 30, 1952.

BRUCE CARLISLE EDENTON, JR.

As an executive of several grocery firms of his region, Bruce Carlisle Edenton, Jr., has attained a position of leadership in Tennessee's food industry. First identified with the J. C. Edenton Company, at Jackson, he is a former president. He is general manager and board chairman of Associate Food Stores of Jackson; president of Piggly Wiggly Kentucky Company; president of Mayfield Supermarket Realty Company at Mayfield; and vice president of Puerto Rico Meat Packing Company in San Juan. He serves as a director of each of these concerns. His home is in Jackson.

Born in that city on February 24, 1919, he is a son of Bruce Carlisle, Sr., and Nell (Benton) Edenton. His mother too was born at Jackson, on April 1, 1890, while his father is a native of Macon. The younger Bruce C. Edenton attended the public elementary school at Jackson, and took his preparatory studies at Riverside Military Academy in Gainesville, Georgia, and Darlington School at Rome, Georgia. He then enrolled at the University of Virginia in Charlottesville, and completed his advanced courses at Babson Institute, Babson Park, Massachusetts, where he was graduated with the degree in Business Administration.

Mr. Edenton began his business career with the J. C. Edenton Company in his native city of Jackson in 1945, serving as vice president and subsequently as president of this firm, which was a wholesale grocery organization with branches in Milan, Humboldt, Ripley, and Brownsville, Tennessee, and Corinth, Mississippi. The company was sold in 1957. He remained active as its president until April 1, 1956, when he took a leave of absence and moved to San Juan, Puerto Rico, to serve as director of the Puerto Rican government's food distribution program. His work in this responsible post called for the organization and direction of a staff to establish a modern food distribution system patterned after United States methods.

He is currently general manager and chairman of the board of Associate Food Stores, of Jackson; president and director of the Piggly Wiggly Kentucky Company at Mayfield; president of the Mayfield Supermarket Realty Company; vice president and director of the Puerto Rico Meat Packing Company in San Juan; and director of the Trenton Wholesale Grocery Company of Trenton.

He is a former director of the United States Wholesale Grocers Association of Washington, D.C., and served on the board of governors of the National American Wholesale Grocers Association of New York. He is past president of the Young Executives Club of the U.S. Wholesale Grocers Assoc. and has been generally active in community affairs. He is past vice president and a member of the board of the Jackson Community Chest; has served as vice president, as president and as board member of the Jackson Young Men's Christian Association; has held the same offices in the Jackson Rotary Club; and is formerly vice president and member of the board of the Jackson Civic Music Association. He is also a member of the board of trustees of Union University. He serves his church, the First Presbyterian of Jackson, as a member of its board of Deacons, and is former president of the Will Thompson Bible Class.

Mr. Edenton is a past director of the Jackson Golf and Country Club. He was a member of Theta Kappa Omega social fraternity, in high school, and in Alpha Tau Omega, which he joined at the University of Virginia. He belongs to the lodge of the Benevolent and Protective Order of Elks, and the posts of the Veterans of Foreign Wars and the American Legion. Currently, he is serving as chairman of the Jackson Chamber of Commerce Industrial Development Committee.

His wartime service was with the United States Navy, in which he spent three and a half years on active duty. Sixteen months of that time he was on sea duty in the Caribbean theater, and at the time he received his honorable discharge, held a commission as lieutenant, junior grade.

On December 17, 1943, at Fairview, Oklahoma, Bruce Carlisle Edenton, Jr., married Jane Speece. She is the daughter of Robert L. Speece, who was born at Belva, Kansas, on July 18, 1894, and his wife the former Mary Topley, born February 1, 1895, at Cleo Springs, Oklahoma. Mr. and Mrs. Edenton, who make their home on Northwood in Jackson, are the parents of three children: 1. Jane Speece, who was born June 23, 1950. 2. Mary Topley, born on September 8, 1951. 3. Bruce Carlisle, 3rd, born October 4, 1952. All of the children were born in Jackson.

ELMER ROY SLOAN

Elmer Roy Sloan of Madisonville has proved his abilities in the several fields of the law, insurance, and general business management. A native of Monroe County, he was born on June 21, 1899, son of Lee Roy and Mary (Hensley) Sloan, both of whom were also born in that county—his father on October 29, 1871, his mother on April 13, 1872.

Mr. Sloan attended Carson-Newman College, where he took his degree of Bachelor of Arts in 1922. In 1926 he received his degree of Bachelor of Laws at Chattanooga College of Law, which also conferred on him the Master of Laws degree two years later. Cumberland University granted him a Bachelor of Laws degree in 1947.

Admitted to the bar of his home state, Mr. Sloan began practice in 1947 at Madisonville and has practiced there since. There he had also entered the general insurance business in 1923. In 1956, he became president of the Con-

E R Sloan

crete Supply Company, Inc., and he is a director of the Fort Loudoun Association and chairman of the Madisonville Industrial Committee.

Mr. Sloan served in the United States Army in both World War I and World War II. In politics, he is an independent, with a past record as a Republican. A charter member of the Hamilton County Young Men's Republican Club, he was at one time its president.

As a lawyer he is a member of the Tennessee Bar Association, and he also belongs to Tellico Lodge No. 80, Free and Accepted Masons, in Madisonville, and Post No. 65 of the American Legion.

In Loudon County, Tennessee, on June 28, 1949, Elmer Roy Sloan married Marie Sheets, daughter of John Robert and Lula (Milligan) Sheets. Mrs. Sloan attended Shorter College at Rome, Georgia, and graduated from the University of Tennessee, where she was a member of Phi Mu and Phi Kappa Phi sororities. Both of her parents were born in Monroe County—her father on September 28, 1878, her mother on November 5, 1880. Mr. and Mrs. Sloan have no children.

JAMES DAVID CAUSEY

One of Memphis' younger professional leaders, James David Causey has practiced law in that city since the beginning of his career in 1950. He is a veteran of service in the United States Air Force.

Born January 31, 1926, at Tolarville, Mississippi, he is a son of Reuben C. Causey, a prominent citizen of Lexington, Mississippi, and constable there for more than twenty years; the elder Mr. Causey now operates a farm on Route 1 near Lexington. James D. Causey's mother, Ena (Gray) Causey, is the daughter of J. A. Gray, who was chairman of the board of supervisors when the Court House was built at Lexington, Mississippi. After completing his studies in local public schools, James D. Causey entered Mississippi Delta State College. In 1950 he received his degree of Bachelor of Laws from the University of Florida. His education was interrupted by service in the United States Air Force, in which he served from 1943 to 1946. He served with a bomber crew and held the rating of sergeant.

Admitted to the Florida bar in 1950 and the Tennessee bar in 1951, Mr. Causey began practice in that year in the city of Memphis, and has his own firm, under the name of Law Offices of James D. Causey, in the Home Federal Building. His practice has been devoted largely to trial work in both State and Federal courts.

He is a member of the following bar associations: American, Tennessee, Memphis and Shelby County, and Federation of Insurance Counsel and of Phi Delta Phi fraternity. In his home city, his memberships include The Tennessee Club, Craft Duck Pond Club and Lonely Heart Hunt Club. His hobby is hunting. He is a communicant of St. Luke's Methodist Church. In politics he is a Democrat.

At Hooks, Texas, on June 6, 1948, James D. Causey married Evelyn Lumbley, daughter of Jesse Lee and Mattie Alice (Sealy) Lumbley. Her father works for the Post Office Department. He is a naval veteran of World War I. Mr. and Mrs. Causey are the parents of two children: James Anderson, who was born on March 7, 1956, and Catherine, who was born on March 5, 1959.

WILLIAM MALLORY MORRIS

For some years William Mallory Morris has been a leader in Tennessee insurance circles. A resident of Memphis, he is the owner of Mallory Morris and Company, with headquarters in the Union Planters Bank Building.

A native of Paris, Tennessee, he was born on October 17, 1902, the son of William Taylor and Mary Laura (Chiles) Morris. His father was a planter and a merchant. After receiving his education through the secondary years in local public schools, Mallory Morris enrolled at Georgetown University for advanced studies in 1920. He left there in 1922 and, from 1924 to 1926, was a student at the University of Tennessee.

Mr. Morris is the owner and head of his own general insurance agency known as Mallory Morris and Company in Memphis. In addition to insurance men's organizations, Mr. Morris is a member of Delta Tau Delta, a social fraternity which he joined as an undergraduate, and of the National Early American Glass Club, the Huguenot Society of Virginia, and the English Speaking Union. He is a communicant of Calvary Episcopal Church in Memphis.

In that city, on November 27, 1931, Mallory Morris married Nell Martin, daughter of M. Lawrence and Bertha (Hogan) Martin. The couple are the parents of two children: 1. William Mallory, Jr., who was born on December 20, 1932. 2. Laura Nell, born February 20, 1949.

NEWTON PERKINS ALLEN

Practicing law in Memphis since 1948, Newton Perkins Allen is a partner in the firm of Armstrong, McCadden, Allen, Braden and Goodman. He has taken a constructive part as a member of local organizations, fraternal and alumni groups, and is a veteran of military service in World War II.

He is a native of Memphis, and was born on January 3, 1922, son of James Seddon and Sarah (Perkins) Allen. His father, too, is an attorney. Newton P. Allen received his elementary and secondary education locally, attending Fairview Junior High School and Central High School. On his graduation from high school he entered Princeton University, and received his degree of Bachelor of Arts there with the Class of 1943. He entered military service in that year and served with the Signal Corps in the Southwest Pacific until his honorable discharge in 1946.

After the war, Mr. Allen enrolled at the University of Virginia, in March, 1946. Graduating there in June, 1948, he received his degree of Bachelor of Laws. While at Princeton, he had been a member of the Charter Club, and at the University of Virginia, he held membership in Sigma Alpha Epsilon, the Raven Society, and Omicron Delta Kappa.

Admitted to the bar of his state in October 1947, Mr. Allen joined the firm of Armstrong, McCadden, Allen, Braden and Goodman in Memphis, of which he is now a member. Its offices are in the Commerce Title Building. Mr. Allen has practiced continuously in his city since July, 1948. He is a member of the Memphis and Shelby County Bar Association, the Tennessee Bar Association and the American Bar Association.

One of his major organizational interests is the Princeton Alumni Association of Memphis. He was its secretary from 1956 to 1958, and served as its president for two years from 1958 to 1960. From 1955 to 1958 he was chairman of its schools and scholarships committee, and has been graduate council representative since 1956. He is also active in the Lions Club of Memphis, in which he has held office as president, vice president and secretary. He is a member of the University Club.

Formerly a communicant of the Calvary Episcopal Church, Mr. Allen served as vestryman while there. He is now a member of the Church of the Holy Communion, also an Episcopal congregation, and served on its vestry from 1957 through 1959 and was secretary during the year 1959.

At Rosedale, Mississippi, on October 4, 1947, Newton Perkins Allen married Malinda Lobdell Nobles of that city. She is a daughter of the late Dr. Eugene Rodman Nobles and Lilian Hardeman (Lobdell) Nobles, and a descendant of Simon Lobdell, an early settler in Massachusetts. Her father, a native of Flora, Mississippi, was a physician and surgeon, a member of the American College of Surgeons, the American Medical Association and the Mississippi Medical Society, and chairman of the Mississippi Chapter of the American Cancer Society. Miss Lobdell, whom he married, was born at Rosedale, Mississippi.

Mr. and Mrs. Allen are the parents of three children: 1. John Lobdell Allen, who was born on September 17, 1952. 2. Malinda Nobles Allen, who was born on December 27, 1953. 3. Newton Perkins Allen, Jr., who was born on April 5, 1960.

RICHARD HENRY ALLEN

Member of the firm of Armstrong, McCadden, Allen, Braden & Goodman, Richard Henry Allen has been practicing in Memphis since he completed his professional training. He is a veteran of wartime service in the Army Air Corps, and takes an interested part in the activities of a number of local organizations.

A native of Memphis, he was born on October 28, 1924, son of James

Seddon and Sarah (Perkins) Allen. His father, too, follows the profession of the law, and he is a veteran of World War I, during which he served in the United States Cavalry.

Richard H. Allen attended local public schools, including Central High School, but after completing one scholastic high school year at Central, he transferred from there to complete his preparatory studies at Webb School in Bell Buckle, Tennessee.

In 1943, at the age of eighteen, he entered the United States Army Air Corps as a cadet. He became a commissioned officer (navigator) in June, 1945 and was separated from the Air Corps Service in 1945.

Following his active military service, which lasted for an approximate two-year period, he then resumed his scholastic education, entering the University of Florida. There he attained his degree of Bachelor of Science in Business Administration, graduating in 1947. For his professional training, he entered the University of Florida Law School, and acquired his Bachelor of Laws degree in 1949. While in Law School, he held the position of Editor-in-Chief of the University of Florida Law Review.

Returning to his native city of Memphis to commence practice, he became associated with the firm of Armstrong, McCadden, Allen, Braden & Goodman, which has its offices in the Commerce Title Building, and in 1952 he became a partner in the same firm.

As a lawyer, Mr. Allen is a member of the following bar associations: American Bar Association; Tennessee State Bar Association; and the Memphis and Shelby County Bar Association, with which latter organization he has been a director and has held the office of secretary during the years 1958-1960. He is a past president of the Memphis and Shelby County Junior Bar Association. During the years 1958-1960 he was a member of the executive council of the ABA Junior Bar Conference, representing attorneys in the 6th Circuit, which is comprised of the states of Tennessee, Kentucky, Ohio and Michigan.

He is a member of Phi Delta Phi legal fraternity and Sigma Alpha Epsilon social fraternity. He is also a member of the University Club, the Saddle and Spur Club and the Rivermont Club in his home city, and he is a communicant of Holy Communion Episcopal Church. Mr. Allen holds a license to practice law in the States of Tennessee and Florida, and is also qualified to practice law before the Supreme Court of the United States of America and the United States Court of Military Appeals.

He presently holds the rank of Captain in the Judge Advocate General's Department of the Army Air Force Reserve.

In his home city of Memphis on June 14, 1945, Richard H. Allen married Minnielee Gordon, daughter of William Bradshaw Gordon and Ann (Bridger) Gordon. Mr. and Mrs. Allen are the parents of two children: 1. Richard Henry, Jr., born on May 5, 1947. 2. Sarah Ann, born November 26, 1951.

Bury B. Brooks

AUBREY BUREN TURNER WRIGHT

Aubrey Buren Turner Wright was born January 11, 1890, the son of William James (1846-1911) and Emma M. (Turner) Wright (1858-1893). Their parents were: Robert and Leticia (Briggs) Wright; and John Thompson and Susan (Box) Turner.

He entered military service in 1915. As a career soldier, he served from private to first sergeant, and was commissioned August 26, 1918. In World War I, he served with the 35th Division in France. After World War I, in 1919, he was assigned with ROTC units as Military Instructor and, in this capacity, served until retirement in 1945. He was promoted to his former commissioned rank on retirement.

He married Patty Smith, December 22, 1919. She was born August 30, 1890, to William Jeff (1858-1944) and Ophelia (Dial) Smith (1857-1900). Her grandparents were: William B. and Elizabeth (Brown) Smith; and Robert Findley and Mary (Russ) Dial. Of this union, the Wrights have a son, William Jeff, born October 17, 1920; and a daughter, Alice Buren, born March 11, 1926. In education, Aubrey B. attended Branham & Hughes Academy; Patty is a graduate of Tennessee College for Women. Both are Presbyterians; and both are law graduates of Cumberland University.

William Jeff Wright, a graduate of Columbia Military Academy, also attended Louisiana State University. Commissioned through ROTC, he served thirty-two months with General Headquarters Pacific Theater in World War II. On December 1, 1947, he was given a regular commission in the United States Air Force. Lieutenant Colonel Wright is a graduate of the Armed Forces Staff College, and is presently assigned to Headquarters United States Air Force, Washington, D.C. In 1952 he married Margie Lou Parker. They have a son, Parker Smith Wright, born April 6, 1954. Margie is a graduate of the University of Oklahoma. By a former marriage, Colonel Wright has a daughter, Sharon Leigh, born January 12, 1946.

Alice Buren Wright has a daughter, Patty Grace (Hartley), born March 25, 1945, by a previous marriage. In 1955 Alice married Lieutenant Colonel Reuben Clark Algood, United States Army. Colonel Algood adopted Patty Grace. Their other daughter, Rebecca Clark Algood, was born September 1, 1957. Colonel Algood is a graduate of Mississippi State; Alice of St. Agnes Academy, Memphis. They are Presbyterians. Colonel Algood served in the Pacific Theater throughout World War II; and since in Alaska, Korea, Japan, and the States. He is on present assignment with Headquarters NATO, Ankara, Turkey.

BERRY BOSWELL BROOKS

One of Memphis' leaders in the cotton industry, Berry Boswell Brooks is also one of the city's most versatile, and internationally known men, with a wide reputation as a cotton merchant, planter, civic leader, world traveler and explorer, naturalist, big game hunter and lecturer. He is without peer among African big-game hunters, and has won honors which have reflected credit on his city and the South.

A native of Senatobia, Mississippi, he was born on February 2, 1902, the second son of Berry Boswell, Sr., and Lena Jane (Salmon) Brooks. His paternal grandparents were the Reverend Joseph Howard and Caroline Anne (Berry) Brooks, his grandfather being a Methodist minister. The elder Berry B. Brooks was a Delta cotton planter, and it was from him, and his brother Hope, that the younger Berry B. Brooks developed his fondness for hunting and fishing. From their Delta plantation, the family moved to Memphis in 1912. There the boy became one of the early members of the Boy Scouts of America, and a First-Class Scout; a member of the Children of the American Revolution, member of the Children of the Confederacy, and drummer for Company A of the Memphis Confederate Veterans of America. He once drummed before President Wilson at the Confederate reunion in Washington, D.C.

Mr. Brooks graduated from Central High School in Memphis in 1920 and attended Washington and Lee University in Lexington, Virginia. As an undergraduate, he was grand procurator of Kappa Sigma fraternity.

On September 8, 1922, he entered the cotton business at a salary of twenty-five dollars per month. He advanced to positions of increasing responsibility over the years which followed, and in 1936 established his own organization, the Berry B. Brooks Cotton Company. This has become one of the most favorably known cotton firms in the South. Mr. Brooks served three terms as director of the Memphis Cotton Exchange. Following his terms as director he was elected first vice president of the Memphis Cotton Exchange, founded in 1873, and automatically assumed the presidency in 1960. This is the culmination of thirty-eight years of service on Front Street in Memphis, the largest cotton market in the world. He has extensive farming interests in Arkansas' Delta lands, and maintains a big operation of registered breeding stock Aberdeen Angus cattle at the Berrybrooks Angus Farm.

Mr. Brooks has been called the dean of the African big-game hunters, and has collected more species of African game than any other American. He led the Berry B. Brooks African Big Game Hunting and Photographic Expeditions in 1947 and 1949. His wife was safari scribe on both expeditions which they made, when they penetrated the tsetse-fly infested country, exploring territory never before reached by white man. Mr. Brooks has thrilled audiences of tens of thousands with the narration of his superb African natural color movies, "Passport to Safari Land," "Africana," and "Back of Beyond." Through his illustrated lectures, he has been the instrument for raising vast sums of money in behalf of charity, for sportsmen's associations, philanthropic organizations, educational and cultural groups. He has made notable appearances before the National Geographic Society in Washington, D.C., in New York, Chicago, Hawaii and throughout the United States.

Mr. Brooks' safari diary, "Back of Beyond," was serialized by Outdoor Life magazine in the months of August, September, October and December, 1951, under the title "Dream Hunt." He served as national president of the Shikar-Safari Club from 1954 to 1956, and holds memberships in the Explorers Club of New York, the Adventurers Club of Chicago and Honolulu, the Camp Fire Club of New York, the Camp Fire Club of Chicago, and the East African Professional Hunters Association of Nairobi, Kenya Colony. He is a life member of the Kenya Wild Life Society, an honorary member of Kiwanis International, member of the West Tennessee Sportsmen's Association, and a director of the Wolf River Watershed Association, the Shelby County Livestock Improvement Association, and the Toothpick Club. He was recently admitted to membership in the Boone and Crockett Club of New York City, founded by Theodore Roosevelt, with membership limited to one hundred members. Mr. Brooks is president of the Tri-State Aberdeen-Angus Cattle Association, member of the Travelers Aid Society, the Buffalo Hunters of America, "Lintheads, Incorporated," charter member of the Rivermont Club, member of the English-Speaking Union, the Tennessee Chapter of the National Society, Sons of the American Revolution, Arkansas Traveler of the State of Arkansas, 1960, member of National Rifle Association of America; Sportsman's Club of America, International, Official Scorer for the Boone and Crockett Club, Official Measurer for Rowland Ward, London, the Crown and Sceptre, Top Hatters, Bumper's Club, Rebounders, Memphi, and the Royal Club of the Memphis Cotton Carnival. He is also vice president of the Memphis Cotton Carnival Association and was chairman of the Hospitality Committee, 1958. As president of the Memphis Cotton Exchange he presented the Maid of Cotton and Cotton Princess to the 1960 Royal Court of the Memphis Cotton Carnival. King Berry of the House of Brooks was King Cotton XXIII of 1957. He reigned in 1957 as king of that year's Cotton Carnival, and set a precedent in carrying out his duties without smoking or drinking alcoholic beverages.

The executive and explorer is a member of the Free and Accepted Masons, higher bodies of the Scottish Rite and Shrine, the Royal Order of Jesters, Memphis Cotton Exchange and of the Memphis Country Club. He is a communicant of St. John's Methodist Church. In World War II, he offered his services, and entered the United States Coast Guard Reserve, being assigned to Port Security as a seaman, first class.

Mr. Brooks is an earnest Bible student, a man of temperate habits and a nonsmoker. Epping Forest Manor, his country estate, is a fitting background for the part the Berry Brooks triumvirate play in social life. They are distinguished hosts, whose guests book lists over sixteen thousand signatures of visitors who have enjoyed their hospitality since 1948. The city of Memphis has honored the three with two receptions at the Memphis Museum of Natural History, and once presented them with a golden plaque. The Memphis Cotton

Exchange has honored them with a testimonial dinner, at which they were given an engraved silver tray.

It was on April 27, 1929, that Berry Boswell Brooks married Virginia Feild Walton of Blytheville, Arkansas, who is the subject of a separate sketch. Their only child, Virginia Walton Brooks, was born June 4, 1933, and on June 29, 1957, became the wife of Allen Martin of Katonah, New York. They have one child, Ann Feild Martin, born in Mount Kisco, New York, April 1, 1959. Mrs. Martin has shared the fame of her illustrious parents, accompanying them on both of the Brooks expeditions, in 1947 and 1959. At the age of fourteen, she became the youngest person in the world to bag an elephant when she assisted her father in collecting seventy-two specimens for the Berry B. Brooks African Hall and Wing of the Memphis Museum of Natural History, containing one hundred and fifty-five trophies of record African game, which her parents donated to the city of Memphis.

Mr. Brooks has hunted the North American continent from Mexico to Canada and Alaska, plus his two African safaris. His hunting objective was to perpetuate record game for the enlightenment, study, and enjoyment of posterity. The Boone and Crockett Club of New York City awarded him a medal for his COUES Deer for 1957 competition and a medal for his Alaska-Yukon Moose in 1960. He has been presented with gold keys to the cities of Memphis and New Orleans. In September, 1958, Mr. Brooks returned to the forty-ninth State, Alaska, for a big game hunt in the Wood River section for record trophies of moose, caribou, and DALL sheep. He again traveled northward in 1959, this time for a successful big game hunt in British Columbia. He is a Gentleman Adventurer, a robust outdoor man of stamina and courage.

Berry Boswell Brooks is listed in the 1950 edition of International Who's Who—And What among Authorities, Experts, and the Specially Informed, 1949-1954, and he is also listed in the eleventh International Edition, 1959, of Who's Who in Commerce and Industry. His family lineage is recorded in "Historical Southern Families" volume 1, by John B. Boddie. He is a biographee in "Who's Who in the South and Southwest," 1956-1958. The greatest honor to be bestowed upon Berry Brooks occurred December 5, 1959 in Washington, D.C., when General James H. Doolittle presented him with the Weatherby Big Game Trophy for 1959 as international sportsman "for his outstanding sportsmanship and great achievements in the hunting fields of the world." Berry Brooks has become a living legend within his own life span.

MRS. BERRY BOSWELL BROOKS

As a community, social and organizational leader, world traveler and explorer of wide reputation, a historian and genealogist, Mrs. Berry Boswell Brooks is acclaimed as the gracious hostess of Epping Forest Manor. Born

Virginia Feild Walton Brooks

Virginia Feild Walton, at Jonesboro, Arkansas, on August 6, 1904, she is the daughter of Allan Walton and Virginia Warren (Feild) Walton. Her father was a leader in civic and business affairs in Mississippi County, Arkansas, until his death in 1919; and her mother married, as her second husband, Henry Clay Knappenberger of Blytheville, Arkansas. Mrs. Brooks is the granddaughter of Henry Allison and Virginia Warren (Capps) Feild, the latter a daughter of Benjamin Henry and Virginia Frances (Butt) Capps of Norfolk, Virginia, and Memphis Tennessee. Mrs. Brooks' paternal grandparents were the late Frederick Bates Walton, namesake of his grandfather, the second governor of Missouri, and his wife, the former Louisa Conway of St. Louis, Missouri. Six generations of Mrs. Brooks' distaff ancestry have lived in Memphis since 1843. Her earliest Virginia forebear to pioneer in Tennessee was Major Joel Dyer, who settled on the Holston River in the Western Territory in 1792, in what is now Hawkins County. There he played host to the Duke of Orleans when he and his brothers were political exiles, following the French Revolution—probably the first Tennessean to entertain King Louis Philippe.

Mrs. Brooks is a graduate of Blytheville High School, and attended Lindenwood College, St. Charles, Missouri. Her family moved from her native Jonesboro to Blytheville, Arkansas, in 1907. There she was married on April 27, 1929, to Berry Boswell Brooks, Jr., of whom a separate biographical sketch accompanies. Their only child, Virginia Walton Brooks, was born June 4, 1933, and is the wife of Allen Martin of Katonah, New York. They have one child, Ann Feild Martin, born April 1, 1959. Mrs. Martin had a unique record as teenage explorer when she accompanied her parents to Africa in 1947.

Mrs. Brooks, too, accompanied her husband on this expedition, and at that time, and again in 1949, acted as safari scribe, foreign correspondent, and public relations director. They succeeded in collecting some unduplicated specimens for the Berry B. Brooks African Hall and Wing of the Memphis Museum of Natural History. Mrs. Brooks herself did the research, identification and classification of the trophies.

Possessing a daring and adventurous spirit, courage and stamina, Mrs. Brooks has led an active and colorful life. As early as 1919, she took her first airplane flight, and she has since flown in all parts of the world. In 1956, she and her daughter took a four-month flight around the world, visiting twenty-seven countries on three continents. Over the years, Mrs. Brooks has visited seventy-eight foreign lands and fifty states. In August and September, 1958, Mrs. Brooks made a seven weeks solo emplanement to fourteen European capitals, with twenty-one adventurous days behind the Iron Curtain, visiting in Leningrad, Moscow, Kiev, and Odessa in the Soviet Union, with excursions to Warsaw and Prague and East Berlin. In the summer of 1959, she again visited Eastern Europe, Asia Minor and the Middle East and was back of the Iron Curtain again, this time in Yugoslavia, Rumania and Bulgaria. As a member of the Hellenic Travelers Club of London, she made an archaeological seminar cruise in the Aegean Sea. In 1960 she attended the Passion Play in Aberammergau, Bavaria.

She is an influential member of no fewer than fifty-eight organizations. She is a charter member of the Shikar-Safari Club, having served as vice president of the Southwestern States, the first lady member to hold office. She was succeeded by her daughter Virginia in 1956. She has promoted the pursuit of genealogy in Memphis. As founder, organizing president and honorary life president of the Memphis Genealogical Society, 1960-1962 Adviser to the President, she shares her own extensive genealogical library with this organization. She is founder and organizing president of the Colonel Richard Lee Chapter of Tennessee, and Honorary National President General, for Life, The National Society, Children of the American Colonists; past first vice president general of the National Society of Dames of the Court of Honor, honorary national trustee for life, founder and organizing president of the Tennessee Society; 1960 President of the State President's Club; former second vice president of the Tennessee Society, United States Daughters of 1812; founder and organizing president of the Star Spangled Banner Chapter of Memphis; past Tennessee president of the National Society of Daughters of Founders and Patriots of America; past national historian, for three terms, of the Huguenot Society of the Founders of Manakin in the Colony of Virginia, honorary president for life, and past historian of the Tennessee Society; founder, organizing president, and honoary president for life of the Captain Nicolas Martiau Chapter of Memphis; past second vice president and curator of the Tennessee Women's Press and Author's Club; ex-president of the Tennessee and Memphis Branches of the National League of American Pen Women; former second vice regent for Tennessee, National Society of Daughters of the American Colonists; founder and organizing president of the Jamestown Chapter of Memphis, Tennessee; past regent and historian of the Fort Assumption Chapter, National Society of Daughters of the American Revolution, past Tennessee chairman of Pioneer Preachers of Tennessee, Tennessee Chairman of Radio and Television, member of D.A.R. Tennessee Belles; Virginia state organizing historian of the National Society of Colonial Dames of the Seventeenth Century; charter member of the Association for the Preservation of Tennessee Antiquities; member of the Virginia and Tennessee Societies of Daughters of Colonial Wars; ex-secretary of the Memphis Society of the Archeological Institute of America; life member of the National Society of the Daughters of the Barons and Runnemede with Orders of Distinction, Knight of the Garter, Knight of the Bath, and Lady of the Garter; Descendants of Lords of Maryland Manors, the Order of Washington, vice sovereign of Colonial Order of the Crown, organizing second vice president, National Order of the Mexican War and past first vice president National Order of the Mexican War, Magna Charta Dames, Americans of

Armorial Ancestry, Americans of Royal Descent, Order of the First Crusade; associate member, The American Museum of Natural History; Sportsman's Club of America, International; West Tennessee Sportsman's Association; House and Garden Club, Society of Descendants of Knights of the Garter, Order of the Plantagenet Society, Colonial Daughters of the Seventeenth Century (organizing member of its Pennsylvania chapter), Order of Descendants of Colonial Governors, United Daughters of the Confederacy, Louisiana Colonials, Huguenot Society of South Carolina, Huguenot Society of Washington, D.C., and member of the Southern Historical Association and the state historical societies of Virginia, Kentucky, Missouri, Arkansas, Tennessee, Alabama, and the Filson Historical Society. Mrs. Brooks is founder of the Tennessee Company of the Jamestowne Society, and first Deputy Governor; member of the Second Church of Christ, Scientist, in Memphis, Tennessee, and of the First Church of Christ, Scientist, in Boston, Massachusetts, member of the Christian Science Association of the pupils of Mrs. Elisabeth Carroll Scott, C.S.B., and is a life long Democrat; member, Memphis Democratic Promotion Club; Tennessee Federation for Constitutional Government; founder and vice president of the Epping Forest Manor Fine Arts Club, and is a member of the National Geographic Society, National Travel Club, Young Women's Christian Association, Memphis Glass Collectors Society, Travelers Aid Society; founder of the "Go-Places-Instead" Club; Memphis Museum Society, Forefathers' Club and English-Speaking Union and "The Royal and Ancient Order of Dinosaur Coprolites." Mrs. Brooks is a patron of the Brooks Art Gallery, and a charter member of the Poetry Society of Tennessee. She was chosen for the designation of Arkansas Traveler by Governor Orval E. Faubus, and was presented a golden key to the city of Memphis by the late Mayor Frank T. Tobey. It was she who composed the City of Memphis marker, erected at the seven major highway entrances to the city. In 1953, she was chosen as one of two outstanding women in America on whom was conferred honorary membership in Kappa Delta sorority. She is a member of the Royal Club of the Memphis Cotton Carnival Association, and served as royal duchess of the Mystic Society of Memphi Court in 1953. She was The Forgotten Woman of 1957 when Mr. Brooks was King of the Memphis Cotton Carnival. She was a member of the Les Miserables Club. She is an avid collector of objet d'art. Mrs. Brooks neither smokes nor drinks alcoholic beverages and has never served them in her home. This renowned hostess has shared her Southern hospitality and collections of world treasures with thousands of friends who visit the Berry Brooks' celebrated country estate, Epping Forest Manor. She has a penchant for chic chapeaux, a Peacock fancier and a devotee of Biblical archaeology.

Mrs. Brooks is the author of the following books: "Laps I've Sat In: Diary of a Pomeranian Puppy" (1933); "Smiling Our Way Thru' Europe" (1937); "Little Mike of Mexico" (1940); "The Musical Album" (1944);

"Screed of Safari Scribe" (1947); "Spate of Safari Scribe" (1949); "The Epoch of Epping Forest Manor" (1950); "The Twentieth Century Youthful Adventurous Huguenot Heroine, Virginia Walton Brooks" (1952); "Virginiana," a family genealogy, (1955); "Splendrous Oriental Flight," a photographic essay of a globe-girdling flight, (1956); "Monograph of Berry Boswell Brooks" (1957). In addition, she has made genealogical contributions to the following publications: Magna Charta, Parts IV and VI; "Lost Links" by Francis and Moore; "Some Maryland Baxters and Their Descendants" by Humphreys; and has prepared twelve Bible records for the Tennessee Daughters of the American Revolution Bible Records Collections. She has also contributed to the following publications: "The Opie Family of Northumberland County, Virginia" by Reverend Opie Lindsay Duvall; "Couper Family Charts" by Colonel William Couper. She also has a record as a journalist. She was foreign observer for the "Cotton Trade Journal" in 1947 and 1949, and was foreign correspondent with the Memphis "Commercial Appeal" in 1949. In 1947, she was foreign correspondent for the Blytheville, Arkansas, "Courier News." She scooped the world on her story of the St. Peter's Basilica Excavations in Rome, date line, May 8, 1947. Her ancestral record is included in many reference works.

Mrs. Brooks' royal lineage is given under "Le Sang Royal" of Annuaire De La Noblesse De France Et D'Europe" volume 88, and in "World Nobility and Peerage" volume 87, 1955, listed under "Distinguished American Families of Established Lineage." She is a biographee in Who's Who of American Women, First Edition; "Living Descendants of Blood Royal" (1960). Listed in the Virginia Social Index, 1607-1957.

Mrs. Brooks' bipolarity of interests has carried her far afield as genealogist, international traveler, antiquarian, Bibliophile, collector of art, diurnal diarist, Egyptologist, gifted letter-writter, home executive and renowned hostess.

EVERETT HOPE BROOKS

For over two decades, Everett Hope Brooks has played a large part in Memphis' important industry, the cotton business. His position is that of office manager of the Berry Brooks Cotton Company. He once served in the Arkansas House of Representatives, and he has taken a lively interest in the organizational affairs of his present home city.

Born at Senatobia, in Tate County, Mississippi, on October 16, 1899, he is a son of Berry Boswell and Lena Jane (Salmon) Brooks. His father, who was born July 21, 1860, at Independence, in Tate County, Mississippi, was at one time sheriff of that county. He later came to the Memphis area, where he became a prominent citizen. He died December 16, 1954, at Brickeys, Arkansas. Lena Jane Salmon, whom he married, was born at Senatobia on January 30, 1871, and died July 5, 1954, in Memphis.

Everett Hope Brooks graduated from Gulf Coast Military Academy at

Gulf Coast, Mississippi, and during 1919-1920, attended the University of Virginia. From 1921 to 1925 he was associated with his father in operating the plantation, "Park Place," at Brickeys, in Lee County, Arkansas. While there, he was elected to represent that county in the Arkansas State Legislature for two terms, beginning in 1925 and 1927. Retiring from public life in 1928, he once again devoted his attention to farm operation, and to a cotton and mercantile business at Brickeys.

In 1938 Mr. Brooks moved with his family to Memphis, and there joined his brother, Berry B. Brooks, in the cotton business. He is still with the same organization, the Berry Brooks Cotton Company, in the capacity of office manager. He retains agricultural holdings and interests in eastern Arkansas and is a member of St. Johns Methodist Church.

He is a member and past president of the Walnut Grove Community Club, and a member of the Western Tennessee Sportsmen's Association, the Memphis Camellia Society and the Hughes Hunting Club. Affiliated with DeSoto Lodge of the Free and Accepted Masons, Mr. Brooks is a member of the higher bodies of the order, including Albert Pike Consistory of the Ancient and Accepted Scottish Rite at Little Rock. A hobby of Mr. Brooks is antiques. His favorite outdoor sports are hunting and fishing.

In Memphis, on January 30, 1924, Everett Hope Brooks married Evelyn Fay Halley. Born August 23, 1903, at Helena, Arkansas, she attended High School at Marianna, Arkansas, and Central Baptist College for Girls at Conway, Arkansas, where she specialized in Art and Music. She is a collector of Art and Porcelains and is a member of the Association for the Preservation of Tennessee Antiquities. Mrs. Brooks is a member of the Baptist Church. In 1933 she served as first woman calendar clerk of the state of Arkansas. Active in many church and club activities in Arkansas, upon moving to Memphis she became a member of Memphis Camellia Society and the Four Season Garden Club, being a charter member and past president of the latter. She is also past president and charter member of Memphis Genealogical Society and is now serving as director of research and a member of the board of directors and Library Committee. Mrs. Brooks is vice president of the Walnut Grove Community Club.

Mrs. Brooks is the daughter of John Snyder and Elizabeth Gertrude (Opp) Halley. Her father was born July 17, 1866, at Rodney, Mississippi, and died May 17, 1926, at Brickeys, Arkansas, while her mother, born January 2, 1875, at Helena, died March 13, 1948, also at Brickeys. The couple were married at Tunica, Mississippi, in November, 1898.

Mr. and Mrs. Brooks are the parents of the following children: 1. Everett Hope, Jr., whose biography accompanies. 2. Bettye Jane, born September 24, 1928, in Memphis. She graduated from Central High School, where she was a member of Chi Sigma sorority and for two years attended the University of Tennessee, at Knoxville where she was a charter member of Delta Gamma sorority. She later transferred to the University of Mississippi. She served in the Royal Court of Crown and Scepter. For four years she served as Arkansas Junior President of the Children of the American Revolution. On December 30, 1948, at the Bellevue Baptist Church in Memphis, she became the wife of William Shaw Bennett, son of Earl S. and Mae (Shaw) Bennett of Caruthersville, Missouri. He attended Westminster College, and graduated from Memphis State College, and served in both World War II and the Korean War, and was awarded the Silver Star. He has served on the staff of the Cotton Trade Journal, and also as police reporter and assistant night editor of the Commercial Appeal. He now heads the Commercial Appeal's Nashville bureau. He is a member of the Newspaper Guild and 30 Club. The couple have two daughters, Katherine Jane Bennett, born December 4, 1957, at Memphis; and Suzanne Brooks Bennett, born July 1, 1959, in Nashville.

Everett Hope Brooks, Jr.

Born in Memphis, the son of Everett Hope and Evelyn Fay (Holley) Brooks, Everett Hope Brooks, Jr., is active in the cotton business in Memphis.

He received his education locally, was graduated from Central High School, and attended the University of Tennessee Extension Course of Memphis and Memphis State College. A veteran of service in World War II, he was a member of the 36th Infantry Division overseas, and the recipient of the Purple Heart. He has since been engaged with increasing distinction in the enterprise that has won the family much prestige in this cotton center of Tennessee.

Robert Lewis Dobbs

Practicing law in Memphis for the past decade, Robert Lewis Dobbs is now a partner in the firm of Dobbs and Sayle, with offices in the Exchange Building. He has concentrated his attention primarily on personal injury claims and cases in criminal law; and he figured prominently in a nationally publicized court action involving the issue of school segregation, occurring in Andersonville County a few years ago.

One of his city's younger members of the bar, Mr. Dobbs was born at Raiford, Florida, on September 26, 1921, and is a son of Lester Daniel and Leila (Gordon) Dobbs. Lester D. Dobbs was for a number of years a captain at the Florida State Prison. Now retired, he makes his home at Gainesville in that state. Leila (Gordon) Dobbs is deceased. Robert L. Dobbs received his early public school education at Raiford, Florida, and graduated from the high school at Lake Butler in that state in 1940. He entered the army while in his last year there. Stationed near Lake Butler, he continued with his classes in the evening to enable him to graduate with his high school class. Continuing with his military service, he was assigned to the infantry, and during the war served in the Hawaiian Islands, elsewhere in the Pacific Theater, and in Japan. At the time of his honorable discharge in November, 1946, he held the rank of first sergeant.

Mr. Dobbs then resumed his education. Entering Cumberland University to prepare himself for a career in the law, he completed his courses there in only two years, graduating with the degree of Bachelor of Laws in 1948.

Admitted to the bar of the state of Tennessee, Mr. Dobbs began the practice of law independently on February 2, 1948. He continued in his own office until the mid-1950s, when the present firm of Dobbs and Sayle was organized, with him as its senior partner. Throughout the years of his practice, Mr. Dobbs has specialized in criminal law and personal injury suits. He is also active in the field of labor and union law.

When, in July, 1957, a trial concerning school segregation, and involving fifteen citizens of Anderson County, began at the Knoxville Federal Court, Mr. Dobbs came into prominence. The defendants were charged with violating a federal injunction growing out of the integrating of the schools of Anderson County. The federal government contended that in this type of proceedings, the defendants were not entitled to trial by jury. This contention, as well as the broad application of the injunctive procedure, was given widespread publicity, and aroused great interest in the legal profession. The attorneys general of several southern states sent representatives to participate in the trial, nineteen lawyers thus assembling to defend the accused. These nineteen selected Mr. Dobbs as chief counsel, although he was the youngest member of the defense staff. His associate throughout the trial was Governor Ross Barnett of Mississippi. The trial resulted in the conviction of six of the defendants, and nine others were exonerated. None ever served a prison term.

Mr. Dobbs is now a member of the advisory staff of Governor Barnett, an exceptional honor for one not a resident of Mississippi. He has been influential in Democratic party councils, although he has never sought elective office. As a lawyer he is a member of the Memphis and Shelby County Bar Association, the Tennessee State Bar Association, and the American Bar Association.

Affiliated with the Free and Accepted Masons, he belongs to the Blue Lodge and to the higher bodies in the Scottish Rite. Holding the Thirty-second Degree, he is a member of Al Chymia Temple, Ancient Arabic Order of Nobles of the Mystic Shrine. He and his family attend the Baptist Church in Memphis.

In a Baptist Church at Lake Butler, Florida, on June 28, 1941, Robert Lewis Dobbs married Eloise Hayes, who was at that time a resident of Lake Butler. She is a daughter of Calvin Brinkley and Annie (McCloud) Hayes. Very prominent in Parent-Teacher Association circles, she is president of the Sherwood association, and was a delegate to the state convention in 1955. Mr. and Mrs. Dobbs have two children: 1. Deirdre, who was born on August 25, 1946. She was selected by Governor Ross Barnett of Mississippi as hostess at his inauguration to office in 1960. 2. Debrough Ann, born on August 19, 1954.

Mr. Dobbs is fond of the out-of-doors, being particularly partial to the sports of hunting and water skiing.

NOAH HAMILTON GRADY

In the course of his long record of achievement and service in Chattanooga, Noah Hamilton Grady established himself as a realtor, and later made distinctive contributions to the development of the city. He was also a leader in the insurance field in southern Tennessee.

Noah Hamilton Grady was born in Hannibal, Missouri, on the day after Christmas, December 26, 1862, son of Joseph and Saredelda J. (Donley) Grady. He married in 1891, and came to Chattanooga on April 1, 1893. He liked the prospects and opportunities of the Tennessee city, despite the fact that business was then affected by the national depression of that year. He remained to become one of its loyal and useful citizens. A contemporary said of him: "Way back in 1893, Mr. Grady was a very handsome fellow, as he always has been. At that time he was about thirty-one years of age and as straight as a ramrod, smiling—a clean-cut man. There was nothing to expect of him but success."

Down the years, Mr. Grady was identified with a variety of enterprises, the longest and most noteworthy being insurance, although he once dealt extensively in real estate and was one of the developers of Lookout Mountain, where he maintained a summer home near Point Park Gate. Formerly he owned almost all of what is now Irving Place. General insurance was his principal business for over a half-century. His first connection in this field was with Glover and Grady, and with the death of Alex S. Glover, the firm became the Grady-Alexander Company, dealers in almost every type of insurance. In the launching of a number of enterprises, Mr. Grady was instrumental in the establishment of the Richmond Hosiery Mills, the Chattanooga Boiler and Tank Company, and the Standard-Coosa-Thatcher Company, and others of lesser importance. At the time of his death he was the oldest living former president of the Chattanooga Chamber of Commerce, to which in earlier days he devoted a great deal of attention and energy. In fact, he was called the "wheelhorse" of the Chamber in the period shortly after the end of the Spanish-American War, and he was head of the organization when the then new city hall was built. He worked effectively in that construction program, and officiated in the laying of the cornerstone.

Mr. Grady was one of the founders of Chattanooga—Lookout Mountain Park, forerunner of the present national park on the mountain. He was an active member of the Mountain City Club, director of the Half-Century Club, and a charter member of the Chattanooga Golf and Country Club. He was at one time chaplain of John Sevier Chapter, Sons of the American Revolution.

Noah H. Grady

On October 20, 1891, Noah Hamilton Grady married Annie Louise Veach, who was born at Adairsville, Georgia, on October 25, 1865, daughter of Colonel James Madison and Julia Ann (Echols) Veach. Her mother was born on August 16, 1836, and died January 4, 1923. Colonel Veach was born on August 14, 1823, and died February 7, 1897. Mr. and Mrs. Grady were the parents of two children: 1. Henry Veach, who was born in Nevada, Missouri, on August 11, 1892, and died in 1918. He married, at Carters, Georgia, in November, 1914, Rebecca LaMar Divine, and they were the parents of two sons: i. Henry Veach, Jr., who married Catharine Collett Smallwood on June 19, 1937. They have four daughters: a. Collett Ann, born August 9, 1938. b. Carta LaMar, born January 19, 1943. c. Cathy, born January 18, 1946. d. Christie, born in December, 1952. ii. Sam Carter, who married, in November, 1939, Evelyn Carroll of Knoxville, Tennessee, and has one daughter, Virginia Louise Grady, born September 22, 1941. 2. Annie Virginia, born in Chattanooga, April 12, 1894. Mrs. Grady passed away on October 21, 1938.

Mr. Grady's death occurred on April 4, 1948, in Chattanooga. Tributes were paid to his business accomplishments, high character, sound citizenship, and generous personality, and among these tributes were the following lines appearing in the editorial columns of a local paper:

In the passing of Noah Hamilton Grady last Sunday morning "The Herald" lost one of its oldest and closest friends. Ever since the day this paper was first issued he has been one of its most constant readers and staunchest supporters.

Mr. Grady was one of the real builders of Chattanooga. He assisted in the establishment of a number of local enterprises of importance . . . At the time of his death he was the oldest living past president of the Chamber of Commerce, an organization to which in his younger years he devoted a lot of his time and energy.

Although eighty-five years of age he never ceased to take a lively interest in public affairs and to keep abreast of the times. He was never one to sit in the chimney corner and dream dreams. Mr. Grady was an amateur artist and spent a lot of leisure time in drawing and painting. The walls of his den at his old Lookout Mountain home were decorated with murals painted by himself.

He was a man of varied interests and talents, whose full resources were placed at the disposal of his community for its betterment.

THEODORE HADLEY MILLER

Deputy county court clerk of Campbell County in Tennessee, and a leading member of the community of Jacksboro, Tennessee, Mr. Miller was born in La Follette, on August 27, 1915, the son of Arron Hobart Miller and of Mae (Roach) Miller. His parents are farmers in the region.

Mr. Miller was educated in the La Follette grade schools and graduated from La Follette High School. He has been active in local politics and now holds the post of deputy county court clerk of Campbell County. A member of the Masonic Lodge, he also holds membership in the Round Table Club. He attends religious services as a member of the Baptist Church.

JOHN ARCH SHULTS, D.D.S.

As a dentist, Dr. John Arch Shults has practiced at Dandridge, Tennessee, since the beginning of his professional career. He completed his training following wartime service in the United States Navy, in the course of which he was in combat areas. He is active in veterans' and professional groups, and in community life generally.

Born February 21, 1924, at Sevierville, Tennessee, he is a son of Arch and Susan Ethel (Evans) Shults. His father was a farmer. Receiving his early education in his native town, Dr. Shults completed his secondary courses at Pittman Center High School, then attended East Tennessee State College in Johnson City. He transferred from there to the University of Tennessee at Knoxville, and following his wartime naval service, completed his professional courses at the university's College of Dentistry in Memphis.

Upon entering the United States Navy, he was assigned to a destroyer, participating in the North African and Sicily invasions, the Anzio Beachhead, and the invasion of southern France. He received his honorable discharge at the conclusion of hostilities and then resumed his studies, receiving his degree in dentistry. He then opened offices for general practice at Dandridge, where he has been since.

He serves on his county's board of health commissioners, and is a member of Delta Sigma Delta dental fraternity. As a veteran of World War II, Dr. Shults holds membership in the local posts of the Veterans of Foreign Wars and the American Legion. He is a communicant of the First Methodist Church at Dandridge.

At Fayetteville, Georgia, on March 16, 1946, Dr. John A. Shults married Pauline Newman, daughter of Nelson and Dolly (Pryor) Newman. The couple are the parents of three children: 1. Joseph Martin, born October 15, 1950. 2. Johnny Rhea, born October 3, 1952. 3. James Lynn, born January 12, 1957.

HOWARD B. GAYLOR

Chief of police of La Follette, and by virtue of his office one of the leading figures in the political and civic life of the community, Mr. Gaylor has been active in local organizations and is a member of Kiwanis International.

He was born in La Follette, the son of Eli Gaylor and of Mary (Trammel) Gaylor. He attended the schools in East La Follette, and during World War II, served with the Military Police attached to the Sixth Armored Division. He was stationed in the European Theater of Operations from 1943 to 1946.

Mr. Gaylor is a member of the Masonic order and attends religious services as a member of the Baptist Church.

He was married in La Follette in March, 1941, to Della Perkins, the daughter of Walter Perkins and of Mamie (Ivey) Perkins.

THOMAS LEE ROBINSON

Thomas L. Robinson was born in Memphis on June 11, 1906, the son of Thomas and Mabel Hurt Robinson. His father held various posts with the Memphis city government for eighteen years and prior to that had been in the cigar manufacturing line, in addition to farming operations.

Thomas Lee Robinson attended the Gordon Grammar School in Memphis and graduated from the Christian Brothers College in 1926, having worked for his father before graduation, for one year. He studied law at the Memphis Law School in 1927-1928. He received his law degree from Cumberland University College of Law in 1929 and entered the law firm of Poston and Polk, moving on to the firm of Brode and Cohen in 1932. In 1934, he formed his own law firm, still operating under the name of Robinson and Robinson. He is a member of the American Bar Association, the Bar Association of Tennessee and the Memphis and Shelby County Bar Association. In college, he joined the Sigma Alpha Epsilon fraternity and, after law school, the Law Fraternity of Delta Theta Phi. He is a member of the Knights of Columbus, a former Esteemed Leading Knight of the Benevolent and Protective Order of Elks, vice president of the Junior Chamber of Commerce in 1932, and a director of the Mid-South Fair during 1933, 1934 and 1935. He was president of the Alumni Association of the Christian Brothers College for three years. He and his family are members of the Colonial Country Club of which he was a director and attorney in 1950 and 1951. He is a member of the Irish Society, the Tennessee and the Lady Luck Clubs, all in Memphis. Mr. Robinson and his family are Catholic in religious faith, attending The Little Flower Church.

Thomas Lee Robinson married Linda Dunlap, daughter of James Lafayette and Margaret Red Dunlap, on October 24, 1929 in Memphis. The Robinsons have two daughters: 1. Peggy Lee (Robinson) Gerber, born July 13, 1931. 2. Patricia Claire (Robinson) Sneed, born February 11, 1933.

HENRY T. FROST

Born in Clarksville on May 15, 1927, Henry T. Frost is the son of the late Henry Frost and Stella (Jackson) Frost. The elder Mr. Frost was a blacksmith and machinist throughout his life. Born in Montgomery County in 1882, Mr. Frost was in turn the son of Henry Frost of Montgomery County; our subject's father died at Clarksville in November, 1947. His wife, Stella (Jackson) Frost, born in Montgomery County in 1901, the daughter of William Jackson of Montgomery County, now makes her home in Clarksville. The Frost and Jackson families are among the early families who settled in Montgomery County and have always been closely connected with community affairs.

Henry T. Frost received his education in the public schools of Clarksville and attended Tennessee Polytechnic in Cookeville from which he graduated in 1952. He entered the army upon graduation and served for four-and-a-half years with sixteen months spent in Korea. He had previously trained at the University of Idaho at Moscow with the Reserve Officers Training Corps for one year. Upon his discharge from service, he returned to Cookeville where he opened the Mozars Restaurant with a partner. He continues in this business to the present time. Mr. Frost is a member of the Junior Chamber of Commerce and the Cookeville Country Club. He is a communicant of the Episcopal Church.

REVEREND LEO CHARLES BALDINGER

In the course of a career effectively devoted to the Catholic priesthood, the Reverend Leo Charles Baldinger has become the spiritual guide of the people of Holy Ghost Parish in Knoxville.

He is a native of Nashville, and was born on June 12, 1909, son of Otto, who is deceased, and Catherine (Corcoran) Baldinger. Receiving a parochial school education, he attended Cathedral Grammar School in his native city, and took his secondary and junior college studies at St. Bernard College, Cullman, Alabama. From there he went to St. Gregory Seminary in Cincinnati, Ohio, for the study of philosophy and concluded his professional training with a four-year curriculum in theology at St. Mary's Seminary, which is also located in Cincinnati.

Graduating there, Father Baldinger was ordained to the Roman Catholic priesthood. He came to Knoxville as pastor of Holy Ghost Roman Catholic Church and continues there as spiritual leader of his parish.

Father Baldinger is a member of the Knights of Columbus.

JOEL VINCENT BELL

In addition to his lifelong activities as a farmer, Joel Vincent Bell has business interests, and has served his home city of Springfield and his region in a number of connections. He serves on several boards.

Born on a farm near Springfield, in Robertson County, on May 11, 1897, Mr. Bell is a son of Robert Lee and Sarah Etta (Bell) Bell. His father too was a farmer. The Bell ancestors came to Tennessee from North Carolina before the Civil War. Immediately after completing his formal education at Springfield High School, Joel V. Bell turned his attention to diversified farming as an occupation. Since that time he has raised livestock and grown grain, tobacco, and field crop seed.

Over the years he has acquired a number of business interests, through

Joel V. Bell

which he has proved himself no less capable in commercial pursuits than in farm management. He has an interest in the Bell Clothing Company in Springfield, and is currently serving as vice president of the Robertson County Grain Co-op, which has an elevator located on Highway 41. He is a member of the board of directors of the Burley Stabilization Corporation, with its main office located in Knoxville. A charter member of the Tennessee Farmers Insurance Company, he formerly served on its board of directors.

He is a member of the board of the Robertson County Fair Association, and is also a member of the board of the Robertson County Livestock Association. A charter member of the Robertson County Farm Bureau, he served as its president from 1937 to 1943. From 1938 to 1948 he was on the board of directors of the Tennessee State Farm Bureau. In 1939, Mr. Bell was appointed organization chairman for securing funds for starting the Highland Rim experiment station. He carried out his duties successfully, and the experiment station has since been built, on Highway 41 near Springfield. He is also a member of the board of trustees of the Jesse Jones Hospital.

Mr. Bell is a Kiwanian, and a member of the Barren Plains Men's Club and the Barren Plains Community Club. He is affiliated with the lodge of Free and Accepted Masons. A communicant of the Springfield Baptist Church, he has served as a deacon, and is past president of the Men's Sunday school class.

In a home wedding on September 20, 1916, Joel Vincent Bell married Carline Cook of Springfield, Tennessee, daughter of George Thomas and Sarah Leota (Sprouse) Cook. The couple are the parents of two children: 1. Joel Edward, born on November 15, 1918. He married Ruby Lipscomb also of Springfield. They have two daughters: Susan Cook, born May 18, 1942 and Judith Ann, born March 14, 1945. 2. Margaret Ann, born on May 24, 1922. She is now Mrs. Burton J. Lucas. They are parents of Mary Anne, born May 30, 1944, and Lee Bell, born May 3, 1946. Mr. and Mrs. Bell reside at Belle Meade Farm near Springfield.

WILLIAM CAREY BATEMAN

Born in Norfolk, Virginia on June 9, 1908, William Carey Bateman is the son of the late Dr. Robert Johnston Bateman, Pastor of the First Baptist Church in Memphis at the time of his death in 1943, and Mae (Ford) Bateman, who makes her home in this city.

He received his early education at the Georgia Military Academy and later attended the University of North Carolina, Wake Forest College and Furman University. He studied law at Oklahoma University and received his Bachelor of Laws degree from this institution.

He established his practice in Memphis shortly after passing the bar and has practiced law in this city since. In World War II, he was a member of the Judge Advocate General staff. Since his return to civilian life, Mr. Bateman has been a member of the well-known Memphis firm of Waldaner, Bateman and Lawrence, with offices in the Commerce Title Building.

He is a Mason and a Shriner and has held high office in both organizations. He and his family are members of the First Baptist Church, the church his father served so faithfully.

On June 10, 1932, he married the former Marjorie Alma Meeker at Beggs, Oklahoma, where her parents, Arthur Augustus and Alma Louise Marian (Acken) Meeker, make their home. William and Marjorie Bateman have four children. They are: 1. William Carey Bateman, Jr., born May 6, 1938; 2. Virginia Mae Bateman, born January 19, 1940, now Mrs. Asa Lefler Stamps; 3. Robert Johnston Bateman, born May 18, 1942; and 4. Marjorie Meeker Bateman, born February 12, 1948.

John Lawson Greer

One of the business leaders in Knoxville, where he is part owner, chairman and treasurer of Brown-Greer Company, and as a director of the Sterchi Brothers Furniture Stores, and the Hamilton National Bank, John L. Greer keeps in close contact with the business life of his native city. He is also a director of the Skyland Life Insurance Company of Charlotte, North Carolina.

John L. Greer, born in Knoxville on January 4, 1898, is the son of Preston Alonzo Greer, school teacher and farmer, and Sarah Mynatt Greer.

He attended school in his native Knoxville before entering the University of Tennessee where he received the degrees of Bachelor of Arts and Bachelor of Laws in 1919. In the meantime he had served as a lieutenant in the Field Artillery during World War I. Upon receiving his law degree, John L. Greer was named treasurer of the City of Knoxville, while also serving as Recorder and Municipal Judge, from 1919 to 1923. Upon leaving public service, he became part owner and operator of the St. James Hotel in Knoxville. In 1925, he sold his interest in the hotel to become a part owner of Brown-Greer Company, of which he is now chairman and treasurer.

He is a member of Sigma Nu fraternity, the Masonic Lodge and the Shrine. He is also a past president of the Southern Bankers Association and a former member of the board of governors of the American Bankers Association. His clubs include the Cherokee Country Club and the Knoxville City Club. He is a member of the First Baptist Church in Knoxville.

Mr. Greer married the former Kathleen Russell Zemp in Knoxville, the home of her parents, Ernest Russell and Kathleen (Hurt) Zemp. Mr. and Mrs. Greer have four children: 1. Sarah Elizabeth Greer, born July 17, 1921, and now married to James Edward Vestal. 2. Mary Nell Greer, born July 30, 1922, now Mrs. William G. Brownlow, III. 3. John Lawson Greer, Jr., born March 19, 1928. 4. William Capers Greer, born November 6, 1936.

ASHER HOWARD

After varied experience in business, industry, teaching, and the wartime service of his country, Asher Howard recently assumed a responsible public post as county judge of Blount County. His court convenes at Maryville, and Mr. Howard is active in the organizational life of that city.

Born at Pathfork, Kentucky, in 1913, he is a son of Britt and America (Lee) Howard, also natives of Pathfork. He received his early education in the public schools, and went on to advanced studies at the University of Tennessee.

In 1940, Mr. Howard joined the Aluminum Company of America, working in its power department until he left for wartime service with the United States Marine Corps in 1943. He was in uniform until 1945, holding the rank of corporal.

In 1946, shortly after his return from the war, Mr. Howard became a High School coach, a position he retained until 1950. Thereafter until 1953 he worked as a salesman.

It was in 1953 that Asher Howard was named to the bench of the county court of Blount County. He has served with distinction as judge since that time.

His memberships include the Fraternal Order of Police, the Optimists, and the lodge of Free and Accepted Masons. His religious affiliation is with the Baptist Church.

In March, 1938, at Pineville, Kentucky, Asher Howard married Mildred Frances Myers, daughter of B. E. and Louise Ramsey Myers.

REVEREND THOMAS JASPER MATTINGLY

One of the widely known and highly respected clergymen of the Knoxville area is the Reverend Thomas Jasper Mattingly, who is pastor of the First Christian Church at East Fifth and Williams Streets. This is a congregation of the Disciples of Christ, in whose denominational affairs the Reverend Mr. Mattingly has long been active.

He is a native of Owensboro, Kentucky, and was born on April 11, 1909, son of Jasper F. and Mary Ella Mattingly. His father was the owner of the Kentucky Sheet Metal Works. Attending the public schools of his native city, Thomas Jasper Mattingly graduated from Owensboro Senior High School. During the years of his youth, he was a paper boy for the Owensboro Messenger Inquirer, and revealed his denominational good will by pumping the organ at Trinity Episcopal Church. Some years after he had completed his high school studies, he enrolled at Transylvania College in Lexington, Kentucky, and took his degree of Bachelor of Arts there in 1934. As an undergraduate there he helped defray the expenses of his education by waiting on tables. He went on to theological studies at The College of the Bible, and there he received his degree of Bachelor of Divinity in 1936.

He was ordained shortly afterwards into the ministry of the Disciples of

Christ. The Reverend Mr. Mattingly is now pastor of the Knoxville Church of that denomination. At the time of World War II, he was absent serving in the United States Army as a chaplain, and he retains a commission as major in the United States Army Reserve Corps.

Mr. Mattingly is a member of the Commission on Military and Veterans Affairs of the Disciples of Christ. In 1950 he received the first annual Citizenship Award conferred by the Kentucky Department of Veterans of Foreign Wars for his work with children and youth. He was delegate from Kentucky to the Midcentury White House Conference on Children and Youth.

In his home city, the Reverend Mr. Mattingly is a member of the lodge of Free and Accepted Masons and the Optimist Club.

In Detroit, Michigan, on October 21, 1937, Thomas Jasper Mattingly married Dorothy Leoene Doub, daughter of Arnold and Mary Doub. The couple make their home at 1212 Oakdale Trail, Knoxville, and they are the parents of three children: 1. Mary Gayle, born in 1939. 2. Betsy Lou, born in 1941. 3. Thomas Jasper, 2nd, born in 1948.

ALLEN McQUARY O'BRIEN

Direct representative to the Tennessee General Assembly from 1954 to 1958 and in the State Senate from 1958 to 1960, and a member of the Tennessee Civil Service Commission in 1953 and 1954, Mr. O'Brien has been active in the practice of law since 1949. He is an active Democrat in politics.

He was born in Springfield, Tennessee, on July 24, 1926, the son of Jake Allen O'Brien and of Katherine (McQuary) O'Brien. His father was an attorney who served as county attorney and he was a member of the Tennessee State Senate from 1942 to 1946. Mr. O'Brien attended the Springfield public schools and graduated from Springfield High School in 1944. He then studied at Milligan College, Milligan, Tennessee; the Central Michigan College of Education in Mount Pleasant, Michigan; and obtained the degree of Bachelor of Arts at the University of Michigan. He received the degree of Bachelor of Laws from Vanderbilt University in 1949. During World War II, he served in the United States Navy from 1944 to 1946. Mr. O'Brien attends religious services as a member of the Methodist Church.

He was married on September 6, 1947, to Ruth Helm, the daughter of James Wallace Helm and of Sammie (Stockett) Helm.

Mr. and Mrs. O'Brien have four children: 1. Michael Wallace, born on June 15, 1948. 2. Patrick Allen, born on September 6, 1949. 3. Jake Allen II, born on May 8, 1955. 4. Kevin, born April 2, 1960.

DON VICTOR WEIGAND

An engineer and designer, the late Don Victor Weigand of Memphis possessed an exceptionally creative mind, as well as managerial talents which he put to effective use as head of his own organization, Weigand Display

Don V. Weigand

and Manufacturing Company. He also rendered useful service to the government in time of war, with the design of devices required by the armed forces.

Born at Burlington, Kansas, on May 24, 1904, he was a son of Charles Francis and Stella (Barnett) Weigand. The family originated in Germany, and the name is derived from the Old High German word "Wigant," meaning hero or warrior. Its bearers, both in Europe and in this country, have been particularly distinguished in science and industrial technology, scholarship, law, and literature. Among them have been a Conrad Weigand, a German historical painter (1842-1897), Sebastian Weigand, also a German painter (1706-1824), and Wilhelm Weigand, German philologist (1803-1881). Immigrants of this name came to this country early in the Eighteenth Century, among them Johann Martin Weigand. However, it was with John Weigand (1810-1865) that Don Victor Weigand's branch of the family first came to this country. He was born in Hesse-Darmstadt, and his first American home was Zanesville, Ohio, whence he moved to Illinois in 1853. He settled on a thousand-acre farm five miles northeast of Mount Sterling, Illinois. His son, Jacob James Weigand, was born near Zanesville, and died August 8, 1911, and he was the father of Charles F. Weigand. There are ties of consanguinity between the Weigands and the Krupp family, famed ammunition manufacturers.

Attending the public schools of Burlington, Kansas, Don V. Weigand graduated from high school there, and he was later a student at the Kansas City Art School in Kansas City, Missouri. Arriving in Memphis in 1929, when he was twenty-five years of age, he immediately organized a business of his own there, the Weigand Sign and Poster Company, with headquarters at 267 Union Street. In 1935 he formed the Weigand Display and Manufacturing Company, which first had its offices at 340 Adams Street. In consequence of the growth of the business, he moved to another location at 1540 Texas Street, Memphis, in 1946. He continued as active head of his firm, at that address, until his death a decade later.

Mr. Weigand's creative efforts were not confined to the display poster and advertising field. At the time of this country's involvement in World War II, he turned his attention to the design and construction of wind tunnels, for use in testing by the United States Navy. So noteworthy were his improvements that the government sent engineers from Washington to study his designs, which were adopted generally by defense-production manufacturers. For a time during World War II, Mr. Weigand was absent serving in the Corps of Engineers of the United States Army.

In his civilian career, he proved himself a master of the techniques of designing all types of displays, which were contracted for and constructed by his company.

As diversion during his hours away from business, Mr. Weigand was fond of fishing and playing golf. He owned a cottage at Horseshoe Lake, where he repaired to engage in fishing and also hunting, over a period of about two decades. He was a Roman Catholic in religious faith, a communicant of Sacred Heart Church, although Mrs. Weigand is a member of the Methodist Church.

She is the former Miss Christine Jenkins of Pontotoc, Mississippi, daughter of Louis N. and Annie (Rackley) Jenkins. Her father was a native of Verona, Mississippi, a cattleman and cattle shipper by carload, a large landowner and planter in Mississippi. Her mother was born in Pontotoc County, that state. The Jenkins family were pioneer settlers of Pontotoc, Mississippi, from North Carolina. The family traces its ancestry back to Paul Revere through the Rivers line. Mr. and Mrs. Weigand were married in Memphis on August 21, 1948. They had no children.

The death of the inventor, designer and business leader occurred in his home city on November 19, 1956, bringing an untimely end to a creative and useful career.

DOUGLAS SPARKS

With news reporting and public relations experience dating from the early years of his career, Douglas Sparks is now editor of the "Daily News Journal," published at Murfreesboro by the Mid South Publishing Company. He has also continued his activity in the public relations field.

A native of Lewis County, Kentucky, he was born in 1913, son of John W. and Florence (Raleigh) Sparks. His father too was born in Lewis County, Kentucky, and for some years has been a building contractor, constructing homes. Douglas Sparks received his public school education in Ohio, and attended Ohio Southern University.

For several years, early in his career, he was on the staff of the International News Service, at Columbus, Ohio. Subsequently, he took a public relations position with the Marine Corporation, with which he remained for four years. There followed a stint as reporter on the staff of the Philadelphia Inquirer.

Removing to Murfreesboro, Mr. Sparks has been public relations man and editor of the Daily News Journal, Mid South Publishing Company, since 1954.

Since making his home there, he has held a number of posts of public trust. He has been director of Civil Defense, a member of the Rutherford County Safety Council, and also a member of the county's Advisory Committee on Welfare. In past years, Mr. Sparks has been an active supporter of the program of the Boy Scouts of America. He is a member of the Kiwanis Club and attends the Episcopal Church. His hobbies are photography and furniture making.

At Orangeburg, North Carolina, in January, 1953, Douglas Sparks married Sheila Vynum. Born in Georgia, she is a daughter of J. W. and Anna Vynum, and her father was a native of Blakely, Georgia. Mrs. Sparks attended schools in that state. The couple have no children.

CLYDE WASHBURN, SR.

After a quarter-century's activity as industrialist in Indiana, Clyde Washburn, Sr., came to Tennessee and entered the oil business there, having holdings in that state and in Illinois as well. Making his home in Memphis, he took a full part in that city's organizational and civic life.

Born at Hopedale, Illinois, on September 10, 1886, he was a son of George and Susan (Beaver) Washburn. His father was born in Indiana and his mother in Illinois. When Clyde Washburn was young, the family moved to Fort Scott, Kansas, and he attended public schools there. He later attended college in St. Louis, Missouri.

Beginning his career in industry, he spent more than a decade and a half with the Hassler Southeast Company, becoming its owner and president, and also represented the Hassler Shock Absorber Company in Indianapolis. He liquidated this business about 1927, and came to Tennessee, where he directed his considerable business abilities toward the petroleum industry. He had holdings in oil properties in Illinois and Tennessee for some years before his death in 1940.

In the 1920s, Mr. and Mrs. Washburn built a beautiful home at 186 East Parkway, where the First Baptist Church now stands. It was one of the showplaces of Memphis.

Mr. Washburn was a member of the Kiwanis Club, the Colonial Country Club, and the Horseshoe Club in his home city, and the Fishing and Hunting Club at Hughes, Arkansas. He was a communicant of St. Mary's Episcopal Church.

At Enid, Oklahoma, on August 16, 1908, Clyde Washburn, Sr., married Daisy Craighead. A native of Fayetteville, Arkansas, she is a daughter of Jonathan Dudley and Virginia Ann (Williams) Craighead. Mr. and Mrs. Washburn became the parents of the following children: 1. Clyde, Jr., who was born in Memphis on October 12, 1925. He attended Snowden School and Central High School. On October 20, 1957, in Memphis, he married Mary Jane McElray. 2. Allen Craig, born December 24, 1928, also in Memphis. He attended the same schools as his elder brother, and also the University of Tennessee. He transferred from there to Boston University, where he took the degree of Bachelor of Science in Aeronautical Engineering. He is now with the Glenn R. Martin Corporation at Orlando, Florida.

Mr. Washburn's death occurred on March 19, 1940.

JACK ERVIN WHITAKER

An active member of the community and a leader in civic affairs, Jack Whitaker in more than a third of a century, has given much of his time to the betterment of Chattanooga while devoting himself to his chosen career—banking.

Born March 28, 1906 in Chattanooga, he is the son of David Erwin and

Minnie (Smith) Whitaker, the father a native of Chattanooga, Tennessee, and the mother of Kennesaw, Georgia. He was educated at the McCallie School in Chattanooga and in 1923 became associated with the Hamilton National Bank, moving up through the various levels until today he serves as chairman of the board. In 1936 he was elected assistant cashier and five years later, in 1941, he was elected assistant vice president. The year 1946 saw his election to the vice presidency of the bank, in 1953 he became vice chairman of the board, and in 1958 he was chosen chairman of the board of directors of the Hamilton National Bank.

Mr. Whitaker has assumed responsibility in enough organizations to satisfy several men's civic and business ambitions. On the business side he is director of the Hamilton National Bank, the Hamilton National Associates, the Hamilton National Bank of Knoxville, Interstate Life and Accident Insurance Company, East Tennessee National Gas Company, Ross Meehan Foundries, Interstate Fire Company, Rutherford Garment Company, Calhoun Garment Company, the Clift-Smith Company Inc., and Tennessee Investors, Incorporated. His posts in civic circles include roles as director of the Chattanooga Chamber of Commerce, the United Fund-Red Cross and the Industrial Committee of One Hundred, and formerly the Citizens Taxpayers Association and the Tennessee Tax Payers Association. He is a trustee of King College, the McCallie School, Evans Foundation, Colsted Foundation, also of Forrest Hills Cemetery and Bachman Homes. His clubs include Chattanooga Golf and Country Club, Lookout Mountain-Fairyland Club and The Mountain City Club. Mr. Whitaker is an elder in the Central Presbyterian Church.

Mr. Whitaker married Elizabeth Ford in Chattanooga on December 27, 1929, daughter of C. L. and Elizabeth (McAfee) Ford; he, a native of Redhouse, Virginia, and she of Cleveland, Tennessee. They have two children: 1. Martha Ann, born on August 1, 1931, now Mrs. B. Lamar Rankin, they have two children: Bruce Lamar, Jr. and Elizabeth Lee. 2. Jack Ervin, Jr., born February 26, 1939, now a student at the University of Chattanooga.

GLAD WOODWARD

Over the past decade, Glad Woodward has been rendering conscientious and effective service as a law-enforcement officer in Anderson County. He is an officer on the police force at Oak Ridge, and is active in organizational and civic life there.

A native of Blount County, Tennessee, he was born on April 16, 1905, son of Dr. David Morgan and Mary Jane (Davis) Woodward. His father, had come to the area from Lee County, Virginia, where he was born on April 14, 1869. Miss Davis, whom he married, was born in Blount County on April 12, 1874. After attending Winona Grammar School, Glad Woodward completed his formal studies at Huntsville High School. For six years he served as a magistrate in Scott County. He then became sheriff of Anderson County, and has been a police officer at Oak Ridge for the past eleven years.

Mr. Woodward saw service for one year in the United States Army, being assigned to the 26th Infantry. He is a member of the lodges of the Free and Accepted Masons and the Fraternal Order of Eagles, and attends the Methodist Church.

At Winona, on June 22, 1933, Glad Woodward married Mae Newport, daughter of Frazier and Betty Newport. Both of her parents are natives of Scott County, where her father was born April 18, 1890, and her mother on May 3, 1894. Mr. and Mrs. Woodward have two children: 1. Carol Sue, born in Scott County on March 12, 1940. 2. Betty Jane, born there on April 10, 1942.

WILLIAM M. BARR

Descendant of one of Tennessee's pioneer families, William M. Barr was born August 12, 1900 in Memphis, the son of William Sevier and Catherine (Marmann) Barr.

He began his business career in 1923, when he entered the Sales and Advertising Department of DeSoto Paint Manufacturing Company. He later joined the Sales Department of John Lucas & Company, of Philadelphia, where he became sales manager, and where he remained until 1936. He returned to the DeSoto Paint & Varnish Company as general sales manager in 1937, and held that position until 1946, but during that period took three and a half years out to serve in the Army of the United States during World War II.

He entered the Army of the United States during the year of 1942 as a Captain, and was discharged as a Lieutenant Colonel in 1946. He served in the Active Reserve of the Army until 1953, when he retired to the inactive reserves, with the rank of Lieutenant Colonel.

In 1946, he organized his own company, W. M. Barr & Company, operating as specialists in the manufacture of paint removers, and paint specialties. Since that time, three other companies have been founded—The Klean Strip Company, King Chemical Company and Klean Strip International. These companies operate in all the states and throughout the world, and their products occupy a major position in their field. Mr. Barr is president of all four companies.

In 1948, Mr. Barr and five other local citizens formed an organization which later defeated the old Crump political machine for the first time in many years, and elected Senator Estes Kefauver to the United States Senate. Three years later, Mr. Barr became co-manager of the Shelby County Committee for Congressman Albert Gore, who defeated the aged Senator Kenneth McKellar and went to the Senate as the Junior Senator from Tennessee. Mr. Barr served one year as Shelby County Election Commissioner and has taken an active citizen's interest in politics since.

He is a member of Park Avenue Lodge of the Masonic Order in Memphis; a member of Colonial Country Club, The Army and Navy Club, and the Tennessee Club. His civic activities include directorships in the Civic Research Committee and in the Memphis Public Affairs Forum. He is a member of St. Mary's Episcopal Cathedral and active in the work of that church.

In Memphis on April 19, 1921, he married Roberta Worden, daughter of William D. and Catherine Strehl Worden. The Barrs have one child, Kathryn Worden Barr, born June 3, 1926.

ARTHUR G. MANN

It may well be that Arthur G. Mann's career in funeral directing is unique in the annals of the profession. One would certainly look far to find another veteran of seventy years' experience in mortuary practice. Turning his attention to this occupation when he was fifteen years old, he has followed it ever since, and established Mann's Mortuary in Knoxville.

He is a native of that city and was born on November 5, 1871, son of Edward Branch and Sarah (Moody) Mann, both natives of Dinwiddie County, Virginia. His father was a business man and a funeral director and with his son founded the Mann Mortuary on March 18, 1884. Edward Branch Mann was also a railroad man and during the Civil War served on the Richmond, Danville Railroad. Arthur G. Mann attended the public schools of Knoxville, and first began his experience in the field of funeral directing with his father in 1884. He has continued in the same profession ever since. During most of these years he has operated his own establishment.

Several other well-known funeral directors in the city began their careers with him. His funeral home is located in the center of town; it has a dignified and impressive appearance, and it is also completely modern in equipment and operation. The present building was built in 1925 and was the first mortuary to be built in the South.

Mr. Mann is a member of the lodge of Free and Accepted Masons and the higher order of the Scottish Rites as well as the Independent Order of Odd Fellows. He is a Rotarian, and a member of the Episcopal Church.

In his native city of Knoxville, on April 26, 1893, Arthur G. Mann married Mabelle Kane, daughter of Patrick and Emma (Wilson) Kane. The couple are the parents of the following children: 1. Edward K., born on February 12, 1894, served in the Navy in World War I. He is married to the former Georgia Rule and they have two children, Edward G. and Patricia J. 2. Hubert Y., born on May 7, 1896. He is married to the former Maida Lane. 3. Helen, born on May 8, 1898. She is the wife of George Wesley Pickle. They have a son, Arthur Harvey.

WALTER CHARLES GILBERTSON

After commencing his career in the profession of funeral directing, Walter Charles Gilbertson turned his abilities to the task of meeting a need which existed in his area for the supplying of the materials required by morticians. Following World War I, he established a successful business, the Gilbertson Funeral Supply Company, with headquarters in Memphis. He was highly regarded throughout the ranks of the profession; and retained and continued to develop to a high degree of efficiency certain skills in embalming, particularly dermosurgery, for which his services were often sought. He was active in civic and lodge affairs in his home city.

He was born there on May 5, 1883, and was a son of John Thomas and Martha Anne (Graham) Gilbertson. His father had come to this country from the Isle of Man off the English coast, and was a son of Sir John Thomas Gilbertson. Miss Graham was born in Memphis. Walter C. Gilbertson attended the public schools of that city, and the Peabody School.

At the outset of his career he chose mortuary science as his profession, and in his early years worked as funeral director for the J. W. Norris Funeral Home and the J. J. Collins Funeral Home, both in Memphis. In 1918 he entered the funeral supply business in that city, founding the Gilbertson Funeral Supply Company. For many years it had its headquarters at 833 McLemore and this address was the center of a thriving business which developed a distributorship for funeral dry goods throughout a tri-state area comprising Kentucky and Illinois as well as Tennessee. The firm also manufactured these products. Mr. Gilbertson remained at the head of his organization until two years before his death.

He was one of the first embalmers in his area to study, perfect, and apply the techniques of dermosurgery, and his proficiency in this field earned him a wide reputation among funeral directors. Even after establishing his manufacturing and distributing firm, he retained his embalmer's license, and was frequently called in for advice and active service in fatality cases in which dermosurgery was required. In these instances he would accept no remuneration. Mr. Gilbertson was a very active member of the Southern Funeral Directors Association, and at one time served as its secretary. He gave freely of his time to elevating the standards of the profession, and to promoting the dignity and the effectiveness of morticians in their respective communities.

Mr. Gilbertson was a life member of the lodge of the Free and Accepted Masons, and a member of the higher bodies of the Masonic order. He also belonged to the Benevolent and Protective Order of Elks. He was a communicant of St. John's Methodist Church. Fond of the out-of-doors, he particularly enjoyed hunting, and was fond of horses, of which he owned several.

In his home city of Memphis, on June 4, 1908, Walter Charles Gilbertson married Alberta Lipford, daughter of Albert Thaddeus and Emma Amelia (Williams) Lipford. Both of her parents were natives of Florida. Mr. and Mrs. Gilbertson became the parents of four children: 1. Alberta Bernice, who is the wife of Frank Orum Waddey. They live in Memphis and are the parents of one son, Walter Orum, who married Viola Marie Bolton. Their children are Karen Lynn and Laura Marie Waddey. 2. Wallace Cornell, who married Mary Virginia Mabry. They live in New Canaan, Connecticut, and have three children: Jon Wallace, Virginia Mabry, and Cynthia Anne. 3. John Thomas, who is a lawyer and a judge, in Knoxville. He married Rosanne Merritt, and their children are John Martin and Robert Mark Gilbertson. 4. Dr. Robert Bruce, who practices in Knoxville. He married Peggy Ruth Mayer and their children are Robert Bruce, Jr., Stephen Andrew, and Thomas Mayer Gilbertson.

A career in which he won distinction in his profession, and among his fellow citizens in all walks of life, came to a close with the death of Walter C. Gilbertson, at his home in Memphis, on December 20, 1956.

THOMAS E. WOODALL

Shortly after his return from wartime military service, Thomas E. Woodall was attracted to the profession of funeral directing, and he is now the owner of the Taylor Funeral Home at Dickson. He has already become well known in professional circles, and is active in both the state and the national morticians' groups. He has held office in the local Chamber of Commerce, and in the group which manages the county fair.

Born May 16, 1921, at White House, in Sumner County, he is a son of Walter Thomas and Clara Elizabeth (Widick) Woodall. His father was for twenty-five years a funeral director at White House. Born in 1886 near Cross Plains in Robertson County, he is now retired and lives at Dickson. He served on the school board of Sumner County for fifteen years, and was its chairman for five years. Mrs. Woodall, who died in September, 1956, at Dickson, was also a native of the Cross Plains area. Her family, the Widicks, were related to the Winfield family, prominent in Civil War history. She was active in the Methodist Church.

Attending the public schools of White House, Thomas E. Woodall took his intermediate studies at Tennessee Polytechnic Institute at Cookeville. From there he went to the University of Tennessee, where he majored in chemical engineering. He enlisted in the United States Army Air Corps in 1942, and served in the Air Transport Command until November, 1946, when he received his honorable discharge. Attaining the rank of captain, he saw action in the Pacific and also in the European Theater of Operations.

Immediately after returning from Air Corps service in 1946, Mr. Woodall entered the restaurant business at Tri-City Airport at Johnson City, and continued in this occupation for two years. Meantime, he was preparing himself for the profession in which he had determined to seek his career. He attended classes at the John A. Gupton School of Mortuary Science in Nashville, and graduated there in 1948.

Mr. Woodall then moved to Dickson, where he bought the Taylor Funeral Home in partnership with his brother. They operated the home for six years,

Henry J. Winkelmann

and at the end of that time the brother sold his interest to Thomas E. Woodall, who has since been sole owner. He is a part owner of the Union Cemetery at Dickson.

In addition to his professional memberships in the National Funeral Directors Association and the Tennessee State Funeral Directors Association, Mr. Woodall belongs to the Chamber of Commerce at Dickson, of which he is a past director. He is a member of the Dickson County Fair Association, and served as its president in 1952-1953. He is a Kiwanian and a member of the American Legion. A Methodist, he is a member of the official board of the church at Dickson. He is an independent in politics.

At Dickson, in 1953, Thomas E. Woodall married Jean Thompson Taylor. Born in that city on February 27, 1921, she is a daughter of DeWitt Talmage and Stella (Thompson) Taylor. Both of her parents were natives of Dickson County, and Mr. Taylor was a funeral director at Dickson from 1909 to 1948. He served in the army in World War I. His death occurred January 9, 1948.

Mrs. Woodall graduated from Dickson High School, and from Middle Tennessee College, where she majored in science and in biology and graduated with the degree of Bachelor of Science. In 1942 she taught school at White House, and for six years thereafter, was a member of the faculty at Dickson High School. She has served as president of the Methodist Church Guild, and was formerly Sunday school teacher there. In past years she worked in the Methodist Publishing House.

The couple are the parents of one son, Thomas Talmage, who was born in Nashville on April 27, 1955.

Henry Tanner Winkelman

As president and general manager of Tri-State Armature and Electrical Works, Inc., at Memphis, Henry Tanner Winkelman heads an organization which has installed the electrical systems for many of the major industries in the city. He has had an exceptional experience record, including connections with the Tennessee Valley Authority and General Electric Company, and performed important government work as a naval officer during World War II.

A native of Memphis, Mr. Winkelman was born at 267 South Belvedere on December 9, 1913, and is a son of Henry Tanner, Sr., and Arra Bell (Cowgill) Winkelman. His father founded the Winkelman Baking Company, a retail and wholesale bakery. He headed this organization, at 93 North Main Street, from 1894 to 1924. In the latter year he built and moved into a new plant at 1553 Madison Avenue, and sold the plant and business to Purity Baking Company in 1928. In addition to being executive head of the bakery, the elder Henry T. Winkelman was director of the Union and Planters Bank and Trust Company. In 1905 he was elected a member of the Memphis Board of Public Works. He was also a member of the Committee on Streets, Bridges and Sewers, and the Hospital Committee. He died in 1938 in Memphis, aged 78 years.

Beginning his education at Bruce Grammar School in Memphis, the younger Henry T. Winkelman completed his courses there in 1927, and graduated from Central High School in 1931. In 1936 he graduated with the degree of Bachelor of Science in Electrical Engineering from the University of Tennessee at Knoxville. He has been a registered engineer in the state of Tennessee since 1950.

Mr. Winkelman's first experience in business came in the summers of 1930 and 1931, while he was still a high-school student. He was employed by the Union Planters National Bank. On entering the College of Engineering at the University of Tennessee, he applied for the co-operative course which involved attending classes during alternate three-month periods, and gaining practical experience in engineering work in the intervening three months. On this basis, he was employed by the Tennessee Valley Authority for four years, and worked on the Norris, Wheeler, Pickwick, and Kentucky dams, and also in the Authority's engineering office in Knoxville—all in the course of various assignments of three months' duration.

On his graduation in June, 1936, he returned to Memphis, and was employed as an electrical distribution engineer by the Memphis Light, Gas and Water Division. In 1940, to further his engineering experience and education, he entered General Electric Company's famed test course, one of the nation's most productive sources of experienced engineers. He was "on test" in Schenectady, New York, where General Electric has its main plant, until 1942. In that year, the company loaned his services to Chrysler Corporation, for which he worked as engineer in charge of the construction of electrical testing facilities at its new Dodge plant in Chicago. These facilities were to be used in the manufacture and testing of aircraft engines for powering the B-29 bombers which made such an outstanding record during World War II.

Mr. Winkelman left the Chrysler plant for two years' service in the United States Navy. With a lieutenant's commission, he served in the Bureau of Ordnance, specializing in electronic gunfire control systems, and was stationed in Washington, D. C. In 1946, following the war, he returned to Memphis and rejoined General Electric Company there as a sales engineer in its Apparatus Department.

On January 1, 1953, he left General Electric to accept appointment as president and general manager of Tri-State Armature and Electrical Works, Inc., which is the largest electrical contractor and industrial electrical equipment shop in Memphis. Founded in 1920, it was managed by L. H. Lanahan who was also president through 1952, and he was succeeded by Mr. Winkelman. Over the years, its growth has roughly paralleled, while actually exceeding, the growth of Memphis as a user of electricity and electrical equipment. It began its existence with three employees and less than one thousand square feet of floor space. Many of its present loyal employees have spent all of their working years with the company, in the course of its growth to an organization using over twenty-thousand square feet of floor space. At its East Butler Avenue plant, it contracts for installations, repairs and maintenance, and is also a sales organization. Its wiring department, which has installed a total of more than three thousand miles of wire on its many jobs, has completed contracts for a large number of the major industrial plants of Memphis and the surrounding area. The largest of these was the installation for Grace Chemical Company, which built its plant in 1955. At the time of writing, the company is working on the electrical system of Memphis' new steam plant. In addition to its wiring department, the company operates efficient repair, rewinding, and trouble-shooting departments, and it is prepared to cope with breakdowns in electrical systems on a twenty-four-hours-per-day basis.

Retaining his professional connections, Mr. Winkelman is a member of the American Institute of Electrical Engineers, the Tennessee Society of Professional Engineers, the Memphis Electric League, and the Engineers Club of Memphis. In the last-named organization, he served as director in 1951 and 1952, and as vice president in 1954. He is a member of Sigma Alpha Epsilon fraternity, and was its president in 1935. His local memberships include the Rotary Club and the Chickasaw Country Club.

He and his family attend the Idlewild Presbyterian Church. He has held office as deacon in this congregation, and was also co-chairman of its committee which, in the spring of 1958, raised a million dollars for a church-expansion program.

Mrs. Winkelman is the former Miss Mary Marguerite Pitner, of Franklin, Tennessee. She is the daughter of Andrew Watson and Maggie Robbie (Cowles) Pitner, and she became the wife of Henry Tanner Winkelman in a ceremony at Franklin on June 11, 1938. The couple make their home at 5501 North Angela, Memphis, and they are the parents of the following children: 1. Henry Tanner, Jr., born on September 21, 1941, in Schenectady, New York. 2. Andrew Pitner, born in Memphis on January 23, 1950. 3. Mary Cowles, born in that city on September 22, 1954. 4. William Robert, born July 7, 1958, also in Memphis.

CHATHAM COFFEE REAMS

Chatham Coffee Reams of Chattanooga, has had a distinguished career in the profession of civil engineering, dividing his years between private enterprise and public service posts. At the time of his recent retirement he had been for twenty-one years with the Tennessee Valley Authority, in charge of important work in hydrological engineering. He has been active in professional and fraternal groups, and is a veteran of World War I.

Born at McMinnville, on October 24, 1890, he is a son of Radford Monroe and Jessie (Coffee) Reams, who spent their lives in that city. There, Radford

M. Reams was owner, editor, and publisher of the McMinnville Standard. Attending the local public schools, Chatham C. Reams graduated from McMinnville High School, then entered the University of Tennessee, where he took his degree of Bachelor of Science in Civil Engineering in 1913.

In that year he began his career with the Morgan Engineering Company of Memphis, remaining with that organization until 1922. He was absent at the time of World War I, serving in the army. He enlisted at Camp Taylor, Kentucky, in May, 1918, and by the time he received his honorable discharge at Fort Sill, Oklahoma, on December 11 of that year, he had attained the rank of second lieutenant in the Field Artillery.

In 1922, Mr. Reams took a position as construction engineer with the Tennessee Electric Power Company. He remained through 1924, and in 1925 became chief engineer with the Conley Frog and Switch Company at Memphis. He became a special representative of the Detroit Fidelity and Surety Company in 1927, and for some months in 1928, was with the Forest Products Chemical Company. Later the same year, Mr. Reams accepted a position as resident engineer with the Tennessee State Highway Department.

He joined the staff of the United States Engineers Office at Chattanooga, in 1931, and worked on design and construction projects with that office and later with the Memphis office of the same government bureau. During 1933 he was employed in responsible engineering capacities by the S. and W. Construction Company.

In 1934-1935, Mr. Reams was engaged in concrete inspection work on the construction of the Norris Dam, and from 1934 until the end of his active career, he was identified with the Tennessee Valley Authority in the capacity of hydrological engineer.

He is a life member of the American Society of Civil Engineers, largest of the nation's engineer groups, a founding member of the Memphis Engineers Club, and he is also a member of the American Legion and the Free and Accepted Masons. In the Masonic order he belongs to the higher bodies of the Scottish Rite, and to the Ancient Arabic Order of Nobles of the Mystic Shrine. His fraternity is Phi Kappa Phi. He takes an interest in competitive sports, particularly football, basketball and baseball.

On December 12, 1923, in Memphis, Chatham Coffee Reams married Avaligne O. Edgington, daughter of Hugh and Catherine (Duduit) Edgington. Her father, who was an attorney in Memphis, was the son of Colonel Thomas Benton Edgington and his wife, the former Catherine Vose Baxter. Colonel Edgington too was an attorney. Mr. and Mrs. Reams became the parents of one son, Benton Edgington, who was born on July 2, 1925. He now holds the rank of Lieutenant Commander in the Submarine Service of the United States Navy. He is Construction Superintendent at Portsmouth Naval Shipyards, New Hampshire. He married Nancy Slaven of Annapolis, Maryland. Their children are: Suzanne Montgomery, Hugh Edgington, and Nancy Redmond.

Mr. Reams has been retired since 1955. He makes his home in Chattanooga.

DAVID BALLON

An attorney practicing in Memphis since the beginning of his career, David Ballon is a partner in the firm of Ballon and Farrar, with offices in the Porter Building. He has been influential in municipal affairs, civic groups and bar associations. He is a veteran of military service in World War II.

The son of William and Frances (Goldstein) Ballon, he was born in Memphis on September 27, 1907. His father was a merchant in that city. Receiving his early education locally, David Ballon attended Lawler Grammar School and Tech High School, then went on to his advanced studies at Washington and Lee University, where he completed his prelegal education. He took his professional studies at Vanderbilt University, where he graduated in 1932 with the degree of Bachelor of Laws.

Admitted to the Tennessee bar, he began his practice at Memphis, joining the firm of Anderson and Leftwich, which became Anderson and Ballon in 1934. With a change in membership, it was renamed Ballon, Graves and Nicholson in 1943; and since 1948 has been known as Ballon and Farrar. Active in the Tennessee Bar Association, Mr. Ballon currently serves on its Board of Governors. He is a member and past director of the Memphis and Shelby County Bar Association, and a member of the American Bar Association.

In September, 1943, Mr. Ballon entered the United States Army for wartime service. As a staff sergeant, he remained in the armed forces until October, 1945.

Mr. Ballon serves on the board of directors of the Mid-South Fair, and in his home city of Memphis he is a member of the Traffic Advisory Commission. In 1940-1941, before he himself entered military service, he served as chairman of the Memphis Plan to provide entertainment and recreation for soldiers and sailors in the city. After the U. S. O. established its nationwide program for the same purpose, it took over operation of this organization. Mr. Ballon's reputation in civic service goes back many years. In 1939 he was recipient of the Distinguished Service Award of the Junior Chamber of Commerce. He is currently president of the Memphis and Shelby County Safety Council; and he is a member and past president of the Memphis and Shelby County Civic Clubs, and a member and past president of the Binghamton Civic Club.

His other memberships include the West Tennessee Saddle Club Association, which he is currently serving as president. He is a member and past president of the Gavel Club, is president of the Cavalier Riding Club, a life member of the council of the Civic Clubs, and a member of Ridgeway Country Club, Phi Epsilon Pi fraternity, and the Legion of Honor of DeMolay. Of Jewish faith, he attends Temple Israel.

At Pine Bluff, Arkansas, on April 29, 1934, David Ballon married Polly L. Weaver, who comes from Lawrenceburg, Tennessee. She is a daughter of John and Katherine (Springer) Weaver. Mr. and Mrs. Ballon have one daughter, Kathie Frances, who was born on September 24, 1943.

EVERETT RICHARD COOK

Since he entered the cotton business in his own name, four decades ago, Everett R. Cook has advanced to a place of leadership in the industry which is recognized throughout the South. He is head of Cook & Co., Inc., Cotton Buyers, in Memphis, and of several other firms, and on a number of occasions he has served his government in consulting capacities. He has held office in a number of organizations of industrialists.

A native of Indianapolis, he was born on December 13, 1894, son of Jesse Everett and Ollie Belle (Shonacker) Cook. Both of his parents were lifelong residents of Indianapolis, where Jesse E. Cook died in 1942, and since that time Mrs. Cook has made her home in Memphis. He was a foreman in the construction industry.

Everett R. Cook received his education in the Memphis public schools. He did not attend college; but in 1954, Southwestern at Memphis conferred on him the honorary degree of Doctor of Laws.

In 1916, when he was only twenty-one years old, Mr. Cook organized his own cotton business at Marianna, Arkansas. His firm was known as Cook and Company until 1950, when it was incorporated under the name of Cook & Co., Inc., Cotton Buyers, with headquarters at Memphis since 1921. In addition, it has offices in New York City, Boston, Atlanta, Houston, Gastonia, Phoenix, Fresno, Ghent, Belgium, Athens, Greece, and Osaka, Japan. Mr. Cook also heads Cook and Cia., S.A., with home office at Sao Paulo, Brazil, which was founded in 1945. He is president of the Cotton Belt Insurance Company, and a partner in Cook and Company of New York City. He serves on the boards of directors of Eastern Air Lines and of Plough, Incorporated. He entered the Signal Corps, United States Army, May 12th 1917, after pilot training in the United States and France. He served as pilot, flight commander and later, commander of the 91st Aero Squadron in France and Germany. He was recalled to Washington to serve in General Mitchell's headquarters in April, 1919, and retired from the service in September, 1919. He has been awarded the Distinguished Service Cross, Silver Star, Croix de Guerre with Palm (France) for services in World War I, and the Legion of Merit and the Legion of Honor (France), for services in World War II.

Mr. Cook served on the United States mission to negotiate Peruvian cotton purchases in 1942. In the same year, he held office as vice president of the Commodity Credit Corporation, an agency of the Department of Agriculture. Later that year, he entered the United States Army Air Corps, in which he was commissioned a colonel. He served as deputy chief of staff of the Eighth and

Emmett R. Cook

Twelfth Air Forces in the United Kingdom, North Africa and Italy, through 1943, and the following year was with the United States Strategic Air Force in the European Theater of Operations. From 1948 to 1953, he held the rank of brigadier general in the Air Force Reserve and is now retired. He was a member of the Reserve Forces Policy Board, Department of Defense, in 1951-1952. Immediately after his return from active service, he held several government posts of importance. In 1944-1945, he served as special assistant to the War Food Administrator, and national chairman of the Agricultural War Boards. He was adviser on wartime economic affairs to the Department of State in 1945, and consultant in 1945-1946.

In 1953, Mr. Cook served on the Rubber Producing Facilities Disposal Commission, and in the same year he was a member of the Tennessee Constitutional Committee. A member of the American Cotton Shippers Association, he held office as its president in 1949/50. He was president of the Memphis Cotton Exchange in 1931, and retains membership in that organization and also in the New York Cotton Exchange, the New Orleans Cotton Exchange and the Liverpool Cotton Association. He also belongs to the Southern Cotton Shippers Association, of which he was president in 1932. In 1931, he was president of the Memphis Cotton Carnival Association.

Mr. Cook's memberships include the Memphis Country Club, Memphis Hunt and Polo Club, the Metropolitan Club of Washington, D. C., and The Brook and India House of New York City. He attends the Episcopal Church, and is a Democrat in his politics.

On June 4, 1919, Everett Richard Cook married Phoebe Willingham. The couple make their home at Germantown, Tennessee, and they are the parents of two children: 1. Edward Willingham, who was born on June 19, 1922. 2. Phoebe, born on March 27, 1926. She is the wife of John L. Welsh, Jr. Mr. Cook has six grandchildren: Edward W. Cook, Jr., Everett R. Cook, 2nd, Barbara Cook, John W. Welsh, 3rd, Edward C. Welsh, and Phoebe Lemoine Welsh.

EDWARD DOSS LYNCH

Since he completed his law training, Edward Doss Lynch has practiced at Maryville, Tennessee, where he has his offices in the Blount National Bank Building; a partner in the firm of Dunn, Felknor, and Lynch. He served in the United States Navy, both in World War II and during the Korean War; and has had varied experience in his state's Department of Public Health, in newspaper work, and in automobile finance and insurance.

Born September 29, 1927, he is a native of Lenoir City, and a son of Fred and Jessie (Graham) Lynch. Both of his parents were born at LaFollette, Tennessee—his father on August 31, 1905, his mother on July 12 of the following year. The lawyer received his early schooling in his native city, attending Nichols Elementary School, and he completed his secondary studies at Maryville High School. He returned to graduate there in 1946, after having spent two years in the United States Navy—one in the Naval Air Force, and one in the Legal Department. He next enrolled at Maryville College, but transferred from there to the University of Tennessee, taking courses at its College of Business Administration. From 1951 to 1953, Mr. Lynch was again absent in naval service, being recalled as a reservist. He was assigned to Recruiting Service during that entire period. He later studied at the University of Tennessee's College of Law, graduating with the degree of Bachelor of Laws in August, 1955.

He was busy in various jobs during his years in law school, being circulation manager of the weekly newspaper, The Maryville Enterprise, for one year, and manager of the finance and insurance department of a local automobile agency the next year. Prior to service in the Korean War period, he worked as senior sanitarian for the Tennessee Department of Public Health for three years.

Admitted to the Tennessee bar, Mr. Lynch began his private practice of law in Maryville in March, 1956. He is a member of the Blount County Bar Association, the Tennessee Bar Association and the American Bar Association, as well as Phi Delta Phi national legal fraternity.

Mr. Lynch serves on the board of directors of Cumberland Memorial Gardens at Corbin, Kentucky. In his home city of Maryville, he is a member of the Junior Chamber of Commerce; a member of the Maryville-Alcoa Civitan Club, which he is currently serving as district governor; and a member of Maryville Post No. 13, American Legion, of which he is past judge advocate. He is a member of Broadway Methodist Church in that city. In his politics he is a Democrat.

On July 13, 1947, Edward Doss Lynch married Doris Lee McDaniel, daughter of John F. and Gladys (Long) McDaniel. Both of her parents were born in Grainger County, Tennessee, her father in 1905, her mother in 1907.

FRED LELAND ALLEN

The oldest living ex-mayor of Knoxville, and a man who embarked on a career in municipal service after retiring from business, Mr. Allen was a stalwart champion of the city manager form of government, fighting to keep public business free from political control. His decision to enter local politics was prompted by his interest in civic improvements. He was one of the leaders in establishing Knoxville's Municipal Airport, and he led city-ordinance drives that drastically improved milk sanitation and smoke-abatement controls. A member of the Democratic party, he constantly fought to keep Knoxville municipal government free from politics, and as friends said of him, "he was always more interested in what he was putting into a thing than what he was getting out of it."

Mr. Allen was born in Opelika, Alabama, on April 4, 1866, the son of George Washington Allen and of Mary Catherine (Wilhelm) Allen. His father was born in Virginia and was of Irish and French descent. Mr. Allen's mother was a native of Columbus, Georgia. He attended the public schools of Atlanta, Georgia, and as a boy carried papers for the Atlanta *Constitution*. He was later promoted to the circulation department, and then moved to Birmingham, Alabama, as circulation manager of the Birmingham *Age-Herald*. He came to Knoxville, as local agent for the Standard Oil Company in 1905, and on his retirement in 1931, he was the area agent for the company.

It was after his retirement that Mr. Allen became active on the Knoxville political scene. He ran for city councilman in 1934 and was elected, and he won re-election in 1938, 1940 and 1946. He served as vice mayor in 1940 and he was mayor in 1946. As a city official, he favored separation of the water and power departments and he wanted the city utilities to be directly under the city manager rather than under a commission. It was through his efforts that the city's water department was organized as a separate department, and he was also largely responsible for the establishment of the Knoxville Utilities Board, and drew the plans for the Utilities Board. His term as mayor was served under the city manager form of government, having been elected presiding officer of the city council by the other members. His title carried with it the prestige of being head of the city's legislative body, and was not primarily an executive post.

Mr. Allen's community activities were many and varied and he was in addition a member of the Rotary Club. His social connections included membership in the Sons of the American Revolution and the Huguenot Society, and he was a Thirty-second Degree Mason and a Shriner. His favorite hobby was reading, especially poetry, and he kept informed on current events. He was a member of the First Baptist Church of Knoxville, served as Sunday School teacher and as superintendent of the Sunday School, and he was also a deacon of the Broadway Baptist Church.

Mr. Allen was married to Elizabeth Anna Welch of Atlanta, Georgia, the daughter of Benjamin Blakely Welch and of Evaline Louise (Marshall) Welch. Her father was a native of Montgomery, Alabama, and her mother was of English-Irish descent. Mrs. Allen died on June 1, 1942.

Mr. and Mrs. Allen had six children: 1. Lizzie Fred, now Mrs. Loy W. Allison of Jacksonville, Alabama. 2. Montine. 3. Mary Catherine, now Mrs. Winstead Cooper of Knoxville. 4. Leland Norcross, married to Dorothy Whitaker and residing in Montgomery, Alabama. 5. Frances Louise, now Mrs. Louise Allen Trotter of Knoxville. 6. Jerome Marshall of Knoxville.

This is the record of the long and distinguished career of Fred L. Allen, who died at Knoxville, on April 11, 1957, at the age of ninety-one. Entering the field of politics after a very successful business career, Mr. Allen was able to use his wide experience and solid judgment for the betterment of the community of Knoxville. A man of rigid honesty and firm convictions, it was said of him that "he hated politics, favoritism and incompetence when it came to running the people's business. He believed in getting the right man for the job and in letting that man operate without political control." He was a distinguished public servant.

Edward Charles Wirotzious

Following a record of valuable experience with the Bureau of Internal Revenue, Edward C. Wirotzious joined a Memphis firm of certified public accountants. On May 1, 1944 he established his own firm; and the present firm of Edward C. Wirotzious & Company, with offices in the Home Federal Building, at 147 Jefferson Avenue, Memphis, was founded in 1955. He is its senior partner.

A native of Louisville, Kentucky, Mr. Wirotzious was born on January 6, 1907, son of Edward and Carolyn (Grampp) Wirotzious. His father, who was born on April 18, 1880, is now deceased. Mrs. Wirotzious was born January 4, 1884. The accounting executive received his entire education in the schools of Louisville. His first professional connection was with the firm of Ernst and Ernst, a nationwide firm of certified public accountants, and he worked in its Louisville office from 1928 to 1938. In August of the latter year he joined the Bureau of Internal Revenue, United States Treasury Department, working in accounting capacities, and continued with the government until December 1, 1941. At that time he moved to Memphis, and his home has since been at 1210 Poppen Drive.

On May 1, 1944, he opened his own accounting firm, which he operated individually until the present firm of Edward C. Wirotzious and Company was established on August 1, 1955. He has since been senior partner of his enlarged organization, which in December, 1958, opened a branch office in the Frank Nelson Building in Birmingham, Alabama. Mr. Wirotzious is professionally certified in the states of Kentucky, Mississippi, and Georgia, as well as Tennessee, and holds membership in the Kentucky, Georgia, and Tennessee Societies of Certified Public Accountants. He is a member of the American Institute of Certified Public Accountants, the National Association of Accountants, and the American Accounting Association.

In his own city, Mr. Wirotzious belongs to the Chamber of Commerce, and the lodge of Free and Accepted Masons. In Masonry, he is a member of the higher bodies, including the Commandery of the Knights Templar; he is a Thirty-second Degree Scottish Rite Mason; and belongs to the Ancient Arabic Order of Nobles of the Mystic Shrine. A member of the Union Avenue Baptist Church, he serves on its Board of Deacons and on its Finance Committee.

In his native city of Louisville, on October 24, 1929, Edward C. Wirotzious married Lillian F. Ashcraft, daughter of Elisha E. and Pauline (Ferguson) Ashcraft. Her father and mother are deceased. Mr. and Mrs. Wirotzious are the parents of one daughter, Lillian Joy, who was born on November 13, 1930. She is the wife of the Rev. James Foster Yates, who is now pastor of the First

Claude A. Armour

Baptist Church at Paragould, Arkansas. They have a daughter, Carol Joy, born May 11, 1958; and a son, John Edward, born July 27, 1959.

CLAUDE ALBERT ARMOUR

After an excellent record as a law-enforcement officer, in the course of which he advanced to the post of Memphis' chief of police, Claude Albert Armour was given additional duties as vice-mayor of the city. He is now commissioner of fire and police as well, and by virtue of the dual post is one of the most influential men in municipal government. He is a veteran of naval service in World War II.

A native of Memphis, Mr. Armour was born on August 21, 1919, and is a son of Edward Freeman and Vera (Strawhan) Armour. His father was a member of the Memphis Fire Department for twenty-eight years, attaining the rank of lieutenant, and he is now retired. Claude A. Armour attended local public schools and graduated from high school in Memphis. He later attended business school and law school, but finding that neither led to a career congenial to him, did not complete his courses at either. He is, however, a graduate of the Federal Bureau of Investigation National Academy.

On December 10, 1941, he began his career in the Memphis Police Department as a patrolman. He remained with the department until September 12, 1942, when he volunteered for service in the United States Navy. In the course of his naval career he held the ranks of coxswain, second class boatswain's mate, first class boatswain's mate, and chief boatswain's mate, the rating he held at the time of his honorable discharge on November 19, 1945. Serving in the Pacific, he was wounded at Okinawa on May 22, 1945. He received the Purple Heart, and two battle stars on his campaign ribbon.

After his naval experience was over, Claude A. Armour returned to the Memphis Police Department as a patrolman. He was promoted to the Detective Division, April 1, 1946, and advanced to lieutenant in that division a month later. On April 1, 1947, he left to attend the Federal Bureau of Investigation National Academy. He was promoted to uniform inspector in the Memphis Police Department on June 1, 1947; but continued his F.B.I. studies, graduating from the school on June 3, 1947.

On February 1, 1949, Mr. Armour was appointed chief of police, and he was reappointed to that post on January 1, 1950. In October of that year, he was appointed vice-mayor and commissioner of fire and police. On November 8 of the following year he was elected to a four-year term to fill both offices; and was re-elected to a second four-year term on November 10, 1955.

Mr. Armour is a member of the International Association of Police Chiefs, the International Association of Fire Chiefs, the F.B.I. National Academy Associates, the Tennessee National Academy Associates, the Tennessee and Mississippi Peace Officers Association, and the Tennessee Peace Officers Association. Besides these connections held as a professional law-enforcement officer, he is a member of the posts of the Veterans of Foreign Wars, the Forty and Eight, and the American Legion. Affiliated with the Free and Accepted Masons, he is a member of the higher bodies of the Ancient and Accepted Scottish Rite, holds the Thirty-second Degree, and is a member of the Ancient Arabic Order of Nobles of the Mystic Shrine (Al Chymia Temple).

Authorship is one of Mr. Armour's accomplishments. He has written articles appearing in several magazines, concerned with problems of noise abatement, traffic safety, and the management of police and fire departments.

Fond of sports, Mr. Armour takes an especial interest in golf, football and professional baseball. He is a Protestant in his religious faith.

At Tunica, Mississippi, on July 2, 1942, Claude A. Armour married Grace McCord, daughter of Thomas James and Patti (Bailey) McCord. The couple are the parents of one daughter, Claudia Diane Armour, born June 8, 1943, in Memphis.

TORRANCE FRAZIER MCEWEN

A law-enforcement officer for the past decade, Torrance Frazier McEwen has spent most of that time as chief of police at Tullahoma. He is active in peace officers' groups, and in fraternal and community life in his city.

Born in Montgomery County, on November 18, 1903, he is a son of James William and Betty (Vandergriff) McEwen. Both parents were natives of Tennessee. His father was born in Robertson County in 1870, and died at Tullahoma in 1946. He was a farmer, and both he and Mrs. McEwen were members of the Church of Christ. She was born in Murfreesboro, and her father, James Vandergriff, was a veteran of the ivil War.

Torrance F. McEwen attended the public schools of his native Montgomery County. Reared on a farm, he chose agriculture as his occupation, and continued in that work until 1935. Most of this time was spent in Montgomery County, although he also farmed in Bedford County.

In 1947, he accepted appointment as deputy sheriff with the Tullahoma Police Department, and the following year was elected chief of police, the position he has held ever since. He is a member of the Tennessee Peace Officers Association, and is currently serving as president of the Middle Tennessee Peace Officers Association.

His lodges are the Woodmen of the World and the Knights of Pythias. He is a Democrat in politics, and a communicant of the Church of Christ.

On February 15, 1925, in Moore County, Tennessee, Torrance F. McEwen married Betty Mullins. Born in Bedford County, Tennessee, on January 23, 1900, she is a daughter of two natives of that county, Mannon and Mattie (Pearce) Mullins. Her father was a farmer. Mr. and Mrs. McEwen are the parents of the following children: 1. Curtis Eugene, born March 4, 1927, in Tullahoma. He served two years in the Navy, being in the South Pacific. He now makes his home in Tullahoma where he is a heavy-equipment operator. He married Ruth Sanders from Moore County, and they are the parents of one child, Jenifer, born in 1957. 2. Ruby, born April 4, 1929, in Tullahoma. She married Bryant Bowden of that city. 3. Thomas Ray, born December 13, 1932, also in Tullahoma. He enlisted in the United States Air Force and spent forty-eight months in the Radar Division. He has also attended State Teachers College at Murfreesboro, and is now an accountant, working for the Air Force at Redstone Arsenal, Huntsville. Thomas R. McEwen married Bobby Jane Tipps, and they have one child, Tim. 4. Mary Frances, born April 17, 1934, in Tullahoma. She married Roy Barton, and they have two children, Roy, Jr., and Melanie Ann. 5. Arey Jene, born January 6, 1940; a high school graduate. 6. Charles Vernon, born August 26, 1953.

Mr. and Mrs. McEwen have had at various times forty-six other children from the Welfare Association in their home and have helped to raise them.

WILLIAM COLONEL ANDERSON

William C. Anderson has practiced at Gainesboro from his early years in the legal profession. He has also distinguished himself in public office as United States attorney, and county clerk and master. He is a devoted and reliable civic, church and organizational worker.

Born at Flynns Lick, Tennessee, on June 5, 1910, he is a son of Philip Jordan and Mary (Manley) Anderson. His father, who was born at Free State Community near Gainesboro, in Jackson County, on September 12, 1884, is likewise an attorney, still in practice with his two sons. He has to his credit more than forty-four years' practice in Gainesboro. For four years, 1907-1911, he served as superintendent of schools of Jackson County. Mary Manley, whom he married, was born August 12, 1889, at Grandville, Tennessee. She taught school for a number of years. This couple became the parents of six children: 1. William C., our subject, and a lawyer at Gainesboro. 2. Garland Draper, also a lawyer, the third partner in the Anderson firm. He served in the European Theater in World War II and was severely wounded, spending seventeen months in the hospital. He received the Purple Heart, Combat Infantry Badge, and European Theater ribbon with battle stars. He held the rank of first lieutenant in the 33rd Division, a component of the Third Army. He was in uniform from 1941 to 1946. 3. Herbert Page, who is in the insurance business at Gainesboro. 4. Philip Jordan, Jr., rancher at Exeter, California. 5. Wayne, a scientist working on naval ballistics missiles at China Lake, California. 6. Russel B., in the real estate business in Nashville.

Attending the public schools of Gainesboro, William C. Anderson went on to advanced studies at Tennessee Polytechnic Institute at Cookeville. On choosing the law for his career, he enrolled at Cumberland University Law School, and there he received his degree of Bachelor of Laws, on his graduation, May 31, 1933. Mr. Anderson taught school for a short time after graduation.

Ever since completing his courses at Cumberland University Law School, Mr. Anderson has practiced at Gainesboro, with the exception of the years 1947-1948. During that period he served as United States attorney for the War Department, with jurisdiction over a district comprising the states of Tennessee and Kentucky. His partners in law practice are his father, and his brother Garland D. Anderson.

Since 1948, Mr. Anderson has held office as Jackson County Clerk and Master. For four years he has served as president of the Jackson County Farm Bureau, and is now its vice president. He is deeply interested in agriculture, owning and operating a prosperous farm on the Cumberland River.

As a lawyer, Mr. Anderson is a member of the American Bar Association and the Jackson County Bar Association. He has military service to his credit—not in wartime, but as a trainee at Citizens Military Training Camp at Fort Oglethorpe in 1927-1928. Among his community and welfare interests for some years has been the crippled children's program, to which he has given consistent and generous support. As a Mason, he is a Master Shriner and secretary of his Temple, and he is also a past worthy patron of the Order of the Eastern Star.

His religious affiliation is with the Methodist Church. He has served his church as district steward, as a member of the finance committee, and as chairman of the board of trustees.

At Centerville, Tennessee, on August 27, 1939, William Colonel Anderson married Doyene Lee. Born at Gainesboro on March 3, 1913, she is a daughter of John and Avo (Rogers) Lee. Her father is a large landowner and a dealer in livestock in Jackson County. Mrs. Lee taught school for about fifteen years at the Jackson County High School. Mrs. Anderson is a member and past president of the Hurricane Home Demonstration Club. The couple are the parents of two children: 1. Patsy Ellen, born July 18, 1944. 2. William Earl, born February 25, 1946. Both children were born in Davidson County, Tennessee.

WILLIAM BRANSFORD MASON

Since 1946, when he established the Memphis Metal Manufacturing Company, William Bransford Mason has become one of the city's most active industrialists, with a wide range of interests. He is president of the above firm at the present time, and also president of six other corporations. He had been active in Democratic politics in Kentucky before coming to Memphis, but in recent years has supported the national Republican candidates.

Born April 13, 1909, at Eddyville, Kentucky, he is the son of the late Rhenier Sanders and Norabel Alexander Stewart (Bradshaw) Mason. His grandparents on his father's side were Judge William Newton Mason, who

W.B. Mason-

was a descendant of John Mason, American Colonist, Governor of New-foundland in 1616 and a founder of New Hampshire, and Frances Jane (Sanders) Mason of LaVergne, Tennessee. His grandparents on his mother's side were Robert Bell and Alice May (Stewart) Bradshaw, whose ancestors came from Scotland in 1734 and settled in Frederick, Maryland, later moving to Virginia and Kentucky. The name William Bransford was bestowed upon him in honor of a close friend of his father, William S. Bransford of Nashville.

Mr. Mason's father, Rhenier Sanders Mason, was an outstanding Kentuckian, former mayor of Eddyville, a Kentucky Colonel, very active in Democratic politics and held many state and federal honorary appointments. He was founder of the Mason Mining Company, Pioneer Rock Asphalt Company, Mason Fluorite Company and The Kentucky Whip and Collar Company, and served as director of the Forest Farmers Association, Eastern Dark Tobacco Association. He was a devout Methodist.

At the age of nine, his parents moved a mile from Eddyville to an old, historical, ante-bellum home, "Mineral Mound" which overlooked the Cumberland River, and showed the scars of a cannon ball fired by a Yankee gunboat in 1862. It was here at "Mineral Mound" on its rolling hills, he was reared with his sister, Louise, now Mrs. G. W. McConnell, and brother, Robert Sanders Mason, now deceased. He has pleasant memories of United States Senators and Governors who visited in his home. The two favorites were Governor, and later United States Senator, A. O. Stanley, who hunted with him on several occasions, and Vice-President Alben W. Barkley whom he drove throughout the country at various times in later years when Mr. Barkley was campaigning for the United States Senate. In 1924, at the age of 15, while attending the Democratic National Convention in New York with his parents, he was honored by casting Kentucky's 26 votes for William Gibbs McAdoo for the presidential nominee on the 76th ballot.

Largely due to his father's various mineral interests in Western Kentucky, William B. Mason became interested in geology at an early age.

In 1927 he graduated from Columbia Military Academy and received most efficient officer award of the Academy. He ranked second in marksmanship and merit awards, and received letters in baseball.

In 1931 he graduated from Vanderbilt University with the degree of Bachelor of Science, having majored in geology and chemistry. He spent several months doing geological exploration work in nearly all the western states. At Vanderbilt he was a member of Phi Delta Theta fraternity, the Owl Club, was business manager of the Vanderbilt Hustler, assistant manager of Cap and Bells, and a member of the staffs of the Commodore and Masquerader.

On graduating from Vanderbilt, William B. Mason joined his brother in forming the Marion Fluorspar Company, which they operated for several years. In 1932, during the depression, he gave his services in helping organize The Eastern Dark Fired Tobacco Grower's Association which created a market for the farmers that is still in existence. He then became associated with his father in the manufacturing and coal mining industries in western Kentucky.

In 1942 he became connected with the Southern Coal Company of Memphis, and the following year joined Reynolds Mining Company. While there, he succeeded in establishing a method of sampling bauxite ore that was acceptable, and was adopted by Metal Reserves, an instrument of the government, as well as by Reynolds Mining Company. The method formerly used had been inconclusive and not representative of the ore. In the fall of 1944, Mr. Mason was sent to Jamaica, British West Indies, where he remained nearly a year as manager of geological exploration work in St. Ann Province. After returning to the states, he went into the industrial sales division of Reynolds Metals Company and was sales manager of the Memphis territory.

In 1946 he resigned from Reynolds and organized the Memphis Metal Manufacturing Company, of which he is now president and owner. He is also president of Crusader Enterprises, Barbecue Ovens, Inc., Outdoor Stoves, Inc., Union Metal Products, Inc., Pioneer Rock Asphalt Company, and Mason Mining Company, Inc. He is manager and part owner of other mineral holdings in western Kentucky. He is co-inventor of several items on which patents have been granted; however, to pick the one favorite, he chooses the coin operated mechanical "Crusader Horse" which has been enjoyed by millions of children.

In 1932, Mr. Mason was appointed by Kentucky Governor Ruby Laffoon to help organize the Young Democratic Clubs throughout the state. He served as an officer of the first state organization and held various offices until 1940 when he resigned. He also helped organize several Lions Clubs in Kentucky and in the past, has been active in Boy Scouts and in organizing Cub Scout troops. He is a member of the Chickasaw Country Club, the Rivermont Club, Sales Managers Club, the Fisher Hunting Club, and the Redman Duck Hunting Club. He is currently serving as president of the Memphis Vanderbilt Alumni Association. A communicant of St. John's Methodist Church, he serves on its board of stewards. His favorite sports are hunting, fishing, and golf.

In 1937, William Bransford Mason married Elizabeth Armantine Redwine, daughter of Judge Robert Worth and Sallie (McAllister) Redwine of Monroe, North Carolina. Judge Redwine was an attorney and legislator, who served in the State Senate for many years. He was president of the Monroe Bank, a graduate of the University of North Carolina and served as a trustee for over thirty years. He was a son of Dr. T. W. and Mary (Clark) Redwine, who had served as an officer in the Confederate States Army. Sallie McAlister, whom he married, was the daughter of John A. and Sarah (Wall) McAlister. Mr. and Mrs. Mason have one son, William Bransford, Jr., who is married to Louise Marley Webb, and who is now attending the School of Engineering at Vanderbilt University. The family's residence is at 241 Lombardy Road, in Memphis.

John R. Billings, D.D.S.

Since he completed his studies in dentistry, Dr. John R. Billings has practiced at Livingston. He has found a profitable avocation in the breeding of Aberdeen Angus cattle. Well known in his profession, he has held office as president in the local dentists' association, and is active in the state and national groups.

Dr. Billings is a native of Oakley Community, in Overton County, and he was born on April 24, 1918, son of Charles Lee and Bessie (Taylor) Billings. His father, who was born in Overton County in 1886, was a farmer and a merchant, who pursued both of these occupations in his native county, where he spent his life. His father in turn was a prominent physician, Dr. Mont Billings, who practiced in the Willow Grove Oakley community, Overton County, for many years. Bessie Taylor, whom Charles L. Billings married, was born in Oakley Community in 1894. Both she and her husband died in 1956.

Beginning his education in the public schools of Livingston, Dr. John R. Billings went on to Tennessee Polytechnic Institute at Cookeville. He then entered the University of Tennessee in Memphis. Throughout his student years he was interested in sports. He had played football and basketball on the local school teams, and served as captain of the football team at Livingston Academy. He also served as captain of his football team at Tennessee Polytechnic.

After graduating from the University of Tennessee with his degree of Bachelor of Science, he began his career as a teacher, on the faculty of Livingston Academy, and coached athletics there as well. He then returned to the University of Tennessee and entered Dental School. Receiving his degree of Doctor of Dental Science in 1950, he has been practicing at Livingston since. Dr. Billings served in the United States Navy from 1941 to 1946. As a chief petty officer, he was assigned to the physical education department's coaching staff, and remained stateside.

Over the years Dr. Billings has taken an increasing interest in agricultural pursuits. He established the Standing Stone Aberdeen Angus Stock Farm, on which he raises Black Angus cattle.

Professionally he is identified with the American Dental Association and the Tennessee State Dental Association, and served as president of his local group.

His nonprofessional memberships include the lodge of Free and Accepted Masons, and he is a member of the higher bodies of the order and of the Ancient Arabic Order of Nobles of the Mystic Shrine. He attends the Methodist Church, and is chairman of its official board. Fond of the outdoors, the one-time star athlete and coach now derives his greatest enjoyment from hunting and fishing. He is a Democrat in his politics.

In his native Overton County, in 1936, Dr. John R. Billings married Ann Robert Clark. She was born in the Windle Community, that county, on March

23, 1918, and is a daughter of John W. and Grace (Averett) Clark. Her father is a sawmill operator and lumber industry executive, who has found a rewarding specialty in the manufacture of golf sticks. Dr. and Mrs. Billings are the parents of two children.

WILLIAM KRAUSS MOODY

Since his admittance to the Tennessee bar two decades ago, William Krauss Moody has been practicing in Memphis, his only appreciable period of absence from the city being at the time of World War II, when he was serving as an officer in the Marine Corps. He has taken an influential part in the affairs of the Republican party in his state.

A native of Memphis, he was born on February 13, 1917, son of Dr. Needham Khan and Clara Nell (Rawles) Moody. His father practiced as a physician in that city. After attending Memphis University School, William K. Moody completed his preparatory studies at St. John's Military Academy in Delafield, Wisconsin, where he graduated. He then enrolled at the University of Virginia in Charlottesville, attended two years and then entered Cumberland University School of Law at Lebanon, Tennessee, for his professional studies, receiving his degree of Bachelor of Laws there in 1938.

Admitted to the practice of law by the Tennessee Supreme Court in 1939, he has practiced at Memphis ever since, with the exception of the World War II period. He is now a member of the law firm of Moody, Nearn and Livingston, with offices in the Porter Building. He is a member of the American Bar Association and of the state and county bar groups.

Enlisting in the United States Marine Corps in December, 1941, Mr. Moody served in the Pacific with the Third Marine Raider Battalion, the Fourth Marine Regiment, on Guadalcanal, Emirau, Bougainville and Gaum. He had entered as a private three days after this country became involved in the war with the attack on Pearl Harbor, and advanced to commissioned officer in the course of the conflict. He now holds the rank of major in the Marine Corps Reserve, and is commanding officer of the Marine Corps Volunteer Training Unit at Memphis.

As a Republican, Mr. Moody has been active in the councils of his party from the early years of his career. He was for four terms national committeeman of the Young Republicans of Tennessee. In 1956 he served as delegate to the Republican National Convention at San Francisco. He is a member of the lodge of the Benevolent and Protective Order of Elks and attends Grace-St. Luke's Episcopal Church.

In his home city of Memphis on November 8, 1947, William Krauss Moody married Ann Forrest Godbold, daughter of Forrest J. and Mamie Esther (Tatum) Godbold. Mrs. Moody, like her husband, is interested in the political program of the Republican party. She is currently Southern Regional Director, and formerly co-chairman of the national publicity committee, and a member of the national executive board, of the Young Republicans National Federation. She is also very active in her church. In August and September of 1959, she was a delegate to the North Atlantic Treaty Organization Youth Conference, visiting all NATO countries as their guest.

The couple are the parents of two children: 1. William Krauss, Jr., who was born on May 14, 1950. 2. Mary Ann Rawles, born August 15, 1952. Mrs. Moody has a daughter by a previous marriage: Charlotte Ann King, who was born on October 18, 1943.

ROBERT NICHOLS BOEHMS

Manager of WHLP Broadcasting Service in Centerville, Robert Nichols Boehms brings to this position a diversified background which includes farming, the automobile service business, and military service, coupled with personal drive and ambition.

He was born in Jones Valley on October 1, 1921, the son of Lewis Kinzer and the late Blanche (Woody) Boehms. His father was born in Hickman County in 1896, the son of Samuel H. and Minnie (Harville) Boehms; he has been a farmer all his life. He served overseas in World War I with the Tennessee Division Field Artillery. His family were among the early settlers in the Little Lot Community, Jones Valley section, having moved there from Murfreesboro. His wife, Blanche (Woody) Boehms was born in Hickman County in 1898 and died in 1937. They were both active in the Leatherwood Methodist Church where Mrs. Boehms was organist and Mr. Boehms was superintendent of the Sunday School.

Robert Boehms received his education in the public schools of Jones Valley, and Shady Grove. After completing his education, Robert Boehms joined his father in operating the farm. In 1942, he joined the army and served overseas with the Ninth Armored Division. A staff sergeant, he holds the Bronze Star and participated in campaigns in France, Belgium, Germany and Austria. He was in the Battle of the Bulge in 1944. Upon return to civilian life, Mr. Boehms farmed for a while and then became manager of the Farm Supply Store in Centerville. He reentered service for a year during the Korean War and after discharge became parts and service manager for the Bratton Motor Company of Centerville. In 1957, after six years with the Bratton Company, Mr. Boehms became manager of station WHLP in Centerville and has continued in this post since. He is an active Knight of Pythias, currently is Master of Arms, and has served in all the chairs. He is a past president of the Lions Club and is its program chairman. He also serves on the board of directors of the Hickman County Farm Bureau, as well as the Young Farmers and Homemakers organization of which he is past president of the County group, and he is the general chairman of the Hickman County Sesquicentennial. Like his parents, Mr. Boehms is a member of the Methodist Church, and makes his home in Centerville.

Tom O'Ryan

Tom O'Ryan is a self-made man who came to this country in 1929 practically without funds, when he was seventeen years old and today is a nationally known leader in the advertising field, an active club member and a dynamic, much-sought-after speaker.

Born in Limerick City, Ireland, on December 1, 1912, he is the son of Edward and Mary (Cusack) Ryan. His father was a retail merchant in Ireland for many years and has the distinction of having served in the Irish Revolution for ten years and was director of a patriot group in Munster Province. Tom O'Ryan attended Blackrock College at Dublin, Ireland, and attended New York University School of Journalism in New York City.

When Mr. O'Ryan arrived in this country in 1929 he was forced to take any kind of work he could find, even to selling vegetables in Brooklyn, New York. But in 1932 things began to pick up when he became affiliated with Saks on 34th Street, and continued with the firm until 1937, when he began his career in the bus advertising business with Barron G. Collier in the New York market. In 1949, he formed his own company, "Tom O'Ryan Advertising Company," concentrating his efforts on development of the merchandising aspects of transportation advertising. In 1950, he joined forces with Joseph H. Batchelder, of Peoria, Illinois, and formed the O'Ryan and Batchelder Corporation. The firm now has fourteen offices throughout the country. In November, 1957 the firm completed their present modern office building in Memphis at 830 Crump Boulevard, the only building of its kind devoted to this advertising. The company employs a total of 190 people.

Through the years he has built a reputation as a proponent of advertising and has spoken before numerous advertising and sales executive clubs throughout the United States. He has in the past held many offices in various clubs and organizations and was a director of the National Association of Transportation Advertising, Incorporated. He also is a director, past president and chairman of the board of Mutual Transportation Advertising, Incorporated. Despite his active business life, he has found time to join and take an active part in the Loyal Order of Moose and the Knights of Columbus, and also is a member of the University Club, the Kiwanis Club, Petroleum Club, Variety Club, Serra Club, National Chamber of Commerce, Sales and Executive Club, Army and Navy Club, and the Advertising Federation of America. Mr. O'Ryan served three years in the New York National Guard. He is a Roman Catholic in religious faith.

He married April 10, 1948, in Memphis, Mary McKeon Fay, daughter of William L. and Marie (McKeon) Fay. The O'Ryans have four children: Emmett Jude, Mary Fay, William Fay, and Thomas Michael.

JAMES BRUCKNER CHASE

Since his return from wartime service as a naval officer, James Bruckner Chase has been active in the business life of Memphis. He is president of Bruckner Chase and Company, Inc., and of Southern Insurance Advisors, Inc., and is also an official of Resort Associates, Inc. He has headed his city's Traffic Advisory Commission, and has held office in other municipal and civic groups.

Born in Nashville on April 4, 1912, he is a son of Irvine Greer and Mattie Lee (McCarthy) Chase. Bruckner Chase received his public elementary and high school education at Peabody Demonstration School in Nashville, where he graduated in 1929. He then entered Vanderbilt University. While there he was pledged to Beta Theta Pi fraternity and was elected its president. He was also business manager and president of the Glee Club, and business manager of the university annual, "The Commodore." He was elected to Omicron Delta Kappa. He graduated cum laude in 1933.

From 1933 until 1942, Mr. Chase was with the Group Insurance Division of Aetna Life Insurance Company. As home office representative, he spent his time in the cities of Hartford, Connecticut; Atlanta; Georgia; Newark, New Jersey; Memphis; and Richmond, Virginia.

On August 27, 1942, he was commissioned a lieutenant, junior grade, in the United States Naval Reserve, and served throughout the war, being separated from active duty on October 5, 1945. He served in the North African operations which gave the Allied forces their first foothold from which to oppose the Wehrmacht, and he afterwards participated in the amphibious invasions of Sicily, Salerno, Corsica, Anzio, and Normandy. He received citations from Major General E. N. Harmon of the First Armored Division, on Anzio Beachhead; and from Admiral Sir Bertram Ramsay, Royal Navy, who commanded "Force Gold" in the Normandy Invasion. When that invasion took place, Commander Bruckner Chase, commanding U. S. S. LST 379, landed General (later Field Marshal) Sir Bernard Law Montgomery on the Normandy beaches, on D Day, June 6, 1944. Awards which he received in the course of his wartime naval service include the Silver Star Medal (which he was awarded on two occasions); the Purple Heart (three times); the Bronze Star with "V"; and the European Theater Medal with five battle stars.

After his return to civilian life, Bruckner Chase made his home in Memphis. There he established the firm of Bruckner Chase and Company, Inc., and has held office as its president since. He is also president of Southern Insurance Advisors, Inc., and secretary of Resort Associates, Inc.

Mr. Chase has served as president of the Insurors of Memphis. He was the first chairman of the Traffic Advisory Commission of the City of Memphis, and has also served as chairman of the City-County Planning Section of the Civic Research Committee. He is vice president of the Family Service of Memphis, and a director of the Memphis Council. He is vice president of the Family Service of Memphis, and a director of the Memphis Council. He was chairman of the

Crusade for Freedom, and has served as president of the Memphis Vanderbilt Alumni Association. He has also been active in the Memphis Cotton Carnival Association, serving on its board of directors; and is likewise a director of the Memphis Sales Executives Club. He is a member of the Memphis Lions Club and has served as its vice president.

As a veteran of World War II, Mr. Chase organized the Army-Navy Club of Memphis, and served as its first president. He has held various chapter, departmental, and national offices in the Reserve Officers Association, and in June, 1956, was elected its vice president for naval affairs. Affiliated with the Free and Accepted Masons, he is a member of the higher bodies of the Ancient and Accepted Scottish Rite, and of the Ancient Arabic Order of Nobles of the Mystic Shrine.

An Episcopalian in his religious faith, he attends the Church of the Holy Communion.

On December 4, 1934, in Nashville, James Bruckner Chase married Isobel Hibbs of that city, daughter of Henry Closson and Agnes (Bryan) Hibbs. The couple are the parents of two children: 1. Eloise Bryan, born in Memphis on July 9, 1938. 2. James Bruckner, Jr., born on July 9, 1940.

Robert Garland Draper

A native Tennessean, Robert Garland Draper began his career auspiciously in his home state by serving a term in the Tennessee State Legislature representing the citizens of Jackson County. For many years he has practiced law at Memphis, being one of the most respected members of its bar, and in the course of that time he has capably filled another public office as Assistant United States Attorney.

Born at Gainesboro, on April 15, 1887, he is a son of William Wallace and Emily (Settle) Draper. His father practiced law at Chattanooga, and at various times held office as Assistant Attorney General of the state at Chattanooga, and as special chancellor at Gainesboro. Robert G. Draper received his early education in the public schools of that city and graduated from Gainesboro High School. He then went to Cumberland University in Lebanon, where he graduated in 1908.

The following year he was elected to the Tennessee State Legislature from Jackson County, serving one term. He then moved to Boise, Idaho, where he practiced law for three years. At the end of that time he returned to Tennessee and opened law offices in Memphis, practicing there ever since. He became Assistant United States Attorney in that city at the beginning of 1933, and served through 1943 a total of eleven years. Long interested in the state's political affairs, he managed the late Cordell Hull's campaign in western Tennessee when the future Secretary of State was candidate for the United States Senate.

In addition to bar associations, R. Garland Draper is a member of the lodge of Free and Accepted Masons and of the Tennessee Club.

Mr. Draper married, first, April 15, 1918, in Memphis, Katherine Glankler, daughter of Frank and Julia (Doyle) Glankler; she died October 26, 1942 in Memphis.

On July 17, 1950, Mr. Draper married, second, Sara Meyers, in Memphis. Children, all of the first marriage: 1. Emily, who married, first, Thomas Carr and they had a son, Thomas, Jr.; she married, second, Donald Lessard. 2. Anne, who is the wife of Robie Macauley and they have one child, Cameron. 3. Garland, a daughter, who is secretary to Senator Albert Gore in Washington, D. C. 4. Robert Francis, who graduated from the United States Military Academy at West Point, and is now a civil engineer. 5. James Wallace, who is manager of the Los Angeles, California, plant of the Hunko Company of Memphis; he married Martha Carroll and they have four children: Catherine, James W., Jr., Blake and Garland. 6. George Edward, who is studying law at Southern Law School.

RALPH H. GODWIN

Ralph H. Godwin's varied career has comprised activity as an airline employee and manager of a funeral home. He is now an official of the First State Bank in his home city of Linden, and also heads an insurance agency there.

Born December 26, 1923, in Perry County, Mr. Godwin is a son of Ralph Holley, Sr., and Katherine (Sharp) Godwin. The elder Ralph H. Godwin, born in the same county in 1891, is now retired from his profession of pharmacy. For thirty-eight years he owned and operated the Godwin Drug Store at Linden. He is a veteran of World War I, with overseas service in the army to his credit, and he has held office as adjutant of the American Legion. He is executive vice president of the First State Bank at Linden, and served in former years as mayor of the city. Katherine Sharp, whom he married, was born in Perry County, in 1898. She is a graduate of Vanderbilt University and is a registered pharmacist.

The younger Ralph H. Godwin attended the public schools of Linden and graduated from that city's high school. At the time of World War II, he served in the United States Navy, and returning to civilian life in 1944, took a position with American Air Lines at Nashville. He remained with the organization for two years, and left in 1946 to assume management of a funeral home, which he successfully operated for three years. It was located in Linden.

Since 1949, Mr. Godwin has held office as cashier of the First State Bank of Linden. While carrying the duties of this office, he established the Godwin Insurance Agency at Linden and retains both business interests at the present time.

Active in the Lions Club, Mr. Godwin formerly served as its president. He is also affiliated with the Free and Accepted Masons, and as a bank official, belongs to the Tennessee Bankers Association. He is a Democrat in politics, and of Christian faith.

In 1946, in his home city, Ralph Holley Godwin took as his wife Miss Kira Dickson. Born in Decatur County in 1926, she is a daughter of L. H. and Bessie Dickson, both of whom are deceased. Mrs. Godwin attended Nashville Business College. She and her husband are the parents of two children: 1. Julia Ann, who was born in 1947. 2. Rosemary Elaine, born in 1955. Both were born in Nashville.

CECIL ELROD, JR.

Cecil Elrod, Jr. has earned an enviable position in the community life of Murfreesboro where he is owner and operator of radio station WGNS.

Born at Cookville, Tennessee, on January 21, 1913, he is the son of Cecil, Sr. and Sarah (Henson) Elrod. Mr. Elrod has been a merchant in Cookville and in Murfreesboro for thirty-five years. Born in Graysville, in 1886, Mr. Elrod has been in the ladies wear business all his life. He is a past president of the Chamber of Commerce as well as of the Rotary Club and the Elks. He is a member of the Board of Stewards of the First Methodist Church in Murfreesboro. A member of an old and respected Tennessee family, he is distantly related to Cordell Hull, and Congressman J. Ridley Mitchell. His wife, born in Livingston, was a teacher in the schools of that city for twelve years. She is active in civic clubs, a member of the State Garden Club, the Antique Club, and of the State Historical Society.

Cecil Elrod, Jr. was educated in the public schools of Murfreesboro and graduated from Georgia Military Academy before entering Vanderbilt University from which he graduated in 1931. He received a commission as a lieutenant in the army after graduating from Georgia Military School and while in service studied radar at Wright Field, Dayton, Ohio. He had charge of, and operated five radio stations while in service. In 1939 he performed a special job for the United States government in Brazil, South America, and then returned to the United States in 1941 to enter service during World War II. He served in the European and Mediterranean Theaters with a captain's commission and received a special commendation for his work. He was discharged in 1946 and returned to Murfreesboro where he built station WGNS, which he has been operating successfully since. He is a member of the American Legion, being a past commander of Bob Brown Post Number Sixteen. He is also chairman of the Middle Tennessee Army Advisory Committee. His clubs include the Elks and the Rotary, which he has served in all capacities except that of president. He is a past president of both the state and local Junior Chambers of Commerce and former member of the United States Junior Chamber of Commerce National Board of Governors. He helped organize the Murfreesboro

United Givers Fund. He is deacon in the Central Christian Church which he and his family attend.

He married the former Betty Garmany in April, 1940, in Chattanooga. Mrs. Elrod, daughter of Henry Knox and Mabel Garmany of Chattanooga, is active in both church and civic organizations. She is a past president of the Garden Club, and the Hospital Auxiliary. Her father is a druggist and is past president of the Tennessee Drug Association.

Mr. and Mrs. Elrod are the parents of : 1. Karen, born in 1943; 2. Susan, born in 1946; 3. Cecil, III, born in 1949; 4. Elizabeth, born in 1954; and 5. David, born in 1956. All of the children were born in Murfreesboro.

Dr. Paul Nowlin Grubb

Pastor of the Faith Temple Church in Memphis, Tennessee, since 1947, Dr. Grubb has been active in the ministry for nearly twenty years, and he is the author of "The End-Time Revival," which was published in 1954.

He was born in Bluefield, West Virginia, on October 10, 1917, the son of Simon Alexander Grubb and of Annie (Thompson) Grubb. His parents were both born in the State of Virginia. His father has a dry cleaning business in Welch, West Virginia. Paul Nowlin Grubb graduated from Gary, West Virginia, High School, and obtained the degree of Bachelor of Arts from Emory and Henry College. He prepared for the ministry at Emory University, where he received the degree of Bachelor of Divinity, 1940, and the degree of Doctor of Divinity was conferred upon him in the same year. He obtained the degree of Doctor of Philosophy at Milton University in 1948.

Pastor at the Methodist Church in Wilcoe, West Virginia, and then at Dickersonville, Virginia, Dr. Grubb then evangelized for eight years through the United States and Canada, preaching in almost every state and province, and he also did missionary work in Europe and in the Caribbean Islands. It was in 1947 that he accepted the pastorate of the Faith Temple Church in Memphis, Tennessee, and the parish is now in the process of constructing an auditorium to seat three thousand persons, and which will serve as a non-denominational evangelistic center. The Faith Temple was first known as the Central Assembly of God and was in the Gage Home on North Trezevant, one of the fine early homes of Memphis. After Dr. Grubb became pastor the name was changed to Faith Temple and the buildings and grounds were purchased and incorporated. Dr. Grubb founded the Bible School at Faith Temple in 1951. The 3,000 seat auditorium was undertaken under the direction of Dr. Grubb and his associates and its construction will be financed entirely by faith contributions. Dr. Grubb is the founder and editor of "Voice of Faith," a monthly publication he began in April, 1950. Dr. Grubb is also active in the Young Men's Christian Association, and in the Memphis Ministers Association.

He was married in Atlanta, Georgia, on April 23, 1940, to Lura Johnson, born on June 28, 1915, the daughter of Joseph Johnson and of Josie (Potts)

Johnson. Her father is a farmer and land owner in Mississippi. Mrs. Grubb is the author of "Living to Tell of Death," which was published in 1946. Dr. and Mrs. Grubb have one son, Paul Thomas Grubb, born November 24, 1944; he is a student at Treadwell High School.

VICTOR HAL HOLMES

A distinguished attorney and jurist of Trenton, Victor Hal Holmes rendered military service to his country in two wars. He later served most capably as chancellor of the Ninth District Chancery Division. He established a family tradition of legal achievement which the succeeding generation has followed.

Born in Gibson County in 1880, he was a son of Abner and Elinor (Waddell) Holmes. His father, who was an attorney practicing in Gibson County, died when Victor Hal Holmes was in his boyhood, and his mother then moved to a farm at Millsboro, Pennsylvania, near Pittsburgh. After completing his public school education, Victor Hal Holmes entered Waynesboro College, where he was a student for two years, leaving to enter military service in the Spanish-American War. Only eighteen at the time, he was seriously wounded in action in the Philippines, being shot through the lung. Upon his return home he was advised to go West for a while and consequently went to Nebraska, where he remained for about three years. In 1903 he returned to his native state of Tennessee and read law in the office of General W. W. Wade in Trenton.

General Wade was attorney-general of the circuit, and Victor Hal Holmes was appointed assistant attorney general in 1905. He later became a member of the law firm of Deason, Elder and Rankin, which became Deason, Elder and Holmes after Captain Quintane Rankin's death. Judge Holmes had been an intimate friend of Captain Rankin, whose tragic murder was one of the causes of the famed Night Riders' Uprising at Reelfoot Lake. Judge Holmes was active in prosecuting the raiders in 1909. The other member of the law firm was Lieutenant Colonel James Deason, of the United States Army. Judge Holmes served on the Mexican border in 1916. During World War I he was commissioned a Major in the Tennessee National Guard. In 1918, Judge Holmes was elected chancellor of the Ninth District, Chancery Division, and served until 1934. In that year he resumed private practice, taking two of his sons into law practice with him, the firm being known as Holmes and Holmes Attorneys at Law. Since his death the brothers have continued their practice under the same name. For many years Judge Holmes taught a Bible Class at the Methodist Church in Trenton.

On October 18, 1908, Victor Hal Holmes married Miss Alice Davidson, and they became the parents of the following children: 1. Richard Davidson, who was born in Trenton on March 28, 1913. A graduate of Columbia Law University at Lebanon, he practiced with his father and brother; and the two brothers still continue in partnership, with offices in Trenton. He is general counsel of the Citizens State Bank, and a member of the Gibson County and Tennessee State bar associations. On November 25, 1937, he married Carolyn Burrow, who was born in Trenton on October 9, 1914, daughter of Banks M. and Carrie (Wade) Burrow. 2. Hal, who married Margarette Harrison and they have a son, Hal, III. 3. James D., who married Nancy Carr; they have two children: James D. and Alice.

Judge Holmes' death occurred at Trenton on April 1, 1956.

Commissioner Donald Murdoch McSween

The head of the Tennessee Department of Employment Security, Commissioner Donald Murdoch McSween took office January 15, 1953, coincident with the inauguration of Governor Frank G. Clement.

A native of Newport in Cocke County, he was born on May 18, 1915, son of the late Circuit Judge W. D. McSween, who was a leading civic and political force in Tennessee at the time of his death in 1945. Judge McSween's wife was the former Miss Rowena Jones.

The Commissioner attended the public schools of Newport and received his higher education at the University of Tennessee, where he was active in all phases of student life. As an undergraduate there, he served as editor of the student publication The Orange and White and as associate editor of the yearbook; he was a member of the Publications Council and the All-Students Council, and was elected to the Scarabbean Senior Honorary Society and Sigma Alpha Epsilon fraternity. Mr. McSween received his legal training at Cumberland University, and was admitted to the Tennessee Bar in 1942. He practiced law in Newport for ten years, with the exception of the period spent in wartime service; he represented the fifth generation of McSweens to follow that profession at the Cocke County seat. He served as city attorney there for four years, 1946 through 1949. He had also served the Tennessee Valley Authority and the Veterans Administration in legal capacities, and served for a time as assistant area director for the War Manpower Commission in East Tennessee. He is a member of the Tennessee and American bar associations. Mr. McSween served with the Signal Corps, United States Army during World War II.

Commissioner McSween was state vice president of the Tennessee Young Democrats the year Governor Clement was president, and up until his appointment in his present capacity, was active in state political circles, serving as state field manager for the Clement campaign in 1952. He has been recognized as one of the country's most progressive Employment Security administrators, and has served as vice president of the Interstate Conference of Employment Security Agencies and as a member of its legislative committee. He is currently chairman of that organization's veterans and military affairs committee. He has been one of the most active agency heads in the country in supporting the International Association of Personnel in Employment Security, the department employee's professional organization, and has served as vice chairman of the International Council for Personnel Development, which has membership from many groups in this country and abroad.

He has pioneered in programs seeking jobs for the physically handicapped, the older workers, paroled prisoners, and returning veterans. Much of his time has been spent in public relations activities in an effort to get over to the people of the state the true meaning and goals of the vast Employment Security program. Since assuming his cabinet post in 1953, Donald M. McSween has devoted himself to the economic problem of the loss of our people, particularly young people, to other states and areas. He has also concentrated his attention, and that of the department, on the creation of new job opportunities within the state.

Following his return from military service, Mr. McSween joined the American Legion, and rose through various offices to that of Department Judge Advocate, which he held in 1946. In 1947 he was elected State Commander, the first from the ranks of World War II veterans. He has served on several national committees of the Legion and is now a member of the National Convention Commission and the State Executive Committee. As Department Commander of the American Legion, he started several new programs including newspaper and radio awards and inaugurated the statewide employer awards program in connection with the hiring of the physically handicapped veterans. He has since served as chairman of the Inter-Agency Committee of National Employ-the-Physically-Handicapped Week.

Commissioner McSween has been active in numerous civic and fraternal enterprises, including work in the Benevolent and Protective Order of Elks, the Lions, Kiwanis, Chamber of Commerce and the Forty and Eight. He was honorary state director of the March of Dimes for several terms and has headed county and sectional campaigns for it, the Red Cross, Cancer Society, Tuberculosis Association, East Tennessee Crippled Children's Hospital, and other drives. In 1947 he was chosen by the State Junior Chamber of Commerce as Tennessee's Outstanding Young Man of the Year for his civic and charitable accomplishments in the preceding year, although he was not a member of the Junior Chamber himself.

Affiliated with the Free and Accepted Masons, he is a member of the higher bodies, including the Knights Templar Commandery, and holds the Thirty-second Degree. He and Mrs. McSween attend the Presbyterian Church.

She is the former Miss Louise Valentine of Newport, Tennessee, and Greenville, South Carolina. The couple have no children. Mr. McSween's offices are in the Cordell Hull Building.

GEORGE MAHAN, JR.

George Mahan's long and distinguished career in architecture has been centered in Memphis. From the early years of the century, he has worked on

ARNOLD SHAPLEY, JR.

GEORGE MAHAN, JR.

the design of a number of the outstanding buildings erected in the area—commercial structures, schools, churches, industrial plants, residences.

A native Memphian, Mr. Mahan was born on April 6, 1887, and is a son of George, Sr., and Jessie (Steel) Mahan. His father was born at Muscatine, Iowa, in 1862, and was brought to Memphis by his parents as a boy. Reared in the city, he was a businessman and musician there for more than fifty years. He was first associated with Oliver Finnie Company of Memphis and later with the Memphis Wholesale Grocery Company, which he managed. Then, for over forty years, he was successfully engaged in the mercantile brokerage business. A communicant of the Second Presbyterian Church for many years, he directed the church choir. He sang bass in the choir and was an ardent devotee of the opera. His wife, the former Jessie Steel was born in Louisville, Kentucky. They were the parents of five children: four sons and one daughter: James Steel, George, Jr., Frank, Angus Campbell, and Jessie Hoyt, George Mahan, Sr., died March 6, 1937, and his wife died in October, 1919.

Receiving his public school education in Memphis, George Mahan, Jr., entered the office of Shaw and Pheil, Architects, at the age of fifteen. While with them, he took courses in architecture and an engineering course offered by International Correspondence School in Chicago. In 1907 he became associated with N. M. Wood, who was at that time one of the leading architects of Memphis. Together, they drew the plans for the Exchange Building in 1909—the largest and most modern office building erected in the city up to that time and for some years afterwards. During the same period, Mr. Mahan also collaborated on the plans for the First National Bank Building, J. J. Broadwell, who later became a partner of Mr. Mahan, was associated with him and Mr. Wood in drawing these plans.

In 1910 the firm of Mahan and Broadwell was organized with Mr. Mahan as senior partner. The firm was one of the most active and highly regarded in the city, and ranked with the leading architectural organizations of the state and the South. They designed the American Savings Bank Building, a majority of Shelby County schools, and many modern business structures in and out of Shelby County, including some in Mississippi and Arkansas. They made a specialty of schools and churches. They drew plans for additions to the Western Tennessee Normal School, now Memphis State University, and a large number of private residences throughout the Delta region. Their work on the Exchange Building won them the contract for the Cotton Exchange Building, which succeeded to the title of finest office building in the South.

Early in 1920, Mr. Mahan opened a branch office in Greenwood, Mississippi, doing all types of commercial architectural projects, and designing schools and public buildings, and many fine mansions of the Mississippi Delta region. This office was closed in 1930. Shortly after the Cotton Exchange Building was completed, he began to practice by himself. In the early years of his independent work, he designed the King Cotton Hotel in Memphis, and remodeled the Brys Department Store, combining six separate buildings into one. He designed many of the high schools of the area, and medical centers including Dr. Campbell's Clinic and the Baldwin-McElroy Clinic. His work also included the Nineteenth Century Club Auditorium, and he planned the first penthouse in Memphis, atop the Manhattan Savings Bank Building and this was his office. He also designed the Skyway Room in the Hotel Peabody, one of the finest supper club rooms in the United States. Other projects which he planned include the C. M. McCord Pumping Station, the $2\frac{1}{2}$ million dollar addition to Memphis Central Police Station, facilities for the Tri-State Lumber Company and for cotton warehouses and cotton compresses.

In 1947, Mr. Mahan was joined by Mr. Shappley, who became a junior partner in the firm in 1956. They have completed the $3,000,000 addition to the St. Joseph Hospital at Memphis and are now engaged in planning the seven story doctors' office building connected with St. Joseph Hospital.

Other structures whose plans have come from Mr. Mahan's boards over the course of the years have been the Fayette County Courthouse at Somerville, the Normal Practice School at Normal, the Dyersburg Methodist Episcopal Church, the Hellenic Orthodox Church in Memphis, the Whitehaven School at Whitehaven, plant for the Saniwax Paper Company, the Union Chevrolet Building, the Children's Clinic in Memphis, LaBlanche Apartments, Moores Studio Building in Memphis, the model home for Chickasaw Gardens, in that city, the Women's Art Building in Memphis, and the School and Church of the Madonna at Frayser Station. The school was remodeled into a monastery and an addition was later added. He designed the residence of Mrs. Frank Crump in Memphis, one of the finest examples of colonial architecture in the South; and also residence of Horace Twiford, Robert Galloway, J. C. Rainer, Dr. Harry Schmeisser, Peter Van Vleet, Curtis King, W. H. Wiley, McKay Van Vleet, W. D. Cannon, Dr. J. B. McElroy, J. N. Magna, Joseph Thomson, O. P. Hurd, Paul Dillard, E. F. Gibbs, C. B. Stout, the J. Everett Pidgeon Homes (Father and Son) and that of John Sneed Williams. These residences are all in Memphis. Clients outside the city who have had Mr. Mahan design their residences are Oscar Bledsoe of Greenwood, Mississippi, Peter Grant of Germantown, Will Hale of Whitehaven, W. R. Humphries of Greenwood, Mississippi, R. E. L. Wilson, Jr., of Wilson, Arkansas, Allen Hobbs of Greenwood, Mississippi, Ferd Rogers and S. B. Dodds, both of Clarksdale, Mississippi, and the Thomas P. Florida and George Florida homes in Osceola, Arkansas.

The following statement of Mr. Mahan expresses his creed as an architect:

Architecture is an art in which effective collaboration is of prime importance. It is not, as are painting, sculpture, and music, the endeavor of a single mind. Only by coordination of effort on the part of client, architect, and builder can the best results be achieved. We feel that we have been particularly fortunate in our association with those who have joined their efforts with ours. . . . Our clients by the high merit of the idea brought to us and our coworkers in the various crafts, and by their sympathetic understanding in its execution, share with us whatever measure of success we have obtained.

Mr. Mahan is a member of the Chamber of Commerce and the Tennessee Club. He is also a member of the American Institute of Architects. He has always taken a constructive interest in Democratic politics, and he attends the Second Presbyterian Church. He is fond of the out-of-doors, particularly hunting and fishing.

On November 25, 1909, in Memphis, George Mahan, Jr., married Emily Smith, who is a native of Gibson County. The couple have two children: 1. Elizabeth Ann, who married E. G. Ballinger of Atlanta. They have a daughter, Nora Gorman. 2. Emily Smith, who married John B. Tomlinson of Jacksonville, Florida. Their children: J. B., Jr., and George M.

ARNOLD SHAPPLEY, JR.

As an architect with experience in a number of large projects, Arnold Shappley, Jr., is now a partner of George Mahan, Jr., in Memphis.

He is a native of Benton County, Mississippi, and was born on June 24, 1927, son of Arnold, Sr., and Era Norene (Holley) Shappley. Both parents were born near Ripley, Mississippi, his father on November 26, 1905, and his mother September 1, 1908. The younger Arnold Shappley received his education through the ninth grade at the White Station School at Memphis, where the family had moved when he was young; and he completed his secondary studies at Memphis Technical High School, where he graduated in 1945. He had served in the Marine Corps, and had begun his professional career, before he completed his advanced training in architecture. Entering the Marines following his graduation from high school, he served for a year, spending some time in the Pacific and in Northern China.

On receiving his discharge in May, 1946, he returned to Memphis, where he joined George Mahan as an apprentice draftsman, and continued in drafting duties until 1951. At that time he left for Oak Ridge, where he worked as an engineering draftsman in the Y-12 plant of the Carbide and Carbon Chemical Company until 1953. Rejoining Mr. Mahan in that year, he is now a partner in the firm. Mr. Shappley took his first advanced courses in architecture and engineering from International Correspondence Schools in 1950. Between 1952 and 1958, he took extension courses at the University of Tennessee and he took Georgia Institute of Technology's refresher course in design in 1953. He is a member of the American Institute of Architects

He and Mr. Mahan recently completed the three million dollar addition to St. Joseph Hospital in Memphis. They are now engaged in work on a seven story office building connected with St. Joseph Hospital. Projects in which Mr. Shappley and Mr. Mahan were associated included: The Florida Brothers homes in Arkansas; the Bank of Wilson in Wilson, Arkansas; the two and a half million dollar addition to the Memphis Central Police Station; the Somerville Bank and Trust Company in Somerville, as well as the Fayette County Jail at Somerville; also the Peoples Bank in Collierville, the Peoples State Bank in Millington as well as that bank's new drive; the C. M. McCord Pumping Station, Memphis; Lee Memorial Hospital in Marianna, Arkansas; Highland View Church of Christ in Oak Ridge, which church is to be used as an example of religious structure in a motion picture being made by A. E. C. and Union Carbide Company; other projects were the Barrettville Bank and Trust Company at Barrettville, the First State Bank of Henderson, Dyersburg Methodist Episcopal Church, the Children's Clinic in Memphis, and a number of commercial buildings, apartment houses and private residences.

Mr. Shappley is a member of the Memphis Athletic Club, and is a communicant of the Berclair Church of Christ.

At Senatobia, Mississippi, on December 5, 1944, Arnold Shappley, Jr., married Kathryn Elizabeth Billingsley, daughter of William and Kathryn (Clark) Billingsley. The couple are the parents of two children: 1. Kenneth Leslie, who was born on May 15, 1955. 2. William Arnold, born June 25, 1959.

CARROLL FRANK FOURMY

Retiring in recent years after a long connection with the firm of Penick and Ford, Ltd., Inc., of New Orleans and New York, Carroll Frank Fourmy entered upon a new cycle of business activity in Memphis, Tennessee. There he joined a new partner, I. Guy Williams, and organized the food brokerage firm of Fourmy and Williams.

Carroll Frank Fourmy was born in Franklin, Louisiana on October 4, 1892. He is the son of James Campbell, (a Civil War Veteran) and Martha Louisiana (Thompson) Fourmy. His father was a planter who owned a sugar plantation in Franklin. There Carroll Frank received his public elementary and high school education. He attended the University of Texas, Austin, Texas, for his advanced studies.

At the time of World War I Mr. Fourmy entered the U. S. Air Corps and was discharged December, 1918, with the rank of sergeant. When he returned to civilian life in 1918, he formed his connection with Penick and Ford, Ltd., Inc. in New Orleans, Louisiana, and remained for thirty-nine years, becoming assistant Southern sales manager and sales manager of the Central South. In the course of this period he lived in several states.

On December 30, 1957, he retired, but being a man of active nature Mr. Fourmy found that complete withdrawal from the business world was distasteful to him. He decided to re-enter the industry with which he was familiar, so organized the food brokerage firm.

A vice president of the Memphis Cotton Carnival, Mr. Fourmy also serves on its board of directors. He is a member of the Kiwanis Club, the Tennessee Club, Petroleum Club and the Rivermont Club. He and his family attend the Second Presbyterian Church.

Mrs. Fourmy, the former Mary Louise Ellis, is the daughter of William Arthur and Minnie Ella (Jarvis) Ellis, both of Petersburg, Tennessee. She attended Randolph-Macon Woman's College, Lynchburg, Virginia and joined Kappa Alpha Theta sorority while there. She is a member of Lisons Book Club, Walnut Grove Garden Club, and the Friendship Circle of Kings Daughters.

The couple were married in Okolona, Mississippi, on April 30, 1919. They are the parents of two children: (1) Joye, who was born in Monroe, Louisiana, on November 28, 1920. She attended Southwestern College, Memphis, Tennessee, and was graduated from Randolph-Macon Women's College in June, 1942.

Joye is the wife of Oliver P. Cobb, Jr., of Memphis. She has two children by a former marriage, Lisa Thompson, who was born on December 2, 1944, and Tommy Thompson, born February 11, 1947.

By her present marriage she is the mother of another child, Carroll Fourmy Cobb, born September 24, 1957.

(2) Carroll Frank, Jr., was born on March 11, 1924, in Little Rock, Arkansas.

He attended the University of Tennessee and graduated with a degree of Bachelor of Laws in 1948. While there he was a member of the Sigma Alpha Epsilon and Omicron Delta Kappa fraternities.

Carroll Frank Fourmy, Jr., married Beverly Stewart. Their children are Carroll Frank, III, born March 6, 1953, Margot Ellis, born February 19, 1957, and Richmond Stewart, born March 28, 1960.

HOMER K. JONES

One of the prominent citizens of Memphis and a respected member of the business community of this city, Homer K. Jones is a native Mississippian, and a former resident of Missouri. He moved to Memphis, Tennessee, in 1906, and has made his home there since.

Born in Mississippi, he was taken by his parents, Millard Fillmore and Martha (Cheshire) Jones, to West Plains, Missouri, when he was two years old. He received his early education in Missouri public schools and later graduated from West Plains College in Missouri. He studied accounting in various business schools. Moving to Memphis in 1906, he established the certified public accounting firm of Homer K. Jones, and has operated this successful business enterprise ever since.

In the early days he specialized in federal taxation matters extensively, and had offices in Washington, D. C., Nashville, Tennessee, Knoxville, Tennessee, New Orleans, Louisiana, and Little Rock, Arkansas. He successfully represented the Piggly Wiggly Corporation in a suit before the federal tax courts—litigation which has been called "one of the largest cases of its kind in the Memphis area." At one time, Mr. Jones employed over one hundred people on his staff. The firm is one of the largest of its kind in Memphis—probably the largest locally owned. At one time, prior to the founding of the Federal Reserve System, Mr. Jones represented all of the leading banks in the city.

Homer K. Jones is a member of the Cotton Carnival Society, the Fifty Club, the Memphis Country Club, Memphis Hunt and Polo Club, the Tennessee Club, and Mud Lake Club. His hobby is hunting. He maintains an extensive shooting preserve in the vicinity of Grand Junction, Tennessee, and there he has a hunting lodge and other facilities for entertaining his guests and members of his organization. He maintains his residence in Memphis, but owns and operates a six-hundred-acre farm at Germantown, Tennessee.

On June 17, 1908, in Memphis, Homer K. Jones married the former Martha Louise Edmondson. She is the daughter of Frazer Titus and Mary (Howard) Edmondson of Memphis. Her family dates back to the days of early Memphis settlement, and her great-grandfather, Frazer Titus, built the first two-story house in the city, according to official Memphis records. Mr. and Mrs. Jones have a daughter, Jacqueline Carey, born March 24, 1916.

RICHARD GORDON HOLLADAY

Richard Gordon Holladay, president of the firm of Marx and Bensdorf, has had a long career in federal housing and in home loans and insurance, not only in the city of Memphis but throughout the state of Tennessee.

He was born in Dresden, Tennessee, on July 30, 1908, the son of the well-known Dresden attorney, Lake Erie Holladay, and Addie May (Hummel) Holladay of that city.

He attended elementary and high school in Dresden before entering Southwestern at Memphis which he attended for two years. He then attended Cumberland Law School in Lebanon, Tennessee, and after passing the bar, practiced law in Dresden from 1930 to 1935 when he joined the Memphis Insuring Office of the Federal Housing Administration as attorney for them in the State of Tennessee. In 1946, he left government service to join the firm of Marx and Bensdorf Inc. in Memphis as vice president and secretary, also serving as secretary of The Home Federal Savings and Loan Association. In 1950, Mr. Holladay was named president of these two firms as well as of the Memphis Fire Insurance Company, and the Securities Investment Company, in which posts he currently serves. Mr. Holladay is a member of the Board of Governors of the Mortgage Bankers Association of America, and is a member of United States Savings and Loan League. A staunch Democrat, he served as Direct Representative to the Tennessee General Assembly from 1933 to 1935. Mr. Holladay is an ardent Mason, a member of F. & A.M. Number 722, a Knight Templar and Shriner, a member of Al Chymia Temple. His clubs

R.G. Holladay

include the Tennessee Club, the Fifty Club, the Petroleum Club and the Colonial Country Club.

He was married to Martha Elizabeth McDaniel on December 21, 1934 at Bemis, Tennessee. She is the daughter of Elmer Finch and Martha Elizabeth McDaniel of Covington, Tennessee. Mr. and Mrs. Holladay are the parents of: 1. Richard Gordon, Jr., born June 29, 1941; 2. Harold Lake, born May 30, 1943; and 3. John McDaniel, born November 16, 1945.

WILLIAM WESLEY WHITE KIRKSEY

In his late seventies, William Wesley White Kirksey operates one of the leading lumber businesses in Tennessee in association with his sons in the firm of W. W. Kirksey and Sons, founded in Bolivar in 1932. He has been associated with the timber industry in Tennessee and in Arkansas since before the turn of the century and has been in business for himself from 1907 when he established the firm of W. W. Kirksey, manufacturing spokes and handles.

He was born in Jonesboro, Craighead County, Arkansas, on February 28, 1882. His father, the late Joseph W. Kirksey, born in East Tennessee, lived most of his life in Arkansas, where he was a farmer. His wife, the late Sarah Helen (Duke) Kirksey and Joseph W. Kirksey are both buried in Jonesboro.

William W. Kirksey attended elementary school in Jonesboro and after completing his primary education, entered the lumber business as an independent cutter for various saw mills. For a time he was associated with an independent operator in Craighead County, Arkansas, but in 1907, he established his own firm, operating it for the next thirty years. In 1919, he opened a branch mill at Millington, Tennessee, and later added mills in Covington and Brownsville. He settled in Bolivar in 1932 where he established W. W. Kirksey and Sons. Mr. Kirksey built up and enjoys one of the finest timber and lumber businesses in Tennessee. He is still active in the business.

He married the former Versie Jane Mills on December 29, 1907 in Jonesboro where she was born on August 26, 1891. Her parents, the late Lonnie and Sally (Pipes) Mills, are both buried in Freemanville, Arkansas, where they lived the latter part of their lives. William Wesley and Versie Jane Kirksey celebrated their Golden Wedding Anniversary, December 29, 1957. They have two sons and daughters: 1. Mary Irene Kirksey (Frost), born November 1, 1908 and the mother of one son, William Kirksey Frost. 2. Elsie Fay Kirksey (Pruitt), born October 1, 1910, the mother of Walter Lee Pruitt, Jimmie Pruitt and Betty Joe Pruitt Wadley, who has a son Luke Wadley, Jr. 3. Estle J. Kirksey, born February 22, 1914, who is the father of Robert E., Carolyn, Marylin, Donna Gene and Mike Kirksey. 4. Russell L., born June 22, 1916, the father of Jane, Charles Lynn, Marjorie Ann and Ted Roy Kirksey.

Herbert Bernard Moriarty, Jr.

One of Memphis's younger professional men, Herbert Bernard Moriarty, Jr., is a member of the law firm of Exby, Moriarty and Goff, with offices in the Commerce Title Building. He is now serving as representative from Shelby County in the Tennessee State Legislature.

Born June 5, 1929, in Memphis, he is a son of Herbert Bernard, Sr., and Kathleen Doyle (Prindaville) Moriarty. His father, a lawyer, was likewise a partner in the firm of Exby, Moriarty and Goff. The younger Herbert B. Moriarty received his high school education at Christian Brothers College; he attended college at Vanderbilt University, where he graduated with the degree of Bachelor of Arts in 1950. He also took his professional courses there, receiving the degree of Bachelor of Laws in 1952.

Admitted to the Tennessee bar, Mr. Moriarty practiced law for a few months before entering the United States Air Force. He remained in uniform until 1954, serving in Texas (Randolph Field) and Alabama (Maxwell Field). He holds the rank of captain at present in the Ready Reserve forces of the Air Force.

Mr. Moriarty resumed his practice with the firm of Exby, Moriarty and Goff. He is licensed to practice before the United States Supreme Court and lower United States courts, the Tennessee Supreme Court and lower Tennessee courts. He was elected to the Tennessee House of Representatives from Shelby County in 1958. He is also a member of the Shelby County Democratic Executive Committee.

In addition to the national, state and regional bar associations (past vice president, Memphis Junior Bar), he belongs to Delta Theta Phi legal fraternity, and to Sigma Chi social fraternity. His local club memberships include the University Club, the Saddle and Spur Club, and the Bachelors' Club of Memphis, of which he is president. He is also president of the Muscular Dystrophy Chapter of Memphis and Shelby County and co-chairman of the Memphis Round Table of the National Council of Christian and Jews. He is also a book reviewer for the Memphis Commercial Appeal, and periodicals. A Roman Catholic, he attends Immaculate Conception Church.

Fountain Ezekial Pitts, Jr.

Mr. Pitts' career includes newspaper reporting, retail selling, twelve years in the Tennessee State Labor Department and the Employment Security Department, and, since 1950, County Clerk for Rutherford County.

Fountain E. Pitts, Jr. was born at Murfreesboro on January 19, 1911, the son of the late Fountain E. Pitts, Sr., and the late Mary Etta (Cowan) Pitts. His father was born in 1869 in Rutherford County and died in Murfreesboro in 1939; he attended Union University and was chief of police in Murfreesboro for eighteen years. His mother, born in Memphis in 1869 and died in Murfreesboro in 1949, was active in Church of Christ organizations.

Mr. Pitts was educated in the public schools of Murfreesboro and while attending Murfreesboro High School worked for the Daily News Banner at Murfreesboro, now called the Murfreesboro Journal. After graduation from school, he worked for the Firestone stores in Murfreesboro and two years later went to work for the State Labor Department. Subsequently he worked for the State Employment Security Department. In 1950, after twelve years in state service, he ran for the post of County Clerk for Rutherford County. He was elected and has since been reelected to this position which he currently holds.

During World War II, Mr. Pitts enlisted in the Army and served from November 1, 1942 to January 5, 1946. He was a sergeant major in the Engineers and saw service in the Asiatic and Pacific areas and holds a battle star for the campaign on Okinawa. He is a member of the Veterans of Foreign Wars, the Rotary Club and the Blue Raider Club. He and his family are members of the Church of Christ in Murfreesboro.

He married the former Jonnie Bailey at McMinnville on September 22, 1946. Mrs. Pitts is the daughter of Louis Bailey who was born in Warren County and is now deceased, and Edith (Jones) Bailey who makes her home in McMinnville. Mr. and Mrs. Pitts have two children: 1. Fountain Ezekial, III, born May 27, 1955; and 2. William Edward, born October 26, 1956. Both children were born in Murfreesboro.

SAMUEL ROBERT RAULSTON

Since he commenced his practice of law, Samuel R. Raulston has had offices in both South Pittsburg and Jasper. He is a veteran of wartime experience in the Army Air Corps; and in his own community he has taken a constructive interest in political affairs.

Born at Jasper, Tennessee, on June 27, 1923, he is a son of Samuel Polk and Lois Aline (Hudson) Raulston. His father too was born at Jasper, on April 11, 1896, and is an attorney with offices there and in South Pittsburg. He commenced his practice in 1921, shortly after his return from wartime service with the Marine Corps. He was in action overseas with this arm of the service, and held the rank of sergeant. He is also a veteran of World War II, during which he served in the Judge Advocate General's Department. Sent again to the European Theater, he held a commission as first lieutenant. Samuel P. Raulston took his degree of Bachelor of Laws at Cumberland University. He is a former county attorney of Marion County. Lois Aline Hudson, whom he married, was born in South Pittsburg on April 13, 1902. She is a music teacher in the Marion County schools, in which she has taught voice and piano for about thirty-seven years. She is a graduate of Chadex Conservatory in Chattanooga, Tennessee. Both Mr. and Mrs. Samuel P. Raulston are active in the Methodist Church.

Attending the public schools of Jasper, Samuel Robert Raulston completed his preparatory studies at Castle Heights Military Academy in Lebanon.

He went from there to military service, enlisting in the Army Air Corps, and was assigned to the 44th Bomb Group, a component of the Eighth Air Force. In action in the European Theater, he attained the rank of staff sergeant, and received the Air Medal and four oak leaf clusters.

Following his return to civilian life, he resumed his studies, and in 1951 received his degree of Bachelor of Laws from Cumberland University. In his earlier student years, he was interested in sports, playing football while in high school and military academy. After his admission to the bar of his state, Mr. Raulston commenced practice of law in South Pittsburg and Jasper, in 1951, and has offices in both towns at the present time. He is in partnership with his father.

A Republican, he is currently serving as chairman of his party. He is a member of the Lions Club. He attends the Methodist Church.

Choosing as his wife Miss Sue Brown of Jasper, Samuel Robert Raulston was married in that city on January 20, 1946. She was born on August 18, 1923, in Jasper, daughter of Newman Holland and Veda Brown. Mr. Brown is a retired merchant, and now lives in South Pittsburg. He was at one time a merchant in Jasper. Mrs. Raulston attended Marion County schools and graduated from the University of Alabama with a degree of Bachelor of Science. She trained as a laboratory technician. For three years she taught school in Jasper. She is also active in the Girl Scout movement, serving as a director of the local council.

Mr. and Mrs. Raulston have three children: 1. Pamela, who was born on April 2, 1948. 2. Susan Holly, born on January 26, 1953. 3. Katha, born May 20, 1954. All of the children were born in Chattanooga.

MAURICE FRANKLIN KEATHLEY, SR.

Maurice Franklin Keathley, Sr., has seen his bakery business grow from a modest home bakery enterprise into an over-a-million-dollar annual business. Incorporated in 1954, Mr. Keathley was elected president and board chairman, the posts he currently holds.

Born in Kenton, on September 9, 1905, he was brought up on the farm his parents, John Franklin and Myra Emma Moore Keathley, owned in this rural Tennessee area.

He attended the public schools in the town of Kenton and then worked on his father's farm until 1928 when he moved to Memphis to work for the Bowers Stores, later to become the Kroger Stores. In 1929, he worked for the Ford Motor Company, and towards the end of the year began a home bakery at 1000 Philadelphia Street. The business, started on a modest scale, grew steadily and developed into an over-a-million-dollar a year business. Today the company occupies a full block, frontage on Young Avenue, where approximately 75 people are employed. While the business was growing, Mr. Keathley and his associates organized the K & M Machine Company to manufacture

M. F. Keathley Sr.

bakery machinery designed to produce quality merchandise at lower cost. Mr. Keathley was elected president and board chairman of this company as well. He is a member of the Independent Order of Odd Fellows, the Lions International, and is president of the Memphis Union Mission. Mr. Keathley is a deacon in the Temple Baptist Church.

He married Ruby Geneva Haskins, daughter of William Edward and Rosa Esther Durham Haskins on August 28, 1924. The Keathleys are the parents of: 1. Maurice Franklin, Jr., born April 23, 1926; now vice president and sales manager of Keathley's, Incorporated. M. F. Jr. married Montie Lee Robertson of Memphis and they have three children, Cheryl, Randy and Robin. 2. Carman Royce, born December 18, 1927; vice president and production superintendent of Keathley's Inc. Carman R. married Louise Drennan of Memphis and they have two children: Carmen Kay and Connie Louise. 3. Royalyn, born February 7, 1933; an attorney in Memphis. 4. Rosamyra, born December 10th, 1934, and died December 27, 1934; and 5. Naymond Haskins, born September 25, 1940.

DAVID OWEN CONDRA

Engaged in a practice of civil law in the city of Nashville, David Owen Condra is one of that community's younger attorneys. He is with the firm of White, Gullett, Phillips and Steele, whose offices are in the L. and C. Tower. He is a veteran of Air Corps service, and takes an active part in bar and fraternal groups, as well as in civic affairs.

Born September 14, 1924, he is a native of Nashville, and a son of Rufus Russell and Bessie Bell (Brown) Condra. His father has been for forty-six years a department head with the Methodist Publishing House in Nashville. David O. Condra attended the public schools of that city, and went for his advanced studies to Vanderbilt University. There he received his degree of Bachelor of Laws. He was with the United States Air Force (Army) for three years, serving overseas as a flying aerial engineer.

Following completion of his professional courses, Mr. Condra was admitted to the Tennessee bar, and began practice in his native city. For the past seven years he has been identified with White, Gullett, Phillips and Steele in general civil practice. He is attorney for the Home Federal Savings and Loan Association. As a lawyer he belongs to the American Bar Association, the Tennessee State Bar Association and the Nashville Bar Association.

In the year 1958 Mr. Condra was a candidate to serve the people of his district in the Tennessee General Assembly.

Since his return from Air Corps service, he has been a member of the American Legion, and his memberships also include Phi Alpha Delta legal fraternity, Kappa Alpha fraternity, Hillwood Country Club, and the lodge of Free and Accepted Masons. In Masonry he is a member of the higher bodies of the Scottish Rite, holding the Thirty-second Degree, and he belongs to the

Ancient Arabic Order of Nobles of the Mystic Shrine. He also holds membership in the Benevolent and Protective Order of Elks. He is a member of the Methodist Church.

Mr. Condra is unmarried. He makes his home at 3907 Brighton Road.

ROBERT H. BADGER, D.D.S.

Robert H. Badger was born in Marion, Indiana, on November 21, 1927, the son of the late Ormus Harwood and Mabel (Givan) Badger. His father, born in 1908, was a musician. After his death in 1941, Mrs. Badger married Dr. J. K. Kaufman and now makes her home in Murfreesboro.

Robert H. Badger attended public schools in Murfreesboro, later graduating from Middle Tennessee State College with a Bachelor of Science degree. He receive his D.D.S. degree from the University of Tennessee in Memphis in 1956, and opened his office in Murfreesboro for the practice of dentistry on January 1, 1957. In February, 1958, he moved to Hartsville, Tennessee, where he is now practicing. He is president of the Kiwanis Club, and he and his family are members of the First Methodist Church in this city. Dr. Badger served in Japan with the Eleventh Airborne Division as a private, first class, from 1946 to 1948.

He married the former Robbie Gregory on June 4, 1950, at Clarksville. Mrs. Badger, born on February 12, 1929, in Trousdale County, is the daughter of W. C. and Grace Gregory. Mr. Gregory, born in 1906, lives at Pulaski, where he is a group manager with the Southern Bell Telephone Company in that city. Mrs. Badger is a graduate of Middle Tennessee College where she majored in English. For six years prior to her marriage, she taught in schools in Murfreesboro, Tullahoma and Memphis.

Dr. and Mrs. Badger have three children. They are: 1. Robert H., Jr., born November 19, 1951; 2. Bettye Lynn, born April 16, 1953; and 3. William Kenneth, born May 29, 1958. All of the children were born in Murfreesboro.

JOHN EARL ALLEN

After a number of years' experience in agriculture and merchandising, John Earl Allen took over his duties as sheriff of Meigs County three years ago.

He is a native of that county and was born on February 11, 1914, son of William Gaston and Artie (Atchley) Allen. Both parents have been lifelong residents of the same county. Attending local public schools, Sheriff Allen graduated from Meigs County High School in 1932. Shortly afterwards he started farming on his own acreage in his native area. His activities as a merchant began in 1941, when he established his store at Decatur, conducting business under the firm name of Allen's General Merchandise.

Mr. Allen was elected sheriff of Meigs County in 1956 and continues to hold this post to date. Reelected most recently, in November 1960, he is the first sheriff ever to be elected to a third term in the history of Meigs County.

He is a member of the Lions Club and the lodge of Free and Accepted Masons, and he and his family are members of the Shiloh Baptist Church.

Miss Lucy Blevins became the wife of John Earl Allen in a ceremony in Meigs County on September 3, 1933. She is the daughter of James Hoyle and Mary Lou (Neal) Blevins. Mr. and Mrs. Allen are the parents of the following children: 1. Charlotte Sue, born on February 21, 1936. 2. John Douglas, born June 1, 1937. 3. Jeanette Lou, who was born on August 13, 1940. 4. Betty Linda, born June 8, 1947. 5. Gail Sandra, born June 17, 1954. All of the Children were born in Meigs County.

SAMUEL FRANCIS COLE

Admitted to the Tennessee bar three decades ago, Samuel Francis Cole practices in Memphis, with offices in the Commerce Title Building. He has taken an active part in public affairs and in Democratic politics, and has served in both houses of the Tennessee State Legislature.

Born in Gibson County on October 19, 1905, he is a son of William Presley and Mary (Reynolds) Cole. He was named for his grandfather, Samuel Francis Cole, and is a first cousin of the late Judge Samuel Cole Williams, who was a Tennessee historian as well as a jurist. William P. Cole too was a native of Gibson County, and followed his career of farming in that county, where he died in 1926. Miss Reynolds, whom he married, was a native of Corinth, Mississippi.

Samuel Francis Cole received his early education in his native Gibson County and graduated from Medina High School there. He then entered Southwestern at Memphis, and took his professional courses at the University of Memphis Law School, where he graduated in 1930 with the degree of Bachelor of Laws.

Admitted to the state bar in that year, he began his practice in Memphis, where he has been since. He was first elected to the Tennessee Legislature for the 1935 term, and served for a total of six years—two terms in the House of Representatives, and one term in the Senate, where he concluded his tenure in 1941.

As a lawyer, Mr. Cole is a member of the State Bar Association of Tennessee, the Memphis and Shelby County Bar Association, and the American Bar Association. He is a member of the Chickasaw Council of the Boy Scouts of America. He is a member of the Tennessee Society of the Sons of the American Revolution and is a past president of the Memphis Chapter of the Sons of the American Revolution; a member of DeSoto Lodge of the Free and Accepted Masons and of the higher bodies of the Scottish Rite, he belongs to Al Chymia Temple, Ancient Arabic Order of Nobles of the Mystic Shrine and is a past president of the Shrine Luncheon Club. Mr. Cole is fond of various sports, and one of his hobbies is floriculture. He and his family are communicants of St. John's Episcopal Church.

On December 6, 1930, in Memphis, Samuel Francis Cole married Elizabeth Law, daughter of the late Alfred and Alma (Hogshead) Law. Mrs. Law
served for many years as Shelby County's first and only woman magistrate
and member of the County Court. Mrs. Cole is a native Memphian and she and
Mr. Cole are the parents of four children: 1. Mary Alma, who was born on
September 4, 1932. She is married to the Reverend James Parker, an Episcopal
clergyman at Peru, Indiana, and they have two children: i. Margaret Parker.
ii. Clare Parker. 2. Samuel Francis, Jr., born on July 26, 1936, and now serving
in the United States Air Force. 3. Betty Law, born March 13, 1943. 4. James
Presley, born April 1, 1945.

WILLIAM ASHMORE REED

William Ashmore Reed, the youngest of nine children, was born to William Keith Reed and Sarah Ann Welch Reed at Pocahontas, Hardeman
County, on May 7, 1882, and died on March 8, 1959, at Memphis.

"Uncle Willie" as he was affectionately known, lived most of his life at
Pocahontas. His formal education was limited to the public schools at Pocahontas and the Normal School, located at Middleton. He was always interested
in the young boys of the town and helped them to get started in their life's
work, using his facilities as stepping stones and encouragement. He was also
instrumental in securing a Junior High School at Pocahontas before the days of
good roads and consolidation. Mr. Reed was a member of the Church of Christ
and a Republican.

Mr. Reed married Mary Magdalene Gatlin, daughter of Albert Galloway
Gatlin and Nancy Keith Gatlin, in November, 1904. To this union were born
three children; Ara, Inez and William Ashmore Reed, Jr. Ara married Enoch L.
Mitchell, head of the History Department, Memphis State University, Mem-
phis, and one of the authors of this *History of Tennessee.* They were married
on February 8, 1930, and have two children, a son, Lieutenant Allan Reed
Mitchell, executive officer, USS Esteem, and a daughter, Mary Katherine
(Kitty) Mitchell, student at Lausanne School for Girls and Central High
School. Ara and Enoch also own and operate the Blue and Gray Book Shop,
one of the outstanding bookshops of the South.

Inez, second daughter, married Chalmers Patton Seabrook, owner of Paint
and Wallpaper stores, Jackson, Mississippi. They have three sons, Chalmers
Patton, Jr., graduate of Vanderbilt University and presently in the U.S. Army;
William Reed Seabrook, student, University of Mississippi, Oxford and Abi-
lene Christian College, Abilene, Texas. David Seabrook attends Junior High
School in Jackson.

William Ashmore Reed, Jr., was born at Pocahontas on September 23,
1917, and died on September 23, 1928, and was buried at Old Bethel Cemetery.

Mr. Reed's paternal ancestors, Thomas, George and Phelps Reed emigrated from Roane, England to the Carolinas and part of the large family

Virginia Gibbons O'Hara

S. E. O'Hara

moved to Giles and Lawrence County, Tennessee, in the earlier days of its history. Richmond Pearson Reed, William Reed's grandfather, a Cumberland Presbyterian Minister, moved to Hardeman County, Tennessee, and served Old Bethel Church on State Line Coach Road near Mattimore Hill. His wife was Kate Green Keith, daughter of William Alexander Keith and Sallie Hampton, and the family heritage names such names as the Wades, Yanceys, Randolphs, Jeffersons and Marshalls of Virginia, tracing descent from Lord Keith, Earl Mareschal of Scotland and from Edward, III of England. Lord Keith was created Earl Mareschal. His grandson, Sir William Keith married Elizabeth Gordon, daughter of Alexander, the first Earl of Huntley, and his wife, Annabelle Stuart, daughter of King James I of Scotland and great-granddaughter of Edward, III of England. In 1715, after the downfall of the Stuart dynasty, to which the Keiths were devoted, their property was confiscated and they were banished. Early in the 18th Century, one of the family, Reverend James Keith, left England and came to Virginia. He married Mary Isham Randolph, daughter of Thomas Randolph.

Mr. Reed's maternal ancestors included the Welch family from England, Mauldin from Ireland, and White from Scotland.

Mr. Reed has two surviving sisters, Mrs. Lois V. Majors, Los Angeles, California, ninety-seven years old, and Mrs. James Shelton (Ipie), Middleton, Tennessee, eighty-three years old.

William Ashmore Reed was Postmaster, merchant and landowner at Pocahontas until his retirement. His wife, Mary Gatlin, died December 1, 1933. The Gatlins lived in Virginia and the Carolinas before moving to Middle Tennessee. Andrew Gatlin married Jane West and moved to Mississippi from near Nashville. To this family was born seven children. Albert Galloway Gatlin, Mary Reed's father, married Nancy Keith, daughter of Sterling Yancey Keith and Eliza Jones. Sterling Yancey was a brother of Kate Green Keith who married Richmond Pearson Reed. Both Andrew Gatlin and Albert Galloway Gatlin served in Forrest's Cavalry from Mississippi in the War Between the States.

Mr. Reed moved to Memphis in 1947 and became a realtor for several years until he became ill. He married Mrs. Bessie Tipler Murray of Lynwood, California, on March 4, 1948, who had been a classmate of Mr. Reed in childhood days at Pocahontas, and she survives him, living at their home at 3637 Johnwood, in Memphis.

Harry Edward O'Hara

In the decade following his return from naval service in World War II, Harry Edward O'Hara acquired valuable experience in industrial connections, and this he has put to good use as a partner in the firm of Allen Bros. and O'Hara, Inc., of which he is treasurer. He holds the same positions in Allen

Bros. Construction Company, Inc. Both are engaged in commercial and industrial building.

A native of Greenville, Mississippi, Mr. O'Hara was born on September 4, 1912, and is a son of William Harvey and Leona Rugg (Foster) O'Hara. His father, who was born at Vincennes, Indiana, on August 25, 1874, was a merchant at Greenville. He died in that city on December 5, 1944. Miss Foster, whom he married at Cairo, Illinois, on November 29, 1899, was born in that city on February 22, 1882. She survives him.

Harry Edward O'Hara attended grade and high schools in Greenville, completing his secondary studies at St. Rose of Lima School in the same city. He began his career as a mortician, and took the State Board of Embalmers examination in Tennessee, being granted his license in 1933. He received his Mississippi license the following year. From 1930 until 1938 he managed funeral homes in Water Valley, Indianola, and Greenville, Mississippi.

Mr. O'Hara left the profession to take a special course in machine tool operations, and was employed by the U. S. Gypsum Company of Greenville, Mississippi, until 1942. He joined the United States Navy as a machinist's mate, second class, in July, 1942, and was later promoted to machinist's mate, first class. Until September, 1944, he was stationed at the Naval Air Station at Millington, Tennessee. He spent one year at sea in the South Pacific Theater of Operations aboard the U. S. "Provo Victory," AK-228, an ammunition ship of the United States Navy. He received his honorable discharge from the Navy on October 31, 1945.

In November, 1945, Mr. O'Hara joined the firm of Hay's Machine Tool Company in Memphis, as its machine tool representative in the Mid-South area, and at the same time he bought a tool and die shop which grew into Precision Tool Company, Inc., and Diamond Plating Company, of Memphis, a manufacturing plant and subsidiary producing ordnance ammunition for the United States Army. Mr. O'Hara joined his own firm in 1950 and served as vice president until the company's assets were sold to the Pace Corporation of Detroit, Michigan, in September, 1954.

In January, 1955, Mr. O'Hara became a partner and treasurer of the firm of Allen Bros. Construction Company, Inc., general contractors. A year later another company was formed under the name of Allen Bros. and O'Hara, Inc., and he is serving as treasurer of this firm. The two companies are located in Memphis, and are engaged in commercial and industrial building both within and outside of the state of Tennessee.

Mr. O'Hara had had military experience before he entered the wartime service of the Navy. He was a member of Battery "A," 114th Field Artillery, 31st Division, Mississippi National Guard, from 1928 until 1941. He is a member of the American Ordnance Association. Affiliated with the Free and Accepted Masons, he belongs to Lelia Scott Masonic Lodge No. 289, is a member of the higher bodies of the Scottish Rite, in which he holds the Thirty-second Degree, and belongs to Al Chymia Temple, Ancient Arabic Order of Nobles of the Mystic Shrine, at Memphis. He is also a member of the Chickasaw Country Club. He and Mrs. O'Hara attend the Mullin Methodist Church.

She is the former Miss Virginia Dawn Gibbons and became the wife of Harry Edward O'Hara in a ceremony in his native city of Greenville, Mississippi, on November 25, 1939. She was born at Morehead in the same state on December 9, 1915, daughter of Rufus Elmer and Bessie Mae (Field) Gibbons. Both of her parents had come to the South from Illinois. Her father was born at Belknap, that state, on May 26, 1891, and died July 28, 1954, in Memphis. Her mother, a native of Grand Chain, Illinois, was born May 8, 1889.

Mrs. O'Hara graduated from Greenville High School in 1934. She was employed by the Department of Agriculture, Extension Service, as secretary and assistant to the county home demonstration agent for Washington County, Mississippi, in 1938. In 1942 she transferred to the War Labor Board, which she served until moving to Memphis in 1944. There she rejoined the United States Department of Agriculture, Cotton Branch, in 1945, and was employed in this government bureau until she resigned in December, 1952. Mrs. O'Hara is past president of the National Federation of Business and Professional Women's Clubs, having held this office in both the Greenville, Mississippi, club (1943-1944), and that at Memphis (1948-1949). She was president of the Memphis Genealogical Society in 1958-1959. She is a member of the National Genealogical Society, is vice-leader of the Rosemary Circle, and held membership in the International Order of Kings Daughters in 1958-1959. She is a member of the Huguenot Society of the Founders of Manikin, a member of the Women's Executive Council, member of the Fort Assumption Chapter of the Daughters of the American Revolution, and a member of the Society for the Preservation of Antiquities. Mr. and Mrs. O'Hara have no children.

MILDRED ELOISE DOYLE

A long and most creditable record as teacher and educational administrator in Knox County has brought Miss Mildred Eloise Doyle to her present post as superintendent of that county's schools, with offices in Knoxville. She holds membership in a large number of educators' groups; and her vital and personal interest in the proper training and guidance of young people is a most constructive force in the cultural life of the area.

She is a native of Knox County, and was born on December 27, 1904, daughter of Charter Elbert and Illia Rutillia (Burnett) Doyle. Her father was a buyer for the Vestal Lumber Company for fifty-five years, and was also prominent in the public life of his region, serving for twenty-five years as a member of the Knox County Quarterly Court.

Miss Doyle attended local public schools and was graduated from Young High School in 1922. She then began her career in teaching, continuing her studies at the advanced level during the summers to enable her to serve more effectively in her professional capacities. She is a graduate of the University of Tennessee, where she took her degree of Bachelor of Science in 1940, and the degree of Master of Science in 1945.

After five years as a teacher in the elementary grades, in the public schools of Knox County, Miss Doyle became principal of the Vestal Elementary School. Beginning to teach at Vestal School in 1925 she became principal in 1929 and continued at the Vestal School until 1945. She then spent one year as supervisor, and in 1946, was named superintendent of Knox County schools.

Miss Doyle is a life member of the National Education Association, and a member and past president of the Tennessee Education Association. She is also a member of the East Tennessee Education Association, Knox County Education Association, the American Association of School Administrators, the Tennessee School Board Association, Tennessee Public School Officers Association, and the Tennessee County Superintendents' Association. She is also a member of the American Association of University Women and the Department of Rural Education, the National Federation of Business and Professional Women's Clubs and the University of Tennessee Alumni Association. Her fraternity is Delta Kappa Gamma, of which she is past president.

In her home city of Knoxville, Miss Doyle is a life member of the Parent-Teacher Association, and a member of the Young Women's Christian Association. She also belongs to the Huguenot Society, and is an honorary member of the Knox County Board of Commissioners. She attends the New Prospect Presbyterian Church.

CARL NICHOLAS STOKES

A native of Memphis who completed his training for his law career there, Carl Nicholas Stokes has to his credit an excellent record in public service as well as in private practice. He is now a member of the firm of Shea and Pierotti, and he has served in recent years on the benches of the city court and the traffic court.

Born on January 26, 1907, he is a son of John William and Edith (Burgess) Stokes. His father was a locomotive engineer, for many years employed by the Illinois Central Railway System. Carl N. Stokes attended Riverside Grammar School and Central High School in Memphis, after which he completed his secondary studies at South Side High School, where he graduated in 1925. In that year, he accepted a position with Illinois Central Railway System, working in its freight department for nearly a decade; and his advanced studies were completed while he was working in this connection. He was a student at Draughon's Business College during 1929-1930, studying accountancy. In 1931 he enrolled at the University of Memphis Law School, where he took his degree of Bachelor of Laws in 1933.

Mr. Stokes began his practice of law in 1934. Early in his career he turned his attention to the responsibilities of public office. He joined the legal department of the Unemployment Compensation Division of the State of Tennessee in 1937; and the following year, interrupted his private practice to devote himself to the duties of city court clerk. He filled that post until 1942, when he enlisted as a private in the United States Army. Assigned to the infantry, he advanced to the rank of captain in the course of the war years. At the time of the war's end in 1945, he was assigned to war crimes prosecutions in Manila, Philippine Islands, as one of the chief prosecutors of certain Japanese generals and others responsible for wartime atrocities.

When he received his honorable discharge from the army, Carl N. Stokes returned to Memphis, and assumed duties as clerk of the criminal court. He served until 1950 when he was appointed to the bench as judge of the city court. He became judge of the traffic court the following year, and served until 1953. At that time he returned to the private practice of law, and has since been a member of the firm of Shea and Pierotti, which has offices at 724 Commerce Title Building in Memphis.

Mr. Stokes is a member of the Memphis and Shelby County Bar Association, the Bar Association of Tennessee, and the American Bar Association. He has held office in a number of the social organizations of which he is a member, being past president of the Sertoma Club, the Gavel Club, the South Side Civic Club, and the Shrine Luncheon Club, all of Memphis. Affiliated with the Free and Accepted Masons, he is a member of McLemore Avenue Lodge No. 715. He is also a member of the higher bodies of the Ancient and Accepted Scottish Rite, and St. Elmo Commandery No. 15 of the Knights Templar. He belongs to Zaman Grotto, and to Al Chymia Temple, Ancient Arabic Order of Nobles of the Mystic Shrine and now serving as Oriental Guide. As a veteran of military service in World War II, he is a member of the posts of the American Legion, the Forty and Eight, and the Military Order of the World Wars.

Active in the Lindenwood Christian Church, Mr. Stokes served as an elder and as chairman of its official board from 1953 to 1956. Since 1954, he has been teacher of the Lindenwood Men's Bible Class.

At the Madison Heights Methodist Church in Memphis, on August 21, 1930, Carl N. Stokes married Laverne Judson, daughter of David Newton and Pearl Judson. The couple make their home at 115 Palisade Street, Memphis, and they are the parents of one daughter, Vicki Laverne, who was born on May 19, 1946.

JACK T. FARRAR, M.D.

Early in his career, Dr. Jack T. Farrar began his practice of medicine at Tullahoma, where he has been since. For the past decade he has served as mayor of the city.

A native of Flat Creek, Tennessee, Dr. Farrar was born on March 20,

1906, son of Clayton and Elizabeth (Thompson) Farrar. His father was born in Bedford County on July 24, 1882, and became a farmer in the region. He was active in the Flat Creek Methodist Church, and served for twenty-six years as magistrate of the 24th District, Bedford County. Elizabeth Thompson, whom he married, was born November 27, 1885, at Unionville. Her father, William Elgin Thompson, was one of a class of six which was the first to graduate from the University of Tennessee following the Civil War. Mrs. Farrar survives her husband and lives at Flat Creek. For the past fifteen years she has taught in the public schools of Shelbyville, and since passing her seventieth birthday, has taught only music. She is a graduate of Sole College, Murfreesboro, and holds the degree of Bachelor of Arts.

Dr. Farrar attended the public schools, and completed his secondary studies at Petersburg Prepartory School. He then entered the University of Tennessee at Knoxville, where he took his degree of Bachelor of Science in 1929. For his professional studies he entered the University of Tennessee Medical School at Memphis, and there received his degree of Doctor at Medicine in 1931.

The first two years following his graduation were spent at Grady Memorial Hospital in Atlanta, Georgia, the first year as an intern, the last as assistant resident physician. He then practiced medicine at Mulberry, Tennessee. He spent the year 1935 at Nashville, where he was associated with Dr. W. D. Haggard. He moved to Tullahoma on January 31, 1936, and established his general practice there. He has lived in the city continuously since that time.

A Democrat, Dr. Farrar was first elected mayor of Tullahoma in 1948, after serving one term as alderman. He has capably headed the municipal government ever since. In addition to public office and his practice of medicine, he is also one of the city's leading business men, being owner of the Goldstein Department Store. He also owns a half interest in the Shelbyville Motor Company at Shelbyville.

As a physician, Dr. Farrar holds membership in the American Medical Association, the Tennessee Medical Association, and the Tullahoma Medical Society. Apart from his professional affiliations, he is a Rotarian and a member of the lodge of Free and Accepted Masons. He attends the Methodist Church. Dr. Farrar was on the National Guard rolls from 1945 to 1956.

At Faunsdale, Alabama, on May 1, 1938, Dr. Jack T. Farrar married Grace McKee. A native of that place, she was born on December 7, 1912, daughter of Hilton and Elizabeth (Wilkins) McKee. Mrs. Farrar is a graduate of the University of Alabama, with the degree of Bachelor of Arts. The couple are the parents of the following children: 1. Jack T., Jr., who was born on July 9, 1939, at Shelbyville. He graduated from Webb Preparatory School in June, 1957, and is now attending the University of Tennessee, majoring in science and chemistry. 2. Elizabeth McKee, born at Shelbyville on February 20, 1943.

JUDGE GENE WALKER

Judge Gene Walker, who has practiced law in Jackson during the past decade, was recently chosen judge of the General Sessions Court of Madison County. He has been a leader in welfare and civic organizations in his home city.

Born September 4, 1917, at Ozark, Missouri, he is a son of Ross Ellis and Eula (Simmons) Walker. His father too was a native of Ozark, born on September 13, 1887, while his mother was born at Springfield, Missouri, on February 14, 1888. The father was a merchant of Ozark and later at Springfield, Missouri. He was formerly in United States Army service. He died in 1939. Gene Walker attended the public schools of Springfield, and graduated from Springfield High School, where he was baseball and football captain and president and valedictorian of his class. He was also football and basketball letterman. He entered Drury College, also located in Springfield, and graduated there in 1939, with the degree of Bachelor of Arts. He then read law in his brother Wayne T. Walker's law office and also clerked in a clothing store in Springfield to help defray the expenses of his education. For his professional training he went to Cumberland University at Lebanon, Tennessee, where he received his degree of Bachelor of Laws in 1948.

On September 14, 1943, Mr. Walker enlisted for service in the United States Army Air Corps, and served until April 8, 1946. Assigned to the 346th Bomb Group, he served in the Pacific.

In 1948, Mr. Walker commenced his practice of law at Jackson as an associate in the office of Pigford and Key. In 1952 he joined the firm of Hall, Martin and Walker, in which he was a partner until 1954, when it became Martin and Walker. This was his professional connection up to his election in September 1958 to the bench of the General Sessions Court of Madison County.

As an Air Corps veteran of World War II, he belongs to and is a past commander of the Veterans of Foreign Wars, and is a director of the V.F.W. Recreation Center. He is also a director of the Polio Foundation and the Young Men's Christian Association. He is a member of the Disabled American Veterans, the Lions Club and the Exchange Club, and as a lawyer holds membership in the American Bar Association, the Tennessee Bar Association and the Jackson-Madison County Bar Association. He attends the First Baptist Church, where he is superintendent of the Adult Department of the Sunday School. He is president of the Junior Bar Association and secretary of the Senior Bar Association.

In recognition of his contributions to his city, Mr. Walker was selected as Jackson's Young Man of the Year for 1952, and in 1954 was chosen Jackson's Man of the Year.

Twice married, Gene Walker chose as his second wife Ione Allen, daughter of Gilbert Lafayette and Mary Lillian (Williams) Allen. Both of her parents are natives of Tennessee, her father having been born at Greenfield on August 12, 1891, and her mother on March 18, 1886, at Bradford. Mr. and Mrs. Walker were married at Springfield, Missouri, on July 8, 1951. They make their home at 14 Windsor, in Jackson. By a previous marriage, Mr. Walker is the father of a son, Eugene Sanford Walker, who was born at Springfield, Missouri, on April 23, 1935.

George Awsumb

As an architect, George Awsumb was highly respected not only in his own city of Memphis, but well beyond the confines of his own state. In particular, he won a reputation for the design of church buildings, of which the Idlewild Presbyterian Church and the Baron Hirsch Synagogue are outstanding examples. A resident of Memphis for four decades, he made a substantial contribution to its present-day attractiveness as a city. An editorial in the Commercial Appeal, reviewing his career, appraised his work in these words:

. . . As an architect he designed and saw to the building of many of the more beautiful and impressive structures which are ours, notably churches and public buildings. He owned and exercised a remarkable ability for combining grace and durability in his work.

Mr. Awsumb was born in the town of Skien, Norway, on July 20, 1880, the son of Sigwart and Amborlena Awsumb. When he was four years old, the family came to the United States, and settled at Whitewater, Wisconsin. There the future architect attended the public schools, and graduated from high school. His first choice of a profession was mechanical engineering, and he began his studies at the University of Wisconsin. Soon, however, the family moved to Eau Claire, Wisconsin, and there he entered the building trade and concentrated his attention on the construction of barns. These barns were not the small ones found in many parts of the country, but huge structures formed with massive beams and rafters held together by wooden dowels. The experience he gained in this work was, he observed later in life, useful to him in planning churches and other large public structures, for there are basic principles in common. His work in construction also fixed his career interest in architecture, a profession which he had decided definitely to follow by the winter of 1901. He undertook his first studies independently, reading and sketching each night by lamplight after the fire had died down. Moving to Chicago the following spring, he entered the University of Illinois, where he took his degree of Bachelor of Science in Architecture in 1906. For two years he worked for various architectural firms, and his work won him the Chicago Architectural Club's traveling scholarship. Going to England, France and Italy, he toured these countries on a bicycle, and learned much concerning the structure of the classic buildings of antiquity.

George Rosemont

On his return, Mr. Awsumb taught for a year at the Chicago Art Institute, then returned to Europe to make a more thorough study of Gothic design and of the continent's famed cathedrals. This tour served to crystallize his determination to concentrate on the design of churches and other public buildings. However, in the course of his years in Chicago, where he remained until 1919, the design of residences remained his major interest. No less an observer than the writer and humorist Ring Lardner drew upon him in depicting a young architect, described in one of his early stories, "Own Your Home," published in the January, 1915, Redbook:

So we been talking to a young architect and he says we can put up a swell two-story house for $2000 and he will draw up the plans and see the house is built O.K. and all we have to give him is 5% of what it costs or $100 and he will look over the whole business and he's a good architect all right because he graduated out of the university and got his office up pretty near the top floor of the Jackson Building. Him and Grace has been figuring out plans for the house all year.

Mr. Lardner's appraisal of Mr. Awsumb as "a good architect" who kept his office "near the top" stood throughout his forty-five-year career. However, Mr. Awsumb left Mr. Lardner's part of the country in 1919, being attracted to Memphis when his design for the Ellis Auditorium won in a competition. In that city he joined the late Charles O. Pfeil, a prominent architect then practicing there, in seeing the building through to completion. In the years which followed, buildings of his design contributed much to the overall beauty of Memphis. The Idlewild Presbyterian Church, one of the best examples of his work, took second prize in the Christian Herald National Competition, and he also received awards for the First (Cloverdale) Methodist Church at Montgomery and the remodeling of the First Methodist Church of Memphis. In addition, he designed Methodist churches for Cocoa, Miami, and Coral Gables, Florida. Among religious edifices in his home city, the Baron Hirsch Synagogue was representative of the high standard of his work. Also locally, he designed the Dermon Building and the Cosmopolitan Funeral Home. At the time of his death he was working on a youth center for Idlewild Presbyterian Church and two Young Men's Christian Association youth buildings. His out-of-town contracts called for plans for the First Presbyterian Church and the Methodist Church at Osceola, Arkansas, the Second Presbyterian Church at Richmond, Virginia, and the C. Arthur Bruce Hall and the Administration Building at LeMoyne College.

His approach to his work, particularly in the design of churches, was one not only of conscientious service but of reverence. At his death, a memorial tribute in the editorial columns of the Memphis Press-Scimitar carried the following comment:

To him a Gothic church was a great symphony in stone, a sweeping wave of rhythmic movement caught at an instant's pause.

The lines of his churches were designed to draw the eyes of the beholder towards the chancel. He believed that ornament is one of the really vital phases of church design. When the ornamentation becomes meaningless, he said, the church is no longer alive.

The symbols were formerly a simple mode of expression for people of a day who could read in no other way and the ancient architects, he believed, placed the figures of the saints in the lower sections where worshippers could be near them and draw spiritual comfort and the fiends and gargoyles were placed high in the steeple and tower, as far away as possible.

In his own design of the great square tower of the Idlewild Presbyterian Church, which has been called "his most magnificent creation," the scheme called for the winged bull of St. Luke on one corner, the winged lion of St. Mark on another, and the symbols of St. Matthew and St. John on the remaining two.

During most of his years in Memphis, Mr. Awsumb headed his own firm, and he took his two sons into partnership with him on their graduation from the University of Illinois, to form the organization known as George Awsumb and Sons. Today the sons remain partners under the same name, with new offices at 2029 Peabody Avenue.

Mr. Awsumb was a member and past director of the American Institute of Architects, and a member of the Church Architectural Guild of America. He held National Architectural Registration. Locally, he was a charter member of the Sertoma Club, the University Club, and Chicasaw Country Club, and was a member and past president of the Egyptians Club. A communicant of Idlewild Presbyterian Church, he served as an Elder.

In Chicago, Illinois, on January 1, 1915, George Awsumb married Ella Wells, a native of Beatrice, Nebraska, and daughter of D. O. O. and Marie (McConnell) Wells. The couple became the parents of three children: 1. Wells, who was born on October 28, 1915. He is a graduate of the University of Illinois. At the time of World War II, he served in the United States Navy with the rank of lieutenant, and was in the North African Theater. On his honorable discharge, he joined his father in the architectural firm. He married Gwendolyn Van Court Robinson, and they have three children: i. George Wells. ii. Carl David. iii. Cathy. 2. Georgianna, born on February 14, 1918. She is a graduate of Southwestern University of Memphis, and studied medical illustration under Dr. Tom Jones at the University of Illinois Medical School. She is the wife of Major Lockwood Ensminger. They have three children: i. Lockwood, Jr. ii. Alan. iii. George. 3. Richard Norman, born on August 4, 1919. He is a graduate of the University of Illinois, and was in the United States Army for four years at the time of World War II. Assigned to the Ninth Army, he took part in the Normandy invasion, and participated in action in the combat areas of Europe. He returned to college for two years after the war, and on completing his courses, joined his father in the architectural firm. Richard N. Awsumb married Kathryn Gibson. They have three children: i. Richard, Jr. ii. John Kenneth. iii. Rebecca.

A distinguished career in architecture ended with the death of George Awsumb on November 24, 1959.

JOHN McCALL HEISKELL

An attorney practicing in Memphis since his return from wartime service in the United States Navy, John McCall Heiskell is now a partner in the firm of Montedonico, Boone, Gilliland, Heiskell & Loch. He has served his country as district attorney, is active in political affairs, and in fraternities and local organizations.

A native Memphian, he was born on March 17, 1913, son of L. Lamar and Ruth (McCall) Heiskell. His father too was an attorney in Memphis and died in 1929. Mrs. Heiskell is still living and has married, as her second husband, L. Y. Williamson.

After attending local public schools and graduating from Central High School, John M. Heiskell went to the University of Tennessee, where he completed both his advanced academic and his law courses and graduated with the degree of Bachelor of Laws in 1936.

Admitted to the bar, he commenced his practice in Jackson, where he remained through 1939. In 1940 he was appointed to a very responsible post for a man of his years, becoming Assistant Attorney General of the State of Tennessee. He continued his duties in that office until 1943, when he entered active service in the United States Naval Reserve, with a commission as lieutenant, junior grade. He was in action in the South Pacific, and participated in the invasions of Iwo Jima and the Philippines.

When he returned to his law practice after the war, Mr. Heiskell came to Memphis. There he became an associate in the firm of Westchester and Bearman. He resigned from this partnership in 1948 to become attorney general of Shelby County, and the performance of his duties in that office occupied his full time until 1955. Then going back to private practice, he joined the firm of Canale, Glankler, Montedonico and Boone and Loch as a full partner; the firm is now known as Montedonico, Boone, Gilliland, Heiskell & Loch.

Mr. Heiskell has remained active in public affairs, and was a delegate to the Tennessee Constitutional Convention of 1959.

In addition to the national, state and regional bar associations, Mr. Heiskell is a member of Phi Delta Phi legal fraternity and of Sigma Alpha Epsilon social fraternity. He also belongs to the lodge of Free and Accepted Masons, and to the Chicasaw Country Club. His favorite outdoor pastime is golf. He and his family attend Grace St. Luke's Episcopal Church.

In his native city of Memphis on January 23, 1937, John McCall Heiskell married Margaret Winchester. Also born in that city, she is a daughter of Lee and Harriet (Bond) Winchester. Mr. and Mrs. Heiskell are the parents of three children: 1. Margaret W., who was born on March 3, 1938. 2. L. Lamar, born on February 5, 1939. 3. Ruth McCall, born November 25, 1948.

DR. LELAND MANN JOHNSTON, SR.

A founder and part owner of Jackson Clinic, a staff member of the Jackson-Madison County General Hospital of Jackson, and a consultant to the Haywood County Memorial Hospital of Brownville, and to St. Mary's Hospital of Humboldt, Dr. Johnston has practiced medicine for twenty-five years and is a member of the visiting staff of the Webb-Williamson Hospital of Jackson. A director of the Tennessee Cancer Society from 1948 to 1952 and of the Tennessee Heart Association since 1953, he has been a trustee of the Tennessee State Tuberculosis Hospitals since 1948, and was counselor of the Tennessee State Medical Society from 1952 to 1957.

Dr. Johnston was born in Hickman, Kentucky, on July 30, 1907, the son of William Anderson Johnston and of Annie Lewis (Mann) Johnston. His father was born in Ripley, Lauderdale County, Tennessee, in 1873, and his mother in Brownsville, Haywood County, Tennessee, in 1889. Dr. Johnston attended the elementary schools in Hickman, Kentucky, graduated from Webb School, Bell Buckle, Tennessee, in 1925, and attended Vanderbilt University for three years. He received his medical degree from Tulane University in 1933.

Assistant resident in pathology at Vanderbilt Hospital, Nashville, Tennessee, in 1934 and 1935, and a resident and instructor from 1935 to 1937, Dr. Johnston was assistant resident in medicine at University Hospital, Ann Arbor, Michigan, in 1937 and 1938, and in 1938 and 1939 he was resident physician at the Maybury Sanitorium in Northville, Michigan. Assistant resident in medicine at Bellevue Hospital, New York City, in 1939 and 1940, he was a physician in the New York State Health Department in 1940 and 1941, and was stationed at the Mount Morris Tuberculosis Hospital, Mount Morris, New York. He was in private practice of medicine at Jackson, Tennessee, from 1942 to 1950 and since 1950, he has practiced at the Jackson Clinic, of which he is one of the founders and part owner.

Dr. Johnston has been active in professional organizations, and he is a Fellow of the American College of Physicians and of the American College of Chest Physicians and he is a member of the American Medical Association. He has been a trustee of Lambuth College in Jackson since 1950, was president of the Tennessee Heart Association in 1956 and 1957, and has been a member of the Jackson Rotary Club since 1942. He was initiated into Phi Kappa Psi fraternity in 1925 and Phi Chi medical fraternity in 1929. He attends religious worship at the First Methodist Church in Jackson, Tennessee.

Dr. Johnston was married in Chattanooga, Tennessee, on June 27, 1936, to Dr. Helen Presley, born in Scottsboro, Alabama, on November 29, 1911, the daughter of Solomon David Presley and of Annie (Boyd) Presley. Her father was born in Scottsboro on October 11, 1878, and her mother in Larkinsville, Alabama, on January 13, 1873.

Dr. and Mrs. Johnston have three children: 1. Annie Lewis, born in Nashville, on June 7, 1939. 2. William David, born in Memphis, on March 11, 1942. 3. Leland Mann, born in Jackson, Tennessee, on July 2, 1947.

LAWRENCE PLUMMER JACKSON

In his role as one of the more influential business leaders of the city of Jackson, Lawrence Plummer Jackson is active head of two firms. One of these, the L. P. Jackson Jewelry Store, is the longest established store of its type in the city, and it has retained its pre-eminence in the retail jewelry field. Mr. Jackson is its owner and operator. He is also president of Kelly Foods, Inc., manufacturers of quality canned meat products, which enjoy wide distribution in this area. Taking an active part in community life, he is a former director of the Jackson Chamber of Commerce.

He is a native of Franklin, Kentucky, where he was born on September 14, 1894, son of the late James Emory Jackson and the former Dora Dee Plummer. His father was born in Madison, Indiana, on July 28, 1850, while his mother, born on March 8, 1858, was a native of Huntsville, Alabama. The family moved to Jackson when Lawrence Plummer Jackson was in the first year of his life; and there, in 1895, his father established the present jewelry store, which has continued under the same family management to the present time.

Attending the city public schools, he graduated from Jackson High School, after which he entered the jewelry store in association with his father. At the advent of World War I, he volunteered for military service and was in the artillery and ordnance department. He held the rank of sergeant.

When the war was over he entered the Illinois College of Optometry, in Chicago, from which he was graduated with the degree of Doctor of Optometry. He was affiliated with the Omega Delta professional fraternity during his college days.

He began the practice of optometry in connection with the retail jewelry store established by his father; and in 1928 assumed responsibility for the management of the store as well. He has been its co-owner and active head since that time. More recently, he was chosen president of Kelly Foods, Inc.

When this country became involved in World War II, and the Tennessee National Guard was incorporated into Federal service, Lawrence P. Jackson entered the newly formed Tennessee State Guard. He was commissioned captain in the Jackson unit.

In addition to being a member and past director of the Chamber of Commerce, he is also a director of the Young Men's Christian Association, which he formerly served as president. He is a past president of the Jackson Rotary Club, a past commander of Post No. 12 of the American Legion, and a member of Launcelot Lodge No. 13, Knights of Pythias, of which he is past Chancellor Commander. He is also a member of Jackson Lodge of the Masonic fraternity and the higher bodies of Masonry. Holding the Thirty-second degree, he belongs to the Ancient Arabic Order of Nobles of the Mystic Shrine, and is a past worthy patron of the Order of Eastern Star. He is also a member of the Benevolent and Protective Order of Elks. He attends the First Methodist Church of Jackson, where he is a member of the board of stewards.

At Bemis, on February 2, 1928, Lawrence Plummer Jackson married Irene Romig Low, daughter of William Ross and Adalene (Romig) Low. Her father was born in Williamsport, Pennsylvania, on September 22, 1861, and her mother at Dewart, Pennsylvania, on September 25, 1873. Mrs. Jackson is now co-owner of L. P. Jackson Jewelers. For eighteen years, including the entire period of World War II, she was treasurer of the local chapter of the American Red Cross, and received a citation when she resigned. She is past president of the John A. Deaver unit of the American Legion Auxiliary; and also past department president of the state of Tennessee. At the present time she is chairman of the department of finance for the same organization. She is a past president of the Jackson Women's Club, and later served the Federation of women's clubs as treasurer and she is a member of the Business and Professional Women's Club. She is also a member of and past matron of the Order of Eastern Star.

Dr. Chester Leon Holmes

A staff member of Jackson-Madison County General Hospital of Jackson, and a courtesy staff member of St. Mary's Hospital of Humboldt, Dr. Holmes has been active in the practice of medicine since 1942, and he is a director of the Little Club and Madison County Tuberculosis Association since 1956; he was a director of the Idaho Tuberculosis Association from 1948 to 1951. He has made many contributions to medical literature, notably "Varicose Ulcers" with F. L. Smith; "Extensive Lymphangioma of the Scrotum, Penis and Adjacent Areas: Report of Case," with D. O. Ferris; and "Pyloric Stenosis Caused by Ingestion of Corrosive Substances" with H. K. Gray. He is also the author of "Electrolyte and Protein Balance in the Surgical Patient," "Surgery for Duodenal and Gastric Ulcers Revaluated," "Common Errors in Diagnosis of Carcinoma of the Lung" and "Pectus Excavatum—A New Surgical Technique."

Dr. Holmes was born in Lexington, Tennessee, on May 22, 1919, the son of Chester Lowe Holmes and of Addie Belle (Hamilton) Holmes. His father was born in Juno, Tennessee, on December 28, 1896, and his mother in Lexington, Tennessee, on August 16, 1900. Dr. Holmes attended Alexander Elementary School in Jackson, Tennessee, from 1925 to 1931, he studied at Jackson Junior High School, and graduated from Brazil High School in Trenton, Tennessee, in 1936. He attended Lambuth College, Jackson, Tennessee, from 1936-1939, where he was vice president of the student body in 1938 and 1939.

Joseph S. Bean

He received his medical degree from the University of Tennessee Medical College in 1942. He then studied at the University of Minnesota Graduate School (Mayo Foundation), Rochester, Minnesota, from 1943 to 1948, and received the degree of Master of Science in Surgery from the University of Minnesota in 1946. Dr. Holmes interned at Baptist Memorial Hospital, Memphis, Tennessee, in 1942 and 1943, and after completing his surgical studies, was on the active staff of St. Luke's Hospital and of St. Alphonsus Hospital in Boise, Idaho, from 1948 to 1951. At the same time, he was consultant in thoracic surgery at the United States Veterans' Hospital in Boise, Idaho, and at the Idaho Tuberculosis Sanatorium, Gooding, Idaho.

He headed the Department of Thoracic Surgery at the Marshfield Clinic, Marshfield, Wisconsin, from 1951 to 1953. Dr. Holmes was commissioned a major and served on active military duty with the United States Army as consultant in thoracic surgery for the European Command and was attached to the Ninety-eighth General Hospital at Neubreucke, Germany, from 1953 to 1955 as chief of the general and thoracic surgery section of the hospital. He resumed his active medical practice in Jackson, Tennessee, in 1955, and is now associated with the Jackson-Madison County General Hospital of Jackson and with St. Mary's Hospital of Humboldt, Tennessee.

Dr. Holmes served as president of the Community Concert Association in Jackson, Tennessee, in 1958. He has been active in professional organizations and is a Fellow of the American College of Surgeons and of the American College of Chest Physicians, a Diplomate of the American Board of Surgery and of the American Board of Thoracic Surgery, and a member of the American Medical Association. He also holds membership in the Alumni Association of the Mayo Foundation for Medical Education and Research and in the American Trudeau Society. His social connections include membership in the Jackson Rotary Club and the Jackson Country Club, and he attends religious worship at the Forest Heights Methodist Church in Jackson, Tennessee.

Dr. Holmes was married in Fulton, Kentucky, on April 16, 1938, to Lorraine M. Wagner, the daughter of Carlyle Lewis Wagner, D.D.S., and of Olive (Van de Plash) Wagner. Her father was born in Sheboygan, Wisconsin, on February 3, 1897, and her mother in Brookfield, Wisconsin, on December 9, 1896.

Dr. and Mrs. Holmes have two children: 1. Terry Jo, born in Rochester, Minnesota, on August 14, 1945. 2. Craig Leon, born in Butte, Montana, on October 5, 1948.

JOSEPH S. BEAN

Joseph S. Bean came to Winchester from Chattanooga, about a decade and a half ago, and there has continued his practice of law. He also has an excellent record as a state legislator, having served in both the Tennessee House of Representatives and the Senate.

He is a native of Franklin County, and was born on March 14, 1908, son of John Crawford and Elizabeth (Sanders) Bean. His father came from Alabama, having been born in Jackson County, that state, on January 3, 1866. A farmer and a stock dealer, he died in Franklin County in 1950. He is survived by his wife, the former Elizabeth Sanders, who lives in Chattanooga. She was born in Madison County, Alabama.

Attending the public schools of Winchester, Tennessee, Joseph S. Bean graduated from Central High School there, and from the University of the South at Sewanee, where he took his degree of Bachelor of Arts. For his professional studies he enrolled at Cumberland University, and there received his degree of Bachelor of Laws in 1932. He received the degree of Bachelor of Business Administration at the same time.

Admitted to the bar immediately after his graduation there, Mr. Bean commenced practice at Chattanooga, where he remained for ten years. He moved to Winchester in 1942, setting up law practice there, and that city has been the center of his professional activities ever since. He has been prominent in political and in civic affairs, as well as in the private practice of law, in which he has won a wide reputation.

A Democrat, Mr. Bean was elected to his first public office only three years after he had graduated from law school. In 1935, he represented Hamilton County in the Tennessee House of Representatives. He was elected state senator from that county in 1939.

He is a member of several bar associations and of Phi Gamma Beta, social fraternity which he joined at Cumberland Law School, and Sigma Delta Kappa. He also belongs to the lodges of the Woodmen of the World, the Independent Order of Odd Fellows, the Fraternal Order of Eagles, and the Benevolent and Protective Order of Elks. His favorite outdoor sport is hunting. He is a communicant of the Episcopal Church.

In Atlanta, Georgia, on July 25, 1941, Joseph S. Bean married Mary Frances Kelley. Born in Birmingham, Alabama, on the day before Christmas, 1918, she is a daughter of Scott and Willie Mae (Evans) Kelley. Her father was born in Marion County, Tennessee, and her mother in Alabama. Mrs. Bean attended East Tennessee State Teachers College in Johnson City, and graduated there with the degree of Bachelor of Science. She taught at Franklin County High School for four years, and at the Clara Carpenter School in Chattanooga for several years. She is now Sunday school teacher and pianist at the Cumberland Presbyterian Church.

She and Mr. Bean are the parents of the following children: 1. Joseph Scott, who was born on August 25, 1942, at Chattanooga. He is attending Sewanee Military Academy, and plays football and basketball there. 2. Jerry Wayne, born September 22, 1944, in Chattanooga. He is active in athletics at school. 3. Daniel Alan, born in that city on February 7, 1948.

GUY BALLARD AMIS

An educator in the early years of his career, Guy Ballard Amis of Lexington has been devoting his attention to business interests for nearly two decades. He heads the Lexington Amusement Company and Lexington Broadcasting Service; is a bank official; has insurance and agricultural interests; and serves on many boards of directors.

Born on a tenant farm near Juno, in Henderson County, Tennessee, on December 11, 1897, he is a son of August Joseph and Bettie (Ballard) Amis. Both of his parents were likewise native Tennesseans. His father was born at Somerville, Fayette County, on April 8, 1869, and his mother on September 2, 1871, at Juno.

Guy B. Amis attended the elementary schools of Henderson County, and received his secondary education at Lexington High School, where he graduated in 1921. He later attended Union University at Jackson, and Draughan Business College. However, in 1922, he began his career in education as a teacher in the Lexington High School, and served on its faculty through 1928. From 1929 until 1933 he taught in the schools of Henderson County, and he then returned to Lexington as superintendent of the city schools there, a position he capably filled until 1941.

At that time, Mr. Amis left the teaching field to enter banking. He joined the staff of the Central State Bank at Lexington as assistant cashier, and has been cashier since 1944. In 1935 he formed the Lexington Amusement Company, Inc., at Lexington, and began to serve as its secretary-treasurer and manager while still teaching. He has held all of these offices to the present time. Since 1955 he has been president of Lexington Broadcasting Service, Inc. He is a director of that company, of the Lexington Amusement Company and of Central State Bank, and also of the Panoply Corporation and Lexington Industrial Improvement Association, Inc. He is vice president and director of West Tennessee Industrial Association, Inc., of Jackson, and a director of Theatre Owners of Arkansas, Tennessee, and Mississippi, which has its headquarters in Memphis. Mr. Amis is also an insurance agent and a farmer.

From 1942 to 1944, Mr. Amis served in the Tennessee State Guard. He is a Rotarian, and a member of the lodge of Free and Accepted Masons. He is a Democrat, and he and Mrs. Amis attend the First Methodist Church of Lexington.

She is the former Miss Alberta Holmes, daughter of Joseph H. and Sallie V. (Wilson) Holmes. Both of her parents were natives of Henderson County, where her father was born in 1869, and her mother in 1867. Miss Holmes became the wife of Guy Ballard Amis in a ceremony at Lexington on December 24, 1923. The couple make their home on Monroe Street in that city. They are the parents of one daughter, Carol Ann, who was born there on November 29, 1929. She is now the wife of William T. Stone. Mr. and Mrs. Stone have a daughter, Sandra Ann Stone.

CHARLES RAYMOND WOMACK

After considerable business experience in various industries, dating back to his early youth, Charles Raymond Womack joined the Southern Supply Company at Jackson some years ago, and has advanced steadily to the presidency. He has been very active in community welfare and civic programs.

Born at McMinnville on July 4, 1905, he is a son of John Watson and Frances Isabel (Denton) Womack. Both of his parents were also natives of McMinnville, where his father was born on July 9, 1869, and his mother on December 18, 1873. Through his mother's line Mr. Womack is descended from the Reverend Richard Denton who came to America from England in colonial times and settled first in Massachusetts and later on Long Island. He was a pioneer Presbyterian church leader and served as pastor of the oldest Presbyterian church in America which is located on Long Island.

Charles R. Womack attended the public schools of McMinnville and graduated from McMinnville High School in 1924. Meantime, for six years before completing his public school studies, he had been working, learning the printing trade while on the staff of the Southern Standard at McMinnville, 1918-1924. When he graduated from high school, he took a full-time position as bookkeeper with the Walker and Smith Lumber Company, also at McMinnville. He remained with that firm for a year, then went to Florida, where for another year he was journeyman printer in Orlando and Miami. He returned to McMinnville in 1926, and took a position as office manager with the Menzies Shoe Company. He was a clerk with the Forest Nursery Company of McMinnville in 1928.

With the year 1929, Mr. Womack established his residence in Jackson, where he joined the Jackson Cooperage Company as a bookkeeper. During the next three years, while working there, he completed courses in higher accountancy offered by LaSalle Extension University, and received his degree from that institution in 1932. Mr. Womack has since studied at Southern University College of Law, where he completed professional courses leading to the degree of Bachelor of Laws in 1944. The same year he was licensed to practice law in the state of Tennessee. However, he has never done so, rather using his law training in the service of his business interests.

Mr. Womack formed his connection with Southern Supply Company at Jackson in September, 1932. He soon joined the management roster of the corporation, being elected secretary in January, 1933. In January, 1939, he became treasurer, while continuing his duties as secretary; and he was named to the board of directors in July, 1949. That same month he was elected first vice president of the company, and he became its president in December, 1955. He is now president and treasurer.

In 1943, Mr. Womack served as director and president of the Retail Credit Men's Association of Jackson. A member of the Jackson Exchange Club, he held office as its president and a member of its board of control in 1948.

He has also served as president of the Council of Community Agencies. He was United States Savings Bond chairman for Madison County from 1950 to 1955.

One of his major interests has been the program of the Boy Scouts of America, an organization to which he has rendered valuable service in various capacities. Since 1955 he has been treasurer, and a member of the board of control, of the West Tennessee Area Council; and he is also treasurer and trustee of the Mack Morris Boy Scout Foundation. He served as chairman of the committee to raise funds to add to the initial donation of Mr. Morris for the purchase of the Boy Scout camp near Camden, Tennessee, now known as Camp Mack Morris. In recognition of his services to the organization, Mr. Womack has been awarded the Silver Beaver.

A Republican in his politics and active in the councils of his party, he was a delegate to the Republican National Convention in 1956.

During 1943-1944, Mr. Womack served in the Tennessee State Guard, holding the rank of corporal. As a man trained in the law, he is a member of the Jackson-Madison County Bar Association. His other memberships include the Fraternal Order of Police, the lodges of the Benevolent and Protective Order of Elks and the Knights of Pythias, and the Jackson Golf and Country Club. He is an earnest worker for his church, the Central Church of Christ in Jackson. For the past twenty years he has served as a deacon there, and he is a former Sunday school superintendent.

In his native city of McMinnville, on July 19, 1929, Charles Raymond Womack married Sally Lee Carver, daughter of Joseph Cephas and Lucy H. (Moreland) Carver. Both of her parents were born in Kentucky, her father on December 13, 1859, and her mother on February 9, 1865. Mr. and Mrs. Womack make their home at 409 Wisdom Avenue in Jackson. They are the parents of two children, both of whom were born in that city: 1. Mary Carolyn, born on December 18, 1931. She married Dr. Harry Corson, 3rd, of Nashville, and they have two children: Mary Corson and Sally Womack Corson. 2. John Winston, born January 9, 1934. He married Annette Moore.

HISTORY OF FREED-HARDEMAN COLLEGE

For almost a century private schools have operated in Henderson. At times some of these have combined whereas others became extinct and new institutions sprang up. The present institution is indebted to its many predecessors for a rich heritage; these institutions pioneered in teacher education, commercial work, and co-education. This spirit has continued through the years.

The first school, The Masonic Male and Female Institute, was established in 1869, and operated until 1884. In 1884 West Tennessee Christian College was organized by a Mr. Inman and Bible became a part of the curricula in addition to secular subjects. Within a few years, the Southern Tennessee Normal College, of Essary Springs, forty miles from Henderson, established in 1889 by A. G. Freed, was united with it. In 1895 Freed became president of this combination. Two years later the name was changed to Georgie Robertson Christian College honoring the deceased daughter of a resident of Crockett Mills, Tennessee, who donated $5,000.00 in her memory. This college flourished and attracted large numbers of students for an additional ten years and then closed.

A. G. Freed, along with N. B. Hardeman, who was on the faculty, severed their connection with the school in 1905. Freed went to Texas to work in a Christian school in Denton. In 1908 he returned to Henderson to assist in launching a new school. In 1906 Georgie Robertson Christian School failed completely. This left an opening for another school and Hardeman was able to persuade Freed to return to Henderson to help organize one. Freed and Hardeman built the present administration building and began operation in the fall of 1908 under the name of National Teachers' Normal and Business College. At that time it was nominally under a board of trustees, although in reality, it was a private enterprise built, financed, and owned by Freed and Hardeman. After ten years a movement was inaugurated by certain members of the Church of Christ in the territory to raise money to buy the school and place it in the hands of a new board of trustees. This was accomplished and in 1919 the school was rechartered by the state of Tennessee under the name of Freed-Hardeman College, with Freed serving as president and Hardeman, vice-president. This arrangement continued until 1923 at which time both men severed connection with the school. W. Claude Hall became president and C. P. Roland became dean. During the two succeeding years efforts were begun to standardize the curricula and to gain accreditation. This was realized in 1925 by receiving approval by the Tennessee State Board of Education as a teacher training institution, and by becoming a member of the Tennessee Association of Colleges. The college has retained its approval and membership in both of these and has also been a member of the American Association of Junior Colleges since 1925. It was one of the first members in the national association of junior colleges. It is fully accredited by the Southern Association of Colleges and Secondary Schools.

In 1925 N. B. Hardeman and Hall C. Calhoun were elected associate presidents. At the close of the session Calhoun resigned and from then to May 24, 1950, Hardeman served as president continuously.

In 1950 H. A. Dixon was selected as president. E. Claude Gardner, Dean-Registrar has served the college as administrator and teacher since 1949.

The college is an endowed, private, non-profit organization. It is not owned or operated by a church or a combination of Churches of Christ. It is under the control of a self-perpetuating board who are members of the Church of Christ. The faculty and the majority of the students are members of the Church of Christ. However, it enrolls students of any religious faith or those who have not affiliated with any religion.

Walter Townsend

During 1957-58 the college celebrated its fiftieth anniversary. All of the college programs were planned around this event. Many special activities were a part of this "year of celebration."

Freed-Hardeman College proposes as the end of all instruction, social contacts and religious emphasis, to develop Christian character and life as the essence of good citizenship in the community and nation. It also strives for a sound academic program, covering the first two years of college in a Christian environment with the Bible as a daily text, taking care to develop the student mentally, socially, physically, and spiritually.

The objectives of education have been variously expressed as: adjustment, development of social efficiency, development of personality, reorganization of experience, and development of one physically, socially, mentally, and spiritually. All of these are accepted as valid toward becoming an educated person.

To each student a threefold obligation is felt. (1) To prepare him for a more complete, full and happy life in personal and family, school and society, civic and spiritual relationships by aiding him in developing moral and religious values. (2) To increase his understanding and appreciation of the world and our cultural heritage through the arts, sciences and humanities. (3) To prepare him to make a living as he makes a contribution to society and to the kingdom of God.

The college offers university-parallel courses, with terminal programs of one or two years in business administration, two years in teacher education, and two or three years in Bible.

In summary, the objectives of Freed-Hardeman College are to inspire every student to be something and to accomplish something worth-while in life.

WALTER CORLEY TOWNSEND

After extensive experience in the hardware and electrical contracting and supply industries, Walter C. Townsend founded the Electric Motor Rewinding and Service Company at Jackson a few years ago, and has been its president since that time. He has taken an active part in trade groups, and in the organizational affairs of his city.

Born at Eastview Farms, Rutherford, Tennessee, on March 11, 1901, he is a son of William Henry and Martha Ann (Corley) Townsend. Both of his parents were likewise natives of Tennessee, his father having been born on the Buffalo River in Perry County on June 14, 1862, and his mother on March 12, 1866, at Yorkville. Walter C. Townsend attended local public schools and graduated from Rutherford High School, going from there to East Tennessee State Normal School.

In 1925 he established the retail hardware business formerly known as Guy-Townsend Hardware Company. Its management remained his major interest until 1937, when he joined his two brothers, Homer and Jesse Townsend, in entering the electrical contracting business. The firm was incorporated in

1946 and at that time he was elected its secretary and treasurer. At the death of his brother Jesse in 1948, he became president, and still holds that position. The name of the firm is Townsend Electric Company.

In 1946 Mr. Townsend established a second business enterprise, a wholesale and electrical supply business under the firm name of Townsend Hardware Company. He has been its secretary and treasurer since its formation. In 1952 he established the Electric Motor Rewinding and Service Company, of which he is the president.

Mr. Townsend is treasurer of the Power and Communication Contractors Association, and a member of the National Electric Contractors Association and the National Industrial Service Association. In his home city he belongs to the Chamber of Commerce, the Knights of Pythias, Lodge No. 192 of the Benevolent and Protective Order of Elks, the Exchange Club and Jackson Golf and Country Club. He is a communicant of St. Luke's Episcopal Church.

On April 25, 1923, at Rutherford, Tennessee, Walter Corley Townsend married Mayanne Walker, daughter of James Claborn and Lee Anna (Anderson) Walker. Her father was born at Kenton, Tennessee, on February 5, 1872, and her mother at Fairview Farms, near Mason Hall, Tennessee, January 1, 1881. Mr. and Mrs. Townsend live at 340 Crescent Avenue, and they are the parents of two children: 1. Walter Corley, Jr., who was born at Jackson on March 6, 1932. 2. Leanne Townsend, born September 29, 1942, also at Jackson.

ELISHA GEE, JR.

A lawyer practicing in Memphis from the early years of his career, Elisha Gee, Jr., is a native of Norfolk, Virginia, where he was born on February 2, 1902. His father, Elisha, Sr., held the position of vice president and general manager with the American Beet Sugar Company at Denver, Colorado. He is now deceased. The younger Elisha Gee lived his early life in Denver, Colorado, from 1908 to 1928, and attended the schools of that city. He completed his preparatory studies at Phillips Exeter Academy in New Hampshire, and then entered Lehigh University in Pennsylvania, graduating there with the degree of Bachelor of Arts in 1924. In 1928 he received his degree of Bachelor of Laws at Harvard Law School.

He established his practice in Memphis in 1928, and has his own firm, with offices in the Commerce Title Building. He specializes in real estate law. During the World War II period, Elisha Gee, Jr., was absent serving in the United States Navy, having been commissioned a lieutenant commander.

Mr. Gee is a member of the following: Memphis, Shelby County, Tennessee, and American bar associations, and of Alpha Tau Omega fraternity. In his own city he belongs to the Memphis Country Club, and he and Mrs. Gee attend the Episcopal Church.

She is the former Mary Snowden Treadwell, daughter of Lawson H. and Mary (Snowden) Treadwell. She became the wife of Elisha Gee, Jr., in a ceremony at Ashville, North Carolina, on September 12, 1925. The couple have no children.

MISS EMMA INMAN WILLIAMS

Miss Emma Inman Williams, who for the past twenty years has taught American history at the Jackson High School, is also widely known in her region as an editor and author. For more than a decade she has edited the Sunday book page of the Jackson Sun, and she has written a full-length history of her county, as well as several articles appearing in the Tennessee Historical Quarterly.

Born at Henderson on October 6, 1906, she is a daughter of Charles Willis and Rhoda (Montague) Williams. In two family lines, she is a descendant of early settlers in the state: the Montagues of middle Tennessee and the Williams family of Savannah, Tennessee. For many generations, her forebears have valued education highly, and many were teachers. Her great-uncle, J. B. Inman, was co-founder with W. G. Savage of the West Tennessee Christian College at Henderson, which was established in the 1870s. Miss Williams' mother, Rhoda (Montague) Williams, was a teacher in the Jackson city schools for thirty-three years. Her aunt, Annie Montague, taught first at Henderson and later at Jackson, and was a teacher for forty years in all.

Miss Williams completed her secondary studies with her graduation in 1924 from Jackson High School, where she was an honor student. Until 1927 she attended Lambuth College, then transferred to Washington University in St. Louis, where she took her degree of Bachelor of Arts in 1928. Some years later, Miss Williams took graduate courses at the University of Chicago, leading to the degree of Master of Arts in 1941 in the field of American history.

She began her teaching career at the Jackson Junior High School, where she taught English from 1928 to 1936. In 1937, she became teacher of American history at Jackson High School, and this important position on its faculty she has capably filled to the present time.

In 1943, Miss Williams began writing a weekly series of historical articles for the Jackson Sun, and continued as a columnist until 1948. In that year she was editor of the two-hundred-page Centennial Edition of the paper. Since 1949 she has been editor of the book page of the Jackson Sun's Sunday edition.

Her historical work titled "Historic Madison; The Story of Jackson and Madison County" is a six-hundred-page volume published in 1946 by the publishing house of McCowat-Mercer as a contribution to Tennessee's Sesquecentennial celebration. Highly regarded by local citizens and by historians in this region and elsewhere, it has been placed in libraries throughout the country. Since it is now out of print, copies which can be located bring a premium price. Miss Williams has had three articles published in the Tennessee Historical Quarterly: "Early Jackson and Madison County" appeared in Volume III in March, 1944; "Letters of Adam Huntsman to James K. Polk" in Volume VI in December, 1947; and "Letters of Elijah Bigelow" was published in the West Tennessee Historical Quarterly. She is now editing the Civil War diary of Robert Cartmell for publication.

Miss Williams held office as vice president of the Tennessee Historical Association in 1957-1958. She is a member of the Southern Historical Association, the West Tennessee Educational Association, the Tennessee Educational Association, and the National Education Association. Locally, she holds membership in the West Tennessee Executives Club, and also belongs to Delta Kappa Gamma teachers' sorority. She is church historian and a member of the First Methodist Church.

BLAIR ARTHUR ROSS

An engineer by profession, Blair Arthur Ross held responsible positions with the United States Engineers during a considerable period of his career, and was later with the National Park Service. One of the useful citizens of the Mid-South, devoted to the preservation and development of its resources, he was superintendent of the Great Smoky Mountain National Park at the time of his retirement, a year before his death. He was a veteran of military service in World War I, and was active in engineering and fraternal organizations.

Born in Knox County, Missouri, on December 16, 1887, he was a son of Albert and Mary (Gifford) Ross. Both of his parents were likewise natives of Knox County, where his father was born in July, 1954, and his mother in November of 1858. The public elementary schools of Knox County provided Blair Ross with his early education, and he graduated from the high school department of the Kirksville Normal School. For his professional training, he entered the University of Missouri, where he graduated with the degree of Bachelor of Science in Civil Engineering; and he remained there for two semesters of postgraduate work.

In June, 1912, Mr. Ross took a position with the Memphis Office of the United States Engineers, and worked there until May, 1917, when he entered military service. Sent to the officers' training camp at Fort Oglethorpe, Georgia, he completed training there before going overseas in September of the same year. He remained until July, 1919. During the war he was in a number of major engagements with Company C of the 29th Engineers, which he commanded as captain. He participated in the Champagne-Marne, St. Mihiel, and second Meuse-Argonne offensives. He received a diploma from General Pershing, and was named an Officier d'Academie.

When he returned to civilian pursuits, Mr. Ross rejoined the United States Engineers Office at Memphis, and remained there until January, 1925, when he was transferred to the New Orleans office. He returned to Memphis in August, 1927. He worked with the Engineers on channel and flood-protection projects on the Mississippi River and its tributaries between the mouth of the

W. Allen Richardson

Ohio and the Gulf of Mexico. A type of project in which he was particularly interested was the concrete bank protection mattress. He wrote several articles on flood control for engineering publications.

In 1940, Blair Ross resigned from the United States Engineers to accept a position with the National Park Service. Named superintendent of Shiloh National Military Park in March of that year, he served until May 1945. At that time he was appointed superintendent of Great Smoky Mountain National Park, a post he most capably filled until his retirement in 1950 for reasons of health.

Mr. Ross was a member of the American Society of Civil Engineers, the Mid-South Engineers, and the Memphis Engineers Club. His nonprofessional memberships included the Lions Club, and the lodge of Free and Accepted Masons, and in Masonry, he was a member of the higher bodies of the Ancient and Accepted Scottish Rite and of the Ancient Arabic Order of Nobles of the Mystic Shrine. He also belonged to Acacia fraternity. He was a Democrat in politics, and he and Mrs. Ross attended the Methodist Church.

She is the former Miss Sarah Alice Murray, the daughter of Thomas Jefferson and Rosa Lee (Pope) Murray. Her father was born in Marshall County, Mississippi, on August 5, 1863, and her mother on May 4, 1869, in Madison County, Tennessee. Mr. and Mrs. Ross were married at Jackson, Tennessee, on October 20, 1925. The couple became the parents of one son, Blair Arthur, Jr., who was born in that city on July 5, 1927. A graduate of the United States Military Academy at West Point, he took his commission in the United States Army Corps of Engineers, and is a veteran of the Korean War. Blair A. Ross, Jr., married Mary Ann Fitts, and they have two children: i. Blair Arthur, 3rd. ii. Elizabeth Blair.

Blair Arthur Ross, Sr., died on April 30, 1951, less than a year after his resignation from his responsible government duties.

WILLIAM ALLEN RICHARDSON

William Allen Richardson studied law in night school while teaching school during the day. After passing the bar examination, he established his practice in Columbia in 1936 and has been professionally active in this community ever since. Best known throughout Tennessee as a legislator, he has served four terms in the Tennessee House of Representatives.

He was born near Bordenham in Giles County on October 8, 1902. His father, Josiah Allen Richardson, was born November 7, 1873 near Stiversville in Maury County. A farmer all his life, he is now deceased. His mother, Lucy Jane (Hickman) Richardson, born December 20, 1876, now lives near Culleoka. Our subject's grandfather, James (Jim) Allen Richardson, served in the Confederate Army. Twice captured, the first time he escaped and was able to rejoin the army of the South.

After graduating from public schools in Culleoka, William Allen Richardson went to Detroit, Michigan, where he worked for the Timken Roller Bearing Company for a short time. He returned to Tennessee where he studied at State Teachers College in Murfreesboro and then taught school from 1925-1927. Moving to Nashville, he sold insurance while attending Peabody College and after graduation returned to school teaching while studying law at night. He received his license to practice law in 1934 and immediately moved to Columbia, where he established his practice. In 1952 he was elected to the Tennessee House of Representatives and reelected three consecutive times. He belongs to the Columbia Chamber of Commerce, the Columbia Civitan Club, the Farm Bureau, and the Junior Order of United American Mechanics.

He married Alvy Holt in Nashville on March 15, 1928. She was born in Culleoka on May 3, 1905, the daughter of Lee and Susie (Mitchell) Holt. Both her parents are deceased.

Our subject is a member of the Church of Christ and his wife of the Baptist Church. Mr. Richardson is a Sunday school teacher. They have three children: 1. William Allen, Jr., born March 20, 1933, is in the Signal Corps, stationed in Korea, having studied engineering at Tennessee Polytechnic Institute prior to entering the service in 1956. He is married to Peggy Bell Ashburn and they have three children—William Allen, III, Autumn Joy, and Nancy Rene. 2. Joseph Lee, born in Maury County April 7, 1938, now attending Martin College in Pulaski. While in high school, he attended the National Convention of Future Farmers of America in Saint Louis. 3. James Holt, born December 31, 1941, a senior in Culleoka High School, where he plays on the basketball team. He attended the State Future Farmers of America Convention recently.

JOHN THOMAS HAMILTON

Jackson's business leader John Thomas Hamilton was interested in the management of a variety of enterprises in his home city. Foremost among these were two restaurants: The Hut, and The Fox Restaurant. He was also part owner of the Battle House Hotel, a dress shop and a camera shop, and had banking interests. He proved himself a valuable citizen of Jackson, deeply interested in its civic, welfare and organizational life.

Born at Charleston, Mississippi, on September 25, 1909, he was a son of John Thomas and Nannie Young (Fox) Hamilton. When he was young, the family moved to Jackson, and he attended the public elementary schools there. He took his preparatory studies at Branham and Hughes Military Academy at Springhill, Tennessee, and Gulfport Military Academy at Gulfport, Mississippi, then entered the University of Alabama at Tuscaloosa for his advanced studies. He also took courses at the Eastman School of Business Administration and Accounting, at Poughkeepsie, New York.

In the early years of his career, Mr. Hamilton worked for Swift and Company at Evansville, Indiana. On the death of his father he returned to Jackson

John T. Hamilton

to assume management of The Fox Restaurant. He remained its president until it was sold in October, 1958, due to his ill health. He was also president and owner of another restaurant, The Hut, Inc.

In 1944 he became one of a group of twenty men who joined forces to acquire ownership of The Battle House Hotel in Mobile, Alabama. In association with two others, he opened a smart dress shop, located in The Battle House, which has attracted discriminating purchasers throughout the area. Mr. Hamilton was also part owner of The Camera Shop in Jackson, which retails all types of photographic supplies. This he sold at the time of his final illness. He also served on the board of directors of the Second National Bank of Jackson. When his untimely death occurred, stockholders and officials of the bank paid him tribute in these words:

Although the youngest director of the bank in point of service, and one of the youngest in years, he nevertheless had made his influence felt in a striking manner and from the time of his election was one of the bank's most able and ardent supporters. . . . His keen perception of the bank's affairs and his knowledge of business principles were of inestimable value. . .

During the World War II years 1944-1945, Mr. Hamilton was absent serving in the United States Navy. He was an honorary member of the Jackson Police Department, and a member of the Chamber of Commerce and the Rotary Club. A skilled golfer, he was medalist of the Jackson Golf and Country Club in 1956. He served on the house committee of this club. His other memberships included the lodges of the Loyal Order of Moose, the Benevolent and Protective Order of Elks, and the Knights of Pythias, and he was also a member of Lodge No. 45 of the Free and Accepted Masons. A member of the higher bodies of the Masonic order, he belonged to the Scottish Rite Consistory, Al Chymia Temple of the Ancient Arabic Order of Nobles of the Mystic Shrine, and the Jackson Shrine Club.

Mr. Hamilton was a devoted worker in his church, St. Luke's Episcopal, and served on its finance board.

In Jackson, on February 22, 1936, John Thomas Hamilton married Frances Lucille Doak, daughter of Harry and Beulah (Boone) Doak. The couple became the parents of two children, both of whom were born in Jackson: 1. John Thomas, Jr., born on January 9, 1941. 2. Stephen Doak, born April 9, 1945.

Mr. Hamilton's death occurred in his fiftieth year, resulting from a disease which he had known for some time would probably be fatal. Nonetheless, he had courageously carried on his full responsibilities. When his life came to an end, the columns of a local paper carried this editorial tribute:

J. T. Hamilton looked death in the eye without flinching.

Relatively a young man, he had known for months that his time on earth was limited.

Internationally recognized specialists were consulted in the hope that something might be done to let him live out his normal existence.

The best they could offer was the hope that weeks might be prolonged into months.

With that knowledge, J. T. Hamilton moved about his daily business in normal manner as long as strength allowed.

He sought to make ample provisions for his family's welfare, hoping to see them settled in a new home.

He sold the profitable Fox Cafe which his father had established lest it prove too difficult an operation for his heirs to manage. He kept the Hut, knowing it is in capable hands.

Through all these months of preparation for death, he retained his warm, smiling manner which had earned so many friends for him. If he was depressed, the public was kept from knowing it.

It is no easy matter for a man to suddenly face death. It must be even more difficult to face that certainty for months. He showed, in his ability to do so without complaint, a fortitude which endeared him even more to his friends.

In J. T. Hamilton's death, Jackson has lost a capable restaurateur, a generous man, a good citizen.

His family has the sincere sympathy of all who knew him.

George Percy Gardner, Jr.

Over a number of years, the George Percy Gardners of Jackson, father and son, have been leaders in the ranks of those modern-day hostelers, the proprietors of motels. George P., Jr., is now the general manager of the George-Anna Motel, an up-to-date sixty-unit establishment at Jackson which has a history of more than three decades of prosperous existence. He has proved himself a leader in his line of business. He was one of the founders and first president of the Tennessee Motel Association, and has held office in national groups as well. His city has found him a willing hand whenever civic and welfare programs are projected.

He is a native of Jackson, and was born on November 26, 1914, son of George Percy, Sr., and Helen Ruth (Kesselus) Gardner. His father began serving the traveling public in 1927, when he erected twenty neat and attractive cottages at the site of the present motel. He too took a significant role in organizing the membership of what was then an infant industry, being one of the founders, in 1932, of the Tourist Court Owners Association, and serving as its first president. Helen Ruth Kesselus, whom he married, was born at Bastrop, Texas, near Austin.

The younger George P. Gardner attended the public schools of Jackson, and after graduation from high school in that city, entered Memphis State College at Memphis. He left there to attend Bowling Green University, at Bowling Green, Kentucky, where he could receive special training in accounting. When he completed his studies in 1936, he immediately joined his father in the operation of the motel, which by that time had been in existence for nine years and was faring quite well. It had been given the name of George-Anna for the founder's son George and daughter Anna, who is now Mrs. Isaac

T. Conner. It has kept the name ever since. Today, Mr. Conner is its assistant manager. George P. Gardner, Jr., assumed increasing responsibility in the operation of the tourists' hostelry, and by the late 1940s had assumed full charge.

Active in the United Motor Court Association, he served on its board of directors in 1939-1940. One of the founders of the Tennessee Motel Association in 1950, he served as its first president. Since that time he has been on its board of directors, and he is also a member of the board of governors of the American Motel Hotel Association. Also a member of the Congress of Motor Hotels, he holds the office of senator in that organization during the current year, 1958-1959.

For many years he has held membership in the Jackson Exchange Club, and has served on its board of control. He has taken responsible roles in fund-raising for charitable causes, including the program of the Jackson Community Chest, and campaigns for the American Red Cross and the Young Men's Christian Association. He has been chairman of the Casey Jones Railroad Museum Committee since the museum was established. Another of his consistent interests has been the Jackson Chamber of Commerce. He served as a director in 1955-1956, and was elected a vice president in 1955. He is currently chairman of the Tourist and Convention Committee of the Chamber, an office particularly appropriate in view of his wide recognition as probably the city's number one host to motoring visitors. Mr. Gardner was a team captain when the first United Fund campaign was held in 1957. He headed the committee for the selection of teams for the Annual Exchange Bowl Game.

His memberships include the lodges of the Benevolent and Protective Order of Elks, Royal Order Moose, the Knights of Pythias, and the Free and Accepted Masons. In Masonry, he is a member of the higher bodies, holding the Thirty-second degree and belonging to Al Chymia Temple, Ancient Arabic Order of Nobles of the Mystic Shrine, in Memphis.

He has also been a most devoted and useful member of the First Baptist Church, active in many phases of its program. He has been at various times superintendent of its Sunday school's intermediate department, junior department, and young people's department.

On June 18, 1938, at Eldorado, Arkansas, George Percy Gardner, Jr., married Ardis Worthington of that city, daughter of John D. and Lena (Teague) Worthington. The couple are the parents of two children: 1. George Percy, 3rd, who was born on October 23, 1939. He is now attending the University of Tennessee at Knoxville. 2. John W., born on August 18, 1942, now completing his high school courses. The family's residence is 423 Poplar in Jackson.

ELMUS CLYDE FITE, JR.

As owner and active head of the Fite-Hutchinson Feed Company, Clyde Fite, Jr., heads an organization which, under various firm names, has continued to serve the people of Murfreesboro for over thirty-five years. He himself has contributed much to its growth and efficiency, as did his father before him. The elder Elmus Clyde Fite, who was born February 29, 1880 near Auburn Town in Cannon County, established the seed and feed business in 1922. Prior to that time, he had engaged in farming. He remained a partner in the business until his death in 1953. He and his wife were active members of the Baptist Church. She was the former Miss Dana Quarles, and was born at Lascassas, Tennessee, in 1890. She died in 1921 in Lascassas.

Their son, the younger Elmus Clyde Fite—who has always used his middle name—was born in Lascassas on September 6, 1914, and received his public school education in Murfreesboro. Graduating from high school there, he attended Tennessee State Teachers College, which is also in the same city, but later transferred from there to the University of Tennessee in Knoxville. He started as a partner in his father's company, where he gained his first business experience in 1933, and after completing his education, began a full-time connection with the organization which has continued to the present time. Originally known as the Fite, Bell and Odom Feed Company when it was first established in 1922, its name was changed in 1930 to Fite and Moore Feed Company. In 1933, the elder Elmus Clyde Fite bought his partners' interests, and renamed the concern the Fite Feed Company. Since his death in 1953, it has borne the name of the two present partners—Fite-Hutchinson Feed Company.

Besides his role in his city's commercial life, Clyde Fite, Jr., has taken a constructive and useful part in municipal government. He has been city councilman from 1946, now serving his thirteenth year, and vice-mayor from 1954 to the present time. He has also served on the Murfreesboro electrical department's board and is currently a director of the city's board of education.

Mr. Fite is also a veteran of World War II. Entering army service in 1941, he served with the 66th Infantry. He remained stateside, being stationed in the southern states, and advanced to the rank of first sergeant. He received his honorable discharge in 1943.

Besides his major business connection with the Fite-Hutchinson Feed Company, Mr. Fite serves on the board of directors of the Murfreesboro Federal Savings and Loan Association. He is currently vice president of the Chamber of Commerce, and is a member of the Stone's River Country Club. He and his family attend the First Baptist Church.

In Murfreesboro, on October 4, 1941, Clyde Fite, Jr., took as his wife Miss Betty Jackson. Daughter of Charlie C. and Laura (Askew) Jackson, she was born at Alexander, Tennessee, on December 10, 1918. The couple have

Clyde Fite

two children: 1. Elmus Clyde, 3rd, who was born on December 5, 1946. 2, Barton Brown, born March 5, 1951. Both children were born in Murfreesboro.

AUTRY CLAYTON EMMERT, M.D.

One of Waverly's younger professional leaders, Dr. Autry Clayton Emmert commenced his general practice of medicine at Waverly, where he is now identified with a recently established clinic. This organization is making a contribution of inestimable value in serving the medical needs of the area.

Dr. Emmert was born on September 11, 1922, in Haywood County, the son of George Autry and Mattie Ruth (Clayton) Emmert. Both of his parents are natives of Haywood County, where George A. Emmert was born in 1887 and his wife in 1902. A merchant, he now has a dry goods store at Alamo, Tennessee, where the couple live. Dr. Emmert received his early education in the public schools of Whiteville and graduated from high school there. As a high school student he played on the basketball team. After graduation, he entered the armed services, but following his World War II service in the Air Corps he studied for three years at Union University at Jackson, Tennessee where he took pre-med work. In 1948 he entered the University of Tennessee, where he took his professional courses and received his degree of Doctor of Medicine in 1952 following training as physician and surgeon.

His wartime service began in 1942. As pilot of a B-26, he served in the Ninth Air Force, was in the European Theater of Operations during much of his time in uniform, and participated in the assault on Germany, the last core of resistance of the Nazi movement. He attained the rank of captain and received the Air Medal and a Presidential Unit Citation. He served until 1946.

After receiving his doctorate from the University of Tennessee, Dr. Emmert commenced his practice at Waverly, in 1952, and has had his offices there ever since. In association with Dr. Arthur W. Walker, he established the clinic in that city in 1953. He is a member of the American Medical Association, the Tennessee State Medical Association and the Benton-Humphrey County Medical Association, as well as Phi Rho Sigma professional fraternity. His social fraternity is Alpha Tau Omega. Dr. Emmert attends the Baptist Church and is a Democrat in his politics.

On April 10, 1947, Dr. Autry Clayton Emmert married Annie Goodwin, in a ceremony at Jackson, Tennessee. She was born at Winter Haven, Florida, on September 2, 1927, and is a daughter of Willard and Eunice (Bell) Goodwin. Her parents now make their home at Jackson, where he is a foreman for the Tennessee Valley Authority. Mrs. Emmert is active in the Baptist Church. She is currently the president of the Women's Study School, and teaches Sunday school at the Waverly church. The couple are the parents of two children: Cynthia Lynn, who was born in Nashville on November 6, 1956, John Clayton, born July 6, 1958 in Clarksville.

ROY HALL

Practicing law in Jackson for the past three decades, Roy Hall is a partner of Homer H. Waldrop, their offices being at 109½ East Main Street. Mr. Hall has held public office as United States Commissioner for the Western District of Tennessee, and he has been active in the councils of the Republican party and in many local organizations.

Born at Lexington, in Henderson County, on December 8, 1896, he is a son of Devalson Gillespie and Susan (Turner) Hall. His father too was a native of Lexington, born on June 30, 1837. His mother was born at Harris Station in Weakley County, on January 16, 1858. Attending local public schools, Roy Hall graduated from Henderson County High School at Lexington in 1917. He then entered Union University at Jackson, but his studies there were interrupted by wartime service in the United States Navy. He enlisted in 1918, and served until February, 1919. He received his degree of Bachelor of Arts at Union University in 1921, and for his professional training, entered Georgetown University School of Law in Washington, D. C. There he graduated with the degree of Bachelor of Laws in 1924.

For three years following his graduation from law school, he was with the firm of I. B. Tigrett and Company, investment bankers. He had been admitted to the bar on August 21, 1924, and on January 1, 1928, he formed a partnership with Homer H. Waldrop to enter the private practice of law in Jackson. He has practiced there since that time.

Mr. Hall was named United States Commissioner for the Western District of Tennessee, Eastern Division, in 1929, and served with distinction until 1934. A Republican, he was a delegate to that party's National Convention meeting in Chicago in 1944, and also to the convention in that same city in 1952. While he has never sought public elective office, he has been prompted to activity in politics by a sense of duty and a desire to serve his state and country.

Mr. Hall is a member of the bar associations, and of Alpha Tau Omega social fraternity, which he joined at Union University. He also belongs to the lodges of the Benevolent and Protective Order of Elks and the Knights of Pythias, and has held various offices, including that of chancellor commander, in the Pythian group. Active in the Jackson Exchange Club, he served as its president in 1932, and he is also a member of the Jackson Golf and Country Club.

As a veteran of naval service in World War I, Mr. Hall has taken a prominent part in the affairs of the American Legion. He has been commander of John A. Deaver Post No. 12; has been vice-commander-at-large two different years; and held office as state commander in 1942-1943.

A communicant of the First Baptist Church at Jackson, Mr. Hall was secretary of the church for several years, and has been for some time a member of the board of deacons.

At Dyersburg, on September 14, 1926, Roy Hall married Cornelia

Slaughter, daughter of John and Elizabeth (Gilman) Slaughter. The couple are the parents of two children: 1. Cornelia, who was born in Jackson on April 24, 1929. She is now the wife of Robert Tiller. 2. Thomas Roy, born in that city on July 30, 1940. The family's residence is on Trenton Road in Jackson.

JOHN HUGHES CHANDLER, M.D.

Since his return from service in the Medical Corps in World War II, Dr. John Hughes Chandler has been practicing at Jackson, specializing in surgery. He was one of five local physicians who, nearly a decade ago, founded the Jackson Clinic, and he also has a distinguished record of service on the staffs of several hospitals.

Born on August 8, 1910, he is a son of John William and Pearle (Hughes) Chandler. Both of his parents were natives of Bells, where his father was born on December 2, 1877, and his mother on February 28, 1887.

Beginning his advanced studies at the University of Tennessee, Dr. Chandler took his degree of Bachelor of Science there, and continued with his professional studies at the University of Tennessee Medical School. There he received his degree of Doctor of Medicine in 1932. From 1933 to 1936, he was on the staff of St. Joseph's Hospital in Memphis, successively as intern and surgical resident. In 1936 he joined the surgical staff of the United States Marine Hospital in New York City, remaining there until 1938. During the next four years, Dr. Chandler acquired experience in teaching, joining the faculty of the University of Tennessee as instructor in thoracic surgery. He was still there at the time he enlisted in the United States Army Medical Corps, in 1942.

Commissioned a captain, he had advanced in grade to lieutenant colonel by the time the war ended. For two years he served in the European theater as chief of a thoracic and abdominal surgical team with the First and Second Auxiliary Surgical Groups. His active service terminated in 1946.

On his release from military service, Dr. Chandler immediately came to Jackson, where he entered the private practice of surgery. In 1950, in association with Drs. Leland Johnston, Baker Hubbard, Paul Wylie, and Henry Herron, he organized the Jackson Clinic. This clinic now has a medical staff of twenty-two physicians. Dr. Chandler is on its surgical staff.

He is also a member of the surgical staff of the Jackson-Madison County General Hospital, and the visiting staff of St. Mary's Hospital at Humboldt, and Lexington-Henderson County Hospital at Lexington. He is surgical consultant at Western State Hospital at Bolivar.

Dr. Chandler is a Diplomate of the American Board of Surgery, and is a Fellow of the American College of Surgeons and Senior Fellow of the Southeastern Surgical Congress. He is a member of the American Association for Thoracic Surgery and the Southern Association for Thoracic Surgery, as well as the American Medical, Southern Medical, Tennessee State Medical and Consolidated Medical Associations.

His local memberships include the Jackson Lions Club, the lodge of the Benevolent and Protective Order of Elks, and the Jackson Golf and Country Club. He is a communicant of St. Luke's Episcopal Church in Jackson.

At Fort Sam Houston Chapel in San Antonio, Texas, on July 9, 1945, Dr. John Hughes Chandler married Jean Marguerite Champion. Her father is Dr. Albert N. Champion, otolaryngologist, who was born at Luling, Texas, in 1890. Miss Winona Byington, whom Dr. Champion married, was born in Windsor, Ontario, Canada, in 1895. Dr. and Mrs. Chandler make their home at 38 Northwood, Jackson. They are the parents of the following children: 1. Marguerita Park, born in Memphis on May 5, 1946. 2. Pamela Alford, born June 23, 1947, in Jackson. 3. Ann Champion, born in that city on January 12, 1950. 4. John Hughes, Jr., who was likewise born in Jackson, on April 25, 1956.

CHARLES ROBERT ELLIOTT

The major career interest of the late Charles Robert Elliott was the wholesale grocery business. He spent most of his years with the J. C. Edenton Company of Jackson, first as secretary and treasurer and later as executive vice president; and he was an official of several other Tennessee grocery distributorships. He took a constructive part in the life of his community, of local organizations, and of his church.

Mr. Elliott was a native of Woodville, Kentucky, and was born on July 20, 1885, the son of Thomas and Mattie (Dance) Elliott. His paternal grandfather was Dr. C. A. Elliott, a highly regarded physician and surgeon who practiced in Paducah, Kentucky, for fifty years. Thomas Elliott was born in that city. Mattie Dance, whom he married, was a native of Woodville.

Receiving his public school education in Paducah, Charles R. Elliott moved to Jackson, Tennessee, in 1905. There he entered Union University and majored in business administration. He began his career in the city as a bookkeeper at Tuchfeld's Dry Goods Store. A few years later he joined the J. C. Felsenthal Wholesale Grocery Company, and remained with that firm for eight years as credit manager.

In 1916 Mr. Elliott formed his connection with the J. C. Edenton Company, a wholesale grocery firm with headquarters in Jackson. In consequence of his previous experience in the same industry, he joined the organization at the management level, as secretary and treasurer. He was later promoted to executive vice president.

In addition, Mr. Elliott was a director of the company, and also a director of Edenton-Lamb Wholesale Grocery Company of Dyersburg, the Trenton Wholesale Grocery Company of Trenton, and the United Wholesale Grocery Company of Lexington.

Active in the Launcelot Lodge of the Knights of Pythias, Mr. Elliott had held office as chancellor commander. He was also a member of Lodge No. 192 of the Benevolent and Protective Order of Elks at Jackson, and of the Free and Accepted Masons, the Jackson Rotary Club, and the West Tennessee Executives Club. He took a full and responsible part in the work of the First Methodist Church of Jackson, being a member of its official board for twenty-five years, and for some time chairman of the church's insurance committee. He was a member of its men's Bible class. His favorite sport was baseball.

On November 6, 1907, in Jackson, Charles Robert Elliott married Katie Jessie McClintock. She is a daughter of David Fletcher and Catherine Maryland (Harper) McClintock. Both of her parents were native Tennesseeans, her father having been born at Atwood on September 10, 1843, and her mother on September 4, 1856, at Jackson. Mr. and Mrs. Elliott became the parents of four children: 1. Robert Fletcher, born in Jackson on March 29, 1909, is a landscape architect, with office in Memphis. Outstanding projects of his were:

The final layout for Newfound Gap in the Great Smoky Mountains National Park and the supervision, for the National Park Service, of the building of it and the park roads from Gatlinburg to Clingman's Dome; supervision, for the National Park Service, of the Virginia half of the Blue Ridge Parkway; site plans for the Receiving and Intensive Treatment Hospital at Western State Hospital, Bolivar, and the design of the fourteen courts for the patients; the design and plans for the new system of roads and parking areas for the Capital Hill in Nashville. 2. James McClintock, born on July 27, 1912. He is now city editor of The Jackson Sun. He married Virginia Shannon of Greenfield. He served in World War II. 3. Mary Catherine, born November 5, 1916. She is now the wife of R. S. Hellmann, M.D., and with their children, Robert Shearer, James Elliott and Mary Catherine, they make their home in Chattanooga. 4. Alexander Harrell, born November 21, 1918. He is assistant secretary and credit manager of Southern Supply Company of Jackson. He was awarded the Bronze Star Medal for meritorious service in France and Germany in World War II. All four children were born in Jackson.

The death of Charles R. Elliott occurred in his home city on August 10, 1954. "In the death of C. R. Elliott," commented an editorial in The Jackson Sun, "this community loses a very fine citizen, one who was deeply interested in its welfare and development, who took his place in all civic undertakings, and who deserved the popularity he enjoyed."

S. DELBERT MASON

With considerable experience in the manufacture of boots and shoes to his credit, S. Delbert Mason is now general manager of the Boot-Ster Shoe Factory at Clarksville. He takes a constructive part in that community's organizational life. His residence there predates his military service in World War II, which took him overseas with the army.

Born in Palma, Kentucky, on January 5, 1920, he is a son of Herman R. and Mattie Dorinda (Sisk) Mason. His father, born in 1898 at Jordan Springs, Tennessee, has been a farmer all his life and now lives in Michigan. Mrs. Mason is a native of Crofton, Kentucky. From his early years, S. Delbert Mason lived in Clarksville. He attended the public schools there and graduated from its high school. In 1937 he began his working career in a connection with the Acme Boot Factory, in his native city. He remained there until he entered active military service. First enlisting in the Tennessee National Guard, he entered the federal service in February, 1941, and served in the army until February, 1946. His unit was a component of the Third Army, and he served in the European combat areas, receiving several decorations. Now in the Active Reserve, he holds the rank of major.

After the war, in 1946, he returned to Clarksville, and became sales manager of the Acme Boot Company, remaining with them until December, 1951. That year he acquired an interest in the Boot-Ster Manufacturing Company and in January, 1952 he became vice president and general manager of the firm. Since that time the business has become a national distributor.

Mr. Mason is a member of the United States Chamber of Commerce and also Clarksville Chamber, the Tennessee Manufacturers Association, the Civitan Club, and the lodge of the Independent Order of Odd Fellows. He is a communicant of the Methodist Church, being chairman of its official board. His favorite outdoor pastime is fishing.

At Tullahoma, Tennessee, on April 17, 1944, S. Delbert Mason married Margaret Turrentine. A native of Clarksville, she was born on August 12, 1923, and is a daughter of Chesley and Grace (Evans) Turrentine. Her father is a native of Montgomery County. Mr. and Mrs. Mason are the parents of two children, both of whom were born in Clarksville: 1. Gary Dean, who was born on August 19, 1950. 2. Steven Robert, born on April 9, 1952.

PAUL HERRIFORD RUSSELL

Paul H. Russell of Jackson is a distinguished figure in his industry. One of the first men to bottle Coca-Cola in the state of Tennessee, he is now, more than half a century later, still active in the production and distribution of this famous Southern product. He is the president and founder of the Jackson Coca-Cola Bottling Plant.

Born on August 25, 1882, at Cleveland, Tennessee, he is a son of William Erskin and Pauline (Herriford) Russell. He attended the public schools of Cleveland, and took his advanced courses at the University of Tennessee, where he graduated in 1903 with the degree of Bachelor of Arts.

Before he had been active long in the business world, he was attracted by the possibilities of the rapidly growing Coca-Cola bottling industry. The product, which had come into existence in the later years of the last century, had commenced its record of rapid growth, resulting from the vision of company

P H Russell

executives, who saw promise in the idea of numerous local production and distribution centers. The preferred status which the beverage enjoys today may indeed be attributable to its unique taste. On the other hand, its system of distribution undoubtedly had much to do with building up an early demand at a rapid rate. In the state of Tennessee, Mr. Russell played his part in this program of stimulating public acceptance. He was one of the very first bottlers of Coca-Cola in the state, having joined the organization in April, 1905. Beginning with a one-horse cart and a one-spout machine, he filled the bottles, went out and sold them, returned to his base of operation where he washed the empties, then went out to make another circuit. This was the system in the early years, and Mr. Russell has seen many changes. He was one of the first distributors in the state to install and use liquid low-pressure twenty-four-spout machines. Today, the latest in equipment, a fleet of trucks, and a large corps of employees help him to maintain the supremacy of the Coca-Cola name in the greater Jackson area. As one of the thirty veterans of the business in the United States, Mr. Russell received special honors at the Fiftieth Anniversary Celebration, which was held in New York on October 4, 1949.

Mr. Russell has taken a deep interest in civic affairs and so has his organization. In 1943, the Jackson Coca-Cola Bottling Plant was winner in the Tennessee scrap-iron campaign. Its president has won personal distinction for his work as chairman of the Community Chest, and in recent years he has proved himself a loyal and effective supporter of the program of the Babe Ruth League and many civic and educational organizations.

Influential in the general business life of his city, Mr. Russell has been a director of the Second National Bank of Jackson since 1916, and now holds office as senior vice president. He is a charter member of the Rotary Club, and a member of the lodge of the Benevolent and Protective Order of Elks, and of Kappa Sigma fraternity. During his college years, he took military training at the University of Tennessee. He is a communicant of the First Methodist Church. One of Mr. Russell's major interests is travel, and he has made extensive trips throughout Europe and the Middle East as well as in various parts of the North American continent.

In his home city of Jackson, on December 3, 1908, Paul Herriford Russell married Laura Jobe, daughter of Andrew Krecker and Annie (Schoolar) Jobe of Columbus, Mississippi. Mrs. Russell has been very active in religious and civic affairs in her home city, and was honored by being named Jackson's Woman of the Year in 1954. She has taught a Sunday school class for over fifty-five years. Mr. and Mrs. Russell, who make their home at 31 Northwood in Jackson, celebrated their golden wedding anniversary on December 3, 1958.

Mr. Russell is truly a pioneer in his field, at the forefront of every forward-moving innovation in the bottling of Coca-Cola and responsible for many of these steps in its progress. As one of thirty veterans of the Coca-Cola industry in the entire country, he can look back over the years to accomplishments that have made the industry what it is today, and know that he has had a part in each of these steps.

His career as industrialist and citizen may well be expressed in Tennyson's words:

He has given the people of his best;
His worst he kept, his best he gave.

WILLIAM CALVIN HUNT

Devoting his career to the tobacco industry, in which he was widely known and respected, William Calvin Hunt of Memphis was a founder and executive of the American Tobacco Trust Company and the American Snuff Company.

Born on a plantation just out of Water Valley, Mississippi, on August 6, 1856, he was a son of Jesse and Anne (Hale) Hunt. His father was the owner of this large plantation, which he had purchased from an Indian named Billy Creek, and to which he accordingly gave the name of the Billy Creek Plantation. He operated the property productively with a large number of slaves. The homestead was burned during the Civil War.

William C. Hunt received his public elementary and high school education at Water Valley. He left home in 1874 to enter the University of Tennessee, where he graduated in 1878 with the degree of A.B. As a student there, he excelled in scholarship, was a star baseball player, played cornet in the band, and joined a Greek letter society. At the time of his death he was the university's oldest graduate.

While at the university, he made the acquaintance of Martin J. Condon, thus forming a friendship which was broken only by death, and which was productive of significant achievements in the tobacco industry. Following their graduation, the two founded a small snuff company in Knoxville. This firm was originally known as Bruton and Condon, and when it had grown into a thriving business, it merged with the Atlantic Snuff Company to form the American Snuff Company. Of this latter organization, Mr. Condon was the first president and Mr. Hunt the first vice president. It achieved a nationwide reputation under their effective leadership. Mr. Hunt earned a reputation as a dominant figure in the tobacco industry, a man with progressive views and a thorough knowledge of his field.

He was a charter member of the University Club and a member of the Memphis Country Club, where he and his business partner were friendly rivals in games of golf. Mr. Hunt held memberships at different times in the Methodist Church of Knoxville, and the Second Presbyterian Church in Memphis, and he continued his helpful support to both churches after he had come to Memphis. He was known and respected as an effective Christian worker, and started a Bible class in his office in the Exchange Building in Memphis.

Twice married, William Calvin Hunt chose as his first wife Miss Minnie Echols of Knoxville. They were married in 1883, and she died six years later after having borne three children: 1. Martin Condon Hunt. 2. Louise, who became the wife of Mr. Toombs. 3. Helen Hamilton. In 1898, in Chicago, Illinois, Mr. Hunt married, second, Miss Love Bright, a native of Jackson and daughter of James E. and Sarah Josephine (Sanders) Bright. They were of the family of the distinguished English statesman, John Bright. Mrs. Hunt belongs to the Wautauga Chapter of the Daughters of the American Revolution, claiming descent from Captain Robert Bright of Virginia. She is a communicant of Calvary Episcopal Church in Memphis. To their marriage the following children were born: 4. William Calvin, Jr., on April 10, 1901, at Knoxville. Enlisting in service in the United States Marine Corps at the time of World War I, he was assigned to overseas duty, and while enroute, died aboard ship while in sight of France. 5. Sarah Josephine, born on July 24, 1906, in Knoxville. She married Frederic Thesmar, and they had two children: Frederic, Jr., and William Hunt Thesmar. 6. John Bright, born in Nashville, December 10, 1910. He lost his life in an automobile accident in 1930. 7. Mary Love born October 14, 1913, in Memphis. She married Selden Humphreys, and they had a daughter, Sallie Love, born October 4, 1935. She later married Frederic Hayley, and their son, William Bright Hayley, was born September 9, 1946.

Mr. Hunt's career in industry was a long and rewarding one, ending with his retirement in 1937. His death occurred on January 2, 1944.

RAY LAWRENCE WHEAT

With past experience in industry and public service, Ray Lawrence Wheat is now manager of the Memphis Municipal Airport. He is a veteran of Air Corps service in World War II.

A native Tennessean, he was born at Parsons on March 2, 1910, and is a son of Joseph and Laura (Lewis) Wheat. His parents were lifelong residents of Parsons and Memphis, and his father was a salesman in the wholesale grain business out of Memphis. Ray L. Wheat attended the public elementary and high schools of Parsons, and on graduating from high school there, entered Memphis State University. He transferred from there to Union University to complete his advanced studies.

During 1934-1935, Mr. Wheat was employed by the Tennessee Valley Authority. He left the government service to accept a position as superintendent with the Smiley Sand and Gravel Company in Atlanta, Georgia, continuing in that connection until 1939. He then went on the payroll of the state of Tennessee, in a responsible post in the Department of Safety. He remained until 1942, when he entered Air Corps service.

As a flight instructor in the United States Army Air Corps, he was stationed at McKellar Field, Jackson, Tennessee, and at Bennettsville, South Carolina. He received his honorable discharge in 1945.

For a short time after his return to civilian life, Mr. Wheat worked as plant manager for the Marquette Cement Company at Memphis. He left to accept appointment as assistant manager of the Memphis Municipal Airport, and after nine years in that position, was named manager in 1954.

Mr. Wheat holds the rank of admiral in the Flagship Fleet of American Airlines. He is affiliated with the Free and Accepted Masons, and is a communicant of the Methodist Church. An ardent sportsman, he is fond of both hunting and fishing.

In 1939, in Jackson, Ray Lawrence Wheat married Wanda Helen Wade, daughter of B. B. and Lala (Gilliam) Wade. Her father is deceased, and her mother has married a second time, her husband being Edgar L. Stansell of Jackson. Mr. and Mrs. Wheat are the parents of one son, Ray Lawrence, Jr., who was born on July 16, 1949. He is attending Colonial Grade School.

CHARLES LEA NEELY

In the years preceding World War I, when Charles Lea Neely commenced his practice of law, he chose Memphis as the site of his professional career. He has been there since, and he has taken a particularly active part in the programs of bar associations and of veterans' groups. He was an artillery officer during the first world conflict. He has served the people of his district in the Tennessee State House of Representatives.

Born at Bolivar, on October 19, 1888, he is a son of Dr. James J. and Julia A. (Smith) Neely. His father, a physician, served in the Confederate States Army. The Memphis attorney attended the public schools of Bolivar, including its high school, and also the Mooney School and the University of Mississippi. There he completed his law training, after which he was admitted to the State Bar of Tennessee and commenced his practice in Memphis.

Elected to the House of Representatives for the term beginning in 1913, he served through 1915. Prior to World War I, when this country was facing difficulties at the Mexican border, Charles L. Neely was in military service there. He served in the First Tennessee Infantry, Company G., and later with Battery B of the 115th Field Artillery. Advancing to the rank of captain, he commanded Batteries B and D and Headquarters and Supply Company. At the time of World War I, he was in service overseas for one year. He remained in the Reserve Corps for thirty-four years.

A member of Post No. 1 of the American Legion and of Post No. 684 of the Veterans of Foreign Wars, Mr. Neely has served as commander of both units. As a lawyer he has been active in the Memphis and Shelby County Bar Association, he has held office as its president; and since 1942 he has been secretary-treasurer of the Board of Law Examiners of Tennessee. He is a member of the Tennessee Bar Association and the American Bar Association.

His nonprofessional memberships include the Tennessee Club, Memphis Country Club, the M. O. W. W., and the Free and Accepted Masons. In Masonry, he is a member of the higher bodies and belongs to the Ancient Arabic Order of Nobles of the Mystic Shrine. He and Mrs. Neely attend Calvary Episcopal Church.

She is the former Ruby Mayes, the daughter of William James and Lida (Dodd) Mayes. The couple were married at Union City on May 20, 1920, and they are the parents of one son, Dr. Charles Lea, Jr., who was born on August 3, 1927. He is a physician. He served with the United States Navy during World War II. He is married to the former Mary Louise Buckbaum and they have a daughter Louise.

ELMER WARREN McGOWAN

After varied experience in business and industry, Elmer Warren Mc-Gowan recently assumed duties in a responsible public office as senior accounting clerk on the staff of Memphis' city treasurer. He has had thorough training in commercial procedures. In his home city he has been active in lodges and in church work.

Mr. McGowan is a native of Memphis, and was born on September 4, 1919, son of Petty Lantz, Sr., and Emma Janie (Osburn) McGowan. His great-grandfather, John W. S. Browne, was a resident of Memphis from 1850, and a member of The Memphis Secession Directory, his name being listed on February 23, 1861 in the weekly edition of the Memphis Weekly Avalanche, predecessor of the Commercial Appeal. He had five daughters: Clara, Fannie, Emma Byrd, and twins Alicent Taylor and Millicent. Alicent lived in Memphis throughout the Civil War, following her marriage to Samuel Petty McGowan. He served in Companies A and F of the First Louisiana Cavalry, Confederate States Army. She was a charter member of the Confederate Dames. The couple moved to Seguin, Texas, and there in 1871 their first son, Edward Browne McGowan, was born. Their second son, Petty Lantz McGowan, was born in 1873. In 1880, Samuel McGowan died from the delayed effects of wounds and maltreatment in federal prisons at Louisville, Kentucky, Camp Chase, Ohio, and Fort Delaware. In 1883 his widow moved back to Memphis and lived there until her death in 1937. On November 17, 1897, she became a charter member of the Sarah Chapman Gordon Law Chapter of the Daughters of the Confederacy, the oldest and largest chapter in Tennessee. Alicent (Browne) McGowan was a descendant of forebears who had come to this country from Bath and Bristol, England, in 1621. They settled in Virginia and later generations moved to Ohio. She was born in Hamilton County, that state, on October 16, 1847. She was one of the founders of the T.E.L. Class, which is now worldwide. Her father, John W. X. Browne, joined a partner, Mr. Borum, in organizing the Browne and Borum Plumbing and Heating Company. He designed and built the bronze fountain in Court Square in Memphis.

Alicent (Browne) McGowan's elder son, Edward Browne McGowan, was an army officer who served in quelling the Philippine insurrection, was in the Spanish-American War, and was with Pershing on the Texas border in 1916. He attained the rank of colonel. His father, Samuel Petty McGowan, was decorated posthumously on January 19, 1931 with the Southern Cross of Honor, by the J. Harvey Mathes Chapter of the United Daughters of the Confederacy.

Petty Lantz McGowan was also a plumbing and heating contractor by occupation. He served as a quartermaster sergeant in the Neely Zouaves at the time of the Philippine Insurrection. He was a registered southern Democrat. At the First Baptist Church in Memphis, on March 7, 1901, he was married to Emma Janie Osburn, Dr. Arthur U. Boone officiating. She was born July 22, 1883, daughter of Captain William Osburn, U.S.N., and Mary Osburn. He had been a shipbuilder for the United States government during the war, and after the birth of his daughter, in Jeffersonville, Indiana, he took his family to Memphis. He was murdered in that city in 1890, and the murderer was never apprehended.

Elmer Warren McGowan attended Idlewild Grammar School and Fairview Junior High School, both in Memphis, and graduated from that city's Central High School. He took commercial courses at Draughon's Business College and at the Memphis College of Accountancy.

He began his career in the military service, being enlisted in Battery B of the 115th Field Artillery from 1938 to 1940. In the latter year he became a personnel clerk in the United States Army, and during the next six years, served in the following succession of assignments: Company E, 53rd Engineer Regiment (Combat); Division Headquarters, Second Armored Division; Ordnance Maintenance Battalions of the Third, Fifth, Eighth, and Fourteenth Armored Divisions; 151st Ordnance Battalion of the Fourteenth Armored Division; 450th Ordnance Heavy Automotive Maintenance Company of the Eighth Air Force in the European Theater; and the 178th Ordnance Depot Company, 29th Infantry Division. He received his honorable discharge in 1946. In 1940, Mr. McGowan had served as secretary to Major General George S. Patton in the Second Armored Division at Fort Benning, and he served as cadre for the organization of armored forces. In his last assignment, he was with the army of occupation at Bremen Enclave, Bremen-Bremerhaven, Germany.

When he returned to civilian life in 1946, Mr. McGowan put his commercial training to use in a position as stock maintenance control clerk (Kardex) with the Graybar Electric Company, Inc. This position he held until 1949, when he left to become a cost accountant with Walker Nurseries. The following year he joined the Leader Specialty Company as bookkeeper and office manager, remaining with that firm until 1952 when he became a claim agent with Roodway Express, Inc. From 1954 to 1958, he was cashier-bookkeeper with the Dean Milk Company.

He left this position on his appointment as senior accounting clerk in the Memphis City Treasurer's Office. This responsible municipal post he has since held.

Mr. McGowan is a member of Stonewall Lodge No. 723, Free and Accepted Masons, and Stonewall Chapter No. 219, Royal Arch Masons. He is a member of the Tennessee Federation for Constitutional Government, and of the Nathan Bedford Forrest Camp No. 215, Sons of Confederate Veterans. He presently holds the office of historian in this camp.

Since 1927, Mr. McGowan has been an active member of the First Baptist Church of Memphis, and members of his family have been communicants of that church since the 1850s. His grandmother, her sister, Miss Emma B. Browne and Dr. A. U. Boone organized the first T. E. L. Sunday school class there. The sister was principal in the Memphis city schools for fifty years. Mr. McGowan is a Democrat in his politics.

At the First Methodist Church in Fort Smith, Arkansas, on April 16, 1949, the Rev. Dr. Fred G. Roebuck officiated at the marriage of Elmer Warren McGowan to Lucy Charlene Smith. She is the daughter of Emmett Eugene and Mattie Elizabeth (Chandler) Smith. Mr. and Mrs. McGowan have no children. They make their home at 35 North McLean Boulevard, Memphis.

MAX HAROLD FREEMAN

One of the younger professional leaders of Memphis, Max Harold Freeman is practicing law independently with offices in the Commerce Title Building. He is a veteran of wartime service in the Merchant Marine, following which he completed his law studies at the state university.

Born August 22, 1924, at Finley, in Dyer County, he is a son of Dr. John Thomas and Lola (Jones) Freeman. As a general practitioner, Dr. Freeman practiced in Dyer County for about thirty years. The public schools of Dyersburg provided Max H. Freeman with his early education, and he graduated from high school there. He took his pre-law studies at Memphis State University, but his advanced education was interrupted by the call to wartime service, and he entered the United States Merchant Marine in 1943. Until 1946, he was serving aboard ships in the Atlantic, the Mediterranean and the Caribbean. As soon as he returned to civilian life, he resumed his studies, and in 1950 graduated from the Law College of the University of Tennessee, at Knoxville, with the degree of Bachelor of Laws.

Admitted to the bar of his state in that year, Mr. Freeman first joined the staff of the claim department of the United States Fidelity and Guarantee Company, with which he remained for three years. At the end of that time he began his private practice of law with offices in the Commerce Title Building.

He is a member of the Memphis and Shelby County Bar Association, the Tennessee State Bar Association, and the American Bar Association.

Mr. Freeman's nonprofessional memberships include both York and Scottish Rite bodies of Masonry and Al Chymia Temple of the Shrine. He is a member of the Union Avenue Methodist Church. He has an extensive library and enjoys reading, and he is also fond of travel. His favorite spectator sport is football.

At Erwin, on October 14, 1951, Max Harold Freeman married Lois Akers. She was born in Knoxville, the daughter of Robert and Lena (Baker) Akers. Her father is assistant auditor for the Clinchfield Railroad.

John Capen Brough, Jr.

An engineer by profession, John Capen Brough, Jr., has his own offices as a consultant in structural engineering in the Porter Building in Memphis. He is a active in a number of professional groups, and also in the civic and organizational life of his city.

Born at Riverside, Illinois, on March 8, 1919, he is a son of John Capen, Sr., and Helen Merle (McFadden) Brough. His father was born in Evanston, Illinois, and his mother in Whitehall, Montana. The public schools of La Grange, Illinois, provided the younger John C. Brough with his early education, and he also attended a junior college located in that city, and continued his advanced studies at the University of Alabama in Tuscaloosa. There he majored in engineering, and completed his courses in 1940.

In that year, Mr. Brough began his career with the State of Alabama Highway Department. He continued in that connection for only a year, and in 1941 joined the staff of the Mobile District of the United States Engineers. In 1945 he resigned to join Harry B. Hunter and Associates, consulting structural engineers, as an associate engineer. After a decade with that organization, he established his own business as a consulting engineer at Memphis. He has specialized in structural engineering. His firm offers their services in several states in the adjoining area and are registered in each state in which they practice.

He is a member of the National Society of Professional Engineers, the Tennessee Society of Professional Engineers, the American Society of Civil Engineers and the American Concrete Institute. In the Tennessee Society of Professional Engineers, he has served as president of the Memphis Chapter, as state director three years, state vice president one year, and he is also a member of the Memphis Engineers Club. He belongs to Theta Xi fraternity.

In his home city, he serves on the Planning Committee of the Civic Research Committee, is a member of the Memphis Chamber of Commerce, and a past president of High Point Civic Club. Greatly interested in work with youth, he has served on the troop committee of the Boy Scouts of America, and on the Memphis and Shelby County Girl Scouts' Camp Planning Committee. A member of St. Luke's Methodist Church, he has served on its board of stewards, and teaches Sunday School for teenagers.

At Tuscaloosa, Alabama, on May 6, 1941, John Capen Brough, Jr., married Martha Allean Jackson. A native of that city, she is a daughter of Samuel Fletcher and Allean (Harris) Jackson. Her father was born in Greensboro, Alabama, and her mother in Jackson, that state. Mrs. Brough is a member of the Eastland Garden Club, the Parent-Teachers Association, and the Memphis and Shelby County Girl Scout Committee. The couple are the parents of two children: 1. John Samuel, who was born on April 2, 1947. 2. Terry Allen, born August 31, 1953.

Samuel Taylor Beare

In addition to managing several business ventures, and filling responsible posts with the federal government, Samuel Taylor Beare has practiced for a number of years as a lawyer, and now heads his own law firm, with offices in the Columbia Mutual Tower in Memphis.

He is a native of Humboldt, and was born on October 18, 1901, the son of Samuel Taylor, Sr., and Evelyn Nelson (Hunt) Beare; his father was founder of the Beare Brothers Ice and Coal Company of Humboldt; born in Aberdeen, Mississippi, he died in Jackson, Tennessee, in 1910. From 1916 to 1919, Samuel Taylor Beare was a student at the McCallie School in Chattanooga, and he continued his studies at Kentucky Military Institute in Louisville, where he graduated in 1922. He then enrolled at the School of Law of Vanderbilt University, where he took his degree of Bachelor of Laws in 1925.

On July 31 of that year, he was admitted to practice in the state of Tennessee, and he has actively followed his profession in the state ever since that time. In the early years he was at Jackson, and while there, held office as secretary and director of the Beare Ice and Coal Company from 1925 to 1932. In 1931 he became president of the Tennessee Ice Manufacturers Association. Mr. Beare served as representative from his district in the 69th General Assembly of Tennessee during the 1935-1936 term. He was United States commissioner at Jackson in 1936, and special attorney on the staff of the Department of Justice in 1937-1938.

Since 1939, he has been practicing law in Memphis. Under the firm name of S. Taylor Beare, Attorney at Law, he conducts a general practice.

As an honor graduate at Kentucky Military Institute, Mr. Beare was captain of A Company there. He held a commission as captain on the staff of the Governor of Kentucky in 1922. As a lawyer he is a member of the Memphis and Shelby County Bar Association and the Tennessee Bar Association.

His fraternity is Sigma Nu, whose Sigma Chapter he joined at Vanderbilt University. He is an honorary member of the local post of the American

Legion, and also an honorary member of the Officers Club at Memphis. A member of the Jackson Exchange Club, he once served as its president; and he belongs to the Young Democrats and the Peabody-Bellevue Civic Club. Affiliated with the Free and Accepted Masons, he is a member of Jackson Lodge No. 45. He is a communicant of Calvary Episcopal Church, and belongs to the Men's Loyalty League of that congregation.

Twice married, S. Taylor Beare chose as his first wife Miss Evelyn Weatherly, whom he married in Jackson, in 1925. To this marriage his three children were born: 1. Samuel Taylor, 3rd. He married Sandra Brown of Jackson, and they have two children: i. Toni Beare. ii. Samuel Taylor Beare, 4th. 2. Evelyn, who is married to Mr. Miller. They have two children. 3. Richard Leslie, who is attending school in Jackson. On October 16, 1942, at Little Rock, Arkansas, Mr. Beare married, second, Betty Carl Boothe, daughter of James Holston and Edna (Cowan) Boothe. Betty (Boothe) Beare received her high school education at Jackson, after which she attended Union University in that city for one year.

Percy D. Haynes

Percy D. Haynes has made a hobby of gun collecting for many years. The only clubs he belongs to have to do with his hobby. As a member of the National Rifle Association, he keeps in close touch with the experts in the gun field, collectors like himself, the master gunsmiths, the hunters and just plain shooters. Then, to share the fun of his hobby with others interested in the same field, he belongs to the Tennessee Gun Collectors Association of which he is president.

Percy D. Haynes, engaged in the oil business in Columbia, was born in Elkhorn, Kentucky, on March 8, 1917. His father, William P. Haynes, was born in Dickenson County, Virginia, on April 15, 1881. He was the first teacher in Dickenson County before moving to Elkhorn. After his marriage, he moved to Tennessee where he settled in Johnson City with his wife, Bertha (Salyer) Haynes, born October 31, 1883 in Elkhorn. Mr. Haynes was also an accountant and wholesale grocer but is now retired.

Percy D. Haynes was educated in the public schools of Johnson City and graduated from Science Hill High School in that city. After his graduation, he worked for the Army Engineers from 1934-1939 at Fort Belvoir, Virginia, as a journeyman ironworker in construction. Later, during World War II, he joined the army and served in the Pacific where he took part in five major campaigns as a harbor craft operator. For his part in the campaigns of the Easter Mandates, Marshall Islands, Ulithi, Leyte and the Philippines, he received a unit citation as well as a Philippine citation for participating in its liberation. Upon discharge, he joined his father-in-law's oil business in Columbia and in September, 1957, bought out the elder man's interests in the firm and continued its operation under the name of Home Oil Company.

Percy D. Haynes

On December 26, 1939, he married in Columbia, Marjorie Westall, born in Jonesboro on February 9, 1913. She is a graduate of Columbia High School, Girls College in Huntington, Alabama, and Dickenson Secretarial College in Nashville. She worked as a secretary in the Home Oil Company before her marriage. She is a teacher in the Sunday School of the First Baptist Church to which both she and her husband belong. Her father, Sam Westall, was born in England in 1879, and was in the oil business most of his life. Retired, he lives in Columbia with his wife, Annie (Wamsley) Westall also born in England in 1878. Mr. Westall is a Thirty-second Degree Mason, past Master of the Lodge, and a Shriner. Percy and Marjorie Haynes have one son, Dennis, born December 29, 1942 in Columbia, attending high school.

WILLIAM WRIGHT MITCHELL, M.D.

In the course of his decade and a half of medical practice in Memphis, Dr. William Wright Mitchell won a favorable professional reputation. He was a man of varied interests and accomplishments.

Born at Olive Branch, Mississippi, on December 31, 1884, he was a son of William Wright, Sr., and Lelia (Rozelle) Mitchell. His father too was born at Olive Branch, while his mother was a native of Mineral Wells, also in Mississippi. After completing his education through the secondary years in the public schools, Dr. Mitchell entered the University of Tennessee at Knoxville. He completed his premedical courses there, graduating with the degree of Bachelor of Arts in 1907. For his professional studies, he entered the College of Physicians and Surgeons of Columbia University in New York City, and took his degree of Doctor of Medicine there in 1911. He passed his internship at Bellevue Hospital in New York. Dr. Mitchell had also completed legal training, receiving a degree of Bachelor of Laws from the University of Tennessee Law School in 1934.

Dr. Mitchell commenced his practice of medicine at Memphis in 1913 and had his offices in that city for many years before his retirement in 1935. After his retirement he devoted his time to business affairs and his language studies, as well as to amateur radio. He was a member of the American Medical Association and the Memphis and Shelby County Medical Associaiton.

His nonprofessional memberships included the Tennessee Club, and the Memphis Country Club. He was a member of Sigma Alpha Epsilon fraternity. Dr. Mitchell took a great interest in amateur radio operation, and had the first "ham" station in Memphis—W 4 E M. He was an accomplished linguist, speaking Spanish and French, and was often called upon to teach courses in these languages at Southwestern in Memphis. He was a communicant of Calvary Episcopal Church. His favorite sport was golf.

At St. Michael's Episcopal Church in Chicago, Illinois, on September 5, 1914, William Wright Mitchell, M.D., married Katie Mitchel. A native of Memphis, she is a daughter of Peter and Mary Katharine (Booker) Mitchel.

She was an organizer, in 1919, of Les Passees, a club interested in charitable work, particularly the operation of the Cerebral Palsy Hospital. She was also a founder of the La Jeunesse, a social club for young ladies in the late teens. She is a member of the Fortnightly Book Club, the Good Earth Garden Club, and the local Better Films Council, and has served as president of all three.

Dr. and Mrs. Mitchell became the parents of the following children: 1. W. Wright, Jr., who was born on July 11, 1915. He married Irene Bruce, daughter of E. S. Bruce, and they have six children: i. Glenn. ii. W. Wright, Jr. iii. Katie. iv. Peter. v. Irene. vi. Florence. 2. Mary Katharine, born September 29, 1916. She married Scott Herron, and has three children: i. Anita. ii. Kay. iii. Scottie. 3. Amelia Martin, born April 18, 1921. She is the wife of Charles H. Davis, an attorney, and they have two children: i. Howard. ii. Myles. 4. Carolyn Rozelle born on January 19, 1925. She married Charles Kittle and their children are: i. Carla. ii. Carolyn. iii. Katie.

Dr. Mitchell's death occurred in Memphis on October 9, 1951. An editorial appearing in a local newspaper made this appraisal of the man and of his place in the community:

All who were fortunate enough to have possessed his friendship, or to have been beneficiaries of his great goodness, will feel keen bereavement as a result of the passing of Dr. Wright Mitchell. He was a man of great sensitivity of soul and one whose many-faceted mind was ever engaged on the quest for greater knowledge in the cultural fields. A successful physician, he learned the law at an age when most are satisfied to stop at further education. He was thoughtful of others and generous with his knowledge and means. He was a good citizen.

Dr. Mitchell was thorough in everything he did, was thoughtful of others, and generous to a fault.

———————

Rowland Hermann Darnell

A lumber industrialist who had interests in the Memphis area, Rowland Hermann Darnell was a member of a family which over a period of a great many years was active in that same business. He was a man of broad culture, widely traveled, and had many civic and organizational interests in Memphis.

Born at Curve, Tennessee, on November 20, 1886, he was a son of Rowland Jones and Mathilda (Taenzer) Darnell. His father founded the business to the management of which Rowland H. Darnell devoted his career; but the family interest in the lumber industry goes still another generation back, his grandfather, Isaac Mark Warner Darnell having followed the same occupation.

When Rowland H. Darnell was young, the family moved to Memphis, and he received his early education in the Memphis University School of that city before entering Cascadilla Preparatory School at Ithaca, New York, and from there he transferred to the University of Virginia, where he completed his advanced studies.

At the outset of his career, he joined the R. J. Darnell Lumber Manufacturing Company, Inc., which his father had founded, and in 1916, after his father's death, became its president. This firm began operations in Memphis, but later had mills at Darnell, Louisiana, and Batesville, Mississippi. Darnell, Louisiana, was founded by Rowland H. Darnell.

Mr. Darnell spent most of his life in Memphis, where he was a member of the Tennessee Club, the University Club, the Hunt and Polo Club, and the Memphis Country Club, and was active in civic affairs. He also belonged to Kappa Alpha fraternity. In religious faith he was a Roman Catholic. A versatile man, he was talented in music, being a skillful violinist. Both he and Mrs. Darnell were fond of travel, and had made extensive trips throughout the United States and Europe.

The couple were married in Memphis on November 28, 1910. She is the former Miss Roberta Able Speed, and is a native of that city, the daughter of Robert Able and Mollie (Jones) Speed. Her father was born in Louisville, Kentucky, and her mother in Mount Pleasant, Mississippi. Mr. and Mrs. Darnell became the parents of two daughters: 1. Roberta Speed, who was born in Memphis on October 2, 1911. She attended Hutchinson School in that city, and Bennett School at Milbrook, New York. Now the wife of H. Douglas Wilson, she lives at Harbor Springs, Michigan. 2. Mollie Darnell, born on September 19, 1913, in Memphis. She too received her education at Hutchinson School and Bennett School. She married Albert H. Mallory, Jr., and is the mother of three children: i. Albert H., 3rd. ii. Robert Speed. iii. Blanche Darnell.

The death of the lumber industrialist occurred on March 17, 1924.

CHARLES HARRIS BROWN

In addition to the valuable service which Charles Harris Brown has rendered to his fellow citizens of Jackson, as a newspaper publishing executive, he has also devoted much time and energy to civic causes. He has been a dynamic force in securing municipal improvements, in carrying out Chamber of Commerce programs, and in the councils of the Democratic party. In a recent year he was recipient of Jackson's Man of the Year Award. Mr. Brown is executive vice president and editor of the Jackson Sun.

He is a native of the city, and was born on January 5, 1887, son of Charles Morris and Minnie (Harris) Brown. His father came from Alabama, having been born near Montgomery, while his mother was a native of Paris, Tennessee. Harris Brown completed his public school education with his graduation from Covington High School in 1906. He then entered Union University at Jackson, where he received his degree of Bachelor of Arts in 1910. In 1946 this university conferred on him an honorory degree of Doctor of Letters.

Between 1906 and 1910, while attending college, Mr. Brown worked part-time on the news staff and in the composing room of the Jackson Sun. As soon as he had completed his courses, he began his full-time connection with the paper and was immediately named its editor. He has continued in that capacity ever since, a total of nearly fifty-five years, in the course of which he has never deviated from high standards in journalism, nor from a spirit of service in bringing objective news coverage to the people of his city and region. Mr. Brown has acquired a substantial amount of stock in his paper. Since 1951 he has been executive vice president of the company which publishes the Sun, while continuing his duties as editor. He also serves on the corporation's board of directors.

For many years, Mr. Brown has served on the board of directors of the Jackson Chamber of Commerce, and he also served on its committee which helped to locate the two-million-dollar central shops of the Mobile and Ohio Railroad in the city in 1925. He served on another Chamber committee which secured the removal of the division headquarters of the Illinois Central Railroad from Water Valley, Mississippi, to Jackson. He likewise served on the Chamber of Commerce committee which obtained the three-hundred-thousand-dollar post-office and the federal court building for Jackson; and on the committee whose efforts were effective in bringing about the construction of the quarter-million-dollar Madison County Courthouse. He has held office as president of the West Tennessee Highway Association, which launched a program for building more farm-to-market roads in the section. For three years, Mr. Brown was chairman of the Chamber of Commerce committee which worked effectively to insure the construction of the four-lane highway on U. S. Route 45 south from its junction with State Highway 18 to the uptown section of Jackson.

Mr. Brown holds office as president of the Madison County Historical Society, which was responsible for the publication of a six-hundred page volume, "Historic Madison," of which fifteen hundred copies were issued, and which has been acclaimed by the State Historical Commission as one of the best county histories ever published in the state.

Active in the councils of the Democratic party, Mr. Brown was chairman of the Madison County Democratic Executive Committee from 1948 to 1950. In that capacity he initiated several reforms which resulted in cleaner elections in the county.

In recognition of his many services to the city and county, he was voted the Jackson Man of the Year Award by his city's civic clubs in 1947.

A member of the Jackson Rotary Club, Mr. Brown is a past president, and has been a director for seventeen years, an international record. He has also held offices in the West Tennessee Executives Club—as president, and as a director for fourteen years. For a decade he was secretary of the Jackson Conversation Club. He is a member of the lodges of the Benevolent and

W.H. Eagle

Protective Order of Elks and the Knights of Pythias. His fraternity is Sigma Alpha Epsilon.

A devoted communicant of the First Presbyterian Church at Jackson, Mr. Brown served as a deacon for fourteen years, and has been an elder of the church since 1945.

At Ripley, Tennessee, on January 5, 1921, Charles Harris Brown married Bess Klutts. She is a daughter of Robert C. and Sophronia (Maness) Klutts. Her father was a native of Salisbury, North Carolina, while her mother was born in McNairy County, Tennessee. Mr. and Mrs. Brown have no children.

PAUL R. COPPOCK

An editorial writer for "The Commercial Appeal," Paul R. Coppock was graduated from Earlham College at Richmond, Indiana, in 1927, and came to Memphis later that year. A continuous resident of the city ever since, he has been a member of the news staff of "The Commercial Appeal" from 1929 and, from 1952 until the present, has been an editorial writer.

In 1946 Mr. Coppock originated The Night Desk, a column of questions and answers with emphasis upon items of regional history. As a member of the West Tennessee Historical Society, he has contributed to its annual "Papers" and has served for several years on its Board of Editors.

WILLIAM HENRY EAGLE

A lawyer by profession, practicing at Knoxville, William Henry Eagle has held public offices in his state for thirty years. He now holds the position of clerk of the Supreme Court and Court of Appeals of Tennessee, with offices in the Supreme Court Building.

He is a native of Sparta, Tennessee, and was born on July 12, 1887, son of John Hibbett and Marcusette (Smith) Eagle. His father was a wholesale feed and grain dealer in Sparta. Attending the public schools of his home area through the ninth grade, William Henry Eagle later took courses at Knoxville Business College, then, deciding upon a career in the law, enrolled at Knoxville College of Law, where he received his degree in 1924.

Mr. Eagle began practice at Knoxville, and practiced in that city until 1929, a member of the firm of Smith, Carlock, Poore and Eagle. In 1929 he was appointed Assistant Attorney General of Tennessee and served until 1943, at which time he was appointed to his present position, clerk of both the Supreme and Appeals Courts of Tennessee.

Over the years, he has capably filled the following positions of public trust in the state government: court reporter, 1912 to 1924; Assistant Attorney General of Tennessee, 1929 to 1943; clerk of the Supreme Court of the state, 1943 to the present time and clerk of the Court of Appeals from 1943, which two positions he presently holds. A loyal Democrat in his politics, he has never sought elective office, despite his outstanding record in appointive posts.

He is a charter member of the Exchange Club of Knoxville, and a member of the Benevolent and Protective Order of Elks and the Golden Cross. He is a member of the First Christian Church in Knoxville, having served as an elder for sixteen years.

In that city, on March 18, 1913, William Henry Eagle married Mary Lucile McBath, daughter of Bartley Russell and Mary (Russell) McBath. The couple are the parents of one daughter, Mary Russell Eagle, who was born on June 18, 1925. She is the wife of George G. Keith, Jr., of Nashville. Mrs. Keith attended Ward Belmont College and graduated from Vanderbilt University. Mr. and Mrs. Keith have three children: George G., III, William Henry and Mary Russell.

REVEREND DR. DONALD HENNING

Dr. Donald Henning, Rector of Calvary Church in Memphis is well-known for his many years of service in the ministry at both religious and educational levels. Since 1949, he has been a leader in civic, social and religious matters in the city of Memphis.

Born in Toledo, Ohio, on April 12, 1907, Donald Henning is the son of Harry William and Pearl Ann (Smith) Henning. His father was for years one of the leading automotive manufacturers in the city of Toledo.

He received his early education in Toledo, later graduating from both Kenyon College and Bexley Hall Seminary in Gambier, Ohio, receiving his Ph.B. and B.D. degrees. Kenyon College granted him the Doctor of Divinity in degree in 1941 and in 1953, he received an honorary L.H.D. degree from Southwestern at Memphis.

Dr. Henning was ordained in 1931, and was immediately assigned to missionary work among the Indians and in rural towns of South Dakota. During his service in this section of the country, he also served as Chaplain to the Episcopal students at the University of South Dakota in Vermillion. In 1937, he was named Rector of Christ Church in Saint Paul, Minnesota, remaining in this post until 1940 when he was elected headmaster of the Shattuck School in Faribault, Minnesota. He entered military service as a Chaplain in the United States Army in 1942 and subsequently spent thirty months in the European Theater of Operations, participating in five campaigns. At the time of his release from active duty in 1945, he was Senior Chaplain of the Military Railway Service in Europe. Upon his return to civilian life in 1945, Dr. Henning resumed his post as Headmaster of the Shattuck School, remaining there until 1949 when he was elected Rector of Calvary Church in Memphis; he continues as Rector there to the present time. He is currently president of the Standing Committee of the Diocese of Tennessee, a member of the Bishop and Council, and he was recently elected a Deputy of the General Convention in Detroit in 1961.

He is a member of the boards of trustees of Kenyon College, the Memphis University School, Lausanne School for Girls and the Memphis Art Academy, and he is a director of the Memphis-Shelby County Red Cross. He was chosen by the National Council of Churches to be one of twelve American representatives with pulpits of Britain during July and August, 1958. Dr. Henning is a member of the Memphis Country Club and of the Tennessee Club.

On June 15, 1931, he married Mary Standish, daughter of William and Nida (Pangle) Standish, at Gambier, Ohio. Dr. and Mrs. Henning are the parents of two sons. They are: 1. Standish, born May 2, 1932; and 2. Kent Standish, born November 14, 1937.

Pi Kappa Alpha Fraternity

The State of Tennessee and some of its leaders have played an important part in the history of the Pi Kappa Alpha Fraternity. Within six years of its founding in 1868, at the University of Virginia, a chapter was established at East Tennessee University, which is now the University of Tennessee at Knoxville. In 1878, Theta Chapter was chartered at Stewart College, Clarksville, Tennessee (now Southwestern-at-Memphis, Memphis, Tennessee). For several years during the trying period between 1880 and 1890 it served as the Grand Chapter of the fraternity, issued charters, and saved the fraternity from disbanding. This chapter also furnished several national officers who had a part in reorganizing and strengthening the fraternity.

For several years the National Office of the fraternity was in Charleston, South Carolina, but it was moved to Atlanta, Georgia, in the 1890s. In 1946, the National Convention voted to accept the invitation from Southwestern-at-Memphis College and from the City of Memphis to located its national offices in that city and erect there its quarter of a million dollar Memorial Headquarters. This decision was based on the combination of historical interest, geographic location, community interest, cultural atmosphere, and economic advantages offered by Tennessee and the City of Memphis.

The fraternity currently has chapters at the University of Tennessee, Southwestern-at-Memphis, Vanderbilt University, the University of Chattanooga, Memphis State University and East Tennessee State College. At one time chapters functioned also at Cumberland University and the University of the South.

It is a tradition that the founders of Pi Kappa Alpha fraternity were former Confederate soldiers whose war-born comradeship was continued in later life by their fraternity membership. Another cherished tradition is that there is a close connection between the Battle of New Market and the fraternity's founding, for it was in this battle that the charge of the students of Virginia Military Academy helped turn the tide.

The first stated meeting of Pi Kappa Alpha was held on March 1, 1868, in Room 47, West Range, at the University of Virginia, a room which was later occupied by President Woodrow Wilson while a student there. Those present at this first meeting were Robertson Howard, James Benjamin Sclater, Jr., Tazewell A. Bradford and Frederick Southgate Taylor. By authority of the Virginia Legislature, Bradford later dropped his last name and legally adopted the name Littleron Waller Tazewell to perpetuate the name of his maternal grandfather. Howard and Sclater were appointed a committee to draw up a constitution and by-laws, and Taylor brought forward the preliminary designs for a badge, afterward completed by William Alexander.

The second meeting of the fraternity was held at Lover's Rock, near the University, with Howard presiding, and Sclater was elected scribe or secretary. Julian Edward Wood and William Alexander were included at this meeting without the formality of initiation and played active parts in organization plans. The constitution was read and adopted and the new fraternity set about accepting and rejecting proposals for membership.

The third meeting was held at 45 East Range and brought the group its first initiate, Augustus Washington Knox. Arrangements were made with a New York firm to produce the fraternity's badge. At the outset, meeting times were irregular as well as the locale, and during the first two years, perhaps seventy-five to a hundred membership proposals were voted upon.

Expansion was considered and already by May of 1868, the first group was to be known as Alpha and "Grand Chapter" of the fraternity. Meanwhile, movement was soon under way to set up chapters at Virginia Military Institute, Emory and Henry College and Randolph-Macon College. It is noteworthy that the fraternity has always considered *men,* and none of the members were mentioned by the University other than in a commendatory way. Within a year, a second chapter, Beta, was founded at Davidson College, North Carolina, and within less than ten years Gamma, Delta, Epsilon, Zeta, Eta and Theta chapters had been chartered on other Southern campuses.

As the fraternity expanded, the problem of government arose, and the fraternity's first convention was held in the famous old Ford's Hotel in Richmond, Virginia, on December 28, 1871. Precedents were established for interchapter relations and for equality among the chapters and other business was handled at the meeting, attended by four members of the fraternity. By 1880, the fraternity had expanded to seven new campuses, nearly two hundred men had been initiated, and an attempt had beeen made to lay the foundation for a truly national fraternity.

The Reconstruction years dealt harshly with the new fraternity, however, and when the second convention was called in December, 1889, at Hampden-Sydney College, there were but four active chapters who elected delegates: Alpha, Iota, Theta and Lambda. These delegates, who became known in the fraternity's history as the junior founders, worked at amending the constitution, restricted chapter expansion to the South, and studied expansion of the fraternity. An executive council was set up for government of the fraternity, with administrative functions, and the chief officer was known as Councilor Princeps. The first Grand Secretary and Treasurer was Robert Adger Smythe, who was to serve the fraternity for more than forty years, until 1933, when he became honorary life President. The first Councilor Princeps was Theron Rice, who was to serve later as Grand Chaplain.

Smythe established the first General Office of the fraternity at his home in Charleston, South Carolina, sought to bolster the fraternity's finances, and set about publishing an official fraternity magazine, to be known as the *Pi Kappa Alpha Journal.* The first number contained th eminutes of the Hampden-Sydney Convention, an editorial and a financial report, and during its first year of existence, six issues of the publication appeared. The magazine stimulated interest in the fraternity, extinct chapters showed signs of revival and from time to time new chapters were founded. Alpha Chapter was revived in 1890, and that same year Mu and Nu Chapters were founded, the first at Presbyterian College of South Carolina and the latter at Wofford College in South Carolina.

In 1891, the *Journal* was replaced by the first issue of *Shield and Diamond,* and the new publication was to become firmly established as the official fraternity publication. During its first year, the new magazine announced plans for a convention to be held in Danville, Virginia, and for the first time official calls were sent out by the Grand Officers. When the Convention met in the law office of Nathaniel Harden Massie, Alpha, in Danville, on December 29, all three grand officers, Daniel J. Brimm, Theta; Joseph T. McAllister, Iota and Alpha; and Robert A. Smythe, Lambda, were present. Alpha, Iota, Nu and Xi sent official delegates and there were unofficial representatives from three or four other chapters. By-laws to the constitution strengthened the Grand Council and an official flag, yell and a flower, the lily, were adopted.

The Knoxville, Tennessee, Convention of 1892 had delegates present from seven chapters, the report showed seventy-five student members in the nine living chapters, and revived the Zeta Chapter at the University of Tennessee. But there were discouraging notes, notably the financial report, which showed a deficit, and McAllister closed the convention by stressing that finances needed urgent attention.

The Richmond Convention of 1893, held at Murphy's Hotel on December 27, saw only three active chapters, Iota, Xi and Pi, officially represented. The constitution was revised and two new officers, Grand High Councilor and Grand Chaplain, were added to the Grand Council to make it a more active working committee. Finances were shown to be precarious still.

1894 saw the *Shield and Diamond* ceasing publication for two years. The Nashville Convention, held in December and attended by two of the grand officers and representatives from only five local chapters, accomplished little of permanent value. The new councilor princeps elected was Robert Randolph Jones, Iota.

It was in January, 1896, that *Shield and Diamond* resumed publication, and the first issue showed some twelve chapters to be active: Alpha, Beta, Zeta, Theta, Iota, Mu, Nu, Xi, Pi, Rho, Tau and Upsilon. Four alumni chapters had been organized, Richmond, Virginia, Memphis, Tennessee, White Sulphur Springs, West Virginia, and Charleston, South Carolina. There seemed to be a revival of interest, and a convention was called for Richmond, Virginia, in July. Meeting in Richmond Woman's College on July 1, were four of the five grand officers, delegates from six active chapters and unofficial representatives from other chapters. The year was to be the turning point for the fraternity. It was out of debt, and at the second Nashville Convention, held in 1897, nine chapters were represented as well as four alumni chapters. This was the fraternity's largest convention to that time. It created the Supreme Council composed of four National Officers to replace the Executive Council. In addition, moves were made to control individual chapters, and power was granted the Supreme Council to levy fines and to revoke charters.

By the turn of the century, Pi Kappa Alpha was on its way to increased growth, and a period of prosperity began, so different from the difficult years which preceded it. The one problem which faced the fraternity was that of expansion, and as it was basically a Southern fraternity, any expansion into the Northern states had always been defeated. But the tide had turned, and it was at the New Orleans Convention, held in 1909, that John W. Hudson, Zeta, moved an amendment to the constitution to the effect that "active chapters shall be confined to reputable colleges and universities throughout the United States." After much debate and discussion, the amendment was passed by a vote of nineteen to six. From this point on, Pi Kappa Alpha could see its future assured. By adhering to the principles of its founders, Pi Kappa Alpha did yeoman service for the cause of fraternalism, did much to heal the wounds of sectionalism, and extended the benefits of college brotherhood the length and breadth of the land.

In the next ten years, the growth of the fraternity had enormous significance. It had become a national organization. Twenty-six active chapters were added, eighteen alumni groups were chartered, fifteen new states had Pi Kappa Alpha chapters, and Alpha-Xi at the University of Cincinnati had the distinction of being the first chapter admitted from the new "Northern extension" territory in 1910. It was also during this decade that the first directory of the fraternity, the Pi Kappa Alpha Fraternity Register, compiled by J. Graham Sale, was published. A thousand copies were distributed and its publication, most valuable and much needed at this point in the fraternity's growth, was independent of any other fraternity fund.

The same period saw a general movement in the country against fraternities, because of abuses in certain instances. The National Interfraternity Conference, of which Pi Kappa Alpha was a member, worked on the problem, but the participation of fraternity men in World War I was proof that the fraternity system was basically sound, and the fraternities weathered the storm. Four hundred members of the fraternity volunteered at President Wilson's call for troops, and of the nearly two thousand men from Pi Kappa Alpha who served during World War I, more than fifty made the supreme sacrifice of their lives. A great number of those who survived were decorated for bravery in action.

The period following World War I was one of great growth for Pi Kappa Alpha. From 1920 to 1933, twenty-seven new chapters were added and several old groups were revived. With nearly eighty chapters in thirty-six states, administration was divided into nineteen districts. Finances, a chancy affair in the early days, now were solidly established. Revenue in 1930 was around $36,000 a year. Payments to the Chapter House Loan Fund in 1930 were nearly $10,000 a year, and the Shield and Diamond Endowment Fund, based on the life subscription plan of 1926, saw the fund increasing $35,000 a year. Conventions were held biennially in this period, in New York, St. Louis, Atlanta, El Paso and Memphis. The New York Convention in 1922 had as honor guest, the only surviving founder and designer of its badge, in the presence of William Alexander, secretary of the Equitable Life Assurance Society. The 1930 convention, in Memphis, demonstrated that state (Tennessee) to be the most popular for conventions with the fraternity.

The Great Depression of the 1930's saw the appearance of the first "History of Pi Kappa Alpha." Its success was such that it went through several editions and conventions voted that all initiates should possess it. Other important fraternity publications included a full and comprehensive directory, published in 1938, song books, a "Pledge Training Manual" a "Parliamentary Law Manual" and an "Etiquette Manual." The "Ritual" was revised to make initiations more impressive, and by 1940 the Shield and Endowment Fund had reached a total of $120,000, a far cry from early days when publishing costs were hard to meet. National conventions were held in New Orleans in 1936, in Los Angeles in 1938, and in Chicago in 1940. The New Orleans Convention dealt primarily with the alumni problem. The Los Angeles Convention registered the largest number of student members and of alumni in the history of the fraternity to date.

The coming of World War II saw Pi Kappa Alpha men again turning to serve their country in time of need. Such men as United States Secretary of Agriculture Claude Wickard, National American Legion Commander Milo Warner, Congressman John Sparkman of the House Military Affairs Committee, and United States Senator Charles O. Andrews of the Naval Affairs Committee, all played an important part in the nation's war effort. More than 15,000 Pi Kappa Alphas served in the Armed Forces, and among them were Generals Courtney Hodges, Commander of the First Army, Dumas, Lowe, Mitchell and Ott. Fraternity members won decorations from the Congressional Medal of Honor to Silver Stars and Presidential Citations. The Memorial

Headquarters was dedicated to the five hundred Pi Kappa Alphas who made the supreme sacrifice in World War I, World War II, and the Korean conflict.

In gratitude to the services rendered by fraternity men who served in the Armed Forces, the Victory Convention, held in the Grand Hotel on Mackinac Island, Michigan, in September, 1946, took up plans for a War Memorial Fund which had been sponsored by General Leroy Hodges, Pi, prior to his death. The Convention not only voted to continue raising money for the Memorial Fund, but also accepted the offer of a site from Southwestern College at Memphis. The Chapter House Fund, increased by an assessment on each member, neared one hundred thousand dollars as the fraternity entered its eightieth year, and the fraternity publication, *Shield and Diamond,* remained in the forefront of outstanding fraternity publications.

By 1948, Pi Kappa Alpha had passed the 35,000 mark in membership and had more than one hundred chapters. Among the big ten national fraternities, Pi Kappa Alpha played an increasing role in interfraternity affairs with active membership on the National Interfraternity Conference Executive Committee and on the Executive Committee of the Fraternities' Secretaries Association.

It was in 1948 that the National Office of the fraternity was moved from Atlanta, Georgia, to Memphis, Tennessee. A National Headquarters Building containing 10,000 square feet was constructed at 577 University Boulevard and was dedicated on September 1, 1954. The National Office staff now consists of an executive secretary, an assistant executive secretary, five field counselors, and six clerical employees. This staff directs the affairs and maintains the records on the undergraduate chapters at Universities throughout the United States. There are 51,000 members who have been initiated into Pi Kappa Alpha and 117 undergraduate Chapters. The net worth of the fraternity now exceeds $1,000,000.

John U. Yerkovich of Portland, Oregon, was elected National President for a two-year term September 3, 1958 at the Washington, D. C. convention, succeeding Grant Macfarlane of Salt Lake City, Utah. The Executive Secretary, Robert D. Lynn of Memphis, Tennessee, was elected in 1946 and continues in that office.

The Pi Kappa Alpha Memorial Foundation, chartered in 1948 as a nonprofit Tennessee corporation, was established by members of the fraternity to serve as an avenue for providing scholarships for worthy college men, creating and maintaining a fraternity museum and library, and providing a Memorial Headquarters with facilities available for the use of cultural, educational and civic organizations. The current president of the Memorial Foundation is J. Harold Trinner of Memphis, Tennessee.

The last surviving founder, William Alexander, could fitly say of Pi Kappa Alpha in 1933: "The spreading oak upon which we look today with wonder and pride could never have grown from the seed of any weed. Its

character proves that it was a genuine acorn which was planted at the University of Virginia more than half a century ago."

Twenty-five years have elapsed since Mr. Alexander uttered these words. They are even more true today.

DAVID ACRON COOPER

A variety of experience in business and educational connections has led David A. Cooper of Knoxville to his present responsible post as president and superintendent of Cooper Institute, Incorporated, which he founded in 1946. He serves on various educational boards, and is active in a large number of educators' groups.

Born in Charlotte, North Carolina, on October 16, 1910, he is a son of David Porter and Roberta (Lewis) Cooper, and grandson of Loyd Winton and Alice (Six) Cooper, and of William A. and Caldonia (Morrell) Lewis. His father was a native of Wythe County, Virginia, and his mother of Jonesboro, Tennessee. David A. Cooper completed his public school education in his native city and graduated from Central High School in Charlotte in 1928. He completed his requirements for the degree of Bachelor of Science in Public Finance and Business Administration at the University of Tennessee in three years, receiving the degree in 1931; in his spare time he worked in the finance office of the University Athletic Association. He continued with graduate studies there, receiving his degree of Master of Science in Accounting in 1934. Thereafter, until 1936, he took advanced courses in business education and social control, also at the University of Tennessee. Mr. Cooper next enrolled at Columbia University in New York City, for studies leading to the degree of Master of Arts in Business Education, which he received in 1938. He completed advanced courses in guidance and personnel at Harvard University in 1939. While in the armed forces, he studied guidance and personnel subjects at Washington and Jefferson College in Pennsylvania, and also attended Army Clerk School at New Orleans, Louisiana, both in 1943. He taught merchandising at Biarritz American University, Biarritz, France, in 1945 and received a citation from the Army for his services.

Mr. Cooper began his business career in accounting and secretarial capacities with the Taylor Grocery Company in his native city of Charlotte, in 1931. He was a visiting lecturer in merchandising at the University of Tennessee in 1946. Mr. Cooper's next position was with the Knoxville Baptist Tabernacle, now the Tennessee Avenue Baptist Church, in the capacity of educational director. In 1931, he began seven years in radio work, in the course of which he was heard over Stations WNOX and WNBJ in Knoxville.

He next entered the teaching profession in Knoxville, teaching business education at Knoxville High School and also at the city's Adult Vocational Evening School. There followed a position with South-Western Publishing Company of Cincinnati, Ohio, which he served as educational representative and special consultant in the Southeast Territory from 1934 to 1939. In the latter year he accepted a connection with the merchandising firm of S. H. George and Sons (now Rich's) as personnel director and assistant general manager.

Mr. Cooper was instructor in merchandising at Biarritz American University following the war, and on his return to this country, in 1946, became visiting lecturer in retailing at the University of Tennessee. In 1946, he became owner and operator of his own business, Dapco Sales and Services; and he is also a public accountant and personnel and business consultant. He is the president and superintendent of Cooper Institute, Incorporated, which was formerly known as Cooper's Institute of Business, Incorporated.

Besides this major career connection, Mr. Cooper has served on the board of directors of the organization known as Teaching Bible in the Public Schools, with offices at Knoxville. He is a past director, and treasurer of Knoxville Mental Health Association; and he has held office as secretary and as first vice president of the Board of Education, City of Knoxville.

Mr. Cooper's military service covered the years of World War II, and he was in the Adjutant General Division, United States Army, for a total of four years, of which three were spent overseas.

As an educator, he is a member of the Knoxville Associated Teachers of Business, and was its first president. He is also a member of the Tennessee Public Accounting Association, the National Society of Public Accountants, the National Association of Tax Accountants, the National Association of Tax Consultants, the National Association and Council of Business Schools, the Tennessee School Board Association, the National Education Association, the Tennessee Education Association, Eastern Commercial Teachers Association, and the Southern Business Education Association. His other memberships include the American Management Association, Alpha Zeta Chapter of Delta Sigma Pi, Beta Chapter of Phi Delta Kappa, and the Association of Evangelical Churches of Greater Knoxville, which he has served as president. Also in his own city, he belongs to the Chamber of Commerce, the Northside Kiwanis Club, and the North Knoxville Business Men's Club. He is a member of Broadway Baptist Church in Knoxville.

At Bonner Springs, Kansas, on October 15, 1941, David Acron Cooper married Agnes Pearson, daughter of James P. and Beulah May (Luther) Pearson. Mrs. Cooper graduated with a Bachelor of Science in Education from the Kansas State Teachers College at Pittsburg, Kansas, and her Master's degree of Science in Commerce from the University of Denver. Mrs. Cooper is director of education at Cooper Institute. She is active in civic, educational and club functions having served as district governor of Quota International on two different occasions. Her father was born at Pomeroy, now Quivera Lakes, Kansas, in 1878, and her mother at Chattanooga, in 1883. Mr. and Mrs. Cooper have one son, David Acron, Jr., who was born on October 4, 1947.

EDGAR HARDIN GILLOCK

With considerable experience in the floor-covering field to his credit, including the management of his own business, Edgar H. Gillock now holds the post of factory representative with Mastic Tile Company of Joliet, Illinois. In addition to this he is also a very able young attorney. He is an alumnus of several higher institutions, and has served in the Army Air Corps and the National Guard.

A native Tennessean, Mr. Gillock was born in Savannah on July 30, 1928, and is a son of Edgar Cherry and Ruth (Hardin) Gillock. His father, who followed the occupation of carpenter during most of his life, is now retired. Edgar H. Gillock attended the public schools of his native Savannah, Tennessee, and graduated from Central High School there in 1947. He then entered the Air Corps; he was later enlisted in the 196th Field Artillery, National Guard, from 1950 to 1951. In recent years he has furthered his education. He took his degree of Bachelor of Science at Memphis State College in 1956; and has completed his requirements for a Master of Arts degree at Memphis State University. He has also received the degree of Bachelor of Laws, at Southern Law University, graduating as Class President in 1959.

Mr. Gillock was trained in the floor covering field with the Memphis Linoleum Company and Linoleum City Company, 1949 to 1952. He then became proprietor of his own business, which he operated as sole owner from 1952 to 1953.

He was active in the Veterans Club of Memphis State College, of which he was vice president, in the Methodist Men's Club, and in the East Frayser Civic Club. Affiliated with the Free and Accepted Masons, he belongs to Lodge No. 746; and his fraternities are Delta Chi Delta (legal), Phi Alpha Theta, Kappa Alpha, and Tau Kappa Alpha. He has served the last-named society as its president. A Democrat in his politics, he is now a candidate for the State Legislature. He and Mrs. Gillock attend Ardmore Baptist Church with their five children.

Mrs. Gillock is the former Miss Joan Frederickson, and is a daughter of Neil Henry and Thelma Elizabeth (Bartholomew) Frederickson. She became the wife of Edgar Hardin Gillock in a ceremony at Marion, Arkansas, on July 3, 1948. Their children are: 1. Debra Ruth, who was born on April 13, 1949. 2. Lee Hardin, born September 18, 1950. 3. Vicky Denise, born March 25, 1953. 4. Laura Elizabeth, born December 10, 1954. 5. Lorri June, born February 9, 1960.

AUGUSTUS LONGSTREET HEISKELL

One of Memphis' veteran attorneys, Longstreet Heiskell has practiced in the city for more than four decades, and is a partner in the firm of Shepherd, Heiskell, Williams, Beal and Wall, which has its offices in the First

National Bank Building. Mr. Heiskell has banking connections and has been very active in local and regional legal circles.

A native of Memphis, he was born on November 4, 1890, son of Frederick Hugh and Gussie (Lamar) Heiskell. His father too had been a lawyer, who served as judge of the Chancery Court of Shelby County at Memphis for thirty years, and was for a decade judge of the Tennessee Court of Appeals, Western Division. Longstreet Heiskell attended the public schools of Memphis and the University of Tennessee, and completed his professional courses at the Law School of the University of Virginia, where he graduated with the degree of Bachelor of Laws in 1914.

Mr. Heiskell has practiced law in his native city since 1914, specializing in trial work. He has represented a number of the larger corporations, and has tried a number of important cases, including some involving several millions of dollars. His first law firm was Anderson, Crabtree and Heiskell, which later changed membership to become Anderson, Heiskell and Davis, a partner being the Hon. Clifford Davis, now and for many years past being a member of Congress from the Ninth Congressional District of Tennessee. Mr. Heiskell later became a member of the firm of Chandler, Shepherd, Owen and Heiskell, whose senior partner was the Hon. Walter Chandler, one-time Congressman and twice Mayor of the city of Memphis. This firm was succeeded by the firm of Chandler, Shepherd, Heiskell and Williams. His present firm, Shepherd, Heiskell, Williams, Beal and Wall, was formed in 1956, and has since engaged in a general practice.

Mr. Heiskell has not held political or public office other than to serve on the legal trial staff of the City of Memphis for many years. He is of general counsel for The First National Bank of Memphis. He is a fellow of the American College of Trial Lawyers, and a member of the American Bar Association, the Tennessee Bar Association, and the Memphis and Shelby County Bar Association. He is admitted to practice in the United States Supreme Court and the State and Federal Courts of many southern states.

His fraternity is Kappa Alpha, and in his own city he belongs to the Memphis Country Club, the Tennessee Club, and the Civitan Club. He and his family attend Idlewild Presbyterian Church in Memphis.

On June 15, 1918, Longstreet Heiskell married Ardeane McNeil, daughter of James Alexander and Ann (Frank) McNeil. The couple make their home at 2171 South Parkway East and they are the parents of two children: 1. Ann, who was born on March 16, 1919. She is now the wife of Albert C. Rickey, and they have one child: Mary Lamar Rickey. 2. Ardeane, born on March 13, 1922. She is married to C. D. (Jack) Jennings. They also have one child: James Longstreet Jennings.

Wayne Prusnell

WAYNE PRESSNELL

Entering the phosphate business in his own name more than a quarter-century ago, Wayne Pressnell of Columbia, Tennessee, is now owner of the Columbia Rock Products Company and the Pressnell Phosphate Company, Inc. He has banking and farming interests as well, and in his civic as well as his business efforts, has proved himself one of the useful citizens of his community.

A native of Mount Pleasant, he was born on February 6, 1903, and is a son of James Pleasant and Era Jean (McAnalley) Pressnell. His father, born on November 14, 1880, at Athens, Alabama, was in the phosphate business, and was manager of the Federal Chemical Company's plant from 1910 to 1936. Coming to Tennessee in 1900, James P. Pressnell lived at Mount Pleasant until 1919, at which time he was transferred to Columbia. He died in 1936. His wife, the former Era Jean McAnalley, survived him until 1950, when she died at Columbia. he was a native of Lawrence County, Tennessee, born on April 16, 1881. Gifted in music, she played a number of instruments. She was active in the Church of Christ. This couple were the parents of six children.

Wayne Pressnell attended the public schools of Mount Pleasant, and later at Columbia, where the family moved when he was sixteen years old. He graduated from Central High School in the latter city. In 1923 he entered the employ of the Federal Chemical Company at Columbia, for which he worked until 1931. At that time he started his own phosphate business, now operated under the name of Pressnell Phosphate Company, Inc. Its headquarters are at 216 West Seventh Street. Since 1952, Mr. Pressnell has also owned the Columbia Rock Products Company at Columbia, Tennessee.

He is the owner of Haynes Haven Farm with his brother, Harry Pressnell, which they devote to raising livestock, buying and selling cattle. He also raises and deals in Shetland ponies. He is respected as one of the capable and progressive business leaders of his city, and in particular has taken a considerable part in its financial life. He is chairman of the board of The First Federal Savings Bank of Columbia, which he formerly served as president; and he serves on the board of directors of the First Farmers and Merchants National Bank.

He was formerly a Kiwanian, and retains membership in the Columbia Country Club and the lodge of the Benevolent and Protective Order of Elks. He is a communicant of the Church of Christ.

At Spring Hill, on May 2, 1922, Wayne Pressnell married Lottie Willee Blocker. Born at Sawdust, near Columbia, on November 16, 1903, she is a daughter of Edwin LaFayette and Hauty Bourban (Eskew) Blocker. Her father, who died in 1947, owned farm property, and also real estate in Columbia. Mr. and Mrs. Pressnell are the parents of a daughter, Kitty Starling, who was born in Nashville on February 11, 1924. She is the wife of Winafred Jefferson Davis of Danville, Virginia. He now works in and has an interest in the Pressnell Phosphate Company. Mr. and Mrs. Davis have two children:

1. Winafred Jefferson, Jr., born September 21, 1946. 2. Starling Pressnell, born October 24, 1952.

QUINTON CLYDE ATCHISON

Quinton Clyde Atchison enjoys an important and responsible position in the town of Rutherford. As the superintendent and principal of that city's elementary and high schools, he commands the respect and confidence of the entire populace through his splendid record in that capacity since 1952.

He was born April 22, 1920 near Milan, the son of Jimmie G. and Ina (Holt) Atchison. His father, a carpenter and World War I veteran of the United States Army, passed away in Milan, at the age of fifty-three. His mother, now sixty, still lives in Milan.

Originally the Atchison family came from Scotland, but for many generations they have lived in Gibson County, Tennessee—William Atchison III and William Atchison, Jr., Quinton Clyde Atchison's grandfather and great-grandfather, were born in Madison County.

Mr. Atchison was educated in the Gibson County public schools and after graduation from high school, worked his way through Memphis State College, Memphis, where he received his Bachelor of Science degree. He then enrolled in the George Peabody College of Nashville, and after some interruption brought about through necessity, he received his Master of Arts from there in 1952.

Like many successful men, Mr. Atchison is justly proud of the fact that he worked his way through college. This gave him a special understanding of the difficulties facing youth and drew him into his particular profession. He first taught school during 1946 and 1947, when financial necessity caused him to interrupt his college training. From 1948 to 1952 he was in charge of the Obion County Schools with headquarters at Obion.

Like others with a long American heritage, Mr. Atchison served three and a half years in the United States Army in World War II. During that time he spent twenty-six months overseas in the European Theater of Operations area. He entered in July, 1942, and was discharged in November, 1945, at Fort McPherson, Georgia.

As superintendent of the Rutherford schools, he takes a wide interest in civic affairs. He is a member of the Woodmen of the World, Lions Club, American Legion, Veterans of Foreign Wars and is also very active in the Parent-Teachers Association. His main hobby is reading and he also likes to work in his home workshop.

On August 28, 1946, Mr. Atchison and Dorothy Ann Stovaugh were married in Humbolt. Mrs. Atchison was born in Humbolt on August 21, 1925, and her parents, Ed and Nanilee (Hayes) Stovaugh still live there. Mr. and Mrs. Atchison are the parents of: 1. Linda Elaine, born October 29, 1950, in Humbolt. 2. Nancy Gaile, born March 16, 1954, in Union City.

Frank Gentry Sorrells, Sr.

Frank Sorrells, Sr., born and raised in a rural community, has devoted the greater part of his life to the teaching of agricultural subjects in the schools of his native state as well as in Mississippi. Over the years, he has achieved an enviable record of public service. Now in well-earned retirement, he devotes much of his time to the enjoyment of his grandchildren, his petroleum interests in Mississippi and to his functions as a member of the board of directors of the Gibson County Electric Cooperative Association, a post he has held for fifteen years.

He was born in Bellville, on September 5, 1890, the son of the late Newton Alexander and Susan Rebecca (McKenzie) Sorrells, both of Lincoln County and members of old established Tennessee families.

Frank Sorrells, Sr. received his early education in his native town. He graduated from Morgan Preparatory School before entering the University of Tennessee at Knoxville. He was graduated in 1917 with a Bachelor of Science degree in Agriculture.

After graduation in 1917, he was appointed a County Agent in Russellville, Kentucky, and in 1918 he left to enter service in the United States Army. He was discharged in 1918 with the rank of second lieutenant, and immediately turned to farm management near Yazoo City, Mississippi, spending almost two years on this assignment before returning to Clarksville, Tennessee, to work in the Department of Entomology and to teach mathematics and coach the football team at Clarksville High School. Leaving this school, he taught vocational agriculture at the Joelton High School for a semester and then was retained by Ashland City High School to teach this subject from 1922 through 1925. While at this school, he also coached the basketball team, turning out some outstanding squads and winning the state championship in 1925. Mr. Sorrells was appointed principal of the high school in Unionville, from 1926 through 1928, and during this period continued to teach vocational agriculture. In 1928, he moved to Trenton where for the next ten years he was instructor in vocational agriculture at Peabody High School. From 1938 to 1950, he served as Clerk and Master of the Chancery Court in Trenton. In 1950, he returned to teaching vocational agriculture, this time in the Springhill, Tennessee, High School and finally retired in 1956 to devote his time to his family, his farming, and oil well interests.

He is a member of the Masonic Lodge Number 86 in Trenton and of the First Presbyterian Church in that city, where he serves as an Elder.

He married the former Margaret Jane Fouche in Yazoo City, Mississippi, on December 20, 1919. Her parents, Thomas Eden and Mae (Royster) Fouche, come of old Mississippi lineage. Mrs. Sorrells was born in Oakland, Mississippi, on October 11, 1899 and was educated in the schools of her native city. Frank and Margaret Sorrells have twin sons, born in Yazoo City. They are: Frank Gentry, Jr., and Dr. Jack Fouche Sorrells, born on December 12, 1920. Dr.

Sorrells married the former Nancy Burrow Kizer of Milan and they have four children. Frank Sorrells married Ella Jane Campbell and they have three children.

ALBERT JACKSON WOODALL, SR.

In the course of his years of practice as a lawyer at Jackson, Albert J. Woodall, Sr., has won an exceptional reputation in public life and civic affairs.

He is a native of Woodville, Alabama, and was born on June 12, 1912, son of Emmett and Annie (Wann) Woodall. His father was a teacher, merchant, and postmaster at Woodville. However, the family moved to Huntsville, Alabama, when Albert J. Woodall was very young, and he attended public school there, graduating from its high school. For his professional training, he went to Cumberland Law School in Lebanon, Tennessee, where he received his degree of Bachelor of Laws in 1935.

Admitted to the bar of the state of Tennessee, Mr. Woodall began practicing at Jackson, where he has since had his offices. He was absent, however, at the time of World War II, serving thirty-four months overseas with the Eighth Air Force in France and England. He received his honorable discharge on January 9, 1946.

As a lawyer, Mr. Woodall is a member of the Madison County Bar Association and the Tennessee Bar Association. For the past decade and a half he has served as field secretary on the staff of Congressman Tom Murray of the Seventh Congressional District. Since his return from World War II, he has taken a vital interest in political affairs. During the 1947-1948 term, he served as president of the Madison County Young Democrats Club. In 1949 he was appointed to the staff of Governor Gordon Browning, with the rank of colonel; and he became a colonel on the staff of Governor Frank G. Clement in 1953. Mr. Woodall was formerly a member of the Madison County Democratic Executive Committee.

Meantime, his record of civic services has attracted favorable attention, and this comment was made by a fellow citizen: "Wide recognition for his professional attainments and fine public spirit has been won. His services to his community and its institutions, his church and many other causes naturally broaden the scope of his constructive influence beyond the immediate limits of his career as a lawyer." In 1958, he served as area chairman for the Cancer Crusade, and during 1960, is serving as general chairman of the Heart Fund for West Tennessee. He is also vice president of the Jackson-Madison County Crippled Childrens Society. One of his major interests has been the program of the Boy Scouts of America. He was organization and extension chairman for the Central District in 1955, 1956 and 1957; and is currently serving as chairman of the organization and extension committee of the West Tennessee Area Council, his current term to end December 31, 1960. He has devoted himself unselfishly and untiringly to organizational work and public speaking on behalf

Eula Hood Hutton.

W. Ed. Hutton

of Scouting. Currently, he is also a member of the executive board of the local council, and chairman of the Madison County sustaining membership enrollment for 1960. In January of that year, at an awards dinner, he received a silver statuette in recognition of outstanding service.

As a veteran of World War II, Mr. Woodall is active in Cocks-Daniels Post No. 1848 of the Veterans of Foreign Wars, and served as its commander during the years 1953-1954. He was state commander of the V. F. W. in 1949-1950. Prior to that, he was junior vice commander of its state organization, 1947-1948; and senior vice commander in 1948-1949. In 1950 he was honored at a "Jack Woodall Night," in recognition of his outstanding work for the advancement of the Veterans of Foreign Wars in his state. He is also a member of the American Legion, and was district commander in 1956-1957.

Mr. Woodall is an associate member of the Fraternal Order of Police, and his fraternity is Sigma Alpha Epsilon, which he joined at Cumberland University. A devoted worker in the Hays Avenue Methodist Church, he is a member of its board of stewards, and is serving as lay leader during 1959-1960. His local memberships include the Jackson Exchange Club, and the lodge of the Benevolent and Protective Order of Elks.

On September 13, 1941, at Mercer, Albert Jackson Woodall, Sr., married Eloise Pope, daughter of W. D., Sr., and Mabel (McGee) Pope. Both of her parents were natives of Mercer, where her father was born on December 5, 1888, and her mother on July 10, 1896. Mr. and Mrs. Woodall make their home at 41 Mimosa Drive. They are the parents of two children: 1. Albert Jackson, Jr., born on December 1, 1946. 2. David Emmett, born December 13, 1951.

WILLIAM EDWARD HUTTON

Over a period of many years, William Edward Hutton has taken a prominent part in the industrial and commercial life of Dickson. At present he operates a retail furniture store at 114 North Main Street. He has capably filled public office as sheriff of his county and mayor of his town, and is now a member of the Dickson Electric Power Board.

A native of White Bluff, he was born on October 13, 1886, son of Thomas Overton and Addie (Eleazer) Hutton. The Hutton family has lived in the area for many years, and William E. Hutton's grandfather, John W., was sheriff of Dickson County from 1854 to 1860. He held that office again from 1872 to 1877. Thomas O. Hutton was a stock dealer and farmer. Addie Eleazer, whom he married, was the granddaughter of Steve Eleazer and Epps Jackson, who founded and operated furnaces and forges which were important in the early-day development of the region's industry: the Hurricane Mills in Humphreys County, Turnbull Forge in Dickson County, and the Laurel Furnace in Montgomery County's Bell State Park.

After his father's death in 1887, when William E. Hutton was a year old, he and his mother, and four older children, made their home with his maternal grandfather, Minor Eleazer, near White Bluff. He spent his boyhood years there until 1900, when Mrs. Hutton married, as her second husband, Dr. W. P. Hunt of Erin. Dr. Hunt too died in 1905, and Mr. Hutton, then only eighteen years old, became head of the household, largely responsible for its support and also for management of affairs, which included raising his half-brother, W. H. Hunt, who was four years old at the time. Mr. Hunt died in February, 1958.

In his early years, William E. Hutton worked for the Warner Iron Company, at Cumberland Furnace, in which firm he held positions as bookkeeper, yardmaster and store manager. In 1908 he became owner and operator of a general store at Cumberland Furnace, and continued active in its management until he entered the race for sheriff of the county in 1934. He was elected, and took office on September 1 of that year, serving until September 1, 1940. From 1943 to 1946, Mr. Hutton was mayor of the town of Dickson. He was elected to the Dickson Electric Power Board on October 24, 1949, and has served as a member since. He established his retail furniture business in 1940, under the firm name of W. E. Hutton Furniture Store, located at 114 North Main Street, Dickson.

Mr. Hutton received his education in the public schools of Dickson County and at Dickson Normal College. On January 29, 1957, he was commissioned a Kentucky Colonel by Governor A. B. Chandler. He is a member of the Chamber of Commerce and a charter member of the Kiwanis Club at Dickson, and was formerly a member of the Lions Club. His other memberships include Iron Lodge No. 503 of the Free and Accepted Masons at Cumberland Furnace, and he is a past master of that lodge, in which he received his fifty-year pin on April 12, 1958. He is also a member of the Order of the Eastern Star in that community. He is a communicant of the Methodist Church.

Twice married, William E. Hutton chose has his first wife Miss Sallie Belle Pentecost. She was among the first of the 4-H Club leaders of Dickson County. An active member of the Methodist Church and Sunday School of Cumberland Furnace, she was also, at the time of her death, Worthy Matron of Iron Chapter No. 233, Order of the Eastern Star. Her father, W. H. Pentecost, was an early and prominent settler in the northern part of Dickson County. Her mother was the former Lizzie Dodson, member of a family who were also among the early settlers in the county. James Christian Dodson, father of Lizzie Dodson, served in the Confederate States Army. Mr. Hutton and Sallie Belle Pentecost were married at Cumberland Furnace on November 9, 1916, and she died on July 1, 1932. They became the parents of the following children: 1. Mary Elizabeth, who was born on October 23, 1917. Trained as an officer in the WAVES at the time of World War II, she served from 1942 to 1945. Following her training at Smith College, Northampton, Massachusetts, she was commissioned an ensign, and at the time of her separation from service held a commission as lieutenant, junior grade. She is the wife of Joseph H. Netherland of Murfreesboro. He served in the United States Navy for three years, entering as a seaman, second class, and concluding his tour of duty as a pharmacist's mate. Both attended Middle Tennessee State College at Murfreesboro, and both took degrees of Bachelor of Science there. They are the parents of four children: i. Joseph H., Jr., born on September 12, 1946. ii. Carol Elizabeth, born on February 13, 1949. iii. Sally Nell, born April 26, 1951. iv. Ed Hutton, born July 8, 1954. 2. Eunice Mae, born June 24, 1919. 3. Helen, who was born on October 15, 1921. She too attended Middle Tennessee College. She married Ben F. McCreary, Jr. He attended the University of Tennessee, and served in the United States Navy during World War II, being in a Seabees demolition squad stateside. They have two children: i. Mary Jane, born March 5, 1945. ii. Edward Fletcher, born August 21, 1947.

On October 6, 1934, William E. Hutton married, for the second time, Eula Hood, daughter of Charles Manliff and Florence (Woodall) Hood. Mrs. Hutton was born at Murray, Kentucky. Both of her parents were descendants of pioneer families of Virginia and Kentucky. Forebears in the Hood, Waterfield (or Warterfield), and Keys lines were recognized for their contributions in the fields of medicine, the law, and religion. Mrs. Hutton's paternal grandparents were Charles R. and Harriet (Waterfield) Hood. Phillip Warterfield, one of her ancestors, came to this country from England in 1740, and settled in Virginia. Two of his sons served in the Revolution, in which one, James, lost his life. The other, Peter, served until the end of the war, then returned to Virginia, married and reared nine children. In 1818 he and his family moved to Kentucky. One of his sons, Cluff Anderson Warterfield, Mrs. Hutton's greatgrandfather, built a Methodist Church and was its first pastor. Both he and his father are buried in the churchyard of his Goshen Methodist Church in Calloway County. Throughout the years members of the families have taken an active part in politics, and have filled both elective and appointive offices at the town, county, and state levels. One, Harry Lee Warterfield, was elected lieutenant governor of Kentucky in 1955.

ANDREW MIZELL BURTON

The founder of the Life and Casualty Insurance Company of Nashville, in 1903; its president from 1903 to 1950; and now holding the title of president emeritus and director; Mr. Burton served as president of an insurance company longer than any other insurance president in the United States, and still actively interests himself in the insurance field. One of the most successful business ventures in Tennessee, Life and Casualty had its modest beginning in a one-room office when Mr. Burton and his secretary, Miss Helena Haralson, began operations. With one thousand dollars each invested, and with an additional twenty-three thousand dollars invested by Dr. J. C. Franklin, a druggist, Guilford Dudley, a business executive, and P. M. Estes, an attorney, Mr.

Burton saw the company grow enormously. Life and Casualty today has a total insurance in force figure of more than one and a half billion dollars in addition to over a billion and a half of accident insurance in force. Its new thirty-story tower building in Nashville is in sharp contrast to Mr. Burton's first office in 1903, whose rental was twelve dollars and fifty cents a month.

Mr. Burton was born in Castalian Springs, Tennessee, on February 2, 1879, the son of John Booker Burton and of Betty (Lafferty) Burton. After some schooling, he began his insurance career at the age of eighteen, becoming an agent for the Traders Mutual Insurance Company of Illinois in 1897. When the license of this company was revoked by the state of Tennessee, in 1903, Mr. Burton sought to find employment for himself and his fifty fellow agents of the company with the Western and Southern Insurance Company. That company's president, W. J. Williams, refused him, but told him: "Young man, why don't you go home and start a company of your own." This Mr. Burton did, and succeeding in raising twenty-four thousand dollars capital to add to the one thousand dollars that he possessed, the new company began operations on September 12, 1903. The one-room office where the company had its start housed both the home and district offices of the new company, with Mr. Burton as claim inspector and sales manager in addition to his title as president, and with Miss Haralson as policy writer as well as secretary, clerk and office girl. The fifty men who had been with Mr. Burton in Traders Mutual made up the first sales force, twenty operating in Nashville, and the other thirty in Memphis, Knoxville, Chattanooga and other Tennessee communities.

The first three years were a struggle to survive, and during the first years, there was only one regular policy form, a sick benefit, non-cancellable policy which paid sick and accident benefits for twenty-six weeks. The first sick claim, for $2.25, was paid to a Negro woman, and the whole agency attended the first payment, later canvassing the street and writing $750.00 of new business on the strength of that first payment. The first policy written was dated September 14, 1903, and had been solicited by Mr. Burton and his father. The weekly premium on this policy was five cents, and the death claim of fifteen dollars was paid on the policy on March 7, 1942. In the first twelve months of existence, Life and Casualty paid $4,504.56 in sick and accident claims and $923.40 in death claims. By 1958, the company reckoned nearly $145,000,000 paid to policy holders and beneficiaries since its organization.

The company could already show a profit by 1906, and at the end of that year profits totaled $6,619.46. The gain dropped to less than $5,000 in 1907, but rose to more than $11,000 the following year. The company had begun operations at a fortunate time since the economic rise of the South, after the hard years of reconstruction, had begun. Local men and local capital were investing in the future of the area. The company's first investment, once profits declared themselves, was an $800 mortgage on land in Nashville.

By 1909, Life and Casualty owned its own home in what is now the Exchange Building. Capital stock was increased from $25,000 to $150,000, and in December of that year the company went on a legal reserve basis, which meant that policies earned money as they matured. In 1910, stock was sold to outsiders for the first time, and the company went outside Tennessee for business for the first time, seeking new customers in Mississippi, and then Louisiana, Arkansas and South Carolina. Operating territory gradually expanded to the present fifteen state area, with Texas being added in 1953, and California in 1955.

In 1912, policy contracts were liberalized and new forms introduced; in 1918 the company began to write standard industrial life policies and in 1919 ordinary policy forms were added. Although large policies have been written by the company, its stock-in-trade is the small-salaried worker in business and industry, and when Life and Casualty began operations, there were few companies catering to this group. The company's activities were climaxed in 1928 by the construction of a five-story home office building and the acquisition of Radio Station WLAC, as well as the announcement that assets had reached the figure of more than eight and a half million dollars.

The depression was not without its effects on Life and Casualty, but it is worth noting that it was in 1931, one of the worst business years in the country's history, that Guilford Dudley, Jr., the present president of the company and son of Guilford Dudley, Sr., one of the founders of the company, wrote more than $1,000,000 life insurance. With such agents, it was not surprising that Life and Casualty weathered the depression, met the years of World War II, and then went on to become a billion-dollar corporation. On February 21, 1956, at the company's annual stockholders' meeting, it was voted to increase the authorized capital stock from ten million to fifteen million, and Life and Casualty could look forward to still more prosperous years ahead. Symbol of its faith in the future is the thirty-floor, four-hundred-and-nine-foot-high tower home office building which is now headquarters for Life and Casualty in Nashville. The tallest commercial structure in the southeastern United States, it is completely modern in every respect and is a beacon to the people of Tennessee.

Mr. Burton grew with the company and the company grew with him. As prosperity came to Life and Casualty, Mr. Burton's interests expanded, notably in the field of philanthropy. In all, he has given away more than two million dollars, notably to Central Church of Christ, in Nashville, and to David Lipscomb College. Another beneficiary of his largesse has been Nashville Christian Institute, a high school and ministerial training school for Negroes, and both he and Mrs. Burton have contributed generously to foreign and domestic missions maintained by the Church of Christ.

Mr. Burton is a member of the National Farm Chemurgic Council and the American Bible Society, he is vice chairman of the board of directors of David Lipscomb College, and he is president of the board of Nashville

Christian Institute. He is a National Council member representing the Nashville Area Council of the Boy Scouts of America. He attends religious services at Central Church of Christ in Nashville, and his hobbies today are fishing, hunting and life in the out-of-doors, a heritage he has kept from his days as a farm boy.

Mr. Burton was married on October 31, 1904, to Lillie Armstrong, and they have seven children: 1. Lillian, now Mrs. Burton Walker of New York. 2. Mizella, now Mrs. Otis P. Grant of Augusta, Georgia. 3. Nelson, a farmer at Estill Springs. 4. Larimore, now in the insurance business at Homestead, Florida. 5. Robert L., of Chicago, Illinois. 6. Louise, now Mrs. W. C. Roberts of Chattanooga. 7. Jean, now Mrs. Charles Clark of Los Angeles, California.

There are nineteen grandchildren and sixteen great-grandchildren.

GUILFORD DUDLEY, JR.

Guilford Dudley, Jr., president of the Life and Casualty Insurance Company of Tenessee, began his career with the company as an agent in 1931 and made a record in Ordinary production which has not been equaled before or since, his production going well over the million-dollar mark his first year in the business.

Mr. Dudley worked in practically every position in the field, including district supervisor, manager, field supervisor, and auditor before being promoted to the home office as agency secretary in 1935. He was later promoted to assistant vice president and manager of the Ordinary Department, and became vice president in 1937. With the exception of four years' leave of absence, 1942 through 1945, when he served in the Naval Air corps, Mr. Dudley held the position of vice president until he was promoted to executive vice president in 1951 and to president in 1952. He was elected to the board of directors in 1946. He received a citation from Admiral W. F. Halsey and a Presidential Unit Citation during his duty aboard an aircraft carrier in the Pacific. He was given an honorable discharge to inactive duty in 1945 as lieutenant commander.

Mr. Dudley is secretary and a member of the executive committee of the Life Insurers Conference, a former trustee of the Life Underwriters Training Council, a former member of the board of the Life Insurance Agency Management Association of Hartford, Connecticut, having served as chairman of the finance committee and the combination company committee. He was also chairman of the Combination Companies Section of the American Life Convention and is now state vice president of the American Life Convention.

In addition to being president of the Life and Casualty Insurance Company of Tennessee, Mr. Dudley is president of three other corporations: WLAC, Inc., WLAC-TV, Inc., and The Casualty Insurance Company of Tennessee.

Mr. Dudley is a member of the board of directors of the Life Insurance

TENN. III—76

Investors, Inc.; the Nashville Chamber of Commerce; the United Givers Fund; the President's Council of American Institute of Management; the National Council of the National Planning Association; and is also Member-at-Large of the National Council, Boy Scouts of America; and a member of the Advisory Board, Bank of Palm Beach and Trust Company in Palm Beach, Florida. He also holds membership in the Thoroughbred Club of Tennessee; the Hillsboro Hounds Hunt Club; the Belle Meade Country Club; The Cumberland Club of Nashville; the Seminole Golf Club; the Coral Beach Club; the Everglades Club; the Bath and Tennis Club in Palm Beach, Florida; the Saratoga Golf Club in Saratoga Springs, New York; and the Turf and Field Club in New York.

A native of Nashville, Guilford Dudley, Jr., was born on June 23, 1907, son of Guilford and Anne (Dallas) Dudley. He received his education at Loomis Institute where he won a letter in football, the Princeton Tutoring School, and Peabody College, and he holds the degree of Bachelor of Arts from Vanderbilt University. At Vanderbilt he was a member of Phi Delta Theta fraternity and was on the varsity football squad.

A well-known sportsman as well as executive, he shoots golf in the low eighties and last year was runner-up in the Tennessee State Doubles Tennis Championship. He currently holds the Men's Doubles Tennis Championship of the Belle Meade Country Club. He is also well known throughout the South as an amateur steeplechase rider. His hobbies are fox hunting and the breeding and racing of thoroughbred horses. The colors of his Northumberland stables have been carried to victory many times by his famous steeplechasers, Hurst Park and Navy Fighter. His stable ranked seventh among money-winning steeplechase stables in the United States in 1957. His Navy Fighter won the Truxton Purse of the Iroquois Memorial Steeplechase in 1955 with Mr. Dudley in the stirrups; and he repeated as a winner of the Truxton riding Here's Why in May, 1958.

Mr. Dudley has two sons and a daughter, Guilford Dudley, III, Robert Lusk Dudley, and Trevania Dallas Dudley. Mr. Dudley is married to the former Miss Jane Anderson of Nashville.

LIFE AND CASUALTY INSURANCE COMPANY OF TENNESSEE

Its more than a half-century of existence makes the Life and Casualty Insurance Company of Tennessee, at Nashville, one of the long-established organizations of its kind distinctively identified with the state; and its record of growth and service over that period mark it as one of the most sound and successful. At the close of 1957, it had one and a half billion dollars of life insurance in force—an increase of one hundred and fifty-three million dollars over the previous year—and it listed assets at the same time totalling over a quarter of a billion dollars. The thirty-story skyscraper in Nashville which houses its home offices is symbol of an organization which has grown steadily, from a substantial foundation of public service.

The company traces its history from September 12, 1903. Its founder, Andrew Mizell Burton, had approached the president of a Cincinnati insurance firm and suggested the opening of a branch office in Tennessee, to provide jobs for fifty salesman thrown out of work when the license of Traders Mutual of Illinois was revoked in Tennessee. Mr. Burton, then twenty-four years old, had been among those of the ill-fated Traders Mutual. When the Cincinnati executives held out no encouragement to him, he determined to go it alone, and opened a one-room office in the Presbyterian Building on Fourth Avenue, North—a room renting at $12.50 per month. He functioned as janitor, as well as manager of the tiny and hopeful organization, whose office staff was completed in the person of Miss Helena Haralson, secretary. The two had their life savings tied up in the uncertain venture; and three other Nashvillans invested capital which brought the firm's capitalization to twenty-five thousand dollars. These three, who with Mr. Burton and Miss Haralson comprised the first board of directors, were Dr. J. C. Franklin, a druggist; Guilford Dudley, businessman and civic leader, and father of the firm's present president; and P. M. Estes, an attorney. Mr. Burton functioned initially as claim inspector and sales manager, and Miss Haralson wrote policies as well as serving as secretary, and clerk in the office. Former agents for Traders Mutual were given jobs selling insurance, twenty of them under T. L. Ligon making up the Nashville sales force, and thirty working in Memphis, Knoxville, Chattanooga, and other Tennessee towns.

The company went through difficult days in its early years, and Mr. Burton instituted sales contests to stimulate business. For several years they wrote only one regular policy form—a sickness compensation policy, non-cancellable, which paid sickness and accident benefits for twenty-six weeks. The first policy written was dated September 14, 1903, the policyholder being Mary E. Church. Another interesting detail of the earliest days of the company's existence is thus recounted in a historical sketch published in The Nashville Tennessean on the occasion of the firm's fiftieth anniversary:

The whole agency organization went out to the neighborhood when the first sick claim, for $2.25, was paid to a Negro woman whose hand had become infected from a snag on a washboard. The sales force canvassed the houses up and down the street and wrote $750 worth of new business on the strength of that claim payment.

In all, in its first twelve months of existence, the company paid out a little over forty-five hundred dollars in sickness and accident claims, and $923 in death claims. A profit of over sixty-six hundred dollars showed on the books for the year 1906—the first year "in the black." The 1907 gain dropped to less than forty-five hundred in 1907, but rose to over eleven thousand in 1908. At about this period the company made a loan of eight hundred dollars on a frame house near the corner of Fourth Avenue, North, and Jefferson Street, thus inaugurating its real estate transactions.

Life and Casualty soon outgrew its first office, but in the phrase of The Nashville Tennesseean article, it has "never wandered far from the neighborhood where it was born." Its second address was a suite of three rooms in a building where the Ambrose Printing Company is now located. In 1909 it became owner of its own home offices when it acquired the building at 307-309 Church Street, now the Exchange Building, and began operations on one of the upper floors. In that year the capital stock of the company was increased from twenty-five to one hundred and fifty thousand dollars. On December 30 of the same year the company went on a legal reserve basis. Through the first seven years of its existence, all stock was held by the five founders. On August 6, 1910, five hundred shares were put on the market at five hundred dollars per share—par value one hundred dollars. In the same year the company began operations outside the state, approaching new customers first in Mississippi and later in Louisiana, Arkansas, and South Carolina. Addition of new state territories has gone on apace over the years, with the addition of Texas, in 1953, bringing the total to thirteen. After 1912, policy contracts were liberalized, and over the years new policy forms were introduced. Cash surrender values were added to the original policy form. In 1918 the company began to write industrial life policies, and the following year added ordinary policy forms. In that year, 1919, ordinary life insurance paid for amounted to over four million seven hundred thousand dollars.

While the company has written policies up to one hundred thousand dollars in value for a single individual, most of its business is drawn from wage earners in business and industry. When it was formed, there were few firms in the South writing such policies.

At the end of twenty-five years of existence, the Life and Casualty Insurance Company erected a five-story home office building on Fourth Avenue, North, and also acquired Radio Station W L A C. In that year the company's assets reached over eight and a half million dollars. In the mid-1950s, the firm gave evidence of its steadily increasing prosperity when it began the construction of the Life and Casualty Tower, whose four hundred and nine feet of height make it the tallest commercial structure in the southeastern United States. For several years past the company has broken each preceding record in increase in insurance in force. The remarkable burgeoning of its volume of trade was the occasion for a remark by Mr. Dudley when the company observed its fiftieth anniversary: "Although it took us fifty years to get the first billion [of life insurance in force] on our books, we expect to get the second billion by the end of 1960, a period of only seven years. We plan to pass the billion-dollar mark of accident insurance in force within the next two years and at that time will set our sights for the second billion in that department too." Mr. Dudley has been president of the company since 1952, and is the subject of a separate biographical sketch accompanying. Other officials are Paul Mountcastle, chairman of the board; A. M. Burton, the founder of the firm who is now president emeritus; and John S. Bransford, Foskett Brown, Henry Neuhoff, P. M. Estes, and J. Truman Ward, directors. Mr. Estes is the son of the P. M. Estes who was one of the first five stockholders and directors of the company, and who was its chief legal adviser until his death in 1945. Mr. Dudley is a son of another of the original directors.

THOMAS HARRIS

Following his return from naval service in World War I, Thomas Harris commenced his practice of law, and, throughout most of the years since, Linden has been the center of his professional activities and his public service. He has been active in city government since Linden was incorporated, and has acquitted himself well in the posts of mayor and city attorney.

A native of Cheatham County, he was born on April 17, 1889, and is a son of William Washington and Rose Elizabeth (Darrow) Harris. His maternal grandfather, Lee Darrow, served with a Tennessee outfit in the Confederate States Army. He was a farmer and spent the last years of his life in Tennessee. His daughter Rose Elizabeth (Darrow) Harris, was born in that state in 1856, and died March 4, 1921. William W. Harris, whom she married, was born in 1853 in Cheatham County. His death occurred in 1927, in his native Cheatham County.

After completing his public elementary and high school education at Ashland City, Tennessee, Thomas Harris entered Cumberland University at Lebanon. There he prepared himself for a career in the law, and in June, 1914, graduated with the Bachelor of Laws degree. He did not, however, commence his practice immediately, but for the next three years, taught in the public schools of Cheatham County.

In November, 1917, he enlisted in the United States Navy, in which he served through World War I and until February, 1919. Within that period, he had to his credit five months of foreign service, and he was also on convoy duty aboard the armored cruiser "Huntington." He held the rating of seaman first class.

After returning to his home area in 1919, and resuming civilian life, Thomas Harris started his practice of law, first choosing Ashland City for the location of his office. In March, 1920, he moved to Linden, where he has practiced ever since. He became city attorney of Linden in 1923 the year it became incorporated, an office in which he served most capably until 1956, when he resigned. In 1958 he was reelected Linden City attorney. He has been Perry County attorney for the past twenty years. He was largely instrumental in having Linden incorporated as a city in 1923, and he served as its mayor

THOMAS HARRIS

MARIE A. HARRIS

for two years. He also served on the building committee for the Perry County Court House.

Mr. Harris holds membership certificate number one in the Merriwether Lewis Electric Co-operative. His interest in this organization has been continuous since it was founded in 1939, and he currently serves on its project council. Besides the law, business and public utilities, Mr. Harris is interested in farming. He owns a farm near Linden, and there he finds a rewarding avocation in general farming, also raising cattle and hogs.

As a lawyer, he belongs to the Tennessee Bar Association. He was formerly a member of the Lions Club and the lodge of Free and Accepted Masons, and he advanced through the higher orders of Masonry to the Thirty-second degree. He has no church affiliation. In politics he is a Democrat.

On January 2, 1925, in Linden, Thomas Harris married Marie Anderson. A native of that city, she was born on September 8, 1906, and is a daughter of Robert and Anna (Plummer) Anderson. Both of her parents were likewise born in Linden. Mr. Anderson passed away in 1914. His widow resides in Linden. Robert Anderson was a merchant there, his store being known as Anderson and Milan.

Mr. and Mrs. Harris have three children: i. Doris, who was born on October 11, 1925. She attended schools in Linden, and Nashville Business College. Married to Mr. H. D. Armentrout of West Virginia, they live in Maryland at the present time, and they have two children: i. Brenda, born in June, 1951. ii. Thomas, born in February, 1954. 2. Robert A., born March 6, 1927. After beginning his education in the schools of Linden, he took his preparatory studies at Battle Ground Academy in Franklin, and was chosen for the Mid-South Basketball Team three years. He later went to Oklahoma Agricultural and Mechanical College, and while there, made the All-American Basketball Team. He played professional basketball for five years. One of his qualifications for the game is his exceptional height. Robert A. Harris married Alexine Banet of Fort Wayne, Indiana, and they have three children: i. Ellen, who was born in September, 1952. ii. Thomas, born in February, 1955. iii. John Banet, born in March, 1959. 3. Rose, born December 13, 1933. She attended the schools of Linden, and Martin College at Pulaski, Tennessee. She took a business course in Nashville. Married to M. H. Paschall of Linden, she is the mother of two children: i. Michael, born in October, 1955. ii. Robert, born September 8, 1957. The family lives in Nashville, where Mrs. Paschall is on the staff of the Tennessee Department of Highways. All of Mr. and Mrs. Thomas Harris' children were born in Linden.

WILLIAM WALLING LUTTRELL

For one of the younger members of Knoxville's circle of business leaders, William Walling Luttrell has had quite a varied career. He worked for one of the largest of industrial corporations, and also acquitted himself well in public office, before opening his own gift shop. He has served as county commissioner of finance and as county court clerk, as well as holding two state posts; and he is a veteran of military service in overseas combat areas in World War II.

Born in Knoxville on January 6, 1918, he is a son of William Eugene and Martha Lee (Walling) Luttrell. His father was for thirty years assistant cashier of the East Tennessee National Bank, and was a member of the Knoxville Chamber of Commerce for eighteen years. William W. Luttrell received his early education in Knoxville public schools, and graduated from Knoxville High School in 1937. For his advanced studies, he entered the University of Tennessee, and there, in 1941, received his degree of Bachelor of Science in Business Administration.

Before he had had an opportunity to begin his business career, Mr. Luttrell was called into service in the United States Army. He served first in the Ninth Division, 60th Infantry, Company I, to which he was assigned in August, 1941. In February, 1942, he was transferred to the 34th Division, which was slated for overseas service. With Company E of its 168th Infantry Regiment, he took part in the invasion of North Africa, from Algiers on through the Tunisian campaign, being with the first troops to arrive there in November, 1942. He was captured by the Nazis near Faid Pass on February 17, 1943, and spent twenty-six months as a prisoner of war. He was separated from the service in October, 1945, holding at that time the rank of captain.

When he returned to civilian pursuits late in 1945, Mr. Luttrell took a position with the personnel department of Aluminum Company of America. He left in August, 1946, however, following his election as Knox County commissioner of finance. He was re-elected to this office in August, 1950. He has since held several other public offices. In January, 1953, he was appointed state director of purchases; and in July of the same year he was named to another state post, that of commissioner of safety. From this latter position he resigned on April 14, 1956. In August of that year, he was elected clerk of the Knox County court, and is still discharging the duties of that office.

Mr. Luttrell acquired his own business, Moore's Gift Shop, in 1955. This he has operated since, concurrently with his duties as court clerk.

As a veteran of World War II, Mr. Luttrell is a member of the posts of the American Legion and the Veterans of Foreign Wars. His fraternity is Phi Gamma Delta. In his home city of Knoxville, he is a member of the Sertoma Club and the lodge of the Benevolent and Protective Order of Elks, and he and his family attend Sequoyah Hills Presbyterian Church.

Mrs. William W. Luttrell is the former Miss Margaret Helen Moore, daughter of John S. and Annie (Love) Moore. She was married to Mr. Luttrell at Macon, Georgia, on December 19, 1941. The couple live on Route 5 near Lenoir City, a suburb of Knoxville. They are the parents of four children: 1. Pamela Love, who was born on June 28, 1946. 2. John Moore, born May 21,

1949. 3. Laura Evelyn, born July 28, 1953, she passed away on October 1, 1957. 4. Samuel Eugene, born June 5, 1956.

LAWRENCE HOWARD ARMSTRONG, JR.

One of Knoxville's business leaders for many years, Lawrence Howard Armstrong, Jr., has concentrated his efforts in the hardware and construction fields. He is currently serving as a trustee of Knox County.

A native of Knoxville, he was born on June 7, 1915, and is a son of Lawrence Howard, Sr., and Clara Van (Davis) Armstrong. His father was a farmer who was also engaged in the hardware business. Attending Knoxville public schools, the younger Lawrence H. Armstrong graduated from high school there in 1933. He entered the hardware business in 1931, joining the Armstrong Hardware Company in the capacity of truck driver. He has headed his own organization, known as Armstrong Hardware and Supply Company since 1948. The store is located at 122 South Central Avenue. In 1950, Mr. Armstrong entered the construction business, operating under the firm name of Armstrong Manufacturing Company. He specializes in home construction. Headquarters of this business is at 122 South Central Avenue. He has built over seventy-five homes in Knox County, the average price of homes being $15,000.

Mr. Armstrong was elected a trustee of Knox County in 1954 and has served two terms, with his office in the Knox County Court House.

His memberships include the Young Democratic Club, the Optimist Club, and the Free and Accepted Masons. In Masonry, he belongs to the Blue Lodge and the higher bodies of the Ancient and Accepted Scottish Rite, holding the Thirty-second Degree. He is also a member of the Order of the Eastern Star, serving as sentinel. He and his family attend Lincoln Park Methodist Church.

In his native city of Knoxville on April 8, 1939, Lon Howard Armstrong, Jr., married Lola Smith, daughter of Charles Leslie and Laura Edith (Irwin) Smith. Mr. and Mrs. Armstrong became the parents of the following children: 1. Judith Marie, who was born on February 1, 1940, and died the same day. 2. Sandra Kay, born October 9, 1941. 3. Brenda Sue, born October 6, 1943; died October 11, 1948.

HONORABLE HAMILTON SANDS BURNETT

Knoxville attorney Hamilton Sands Burnett has served for the past decade as associate justice of the Tennessee Supreme Court. A native of Jefferson County, Tennessee, he was born on August 20, 1895, son of Jesse M. and Carrie (Sands) Burnett. His father was a Baptist minister, who in the course of his career, served as pastor of churches and as president of Carson-Newman College.

Judge Burnett attended the public schools of Jefferson County, then entered Carson-Newman College, where he graduated in 1916 with the degree of Bachelor of Arts. For two years he studied law at the University of Virginia, and was admitted to the Tennessee bar in 1924. In 1948, his alma mater, Carson-Newman College, conferred on him the honorary degree of Doctor of Laws.

Judge Burnett commenced his practice in 1920, at Richmond, Virginia, and has practiced at Knoxville since 1925. His first experience on the bench began when he was elected circuit court judge of Knox County in 1934. In August, 1942, he was elected judge of the Court of Appeals. He was appointed associate justice of the Supreme Court of Tennessee in 1947, to fill a vacancy caused by the death of Chief Justice A. W. Chambliss. He was elected to fill the unexpired term in 1948, and was elected to a full term in 1950.

Judge Burnett is a veteran of World War I.

A Kiwanian, he formerly served as president of the club in Knoxville. He serves on the boards of directors of the East Tennessee Fair Association and the Young Men's Christian Association, and was a director of the International Young Men's Christian Association. He was a vice president of the Holston Hills Country Club, and is a member of the post of the American Legion and the lodge of Free and Accepted Masons. He and Mrs. Burnett attend the First Baptist Church of Knoxville.

His first wife was the former Miss Mary Griffin, daughter of James Knox and Adeline (Hooper) Griffin; she and Judge Burnett were married in a ceremony at Knoxville on October 10, 1923. The couple became the parents of three children: 1. James Knox, born July 19, 1925. 2. Adeline Sands, born December 12, 1926. 3. Hamilton Sands, Jr., born January 22, 1928. Mary Griffin Burnett died in November, 1952. Judge Burnett married her sister, Margie (Griffin) Beaunard, widow of A. K. Beaunard in October, 1953. Judge and Mrs. Burnett live on Kingston Park Drive in Knoxville.

ZEBOIM CARTTER PATTEN

Following a varied business career which has included insurance, real estate and banking activities, Cartter Patten of Chattanooga was recently elected to membership in the House of Representatives, State of Tennessee, from Hamilton County. He is past president of Ridgedale Bank and Trust Company, which is now merged with the Hamilton Bank, of which he is a director; is board chairman of the First Federal Savings and Loan Association; and has broadcasting, timber and horticultural interests.

Born on Lindsay Street in Chattanooga on February 2, 1903, he is a son of Zeboim Cartter, Sr., and Sarah Avery (Key) Patten. His maternal grandfather, Judge David McKendree Key, was a United States senator, served as Postmaster General under President Rutherford B. Hayes, and was United States District Judge for East Tennessee. The elder Zeboim Cartter Patten was president and founder of the Volunteer State Life Insurance Company.

After attending The Baylor School and Asheville School for Boys, the

CARTTER PATTEN FAMILY

younger Cartter Patten entered Cornell University in Ithaca, New York, where he graduated with the degree of Bachelor of Science in 1926. He was a member of Chi Phi fraternity.

Beginning his business career with the Volunteer State Life Insurance Company in 1928, he was first assistant treasurer, and in the course of the next decade, advanced to the vice presidency. He resigned from that office in 1938, but has remained a member of the board of directors. In 1938 he became owner of the Hotel Key, and also of the Horseshoe Properties. This latter is a 20,000 acre tree farm on Walden's Ridge and one of the pioneer efforts of its kind in Tennessee. He owns Ashland Farm, a colonial residence with extensive naturalized gardens south of Chattanooga.

His first venture in political affairs came in 1958 when he was elected representative from Hamilton County. As a member of the House of Representatives, he currently serves as vice chairman of the Committee on Conservation, and as a member of the Business, Education, Local Government, and Military and Veterans' Affairs Committees.

Mr. Patten is a trustee of the University of Chattanooga. He has taken a constructive interest in forest conservation, and is also a student of Tennessee history, and the author of a history of Tennessee called "A Tennessee Chronicle," which was published in 1953. He was a founder and the first president of the Chattanooga Area Historical Association, and is a member of the Tennessee State Historical Commission.

He is a member and past president of Chattanooga, Incorporated, and a member of the Mountain City Club, Fairyland Club, and Signal Mountain Golf and Country Club. He and his family are members of St. Paul's Episcopal Church where he has served as junior and senior warden. They have a summer home on a lake near Penobscot Bay in Maine.

In Nashville, on August 18, 1931, Cartter Patten married Elizabeth Nelson Bryan, daughter of Dr. Worcester Allen and Emma (Berry) Bryan. Mrs. Patten is a graduate of the University of Chicago. In Chattanooga she has served as president of the Junior League, and is currently president of the Tennessee Society for the Preservation of Antiquities. The couple are the parents of four children: 1. Sarah Key, who was born on September 23, 1932. She is a graduate of Vassar College and is the wife of Phillip Gwynn, who is a graduate of the United States Military Academy at West Point. The couple have a son, Howland Bennett Gwynn. 2. Emma Berry, born August 13, 1935. She too has graduated from Vassar College. 3. Zeboim Cartter, 3rd, and 4. Worcester Allen Bryan, twins, who were born on September 25, 1940. Zeboim Cartter Patten, 3rd, is attending Princeton University, while Worcester A. B. Patten is a student at Cornell University.

John McCauley Dickson

John McCauley Dickson was born of Scottish and Scotch-Irish ancestry on June 14, 1842, in Dickson County, Tennessee. His parents were James and Mary (McCauley) Dickson, and he was a grandson of Joseph and Martha (Cowan) Dickson and of John and Mary (Moore) McCauley. His grandparents came to Tennessee and settled in Montgomery County about 1800. Their wills are recorded in the county clerk's office there.

When he was thirteen years of age, John McCauley Dickson united with the Methodist Episcopal Church, South. On May 14, 1861, he volunteered for military service and joined the Confederate States Army at Nashville, Tennessee, being assigned to Company C, 11th Tennessee Regiment, Infantry. He was promoted to corporal, and the muster roll of January and February, 1864, show him present in that rank. He was twice wounded, being admitted to Floyd House and Ocmulgo Hospital, Macon, Georgia, on November 9, 1864; and to Way Hospital, Meridian, Mississippi, on March 27, 1865. No records of capture or parole have been found, and the supposed date of his discharge was March 27, 1865.

On his return home at the close of the war, he learned that his father, James Dickson, had died December 3, 1863, and a sister, Harriet Eliza Dickson, had died shortly after the Battle of Fort Donelson. John lived with his mother and brothers and sisters until his marriage to Martha Euphrasia Batson on February 5, 1868. She was the daughter of Stephen Carney and Armin Maria (Williams) Batson, and granddaughter of Thomas Batson, who migrated from County Down, Ireland, and who married Elizabeth Ives. Her maternal grandparents were William Williams, of Welsh descent, and Sicily Mabry (Tisdale) Williams. They came to Tennessee in 1825 from Lunenberg, Virginia. The Batsons came to Tennessee about 1800. These two families settled in Montgomery County. Thomas Batson's will is recorded in the county court clerk's office. Administration of the estate of William Williams is found in the court records.

In 1869 John and Martha Dickson bought a farm and built a home in the 16th District of Montgomery County. They were the parents of fourteen children, seven sons and seven daughters. All were born at this home except Eula, the oldest, who was born at the home of her maternal grandparents. Thirteen grew to maturity, Maria Stephena dying at the age of four. The children: 1. Eula, who was born on January 2, 1869, and married, May 21, 1890, Edgar Randolph Gannaway, son of a Methodist minister. They were the parents of four sons and two daughters. Eula died on May 29, 1949. 2. James Carney, born May 7, 1870. On March 7, 1910, he married Mrs. Elizabeth Jane (Matthews) Hagewood, and they were the parents of one daughter and one son. Carney Dickson was a farmer, and was active in the Masons, the Independent Order of Odd Fellows, and Modern Woodmen of America. He was a faithful member of the church. His death occurred December 11, 1921. 3. John Keener, born December 26, 1871. He was married, on December 27, 1898, to Etha Linda Harper, and was the father of one daughter and three sons. His second marriage was to Mrs. Pearl (Tucker) Sandford. Keener Dickson was a farmer and teacher, and served for twenty-seven years on the county board of education, being its chairman for several years. For many years he taught Sunday school. With the exception of a three-year period, he has served as county surveyor since 1904. His son John Irwin Dickson is a Methodist minister, a graduate of Vanderbilt University with the degree of Doctor of Divinity. A member of the Tennessee Methodist Conference, he is now serving his seventh year as pastor of the Franklin, Tennessee, Methodist Church. Another son, Lewis Harper Dickson, is a graduate of the University of Tennessee, where he received the National Cotton Council Fellowship and the Farm Foundation Fellowship. He was the first student there to receive two fellowships, and he used them for a year's study at Cornell University. He served as assistant agronomist at the University of Tennessee, and is now Head of Extension, Methods and Research there. 4. Grafton, born October 24, 1873; married, December 30, 1913, to Gertrude Adeline Harned. He was the father of two sons and one daughter. He was a teacher, merchant and farmer, and was also a good student, and the best singer in the family, possessing a fine tenor voice. His son, John Edward Dickson, served in the army in North Africa and Italy during World War II. Grafton Dickson died February 8, 1946. 5. Felix Grundy, born March 9, 1876. He was married on December 17, 1907, to Ilma Pearl Mayfield, and his death occurred on July 25, 1954. He attended Vanderbilt School of Theology, and was a preacher in the Tennessee Conference of the Methodist Church. He served as pastor of several circuits. As a student of Greek he was said to be the best in the Tennessee Conference. He was a Mason, and a good song leader. Reverend Felix G. Dickson was the father of three daughters and two sons. All of his children attended college. A daughter, Virginia, is a poet, some of whose verses have been published. His grandson, John Paul Dickson, Jr., is completing courses at Vanderbilt University. His son, Felix Grundy, Jr., was an Air Corps pilot during World War II, flying many missions over Europe. 6. Maria Stephena, who was born December 23, 1877, and died October 17, 1881. 7. Eskew Batson, born September 13, 1879. He was married, on January 6, 1926, to Ella Belle (Stanfield-Newbern) Boswell, this being his first and her third marriage. He was the father of one daughter, Dorothy, who is a graduate of Vanderbilt University. At the time of his death on February 28, 1958, E. B. Dickson was part owner, vice president and bookkeeper of Elder-Conroy Hardware Company at Clarksville. He was a director of the First National Bank and Southern Trust Company, a member of the Clarksville Power Board, and a member of the Kiwanis Club, Clarksville Golf and Country Club, and the Free and Accepted Masons. A communicant of the Madison Street Methodist Church, he had served as its treasurer for forty-three years, and attended its Men's Bible Class. 8. Ann Eliza, born August 17, 1881; married on August 23, 1904, to Alexander (Sandy B.) Bradshaw Harris, deceased, who was postmaster at Cunningham, Tennessee. Before her marriage, Eliza Dickson taunght in the public schools of Montgomery County, and has played and taught piano, reed organ and electric organ. She is gifted at writing poetry. She is now demitted from active membership in the Order of the Eastern Star, in which she held good standing, but continues active in the Women's Society of Christian Service of the Southside Methodist Church. She is the mother of one son and seven daughters, and lives at her home in Cunningham, Tennessee, with her oldest daughter, Sallie Martha Harris. Sallie received her Bachelor of Science degree in Education at Austin Peay State College, and her degree of Bachelor of Library Science at Peabody College for Teachers, Nashville, these being the equivalent of a Master's degree. She is presently librarian at Montgomery County Central High School in Cunningham. Another daughter, Mrs. Mary Nell Workman, is a graduate of Austin Peay State College and teaches in the Montgomery County elementary school system. 9. Luther Stephen, born September 14, 1883; died unmarried March 25, 1920. He was a good mathematician, and possessed a splendid baritone voice. 10. Martha Elizabeth, born January 18, 1886. She was married October 10, 1954, to Thomas Polk Smith, a tobacconist. For several years she taught in Montgomery County schools, and from 1927 to 1953 was employed in the solicitor's office of the Department of Agriculture. She is active in the church and in W. S. C. S., and her hobbies are antiques and genealogy. 11. Willie Elnora, born November 15, 1888; died unmarried, June 22, 1919. She was devoted to her church, and highly regarded by everyone in the community. 12. Mary Catherine, born August 20, 1890. Married on April 25, 1914, to Samuel Anderson Weakley, an engineer with the United States government, she is the mother of one daughter, Mary Sue, a graduate of Brennan College, Gainesville, Georgia. Mrs. Weakley studied nursing for one year at Barr's infirmary, a private hospital in Nashville, before her marriage. She is active in the church and W. S. C. S., the Eastern Star, and General Felix Jollicoffer Lodge No. 1430, United Daughters of the Confederacy. he has a good alto voice. 13. Louise, born May 26, 1892; married on April 11, 1925, to Joseph Earl Townley, a pharmacist. She taught in rural schools and was employed for eight years at the Dickson-Sadler Drug Company before her marriage. She was formerly a member of the Students Club, and served two years as historian of the Tennessee Federation of Women's Clubs. She is now active in her church, in W. S. C. S., and in the Silver Cross Circle of the International Order of Kings Daughters and Sons. Mr. Townley died November 28, 1952. 14. Garland, born September 17, 1895; married on November 4, 1944, to Mrs. Katie Burke of Detroit, Michigan. He passed away November 16, 1958. For a number of years he was with Bohn Aluminum and Brass Company of Detroit,

Bessie Rye Weems

Joseph Burch Weems

Agnes Work Shipp

J. A. (Dock) Shipp

Weems

Shipp

Judge Joe B. Weems

Dockie Shipp Weems

Col. Mary Catherine Weems,
W. A. A. C.

Capt. Joseph Burch Weems, III,
U. S. A.

Comm. James A. Weems,
U. S. N.

Violetta Chapman Weems

Brig. Gen. George Hatton Weems
U. S. A.

married Ann Elizabeth Borchett of Virginia, cousin of Theodore Roosevelt's mother who was a Miss Bullock.

Phillip Van Horn Weems, (son by 2nd marriage) who never married, was wounded at Missionary Ridge and then killed near Atlanta, Georgia, during the War Between the States. He carried the rank of major at the time of his death on July 24, 1864. He was buried at Griffin, Georgia, but his remains were removed to Hickman County after the war.

Joseph Burch Weems, who came to this county with his father, served in the Mexican War under Captain Whitfield and was active in the political affairs of Hickman County for many years. He served in the Forty-fourth Tennessee General Assembly in 1885 as representative. He married Mary Ann Brewer, sister of Senator Sterling Brewer of Dickson County.

When William Loch Weems moved to Bon Aqua in 1839, his property on Dunlap Branch came into the possession of his son, Nathaniel C. Weems, who married Eleanor Ann Hatton. Prior to the War Between the States he was one of the leading farmers and land owners of this county. He also owned land in Montgomery County.

The children of Nathaniel C. Weems and Eleanor Hatton Weems were Joseph Burch Weems, Fannie Weems, Susan Weems, Violetta, who married a Gennett, Nathaniel C., William Loch, Elizabeth and Minna.

Elizabeth married William Cook, their son, William Loch Cook, served as Judge of the Supreme Court of Tennessee until his death a few years ago. William Collier Cook, son of Judge Cook, at one time served as Attorney General of Tennessee.

Minna Weems married a Mr. Cunningham and her son, John Cunningham, served as County Judge of Montgomery County for several years. James C. Cunningham, grandson of Minna Weems, is a prominent attorney and political leader at Clarksville. He at one time served in the Tennessee Legislature.

The descendants of Joseph Burch Weems and his wife, Mary Elizabeth Rye Weems, are George Hatton Weems, Brigadier General in the United States Army; Thomas Nathaniel Weems, who married Lillian Pentecost; John Calvin Weems, who married Euvalla Nicks; Violetta, who married John Alvin Slayden of Waverly; Joseph Burch Weems, who married Dockie Ann Shipp; and Philip Van Horn Weems, who married Margaret Thackeray.

Philip V. H. Weems is a retired Captain of the U. S. Navy and heads the Weems System of Navigation at Annapolis, Maryland.

*   *   *

About the same time that the Weems clan came to America from Scotland, Andrew Work, born in Ireland, emigrated to America. He was the grandfather of Robert Jefferson (Doogs) Work. R. J. Work's father was John Ford Work. His mother was Nancy Ellen Jones.

Robert Jefferson Work had the Irish fighting blood in his veins and a deep love for the Confederacy in his heart. He was the first private to volunteer from his county. He said he was eighteen years old—and he looked it—but he was only sixteen when he enlisted for the Lost Cause.

R. J. Work entered service in the Confederate States Army May 14, 1861, as a private in Company "H," 11th Tennessee Regiment, Infantry, of Tennessee Volunteers.

He was honorably discharged from service at Tuscumbia, Alabama, December 1, 1864, as second Lieutenant, Company "H," 11th Tennessee Regiment of Tennessee Volunteers. He was a member of Camp No. 334, United Confederated Veterans, and he received a Cross of Honor. He was a confederate prisoner from the State of Tennessee, and he was wounded at Murfreesboro.

After the war he married Melissa Bingham. To them nine children were born.

AGNES WORK SHIPP (Jan. 17, 1866-Feb. 6, 1913)

Agnes Work Shipp was the only woman ever to be elected Superintendent of Education in Dickson County. She was one of the first women to be elected to this office in Tennessee, and one of the first in the United States to claim that distinction.

She was the eldest of nine children. Agnes Work was born in a log house on the shores of Piney in Dickson County. Her mother, Melissa Tennessee Bingham, was a cultured lady with a keen intellect. Melissa Bingham had been reared in Shady Grove which boasted the finest schools and churches in the district. "Aunt Tennessee" as she was called, taught school, and she saw that her family received proper "schooling." Five of her daughters were teachers, but it was in Agnes Ann that the Torch of Education burned brightest.

Agnes Work attended the subscription and free schools near her home. Later she was a student at the old Dickson Academy at EdgeWood and at Dickson Normal College. She stayed in the home of Dr. Henslee in Dickson and tutored his invalid son, the Honorable Pitt Henslee, father of Lipe Henslee. This enabled her to attend Dickson College. After teaching several years, she married J. A. (Dock) Shipp of Hickman County.

SHIPP FAMILY

Shipp's Bend, just below Centerville on the north side of Duck River, was first settled by a man from England, Josiah Shipp, for whom the bend was named. His wife was Esther Joyce. Shipp settled here in 1806 with his three sons—William, Josiah and Zid, and three daughters—Polly, Sally and Esther.

William married Bethenia Griner. They had six sons and three daughters. The sons were Dr. John Shipp, Horton, Ira, Albert, Robert, and Moore.

J. A. (Dock) Shipp was a son of Albert Shipp who married Catherine Shouse. They had four children—William, Maggie, Abbie and "Dock."

Dock Shipp was a farmer, a school teacher, and clerked in a Pinewood store. Above all else he was a Christian gentleman. He lived only 4 months and nine days after his marriage to Agnes Work. He died of typhoid fever August 11, 1893.

Agnes Shipp came back from Shipp's Bend after her husband's death and opened a country store across the road from her childhood home. She was also appointed postmistress at Redden, Tennessee. The post office was located within the store.

When her child was born—a girl—she was named Dockie Ann for her father's nickname and her mother's middle name.

Agnes Shipp served Dickson County as Superintendent of Education from 1895 until 1897. She had to travel on horseback to reach the schools and in some communities tether the horse, walk a mile through corn fields, cross streams on rickety foot logs to finally reach her destination. Regardless of almost impassable roads, however, the Torch of Learning kept alight, and Agnes Shipp gave many of Dickson County's future leaders training and confidence and the desire to serve and make the world better.

Agnes Shipp felt that her daughter who was four needed her guidance; therefore, she sold the store—her mother became the Redden postmistress—and Agnes Shipp built a modest house in Dickson, taught a private school in her home, and "took in boarders" to keep the wolf from the door.

Her father, R. J. Work, had always been prominent in politics. He served in County Court and as Representative from Dickson County from 1891 until 1893, so in 1899 Agnes Shipp aspired to the office of State Librarian of Tennessee. The librarian was chosen by the vote of the state legislators. Agnes Shipp canvassed tirelessly, and two days before the vote was taken felt that she would win—but only by one vote. She felt that she could rely absolutely on the promises of that many.

One of her ardent supporters was Senator J. A. Clement of Benton County. He promised her not only his vote but his influence. He secured for her the support of Benton County's other representative.

Election day dawned. The vote was taken. Agnes Shipp seeemed the favorite to win but she lost by one vote—she often wondered what two good men and true had broken their vow.

No one was more sympathetic than the Senator from Benton County. In fact, he made numerous trips to Dickson to banish her disappointment, and, as all good stories end, they were married and lived happily ever afterward. Four children blessed their union: Robert Samuel, born November 6, 1900, married Maybelle Goad of Kentucky, August 20, 1919. He is an attorney and served temporarily on the Supreme Court of Tennessee in May, 1955.

He is now Mayor of Dickson, the father of three children, the eldest being Frank G. Clement, Governor of Tennessee from 1952-58.

Jesse Archibald, born June 15, 1902, now deceased, married Marguerite Johnson of Florida. He was also an attorney and served in the Florida Legislature for twelve years. He was the father of two sons.

Joseph Malcolm, born December 7, 1903, and died June 6, 1957. He was a pharmacist and was owner of an insurance agency. He was married to Earline Lockhart, February 17, 1924, and they had two children, one son and one daughter.

Ida Agnes Clement, born March 14, 1907, married Carl Tolbert Nicks of Dickson. They have two daughters. Mrs. Nicks is an outstanding musician and church leader. She is a well-known teacher and business woman.

Some years after their four children were born, the Senator confessed he upset the "librarian applecart." He had fallen in love with the widow Shipp, and as he said to the other Benton representative, "I am going to try to win her, and what chance would I, a poor widower with six children, have with a woman in high office? Vote against her! So will I—then maybe—." Well, yes the Lady lost the race but the Senator won the Lady!

And the Lady, Agnes Shipp Clement, was the grandmother of the Honorable Frank G. Clement, Governor of Tennessee from 1952-1958.

Dockie Ann Shipp Weems (Feb. 22, 1894)

And now let us return to the daughter born to Agnes Shipp and her first husband, "Dock" Shipp.

Although the daughter, Dockie Shipp was born on February 22, and although she was married to a Weems, if not a "parson," Dockie Ann never received the sobriquet applied to George Washington because Dockie had a vivid imagination, and she often saw things that weren't really there— leprechauns, fairies flitting in the tree tops—and knights in shining armor charging right out of the sky. Her vivid imagination linked with a precocious memory was put to advantageous use in the fields of drama and speech.

She began teaching early, but she was qualified even earlier.

At the age of eleven, she held a certificate enabling her to teach anywhere in Dickson County. At fourteen years of age another certificate permitted her to teach primary subjects anywhere in Tennessee. At fifteen years she became certified to teach the secondary subjects anywhere in the Volunteer State. At sixteen years of age she received a Bachelor of Science degree from Dickson Normal College; at this time she also received a diploma in Music from the same college. During World War II, while her children were in uniform, she attended Austin Peay State College, Clarksville, Tennessee, and George Peabody College receiving the Bachelor of Science degree from the former and a Master of Arts degree from the latter.

At the age of sixteen she began teaching in the primary grades of her

Alma Mater, but she still pursued her speech and drama courses and at eighteen years of age she received her Bachelor of Oratory degree from Vanderbilt University School of Speech.

After her graduation from Vanderbilt she did Chautauqua and Lyceum work, but the teaching virus burned hot in her veins. She succumbed to its deadly fever and taught ever after. Teachers, preachers, attorneys-at-law, physicians, politicians—talent in the raw—she took this human clay and out of it molded character. She was a member of the Church of Christ and taught a Sunday School class for twenty years.

She loved her work. She worked unceasingly. National honors were won by her students and herself winning the National Coaches Contest in 1939. Yet, in the natural course of existence "Miss Dockie" was not an unusual person; however, the following incidents are a bit unusual.

Miss Dockie loved devotedly her stepfather, Senator J. A. Clement, and as she would say, Papa Clement was an unusual person. She also loved her "in-laws" and during World War II she edited *Weemsana,* a family newspaper which gave much favorable publicity to the Weems clan. The family publication was recognized over the Blue network in "Time Views the News":

"TIME VIEWS THE NEWS" RECOGNIZES WEEMSANA ON AIR

(As broadcast by "Time Views the News" on Blue Network Nov. 2, 1944)

And now we're going to take a couple of minutes to tell you about one of the fightingest American families there is—the Weemses. They've got so many family members in the armed services that they publish a family newspaper about themselves, every couple of months, a nice little tabloid called "Weemsana." Time Correspondent William Howland, in Atlanta, Georgia, sent us a copy today, and while we grant you this isn't hot spot news—well, anyway it's good Americana.

There are more than fifty members of the Weems family in the service. They've got top-notchers and buck privates, and there are WAVES and WACs among them. Among the topflight Weemses is Brigadier General George Hatton Weems, who is assistant commandant at the Infantry School in Fort Benning; and over in London is Major Mary C. Weems, who has charge of WAC personnel in the London area.

In Dickson, Tennessee, is the civilian, Mrs. Dockie Weems, who edits this novel newspaper, all devoted to the doings of one highly military family. The paper was started at Fort Leavenworth, Kansas, back in January, 1943, by William Slayden, whose mother was a Weems. He became a Lieutenant Colonel and when he was sent overseas, Aunt Dockie took over the editorship.

The family paper, by the way, seldom refers to anybody by a last name—it's always "Mary Kate," or "Susie Anne," or something like that. And as Correspondent Howland says, "the paper is as homey as the aroma of frying sausage from a Weems kitchen in Tennessee."

Back in the days of 1861, or thereabouts, Joseph Burch Weems, of Tennessee, joined the scouts of Confederate General Nathan Bedford Forrest. General Forrest is the man who said, "get there the fustest with the mostest." . . .

Well, ever since then, whenever there's a war, the Weemses are trying to get there "fustest with the mostest relatives."

In the normal course of events, a woman is born; she marries; she rears a family. So, Dockie Ann Shipp was born February 22, 1894, in Dickson County. She married Judge Joe B. Weems, June 2, 1915, in Dickson, Tennessee, and in Dickson, Tennessee, she reared her family of four (one died in infancy)—two sons and two daughters—all serving their country in uniform during World War II.

JUDGE JOE B. WEEMS

Judge Joe B. Weems, son of Joseph Burch Weems and Bessie Rye, was born July 2, 1887, at Southside, Tennessee, and died April 29, 1950. He was one of eight children; two of whom died in infancy. The children were orphaned at an early age. Judge William Loch Cook ("Cousin Loch") assumed their guardianship, secured a housekeeper and kept the family together.

Joe B., as he was affectionately known, received his early education in the public schools. As a young man, he was a carpenter, insurance salesman, and later received his law degree from Cumberland University, Lebanon, Tennessee. He settled in Dickson to practice law and entered the law office of the late Senator J. A. Clement. Subsequently, Joe B. entered private law practice, distinguishing himself in Chancery Court.

He served as County Judge of Dickson County from 1918 to 1934. His tenure of office was emphasized by outstanding progress in rural roads and bridges, from the "toll gate" stage to the present state highway system. It was while he was County Judge that the old Dickson Normal College and grounds were purchased and converted into the existing high school plant.

Joe B. Weems was a man of varied talents: Judge, attorney, surveyor, inventor, artist, historian and an organizer and developer of natural resources. He was a pioneer in the oil exploration in Dickson County. Woodcarving became his hobby. This interest inspired the invention of the "Weems knife" which was used in his carvings and the organization of the Weems Manufacturing Company to produce and market this knife. His wood carvings are currently exhibited in the State Museum in Nashville, Tennessee.

Judge Weems was a charter member of the Dickson County Chamber of Commerce and served as first secretary. He was influential in procuring and developing Montgomery Bell State Park.

A member of the Methodist Church, he was superintendent of the Sunday School and teacher of the Pioneer Bible Class.

On June 2, 1915, Judge Weems married Miss Dockie Ann Shipp, stepdaughter of Senator J. A. Clement. They had five children: Mary Catherine, Joseph Burch, James A., Violetta Chapman, and David who died in infancy.

"Christian Gentleman" best fits his character. Not only was he a devout Christian throughout his life, he was also a man with a keen sense of personal honor. One who knew him intimately knew him to be above petty acts. His mind and character operated on a high plane. If he had a fault, it was that of too much generosity, perhaps where it was not fully deserved. He gave freely of his time and substance to the destitute as well as to his family and friends. He had vision, imagination and ability. He was not only a capable lawyer, but one who could be trusted. His most typical trait was his lifelong willingness to help others in need, whoever they might be.

JOSEPH BURCH (BILLY) WEEMS III

Joseph Burch Weems, III, (Billy) was born in Dickson, Tennessee, January 19, 1918. His parents were Judge Joe B. Weems and Dockie Shipp Weems. He received his early education in the public schools and attended Tennessee Polytechnic Institute at Cookeville, Tennessee. He married Mary Emma Bayer of New York, April 23, 1938. They have four children: Eleanor Ann, born December 8, 1938; Joseph Burch IV, born October 21, 1941; Janet Day, born September 15, 1945; and James A., born November 21, 1950.

Joseph B. Weems, III, entered the United States Army September 22, 1942, was commissioned in the Air Corps December 5, 1943, advanced to first lieutenant July 24, 1945, and has seen service in Newfoundland, Alaska and Korea. He is presently a Captain in the United States Air Force and stationed in Oklahoma City, Oklahoma.

VIOLETTA CHAPMAN WEEMS

Violetta Chapman Weems was born September 2, 1922, in Dickson, Tennessee. Though she was the "latest" surviving child in Judge Joe B. Weems family, she was by no means the "leastest" in ability and physical attractiveness. In high school she was outstanding in speech and dramatics winning numerous cups and medals including four national medals. At the age of sixteen she was chosen "Miss Tennessee" in a beauty contest. Talent played a part in this event also.

After graduation from high school she attended Northwest State Teacher's College, Maryville, Missouri. Her sister, Mary Catherine, was a member of the faculty.

Then came the call of the stage and New York. Stock companies and the Roxy Theater gave her experience and finally *Connecticut Yankee,* a Broadway hit, gave her the needed boost.

After playing in *Connecticut Yankee,* she joined the USO and toured United States Army and Navy camps for a year, then donned her uniform for overseas service, and December 25, 1944, found her entertaining the troops in New Guinea. There she played Milne Bay, Ora Bay, Finschafen, Lae, Nadzab, Hollandia, Biak, the Admiralties; Los Negros, Manus—Numfior, Wendi, Oui, etc., and the Philippine Islands, She returned home on October, 1945.

After returning home, a call from Warner Brothers Motion Picture Studios persuaded her to return to the coast, but before signing a contract, she was persuaded to return to New York by Commander Malcolm Stewart Ragan whom she married April 22, 1946, in New York.

They have three children: Carol Burch, born August 15, 1947; Robert Malcolm, born March 24, 1949, and Ann Deshon, born November 15, 1958.

At the close of the war, was published an interesting book entitled *With Love, Jane* by Alma Lutz which contained letters from American women on the war fronts—"Women With Guts." Included in the publication were letters by Major Mary C. Weems and her sister, Violetta C. Weems (USO).

JAMES A. WEEMS

Born October 24, 1920, and educated in the Dickson public schools, James A. Weems attended Cumberland University and received his Bachelor of Arts degree from Vanderbilt University, Nashville, Tennessee. While at Vanderbilt he was president of the Independents (non-fraternity organization); won the Founders Medal in oratory; State Intercollegiate Championships in oratory; the Seabury Peace Award, and the Frank K. Houston Oratorical award.

James A. Weems enlisted in the United States Navy July 1, 1941, commissioned Ensign on January 16, 1942, Lieutenant (j.g.) March 1, 1943, and advanced to Senior Lieutenant April 1, 1944. He served at Naval Operating Base, Reykjavik, Iceland; Mine and Bomb Disposal Unit, Pearl Harbor, Hawaii; United States Acorn Unit No. 14, Tarawa; ComAirPac, Hawaii; Mine Assembly Base, Oahu, T. H.; and on the USS Bennington CV-20. Leaving the United States for overseas duty he served in Iceland, South America, Hawaiian Islands, Ellis Islands, Gilbert Islands, Marshall Islands, Mariannas, Philippine Islands, Iwo Jima, Okinawa, and Japan. He was awarded the American Defense Service Ribbon, American Theater Ribbon, European Theater Ribbon, Asiatic-Pacific Theater Ribbon (with 4 bronze stars), World War II Victory Medal, the Navy-Marine Corps Medal for heroism, and three official commendations for gallantry. He fought in the campaigns of Tarawa, Iwo Jima, Okinawa and the carrier raids on Honshu, Japan, from February, 1945, through August, 1945.

James A. Weems was retired in May, 1959, as Lieutenant Commander, USNR.

Following his terminal leave, he attended the University of Virginia, Charlottesville, Virginia, where he received his Bachelor of Laws degree and the following honors: Editorial Board, Virginia Law Review; Raven Society; Order of the Coif. Upon graduation he was associated with the law firm of Hunton, Williams, Anderson, Gay and Moore, Richmond, Virginia. Returning to Dickson, Tennessee, he entered law practice with his father, the late

Judge Joe B. Weems, and in 1950 was elected County Judge of Dickson County, and, at that time, was the youngest Judge in the state of Tennessee.

Under Judge James A. Weems' administration a one million dollar school construction program was accomplished; past bonded indebtedness cancelled; a public health center erected; and many rural bridges built.

Judge James A. Weems married Joene Elizabeth Robbley, of Dauphin, Manitoba, Canada, on May 9, 1944, and they have three children: Jamey Ellen Weems, born September 26, 1946; and twins, Shipp Robbley Weems and Lindsay Pat Weems, born March 28, 1948.

Mary Catherine Weems-Fullbright

Mary Catherine Weems, named for her grandmother Weems and great-grandmother Shipp, was the eldest child of Judge Joe B. Weems and Dockie Shipp Weems. Born in Dickson, Tennessee, March 18, 1916, she was educated in the public schools of Dickson County, attended Austin Peay College and Louisiana State University and received her degree from George Peabody College in Nashville, Tennessee. She won national honors in speech in high school. She majored in physical education and taught in Louisiana and the Northwest State Teachers College in Maryville, Missouri, before entering the army.

Mary C. Weems entered the W.A.C. August 1, 1942, commissioned 2nd Lieutenant September 26, 1942, 1st Lieutenant December 24, 1942; Captain April 13, 1943, and advanced to Major April 15, 1944. Major Weems served at Fort Des Moines, Iowa; First WAC Training Command, Second WAC Training Command, Daytona Beach, Florida; Washington, D.C.; Headquarters London, England, and Paris, France, and Headquarters, Frankfurt, Germany. She departed from the United States December 15, 1943, seeing service in Scotland, Wales, England, France, Belgium, Germany, Austria, Switzerland and Italy and returned to the United States November 19, 1945. She was awarded the American Theater Ribbon, European Theater Ribbon, World War II Victory Medal, WAC Ribbon and the Bronze Star Medal. She served in the battles of Normandy and Northern France. She was separated from the service at Fort Bragg, North Carolina, November 24, 1945, terminal leave to expire February 8, 1946.

Mary Catherine Weems married Lex J. Fullbright of Birmingham, Alabama, on August 20, 1943.

She and her husband were recalled to service during the Korean War, and both attained the rank of full Colonel.

Mrs. Fullbright now teaches speech, dramatics and physical education at the Foley High School, Foley, Alabama. Her husband operates a colony of vacation cottages at Gulf Shores, Baldwin County, Alabama.

Mary Catherine Weems was the youngest WAC officer ever to achieve the rank of Lieutenant Colonel and was the third highest ranking WAC officer at the close of World War II.

Brigadier General George Hatton Weems, U. S. Army Retired was the son of Joseph Burch Weems and Bessie Rye. He died of throat cancer at the U. S. Army Hospital, Fort Campbell, Kentucky, at 9:50 P. M. on February 25th, 1957, at the age of 65. He was born on a farm in Montgomery County, Tennessee, September 27, 1891, and was orphaned at eleven years of age. In addition to the Walnut Grove School in Montgomery County, he attended Waverly High School, Waverly, Tennessee, and Southwestern Presbyterian University at Clarksville, Tennessee. After a short period of teaching in a country school, he entered the United States Military Academy at West Point, where he made the wrestling and football teams and graduated with the first war class, April 20, 1917.

Upon graduation, he was commissioned a 2nd Lieutenant of Infantry and assigned to the 9th Infantry Regiment at Syracuse, New York. On September 5, 1917, he sailed for France with this regiment.

He commanded a Machine Gun Company of the 9th Infantry during the occupation of a trench sector near Verdun from March 15 to May 2 ,1918. He then was engaged at Chateau Thiery until July 1918, when he joined the drive on Vaux in the capture of which he distinguished himself by extraordinary heroism in action, for which he was awarded the Distinguished Service Cross. Following this service he was sent to Langres, France, on July 15, 1918, and served as an instructor at the Army Candidates School until November 26, 1918, after which he rejoined the 9th Infantry on the Rhine and entered Germany, where he remained with the Army of Occupation until July 19, 1919. He then returned to the United States.

He commanded the 4th Machine Gun Battalion at Camp Travis, Texas, from September 1919 until August 1920, when he was transferred to Fort Benning, Georgia, as an instructor, serving there until the fall of 1922 when he entered the Infantry School at Fort Benning, and was graduated in June, 1923.

For the following four years he was Professor of Military Science and Tactics at Davidson College, North Carolina. He was graduated from the Command and General Staff School, Fort Leavenworth, Kansas, in 1928, then was assigned to duty as company tactical officer at West Point, New York. He was transferred to Langley Field, Virginia, as an instructor in Infantry tactics at the Air Corps Tactical School from July 1, 1929, until August 15, 1933. He was graduated in June, 1934, from the Army War College, Washington, D. C., and in August, 1934, from the Chemical Warfare School at Edgewood Arsenal, Maryland.

He then was assigned to the 22nd Infantry and became Post Executive Officer at Fort McClelland, Alabama. In September, 1935, he was transferred to Fort Sam Houston, Texas, for service with the 2nd Division. In May, 1939 he was assigned to Port-au-Prince, Haiti, as Chief of the U. S. Military Mission.

In June, 1941, he was assigned as commanding officer of the 22nd Inf. Regt. of the 4th Division, Fort Benning, Georgia, and in March, 1942 he became Assistant Commandant of the Infantry School at Fort Benning. He remained there until July, 1945, when he was assigned on temporary duty to the office of the Assistant Chief of Staff, Operations Division, War Department General Staff, Washington, D. C., in preparation for an assignment to special duty in the Philippine Islands. While Assistant Commandant of the Infantry School, in November, 1944, to January, 1945, he was sent to the European Theater of Operations as special observer for the Ground Forces.

He returned to the States in November, 1945, and was later assigned as President of an Officers Interview Board at Camp Blanding, Florida. In May, 1946, he was assigned to duty with the United States Representation on the Allied Control Commission for Hungary as Chief of the United States Delegation. He was stationed in Budapest and served with British and Russian counterparts on the Control Commission in directing the affairs of occupied Hungary. During the latter part of 1947 the Allied Control Commission was discontinued and General Weems was assigned to the European Command in Germany as U. S. Army Provost Marshal General with station in Frankfurt, Germany.

He returned to the States in 1950 and was assigned as Chief of the Military District of Georgia with headquarters at Atlanta. He served in this capacity until his retirement at the age of 60, on September 30, 1951.

Upon retirement, General Weems made his home in Waverly, Tennessee with his sister, Mrs. J. A. Slayden. He devoted his time to management of his personal affairs and the activities of the G. H. Weems Educational Fund. In 1955 his health began to fail and he received extensive treatment at Walter Reed Hospital in Washington and the U. S. Army Hospital at Fort Campbell.

For bravery in World War I, he was awarded the Distinguished Service Cross with a citation as follows:

For extraordinary heroism in action at Vaux, France, July 1 to 2, 1918. In command of Machine Gun Company, 9th Infantry, he personally took charge of his advanced positions and manned captured enemy machine guns on an exposed flank of the battalion. By his coolness and daring in fearlessly exposing himself to the enemy fire in order that he might personally direct the fire of his guns, he succeeded in breaking down the counter attack of the enemy upon the exposed flank of the battalion.

He was also awarded the Silver Star with two citations, the French Croix de Guerre with a corps citation, and the Italian Order of the Crown, for World War I bravery. The Government of Haiti awarded him the National Order of Honor and Merit in 1941. For services in World War II, he was awarded the Brazilian Order of Military Merit with the following citation:

Brigadier General George H. Weems performed exceptionally meritorious service as Assistant Commandant of the Infantry School, Fort Benning, Georgia, from March, 1942 to July, 1945, during a period when the command was nearly tripled in size. He displayed unusual professional ability in organizing, supervising and prescribing policies governing the activities of the academic department, approaching all problems with an extremely practical viewpoint. His ability to visualize the effect of combat development upon doctrine resulted in completely modern instruction. His forceful personality and outstanding leadership left their impress upon thousands of graduates. In the preparation of up-to-date instructional material and its dissemination to all Infantry regiments, Gen. Weems made a substantial contribution toward raising the professional standards of the entire infantry arm.

He was the recipient of the Algernon Sidney Sullivan Award for 1943 at Davidson College, North Carolina. He was a member of the Alpha Tau Omega Fraternity.

General Weems was never married, yet his love of family life was one of the dominant traits of his character. Behind his precise military manner and at times stern exterior, was the warm heart of a real humanitarian with a keen interest in his fellow man. To his military associates he was affectionately known as "Daddy" Weems, a nickname well chosen, as it signified a man ready to lend a helping hand. He was always "Uncle General" to his many nieces and nephews, and the advice and assistance which he extended his nieces and nephews throughout his life is second only to his highly successful military career as the most outstanding tradition of his life. Prior to 1938, he had "loaned" several thousand dollars to his nieces and nephews to enable them to pursue their education. When it was suggested to him that these outstanding loans be used as a revolving fund for educational purposes as a memorial to his parents, he accepted the idea and together with his brothers and sister established the G. H. Weems Educational Fund on 1 January, 1939. The Fund was originally designated to assist Weems descendants in securing an education and for cultural assistance, but due to General Weems' great interest in young people in general, the Fund was broadened, to include all deserving youth seeking an education and a more useful life.

By terms of his will General Weems left the bulk of his considerable estate to the G. H. Weems Educational Fund, and Trustees have accepted the responsibility of management of this Fund as a trust and a challenge to help worthy youth in the same fine tradition of General Weems' life and as a living memorial to his splendid character and far-sighted abilities.

It was General Weems' idea that *Weemsana,* a family newspaper, be published.

Weemsana was recognized over the Blue Network in "Time Views the News." *Time* and *Life* magazines asked for material for stories. *Saturday Evening Post* carried articles about its members. A Writer's Service asked for information and permission to write articles concerning *Weemsana,* feeling that it deserved editorial comment in national and international magazines.

"The Weems clan only did its duty as thousands of others. They were a prolific group. They possessed some leaders with initiative. They did something with the family loyalty and pride. They established an Educational Fund for the family. They developed a newspaper to keep their people informed— to weld them together. People with more have done less. Maybe it could be said, 'The Weemses got there fustest with the leastest.' . . . Anyway they are getting there, beyond the average, yes, with a few stellar lights and potenial greatness showing in this younger generation. This writer is not a Weems. I see their weaknesses. I see their strengths, but they have a family loyalty that is almost fanatical, even so, worthy of emulation."

Amon Carter Evans

Vice president and director of Tennessee Newspapers, Inc., Amon Carter Evans is one of Nashville's young men who has already gone far in his chosen field, publishing.

Born August 4, 1933, in Washington, D. C., he is a son of Silliman and Lucile (McCrea) Evans. His father, a distinguished newspaper publisher and president of the Nashville Tennessean, is the subject of a biography in this work. Amos C. Evans attended the public schools of Nashville and graduated from Columbia Military Academy at Columbia, Tennessee. He began his advanced studies at Texas Agricultural and Mechanical College, and after attending there for a while, transferred to the University of Tennessee at Knoxville. There he was a student for two years.

Coming to Nashville in 1953, Mr. Evans began his newspaper career working as a reporter on the staff of the Tennessean. In 1955 he was named vice president of Tennessee Newspapers, Inc., which he also serves as director of promotion.

Mr. Evans is also vice president, director, and chairman of the board of controls of the Newspaper Printing Corporation. He is president of Tennessee Promotions, Inc. A member of the American Newspaper Publishers Association and the Southern Newspaper Publishers Association, he has been active on various committees of both, including the labor committee.

In his home city, welfare causes have received Mr. Evans' active and effective support. He is a director of the Tuberculosis Association of Davidson County, and a director and member of the executive committee of the Nashville Big Brothers. He is a member of that city's Junior Chamber of Commerce and Kiwanis Club. He and his family attend the Methodist Church. Mr. Evans has been a member of Alpha Tau Omega fraternity since his days at the University of Tennessee.

On February 23, 1951, at Longview, Texas, Amon Carter Evans married, as his first wife, Donnalyn Louise Knight. She was born in Los Angeles, California, but immediately afterwards her family moved to Senora, Kansas, where she was reared and attended school. She graduated from Texas Christian College in Abilene. To this marriage two daughters were born: 1. Janet Lynn, on November 23, 1953. 2. Celia Ann, born August 16, 1956. Mr. Evans married, second, on December 17, 1958, Carol Mae Haynes Robinson of Nashville.

SILLIMAN EVANS

One of the South's distinguished publishers, Silliman Evans had been president and publisher of The Nashville Tennessean for nearly two decades prior to his death. In acquiring this paper in the 1930s, he returned to his first love among occupations, for while still a relatively young man he had become a top executive in airlines, and later in the insurance field. Residents of his state associate his name with a high standard of journalism and of public service.

He was a native of Joshua, Texas, and was born on April 2, 1894, son of the Reverend Columbus Asbury and Alice (Silliman) Evans. His paternal grandfather, G. Henry Evans, was a Mississippi farmer who lost his life serving the Confederate cause. His maternal grandfather, Abraham Silliman, was a native of Connecticut who went to Texas with Stephen Austin, and organized the first Masonic lodge in the Lone Star State. The Reverend Columbus A. Evans was a farmer and schoolteacher in Mississippi in his early years, giving up these occupations to enter the ministry of the Methodist Church. He went to Texas where he became a circuit-riding preacher, serving congregations throughout the eastern part of the state. He had been previously married, and had five children, before marrying Alice Silliman. Silliman Evans was one of five more children born to the second marriage.

Quite naturally, the future publisher had to learn to face adversity and accept responsibility early in life. With a large family, and the pitifully inadequate income paid to frontier clergymen, the Reverend Columbus Silliman had to move frequently from one charge to another. When one of these removals occurred, the household effects were transported by horse and wagon, on which the boys rode with their father, while the mother, sister, and youngest children traveled by train. Silliman Evans got a paying job as soon as he could do so. Appropriately enough, his early jobs were peddling newspapers and taking subscriptions to The Saturday Evening Post. At the age of thirteen he took a position as apprentice, or printer's devil, on the DeLeon Free Press, a weekly newspaper published in Comanche County, Texas. Later, as a reporter, his duties consisted of meeting the train each day and learning who was arriving in or leaving the town. He attended school during the daytime, and worked for the newspaper afternoons and evenings.

By the time he was ready for high school, the family lived in Fort Worth. Despite precarious family finances, he managed to obtain a sound education, entering the preparatory school at Polytechnic College, which later became

Texas Wesleyan. He had to walk three miles each way between his home at Riverside and his classes. He continued his interest in journalism as a student, writing for the Poly Parrot. His ambition at that time was to get on the staff of the Fort Worth Star-Telegram, but it was several years before this ambition was realized. However, when his father's ill health compelled him to leave Polytechnic at the end of two years, he immediately went into newspaper work. His only formal education thereafter was an eight-week course at Brantley-Draughan Business College. However, he was always an avid reader, even getting through his father's eight volumes of the sermons and hymns of John and Charles Wesley. The fact that he was well-read, plus his mastery of typing and shorthand, enabled him to secure a position with the Fort Worth Record. By taking a review of a prominent minister's sermon to the editor of this paper, he got an offer of a position at $12.50 per week, and began his duties serving as secretary to the famed editor, Hugh Nugent Fitzgerald. He soon became a reporter. However, the fact that the Record was a "wet" brought some discomfort to him and his father, so he soon invested one hundred dollars of his meagre savings in a paper favoring temperance which was being founded in Waco. There he was made managing editor, but since the staff was small, his duties included reporting, news writing, and copy reading. He learned much through a private system of taking a stack of his own papers onto the street, selling them, and observing readers' reactions.

After a short time at Waco, Silliman Evans moved to Houston, where he worked on the staff of the Telegram as city hall and general reporter. An executive of the United Press observed his work and offered him a position in Chicago. There he worked as reporter and desk executive for United Press and later for International News Service, gaining "big league" newspaper experience. Making $22.50 a week, he was sending money home and paying medical expenses which had accumulated during a previous bout with yellow jaundice. While trying to get a raise from the editor, he was fired and returned to Fort Worth, where he became managing editor of The Record. Shortly afterwards the paper changed hands, and he then went to Dallas, joining the Morning News as a reporter.

As soon as this country entered World War I in 1917, he left to enlist in the 133rd Field Artillery, a unit of the 96th Division, a Texas National Guard outfit. Standing guard the first night, he talked a friend into starting a newspaper. The officers approved, and on August 15, 1917, The Reconnaissance first made its appearance at Camp Blair, Texas. Silliman Evans was named its editor, but at this juncture he failed to pass a critical examination for continued service in the army. Going to Washington, D. C., he applied for a position in the diplomatic service, and was soon on his way to Copenhagen, where he became clerk in the code room at the American Legation. In the summer of 1918 he was sent home for reasons of health. Being out of funds, he wired the managing editor of the Dallas Morning News for money, received it, and went to that city. His return trip was made at such a time that he was among those falling under suspicion of smuggling the Russian crown jewels into this country, but he was soon cleared. He remained with the Morning News only a short time, then returned once again to Fort Worth where he realized his boyhood ambition of working for the Star-Telegram. He began his connection with that paper as a copy reader, and after a year became a reporter. He was given the assignment of traveling throughout all of Texas' two hundred and fifty-four counties to help build the paper's circulation. He had long taken an interest in political affairs, and soon the covering of politics and government activities became his major assignment. In the course of the decade he spent with the paper, he won a reputation still remembered in Texas. He was named manager of the Star-Telegram's bureau in Washington, D. C., and from the time he arrived in that city, figured prominently in the Democratic National Conventions.

On December 1, 1928, Mr. Evans resigned from the Star-Telegram and from newspaper work to become vice president of the Texas Air Transport Company, and concurrently president of the T A T Broadcasting Company, operating Station K F B Q. He was also public relations officer for all the A. T. Barrett enterprises. Having acquired enough franchises and fields in other states, Texas Air Transport Company became Southern Air Transport Company in 1929. He continued as vice president of the new firm; and when it was sold to American Airways shortly afterwards, became vice president of that organization. Transferred to New York, he became assistant to the president.

Interested as ever in politics, he left the airline to serve as manager for his fellow Texan, John Nance Garner, in the Presidential campaign of 1932. He was influential in securing Garner's selection as vice presidential candidate. Mr. Evans permanently resigned his position as vice president of American Airways in March, 1933; but when it became American Airlines in 1936, he was named to its board of directors, a position he held until his death. Following his effective work in the election, he was named Fourth Assistant Postmaster General under James Farley in 1933 and served through 1934. The Post Office Department was expanding rapidly during this period, and Mr. Evans had over three hundred and twenty million dollars' worth of construction projects under his direction.

On April 27, 1934, he resigned as Assistant Postmaster General to accept appointment as executive vice president of the Maryland Casualty Company. This insurance firm was on the verge of bankruptcy at the time—a fate from which his timely and energetic efforts saved it. He reorganized the company and on June 11, 1934, was elected its president. He presided over this organization for three years, bringing it back into the black.

However, Mr. Evans' heart had always been in the newspaper business, and having achieved gratifying success in other lines, he determined to resume his publishing career. In January, 1937, he purchased The Nashville Tennessean; and in April of that year the native Texan moved his home to Nashville to begin his active duties in directing the newspaper. This remained his major interest for the rest of his life, a productive period of nearly two decades. Throughout that time he adhered to the code which he established for the paper, one which has been rigorously followed ever since: "The news colums shall be fair and accurate, the editorial columns shall be honest and just." The paper has been an ardent champion of the Tennessee Valley Authority. It played its part in destroying the power of the Crump machine, and in abolishing the poll tax, through its courageous and well-directed campaigns. For a period of two years, Mr. Evans divided his time between the Tennessean and the Chicago Sun, being the first publisher of the latter paper and going to Chicago frequently in the course of his duties. However, he resigned as publisher of the Sun in 1944.

He remained on the board of directors of the Maryland Casulty Company and American Airlines. His memberships included the Fort Worth Club, the National Press Club of Washington, D. C., the Cloud Club of New York, and the Chicago Athletic Club, Racquet Club, Tavern Club, Chicago Club and Union League, all of Chicago, as well as the Belle Meade Country Club in Nashville. Affiliated with the Free and Accepted Masons, he belonged to the Corinthian Lodge in that city, where he was also a communicant of the Brentwood Methodist Church. Among the honors which had been conferred on him was the Brazilian Order of the Southern Cross.

On November 20, 1923, at Cisco, Texas, Silliman Evans married Miss Lucile McCrea, who was born at Roby, Texas, on November 12, 1902, daughter of Judge L. H. and Celia A. McCrea. She received her education at Kid Key, Sherman, Texas. Mr. and Mrs. Evans became the parents of two children, Silliman, Jr., and Amon Carter Evans, both of whom have biographies on these pages.

Mr. Evans' death occurred on June 26, 1955, in Fort Worth, Texas, where he had been attending the funeral services of a friend, Amon G. Carter, also a newspaper publisher. In the present brief record of his career and achievements, it will be noted that, despite the positions of high honor and responsibility which he held in corporate and government connections, the greater part of the narrative concerns his work in newspaper publishing. It is likely that that is the way he would have wished it. He was a newspaper man first and last, whose abilities could be put to most effective service in establishing high standards of journalism in those papers which employed him, or which he published. It is as a devoted and distinguished leader in this field that Tennesseans will always first think of him.

SILLIMAN EVANS, JR.

One of the South's younger leaders in newspaper publishing, Silliman Evans, Jr., is now publisher of The Nashville Tennessean. He began his career with the Sherman, Texas, Democrat, and has also published a paper in Florida. He is a veteran of Air Corps service in World War II, and takes a considerable interest in the organizational and civic life of his city.

Born on January 23, 1925, at Fort Worth, Texas, he is a son of Silliman Evans, well-known southern newspaper publisher whose biography also appears on these pages, and his wife, the former Lucile McCrea. After completing his preparatory education at the Tennessee Military Institute at Sweetwater in 1942, the younger Silliman Evans entered Vanderbilt University in Nashville. He left there to enter flight training at Chapman Field, Miami, with the Embry-Riddle Aviation Company. He received his commercial pilot's license and entered training with American Airlines, becoming a pilot with them. He resigned to enter the United States Army Air Corps, being commissioned a first lieutenant. He served in the ferrying command and later in the Air Transport command, and was released from active service in 1946.

Mr. Evans then entered the University of Miami for a year's study, and at its conclusion, in 1947, he went to Sherman, Texas, becoming associated with The Sherman Democrat. He resigned from that paper to return to Nashville in 1947, and join the staff of The Nashville Tennessean as assistant to the publisher. In 1953 he went to Florida to become publisher of the Lake Worth Leader, which he published until he returned to Nashville in 1955. Since that time he has been publisher of The Nashville Tennessean. Mr. Evans' experience with this paper dates back many years. During summer vacations while attending school he had held various positions there.

Mr. Evans is a member of Sigma Alpha Epsilon fraternity, and belongs to the Free and Accepted Masons, being a member of Observance Lodge No. 686 and of the higher bodies of the order, including Al Menah Temple, Ancient Arabic Order of Nobles of the Mystic Shrine. His other memberships include the United States Power Squadron, the Air Force Association, the Propeller Club of the United States, the Quiet Birdmen, Colemere Club, Belle Meade Country Club, the Blue Grass Country Club, and the Richland Country Club. He is a member of the Episcopal Church.

At Sherman, Texas, on April 7, 1947, Silliman Evans, Jr., married Mary Frances Totten, daughter of Jess M. and LaRue (Ranson) Totten. The couple make their home on Bluegrass Drive in Hendersonville. Mrs. Evans attended Randolph-Macon College and the University of Texas. She was society editor of The Sherman Democrat prior to her marriage.

Robert Greene Lee

Robert Greene Lee has devoted his life to the service of the Lord. He was a pastor in rural churches until 1918, later being called to pastorates in Edgefield, South Carolina; New Orleans, Louisiana; and Charleston, South Carolina. Since 1927, he has served as pastor of the Bellevue Baptist Church, Memphis.

Robert G. Lee was born near Fort Mill, South Carolina, on November 11, 1886. His parents, David Ayers Lee and Sarah Elizabeth (Bennett) Lee, were native South Carolinians; and his father was a farmer all his life.

Mr. Lee was educated in the rural schools of South Carolina, later graduating from Furman University in Greenville, South Carolina, and the Chicago Law School in Chicago, Illinois. He also studied at Tulane University in New Orleans, but received no degree. Robert Greene Lee holds honorary degrees from Union University—D.D. 1929, LL.D., 1934; Furman University—D.D., 1937; Stetson University—D.D., 1948; Baylor University—LL.D., 1954; Bob Jones University—Litt.D., 1938; Houghton College—Litt.D., 1952; Howard Payne College—LL.D., 1956.

Dr. Lee belongs to no clubs or societies, devoting all his time to his flock and to Baptist Church organizations. For years he was a member of the Executive Committee of the Tennessee Baptist Convention; president of the Tennessee Baptist Convention for four terms; president of the Southern Baptist Convention for three terms; and Colonel on the staff of Governor Jimmie Davis of Louisiana and later Colonel on the staff of Governor Strom Thurmond of South Carolina.

As an author, Dr. Lee has written the following books: "From Feet to Fathoms," 1926; "Lord, I Believe," 1927; "Beds of Pearls," 1930; "Whirlwinds of God," 1932; "Grand Canyon of Resurrection Realities," 1937; "Lee Lines," 1937; "A Greater Than Solomon," 1935; "This Critical Hour," 1942; "The Name Above Every Name," 1938; "Pulpit Pleadings," 1948; "Pickings," 1938; "Bread from Bellevue Oven," 1947; "The Sinner's Saviour," 1950; "For the Time of Tears," 1949; "The Bible and Prayer," 1950; "Glory Today for Conquest Tomorrow," 1941; "Rose of Sharon," 1947; "Be Ye Also Ready," 1944; "Proximities of Calvary," 1940; "Yielded Bodies," 1954; "Great Is The Lord," 1955; "Modern Illustrations for Public Speakers," 1955; "Bible Fires," 1956; "Bought by the Blood," 1957; "Seven Swords and Other Sermons," 1958; "The Place Called Heaven," 1959. In addition, he has written many articles and poems for several periodicals.

He married the former Bula Gentry in Greenville, South Carolina, on November 26, 1913. A native of South Carolina, Mrs. Lee is the daughter of Daniel David and Martha Jane (Holland) Gentry. Dr. and Mrs. Lee have two children: they are: Bula Gentry, born January 2nd, 1917, and an adopted son, Roy DeMent Lee, born April 19, 1925. Their daughter married Captain Edward R. King of the United States Navy. To this union were born three children—Bettye Lee King, Robbye Lee King, and Edward Lee King. Roy DeMent Lee is married and has two sons—Robert Greene Lee and Richard Lee.

JIMMY STROUD

The Memphis Union Mission, a landmark of Christian achievement in Memphis, is a monument to the devotion and herculean efforts of James

Stroud. Coming to the city in 1945, Jimmy Stroud—as he is much better known among Memphis residents—launched courageously into a seemingly impossible assignment which has had its constructive effect in the lives of men far beyond the confines of the mid-South metropolis.

He was born at Lee, Florida, on June 17, 1915, son of Frank and Olive Stroud. His father, after some years as depot agent with the Seaboard Air Line Railroad, became a rural mail carrier, an occupation which he followed for twenty-nine years until his death in 1941. Jimmy attended local schools, and gained early working experience in such tasks as janitorial work in the school building. When he reached high school age, he traveled the eight miles to the county seat at Madison, graduating there in 1934. He excelled in baseball, playing in the South Georgia and North Florida leagues. He also played half-back position on his school's football team. At this period, he also demonstrated a talent for music, possessing a voice of excellent quality.

After graduation from high school young Jimmy was for a time undecided whether to follow his interest in osteopathy to a professional career, or prepare for Christian service. He had "sown his wild oats" in his day, but the strong moral influence of his mother had prevailed, and it prevailed now in the formation of his decision to enroll at a Christian school. The institution chosen was Asbury College at Wilmore, Kentucky. His year at this Methodist college did not have the immediate effect of converting the fun-loving youth into a Christian worker; rather, the goal was arrived at by indirection. One of his classmates was Eddie Withrow, son of Pat Withrow, founder and director of the Union Mission at Charleston, West Virginia. It was probably the influence of Pat Withrow which determined the course of his dynamic career of service. The book titled "Mud 'n' Mercy in Memphis," which recounts Mr. Stroud's achievements at Memphis Union Mission, tells the story of their encounter in these words:

When classes were over at the end of the school year, Jimmy accepted Eddie Withrow's invitation to spend the summer in Charleston. He had nothing else to do and liked the idea of being in a large city. When Eddie Withrow said to Jimmy, "Meet my dad," something clicked and Jimmy knew he had a lifetime friend. Radio newscaster Lowell Thomas once described Pat Withrow as "one of the most picturesque characters of our day—a dynamic, irrepressible and indomitable spirit who deserves the cooperation of everyone." Jimmy knew one thing for sure: this man was real. There was nothing phony about him. (Today his rescue mission in Charleston is one of the largest in the world, with some $750,000 in assets, 17 departments and an average of 50 workers on the payroll.)

In his early days in the city, Jimmy played on the Owen-Illinois Glass baseball team, and worked at odd jobs in the mission. It was there that his definite commitment to Christianity took place on September 14, 1935. He stayed out of college that fall to continue at the mission at a salary of twenty —later thirty—dollars per month plus room and board. Once again he was

AMON CARTER EVANS
SILLIMAN EVANS JR.

PLAQUE OF
SILLIMAN EVANS

LUCILE MCCRAE EVANS

faced with a decision, this time as to the direction which his Christian service should take—whether to remain in mission work, become an evangelistic song-leader, or prepare for a career in osteopathy, serving his fellows through the medium of a profession. Mission work won the decision. "The next few years under Withrow," writes his biographer Mel Larson, "were Jimmy's 'college education' for his life career. Withrow was the best of teachers. Jimmy saw every possible phase of mission work and he thoroughly enjoyed working there even as he realized that God was preparing him for an effort in some other city." In June, 1944, he came into prominence as a song leader at memorial services for World War II hero Colin Kelly, who had come from his own home town in Florida. It was also in 1944, at the Salem Baptist Church at Winston-Salem, North Carolina, that he was ordained to the ministry.

The following year he began seeking contacts for a mission of his own. He went in February, 1945, to Greenville, South Carolina, where he met with a committee of religious and civic leaders; but he did not sense there the wholehearted response which he believed to be a vital ingredient in the success of a mission. When he returned to Charleston, Mr. Withrow handed him a letter from one T. Walker Lewis of Memphis, who was interested in seeing a mission founded there. It is recorded that within four hours of the time Mr. Stroud walked into Mr. Lewis' office, the Memphis Union Mission had come into being. The project won the support of many other enthusiastic community leaders, Mr. Stroud was named superintendent, and all hands went to work to find a suitable location in the center of the city.

The rest of the Union Mission history is quite well known to Memphians. Over the intervening years, Mr. Stroud's energy, foresight and faith have brought into being an institution which today has assets and holdings valued at three hundred and twenty-five thousand dollars. Its work is carried on by eighteen different departments. There are dormitories for both men and women; and as a part of the program, weekly classes are conducted at the Shelby County Penal Farm, and a twenty-four-hour-a-day telephone ministry is maintained. An evangelistic campaign is held annually in the Christian Youth Auditorium, which in itself represents a one-hundred- and eighty-five-thousand-dollar investment, and is the first of its kind in America. There, Youth for Christ rallies have been conducted weekly since 1945. Another phase of the work is the "Biblemobile,"—probably the first chapel-on-wheels, which contacts high school and college groups.

Still another vitally important aspect of the program is being carried on at Mud Island. This is a rehabilitation center for alcoholics; and hundreds of its "alumni" have left at the end of a twenty-nine-day period to return to useful lives.

The dynamic nature of the work, and its effectiveness, have attracted considerable publicity. The book "Mud 'n' Mercy in Memphis" gives a full account of the program. Written by Mel Larson, it has a foreword by Dale Evans

Rogers, who with her husband Roy Rogers has given most effective support to the Union Mission program. The book was published in 1955 by the Zondervan Publishing House of Grand Rapids, Michigan. In December, 1953, a forty-five-minute sound motion picture, in color, was produced by Westminster Films of Pasadena, California, portraying the work of the organization. It has been shown in churches and before various groups in all parts of the country.

Mr. Stroud has taken a lively and constructive interest in community affairs in Memphis. He has brought to the city some of the nation's foremost preachers, teachers and lecturers. In 1946, and again in 1949, he was nominated by the Rotary Club, the Civitan Club and the Cooperative Club to receive the Distinguished Service Award as the outstanding young man of Memphis in those years. He is often called on to appear as a speaker. He has been a guest on the Old Fashioned Revival Hour broadcast, and has appeared before Bible conference groups. His own religious affiliation is with Bellevue Baptist Church in Memphis.

At Charleston, West Virginia, on June 17, 1941, James Stroud married Dortha E. Bailey, daughter of C. J. and Matilda Bailey. The couple are the parents of three sons: 1. James Andrew, who was born on April 11, 1943. 2. Thomas Ramar, born on March 12, 1944. 3. Paul Markham, who was born on January 26, 1947. The family make their home at 4645 Lorece Avenue, Memphis.

RUTH HENLEY DUNCAN

Mrs. Isaac Greenwood Duncan, of 35 Belleair Drive, in Memphis, nee Ruth Henley, was born in Maury City, December 13, 1908, the daughter of the late Milton Robertson Henley and Lucy Feild (Gibbons) Henley. Her father, born August 5, 1884, in Crockett County, was a merchant and landowner, who died March 15, 1920; he married, January 5, 1908, Lucy Feild Gibbons, who was born October 29, 1889 in Maury City, where she now resides; she is the daughter of William Emmett Gibbons and Willie Victoria (Foster) Gibbons. The Gibbons family lived in Lauderdale County, Alabama, and in Giles County, Tennessee. William Emmett Gibbons was born November 27, 1849 and died May 25, 1896, having married, September 17, 1884, in Crockett County. Willie Victoria Foster, who was born February 21, 1863, in the home of her grandparents in Anderson, Alabama; she died March 9, 1938. Her parents were William Tindall Foster and Lucy Ann (Boothe) Foster and her grandparents were Booker Foster and Lucinda (Tindall) Foster. William Emmett Gibbons removed to West Tennessee shortly after The War Betweeen the States and engaged in business with his older brother Hiram Franklin Gibbons, who had fought in the war in the 20th Tennessee Cavalry. His father, John Quincy Gibbons, was a member of General Brown's famous brigade which was made up in Pulaski, Tennessee, and distinguished themselves in the heavy battles around Dalton, Georgia. Originally this was the

Ruth Henley Duncan

37th Infantry. W. E. Gibbons was an early merchant in Maury City, a civic-minded man, and belonged to the Free and Accepted Masons, being a member of Forked Deer Lodge. He, with other Masons, was instrumental in starting the first public school in Maury City, before parents engaged private tutors who lived in their homes to instruct the children.

Mrs. Duncan was reared in Maury City, graduated from Crockett High School (now called Maury City High School) at 17 years of age, is an alumna of the Jackson School of Business Administration as well as of the Second Genealogical Institute conducted by the American University, Washington, D. C. Mrs. Duncan married, first, William Joseph Godwin, on July 20, 1929, in Memphis; she married, secondly, Dr. I. G. Duncan, noted surgeon and urologist of Memphis, on December 14, 1952. Mr. Godwin was born June 21, 1902; he was a prominent florist and business man, vice president and manager of Southern Wholesale Florists and co-founder of this firm in 1932. He died November 18, 1950. He graduated from Mississippi Heights Academy, Blue Mountain, Mississippi, and was an alumnus of the University of Mississippi in Oxford. He entered the florist business in 1918 and became a director in the Southeastern Florists Association and a leader in the floral industry in the South and Southwest at the time of his death. He was the only son of Lee Godwin, prominent business man and philanthropist of Blue Mountain, Mississippi, and his wife, Alice (Goudy) Godwin. Lee Godwin was president of the bank in Blue Mountain and founded the first bank at nearby Ashland, in Benton County, Mississippi; he died January 11, 1929.

William Joseph Godwin and Ruth (Henley) Godwin became the parents of a daughter, Betty Jo Godwin, who was born January 5, 1932 in Memphis. She has distinguished herself in the Fine Arts. She received her early education and graduated with honors from Miss Hutchinson's School in 1950. She was selected as the most talented in a class of 66 students, was in "Who's Who in the Senior Class" and served as Art Editor of the school publication "The Lantern." Miss Godwin received a Bachelor of Fine Arts degree from the Memphis Academy of Arts in 1954 and was crowned Queen of the Beaux Arts Ball at the February event the same year. She presented her bronze portrait of Dr. Marshall Wingfield to the West Tennessee Historical Society in April 1955, honoring his eighteenth year as president. She received her Bachelor of Science degree from the University of Tennessee in Knoxville in 1957, two years after her marriage on September 7, 1955 to William Heiskell Mitchell, a native of Columbia, South Carolina, who attended the Citadel and graduated from the University of Tennessee, majoring in Electrical Engineering. Miss Godwin is a Life Member of the Art Fellowship of the Memphis Academy of Arts, a member of the National League of American Penwomen for outstanding art work, and the Association of American University Women. She restored the ancient painting and portraits which hang in the Knox County Court House, in 1959, and drew the pen and ink sketch of "The James White

Fort," which the United States Government plans to reconstruct in the near future. She has exhibited in Brooks Memorial Art Gallery and the Audiger Gallery in Knoxville, sponsored by the National League of American Pen-women and the Smithsonian Institution in Washington, D. C. Mr. and Mrs. Mitchell live in Winston-Salem, North Carolina, where Mrs. Mitchell is on the faculty of the Art Council and Mr. Mitchell is associated with Western Electric.

Mrs. Duncan was the First Life Member of the West Tennessee Historical Society in 1947 (West Tennessee Historical Papers, Volume L), and serves on the Executive Committee. She is a Life Member of the Tennessee Historical Society and has served as Corresponding Secretary two years; she is now vice president for the State Society-at-Large. She is a member of the East Tennessee Historical Society.

Mrs. Duncan was elected the second president of the Memphis Genealogical Society, November 6, 1951, and served until November 6, 1953, and during her two years as president, chartered this research group, which holds the distinction of being the first chartered research group engaged in the study of Genealogy in the State of Tennessee. During her presidency, funds were raised for the purchase of a micro-reader and the first census on microfilm was presented to Cossitt Library for the benefit of the public in the field of research. Many census records have been donated by the Memphis Genealogical Society to the library since 1952. This group, which began with a small membership, has grown to number 473. At the present time Mrs. Duncan serves the Memphis Genealogical Society as Research Director. She was an organizing member of the State Society, Dames of the Court of Honor and the Daughters of the American Colonists; she is a past National Recording Secretary of the Children of the American Colonists, and her daughter, Betty Jo (Godwin) Mitchell, is a past State President of the Children of the American Colonists, and served as National Chaplain of this society. Mrs. Duncan is a member of the National Society, Daughters of the American Revolution, the English Speaking Union, the Society for the Preservation of Tennessee Antiquities, United Daughters of the Confederacy, and is serving on the State Advisory Council of the Civil War Centennial Commission. Mrs. Duncan is an antiquarian, and devoted to Southern History, especially the early history of Tennessee and the South. She has recently (West Tennessee Historical Papers, Volume XIV, 1960) found and edited much data with reference to Tennessee and West Tennessee history. She is a past president of the State Branch of the Huguenots of Manakin, in the Colony of Virginia and holds a life membership in this organization. She is a lineal descendant of Lieutenant John S. Henley, Sr. (see Governor John Sevier's Commission Book published by the Tennessee Historical Society), an early Methodist minister and Revolutionary soldier, who settled in Washington County, Tennessee, when the state was known as "The Territory South of the Ohio" (see five volumes,

"Holston Methodism" by R. N. Price). Mrs. Duncan is also a descendant of Robert Abernathy, who migrated from Scotland to Tidewater Virginia, was a landowner by 1665 (Nugent's Cavaliers & Pioneers, page 544), and was a descendant of Lord Salton and King David of Scotland. Her great-great-grandparents, Charles Boothe and Lucy Ann (Abernathy) Boothe, were devoted members of the Methodist Episcopal Church South and are mentioned in "Methodism in Tennessee" by McFerrin. She is a lineal descendant, on the maternal side, of such noted Patriots of South Carolina in the Revolutionary War as Justice John Gaston of Chester County, South Carolina, in whose home the patriots met to complete strategic plans. John Gaston had nine sons who fought in the Revolutionary War, and this line can be traced back to Hugh Capet, the first King of France, and to Colonel William Massey, Comptroller for South Carolina, who was imprisoned at St. Augustine, Florida, for two years during the Revolutionary War; the line also goes back to Robert Tindall, gentleman planter, who was too aged to fight, but furnished many supplies for the troops of the Continental Army. Mrs. Duncan was baptized at the age of ten years in the Methodist Episcopal Church in Maury City, Tennessee, in the church her maternal grandmother helped to found. Mrs. W. E. Gibbons was a Charter member of this church, as was her oldest daughter, Dennie Gibbons. Three pews are dedicated to the W. E. Gibbons family in this church, one honoring Lucy Feild Gibbons Henley, and two dedicated to the memory of Mrs. W. E. Gibbons and Dennie Gibbons Mays.

Mrs. Duncan is a genealogist and devotes much time to historical research as well as other local and civic projects and patriotic organizations. She is a democrat and believes in States Rights.

Grover Newton McCormick

For half a century, Grover Newton McCormick has been practicing law in Memphis. In the course of that time he has capably represented a number of corporate interests, and he represented the people of his district for two terms in the Tennessee State Legislature.

A native of Brighton, in Tipton County, Mr. McCormick was born on December 22, 1885, son of George Newton and Nancy (Moffatt) McCormick. His father, who was born in Chester, South Carolina, arrived in Tennessee with his parents when he was eight years of age. They settled in Tipton County, where George McCormick engaged in farming until his death in 1913, at the age of seventy-three. Nancy Moffatt, whom he married, was a native of Tennessee, and she died in 1914.

Grover Newton McCormick was reared on his father's farm and attended local elementary and high schools. He began his advanced studies at Erskine College, a Presbyterian institution, where he graduated with the degree of Bachelor of Arts in 1908. Having decided upon a career in the law, he then enrolled at Cumberland University in Lebanon, and there he took his Bachelor of Laws degree in 1910.

Admitted to the Tennessee bar, Mr. McCormick came to Memphis to open his law offices. Early in his career, he developed a sizeable private practice, and also assumed duties as local counsel for the Hartford Accident and Indemnity Company of Hartford, Connecticut and for the Norwich Union Indemnity Company of New York.

Mr. McCormick was first elected to the Tennessee State Legislature for the session beginning in 1913, and at the end of two years he was returned to office, serving with distinction for another session. He was chiefly responsible for securing passage of the Fire Prevention Act of 1913.

In 1916 he left to enter military service and was sent to the Mexican border with Company I of the First Tennessee Regiment. He continued his military service into World War I, when he was stationed at Camp Taylor in Louisville, Kentucky.

Mr. McCormick is a member of the American Legion, the Chamber of Commerce, the City Club, and the University Club.

E. W. HALE, SR.

A veteran of over fifty-two years' experience in the public affairs of Memphis and Shelby County, E. W. Hale, Sr., had no peers as an influence in the political life of the area. He was for more than three decades chairman of the Shelby County Commission, and in that capacity did much to put local government on a sound basis, and to restore a high standard of ethics. He was a successful businessman, head of the J. W. Hale and Son Mercantile Store.

Born at Oxford, Mississippi, on January 4, 1875, he was the son of J. W. and Mattie Jane (Dean) Hale, and a descendant of an old North Carolina family. His grandfather, J. W. Hale, was also born at Oxford, and became a planter there. His son, also named J. W., was born there in 1850 and died in 1938. He became a merchant and planter of Whitehaven, Tennessee. Mattie Jane Dean, whom he married, was born at Oxford in 1850 and died in 1934. She was a daughter of Elijah Willis Dean, who moved from his native state to Whitehaven, Tennessee, about 1875 and became a merchant. J. W. and Mattie Jane (Dean) Hale were the parents of three children: 1. Maggie, who married W. E. Davis of Memphis. 2. E. William, the subject of this biography. 3. Rosa, a resident of Whitehaven.

The family moved to Tennessee and settled at Whitehaven when E. W. Hale was five years of age. At the age of eighteen, he became a partner of his father in the general mercantile business after his disability was removed by the Courts; he became a full partner in the firm of J. W. Hale & Son at the corner of Highway 51 and Whitehaven-Capleville Road. It remained his major private interest for the duration of his career. However, he also had a

E & r Hale

lifelong interest in farming. Owning considerable acreage in the Whitehaven area, and a farm south of Forest Hill, he had also owned property in Mississippi, although he had sold most of this before the end of his life. He was active at various times as cotton ginner, dairyman and real estate developer.

Mr. Hale, who had received his education in the Whitehaven schools, began his career in politics in 1906, when he became candidate for magistrate of the Twelfth District. He was later appointed to the County Board of Education; and in 1911 resigned to run for the office of Shelby County Commissioner when the county initiated the new commission form of government Thus began a record of forty-four years of effective public service as commissioner. Assuming his duties on January 1, 1912, he remained a dynamic influence in county affairs thereafter until his retirement, effective January 1, 1956. In a review of his career appearing in The Commercial Appeal at the time of his death, his qualities as a man, and contributions as a public servant, were assessed in these words:

Mr. Hale steered the county to its present growth as a metropolitan area in a quiet, unassuming manner. Backing his calm demeanor was a ready decisiveness when a decision was called for, a keen ability for analysis and a sparkling sense of humor.

Mr. Hale authorized the spending of millions of dollars of county taxpayers' money only after he was convinced such expenditures were warranted. His reputation among county office-holder associates and Memphis businessmen was that each county dollar must return "at least" a dollar in value and benefits. . . . He assumed conservation of the taxpayers' funds as a basic obligation of the county commission chairman. . . .

Mr. Hale held a broad concept of the county's needs as particularly evidenced by the secondary road system and the schools here. He was alert to the public wish and attitude on county matters and was guided thereby. Thus when the controversy arose as to the need for voting machines, Mr. Hale accepted the public's stand in the matter. . . .

His efforts over the years no doubt had their effect in keeping his county's tax rate the lowest in the state; and Memphis can boast a tax rate far below that of comparable cities, in the South or elsewhere.

One of the most significant of his achievements—"perhaps the biggest and most important thing he did," in the words of a Press-Scimitar journalist —was establishing the Shelby County Penal Farm, which has sparked progress in agriculture and in raising livestock standards not only in the county but throughout the Mid-South. When by the early 1930s the county had purchased eighteen hundred acres of its present five-thousand-acre holdings, he advanced the idea of the Penal Farm's developing its own herd of purebred dairy cows, and promoted the expenditure of $34,000 for Jersey cattle. This move met with some opposition at the time, but it has many times over proved its validity in the intervening years. He was adamant against the cutting of salaries of teachers and other public employees during these same difficult depression years. He was largely responsible for envisoning and promoting the city's and county's port and harbor development. He was also instrumental in bringing major industries to the county, Firestone, International Harvester, DuPont, Grace and other plants representing firms attracted here largely through his efforts. His qualities in working with people, and in securing results for the benefit of his county, have been appraised in these words, in The Commercial Appeal article:

Mr. Hale's skill as a businessman and his application of this craft to the county government was complemented by his adroitness in politics. He was dominant in the county phase of the Shelby organization's political skillfulness. . . . The top levels of county government often remarked with admiration on Mr. Hale's ability to retain outstanding men at county posts at much lower salaries than had been made available to them elsewhere. The explanation . . . was that the introductory respect which Mr. Hale first drew developed shortly into loyalty, and then progressed to a deep affection for the county leader.

Mr. Hale never wanted "yes men" working with him for the county. He sought opinions, and when they differed from his he was never satisfied until he had probed thoroughly the other's reasoning. . . . Mr. Hale received the respect of all who knew him well, and he gave a like degree of respect in return.

Following his resignation from the county commissioner's office, Mr. Hale was active in political affairs only at the time of Prentice Cooper's candidacy for governor in 1958. He had previously been a staunch supporter of Mr. Cooper when he became governor in 1939. In the 1958 campaign, however, Mr. Cooper withdrew to enter the race for United States Senator.

Mr. Hale remained a resident of the Whitehaven area throughout his life, with the exception of some time spent in Tucson, Arizona, in the mid-1950s.

At Germantown, Tennessee, on the nineteenth day of July, 1905, E. W. Hale, Sr., married Miss Emma Turner Kimbrough, daughter of Albert Graham and Willie Anderson (Pettus) Kimbrough, Sr. The couple became the parents of two children: 1. E. W., Jr., who was born on July 12, 1907. A lawyer, he is currently serving as county attorney. A biography of him accompanies. 2. Alberta Kimbrough Hale, who was born on April 18, 1912, and is the wife of Russell Lyle of Whitehaven.

The death of this valued public official occurred on December 16, 1959, at Baptist Hospital in Memphis, following a long bout with a respiratory ailment. County leaders were unanimous in praising his achievements, his contributions, and the qualities of the man himself. "Mr. Hale set a shining example of sobriety and efficiency in public office," remarked one of the present commissioners. "He had the rare quality of achieving greatness while retaining complete modesty." Another of the commissioners concurred in this view: "Mr. Hale had at all times been big enough to remain more or less in the background—the mark of a true patriot and statesman, and he was both."

A corporation executive said of him, "Will Hale's sterling character and unselfish devotion to his responsibilities as a county official stamped him as one of the great leaders and an outstanding citizen of Shelby County." "To me," remarked the superintendent of county schools, "his outstanding qualities were honesty, integrity and fairness and his uncanny ability to analyze a situation and get straight to the problem." A member of the Planning Commission spoke for many when he expressed "a deep sense of loss at the passing of a valued friend, a gentleman of the old school, and a conscientious and devoted worker for the public good."

Mr. and Mrs. Hale were members of the Whitehaven Baptist Church. He was active in Masonry and in that Order had advanced to the higher degrees as shown in the fact that he was a member of the Ancient Arabic Order of Nobles of the Mystic Shrine.

Mr. Hale's life is aptly summed up by the following editorial which appeared in The Commercial Appeal the day following his death:

"He Plowed Deep—Straight"
In his ode to the plow, Richard Henry Horne adjured the plowmen:
    Ye rigid Plowmen! Bear in mind
    Your labor is for future hours.
    Advance! spare not! nor look behind!
    Plow deep and straight with all your powers.

As we thought upon the passing of E. W. Hale—of many years of observation of the man and his ways, his governmental leadership of Shelby County, his dedication to endeavors which were for the common good, his integrity and courage, Horne's words came back as a bell to the mind to mark Will Hale's leave-taking.

He was essentially of the soil—the son of a farmer and a plowman at heart. The furrow of his life's work is long. With all his power he plowed it "deep and straight."

It has strong conviction's depth. It has the straightness of true integrity.

He labored for the future through championship of the public school system and the children who are its beneficiaries.

He built for the agricultural Mid-South's future by developing Shelby County Penal Farm's famed registered stock pool of Jersey cattle and swine and making it available to the farmers and stock-growers of this area.

He dared advance. As Chairman of Shelby County Commission he was one of the original sponsors of the skill-developing port project in which Memphis and Shelby County are equal partners.

Will Hale had that builder's vision which enables a true leader to look at far civic horizons. He used it in his unremitting support of the port facility.

He was no dissembler. There was no shading to his "yes" and his "no." There was no equivocating or bending with the political winds once he had spoken the word.

There was a lot of ruggedness in Will Hale which even advanced age could not soften. He had an extraordinary regard for what is called the "taxpayer's dollar." He demanded a dollar's return for every dollar spent. He expected a full and honest day's work from every county employe. He gave far more than a full day all of his active years.

He believed that the taxpayers are entitled to an accounting for funds expended. He took great pride in advertising Shelby's annual audit reports in the county's newspapers. His was the pride of conscientious stewardship.

He was a neighborly man and one softly spoken. Those who found him stern saw only the facade which hid a ready smile.

He expected loyalty from his associates but returned it in even greater measure. He paired it with honesty.

It could not be written of Will Hale that at 84 he was "of the past." He was, despite a respiratory impairment, decidedly of the present and of that future to which his furrow had been plowed.

He kept in touch with government, he conferred with devoted officials and friends, he advised, he suggested. It took death to terminate his interest in the county and city he so dearly loved and to whose progress he had contributed so much.

Will Hale leaves a builder's mark on many things vital to a great tomorrow and our civic well being as his hands give up the plow and he turns homeward.

E. W. HALE, JR.

Since his admittance to the bar, E. W. Hale, Jr., has distinguished himself in private practice in Memphis. Continuing in a family tradition of public service, he has been capably serving for several years past as county attorney.

Mr. Hale is a native of Whitehaven, in Shelby County, where he was born on July 12, 1907, son of E. W. Sr., and Emma (Kimbrough) Hale. His father, who had a distinguished record in public service, is the subject of a separate biographical sketch accompanying. Mrs. Hale died March 5, 1954. The younger E. W. Hale first attended Whitehaven School, then Memphis University School, and transferred from there to the McCallie School in Chattanooga, where he was recognized for his accomplishments in his scholastic activities, including president of the Student Council, and president of his graduating class in 1926. He entered Washington and Lee University, Lexington, Virginia, while there was manager of the Troubadours, a University organization which produced dramatic productions, musicals and other entertainment, served on the business staff of Ring Tum Phi, University paper. He was a member of Phi Delta Theta, social fraternity, Pi Delt Epsilon, honorary journalistic fraternity, and received his degree of Bachelor of Arts in 1931. Before going on with his law studies, he spent three years with the Memphis Light and Power Company. He then enrolled at George Washington University, Washington, D. C., where he graduated with the degree of Bachelor of Laws in 1938. While attending law school, he held a position in the library of the House of Representatives, being engaged in research work for members of Congress. He was a member of "Little Congress," whose

E. W. Hale Jr

membership was composed of administrative personnel to the members of the House of Representatives and the Senate.

Admitted to the bar of his state in 1937, Mr. Hale commenced practice as soon as he left the University, opening offices in Memphis. There he has since won wide recognition as a practicing attorney.

He has consistently taken a vital and helpful interest in civic affairs. He participated in all war bond campaigns during World War II, and served as vice chairman of the Shelby County War Finance Committee from 1941 to 1945. In past years he was active in the Young Democratic Clubs of Memphis and Tennessee, serving at one time as national committeeman for the State of Tennessee.

On February 2, 1939, Mr. Hale took office as a member of the Tennessee State Board of Supervisors of Elections, having been elected by the General Assembly of Tennessee. He was elected for six terms in all—a total of twelve years, and of that period he served the first seven years as secretary, and the next five as chairman of the board. He assumed duties in his present public office, that of county attorney, on January 1, 1956.

As a lawyer, Mr. Hale is a member of the Memphis and Shelby County Bar Association, and has served on its board of directors. He is also a member of the Bar Association of Tennessee, and the American Bar Association. Among his community interests, he has served since 1939 as a director of the Cossitt Library. After a number of years as director, vice president, and grand marshal of parades of the Memphis Cotton Carnival, he was elected its president in 1947. The fourteenth man to serve in that office, he staged a most effective show at "The South's Greatest Party" in that year.

Mr. Hale is a member of the board of the Shelby County Chapter of the American Cancer Society, and the Shelby County Chapter of the Tennessee Society for Crippled Children and Adults. He was formerly a member of the Shelby County Chapter of Muscular Dystrophy Associations of America, and the Infantile Paralysis Foundation.

Long a member of the Navy League of America, Mr. Hale has served as judge advocate of its Memphis Council. His other memberships include the Tennessee Historical Society, the University Club of Memphis, The Tennessee Club of that city, and the Executives Club, also of Memphis.

Mr. Hale makes his home in Whitehaven, where he has farming interests. In this respect he adheres to family traditions of long standing. His grandfathers on both the paternal and maternal side were cotton growers. His maternal great-grandfather established the plantation known as "Cotton Plant," and the antebellum home on this estate was one of the show places of Shelby County until it was destroyed by fire.

On May 22, 1948, E. W. Hale, Jr., married Miss Era Mae Causie, daughter of Mrs. Mary Ella Causie, and the late John William Causie.

John Walter Canada

A nationally noted corporation lawyer who practiced in Memphis from the turn of the century until his death in 1944, Colonel John Walter Canada has left his influence upon the organization which he headed, and upon the business and community life of his city. He was an official of several corporations; and his pioneer work in the creation of airport facilities for his city will place future generations much in his debt.

Colonel Canada was born on a farm near Whitehaven, on December 27, 1876, son of William Wilks and Sallie Thomas (Brewster) Canada. Mr. and Mrs. William Wilks Canada had two other children, William Wilks Canada and Mrs. Carrie Canada Daly, both of whom are deceased. His mother's grandfather, John Dunlap Brewster, was not only the first of this family to settle in the region, but his home, Lambert Logs, is the oldest residence still standing in Shelby County. It is now being maintained by the Tennessee Society for the Preservation of Antiquities, and will be moved to a site in the Riverside Park area in Memphis.

John Walter Canada attended the Memphis public schools and Memphis Military Institute, where he graduated in 1895. He then matriculated at Millsaps College, Jackson, Mississippi, where he received the degree of Master of Arts with the Class of 1897. At the same time, he was pursuing his law studies there under the direction of Judge Edward Mayes. After receiving his law diploma he returned to Memphis, and in January, 1898, was admitted to the bar. Early in his career he served the interests of the railroads, being General Attorney of the Missouri Pacific Railroad, and vice-president and general counsel of the Union Railway Company from 1905. In addition to his general law practice with the firm of Canada, Russell & Turner, he held office as general counsel and member of the executive committee and board of directors of Union Planters National Bank and Trust Company, and of Plough, Incorporated, and as general counsel of the Arkansas & Memphis Railway Bridge and Terminal Company and Memphis Union Station Company. He was general attorney for Tennessee for the Missouri Pacific Railroad Company, and attorney for the St. Louis Southwestern Railway Company. He was vice-president as well as general counsel of the Union Railway Company, and was solicitor for the Frisco System in Tennessee and Mississippi.

Shortly after he had begun his law practice, this country became involved in the Spanish-American War, and he entered the United States Army. Commissioned a first lieutenant, he served in Company L of the Fourth Tennessee Infantry, receiving his commission from Governor Robert L. Taylor. Later promoted to captain, he served with his company in Cuba. He was mustered out at Savannah, Georgia, in March, 1899, and resumed his law practice in Memphis. However, he retained his interest in military matters, and was active in the Reserves with the Second Regiment, Tennessee National Guard. He served

Colonel John W. Canada

Virginia Ware Broaddus Canada

for a time as lieutenant colonel, and was later promoted to colonel—the youngest man to hold that rank in the state guard unit at that time.

Unquestionably the man who did more than anyone else to bring airport facilities to Memphis, Colonel Canada traced his own interest in aeronautics back to the mid-1920s. In 1927, at the age of fifty-one years, he learned to pilot an airplane at the old Armstrong Field near Millington, receiving instruction under the late Captain Vernon Omilie. He went ahead to obtain a government license as a private pilot, and was among the first owners of a private plane in his city. For a time he maintained a private flying field at his home, Adanac Lodge, on Hollyford Road, and flew his Stinson plane on many trips throughout the United States. Not only was he the leading spirit in bringing the first public airport to Memphis, but he also played a conspicuous part in bringing air-mail service to the city. He was copilot on the first air-mail plane flying into Memphis on June 15, 1931, and was presented with a gold spark-plug from the plane as a memento of this occasion. In 1929, Mayor Watkins Overton appointed him chairman of the Memphis Airport Commission, and in that post he exerted leadership in the creation of the Memphis Airport, serving until the duties of the commission were taken over by a city organization in 1937.

As an attorney, Colonel Canada concentrated his attention on civil law, and made a lasting impression at the bar of his state, both through his legal ability, and for his individual personal charm, character, and integrity. He was a member of the Memphis and Shelby County Bar Association, the State Bar Association of Tennessee, and the American Bar Association.

Colonel Canada was an organizer and charter member of the old Memphis Aero Club, and he held membership in the University Club, the Tennessee Club, Memphis Hunt and Polo Club, and the Memphis Country Club. His fraternity was Kappa Alpha. He attended the Episcopal Church, and was a Democrat in politics. One of his major avocational interests was horticulture, agriculture and stock-raising, and he successfully operated a cattle ranch near Sardis, Mississippi, on which he raised blooded stock. He and Mrs. Canada shared an interest in gardening and floriculture. With its large plantings of tulips and daffodils, their residence was one of the show-places of Memphis. Their daffodils won many prizes in flower shows.

Mrs. Canada is the former Mrs. Virginia Ware Broaddus Moore, having one daughter, Virginia Adair Moore, now Mrs. Stanley Law Snow. Mr. and Mrs. Snow have two children, Esther Virginia and Spencer Law. Mrs. Canada is the daughter of Eugene Llewellyn and Carolyne Virginia (Ware) Broaddus. Through her mother she is descended from the Ware family, pioneer settlers in Louisiana and Mississippi. She became the wife of Colonel John Walter Canada on March 16, 1934.

Colonel Canada was married, first, on December 31, 1903, to Emma Berry of Franklin, Tennessee, an accomplished musician and singer, and to that marriage, one son, John Walter, Jr., was born. He is married and has three children, Patty, Mary and Joan.

As Virginia Broaddus, Mrs. Canada attended Belmont College, in Nashville, for two years, and continued her education for the next two years at Randolph Macon Woman's College in Lynchburg, Virginia. Here she was a member of Chi Omega sorority, of S.T.A.B. Secret Society, the Drama Club, and the Y.W.C.A.

Mrs. Virginia Canada is active in garden circles in the South, and makes her home at Adanac Lodge on Hollyford Road. Mrs. Canada belongs to the Garden Club of America and has served as president of the Memphis Garden Club and chairman of the Southern Zone of the Garden Club of America. She also belongs to the Dilettantes, the Contemporaries and is an active member of the Daughters of the American Revolution. The Memphis Chapter of the English Speaking Union was organized by Mrs. Canada in 1953, and she served as the first president of the chapter in Memphis. The organization meeting was held at Adanac Lodge. Mrs. Canada is a member of Calvary Episcopal Church.

The death of the eminent lawyer and corporation executive occurred on June 11, 1944.

Bernard Louis Foy

From the early days of the Tennessee Valley Authority's existence, Bernard Louis Foy has served this vast and complex federal organization as a librarian. He is now technical librarian, supervising the technical library services needed by the Authority's employees in Chattanooga and Knoxville, and at Wilson Dam, Alabama. He is active in many librarians' groups, and also in the affairs of Knoxville, where he makes his home.

A native of Merom, Indiana, he was born on September 19, 1911, and is a son of Louis Calvin and Bessie Blanche (Darnell) Foy. His father was a lumberman. Bernard L. Foy attended the public schools of his native region and went on to his advanced studies at Indiana University. Following his entering Indiana University in the fall of 1929, he secured employment in its library, and continuing his work there throughout his undergraduate years, came to the decision of following librarianship as a career. He took his degree of Bachelor of Arts in 1934.

Lack of funds prevented his enrolling at the University of Illinois until 1935. At that time he obtained a position in the university's library, and entered the University of Illinois Library School. Following graduation there, with the degree of Bachelor of Science in Library Science, he accepted appointment on the library staff and attended the graduate library school.

In February, 1937, he accepted employment with the Tennessee Valley Authority as order librarian in its technical library. In 1941 he was named reference librarian, and in 1942, technical librarian. In the latter position, he supervises the technical library services required by the staff of the Tennessee Valley Authority, at Chattanooga and Knoxville, Tennessee, and also at Wilson Dam, Alabama.

Mr. Foy has been responsible for the compiling of yearly supplements to the "Indexed Bibliography of TVA," a check list of over twelve thousand references to magazine articles written about the Authority; and he has also compiled a "Bibliography for the TVA Program," which contains a selected list of books, documents, pamphlets, and magazine articles describing the various TVA programs. This publication is revised annually.

Active in the Tennessee Library Association, Mr. Foy was its president in 1955-1956. He is a member of the American Library Association, the Special Libraries Association, the Southeastern Library Association, the East Tennessee Historical Society and the Technical Society of Knoxville. In 1951-1952, he served as chairman of the Knox County Library Board. He is chapter consultant for the Oak Ridge Chapter of Special Libraries Associations.

Mr. Foy has served his home community in many capacities over a number of years. In 1943, he was chairman of the Victory Book Campaign for Knox County. He was president of the Knoxville Male Chorus in 1947-1948, and president of the Meadow Hills Community Association in 1948-1949. He is a Kiwanian, and his fraternity is Sigma Alpha Epsilon. He and his family attend the Second Presbyterian Church, and he is serving as a ruling elder of the congregation at the present time.

In Knoxville, on June 4, 1938, Bernard L. Foy married Evelyn Maudlin, daughter of John and Orpha Anne (Kellam) Maudlin. The couple are the parents of two children: 1. Evelyn, who was born on April 9, 1941. 2. David Louis, born May 10, 1943. The family lives at 400 Barclay, Southeast, Knoxville.

Honorable James Whitman Dance

With a long and successful career as a business man behind him, James Whitman Dance was elected in 1954 as mayor of Knoxville and took office in 1955. His previous experience in public affairs included service as county clerk and clerk of court, and he was long active in some of the city's better-known organizations.

The mayor was born at New Market, Tennessee, on June 10, 1897, son of John L. and Mattie (Ault) Dance. His father was a Baptist minister. As there were seven children in the family, and ministers' salaries are traditionally slender, James Dance early became acquainted with hard work and responsibility. As a boy he delivered newspapers, and worked at a variety of odd jobs. In 1916 he graduated from Central High School in Knoxville, and thereafter held positions as truck driver, clerk, and salesman until 1918, when he entered the army. He was assigned to the newly organized Army Air Force, which had come into existence as a branch of the Signal Corps, and served as a private until 1919.

On his return to peacetime pursuits he worked in a bank and as a salesman, and then, in about 1925, founded his own dry cleaning establishment. This he continued to operate successfully for thirty years.

In his first contest for public office, Mr. Dance was defeated. This was when he ran for county court clerk, in 1938. However, in 1939, he took office as deputy clerk, and served most capably for three years. In 1942 he was elected county clerk, an office which he filled for three four-year terms. He had just been elected to a fourth term when his name was put in nomination for mayor of Knoxville, and he was elected, taking office in 1955. Directing the affairs of a city of more than a hundred and twenty-five thousand people, he gave evidence of the same qualities of leadership and practical grasp of affairs which earned him success in business, and he also gave his city a conscientious and high-minded administration. The death of the business leader and public official occurred on April 12, 1959.

As a veteran of World War I, Mayor Dance was a member of the American Legion, and he also belonged to the Exchange Club and the lodges of the Benevolent and Protective Order of Elks and the Junior Order of United American Mechanics. He was a communicant of the Fifth Avenue Baptist Church.

In Knoxville, on September 27, 1920, James Whitman Dance married Mary Johnson, daughter of Samuel E. and Laura (Williams) Johnson. Mrs. Dance attended the University of Tennessee. She played on the girls' basketball team, winning her letter. Mrs. Dance was for some years associated with her husband in business. The couple became the parents of the following children: 1. Jack, who was born December 9, 1921. He entered college but resigned to enlist in the United States Navy for service in World War II. 2. Mary Jane, born July 29, 1923; she is the wife of Robert Jeffries; they have two children: David Whitman and Douglas Neal. 3. John L., born January 7, 1925; attended Milligan College at Johnson City, Tennessee; he played semi-pro baseball with the St. Louis Cardinal Farm League; he married Gertrude Human; they have three children: Rebecca Starr, John Forrest and William Bedford.

CHARLES HOWARD BOZEMAN

Honorable C. Howard Bozeman's experience in the profession of the law has brought him into contact with the three phases of teaching, practice, and service on the bench. Over the past decade, he has served as county judge for Knox County, Tennessee.

He is a native of Knoxville, and was born on June 27, 1918, one of three children born to Art C. and Mary (Aonwine) Bozeman. He has a brother, Dr. Samuel R. Bozeman of Indianapolis, Indiana, and his sister, Mary Kathryn Bozeman died in January, 1958. C. Howard Bozeman attended local public schools and graduated from Knoxville High School in 1936. He began his advanced studies at the College of Business Administration of the University of Tennessee, in pre-law and then transferred to the university's College of Law. There he graduated, with the degree of Bachelor of Science in Business Administration in 1941 and Bachelor of Laws, in 1943. He is also a Public Accountant.

At the University of Tennessee, he held an administrative position under the dean of students, and he was also auditor for three years there, 1943 to 1946. From 1946 to 1948, he taught accounting and business law at the university. Since 1946, Mr. Bozeman has been a practicing attorney and accountant in Knoxville. He is a partner in the firm of Stone, Bozeman, Hoch & Stockton in the Hamilton Bank Building in Knoxville. He was first elected county judge in 1948, and in 1950 was re-elected to a term expiring in 1958.

As a lawyer, Mr. Bozeman belongs to the Knox County Bar Association, the State of Tennessee Bar Association, and the American Bar Association. A member of the Tennessee County Judges Association, he formerly served as its president. He is a member of the board of directors of the Tennessee County Services Association, is state chairman of the Tennessee Commission on Youth Guidance, and has served as vice chairman of the Metropolitan Planning Commission. He is treasurer of the Holston Chilhowee Recreation Commission, and he is an ex officio member of numerous civic organizations.

Affiliated with the Free and Accepted Masons, he is a member of Shekinah Lodge No. 524, and of the higher bodies of the Ancient and Accepted Scottish Rite, holding the Thirty-second Degree. He is also a member of the Sertoma Club. He is a Democrat, and a teetotaler, and a communicant of the First Baptist Church.

On June 14, 1944, C. Howard Bozeman married Barbara Ann Newman, a native of Knoxville and daughter of Russell A. and Georgia (Montgomery) Newman. She has a brother, Lieutenant Russell A. Newman, Jr., of Lenoir City, and a sister, Mrs. J. W. Morton of Knoxville. Mr. and Mrs. Bozeman are the parents of four sons: Barry, Charles, David and Samuel. The family's residence is at 4801 Parva Road, Knoxville.

Poet Dean (P.D.) Cate

Following a number of years of varied business experience, Poet Dean (P.D.) Cate opened his own agency, the Cate Realty Company, in 1945. This is a Knoxville organization, with offices at 713 Market Street. Mr. Cate has long been active in the organizational and civic life of that city.

Born in Sevier County on July 24, 1897, he is a son of Samuel Wesley Gilbert and Lucy Adaline (Henry) Cate. His father was a farmer, who once served as sheriff of Sevier County. In the public schools of that county, Poet Dean Cate received his early education, and he later attended Draughan's Business College in Knoxville.

From 1917 to 1929, Mr. Cate was credit man for C. M. McClung and Company. He left to enter the real estate and construction field with the Schubert Lumber Company. With a background of more than a decade and a half of experience with this organization, in buying, selling and handling real estate, Mr. Cate opened his own office, Cate Realty Company, in 1945, and its management has been his major business interest since that time.

Mr. Cate is a member of the Knoxville Real Estate Board, the National Association of Real Estate Boards and the American Numismatic Association. He is a Republican and has served on the Knoxville Tax Board. He also belongs to the City Club and the Kiwanis Club, and the lodges of the Free and Accepted Masons and Benevolent and Protective Order of Elks, and is a member of the Sons of the Revolution. He is a Methodist in religious faith, while other members of his family attended the Episcopal Church.

At Dandridge, Tennessee, on February 18, 1922, P.D. Cate married Anne Marie Hutchinson, daughter of Richard S. C. and Carrie (Marshall) Hutchinson. Mrs. Cate was born in Denver, Colorado, came to Tennessee as a child, attended the University of Tennessee and was a member of Delta Delta Delta sorority. She is a member of the Daughters of the American Revolution. Mr. and Mrs. Cate have a son, Dean, born March 28, 1925. He attended the University of Tennessee. He is a Sigma Chi member. He served in the U.S. Army during World War II with a paratroop division. He now is associated in real estate business with his father. Dean Cate is married to Miss Lou Hopkins; they have four children: Cooper Dean, born December 8, 1947; Canby, born August 8, 1950; Marshall Wadsworth, born October 24, 1955, and Patrick David, born February 8, 1957. P.D. Cate's grandfather, Abraham Cate, and his twin brother Isaac, served in the Union Army in the Civil War.

FREDERICK MALCOLM CULP

A teacher of history at Peabody High School, Frederick Malcolm Culp has won a wide reputation in his field. He has written and lectured extensively, and was recently elected to the presidency of the Gibson County Historical Society.

Mr. Culp is a native of that county, born at Edison on December 31, 1927, and is a son and one of three children of Fred and Carrie (Childress) Culp. Both parents are native Tennesseeans. His father was born in Wayne County on June 2, 1885, and his mother on January 7, 1891, in Perry County. Attending the public schools of his native place, Frederick M. Culp went on to Peabody High School at Trenton, where he graduated in 1946. He then enrolled at Lambuth College, where in 1950 he received his degree of Bachelor of Arts.

Since that time, Mr. Culp has been a teacher or educational administrator in the public schools of Gibson County. For four years he was principal of the

Wellsview Elementary School, then joined the faculty of Peabody High School as a teacher of history, the position he has since held.

Mr. Culp was vice president of the Gibson County Historical Society prior to his recent election as its president. In collaboration with other members of this society, he is now engaged in the writing of a county history. He is also interested in genealogy. Among his own forebears were North Carolina planters and slaveholders. Henry Culp who came from that state to Wayne County, Tennessee, and William Buchanan Culp, his son, who was born in that county. A son of William B. was Dr. Edward Malcolm Culp, who practiced at Clifton, Tennessee, and he was a twin brother of Fred Culp of Trenton, a landowner and merchant and father of our subject. Carrie Childress, whom he married, was the daughter of Crockett Childress, and the granddaughter of John Childress who served in the Confederate States Army.

Mr. Culp has lectured extensively, and a number of local groups have heard his illuminating papers on the region's history and the men who made it. He is a member of the Tennessee Education Association and the Gibson County Teachers' Association. Apart from his professional connections, he is a member of the lodge of the Woodmen of the World. Active in the Oak Grove Methodist Church, he has been a teacher in its Sunday school and a lay leader.

Mr. Culp is unmarried. He makes a home for his mother and they reside on Route 1 near Trenton.

ROSCOE JAMES HACKNEY

As head of the R. J. Hackney Lumber Company, with headquarters in Memphis, R. J. Hackney was a vital factor in his city's commercial and industrial life for many years prior to his retirement in the early 1930s. He devoted his career to the lumber industry, and had large holdings in several southern states.

Born at Shelbyville, Indiana, on July 22, 1883, he was a son of Judge Leonard J. and Ida Louise (Pudney) Hackney. Judge Hackney was a prominent attorney and Judge of the Supreme Court of Indiana. He left Indiana to serve as general counsel for the Big Four Railroad at Cincinnati, Ohio. R. J. Hackney began his education in the public schools of his native place, and later attended schools in Indianapolis. Concluding his preparatory studies at Culver Military Academy, he entered Cornell University at Ithaca, New York, but left college before graduating, to begin his career.

At the outset of his career, he became interested in the development and effective use of timberlands in southern Arkansas. In 1911 he came to Memphis, where he became a partner in the Brown and Hackney Lumber Company. This firm was the predecessor of the R. J. Hackney Lumber Company, of which he was owner. It had its headquarters in the Commerce Title Building, and mills in Louisiana and Arkansas. Mr. Hackney remained at its head, providing effective executive leadership, until his retirement in 1932. For some years he served on the board of directors of the Memphis Commercial Appeal. From his retirement, however, he gave all his time to private affairs and investments.

Taking a vital interest in organizational life in his area, Mr. Hackney was a member of the Horseshoe Lake Club, Wapanaka Hunting Club, the Tennessee Club, Memphis Country Club, Polo Club and the Fifty Club, the Five Lakes Club, and Oakdonic Duck Club. He also belonged to Delta Kappa Epsilon, and to Phi Delta Phi legal fraternity. Fond of outdoor sports, he particularly enjoyed hunting, fishing, and horseback riding. He was a communicant of the Presbyterian Church.

On September 6, 1911, at Cincinnati, Ohio, R. J. Hackney married Frances Burnet, daughter of Edward W. and Alice (Dana) Burnet. Mrs. Hackney's family was in the insurance business in Cincinnati, Ohio. The Burnets were one of the pioneering and leading families of Cincinnati and they and the Danas have been closely identified with Cincinnati history. Mrs. Hackney is a member of the Memphis Garden Club. The couple made their home at 549 Goodwyn Street, Memphis, for many years before his death, which occurred on August 15, 1959.

JOHN COSTEN

Practicing law in Memphis for the past two decades, John Costen recently occupied new offices in the Sterick Building. Although a member of several partnerships in the past, he is now practicing independently. He has business interests, and served two terms in the Tennessee State House of Representatives from Shelby County.

A native of McKenzie, he was born on May 1, 1916, and is a son of John R. and Mamie (Burns) Costen. His father too, who is now deceased, was born in McKenzie, while Mrs. Costen was born at Trezevant. The elder Mr. Costen was a cotton merchant at McKenzie, served as Mayor for three terms and was a Spanish-American War Veteran. John Costen received his early education in the public schools, and began his advanced studies at Bethel College. He transferred from there to Vanderbilt University, where he received his degree of Bachelor of Arts in 1937. The following year he completed his professional training at Cumberland University Law School, where he was a member of the Barristers Club and Jackson's Temple, Honorary Scholastic societies, receiving his degree of Bachelor of Laws there in 1938.

In 1939, Mr. Costen was admitted to the Tennessee bar, and he began his active career in practice as a member of the firm of Costen, Crabtree and Costen. He remained with this organization until 1955, and thereafter until 1958, was a member of the firm of Taylor, Costen and Taylor. In 1958 he opened his own offices for independent practice as John Costen, attorney at law. In 1959 he moved to his location in the Sterick Building. He specializes in business and corporation law.

A member of the board of directors of the Security American Life Insurance Company of Tennessee, Mr. Costen is also serving as its secretary. He was United States Commissioner for the Western District of Tennessee, Western Division, in 1945. His first term as a member of the Tennessee State Legislature began in 1943 and ran until 1945. Having been re-elected by his constituents in Shelby County, he remained in the House of Representatives until 1947.

As a lawyer, he belongs to the Bar Association of Tennessee, and served as president of its Junior Section during 1945-1946. He is also a member of the Memphis and Shelby County Bar Association, the American Bar Association, and the American Judicature Society.

Mr. Costen's nonprofessional memberships include the Petroleum Club and the Memphis Executives Club. He was formerly a member of the Chicasaw Country Club. His fraternity is Alpha Tau Omega. He is a communicant of the Second Presbyterian Church, and is vice president of the Men's Bible Class.

At Pine Bluff, Arkansas, on January 18, 1948, John Costen married Virginia Ann Sloss. She is a native of that place, and the daughter of Joseph and Emma (Dewoody) Sloss. Mrs. Costen is a member of the Josephine Circle and is currently serving as its treasurer. She also belongs to Le Bonheur Club, and is active in women's groups at the Second Presbyterian Church. The couple are the parents of two children: 1. Sandra, who was born on October 31, 1951. 2. Susan, born on September 16, 1954. Both of these children attend Miss Hutchinson's School.

Robert Edwin (Buster) Williams

As a dealer in phonograph records with thirty years' experience, Robert Edwin Williams of Memphis has more recently been manufacturing records in his own right. He has also become active in the petroleum industry. At the present time he heads the Music Sales Company, Plastic Products Company, Coldwater Industries, Coldwater, Mississippi, R. E. Williams Drilling Company, and R. E. Williams Oil and Gas Company, all with headquarters in Memphis.

He is a native of Enterprise, Mississippi, and was born on January 14, 1909, the son of Zan and Amanda (Thompson) Williams. Attending the public schools of his native community and graduating from high school there, he was later a student at the University of Alabama.

Mr. Williams has been active in the music business for the past thirty years. A wholesale distributor of phonograph records, he heads his own firm, Music Sales Company, with offices at 1117 Union Street in Memphis. About a decade ago, he turned his attention to manufacturing records, and in that aspect of his operations, has formed another organization, Plastic Products Company, whose offices are at 1746 Chelsea. He recently erected a plant for the manufacture of the records at Coldwater, Mississippi.

It was also about ten years ago that he entered the petroleum industry, which has been one of his major interests since. His two firms, the R. E. Williams Drilling Company and R. E. Williams Oil and Gas Company, both have their offices in the DuPont Building in Memphis.

In December, 1941, Mr. Williams entered the United States Army Air Corps as a private, and advanced in rank to first lieutenant while serving as an airplane pilot and glider pilot. He received his honorable discharge in 1946.

Mr. Williams is a member of the Tennessee Club, the Chicasaw Country Club, and the Sportsmen's Pilot Association. Also affiliated with the Free and Accepted Masons, he is a member of the higher bodies, holding the Thirty-second Degree, and he belongs to the Ancient Arabic Order of Nobles of the Mystic Shrine. He is a communicant of St. John's Episcopal Church.

At Victorville, California, on March 3, 1943, Robert Edwin Williams married Marilyn Triolo. She was born in Los Angeles, California, daughter of Raymond Lewis and Erma (Edwards) Triolo. Her father was a native of Chicago, Illinois, while her mother was born in Stockton, California. Mr. and Mrs. Williams are the parents of three children: 1. Robert Edwin, also born in Stockton, California, on December 10, 1944. 2. Marilyn Virginia, born in Memphis on August 12, 1950. 3. Sue Zan, born in that city on July 22, 1952.

JAMES OZRO GARNER

For more than two decades James O. Garner has practiced law in Memphis, with the exception of three years' absence while serving in the United States Navy during World War II. He is a member of the firm of Garner and Batchelor with offices in the Commerce Title Building.

A native of Pulaski, he was born on May 7, 1914, son of John Daniel and Ethel Edna (Cooper) Garner. Both of his parents were born at Helena, Arkansas. James O. Garner attended the public schools of his native city, graduated from Central High School there, then entered Tennessee State College at Murfreesboro. He completed his professional studies at Cumberland University Law School, where he graduated with the degree of Bachelor of Laws in 1936.

Admitted to the bar of his state, Mr. Garner's first law connection was in the firm of James O. Garner and Associates. He left for active service in the United States Naval Reserve in 1942, and served through 1945, holding a commission as lieutenant, and spending considerable time aboard the U. S. S. "Augusta" in European waters. When in 1946 he resumed his law practice in Memphis, he formed a new partnership, Garner and Harrison. In addition to his professional activities, he is president and director of the Monticello Insurance Company.

Mr. Garner is a member of the Federation of Insurance Counsel and the American Judicature Society, as well as the national, state and local bar associations, and the International Bar Association. He also belongs to the Counsellors, honorary legal fraternity, and to Sigma Alpha Epsilon. His nonprofessional memberships include the Seldon Society of London, England, and the Lions Club and Petroleum Club in his home city. He is a communicant of St. John's Methodist Church.

At Quincy, Florida, on November 1, 1941, James O. Garner married Mae Random Dunaway of that city, daughter of Roy A. and Mae Jones Dunaway. Mrs. Garner is a member of Les Passes, Chicasaw Bluff Chapter of the Daughters of the American Revolution, the Goodwill Auxiliary, The Memphis and Shelby County Bar Association (Ladies) Auxiliary, the Metropolitan Garden Club, and the Mid-day Study Club. The couple are the parents of the following children: 1. Sandra Louise, who was born on September 13, 1942. 2. James O., Jr., born at Quincy, Florida, on July 24, 1943.

LEE FORLINE WARE

From the time of his return from military service in World War I, Lee Forline Ware was engaged in the cotton brokerage business in Jackson. During the last two decades of his life he headed his own firm. A constructive civic leader, he took a full part in the programs of the Chamber of Commerce and of welfare groups.

He was a native of Moscow, Tennessee, and was born on June 5, 1897, son of Richard Nathaniel and Mary Adelia (Matthews) Ware. His father had come from Virginia, having been born near Richmond, in Chesterfield County, on September 24, 1858. Miss Matthews, whom he married, was born on July 13, 1862, in Fayette County, near Macon, Tennessee. Lee Forline Ware received his education in the public schools of that county. He began his career as a ticket agent for the Southern Railroad at Florence, Alabama. This position he held until World War I, when he volunteered for military service.

He entered the United States Army on May 3, 1917, at Nashville, and was first assigned to the Field Artillery as a private. Later assigned to the 115th Field Artillery, he served as a telegraph operator with this unit, which was a component of the 30th Division. With the headquarters battery of his outfit, he served overseas from May 3, 1918, to April 20, 1919, and participated in the Meuss-Argonne and the St. Mihiel offensives. After the end of the conflict, he was with the army of occupation in Luxembourg for two months.

After his return to civilian pursuits, Mr. Ware began his uninterrupted career as a cotton broker in Jackson. He first joined the firm of L. W. Weil and Company, a Montgomery, Alabama, firm which he served as a representative in his home city. The organization was later succeeded by Clark and Kahn, which he continued to represent at Jackson until 1937. In that year he resigned to enter business for himself under the firm name of L. F. Ware, and he continued to head his own organization most effectively until the end of his life.

When this country was threatened with involvement in World War II, Mr. Ware was named chairman of the Jackson Selective Service Board, and served the government devotedly in that capacity as long as he lived. For his valuable work during the World War II years, he received citations of merit. As a veteran of the first world conflict, he was a member and past commander of the John A. Deaver Post of the American Legion at Jackson, and was also a member of the post of the Veterans of Foreign Wars. Also a member of the Forty and Eight, he held office as chef du train, the title being synonymous with post commander. In consequence of federal recognition, he was appointed major in the Adjutant General's Department of the National Guard of the United States in 1937.

Chamber of Commerce work claimed its due share of Mr. Ware's attention during the mature years of his life. He had been president and a director of the Jackson Chamber of Commerce, and at the time of his death was chairman of the Industrial Committee of the Greater Jackson-Madison County Association. Deeply interested in welfare work, he was former divisional chairman of the Jackson-Madison County program to fight infantile paralysis. Another of his interests was political affairs, and he was always deeply concerned with the problems of good government. He was past chairman of the Madison County Democratic Executive Committee, and had been active in all city and state election campaigns, although he never sought nor accepted candidacy for public elective office himself. He was past chairman of the Tennessee State Election Commission, and a former member of the Madison County School Board. He had also served as a colonel on the staff of Governor Gordon Browning.

Outstanding among the public causes which Mr. Ware served was the American Red Cross. A resolution passed by the local chapter at the end of his life reviewed his achievements on behalf of the organization:

During the flood of 1937, when thousands of refugees came into Jackson, Lee Ware quickly organized the disaster service for the care of these unfortunate people. Through his ability to handle difficult situations, these people were fed, housed and their misfortunes made easier to bear. For his outstanding work at this time he was highly commended by the American Red Cross in Washington.

Later, for a number of years, he served as co-chairman for the local Red Cross in its campaign for funds. The amounts of money raised in these annual campaigns were large, due to the war emergency. He also served as local chapter chairman, and though having many other duties, he never failed to respond to a call for help by the Red Cross.

Mr. Ware was a former campaign director of the Jackson Community Chest, and had served on its board of directors in 1946. He was a member of the Madison County Farm Bureau, and the lodges of the Free and Accepted Masons and the Knights of Pythias. He also belonged to the Conversation

From a portrait in oils by G. Edwin Shofner

Marshall Wingfield

Club of his home city; and as a member of the Jackson Golf and Country Club, was president at the time of his death. His favorite sport was golf.

Mr. Ware also proved himself an effective and loyal worker for his church, the First Methodist of Jackson. He served as a member of its official board, was active in its Men's Bible Class, and was chairman of a building committee which raised a large sum for the construction of a church annex. A resolution passed by the official board of the church at the time of his death paid Mr. Ware this tribute:

During the last few weeks of his life he threw himself unreservedly into the building program of his church. As chairman of the Finance Committee of the building committee, he inspired not only the members of the committee but also the entire Official Board and membership of the church to build adequately not merely for the present but also for future needs. He gave unsparingly of his thought, his time, and his energy to the accomplishment of this goal, and it is to him perhaps more than to any other lay leader of the church that credit is due for a most encouraging campaign for funds to build the kind of church he had dreamed of and desired and worked for so diligently. . . . In the death of Lee Ware we have lost the services of one of our most valued members. . . . The First Methodist Church of Jackson, Tennessee, is bereft of one of its best friends and finest characters. . . . This community has lost one of its very best and most honorable citizens.

An earnest worker in the cause of higher educational opportunities, Mr. Ware had also aided Lambuth College in its financial campaigns.

At Jackson, on November 27, 1926, Lee Forline Ware married Mabel *Winnefred* McClintock. She is a daughter of two natives of Tennessee: David Fletcher McClintock, who was born at Atwood on September 10, 1843, and Kate Maryland (Harper) McClintock, born September 4, 1856, at Jackson. Mrs. Ware was a teacher in the public schools in Jackson at the time of their marriage. They became the parents of one daughter, Mary Catherine, who was born at Jackson on January 8, 1932. On August 22, 1953, she became the wife of Dr. Ben Fred House of Alexander City, Alabama. The couple have two sons: i. Ben Fred, Jr., born in Birmingham, Alabama, on May 25, 1956. ii. Lee Harrell, born May 14, 1958, at Sumter, South Carolina.

The death of Lee F. Ware in his fiftieth year, on January 16, 1947, represented a severe loss to the community, which had come to rely on him heavily for his selfless and effective work as a business leader, civic and political worker, and servant of the church and of welfare causes.

Dr. Marshall Wingfield

Born in Franklin County, Virginia, February 19, 1893, Marshall Wingfield, D.D., Litt.D., is the oldest of the twelve children of Tazewell Tarleton and Mary (Motley) Wingfield. His wife, Marie Gregson, is a daughter of the late James C. and Gertrude (Hoagland) Gregson of Cincinnati. Her twin sister, Anita Gregson, retired in 1960, after thirty-six years as Presbyterian missionary in India and Pakistan. Mrs. Wingfield, like her husband, is an ordained minister. They live at 233 South Watkins Street, Memphis.

Dr. Wingfield's formal education was often interrupted by illness, yet he completed the usual studies without the ordinary procedure and external awards and gained recognition in the most scholarly circles. Tutored by his physician, Dr. R. N. Younger, during a long illness, he was qualified to enter college when, in 1910, he matriculated in Johnson Bible College near Knoxville, Tennessee. Here one could make unusual self-help arrangements and have fellow students from all over America. Many of Dr. Wingfield's school mates went on to distinction, among them T. C. Miller to Admiralty in the United States Navy and Oren E. Long to the United States Senate. When illness struck again at the end of 1912, and a stay in New Mexico was prescribed, even there Dr. Wingfield's studies were continued by unusual help from the New Mexico Military Institute in Roswell. After recovery and an interim ministry, he entered Texas Christian University's Brite College of the Bible for his seminary studies. Refresher courses were almost a passion in Dr. Wingfield's earlier years and include four summers in Union Theological Seminary, New York; four spring sessions in Vanderbilt University and two summers in the University of Chicago. The degree of Doctor of Divinity was conferred upon him by Lincoln Memorial University of Tennessee in 1947, and the degree of Doctor of Literature by Erskine College of South Carolina in 1951. As critic judge for the Pacific Forensic Conference, Dr. Wingfield served in debates at the University of Idaho and Washington State College, 1927-30. He was trustee of Southern Union College 1953-57. He has given baccalaureate sermons and commencement addresses in many colleges and universities and served as Religious Emphasis Week leader in even more.

Ordained a minister of the Christian Church, November 10, 1912; pastorates in Virginia, Idaho and Mississippi before serving First Congregational Church of Memphis, 1937 to retirement in 1958; delegate to World Christian Endeavor Convention, London, 1926; president State Convention Christian Churches in Mississippi, 1936; interchange preacher between England and United States 1926, 1927, 1930; co-founder Institute of Religious Education at University of Idaho, 1929; director Seminary Foundation of Vanderbilt University, 1946-49; moderator Kentucky-Tennessee Conference of Congregational Churches, 1939-40; corporate member American Board of Commissioners for Foreign Missions, 1940-42; president Memphis Ministers Association (all denominations) 1943-44; delegate to Federal Council of Churches' Study Conferences on Just and Durable Peace, Delaware, Ohio, 1942, and Cleveland, 1945; visited United States military installations with priest and rabbi speaking for inter-group understanding; 1945; delegate to Congregational General Councils 1940,1952, and to 6th International Congregational Council, 1949; preacher for interdenominational union church services in Boston six weeks of summer, 1947; president Memphis Council of Churches, 1946-47, 1953-59;

inaugurated radio (WMPS) program of religious news in 1945 and still (1960) conductor of it; delegate to Constituting Convention National Council of Churches, Cleveland, Ohio, 1950; preacher for the American Church in Paris, April 1951; supply minister in Portland and Hawaii, 1958; interim pastor First Congregational Church, Portland, Oregon, 1959; most interesting assignment: preaching for the Nez Perce Indians of Idaho, through an interpreter, August 16, 1936.

Dr. Wingfield is author of the following books: A History of Caroline County, Virginia, 1924; Forces of Destiny, 1932; Translating Christmas and other Poems, 1933; Nostalgia and Other Poems, 1937; Hills of Home, 1938; The Marriage Bonds of Franklin County, Virginia, 1939; The Deathless Preacher, 1942; Literary Memphis, 1942; The Shrine in a Temple, 1943; Boston Sermons, 1947; An Old Virginia Court, 1948; The Life and Letters of General A. P. Stewart, 1954; Strangers First, 1958; Leila Scott's First Century, 1960.

In addition to the foregoing, Dr. Wingfield is co-author of or contributor to other books as follows: History of Henry County, Virginia (with J. P. A. Hill) 1925; American Poetry Anthology, 1927; Windows and Wings, 1928; Harmony of Voice Methods (a text book), 1931; Washington Sermons, 1932; Christmas Lyrics, 1936; American States Anthology, 1936; Year Book of Contemporary Poetry, 1936; American Voices, 1936; American Lyric Poetry, 1936; The Crown Anthology of Verse, 1937; The World's Fair Anthology of Verse, 1938; Strength for Service, 1942; Worship Highways, 1943.

A list of Dr. Wingfield's writings made when Erskine College conferred the degree of Doctor of Literature on him in 1951 recorded nearly one hundred other items, including monographs, magazine articles and introductions to the books of other authors. Other literary activities include initiation on February 22, 1941, of a radio (WMCA) program, The Voice of Books, and the review of a book every week; Mid-South correspondent, The Christian Century, 1940-1955 and Religious News Service 1943.

Dr. Wingfield's address on George Washington was published in a volume of thirty-four prize-winning sermons by the George Washington Bicentennial Commission, 1932; he made the dedicatory address June 3, 1941, when Beauvoir was set apart as a Southern Shrine; was lecturer for World Affairs Forum, University of Tennessee, 1942; received the Pro Bono Publico award for promoting inter-group understanding in Memphis, 1944; made the address in Biloxi, Mississippi, dedicating the Jefferson Davis highway June 3, 1945; lectured on Atomic Fission Tomorrow before the Daughters of the Confederacy in Arkansas, read into the Congressional Record, December 13, 1945; a Memphis thoroughfare named Wingfield Road in his honor, 1946; appointed member of Second National UNESCO Conference in Cleveland 1949, by the U.S. Secretry of State and his address at this conference published in Liberty Quarterly, volume 44, No. 3, 1949; his address May 23, 1949, dedicating

Booker T. Washington's birthplace as a Virginia shrine was published in Vital Speeches of the Day, June 15, 1949; his lecture on R. E. Lee, Memphis, January 19, 1953, was published in Vital Speeches of the Day, February 15, 1953; he was given citywide testimonial dinner 1952 in recognition of ministry of reconciliation in Memphis; and he was a member of President's Committee for Traffic Safety and delegate to Southern Regional Traffic Safety Conference, 1958.

On the services of his grandfather, Pinckney Greene Wingfield of the Tenth Virginia Cavalry, C.S.A., Dr. Wingfield early joined the Sons of Confederate Veterans, served as camp commander and as state commander in both Mississippi and Tennessee; chaplain-in-chief, historian-in-chief and commander-in-chief. In the historian's office he was succeeded by noted editor-author, Douglas Southall Freeman. He was sponsor for restoration of Stratford, birthplace of R. E. Lee, 1935; awarded Distinguished Service Medal by the S.C.V., 1938; commissioned member of staff of J. N. McCord, Governor of Tennessee, 1945, aide-de-camp with rank of colonel; on staff of General J. W. Moore, 1950, aide-de-camp with rank of colonel; on staff of General J. F. Howell with rank of colonel; Memorial Day address in Amphitheatre of Arlington National Cemetery, 1946, read into the Congressional Record June 24, 1946; speaker in Elmira, N. Y., June 6, 1946, at first locally-sponsored meeting ever held at the North for honoring Confederate dead; addresses in 1948, 1950 and 1951, to cadets of Flight Training Course, Naval Air Station, Pensacola, published with introduction by Admiral J. W. Reeves, chief of Naval Air Training Command; Wing (Tenn.) chaplain of Civil Air Patrol of United States Air Force, 1956, with rank of lieutenant colonel; received annual citizenship award from Post 684, Veterans of Foreign Wars, April 4, 1956.

Dr. Wingfield was co-founder of Gailor Hall Home for Boys in 1939 and board chairman 1941-47; co-founder and first secretary of the Memphis Interracial Commission May 5, 1940; member national panel of American Arbitration Association since 1942; life member of the boards of the Y.M.C.A., and the Salvation Army in Memphis; member Community Fund Council; director of the Memphis branch of the American Cancer Society; founder of the Memphis Round Table, 1944; Memphis Council of Social Workers, president 1944-45; and organizer and first chairman, Memphis unit, American Christian Palestine Committee, March 1947. On April 30, 1960, he received the Citizenship Award of the Newspaper Guild of Memphis—"Because you have practiced what you preached—the Gospel of Hope."

Member of the Alpha Epsilon chapter of Kappa Alpha, Memphis, frequent convivium speaker and author of the Lee section in the current Pledge Manual, he also holds all Mason degrees in both Scottish and York Rites, including the honorary Thirty-third Degree and Red Cross of Constantine; Wise Master of Calvary Chapter, Knights Rose Croix; Master of Memphis

Katharine Vincent Black   *Roy Watterson Black*

Masonic Veterans Association, 1950; chaplain of Al Chympia Temple, A.A.O.N.M.S., 1938-1948; chaplain of the Imperial Council of the Shrine under Frank S. Land, 1955; chaplain oft he Grand Lodge (F. & A.M.) of Tennessee in 1955. As proxy of Grand Master R. L. Allen, who was ill, Dr. Wingfield laid the cornerstone of the temple of McLemore Avenue Lodge, No. 715, on December 30, 1954.

His historical interests include: President Monroe County (Miss.) Historical Society 1931-36; president West Tennessee Historical Society since 1937; member Tennessee Historical Commission since 1939 and of its executive committee since 1941; Ninth District (Tenn.) representative in Southwest Territory Commission, 1940; appointed member Tennessee's Civil War Centennial Commission, 1959; his papers in various historical journals would make a considerable volume.

He has led study groups through Europe 1926, 1927, 1930, and study group through Alaska 1928; member of the American Christian Palestine Commission study group which traveled in and reported on conditions in the Middle East in 1951.

His clubs are: The Tennessee; The Egyptians, president 1955-56; The Cross-cut, president 1941 and 1955; The Executives; Sertoma, president 1945-46; Gavel; Agricultural.

Other biographical sketches have appeared in all editions of "Who's Who in America" since 1938; "Who's Who in the Churches, " edited by E. W. Thornton, Cincinnati, Ohio, 1929; "Who's Who in the Clergy, edited by J. C. Schwarz, New York, N. Y., 1935; "Biographical Encyclopedia of America," New York, N. Y., 1940; "Biographical Encyclopedia of the World," Institute for Research in Biography, Inc., New York, N. Y., 1940; "Religious Leaders of America," New York, N. Y., 1941; "American Authors and Books," 1640-1940, edited by W. J. Burke and Will D. Howe, New York, N. Y., 1943; "The Southerner," Southern Editors Association New Orleans, La., 1945; "World Biography," Institute for Research in Biography, Inc., New York, N. Y., 1948; "Who's Who in the South and Southwest," The A. N. Marquis Co., Chicago, 1952; also an introductory sketch in "An Old Virginia Court" (1948), by the late Karl F. Eaheart, Jr., chaplain in the United States Army.

Roy Watterson Black

By occupation, Roy W. Black has been for some years a dealer in farm machinery at Bolivar. There he has been prominent in municipal affairs as alderman and mayor, and among his many interests is regional history. He serves on the executive committee of the Tennessee Historical Commission.

Of Scotch-Irish descent, he was born near Toone, in Hardeman County, Tennessee, on March 3, 1896, son of James Hardy and Sarah Frances (Walton) Black. His forebears had settled in North Ireland following the Covenanter Rebellion, and a later generation migrated to the American colonies. They settled first in Pennsylvania, whence they moved to South Carolina and ultimately to Tennessee. The family lineage follows this biography.

Roy W. Black attended state and county public schools, but did not seek a college education. Reared on his father's farm, he remained there until March, 1918. Then attracted to business, he entered the employ of T. E. Anderson, later Anderson and Yarbrough, automobile dealers operating a Ford agency at Bolivar. This firm was later renamed the Bolivar Auto Company. Remaining with the organization for eleven years, Mr. Black advanced to the position of shop foreman.

Leaving the company on May 1, 1929, he organized the Black Auto Company, which he managed and directed. In October, 1939, under the firm name of Black Farm Equipment Company, he became a dealer in the International Harvester Company's line of farm equipment. He has held this franchise since, and the firm has enjoyed steady growth to its present status as one of the largest of its type in the area. Its present location is 202-206 South Water Street, Bolivar.

Mr. Black rendered military service to his country at the time of World War I. Enlisting on May 6, 1918, he went to Camp Buell, Kentucky, and was transferred from there to the Field Artillery training center at Camp Taylor, on July 13, 1918. He remained there until September, when he was assigned to the School Detachment, Field Artillery Brigade Firing Center, at Camp Knox. He was promoted to sergeant, January 24, 1919, and was instructor at the French Liaison Signal School from September 24, 1918, to March 14, 1919, when he received his honorable discharge from the army.

In January, 1929, he began his long record of public service to his city as councilman, and continued in that office until, on July 27, 1937, he began his tenure as mayor of the city of Bolivar—the first Republican ever elected to that office. He remained at the head of his city's government until January, 1945. His administration was a capable and conservative one, in the course of which the city's indebtedness was greatly reduced. Bolivar, incidentally, is the seat of Hardeman County.

At the time of the disastrous Mississippi River flood in 1937, Mr. Black rendered additional services of a vital nature as chairman of flood relief for his county, under the federal government. He continues his role of leadership in his home community at the present time. He has served as a member of the board of directors of the Bolivar Chamber of Commerce, and on various industrial and welfare committees, and he is a past commander of the city's post of the American Legion.

Mr. Black's trade associations include membership in the Mid-South Implement Dealers Association. His dominant avocational interest, genealogy and local history, finds expression in several organizational memberships. He serves on the executive committee of the Tennessee Historical Commission, which has its headquarters at Nashville; and is representative from the Bolivar area on that committee. He is a member of the Society of Genealogists of London, and of the North Carolina, Virginia, and Tennessee Historical Societies. For a number of years he has been engaged in a project of gathering and compiling source material for a history of Bolivar and the Big Hatchie country. He is a probate and research genealogist, and is also a collector of rare and out-of-print historical works, and of records, relating to Tennessee and the Mid-South. A review of his career in "Library of American Lives" has paid tribute to his efforts in these words:

Mr. Black is acknowledged to be one of the few men in his region who have sincerely and wholeheartedly devoted themselves to the development of matters pertaining to the rescue and preservation of matters of historical and genealogocial interest to Tennessee and the Mid-South area, aiding and assisting worthy persons seeking matters of their knowledge, and quite often without remuneration.

In recognition of his interest in this field, he is listed in Vol. 6, Marquis "Who's Who in the South and South West."

A communicant of Cumberland Presbyterian Church of Bolivar, Mr. Black is now senior member of its board of elders, and also clerk of the session and treasurer. From 1932 to 1945, he served as Sunday school superintendent. He served his denomination as commissioner to the General Assembly of 1938, 1947, and 1952. Also in 1938, he was elected a member of the Educational Endowment Commission of the Cumberland Presbyterian Church, and as vice president of that commission, which later, from 1941 to 1951, he served as president. In 1959 he was appointed chairman of a committee to prepare the history of Madison Presbytery for inclusion in a new history of the denomination.

Near his home city of Bolivar, on November 10, 1921, Roy Watterson Black married Katherine Eugenia Vincent, daughter of Joseph Hiram and Eugenia Helen (Whitten) Vincent. To their marriage four children have been born: 1. Howard Vincent, on October 6, 1922; married, March 26, 1944, Nell Janet (Boone) of Jackson. Child: (a) Cynthia Katharine, born at Jackson, August 13, 1948. 2. Joseph Amos, born October 21, 1926; married June 20, 1948, Mary Will (Conley) of Alamo. 3. Katharine, born September 8, 1934; married, June 11, 1953, James Norris Bush of Silerton. Children: (a) James Norris, Jr., born October 3, 1954, Las Vegas, Nevada. (b) Kenneth Black Bush, born June 29, 1959, Meridian, Mississippi. 4. Roy Watterson, born March 4, 1936; married May 29, 1959, Bonnie Sue (Thomas) of Jackson.

The Black and intermarrying lineages follow:

BLACK

I. *Robert Black, Sr.,* a yeoman, was born probably in North Ireland and emigrated to the American Colonies in the first half of the eighteenth century. He settled first in Pennsylvania and then removed to the York District of South Carolina where he died about October 9, 1779, the date of his will. (Will Book, York, 1770-1815.)

He married Agnes   and they had among six children, a son, *Robert, Jr.,* of whom further.

II. *Robert Black, Jr.,* son of Robert, Sr. and Agness Black was born about 1750 in Pennsylvania. He died about 1811, presumably in South Carolina or Georgia.

His wife's name is believed to have been Mary but her surname has not been found.

They had issue, among others *John,* of whom further.

III. *John Black,* son of Robert, Jr. and Mary Black, was born in Chester District, South Carolina, on Christmas Day, 1778, and died in Madison County, Tennessee, in February, 1838. He married first, in 1799, Abigail, daughter of Robert and Peggy Bailey of Union District, South Carolina. He married, second probably a widow, Mrs. Mary Ann Smith, by whom he had two children.

Of the eleven children of the first marriage, the third was *Amos,* of whom further.

IV. *Amos Black,* son of John and Abigail (Bailey) Black, was born January 20, 1804, in Union District, South Carolina. He removed westward to Tennessee and died in Hardeman County, September 3, 1877.

He married, first, September 25, 1825, Lucy Foster, born April 1, 1808 in Union District, South Carolina, died March 23, 1857 in Hardeman County, Tennessee; she was the daughter of Robert and Sarah Foster. Amos married, second, Jane N. Stephens, by whom he had one daughter.

Of the ten children by the first wife, the fourth was *James Right,* of whom further.

V. *James Right Black,* son of Amos and Lucy (Foster) Black, was born October 5, 1832 in Union District, South Carolina and died July 10, 1912 in Hardeman County, Tennessee. He came to Tennessee with his parents in 1836, the family settling first in Madison County. In 1853 they removed to Hardeman County, where, on October 1, 1857, James Right Black married Mary Angeline Gibson, daughter of George Stewart and Nancy (Henson) Gibson and granddaughter of Jesse Gibson (born in 1777 in Virginia, died in 1847 in Kentucky) and Elizabeth (Parmly) Gibson (born in 1784 in South Carolina, died in 1854 in Hardeman County, Tennessee). Jesse Gibson and Elizabeth Parmly had been married in 1799 in Knoxville, Tennessee.

Ten children were born to James Right Black and Mary Angeline (Gibson) Black, the fourth being *James Hardy,* of whom further.

VI. *James Hardy Black,* son of James Right and Mary Angeline (Gibson) Black, was born January 13, 1865 near Toone in Hardeman County, and died November 8, 1938 near Bolivar. He married, February 27, 1895, Sarah Frances Walton (see *Wallton-Walton* VII).

Issue:

1. *Roy Watterson,* q.v., married Katharine Eugenia Vincent (see Vincent).
2. Homer Walton, who married Fanny Hughes Robinson. Issue.
3. Roscoe Hardy, married Novie Garrett. Issue.
4. Ira Wood, married Lilly Mai Reid. Issue.
5. Orien Francis, married Emodine Brumblow. No issue.
6. Ethel Maryann, married Estil Jason Kirksey. Issue.
7. Sarah Gretchen, married Clyde Glasscock. Issue.

VINCENT

I. *Willis Vincent,* earliest proven ancestor of this Vincent line, was born before 1760; he married, first, before 1778, Julia Powell; he married second, in Granville County, North Carolina, October 19, 1781, Rachel Vincent, born Aprli 25, 1755.

Issue, three sons and several daughters, but by which wife is not known (except for Burkett). A son by his first wife was *Burkett,* of whom further.

II. *Burkett Vincent,* son of Willis and Jane (Powell) Vincent, was born about 1779, perhaps in Halifax County, North Carolina (where his father Willis was listed in the 1790 census). Burkett was living in 1841. He was a planter and owned several farms in Halifax County. He married probably in Halifax County, North Carolina,

Elizabeth Rose. Issue, all born in Halifax County, ten children, including three sets of twins. The sixth child was *Hiram,* of whom further.

III. *Hiram Vincent,* son of Burkett and Elizabeth (Rose) Vincent, was born in Halifax County, February 15, 1814; he died in Hardeman County, Tennessee, December 15, 1893; he married in 1847 probably in Halifax County, Katharine Saludia Shearin (see Shearin VI). Following their marriage they, with a caravan of several families, including relatives and friends, set out on a more than six hundred mile journey to Hardeman County, Tennessee, in the fall of 1847. Issue, all born in Hardeman County, ten children, the seventh being *Joseph Hiram* of whom further.

IV. *Joseph Hiram Vincent,* son of Hiram and Katharine Saludia (Shearin) Vincent, was born in Hardeman County, September 8, 1860, and died there October 3, 1949; he married in Hardeman County, December 11, 1881, Eugenia Helen Whitten, who was born in Chickasaw County, Mississippi, August 15, 1864 and died in Memphis, November 24, 1944. She was the daughter of Coleman Carlyle Whitten and Caroline (Henley) Whitten and granddaughter of Levi Whitten and of John Baxter Henley, of South Carolina.

Issue:

1. Minnie Lenora, born November 17, 1882; died March 14, 1952; married Walter Elmer Stone; issue.
2. Victor Ernest, born July 22, 1884; married Myrtle Womack, of Star City, Arkansas; issue.
3. Ethel May, born February 23, 1886; married Raven Baird Long; issue.
4. James Franklin, born March 6, 1888; married Myra Katherine Newson; issue.
5. Floyce Edna, born February 20, 1890; married Orion Parker; issue.
6. Velma Pearl, born January 14, 1892; married Jesse Pitser Blalock; issue.
7. Alice Beatrice, born July 18, 1893; married James Robert Avent; issue.
8. Joseph Hubert, born April 28, 1895; died February 19, 1950; married, first, Emma Gertrude Avent, sister to James Robert Avent (above); issue; married, second, Lillie Wade Ross; no issue.
9. *Katharine Eugenia,* of whom further.
10. Bertha Irene, born March 4, 1900; married Lawrence Reeves Long; issue.
11. John Iver, born April 28, 1902, married, first, Lois Elizabeth Long, sister to Raven Baird Long (above); issue; married, second, Mrs. Mary Cornelia (Stewart) Harris, widow of William A. Harris.
12. Cecil Vaughan, born October 3, 1904; married Erma Ethel Patton; issue.
13. Morris Olan (Biggie), born May 31, 1907; married Ruby Smalley; issue.
14. Mildred Olene, twin to Morris Olan), married Leonard Partridge; issue.

V. *Katharine Eugenia Vincent,* daughter of Joseph Hiram and Eugenia Helen (Whitten) Vincent, married Roy Watterson Black (q.v.).

WALLTON-WALTON

I. *George Wallton,* as the name was then spelled, was born probably in Virginia but possibly in Maryland about 1680-1683. He died before October 31, 1766 (Will and Deed Book 3, p. 517, Brunswick County, Virginia).

He married about 1705, Elizabeth Rowe, who was born about 1685/6 probably in Virginia and died before July 24, 1775 (Will Book 4, pp. 444-446, Brunswick County, Virginia).

They had five children, the youngest being *Isaac Rowe,* of whom further.

II. *Isaac Rowe Wallton,* son of George and Elizabeth (Rowe) Wallton, died before July 22, 1770 (Will Book 4, pp. 29-31, Brunswick County, Virginia). He married, about 1731/32, Elizabeth Ledbetter, daughter of Henry, Jr. and Edith (Williamson) Ledbetter, the latter a daughter of John Williamson whose will was proven in 1732 in Surry County, Virginia. Elizabeth (Ledbetter) Wallton outlived Isaac thirty-one years and died in 1801, having married second, James Rawlings of Greensville County, Virginia.

Isaac Rowe Wallton served as Burgess in eight sessions of the Virginia Legislature 1761-65, representing Brunswick County.

Issue of Isaac Rowe and Elizabeth (Ledbetter) Wallton, nine children, the fifth being *Drury,* of whom further.

III. *Drury Walton,* who spelled his name with one "l," son of Isaac Rowe and Elizabeth (Ledbetter) Wallton, was born about 1761 in that part of Brunswick County, Virginia, that in 1781 became Greensville County. He died in 1810 in Sumner County, Tennessee (Will Book 1, p. 137).

He married September 27, 1785, Grace Ingram (see *Ingram* V). They had eight children, the oldest being *Mabry,* of whom further.

IV. *Mabry (Maberry) Walton,* son of Drury and Grace (Ingram) Walton, was born October 7, 1785, in Greensville County, Virginia. He was killed by lightning in Hardeman County, Tennessee on July 16, 1851. He married in Sumner County, Tennessee, February 23, 1809. Martha Exum (see *Exum* VI). They had ten children, the eldest being *John Ingram,* of whom further.

V. *John Ingram Walton,* son of Mabry and Martha (Exum) Walton, was born July 4, 1810 in Sumner County, Tennessee and died in 1877 in Hardeman County.

He married in Hardeman County, December 27, 1838, Elizabeth Teague, daughter of John C. Teague. She died September 15, 1902 in Hardeman County.

They had among twelve children, the sixth, *Joseph Gray II,* of whom further.

VI. *Joseph Gray Walton II,* or, as he was called, Joseph Gray, Jr. (he was named for his father's brother, Joseph Gray Walton, "Sr."), was born June 27, 1847 in Hardeman County and died March 23, 1904 in the same county.

He married, first, January 4, 1872 in Hardeman County, Henrietta Frances Barham, who died in October 1876; she was the daughter of Edwin J. (Jack) I. and Susan (Cooper Barham). He married, second, March 12, 1879, in Hardeman County, Temperance Ann Ruffin, by whom he had issue three children. Of the three daughters by the first marriage the second was *Sarah Frances,* of whom further.

VII. *Sarah Frances Walton,* daughter of Joseph Gray II (or "Jr.") and Henrietta Frances (Barham) Walton, was born December 16, 1873 in Hardeman County and died in the same county January 1, 1945. She married James Hardy Black (see Black VI).

EXUM

I. *Thomas Exum (Axum),* the first of his line to come to the American Colonies, is presumed to have come about 1640, but it is certain that he was here before January 30, 1646 when a Norfolk County, Virginia, record mentions a brother, Richard Exum. He married Ann, surname unknown and they had issue, probably among others, *William,* of whom further.

II. *William (I) Exum,* son of Thomas and Ann Exum, was probably born in England and died in Isle of Wight County, Virginia, before February 10, 1700/01 (Will and Deed Book 2). He married Jane   . Issue, according to his will, three children, the second being *William,* of whom further.

III. *William (II) Exum,* son of William (I) and Jane Exum, died before August 22, 1720 (Will Book 2, p. 51, Isle of Wight County, Virginia). The name of his wife is unknown. According to his will he had four sons, the second being *William (III),* of whom further

IV. *William (III) Exum,* son of William (II) Exum, died before December 9, 1756 (Will Book 1, pp. 210-211, Southampton County, Virginia). He married by 1745, Patience Purcell, daughter of Arthur Purcell; she died before December 8, 1774 (Order Book 6, p. 395). Issue, according to his will, ten children, the eighth being, *Arthur,* of whom further.

V. *Arthur Exum,* son of William (III) and Patience (Purcell) Exum, was born about 1750 in Isle of Wight County, Virginia, died in Davidson County, Tennessee in 1819 (estate records); married, first, Mary Simmons; married, second, about 1779, in North Carolina, Elizabeth, whose last name is not known; married, third, September 12, 1805, Sarah Davidson, in Sumner County, Tennessee (Marriage Book 1, p. 22); she died before October 25, 1831 in Davidson County, Tennessee. Issue by first wife, three children. Issue, by second wife, seven children. Issue, by third wife, three children. A daughter of the second marriage was *Martha,* of whom further.

VI. *Martha Exum,* daughter of Arthur and Elizabeth Exum, was born in Southampton County, Virginia, February 1, 1787 and died in Hardeman County, Tennessee, May 16, 1868; she married Mabry Walton (see Walton IV).

INGRAM

I. *John Ingram,* the founder of the family in America, was born in England and came to the Colonies, settling in Virginia before 1652. He died before November 20, 1654 in Northumberland County, Virginia (Record Book, 1652-1657, pp. 48-49). He married Jane   , who survived him and married Thomas Hopkins. Issue, named in his will, three children, the second child and only son being *Thomas,* of whom further.

II. *Thomas Ingram,* son of John and Jane Ingram, died before May 21, 1707 (Record Book, 1706-1720, pp. 21-22). He married Katherine, a sister of Thomas Winter. Named in his will were four children, the second being *Charles,* of whom further.

III. *Charles Ingram,* son of Thomas and Katherine (Winter) Ingram, died between August 10, 1754 when his will was dated, and February 11, 1760, when it was proved in Northumberland County (Book 5, 1758-1762, pp. 174-175). He married, first, about 1701, Elizabeth Dameron, born about 1681 in Northumberland County, daughter of George Dameron and granddaughter of Lawrence Dameron, the founder of his family in America. Charles Ingram married, second, before January 27, 1741, Mary Waddy, daughter of Benjamin and Jane Waddy. Of the nine children named in his will, though by which wife is not known, the seventh was *Joseph,* of whom further.

IV. *Joseph Ingram, Sr.,* son of Charles Ingram, died between October 2, 1793 and December 23, 1793, the dates when his will was made and proved (Will Book 5, pp. 519-521, Brunswick County, Virginia). He married, first probably Franciana Gaskins; married, second, but the name of this wife is not known. He had eleven children altogether the last three of whom were by his second wife. The sixth child by the first wife was *Grace,* of whom further.

V. *Grace (or Gracy) Ingram,* daughter of Joseph, Sr. and Franciana (Gaskins?) Ingram, was born September 17, 1759 in Brunswick County (Albemarle Parish Register, p. 32, Surry County, Virginia) and died in 1836 in Sumner County, Tennessee. She married Drury Walton (see Walton III).

SHEARIN

I. *Joseph Shearin (Shearing),* the first of the family now known, was born about 1687; he lived in Brunswick County, Virginia, but later removed to Granville County, North Carolina, where he made his will on September 5, 1751; that document was proved September 5, 1752 and names, among other children, *John,* of whom further.

II. *John Shearin* or *Shearing,* son of Joseph Shearin or Shearing, was born about 1709 and died in Warren County, North Carolina, in 1795 (Will Book 8, pp. 172-174). He was in Brunswick County, Virginia, in 1732/3 where on February 1st of that year his Negro slave boy was adjudged to be ten years old. He had among five sons and nine daughters, *William,* of whom further

III. *William Shearin,* son of John Shearin or Shearing, married Elizabeth Colclough, daughter of William Colclough, granddaughter of Benjamin, great-grand-daughter of Robert and great-great-granddaughter of Matthew and Mary (Warner) Colclough. After William Shearin's death, Elizabeth (Colclough) Shearin married, second, before July 30, 1801. Peter Glasscock of Warren County, North Carolina. A son of William and Elizabeth (Colclough) Shearin, was *John,* of whom further.

IV. *John Shearin,* son of William and Elizabeth (Colclough) Shearin, married, first, Rebecca Walker; married, second, Elizabeth Burrow; both wives were of Warren County, North Carolina; Elizabeth (Burrow) Shearin outlived her husband as is shown in a petition dated March 17, 1827 to sell his land (Deed Book 25, page 222), "Elizabeth Shearin, wife of John Shearin, Ruthy Shearin, William Shearin, James Burrow and his wife Polly (Shearin) and all above for Arrina Shearin under age . . . widow and children of John Shearin . .. land . . . left to said John by his father William Shearin, subject to life. . . ."A son of John was *William G. Shearin,* of whom further.

V. *William G. Shearin,* son of John Shearin, was born in Warren County, North Carolina, in 1803; he married, November 14, 1827, his second cousin once removed, Rebecca Shearin, who was born in 1808-09 in Warren County, North Carolina, and died about 1870 near Bolivar, Tennessee; she was the daughter of Thomas Shearin (born about 1786 in Warren County; died there before November, 1849) and his wife Mary (Durham) Shearin; granddaughter of Frederick (a Revolutionary pensioner) and his wife Mary (Walker) Shearin of Warren County, North Carolina; great-granddaughter of Joseph Shearin (born in Brunswick County, Virginia, died in Warren County, North Carolina) and his wife Amy (   ) Shearin. This Joseph was a brother to William Shearin of Generation III above. William G. and Rebecca (Shearin) Shearin had eight children, the eldest of whom was *Katharine Saludia,* of whom further.

VI. *Katharine Saludia Shearin,* daughter of William G. and Rebecca (Shearin) Shearin, was born in 1828, died in 1867; married, in 1847, Hiram Vincent (see Vincent III).

MALCOLM WELLS VINCENT

Malcolm W. Vincent's rise to prominence in his banking career has been steady and rapid. His proven leadership and executive ability prompted his fellow townsmen to elect him to the Bolivar City Council and later to the office of Mayor of this city.

Born near Bolivar, November 13, 1914, he is the elder of two sons born to William Hiram and Nellie Pearl (Wilkinson) Vincent. Primarily a farmer, William Hiram Vincent has also been associated with carpentry and bridge construction in his native Hardeman County. Nellie Pearl (Wilkinson) Vincent decends from John Benjamin and Sileta (Gay) Wilkinson. He was born in 1802 and his wife, Sileta Gay, was born in 1809, both in North Carolina. They were the parents of ten children of whom John Andrew Jackson Wilkinson, the ninth child, was born December 5th, 1847, died May 19, 1927 and married January 16th, 1872 Nellie J. Reeves who was born August 5th, 1854 and died November 10, 1897; both were born and died in Tennessee. John Andrew Jackson and Nellie J. (Reeves) Wilkinson were the parents of the following children of whom seven lived to maturity and married, Mamie S., George Robert, (an infant), Lizzie M., Jack Tate, Jennie Lou, (an infant), Hessie (Clessie) Lee, Nellie Pearl (mother of subject) and Hardin Rufus. The ninth child, Nellie Pearl Wilkinson married William Hiram Vincent. They were the parents of Malcolm Wells Vincent.

The father, William Hiram was born near Bolivar, February 27, 1888 and Nellie Pearl, his wife, was born, also near Bolivar, July 31, 1889. They were married April 16, 1911 and reside near Whiteville, in aforesaid county. Their other son Jack Tate, and wife Kathleen (Crowley) Vincent reside with them.

The Vincent forebears were seated in England by the mid-13th century, and members of this family were in Virginia by the mid-17th century.

The proven line of William Hiram is through Willis Vincent (born before 1760 and his wife, Julia Powell (Willis married second, October 19, 1781, Rachel (   ) in Granville County, North Carolina). The known children of Willis are three sons: Burkett, Noah and Stephen. There were some daughters, though their names are not known.

Next in William Hiram's line was Burkett Vincent (born c-1779) by

Malcolm Vincent Jr.

Grace Elizabeth Baker Vincent

first wife Julia Powell; married (c-1810 Halifax County, North Carolina) Elizabeth Rose among their ten children was Hiram Vincent, born February 15, 1814 in Halifax County, died December 15, 1893 in Hardeman County, Tennessee; grandfather of William Hiram Vincent, father of our subject.

Hiram Vincent married in 1847 Katharine Saludia, daughter of William G. and Rebecca (Shearin) Shearin of Warren County, North Carolina. Soon after their marriage Hiram and his bride, in company of a caravan of relatives and neighbors began their long journey of more than 600 miles to Hardeman County, Tennessee, where they settled near Bolivar.

Of their ten children, only three reached full maturity and married: (a) Mary Frances (October 11, 1849-October 18, 1927) married Joe Wellons and removed to near Jonesboro, Arkansas and left issue. (b) Joseph Hiram (September 8, 1860-October 3, 1949) q.v. (c) Thomas Anthony born August 13, 1862, died May 7, 1951, married, first, January 26, 1882 Georgia Annie Largent born March 26, 1866, died December 25, 1910 in Fayette County, Tennessee, daughter of William Largent and Lucy Ann (Everette) Largent, who had five children: Jess, Mollie, Georgia Annie (grandmother of subject) Fannie and Ada. Thomas Anthony Vincent was the father of fifteen children by his first marriage of whom ten lived to maturity; Ida May, Florence Wilma, Alice Nora, William Hiram, (father of subject) Booker Lee, Iler, Joseph Lester, Jesse Alvin, Lucy Ella, Marcus Leon, Edna Estella, Thomas Aubrey, Virgie Pauline, Euel Austin, and Knoxie Lorina. Thomas A. Vincent married as his second wife, Mrs. Hattie (Newsom), widow of Benjamin Pirtle, by whom he had three daughters, Inez, Gladys and Mabel. His second wife had one daughter by her first marriage, Alma Pirtle.

Malcolm W. Vincent attended grammar school in Whiteville, graduating from high school there in 1933; following this with one year of business school.

He began his business career as bookkeeper for the Black Motor Company in Bolivar September 10, 1934; the company was owned and operated by Roy W. Black. On February 10th, 1941 he joined the Hardeman County Savings Bank as bookkeeper.

Answering the call to active military duty, he left the bank—on a leave of absence—to serve in the United States Army for the duration of World War II, serving from July 1, 1943 to March 5, 1946, with overseas duty from December 1944 to September 1945. His tour of duty extended to England, France and Belgium. Decorations and citations for military service were the American Service Medal, Good Conduct Medal, European African Middle Eastern Service Medal with one Bronze Star and World War II Victory Medal. He was assigned to the 165th Finance Disbursing Section while serving in the European Theater of Operations and honorably discharged as a Technician Fifth Grade from the service at Fort McPherson, Georgia, on March 5th, 1946.

He is a member of the American Legion Post 84 and Veterans of Foreign Wars, James David McAnulty Post 2949.

Returning to Bolivar he resumed his position at the bank as teller, moving into the position as an assistant cashier one year later. In 1949 he became a director and then was appointed cashier in 1952; he was named executive vice president on July 1st, 1956 and has held this position since. In May 1952 he was elected for a three year term to the Executive Council of the Tennessee Bankers Association.

He served as a member of the Bolivar City Council, January 1947 to January 1949 and two years later as Mayor, January 1951 to May 31, 1957. During the interim (1949-1950) between his services as alderman and mayor he served as secretary of the City Public Utility Board.

During his tenure of office as mayor he appeared before the Federal Power Commission in Washington, D. C. to petition for natural gas for the City of Bolivar in May 1953. Also in this same year street paving for the entire City of Bolivar was completed. In 1954 the first City Hall was erected in which was quartered the city jail, fire department and the Bolivar Electric Department.

A major improvement in the Water and Sewage System of Bolivar was completed in 1956, the first of importance since the original installation in 1928.

The City Charter in which Bolivar was classified a City instead of Town, along with other major revisions was enacted by the State Leglsiature in 1953.

He was chosen "The Small Town Mayor of the Year" by the Tennessee Municipal League at the State Convention held at Nashville in May 1954.

On July 6, 1953 he became a member of the Bolivar Rotary Club and also has served as president of the Bolivar Chamber of Commerce. He is a director and secretary of the Bolivar Development Corporation.

For the past twelve years he has served as a member of the Board of Elders of the Bolivar Cumberland Presbyterian Church being ordained on July 27, 1947.

Malcolm Vincent and Grace Elizabeth Baker, born August 2, 1915— married in Memphis, Shelby County, Tennessee on May 15th, 1937. Her father, William Burr Baker, was a farmer, County Road Commissioner and School Commissioner of Hardeman County and Elder in the Whiteville Cumberland Presbyterian Church. He was born June 11th, 1867 and died on January 13, 1937; married December 30th, 1902 Blanche Newsom who was born March 1st, 1881.

William Burr Baker's father, Reverend Samuel Baker, was born in Sampson County, North Carolina on December 12, 1818 and died July 22, 1881 in Hardeman County, Tennessee. He married December 23rd, 1847, Christiannia Amanda Parker of Giles County, Tennessee. She was born May 24, 1828 and died April 15, 1907 in Hardeman County, Tennessee. She was the daughter of Zachariah, son of Jeremiah Parker. Zachariah was born November 19, 1787 and died April 1, 1870 in Giles County, Tennessee. His wife was Christiannia Benthal, daughter of Matthew Benthal. She was born June 14, 1791 and died December 23, 1870.

Reverend Samuel Baker and his wife were the parents of six children: Thomas Jefferson, Mary Elizabeth, Martha Marcella, Amanda Alice, Samuel Berry and William Burr, father of Mrs. Vincent.

Blanche (Newsom) Baker's father, Milton Franklin Newsom, born March 15, 1852 and died June 27, 1903. He married December 22, 1874, Sallie Ruddle who was born April 15, 1850, died May 16, 1911, daughter of Robert K. and Dorothy Jane (Hankley) Ruddle.

Milton Franklin Newsom was the son of Micajah James Newsom, who was born October 20, 1826 and died June 19, 1873. He married, October 29, 1846, Mary Catherine, daughter of Wallace Cosbey; she was born April 25, 1825 and died August 24, 1890.

William Burr and Blanche (Newsom) Baker were the parents of twelve children: William Franklin, Samuel Earl, Roy Newsom, Edward Bryan, Noel, twins (boy & girl), Charlie, Lebert Ruddle, James Eldred, Grace Elizabeth and Eleanor.

J. (JACK) MILLARD SMITH

For more than a decade, J. (Jack) Millard Smith served with distinction as president of Memphis State University. He came to the post from the office of director of instruction of the Memphis schools. He takes a consistent interest in the programs of educators' organizations.

Mr. Smith is a native of Stantonville, and was born on March 10, 1895, son of James Andrew and Annice (Hurley) Smith. After completing his secondary studies in local public schools, he entered Memphis State College. In his senior year there, he was recipient of the fifteen-hundred-dollar General Education Board Scholarship. He received his degree of Bachelor of Science in 1929. The following year he completed courses at George Peabody College for Teachers, leading to the degree of Master of Arts.

Before completing his college courses, Mr. Smith had taught in the public schools of Tennessee, and he continued teaching at the public school level until 1933. In that year he was appointed dean of Memphis State College. Called away from that post to serve as Tennessee Commissioner of Education in 1938, he capably filled that position for a year, then assumed duties as president of Tennessee Polytechnic Institute. Mr. Smith headed that institution until 1940, when he became director of instruction for the Memphis public schools. He held his position as President of Memphis State University from August 1946 until February 1960 and resigned as president of Memphis State University on February 5, 1960, to accept an appointment from the U. S. Commissioner of Education as his representative for Region IV, with headqaurters in Atlanta, Georgia.

Mr. Smith served on the council of the Tennessee Education Association, and he is a member of the American Association of School Administrators. A veteran of World War I, who served in the 40th Engineers in the 2nd Army Theater of Operations, he is a member of the American Legion. His fraternity is Phi Delta Kappa and he is a member of the lodge of Free and Accepted Masons and of the higher bodies of the Ancient and Accepted Scottish Rite. He and his family attend the Methodist Church. The educator is a Democrat in his politics.

On June 21, 1917, Mr. Smith married Linda Dunn, daughter of Dr. and Mrs. William Dunn, of Cedar Hill. They have one son, Dr. Will Dunn Smith, born on July 18, 1918.

FRED OGLE BERRY

Over the years, members of the Berry family have rendered efficient, devoted, and highly capable service to the people of Knoxville as trained morticians and funeral directors. Fred Ogle Berry is now president of the Berry Funeral Home, at 3704 Chapman Highway. In addition, he has been a pioneer in airplane ambulance service, having established the first such service in the United States in 1947.

Mr. Berry is a native of Knox County, and he was born on November 6, 1912, son of Ralph Lawson and Myrtle Ethel (Henderlite) Berry. His father, in addition to his profession of funeral directing, was a farmer, and also conducted a successful business, quarrying molding clay which he shipped to all parts of the South. The Berrys were among Tennessee's earliest settlers, and there still remains in the family an intact land grant of some two hundred acres which became the property of their forebears before Tennessee was admitted as a state. This grant is in the Fourteenth District of Knox County, in the Mount Olive community. Fred O. Berry has a maternal ancestor who was a sister of General John Sevier.

Attending the public schools of Knoxville, Fred O. Berry graduated from Young High School in that city in 1933. He decided early in life to follow his father's profession, and to train for his career, entered the Gupton-Jones College of Mortuary Science at Nashville, graduating there in the fall of 1933 with his license as a mortician.

Immediately afterward, he began his career with the Ralph L. Berry Funeral Home in Knoxville, which was managed by his father. They operated this funeral home until 1936, when Ralph L. Berry resigned as its head and established the Goodwill Funeral Home, located at 1406 South Gay Street. In this he was joined by his cousin, Edward S. Weigel, as well as his son Fred. They remained partners, with Ralph L. Berry as president, until the latter's death in 1951. Meantime, in 1938, the name was changed to its present form,

Fred O. Berry, Sr.

Berry Funeral Home. Over the years, additional partners have joined the organization. Earl H., another son of the founder and brother of Ralph L., Jr., became a member in 1941. In 1948 the firm was re-established at its present location, a new building of modern design with all the facilities to enable them to render the highest standard of service. Since 1946 Berry Funeral Home has been a corporation. Ralph L. Berry, Sr., was president until his death, and during that period, Mr. Weigel was vice president and Fred O. Berry secretary-treasurer. The latter became president and general manager on March 8, 1951, and Ralph L., Jr., is secretary-treasurer. Two sons of Fred O. Berry have joined the organization in recent years: Fred O. Jr., in 1955 and G. Edward in 1957. They, and all others connected with the operation of the funeral home, are licensed embalmers. The funeral parlors are of impressive design and the entire establishment has the latest and most suitable equipment. Ambulances and cars are of the latest design. The organization renders the highest quality service, responsive to the requirements of all who come to its doors in time of trouble. It is an impressive and dignified funeral home, capably managed.

At the time of World War II, Fred O. Berry was absent serving in the United States Navy Air Force. He became a captain in the 394th Graves Registration Company, which served in the South Atlantic Command.

It was in 1947 that Mr. Berry established the first airplane ambulance service in the United States. This has since been adopted for use in many states. The pilot with the Berry organization was trained in airplane ambulance service in World War II, and has had many hours of flying time.

Mr. Berry himself is a licensed airplane pilot. He has excellent vision despite the anomaly of having one completely blue eye and one completely brown eye.

He has taken an interest in civic affairs in his home city, and he is a member of the Free and Accepted Masons, belonging to the higher bodies of both the York and the Scottish rites. He is also a member of the lodge of Benevolent and Protective Order of Elks. He is a communicant of the Second Methodist Church in Knoxville.

Twice married, Fred Ogle Berry chose as his first wife Miss Georgia Rule, daughter of Mr. and Mrs. Frank Rule. They were married in Maryville, Tennessee, on March 27, 1934. To this marriage all of Mr. Berry's children were born: 1. Fred Ogle, Jr., on October 28, 1936. He attended Gupton and Jones Mortuary College in Nashville, and graduated from Dallas Institute—Gupton and Jones Mortuary College after it had been formed from the merger of the two preceding organizations. The younger Fred Berry served in the army, and is now in the Reserve Corps. He married Marilyn Brooks, and they have a daughter, Kimberlin. 2. G. Edward, who was born on February 3, 1938. He too is a graduate of Dallas Institute—Gupton and Jones Mortuary College. He, as well as his older brother, is associated with the father in the operation of the Berry Funeral Home. G. Edward Berry married Shirley Mizel. 3. Nancy

Clara, who was born on December 26, 1940. She married John Scott. 4. David Andrew, born November 6, 1942. He is attending high school.

Fred O. Berry married, second, Ruth Le Coultre, a native of Knox County, Tennessee. Their marriage took place on December 26, 1943. She is the daughter of L. M. and Mary (Truan) Le Coultre.

HAM PATTERSON

With nearly a quarter-century's experience in law practice in Memphis to his credit, Ham Patterson now has his offices in the Columbia Towers Building. He is a veteran of military service in World War II, during which he served as an artillery officer.

A native Memphian, he was born on August 28, 1911, and is a son of Malcolm Rice and Mary Russell (Gardner) Patterson. He received his early education at Memphis University School, later completing his preparatory studies at Tennessee Military Institute. Appointed to the United States Military Academy at West Point, New York, he was a student there for three years. However, he abandoned his plans for a military career in favor of the law, and enrolled at Cumberland University in Lebanon, where he graduated in 1934 with the degree of Bachelor of Laws.

Admitted to the bar of his state, he commenced his general practice in Memphis the following year, and has continued his professional career in that city ever since, with the exception of the years of World War II. He enlisted for service in 1941, and in consequence of his record of military training was commissioned a captain in the Field Artillery. Serving as a battalion commander in combat units, he was in service until 1945, and spent most of that time in the European Theater of Operations.

He is a member of the national, state, and local bar associations. He has no lodge or club memberships, but is an active communicant of the Idlewild Presbyterian Church.

At Hernando, Mississippi, on December 20, 1949, Ham Patterson married Donna Rey Neil, a native of Illinois. The couple are the parents of one daughter, Margaret Rice Patterson, who was born on July 19, 1951.

JOSEPH MARCUS LAWSON

Recognizing a requirement of industry, and combining imagination and business acumen in satisfying such a need, have been the mainsprings of many a successful manufacturing enterprise. The Lawson Stacker Company of Memphis illustrates the point. A little over a decade ago, Joseph Marcus Lawson, drawing upon his observation of the lumber industry, devised a stacking machine which he has proceeded to mass-produce for a ready and widespread market.

Mr. Lawson is a native of Pike County, Alabama, and was born on Sep-

tember 13, 1901, son of Vernon Davis and Lizzie Mae (Caraway) Lawson. His father was a lumberman and sawmill operator, who also engaged in farming in Pike County where his forebears had been pioneer settlers. Vernon D. Lawson was active in Democratic politics, and served on the county school board for many years. He and his wife the former Lizzie Mae Caraway were the parents of eleven children: 1. Fanny Esther. 2. Joseph Marcus. 3. Katie Lee. 4. Willie Robert. 5. Laurie. 6. Vernon Davis, Jr. 7. John Wainwright. 8. Lizzie Mae. 9. Adam Ray. 10. Sarah. 11. Lyra. The elder Vernon D. Lawson died in 1953 at the age of seventy-two years. Mrs. Lawson was sixty-two when she died in 1942.

Receiving his public school education in Pike County, Joseph M. Lawson graduated from the high school at Troy, Alabama, in 1921. Mechanically inclined from his boyhood, he gained valuable experience working around his father's sawmills. He was only twelve years old when he made a major repair on mill machinery. He was naturally attracted to engineering, and it was his intention to study at Alabama Polytechnic Institute at Auburn. However, the family met with financial reverses, and, after leaving high school, he had to go to work. He took a position teaching school, which enabled him to alternate semesters between teaching duties and attending Troy State Normal School. He taught at Chilton, Alabama, for two years, and in Bullock County for one year, followed by two more years in Geneva County.

After his graduation from Troy State Normal School, Mr. Lawson continued his studies at the University of Alabama, where he graduated with the degree of Bachelor of Science in 1927. In both high school and college, he played baseball and basketball, and he coached these sports throughout his teaching career. The subjects he taught were science and mathematics. He also planned courses of concurrent study that eventually earned him an engineering degree.

In 1927 Mr. Lawson accepted appointment as principal of the Tanner, Alabama, High School. Two years later he was named superintendent of the schools of Limestone County, where he served for four years. From there he went to Columbiana, Alabama, in 1933, to assume duties as principal of the high school, also serving as superintendent of the city schools. In 1935 he ended his teaching career and became educational advisor in the Civilian Conservation Corps.

He first came to Memphis in 1941, as a consultant in the production of furniture, work for which his early experience had well prepared him. The following year, with this country at war and defense production booming, he took a position in the production engineering department of the McDonald Aircraft Corporation. He worked there until 1944, leaving to join a staff of consulting engineers in the woodworking department of Management Service Company at Memphis. During that period, he studied engineering in furniture factories, sawmills, planing mills, and similar plants throughout the eastern

United States, planning layouts, developing special equipment, and working on related problems.

This was ideal preparation for the launching of his own enterprise, and, in 1949, he designed and built the first automatic lumber stacker. Patenting his invention, he put it into immediate production. Within one year's time it was in such wide demand throughout the lumber industry that he resigned from Management Service Company and founded the Lawson Stacker Company in Memphis, which officially began its existence on July 1, 1950. The first plant was on the grounds of the Memphis Hardwood Flooring Company. It outgrew quarters there, and, in 1956, a new plant and office were opened at 540 Weakley Avenue. At that location, today, is a separate building for development work, a shipping and receiving warehouse, and the fabrication and machine shop. The company produces various items of equipment, but all used for the same general purpose—the rapid and efficient stacking of lumber. These items include the Lawson platform lumber hoist, an unstacker, a combination stacker and unstacker, automatic loaders, stack placers, and automatic course makers. It is possible, by the use of such equipment, for lumbermen to stack up to thirty thousand board feet per man per day—as has been proved at a number of plants throughout the South. The equipment has also been installed in such distant states as New York, New Mexico, and Washington, and in Canada. Through increased efficiency it is having a revolutionary effect on the lumber industry.

Mr. Lawson is a member of the Memphis Engineering Club, Pi Mu Epsilon and Kappa Delta Pi fraternities, and the Lions Club, and he was formerly a Rotarian. A communicant of the Idlewild Presbyterian Church, he serves on its board of deacons. His hobby is woodworking, and he has taught this subject. He is also fond of hunting and fishing. In politics he is a Democrat.

At Athens, Alabama, on June 14, 1931, Joseph Marcus Lawson married Gladys Clower, daughter of William Lafayette and Maggie (Herring) Clower. The couple are the parents of one son, Joseph Herring, who was born on August 19, 1932, at Athens. He is a graduate of Central High School in Memphis and of Southwestern University, and he spent three years in the United States Navy as a lieutenant. He is now studying law at Tulane University.

JERRY S. JOHNSON, M.D.

One of Gainesboro's younger professional men, Dr. Jerry S. Johnson has practiced there since he completed his internship. He is a veteran of naval service in World War II, and takes a lively interest in community life, as well as in the programs of his profession.

Born November 30, 1925, at Flynns Lick, Dr. Johnson is a son of Oliver Lee and Olga (Simpson) Johnson. His father, who was born at Whitesbend Community, near Fort Blunt in Jackson County, on May 20, 1894, was a mer-

John Samuel Poindexter

chant at Flynns Lick, and also followed the occupation of farming. In 1930 he served the people of his district in the Tennessee State House of Representatives. He was active in civic affairs. His death occurred at Flynns Lick on May 1, 1952. Mrs. Johnson, the former Olga Simpson, survives him, and lives in Gainesboro. She was born near Waverly, in Humphreys County, on May 2, 1902.

Beginning his education in the public schools of Gainesboro, Dr. Johnson later attended Tennessee Polytechnic Institute at Cookeville, and subsequently was a student at Vanderbilt Pre-Medical School at Nashville. For his professional studies he entered the University of Tennessee at Memphis, where he graduated with the degree of Doctor of Medicine, in December, 1953. Dr. Johnson's studies had been interrupted by service in World War II. Enlisting in the United States Navy in June, 1944, he served until 1946, and was in action in the Western Pacific, China, Russia, and the South Sea Islands. Serving as signalman and communications man with an amphibious outfit, he held the rank of yeoman, and he received a Presidential Unit Citation.

After he had received his degree in medicine, Dr. Johnson took his internship at Knoxville General Hospital, remaining there for two years. Since 1955, he has conducted a general practice of medicine at Gainesboro. He is a member of the American Medical Association, the Tennessee Medical Association, the Jackson County Medical Association, and the Academy of General Practice.

Apart from his professional connections, he belongs to the Lions Club and the Jackson County Sportsmen's Club. Fond of the outdoors, he is especially partial to hunting and fishing. He is a communicant of the Church of Christ. In politics, he is nonpartisan.

In his native town of Flynns Lick, on December 28, 1948, Dr. Jerry S. Johnson married Christine Smith. She, too, was born in that place on November 25, 1928, daughter of Robert Bough and Ara (Chaffin) Smith. Her father was a schoolteacher and a minister of the Church of Christ, and also a farmer. He is deceased, but Mrs. Smith survives and makes her home at Cookeville. Dr. and Mrs. Johnson have three children: 1. Jacquelyn Lee, born October 14, 1949, in Nashville. 2. Jerry Richmond, born in Memphis on May 30, 1952. 3. Don Oliver, born in Knoxville on January 23, 1955.

JOHN SAMUEL POINDEXTER

One of the major figures in the Coca-Cola beverage interests in the South, John Samuel Poindexter was for many years treasurer of the Savannah Coca-Cola Bottling Company, although he was a resident of Chattanooga, Tennessee, throughout most of his mature life. In addition to his major occupation, he had banking and commercial interests; was well known as one of the city's most constructive workers in civic causes; and was everywhere respected as a man of integrity and ability.

Mr. Poindexter, who first came to Chattanooga in 1899, was a native of

Forest, Virginia, having been born there on February 8, 1874, son of Richard Watts and Mary Ellen (Lee) Poindexter. Among his forebears, were some of the more prominent of colonial Virginia gentlemen. In the paternal line, he was descended from George, Seigneur of Poingdestres, Isle of Jersey, in the sixteenth century, and from his great-greatgrandson, George Poingdestre, third son of Thomas and Elizabeth (Effard) Poingdestre, who came to America and settled in Virginia. It was a descendant, John of the eighteenth century, who first spelled the name in its present form. John married Christian Gissage, or Gizzage, and from them the line of descent runs; Joseph and Elizabeth James (Kennerly) Poindexter; Samuel and Anne Poindexter (Slaughter) Poindexter; Dabney and Mary Eliza, or Elizabeth (Watts) Poindexter; and Richard W. and Mary Ellen (Lee) Poindexter, the parents of John S. Poindexter. Richard W. was born on October 8, 1823, and died April 9, 1900. He lived near Forest Depot, Virginia, and served in the Confederate States Army, Company G, Eleventh Regiment, Virginia Infantry. Mary Ellen Lee, his second wife, was the daughter of John Calhoun and Catherine (Newell) Lee.

John S. Poindexter attended Randolph Macon and concluded his studies a short time before he moved to Chattanooga, just before the turn of the century. His first business connection was with the Chattanooga Medicine Company. In 1905 he became interested in the Coca-Cola bottling business, which had been founded at Atlanta a few years before and had made rapid strides in winning public acceptance for its beverage product. A short time after he joined the firm, he was transferred to Savannah to develop the Coca-Cola interests there. In 1912, however, he returned to Chattanooga where he made his home until the end of his life. He remained secretary and treasurer of the Savannah Coca-Cola Bottling Company. Local business interests included the vice presidency of Arrow Transfer Company, and directorship of the Commercial National Bank, both of Chattanooga. He was a director of several other corporations.

Mr. Poindexter was a member of the Mountain City Club and the Chattanooga Golf and Country Club. For a number of years he took a constructive part in Community Chest campaigns, and was everywhere recognized as a devoted supporter of his city. He was also a loyal churchman. While he retained his nominal membership in the Shiloh Methodist Church of Forest, Virginia, it was the First Presbyterian Church which he attended while in Chattanooga. He was a member of the Men's Bible Class, and gave his earnest support to the church's entire program.

On November 30, 1904, John Samuel Poindexter married Ellen Sharp. They became the parents of three children: 1. Jane, who was born on December 24, 1906. She married, first, Paul S. Steward, and they had a daughter, Pauline Schryber Steward. She married, second, E. Armand Hunter, of Savannah, Georgia. 2. Mary, who was born December 30, 1914, and is now the wife of Winburn B. Willingham. They had four children: i. Eleanor Willingham, who married Harold W. Powell and is the mother of Harold W., Jr. ii. Winburn B. Willingham, Jr. iii. Ann Crosby Willingham. iv. Jane Poindexter Willingham. 3. John S., who was born on October 15, 1908. He married Katherine Rawlings and resides in Savannah, Georgia. They have two children, John S. III and Margaret (Rawlings) Poindexter.

Mr. Poindexter's death occurred on June 21, 1936, and deprived his city and his industry of capable and devoted leadership. His efforts were consistently directed toward the attainment of worthwhile goals.

Pollyanna Creekmore

After brief experience in teaching and having completed her professional library education, Pollyanna Creekmore assumed duties as Librarian of the Calvin Morgan McClung Historical Collection a little more than a decade ago.

Born at Jellico, in Campbell County, Tennessee, on September 23, 1920, she is the daughter of Lewis Millard and Dillie (Creekmore) Creekmore. Her paternal grandparents were Rhucanvy P. and Mary (Lay) Creekmore, while her maternal grandparents were Green Berry and Elizabeth (Chitwood) Creekmore. Both grandfathers were direct descendants of Edmund Creekmore, who came from County Norfolk, England, to Norfolk County, Virginia, in 1650, where he married Jane Wood. Several generations later, about 1787, Robert Creekmore and his wife, Elizabeth Batchelor, went to Nash County, North Carolina, and in 1816, this couple moved to that part of Knox County, Kentucky, now Whitley County, where Robert Creekmore died in 1824. It is through the son, Ballentine Batchelor Creekmore, who married Mary Brown, that Miss Creekmore's lines descend.

Attending the Knoxville public schools, Miss Creekmore completed her secondary studies at Knoxville High School in 1938. She attended the University of Tennessee, where she majored in history, and graduated with the degree of Bachelor of Arts in 1942. At the University she worked as a student assistant in the office of the College of Education and in the Department of History. Twice (1941, 1942) she was awarded the Mrs. J. Harvey Mathes D.A.R. Award in American History.

After teaching the school year, 1942-43, at Greenback High School, Loudon County, Tennessee, she accepted a position as library assistant at the Lawson McGhee Library, the public library of Knoxville. She later attended the School of Library Service of Columbia University for graduate study. There she received her graduate degree of Bachelor of Science in Library Service in 1947.

Since 1947 she has been the librarian of the Calvin Morgan McClung Historical Collection, a collection of historical and genealogocial materials relating to Tennessee and the old Southwest. Since 1948 she has served as secretary of the East Tennessee Historical Society, which makes its headquarters in the library.

Miss Creekmore is active in professional library, historical, and genealogical organizations. She is a graduate of the American University's Institute of Genealogy (1956) and is a member of the American, Southeastern, and Tennessee Library Associations, the East Tennessee, the Tennessee Historical Societies, the Association for the Preservation of Tennessee Antiquities, the National Genealogical Society, the Fort Loudoun Association, and The Tennessee Woman's Press and Authors Club. She is a contributor to historical and genealogical publications, the compiler and publisher of the series, *Tennessee Marriage Records,* and other compilations of Tennessee records. She is a member of the First Baptist Church of Knoxville, and makes her home in that city.

STANLEY JOHN FOLMSBEE

Dr. Folmsbee was born on a farm near South Valley (Otsego County), New York, November 29, 1899, son of Arthur and Clara Somers Folmsbee. Many of his English, Irish, Dutch, and German forebears settled in New York before the American Revolution. His parents moved to Delaware when he was twelve and he was graduated from Bridgeville High School in 1918. He obtained the A.B. degree from Dickinson College (Carlisle, Pennsylvania), 1922, and the A.M. and Ph.D. degrees from the University of Pennsylvania in 1926 and 1932.

He taught history and English at the Columbia (Pennsylvania) High School, 1922-1924, and history and civics at the Smedley Junior High School (Chester, Pennsylvania), 1924-1925. From 1925-1928 he was a graduate student and assistant instructor of history at the University of Pennsylvania. He came to the University of Tennessee in the fall of 1928 and has been teaching history at that institution since that time. Occasionally he has served as acting-head of the Department. Since 1934 he has taught the course in the history of Tennessee.

His publications include: *Sectionalism and Internal Improvement in Tennessee, 1796-1845* (1939); co-editor, *Tennessee Social Science Maps* (1940); four chapters of Mary U. Rothrock (ed.), *The French Broad-Holston Country* (1946); *Blount College and East Tennessee College: the First Predecessors of the University of Tennessee* (1946); co-author, articles on Tennessee in *Encyclopedia Americana* (1949), and *World Scope Encyclopedia* (1950); co-author, *The Story of Tennessee* (1952, 1954, basic school textbook); and numerous articles and many book reviews in such periodicals as the *Journal of Southern History, Tennessee Historical Quarterly,* the East Tennessee Historical Society's *Publications,* and in daily newspapers. He prepares each year an article, "Principal Events in Tennessee," for the *Americana Annual* (Supplement of the *Encyclopedia Americana*).

He is a Past President of the East Tennessee Historical Society and since 1936 has been Managing Editor of its annual *Publications.* He is a member of the Board of Editors of the *Tennessee Historical Quarterly* and has been a

Stanley J. Folmsbee

terly, North Carolina Historical Review, and other journals. His *History of Dickson County, Tennessee* was published in 1956 by the Tennessee Historical Commission and a county historical society. He is author, in collaboration with Oliver P. Chitwood and Frank L. Owsley, of three college manuals to accompany the widely-used Chitwood and Owsley texts in American history.

Professor Corlew married Mary Saille Scott on June 16, 1950. They have two sons, Robert Ewing III, born in 1952, and Daniel Scott, born in 1955.

Enoch L. Mitchell

Chairman of the History Department of Memphis State University, Enoch L. Mitchell has been a student of Tennessee history for the past thirty years. For seventeen years he has offered courses in this field at Memphis State.

Professor Mitchell received his Bachelor of Science degree at Memphis State and his Master of Arts degree from George Peabody College. He has done additional graduate study at Peabody.

He has published in the *Tennessee Historical Quarterly,* "Robert Whyte, Lawyer, Jurist, Agrarian." He has also edited for this publication, "The Letters of a Confederate Surgeon to his Wife," "Nicholas M. Long, Liberal Theologian," and "The Role of George Washington Gordon in the Ku Klux Klan" appeared in the *Publications* of the West Tennessee Historical Society. Professor Mitchell has reviewed books for the *Journal of Southern History, The Tennessee Historical Quarterly,* and for several newspapers.

Enoch L. Mitchell was born November 27, 1903, in Guntown, Mississippi, the son of Elbert A. and Margaret Bryson Mitchell. He moved as a boy to Somerville, Tennessee. He served as County Superintendent of Education from 1932 to 1938 in Fayette County. He is married to the former Ara Reed of Hardeman County. Professor and Mrs. Mitchell have two children, Allan R., a graduate student at Iowa State College, and Mary Kathryn, a junior high student in Memphis. Professor and Mrs. Mitchell live at 3560 Watauga Avenue, Memphis.

Mr. Mitchell is on the board of directors of the Memphis Public Affairs Forum, an organization which he served for two years as president. He is a member of the Editorial Board of the *Tennessee Historical Quarterly,* a member of the executive committee of the West Tennessee Historical Society, secretary-treasurer of the Tennessee Education Association, Western Section, and a communicant of the Protestant Episcopal Church.

---

member of the Board of Editors of the *Journal of Southern History.* He has served as Chairman of the Program Committee of the Southern Historical Association for the 1957 meeting. He is also a member of the Tennessee Historical Society, the West Tennessee Historical Society, the Mississippi Valley Historical Association, and the American Historical Association.

Dr. Folmsbee is a member of the Sigma Chi and Phi Beta Kappa fraternities. He is a Past President of the Knoxville Exchange Club and a choir member in the Methodist Church. He is a board member of the Blount Mansion Association and Credentials Chairman of the Tennessee Society, Sons of the Revolution. He married Ocie Buckner of Chester, Pennsylvania, in 1927; they have no children.

ROBERT E. CORLEW II

Dr. Corlew was born March 24, 1922, the son of Robert Ewing and Mary Ann Leech Corlew, at Charlotte, Tennessee. Both his father's and his mother's forebears were among the first to settle in Tennessee, his father's having fled France shortly after the Revocation of the Edict of Nantes to escape religious persecution. He was graduated from Austin Peay State College, Clarksville, after which he served in the Army Air Forces, in this country and in North Africa and Southwest Asia. After returning from military service he taught mathematics at Dickson High School, studied law at Vanderbilt, and then entered the Graduate School of that University, from which he received the Master of Arts degree in 1949. At Vanderbilt he studied under the distinguished Southern historian, Frank L. Owsley, and wrote a Master of Arts thesis on slavery in central Tennessee. In 1954 he was graduated with a degree of Doctor of Philosophy at the University of Alabama, there also studying under Professor Owsley who in the meantime had left Vanderbilt to establish a new graduate program at Alabama. His doctoral dissertation covered the three decades of Tennessee development following the Civil War, with emphasis upon problems faced in Negro readjustment.

Dr. Corlew joined the staff at Middle Tennessee State College, Murfreesboro, in 1949, and has taught at that institution continuously, except for two years of graduate study at the University of Alabama. While at the Murfreesboro institution he has developed two courses in Tennessee history, one of which is a graduate seminar.

Professor Corlew for some years has been interested in the organization of historical societies on the county level, and has been instrumental in the organization of several such societies now in the state. He is a member of the Executive Committee of the Board of Trustees of Bethel College, of Phi Alpha Theta honorary fraternity, the Southern Historical Association, the Tennessee Historical Society, and other historical and professional organizations. He is a member of the Cumberland Presbyterian Church.

He has published articles and reviews in the *Tennessee Historical Quar-*

PERSONAL AND FAMILY INDEX

(See Historical Index in Volume II)

INDEX

A

Acroyd, Walter Leslie, 561
    Winifred Murrel (Franklin), 562
Alexander, David Almon, 538
    Hazel (Brock), 489
    Jane (Bagley), 539
    Lucille Celeste (Rice), 107
    Ridley Harris, 106
    Vance Jackson, 488
Allen, Dorothy (Strickland), 337
    Elizabeth Anna (Welch), 747
    Fred Leland, 746
    John Earl, 778
    Lucy (Blevins), 779
    Malinda Lobdell (Nobles), 709
    Minnielce (Gordon), 710
    Newton Perkins, 708
    Phyllis (Blanchard), 516
    Purnie Ann (Poole), 562
    Richard Henry, 709
    Sidney Gerald, 562
    Thomas Carelton, 337
    Thomas H., Major, 513
American Investors Corporation, 663
Amis, Alberta (Holmes), 797
    Guy Ballard, 797
Anderson, Doyene (Lee), 752
    Jesse Andrew, 363
    Jo Harris, 72
    Mable Robertson (Coleman), 364
    Nell (Davis), 73
    William, Colonel, 751
Andrews, Caroline (Pound), 165
    Elizabeth Lenoir (Key), 537
    Garnett, Sr., 536
    J. Garnett, 165
Armour, Claude Albert, 749
    Grace (McCord), 750
Armstrong, Dwight Mitchell, 607
    Ellen (Barton), 608
    Lawrence Howard, Jr., 859
    Lola (Smith), 859
Atchison, Dorothy Ann Stovaugh, 844
    Quinton Clyde, 844
Atkinson, Amelia (Appleton), 359
    William Rudolph, 358
Awsumb, Ella (Wells), 790
    George, 788

Aydelott, Alfred Lewis, 138
    Hope (Galloway), 139
Ayres, Margaret Metcalf (McNeill), 362
    Willis Edward, 361

B

Baber, Martha Louise (Gullett), 269
    Rodney Derrick, 268
Badger, Robbie (Gregory), 778
    Robert H., D.D.S., 778
Baenziger, Mary (Kuser), 630
    Walter John, 629
Baldinger, Leo Charles, Reverend, 726
Ballon, David, 743
    Polly L. (Weaver), 744
Barker, Edward, M.D., 307
    Joseta (Ervin), 307
Barnes, Chester Lewis, 491
    Elizabeth Cecile (Taliaferro), 491
Barnett, Mary B. (Stewart), 184
    Thomas Odell, 183
Barr, Roberta (Worden), 736
    William M., 735
Barret, Paul Weisiger, 125
    Sarah L. (Dickey), 125
Barringer, Josephine (Davenport), 289
    Lewis T., 288
Barth, Elizabeth Pike (Ellicott), 263
    Theodore Nott, Rt. Reverend, 262
Bass, Fran M., 141
Bateman, Marjorie Alma (Meeker), 728
    William Carey, 727
Bates, Rosalie (O'Shaughnessy), 351
    Samuel Ogden, 350
Bean, Joseph S., 795
    Mary Frances (Kelley), 796
Beare, Betty Carl (Boothe), 826
    Evelyn (Weatherly), 826
Beasley, Jesse Walker, 547
    Katherine (Halliburton), 548
Bejach, Ailene (Oliver), 534
    Lois (Dilliard), 533
    Wilena (Roberts-Lanning), 534
Bekemeyer, Martha (Barrier), 466
    William Bernard, 466
Bell, Carline (Cook), 727
    Irene (Johnston), 473
    Joel Vincent, 726
    Roy Edgar, 472

Berry, Fred Ogle, 926
 Georgie (Rule), 927
 John William, 502
 Mary Christine (Black), 502
 Ruth (Le Coultre), 928
 Walter Mack, 407
 Walter Mack, Mrs. (Ruby Caroline
  Davis Berry), 406
Billings, Ann Robert (Clark), 755
 John R., D.D.S., 755
Bird, Agnes (Thornton), 184
 Frank Babington, 184
Black, Katherine Eugenia (Vincent), 917
 Roy Watterson, 915
Black Family, 917
Blackwell, Lucy White, 618
Blalack, Adelaide (Fisher), 372
 Bruce, 371
Blanchard, Eugenia Maude (Armistead),
 254
 Jerred G., 253
Bland, John Dietrich, 377
 Virginia Marie (Gavin), 377
Blend, John Francis, 625
 Patsy Joyce (McClaugherty), 626
Blount, James E., Sr., 550
 Margaret Eugenia (Spillers), 550
Bobo, James Herbert, 262
Bodine, Mary Budd (Stewart), 477
 Richard Hill, 477
Boehms, Robert Nichols, 757
Bomer, Edwin Jefferson, 286
 Frances (Meeks), 287
Bondurant, Chester Reid, 353
 Julian Beasley, 347
 May Louise (Harwood), 348
 Merle (Mauldin), 354
 Theo Louise (Miller), 354
Boren, Carolyn Duval (Moore), 253
 James Lewis, 253
Bowe, Annie Mai (Thomas), 482
 Clarence Edward, 481
Bowling, Irma Mary (Kerby), 54
 Winston Turley, 53
Boyd, Angelena (Moore), 636
 Frank Rolland, 636
Bozeman, Barbara Ann (Newman), 903
 Charles Howard, 902
Bradshaw, Frances (Holmes), 311
 William Guy, 310
Brandon, Elvis Denby, Jr., 214
 Helen Holt (Deupree), 216
Branscomb, Harvie, Dr., 8
 Margaret (Vaughan), 9

Brehm, C. E., Dr., 9
 Ruth (Dapp), 10
Briggs, Muriel Lea (Moore), 693
 Raymond Marshall, 692
Briley, Clifton Beverly, 132
 Dorothy (Gordon), 133
Brinkley, Hugh Montgomery, 108
 Olivia Brevard (Langford), 111
Brint, Douglas Laverne, M.D., 383
 Martha Ruth (Harwell), 385
Broderick, John P., 290
 John P., Mrs., 290
Brooks, Berry Boswell, 711
 Berry Boswell, Mrs., 714
 Evelyn Fay (Halley), 719
 Everett Hope, 718
 Everett Hope, Jr., 720
 Judd, 540
 Rena May (Schweikerd), 544
 Virginia Feild (Walton), 714
Brough, John Capen, Jr., 824
 Martha Allean (Jackson), 825
Brown, Bess (Klutts), 831
 Charles Harris, 829
 Dorothy Maurine (Neel), 462
 Ethel Rosalie (Moore), 268
 Jane Roark (Hensey, 137
 Louise (Lewis), 24
 Lytle, Major General, 20
 Richard Bates, 267
 Robert Eugene, 461
 Roy Hogan, Jr., 136
Broyles, Charlie Lou (Barker), 56
 John McDougal, 56
Bruce, Majorie Rutter (Ewing), 490
 Russell Miller Dewey, 489
Bruton, Blanche (Weakley), 628
 Jack Meredith, 627
Bryan, Grace (Marrow), 335
 Marvin Allen, 334
Buckman, Flora Mertie (Williger), 332
 Stanley Joseph, Dr., 331
Buckner, Bernice (Reed), 552
 Elmer Thomas, 551
Bugg, Colden Sparkman, D.D.S., 252
 Elizabeth June (Vogt-Stark), 253
Burch, Barbara S. (Smith), 376
 John C. Brown, 375
Burnett, Hamilton Sands, Honorable, 859
 Margie (Griffin) Beaunard, 860
 Mary (Griffin), 860
Burrow, Aaron Knox, 1
 Evva Agee, 464
 Catherine (Walter), 4

James Weldon, 462
Burton, Andrew Mizell, 849
   Lillie (Armstrong), 852

C

Cain-Sloane Company, 664
Caldwell, Albert Sloo, 616
   Cordelia (Jameson), 618
   Elizabeth Vaughan (Sullivan), 100
   Frank Bevis, 99
   William Addison, Jr., 101
Callaway, Grace Elizabeth (Cuyler), 186
   Lea, M.D., F.A.C.S., 184
Campbell, James Marion, 202
   Minnie Mai (Bond), 204
Canada, Emma (Berry), 899
   John Walter, 898
   Virginia Ware (Broaddus) Moore, 899
Canale, Dorothy (Stoltzenberg), 286
   John Ford, 284
Canepari, Della (Robilio), 638
   Joseph F., 637
Cannon, Margaret (Wilson), 355
   William Dunlap, 354
Caradine, Nancy Kathleen West (Mc-Millan), 217
   Robert Sidney, 216
Carter, James Roy, Jr., 650
   Rosalie, D.D.S., 539
   Virginia Eloise (Fraley), 651
Cartwright, Betty Goff (Cook), 322
   James Buford, 322
   Martha (Kennedy), 126
   Thomas Blount, 126
Cate, Anne Marie (Hutchinson), 904
   Poet Dean (P.D.), 903
Cathey, Frances Charlotte (Heck), 271
   Oliver Edward, 270
Catmur, Eric Alan, 642
   Margaret Croft (Owen), 643
Caudill, Ethel Fern (Alderton), 72
   Robert Paul, Dr., 69
Causey, Evelyn (Lumbley), 708
   James David, 707
Chamberlain, Gay (McFarland), 633
   James W., 632
Chandler, Jean Marguerite (Champion), 814
   John Hughes, Dr., 813
   Marguerite (Johnson), 340
   Robert Owen, 339
Charlet, James Edward, 155
   Martha Elloise (Caldwell), 156

Chase, Isabel (Hibbs), 760
   James Bruckner, 759
Clagett, Alf E., 500
   Linda Tom (Primm), 501
Cobb, Charles Pittman, 341
   Ruth Marie (Moore), 341
Colbert, Maryelinor (Conly), 387
   William Campbell, M.D., 386
Cole, Elizabeth (Law), 780
   Samuel Francis, 779
Collierville, History of, 674
Condon, Alice (Berry), 469
   Marguerite Piazza (Luft), 470
   Martin J., 3rd, 468
   William James, 469
Condra, David Owen, 778
Cook, Evelyn (Terhune), 283
   Everett Richard, 744
   Everett Whitman, 282
   Jesse Burns, 321
   Myrtice Margaret (Goff), 321
   Phoebe (Willingham), 745
Cooke, Betty Lee (Foster), 244
   Carter Gale, Dr., 244
Cooper, Agnus (Pearson), 840
   Argentine (Shafner), 505
   David Acorn, 839
   William Prentice, 505
Cope, Mary Kate (Smith), 55
   Quill, Ed. D., 55
Coppock, Paul R., 831
Corbin, Ladye Mai (Rigsbee), 159
   Tinnon Booke, 159
Corlew, Mary Sallie (Scott), 936
   Robert E., II, 935
Costen, John, 906
   Virginia Ann (Sloss), 907
Cotros, Catherine (Stamati), 632
   George, 630
Coward, Mary (Jones), 122
   Sam B., 121
Cox, Allen E(stes), Jr., 703
   Hortense (Beare), 704
Crafton, Dorislyn (Parker-Jones), 305
   Eugene Calhoun, Jr., Dr., 304
Creekmore, Grace (Blalock), 324
   Marion Virgil, Sr., 323
   Pollyanna, 933
Creighton, Andrew Donelson, 671
   Emma Joe (Stout), 672
Crownover, Arthur, Jr., 337
   Augusta (Maddox), 339
Crump, Bessie Byrd (McLean), 557
   Edward Hull, 555

Crutcher, John Flowers, 571
  Minna Watson (Smith), 572
Culp, Frederick Malcolm, 904
Cunningham, Anne (Rudolph), 574
  James C., 573
Currey, Brownlee Owen, 474
  Frances Elizabeth (Hampton), 476

D

Dance, James Whitman, Honorable, 901
  Mary (Johnson), 902
Darnell, Roberta Able (Speed), 829
  Rowland Hermann, 828
Daves, Blanche Lelia (Hipps), 519
  Gene Carroll, 517
Davidson, Charles Whitten, Jr., 192
  Ethel Marie (Mangum), 192
Davies, Frances Ina (Stewart), 417
  Gillie Mertis, 417
Davis, Eleanor Katheryn (Long), 198
  Nellie Lee (Dunn), 507
  Richard Edward, 506
  William Sidney, 197
Dean, Orville Cole, 218
  Thelma Ethelyn (Percy), 219
Deaton, Clarence Dudley, Jr., 563
  Elouise (Thomson), 563
Deen, Mary Virginia (Culp), 281
  Webb Lowery, 281
Dement, David Barton, Jr., 644
  Marie (Reed), 645
Derryberry, Joan (Pitt-Rew), 296
  William Everett, 295
DeWitt, John Hibbett, Jr., 657
  Sykes (Hewett), 658
DeWooten, Cora Belle (Sides), 524
  Spencer, Jr., 523
Dickinson, John Overton, 166
  Kate Orme (King), 166
Dickson, John McCavley, 862
  Martha Euphrasia (Batson), 862
Dilatush, Katherine Lippincott (Cad-
    wallader), 243
  William Henry, 242
Dobbs, Eloise (Hayes), 721
  Robert Lewis, 720
Dodson, Kemper Harlan, Jr., 113
  Virginia (Sturdivant), 114
Donelson, Janice (Ost), 402
  Lewis Randolph, 3rd, 402
Dossett, Burgin Estel, 509
  Nell (Jennings), 510
Dougherty, Daniel Louis Michael, 378

Florence Mabee (Boone), 183
  John H. Sr., M.D., 182
  Minnie L. (Beck), 378
Doyle, Mildred Eloise, 783
Dudley, Guilford, Jr., 852
  Jane (Anderson), 853
Duffey, Mary (Mockbee), 553
  William Gideon, 553
Dunavant, Dorothy Thomas (Knight),
    220
  William Buchanan, 220
Duncan, I. G., Dr., 889
  Ruth (Henley), 888
  William Joseph Godwin, 889
Dunlap, John Troy, Jr., 698
  Martha Eleanor (Boyd), 699
DuVall, Callie Lois (Davis), 429
  Lloyd Richard, 428
Draper, Katherine (Glankler), 761
  Robert Garland, 760
  Sara (Meyers), 761
Drinkard, Donald, 638
  Helen C. (Polson), 639

E

Eagle, Mary Lucile (McBath), 832
  William Henry, 831
Edenton, Bruce Carlisle, Jr., 705
  Jane (Speece), 706
Egle, Irene (Sights), 685
  John U., 684
Elliott, Charles Robert, 814
  Katie Jessie (McClintock), 815
Elrod, Betty (Garmony), 763
  Cecil, Jr., 762
Emmert, Annie (Goodwin), 811
  Autry Clayton, Dr., 811
Estep, Elizabeth Gladys (Gillespie), 280
  James Dallard, Jr., 279
Evans, Amon Carter, 879
  Brunelle Jennings, 682
  Carol Mae Haynes (Robinson), 880
  Donnalyn Louise (Knight), 879
  Elmer Sue (Ross), 683
  Lucile (McCrea), 883
  Marion Griffin, 544
  Mary Francis (Totten), 884
  Phoebe Olivia (Grosvenor), 545
  Silliman, 880
  Silliman, Jr., 883
Exum Family, 920
Ezell, Mary Belle (Thomason), 656
  Noland Wilson, 656

F

Farrar, Clarence Hamilton, M.D., 606
    Frances (Vance), 607
    Grace (McKee), 786
    Jack T., M.D., 785
    Mabel Frances (Phillips), 584
    Mac, Judge, 584
Farris, Jimmie D. (Wall), 274
    William Walter, 274
Fayette County Free Library, The, 675
Ferguson, Elbert Reginald, 333
    Martha Elizabeth (Smith), 334
Figuers, Alice Amos (Overton), 440
    DeWitt Sherrell, 440
Finney, Elizabeth (Ridley), 91
    John Wesley, 89
    Vellone E. (Palmer), 90
Fisher, Dorothy Emerson (Evans), 484
    William Henry, Jr., 483
Fite, Betty (Jackson), 810
    Elmus Clyde, Jr., 810
Fitzhugh, Gertie (Riggins), 486
    Scott Preston, 484
Fleming, James Surran, M.D., 57, 61
    Josephine (Cliffe), 113
    Ruth (Malcolm), 59
    Ruth Malcolm (Mrs. James S.), 60
    Samuel Milton, 112
Flinn, Beulah A. (Smith), 410
    James Douglass, 409
Folmsbee, Ocie (Buckner), 935
    Stanley John, 934
Fortner, Johnye, (Phillips), 295
    William Harold, O.D., 295
Fourmy, Caroll Frank, 770
    Mary Louise (Ellis), 771
Fowler, Frederick Thomas, 349
    Willie Pearl (Inman), 350
Foy, Bernard Louis, 900
    Evelyn (Maudlin), 901
Frame, Bessie Lee (Brown), 128
    J. Bill, 127
Frank, George Landis, 249
    Nell (Jackson), 250
Frazer, Anita (Lewis), 27
    James Stokes, 25
Frazier, Alfred, Honorable, 309
    Eula Jean (Armstrong), 310
Freed-Hardeman College, History of, 799
Freeman, Gilbert L., 569
    Lois (Akers), 824
    Lynn Barrett, 139
    Max Harold, 823

    Nelle (Brake), 570
Frost, Henry T., 725
Fulenwider, Georgia Deborah (Crowson), 603
    Julian, 600
Fuller, Jeanne (Gordon), 666
    Richard Duke, 665
Fulton, David Franklin, 520
    Ruth Cornelia (Hill), 520
Fults, Chester Lawrence, 634
    Marjorie (Gardner), 635

G

Gilberston, Alberta (Lipford), 737
    Walter Charles, 736
Gillespie, Clarence Earl, M.D., 355
    Dixie Ruth (Denton), 356
Gilliland, Elizabeth Irwin (Jordan), 622
    Frank Marshall, 620
Gillock, Edgar Hardin, 841
    Joan (Frederickson), 841
Gobbel, Luther Lafayette, Dr., 206
    Marcia Rachel (Russell), 208
Godwin, Kira (Dickson), 762
    Ralph H., 761
Gooch, Boyce (Alexander), 374
    Cecil Milton, 372
Goodlett, Frank L., 558
    Sue Neblett (Ely), 560
Gore, John Barnett, 599
    Kathryn (McGinness), 600
Grady, Annie Louise (Veach), 723
    Noah Hamilton, 722
Graham, Edgar Jones, 574
    Kate (Nunnelly), 575
Galloway, Alexander Broadnax, 10
    Elise Chilton (Harrison), 11
Gamble, Minnie May (Snider), 413
    Robert McDuffie, 411
Gardiner, Laurence Bridges, 435
    Lillian Jeanette (Johnson), 438
Gardner, Ardis (Worthington), 809
    George Percy, Jr., 808
Garner, James Ozro, 908
    Mae Random (Dunaway), 909
Garrett, Alleen (Lane), 153
    Dorothy (Roddy), 605
    Ernest Boyd, 152
    Horace James, 604
Gattas, Fred Patrick, 423
    Hollie Eugenia (Wood), 424
Gaylor, Della (Perkins), 725
    Howard B., 724

Gee, Elisha, Jr., 802
　　Mary Snowden (Treadwell), 802
Gentry, Lon Glenard, 685
　　Myrtle Ruth (Daniel), 686
Gettys, Adaline (Oehler), 181
　　Richard Emmett, Jr., 181
Grant, Charles William, D.D., 271
　　Mary Anna (Edwards), 272
Graves, Anna Sue (Stephens), 308
　　Argyle, 308
　　C. Edwin, 306
　　Elizabeth Ann (Dillon), 309
　　Joe Gayle, 308
　　Nettie J. (Martin-Smith), 307
Greer, John Lawson, 728
　　Kathleen Russell (Zemp), 728
Grubb, Lura (Johnson), 763
　　Paul Nowlin, Dr., 763
Grumbles, Virginia Frances (Cook), 330
　　William Henry, 329
Guinn, Bob, 511
　　Martha (Shaw), 511

H

Hackney, Frances (Burnet), 906
　　Roscoe James, 905
Haglund, Joan May Wellington (Rowe),
　　346
　　Louis Howard, 345
Hale, E. W., Jr., 896
　　E. W., Sr., 892
　　Emma Turner (Kimbrough), 894
　　Ena Mae (Causie), 897
Hall, Cornelia (Slaughter), 813
　　James Wilson, Dr., 691
　　Jo (Young), 692
　　Roy, 812
Halliburton, Nelle (Nana), 16
　　Richard, 11
　　Wesley, 14
Hamilton, Frances Lucille (Doak), 807
　　John Thomas, 806
Hanafee, Alice (Taylor), 670
　　Anna Mildred (Tracy), 669
　　William Conrad, 668
Handly, Edith (Madden), 64
　　Gustave Miller, 63
　　Vivian (Hagler), 64
Hanover, Helen F. (Lerner), 141
　　Jay Alan, 140
Harder, Bonnie B. (Kirk), 564
　　Edmund Green, 564
Harris, Ewing Jackson, 208

James Lawrence, 194
　　Lena Sue (Hartman), 209
　　Marie (Anderson), 857
　　Martha Jane (Gurley), 195
　　Thomas, 856
Harrison, David Lawrence, Jr., 211
　　Madge (Madden), 212
Harrover, Elgria (Brown), 165
　　Roy Perkins, 163
Harsh, David Newby, 256
　　Helen Russ (Westervelt), 257
Hart, Elizabeth (Lacy), 172
　　John P., 171
Harvey, Abner Brown, 527
　　Elizabeth Senseney, 528
　　George, Jr., M.D., 455
　　Rosa Marion (Fox), 456
Hasselle, Anne (Williford), 426
　　Robert Marcon, 425
Hastings, Alice Ewing (Long), 89
　　Walter Darlington, Sr., 88
Hatcher, Charles Phillips, 521
　　Olivia ("Olive") Hill (Dobbins),
　　521
Hayes, James Ernest, Dr., 237
　　Vesta Lee (Ready), 238
Haynes, America (Smith), 38
　　John Lawrence, Colonel, 37
　　Marjorie (Wistall), 827
　　Percy D., 826
Hazlewood, Ben Primm, 87
　　Lennie Jane (Sanders), 88
Heiskell, Ardeane (McNeil), 842
　　Augustus Longstreet, 841
　　John McCall, 791
　　Margaret (Winchester), 792
Henning, Donald, Reverend Dr., 832
　　Mary (Standish), 833
Henry, Donald Eugene, 280
　　Elizabeth (Jones), 620
　　Harry Edward, 619
　　Joe W(alter), Sr., 591
　　Louise (Ward), 591
　　Peggy (Leathers), 281
Herron, Addie Lucille (Duncan), 409
　　Henry Harrison, M.D., 408
　　Marian (Rice-Tarbet), 422
　　Stanford Morton, M.D., 420
Heuberger, Edith Agnes (Sugliano), 405
　　Leonard, 404
Hicks, Albert T., 353
　　Effie Mae (Wilde), 75
　　Hanorah (Bresnaham), 353
　　Hugh Webb, 74

Hill, Elizabeth Eloise (Wilkes), 513
    Frances Crump (Butler), 273
    Frank Fontaine, 584
    Henry Garland, M.D., 272
    Henry Harrington, Dr., 511
    Kenneth Horace, 643
    Lizzie (Willins), 586
    Mary Louise (Karsch), 644
Hoehle, Edward Eugene, Sr., 212
    Grace Hortense (Sams), 213
Hoehn, Agnes Elizabeth (Forbes), 688
    Theodore William, 687
Hohenberg, A(dolph) Elkan, 387
    Dorothy (Kayser), 388
Holladay, Martha Elizabeth (McDaniel), 773
    Richard Gordon, 772
Holmes, Alice (Davidson), 764
    Chester Leon, Dr., 794
    Lorraine M. (Wagner), 795
    Victor Hal, 764
Holt, Andrew David, Dr., 62
    Martha (Chase), 63
Hooker, Eugenia Wimberly (Fort), 115
    John Jay, Jr., 114
Houston, Frances (Martin), 397
    George McKnight, 396
Howard, Asher, 729
    Mildred Frances (Myers), 729
Howe, Carl O., Jr., 277
    Katharine (Kittrell), 278
Howie, Bertha Elizabeth (Garner), 320
    William Kenneth, 319
Hubbard, Elizabeth (Beesley), 642
    George Baker, M.D., 641
Hughes, Elizabeth Kertley (Leavell), 259
    Thelma Louise (Heuberger), 406
    William Frierson, 258
    William Lee, 405
Humbrecht, Carolyn Lucille (Shackelford), 129
    Howard Alexander, 128
Humphrey, Eleanor (Wynne), 423
    Turk, 422
Hunt, Jack Wilson, 274
    Lillie Mae (Breland), 275
    Love (Bright), 819
    Minnie (Echols), 819
    William Calvin, 818
Hutton, Eula (Hood), 849
    Sallie Belle (Pentecost), 848
    William Edward, 847

Hyder, Albert, E., 117
    Ann (King), 118

I

Immaculate Conception, Church of the, 676
Ingraham, Frances Rose (Thomason), 150
    Frank Calvin, 148
    Harold Edward, Dr., 146
    Sybil (Ley), 148
Ingram, Marguerite Ada (Peal), 294
    Minyard Dee, M.D., 293
Inman, Elizabeth (Griffey), 529
    William Oliver, 528

J

Jackson, Irene Romig (Low), 794
    Lawrence Plummer, 793
Jamison, Angelee (Cochran), 587
    C. B., D.D.S., 586
Jennings, Elizabeth (Chenault), 155
    Lyndon B., 154
Jeter, Thomas Walker, Jr., 410
    Vadis (Norris), 411
Johnson, Christine (Smith), 931
    Dixie Belle (Dragoo), 249
    Jerry S., 931
    Lester Eugene, 249
    Linton Carroll, Reverend Dr., 127
    Marian Charlton (Sullivan), 530
    Ruth Louise (Masser), 127
    Seale, 529
Johnston, Helen (Presley), Dr., 792
    Leland Mann, Sr., Dr., 792
Jones, Catherine L. (Sommer), 640
    Eleanor (Johnston), 508
    Homer K., 771
    Lelia (Gray), 360
    Louise Berlin, Mrs., 239
    Martha Louise (Edmondson), 772
    Mary Lou (Stephenson), 293
    Paul Tudor, 240
    Robert Floyd, 291
    S. Walter, 639
    Stephen Kent, 507
    Walk Claridge, Jr., 359

K

Kearney, Merlin Francis Xavier, Rt. Reverend, 403
Keatheley, Maurice Franklin, Sr., 776
    Ruby Geneva (Haskins), 777

Kelsey, Ella Katharine (Dudney), 317
    Richard Forrest, M.D., 317
Kenworthy, Ellen Douglas (Gailor), 398
    Stonewall Shepherd, 397
Kincaid, Beulah C. (Chance), 536
    Robert Lee, 535
King, Clarence Gregg, Colonel, 168
    John Smith, Jr., 458
    Lillian (Turner), 170
    Marion Elizabeth (Canale), 458
Kinton, Helen (Davis), 313
    William Robert, Jr., 313
Kirksey, Versie Jane (Mills), 773
    William Wesley White, 773
Klinck, John Crump, 695
Klutts, William Alonzo, 28

L

Ladd, Forrest, 624
    Harriet Virginia (Worshum), 625
Lake, Donelson Martin, 366
    Gene (Ellis), 367
Langford, Bennie Frank, 102
    Katy Jo (Smith), 103
Larkins, Clarence E., 568
    Marjorie (Parks), 569
Lawson, Gladys (Clower), 930
    Joseph Marcus, 928
Laycook, Lois Graden, Sr., 96
    Ovie (Gross), 99
Leach, Lena (Wetzler), 300
    William Harvey, 300
Ledbetter, Marshall, 555
    Mary Alma (Greer), 555
Lee, Aida (de Leon), 472
    Bula (Gentry), 885
    John Davis, 241
    Robert Edwin, 471
    Robert Greene, 884
Leonard, Marie Elizabeth (Sharp), 68
    Robert Hobart, 67
Lewallen, Celdon (Medaris), 222
    William Buford, Judge, 221
Lewis, Eugene Castner, 17
    Pauline (Dunn), 20
Liddell, Frank Broughton, 378
    Rebecca (Lott), 379
Life and Casualty Insurance Company of
    Tennessee, History of, 853
Lindsey, Edward M., 524
    Virginia (Freeman), 525
Lipsey, Margaret (Storey), 634
    Ralph Walton, 633
Livaudais, Lois Loucille (Williams), 180

West, 179
Lockmiller, Alma Elizabeth (Russell), 31
    David Alexander, Dr., 29
Logsdon, Bernice Elizabeth (Wheeler),
    284
    LeRoy Williams, 283
Long, John R., Jr., 426
    Sarah Ann (Norton), 428
Lowrance, Edward Martin, 704
    Patricia (McPhillips), 704
Loyd, Avaline (Miller), 684
    L. W., 683
Luttrell, Margaret Helen (Moore), 858
    William Walling, 857
Lynch, Doris Lee (McDaniel), 746
    Edward Doss, 745

M

Macdonald, Helen Elizabeth (McCarthy),
    237
    James Clark, 236
MacFarland, Lonsdale Porter, Jr., 201
    Perre Coleman (Hutton), 202
Maclellan, Kathrina (Howze), 161
    Robert Llewellyn, 160
Maddox, Doris Virginia (Edmonson), 86
    Maurice Hunt, 85
Magee, Edith May (White), 402
    Robert Stewart, 401
Magevney, Hugh Michael, Jr., 468
    Irwin (Leatherman), 468
Mahan, Emily (Smith), 769
    George, Jr., 766
Major, Georgia Bell (Tidwell), 593
    Samuel Chester, 592
Mallory, Barton Lee, 478
    Frances (Nelly), 480
Malone, Gayle Ingram, 464
    Mary Elizabeth (Beasley), 465
Mann, Arthur G., 736
    Mabelle (Kane), 736
    William Cheairs, 161
Manogue, Betty Perry (Riddick), 269
    Edith Lyle (Reid), 269
    Raymond Edward, 269
Marks, Dempsey Hunter, 590
    Julia (Wilcox), 591
Martin, LeRoy Albert, Dr., 31
    Ruth (Duckwall), 32
Mason, Elizabeth Armantine (Redwine),
    754
    Margaret (Turrentine), 816
    S. Delbert, 815
    William Bransford, 752

Mattingly, Dorothy Leoene (Doub), 730
    Thomas Jasper, Reverend, 729
Maxey, Mary Kate (Stone), 547
    Tony Black, 546
McCain, Elizabeth Adaline, 235
McCalla, Lacye (Wheeler), 214
    Robert Clark, 214
McCallum, Edward P., Jr., 250
    Raimelle (Musick), 250
McCammon, Ammons Funeral Home,
    The, 686
McCord, Jim Nance, 119
    Sula Tataum Sheeley, Mrs., 120
    Vera (Kercheval), 119
McCormick, Grover Newton, 891
McCrady, Edith M. (Dowling), 33
    Edward, Dr., 32
McElroy, Randall James Denison, 234
McEwen, Betty (Mullins), 750
    Torrance Frazier, 750
McGaughran, Emmett Patrick, 688
    Maude (Carpenter), 688
McGowan, Elmer Warren, 821
    Lucy Charlene (Smith), 823
McGregor, Eleanor (Anderson), 390
    Paul Michael, 389
McHugh, Howard Vernon, 311
    Ruble E. (Milburn), 311
McKenzie, Mayme (Fike), 177
    Roy Edgar, 176
McNabb, Earl Anderson, 153
    Mary Tom (Duncan), 154
McSween, Donald Murdock, Com-
    missioner, 765
    Louise (Valentine), 766
McTeer, Anna Belle (Tedford), 188
    William A., 189
Methodist Hospital, 673
Millard, Beulah Bell (Long), 276
    Walter John, Rev. Dr., 275
Miller, Harry Ray, 364
    Loye Wheat, 34
    Margaret Lucille (Perkins) (Mrs.
      Harry R. Miller), 364
    Sara Vance (Davis), 34
    Theodore Hadley, 723
Miller-Hawkins School, The, 365
Mitchell, Annie Bogardus (Tracy), 433
    Ara (Reed), 936
    Edward Dana, M.D., 432
    Edward Dana, Jr., M.D., 434
    Elizabeth (Capps), 435
    Enoch L., 936
    Katie (Mitchel), 827

William Wright, Dr., 827
Montgomery, Ada (Donaldson), 246
    Frank, 245
    Joel Alma, 332
    Mary Lou (Blue), 333
Moody, Ann Forrest (Godbold), 756
    James Duke, 195
    William Krauss, 756
Moore, Barabara Jeanice (Byrne), 501
    Dorothye Adaline (Nyquist), 649
    Francis Lee, 226
    Nancy Evelyn (Kitchen), 168
    Richard Lawson, Jr., 167
    Thelma Mae (Armstrong), 227
    Thomas David, M.D., 645
    Tom White, 501
Moriarty, Herbert Bernard, Jr., 774
Morris, Nell (Martin), 708
    William Mallory, 708
Morrison, Janie May (Guthrie), 595
    John Franklin, Jr., 593
Moss, Golda (Siler), 145
    W. F., 144
Muller, Georgia Ellie (Kittrell), 108
    Herman James, 107
Murphy, Elizabeth (Shewmake), 85
    Ovie Mildred (Wright), 85
    Slater Abraham, Rev. Dr., 82
Murrah, Corine (Falls), 395
    William Fitzhugh, 393

N

Neal, Roberta (Conditt), 596
    Sam, 595
Neely, Charles Lea, 820
    Ruby (Mayes), 821
Neese, Fred Talley, 356
    Martha (Morris), 357
Nelson, Emmet Henderson, 224
    Emmet Henderson, Mrs., 224
Nesbitt, B. Francis, O.D., 611
    Fay (Bishop), 612
Nevils, G. Howard, 288
    Thelma (Brooks), 288
Niceley, Eugene Park, M.D., 186
    Virginia Dare (Whisman), 187
Nichols, James Doddridge, 246
    Louise Alston (Thweatt), 248
Nicks, Carney B., 548
    James Henry, 567
    Jane (Reeves), 549
    Maxine (Beard), 568
Noble, Bess C., Mrs., 278

Northington, Arch Ewing, 330
    Lillian (Harris), 331

O

O'Brien Family, 368
O'Brien, Allen McQuary, 730
    Allene (Gaia), 474
    Ruth (Helm), 730
    Thomas Francis, 473
O'Donnell, Mary Frank (Hennington),
    261
    William McGehee,, Reverend, 260
Ogilvie, Clarence Cooper, 588
    Jessie Clay (Wright), 590
    Myrtice (Goff), 590
O'Hara, Harry Edward, 781
    Virginia Dawn (Gibbons), 783
Oldham, Hugholene (Wells), 199
    John Newton, 198
Orgill, Catherine (Dean), 34
    Edmund, 34
O'Ryan, Mary McKeon (Fay), 758
    Tom, 758
Overton, Harriet Virginia (Maxwell),
    447
    Helen (Parker), 455
    John, 360
    John, Colonel, 446
    John, Jr., 452
    Mary Elizabeth (Bell), 361
    Matilda (Watkins), 452
    Rachel (Harding), 447
    S. Watkins, 452

P

Paddison, Norwood Giles, Jr., 385
    Shirley Elizabeth (Ham), 385
Parker, Lois (Hargis), 396
    William, 395
Partee, LaVerne (Flippin), 298
    Willis Hunter, Sr., 298
Patten, Elizabeth Nelson (Bryan), 861
    Zeboim Cartter, 860
Patterson, Agnatius, Jr., 159
    Annie Lee (Norris), 160
    Donna Rey (Neil), 928
    Ham, 928
    Robert Franklin, Sr., 297
    Sara Emylin (Jones), 297
Patty, Hubert David, 190
Paullus, Bessie M. (Settle), 579
    George Earl, Sr., M.D., 578
    George Earl, Jr., M.D., 579

Margaret (Pickens), 581
    Mary Elizabeth (McDavid), 580
    Wayne Settle, D.D.S., 580
Peabody, Hotel, 666
Peeler, Nancy (Bradley), 578
    William James, 577
Pepper, Alella Diane (Reynolds), 329
    John Robertson, 2nd, 327
Perkins Family, 444
Phelan, Stephen Rice, 228
Phillips, Thomas Lee, 456
    Thomas Lee, Mrs., 456
    Virginia Denise (Caya), 457
Pickens, John Martin, 390
    Loula May (Pearson), 391
Pidgeon, Frank C., 391
    Pallas (Johnson), 393
Pierantoni, Anthony, 312
    Stella (Murino), 312
Pierce, Alma Louise (Switzer), 125
    William Franklin, 124
Pigford, Clarence E., 413
    Sally Branford (Person), 416
Pi Kappa Alpha Fraternity, History of,
    833
Pinkerton, Estelle (McCombs), 538
    Joe Anderson, 538
Pitts, Dooley (Ferguson), 210
    Fountain Ezekial, Jr., 774
    Jonnie (Bailey), 775
    Justin, 210
Poindexter, Duke, 191
    Ellen (Sharp), 932
    John Samuel, 931
    Joy (Roberson), 191
Porch, Davis Scott, Jr., 576
    Marie (Stone), 576
Porter, James Martin, 158
    Virginia Lee (Patton), 159
Powers, Helen (Hill), 611
    James Morris, D.D.S., 610
    Sue McFall, Dr., 263
Pressnell, Lottie Willee (Blocker), 843
    Wayne, 843
Preston, Effie B. (Case), 36
    Howard Payne, 35
Price, Anderson Lacy, 93
    Nellie Vesta (Mays), 96
Pride, Marguerite (Warner), 252
    William Thomas, M.D., 251
Prince, Audrey (Parker), 226
    Roland, 225
Proctor, Frank Scott, 655
    Patty Brown (Harvey), 656

Putnam, Carolyn (Brasfield), 306
    Lyle Lee, 305

Q

Quarles, Robert Thomas, Jr., 193

R

Rainer, Dorothy Gwyn (Cooke), 424
    James Connell, Jr., 424
Raulston, Samuel Robert, 775
    Sue (Brown), 776
Reams, Avaligne O. (Edgington), 742
    Chatham Coffee, 741
Reed, Forrest F., 342
    Katherine Ruth (Mueller), 344
    Mary Magdalene (Gatlin), 780
    William Ashmore, 780
Regan, Martina Elizabeth (Shea), 144
    Richard John, 142
Reynolds, Christine C., Mrs., 122
    Richard Herman, 123
Rhodes, Alice (Archer), 5
    Peyton Nolle, Dr., 5
Rice, Edna Earle (Curdts), 655
    William Russell, Sr., 654
Richardson, Alvy (Holt), 806
    Ann (Mussenden), 494
    Lillian Alpine (Wesson), 496
    St. George Tucker, 492
    Thomas Walker Gilmer, 494
    William Allen, 805
Ridenour, Alice Ruth (Dockery), 224
    James Carson, Sr., 223
Riechman, Gladys (Fox), 533
    John August, 531
Roberson, Caroline (Allen), 178
    Lee, D.D., L.L.D., 178
Robertson, Caffey, 103
    Louise Patterson (Le Master), 104
Robilio, Angelina (Ponzano), 679
    John Pietro, 679
Robinson, Aaron Balbew, 75
    Agnes Maureen Jefferson (Branch),
    76
    Barbara Ann (Bright), 131
    Edward Gale, 130
    Garner, 129
    Henrietta Estelle (von Niedhauser),
    130
    Linda (Dunlap), 725
    Thomas Lee, 725
Robison, Daniel Merritt, Dr., 39
    Dorothy May (Battenfield), 40

Roller, Nettie (Kociencki), 526
    Paul E., 525
Roper, Estelle (Brassil), 403
    Eugene A., Jr., 403
Rose, Frank Lee, 65
    Mae (Bowers), 66
Ross, Blair Arthur, 804
    Jones Wesley, 156
    Louisa (Malone), 157
    Sarah Alice (Murray), 805
Rothrock, Mary Utopia, Dr., 40
Rucks, Edward Lindsey, 694
    Elizabeth Ann (Ross), 695
Russell, Laura (Jobe), 817
    Lawrence Millard, 690
    Martha Katherine (Exum), 93
    Paul Herriford, 816
    Ruth (Breeding), 691
    Simpson, 91

S

Sanford, Fay Gray, 357
    Frances Lillian (Howell), 357
Saulsberry, Alfred Woodrow, 230
    Helen Margaret (Carr), 231
Schadt, Harry Elmer, Sr., 210
    Teresa Helene (Murphy), 211
Schaeffer, Joseph Henry, Jr., 681
    Opal (Jack), 682
Scott, Cleo (Meador), 175
    George Ryland, Jr., 172
Seay, Frances Anne (Ragsdale), 318
    Hilma Ruby (Wilson), 188
    James Irby, 187
    James Irby, Jr., 318
Seelbinder, Arthur, 487
    Clara Elizabeth (Owen), 488
Sellari, Anita (Pellonari), 678
    Artiode, 676
    Ernesta (Giancarli), 678
Servier, Dottie Ann (Mapes), 57
    Lewis Valentine, III, 56
Shappley, Arnold, Jr., 769
    Kathryn Elizabeth (Billingsley), 770
Sharp, Sarah (Robinson), 42
    Vernon Hibbett, 42
Shea, Catharine (Flanagan), 700
    Gwyn (Rainer), 702
    John Joseph, M.D., 699
    John Joseph, Jr., M.D., 701
    Martin Flanagan, 702
Sheahan, Frances Catherine (Riling), 597
    Robert Francis, 596
Shearin Family, 921

Sheftall, John Parry, 670
　　Lillian (Warner), 671
Shelton, Ann Anderson (Roess), 498
　　Hugh Todd, Jr., 497
Shepherd, Aud Lee, 231
　　Hazel Belle (White), 232
Sherrell Family, 445
Shields, Arlie (Cox), 604
　　David William, Jr., 603
Shipp Family, 868
Shipp, Agnes W., 868
Short, Morgan Keith, 628
　　Rosita (Scheyer), 629
Shorter, Carl William, 653
　　Jo Ann (Franklin), 654
Shults, John Arch, D.D.S., 724
　　Pauline (Newman), 724
Slavick, Henry William, 325
　　Lenore (O'Hara), 327
Sloan, Elmer Roy, 706
　　Eugene Holloway, 135
　　Lillian (White), 136
　　Marie (Sheets), 707
Smith, Charles Donovan, II, Captain, 48
　　Dayton William, 232
　　Esmeralda (Robinson), 44
　　J. (Jack) Millard, 925
　　James Alfred, 145
　　Jane (Cutting-Smart), 49
　　Josephine Lorraine (Kreis), 146
　　Justine Holdway, 232
　　Laura (Simmons), 44
　　Linda (Dunn), 926
　　Margaret Anne (Laws), 48
　　Mary Louise (Day), 46
　　Robert Day, 47
　　Walter Lane, 45
Smith-Vaniz, Louise (McDowell), 499
　　William Reid, 498
Snowden, Lily Lucile (Berwick), 117
　　Thomas Day, 115
Sorrells, Frank Gentry, Sr., 845
　　Margaret Jane (Fouche), 845
Sowell, Dorothy (Gray), 554
　　F. C., Jr., 111
　　Frank Freeman, 554
　　Kathryn Agnes (Dowd), 112
Spain, Harrison Milburn, Jr., 379
　　Mary Virginia (Jefferies), 380
Sparks, Douglas, 732
　　Sheila (Vynum), 732
Spence, Dorothy Mae (Wynne), 167
　　Oliver M., 167
Sprunt, Barbara (Hood), 152

Hugh Hamilton, 150
Stevenson, Eldon, Jr., 324
　　Sarah (Shannon), 325
Stokely, James R., Jr., 45
　　Wilma Dykeman (Mrs. James R.
　　　Stokely, Jr.), 44
Stokes, Carl Nicholas, 784
　　Laverne (Judson), 785
Stoltz, James R., 522
　　Virginia Claire (Moore), 522
Stout, Annie Morton, 77
Stroud, Dortha E. (Bailey), 888
　　Jimmy, 885
Sullivan, Herbert Dean, 429
　　James Hartmon, 199
　　Louisa Agness (Johnson), 200
　　Mary Josephine (De Ford), 430
Swann, Floreine (Barber), 137
　　Margaret Fanchon (Guthrie), 179
　　Samuel L., 178
　　William Earl, 137

T

Tallent, Juanita (Norris), 698
　　William Charles, 697
Taylor, Abner, Utley, Jr., Brigadier
　　　General, 79
　　Andrew Thompson, Judge, 6
　　Betty Jo (McClain), 7
　　Billy Holt, 693
　　Gladys Frances (Fite), 80
　　James Alfred, 383
　　Joann (Margrove), 694
　　Karolyn (Fox), 383
　　Robert Campbell, 139
　　Sarah Robinson (Sharp), 140
Thayer, Frederick Thomas, Jr., Colonel,
　　661
　　Katherine (Chiles), 662
Thomas, Harlan Whitney, 649
　　Vergie (Bryant), 650
Thompson, Christine (Burt), 588
　　John Robert, Jr., Dr., 626
　　Judson Allen, Sr., 367
　　Lawrence K., 612
　　Lawrence K., Mrs., 614
　　Lena Frances (Wilde), 627
　　Nelse Caldwell (Rockwood), 614
　　Thurman, 587
　　Wayne (Howlett), 368
Thorn, Edward Stanton, 276
　　Sarah Ross (Greer), 277
Todd, Andrew Lee, Jr., 503
　　Martha (Fox), 503

Williams, Fred Madison, Jr., 175
  John Lomar, 652
  John Sneed, Jr., 336
  Lynn Dinkins (Robinson), 336
  Marilyn (Triolo), 908
  Mary (Lake), 653
  Mary Virginia (Campbell), 176
  Robert Edwin (Buster), 907
  Wray, 133
  Velma Elizabeth (Fleming), 180
Wilson, La Nelle (Montgomery), 382
  Margaret (Hooks), 241
  Marshall Anderson, 189
  Robert Burke, 381
  Rollin Virginius, Jr., 240
  Zelma (Tadlock), 190
Windrom, Tom Aisthorpe, 345
Wingfield, Marie (Gregson), 911
  Marshall, Dr., 911
Winkelman, Henry Tanner, 739
  Mary Marguerite (Pitner), 741
Wirotzious, Edward Charles, 748
  Lillian F. (Ashcraft), 748
Wisdom, Eva Mae (Cox), 400
  Ray Meriwether, 399
Wiseman, Chester Leroy, 376
  Margaret Ethel (Bittner), 377
WJZM Station, 671
Wolf, Daniel Brandeis, 466
  Marcia (Silverstone), 467
Womack, Charles Raymond, 798
  Frederick Isaac, 557

  Marian Catherine Talley, 558
  Sally Lee (Carver), 799
Woodall, Albert Jackson, Sr., 846
  Eloise (Pope), 847
  Jean Thompson (Taylor), 739
  Thomas E., 738
Woodard, Dorothy (Carter), 520
  James Edward, D.D.S., 519
Woodmansee, Norman S., 289
  Rosalyn (Peeples), 290
Woodward, Glad, 734
  Mae (Newport), 735
Wrape, James Wyse, 459
  Lila (McGehee), 459
Wright, Aubrey Buren Turner, 711
  Patty (Smith), 711
WSM, History of, 659
Wunderlich, Alvin, Jr., 219
  Marjorie (Jennings), 220
Wylie, Paul Eve, Dr., 7
  Virginia (Fischer), 8

Y

Yarnell, John D., Judge, 222
  Mary Louise (Denton), 222
Yeates, Elise (Lankford), 399
  Zeno L., 398
Yelton, Catherine (Haile), 632
  Guy E., 632
Youmans, John Barlow, M.D., 52
  Lola Dea (Williams), 53

Townsend, Mayanne (Walker), 802
    Walter Corley, 801
Traughber, Helen (Gallagher), 582
    J. Thomas, 582
Treadwell, Mary (Kuebler), 201
    Timmons Louis, III, 200
Trippeer, Richard Allen, 351
    Ruth (Mason), 352
Trumbo, Dorothy Mae (Tedder), 681
    Leroy Clyde, 680
Tual, Blanchard Selden, 238
    Mabel (West), 239
Turner, Anna Lee (Myer), 599
    Elinor (Ragland), 245
    Louise Fleming (Frierson), 303
    Norfleet, 244
    William Bruce, Judge, 301
    William Hubert, 598

U

Utley, Buford Cecil, 460
    Martha Louise (Pyron), 461

V

Valentine, John Jackson, 348
    Virginia (Townsend), 349
Van Vleet, Angus McKay, 382
    Harriet Huger (Smith), 383
Venable, Joyce Mae (Carter), 347
    William Franklin, 346
Vettel, Charles Theodore, 227
    Mary Helen (Nicely), 228
Vincent, Grace Elizabeth (Baker), 924
    Malcolm Wells, 922
Vincent Family, 918

W

Walker, Gene, Judge, 787
    Ione (Allen), 788
    James Buchanan, 3rd, 526
Wallace, Elizabeth Ann (Belote), 260
    James Ashford, M.D., 259
Wallis, Emma Lou (Mays), 82
    William Carman, 81
Wallton-Walton Family, 919
Walters, Herbert S., 50
    Sarah Ruckman Lockridge, Mrs., 50
Ware, Lee Forline, 909
    Mabel Winnefred McClintock, 911
Waring, Grace Titus (Ford), 567
    Roane, Colonel, 565
Warr, Everett, 316
    Otis Sumter, Dr., 266
    Vivian Louise (Barnett), 266

Washburn, Clyde, Sr., 733
    Daisy (Craighead), 733
Wax, Helen (Goldstream), 336
    James Aaron, Dr., 335
Weatherly, Dalton (Greenwood), 530
    John Henry, 530
Webb, Christine Hope (Glenn), 316
    Edward Frierson, 314
    Mary Julia (Dossett), 106
    William Robert, 3rd, 105
Weems Family, 866
Weems, Dockie Ann (Shipp), 870
    George H., Brig. Gen., 876
    James A., 874
    Joe B., Judge, 872
    Joseph B., III, 873
    Violetta C., 873
Weems-Fullbright, Mary C., 875
Weigand, Christine (Jenkins), 732
    Don Victor, 730
Weiss, Clarence Bernard, Dr., 272
    Mae Emma (Keller), 272
Westergaard, Richard Brown, 170
    Ruth (Hanna), 171
Wheat, Ray Lawrence, 819
    Wanda Helen (Wade), 820
Wheeler, Martha Carolyn, 284
Whitaker, Elizabeth (Ford), 734
    Hewlett (McReynolds), 67
    Jack Ervin, 733
    Mark Boone, 66
White, Anne Meriwether (Hurt), 381
    James Charles, 51
    Thomas Jefferson, 381
    Vera J. (Wynkoop), 52
Whited, Hazel Inez (Speight), 120
    Sam T., 120
Whitesell, Ralph D., 583
Whittington, Earle Ligon, 370
    Margaret (Moore), 371
Wilhelm, Ruby C. (Cottrell), 256
    Walter Linden, M.D., 254
Wilkerson, Jeanne (Everett), 341
    William North, 340
Wilkes, Carlton Neely, 380
    Gladys (Bell), 381
Wilkinson, Clara (Rockholt), 300
    William Baker, 299
Williams, Arthur Boutillier, M.D., 503
    Cecil Frederic, 658
    Emma Inman, 803
    Emma Irene (Arnold), 505
    Emory Lee, 180
    Eunice Margaret (Cardwell), 659

St George Richardson

1. Ann Marie, who was born in Memphis on January 14, 1931. She married Robert Eugene Torti, and they have two children: Cecile Lenoir and Robert Eugene, 2nd. 2. Melissa Cecile, born May 24, 1953.

Mr. Barnes' death occurred at the Baptist Hospital on March 13, 1959.

St. George Tucker Richardson

A civil engineer by profession, St. George Tucker Richardson of Memphis gained an outstanding reputation as "the best surveyor of county property in Mississippi, Arkansas and Tennessee," and was a recognized expert on the original lines of the Mississippi River. It was said of him by a high-ranking government official that as a tracer of old property lines along the river, he was without a peer in the nation. He had held office in engineers' groups, and was held in high regard both by members of his profession and by fellow citizens.

Born in Memphis on April 1, 1882, he was a son of Robert B. and Lucy Beverley (Tucker) Richardson. His father too was a native of Memphis, and belonged to one of the state's distinguished families, whose members had excelled in various professions. Also a civil engineer, Robert B. Richardson had assisted in laying out the Mexican-Central Railroad about 1880, and shortly afterwards came to Memphis, where he entered private practice of his profession. He was actively engaged in civil engineering and surveying in Shelby County, Tennessee, and at many other locations on the Mississippi River until his death in 1905. Lucy Beverley Tucker, whom he married, was born in Charlottesville, Virginia. A member of the family was the first law professor of the University of Virginia.

St. George Tucker Richardson, who was known among his friends as "Saint," received his early education in the old Lake Street School in Memphis and during the early years of his father's life, was actively engaged in assisting him in engineering work. For two years he attended the University of Tennessee, taking the engineering courses there. He left his studies in 1901 to accept a position as surveyor for the land department of the Yazoo and Mississippi Valley Railroad, surveying its lands through the Yazoo Delta of the Mississippi from Memphis to Vicksburg. In the spring of 1905 the county court of Shelby County elected him county surveyor, a position he held from that time until 1927. During a large part of that period he also served as county engineer. He was able to arrange his work so that he could concurrently carry on a private practice.

Between 1905 and 1924 he practiced without interruption in Memphis, making surveys and doing general civil engineering work. Early in his practice he was employed to make some surveys on lands bordering on the Mississippi River and upon the islands in that river. He subsequently did a great deal of surveying and engineering in the same areas, from Forked Deer Island in Tipton County, Tennessee, to below Vicksburg—a stretch of nearly five hun-

who was born on September 13, 1926. He is a graduate of Southwestern University, where he joined Sigma Alpha Epsilon fraternity. He served in the United States Army Air Corps in World War II. 2. Martin Ainsworth, born May 15, 1929; a graduate of Vanderbilt University, where he joined Alpha Tau Omega fraternity. As a lieutenant junior grade, in the United States Coast Guard, he served during the Korean War. The family home is at Dyersburg.

CHESTER LEWIS BARNES

A pioneer in the trucking industry in the Mid-South, Chester Lewis Barnes founded the Southern Forwarding Company of Memphis in 1933, and remained its president thereafter. He was an influential figure in the industry, and also in the life of his city.

Born on February 25, 1893, he was a native of Barnes Ridge, which is near New Madrid, Missouri. His parents were Alexander and Ludie (Frick) Barnes. His father is deceased, but his mother survives and makes her home in California. Her father, a civil engineer, came to this country from Germany, and she was born here.

Chester L. Barnes attended the public schools of Hickman, Kentucky, and graduated from Valparaiso Indiana Business School near Chicago, Illinois. He also took courses at the University of Kentucky. He began his business career with the Mengel Lumber Company at Hickman, remained with that organization for about ten years, then left to join the staff of the American Red Cross. For a period of five years he served on its disaster staff.

Mr. Barnes was a resident of Memphis from 1922, and in 1933 he established his own firm, the Southern Forwarding Company, there. The concern acts as a common carrier between Memphis and Louisville, Kentucky. Its offices are at 728 Alston. Its founder was a member of the Associated Transportation Club and the Traffic Club.

A veteran of World War I, he had served in an artillery unit with the rank of lieutenant. After the war, Mr. Barnes learned to fly, and when he became head of his own firm, used a private plane in business. During World War II, he gave a day a week to the Coast Guard Auxiliary Temporary Reserve Unit.

Besides his memberships in trade organizations, Mr. Barnes was a member of the Rivermont Club and the Caney Slough Fishing Club at Whitehall, Arkansas. He was an Episcopalian, although Mrs. Barnes attends the First Baptist Church.

She is the former Miss Elizabeth Cecile Taliaferro, and was born in Harrisonburg, Louisiana, daughter of Judge Robert Monroe Taliaferro. Her father was an attorney and judge of the Second Circuit Court of Appeals at Shreveport, Louisiana. He married Emma Cecile Holloman, who like himself was a native of Harrisonburg, Louisiana. Mr. and Mrs. Barnes were married in that city on January 1, 1930, and they became the parents of two daughters:

entered the army. He served with Headquarters Detachment, 16th Battalion, Twentieth Regiment of Engineers.

In 1919, following his return from military service, Mr. Bruce began his newspaper career as editor of the Summer County News, in his native city of Gallatin. He remained there until 1922, when he became city editor of the Evening Medium, at Abbeville, South Carolina. He came to Dyersburg in 1923, to serve as city editor of the State Gazette, but left the following year for North Carolina, to serve on the staff of the Statesville Morning Ledger at Statesville, also in the capacity of city editor.

Mr. Bruce was managing editor of the Financial Journal and the Florida Pictorial Magazine, and also vice president of the Financial Journal Publishing Company, at St. Petersburg, Florida, from 1925 to 1928. He then resigned from that editorial and executive post to return to Dyersburg as managing editor of the Daily State Gazette. He has held that position since 1928; has been president of the State Gazette Publishing Company since 1942; and was president of Radio Station WDSG before selling his interest in the station in 1959.

As an author, Mr. Bruce has written a number of short stories, among which the best known are "From Sealed Lips" and "Mystery of the Missing Schooner." He has also written a humorous book of nonfiction titled "Weep No More for Me."

Active in the political and public life of his community and county, Mr. Bruce has held office as member of the Dyer County Democratic Executive Committee, and as secretary of the Dyer County Democratic Primary Board. From 1932 to 1936 he served on the staff of Governor Hill McAllister. He has been foreman of the Dyer County Grand Jury, and was for six years chairman of the Selective Service Board during the World War II period. He served as a member of the City Planning Commission for several years. He is a member of the sponsoring Committee of Christian Children's Fund, North American Division, and past president of the Dyer County Chapter of the University of Tennessee Alumni Association.

Mr. Bruce's memberships include the American Legion, and he was the first man to serve as adjutant of the post at Gallatin. He also has served as historian of the Dyersburg post of the Legion. His other memberships are the Rotary Club and the lodge of Free and Accepted Masons, the Dyersburg Country Club and the Methodist Church.

On June 18, 1924, in Gallatin, Russell M. D. Bruce married Marjorie Rutter Ewing, daughter of Joseph Harlan and Maria Louisa (Rutter) Ewing. Mrs. Bruce attended Vassar College, and transferred from there to Vanderbilt University in Nashville, where she graduated. She joined Delta Delta Delta sorority. She completed her secondary studies at Miss Allison's at Nashville, and did postgraduate work at Peabody College.

Mr. and Mrs. Bruce are the parents of two children: 1. Russell Ewing,

Memphis, nineteen of them as president, and from 1952 to the present, as Chairman of the Board. His fine sense of the business needs of his native state, his management and executive ability make him one of the outstanding senior members of the banking industry in the state of Tennessee.

He was born in Jasper on July 23, 1884, the son of Sam Houston and Emma Caroline Alexander. His father was a merchant and banker throughout his life and it was through him that Vance Jackson Alexander developed his interest in business and banking.

He attended Pryor Institute in his home town of Jasper before entering Vanderbilt University from which he graduated in June, 1906.

His first post in banking was with the Marion Trust and Banking Company in Jasper. Beginning in July, 1906, as cashier, he remained with this institution until January, 1910. His next move was to the Cumberland Valley Bank in Nashville as assistant cashier. In 1912, he was appointed cashier and a vice president, remaining with this bank until 1918. He joined the American National Bank of Nashville as a vice president in 1918 and continued with them to 1933, serving as executive vice president from 1927. In 1933, he was named president of the Union Planters National Bank in Memphis and has been with this outstanding institution since, the last seven years as chairman of the board. Devoted and tireless in his work, Mr. Alexander has little time for outside activities. His clubs are, the Tennessee Club and the Memphis Country Club. He considers himself a Democrat, but always votes for the man and not for the party.

On April 15, 1909, he married the former Hazel Brock in Chattanooga, a native of that city. They have two children: Hazel Peggy Alexander; now Mrs. George Webb of Memphis; they have a son Vance Webb. Vance Jackson Alexander, Jr. Married Betty Russell of Blythville Arkansas and they have four children: Mike Alexander, Hazel Brock Alexander, Vance Alexander, III, Betty Alexander.

RUSSELL MILLER DEWEY BRUCE

A lifelong career in journalism and publishing has taken Russell Miller Dewey Bruce to various cities of the South, and he has filled responsible posts on a number of leading papers. For the past three decades, he has been managing editor of the Daily State Gazette at Dyersburg, and he is also president of the State Gazette Publishing Company. He is a former radio broadcasting executive and an author.

Born at Gallatin, On October 10, 1896, Russell Miller Dewey Bruce is a son of James Francis and Sarah Adeline (Hullet) Bruce. His father was a building contractor. The future editor and publisher completed his secondary studies at Hawkins Preparatory College for Boys at Gallatin, being valedictorian of his graduating class there. He then entered the University of Tennessee at Knoxville, and was an engineering student there at the time he

first man to hold the office of president of the Bellevue-Peabody Civic Club. He was a member of the University Club and the Tennessee Historical Society. Mr. Seelbinder will long be remembered for his sympathetic understanding and for his generosity to those in need. Many young people were able to complete their education through his financial assistance. And many a medical and hospital bill was marked "Paid in full" through his generosity. He was a communicant of Grace-St. Luke's Episcopal Church and a charter member of the Character Builders Bible Class. Mrs. Seelbinder is a member of Second Church of Christ, Scientist.

She is the former Miss Clara Elizabeth Owen, and was born at Selma, Alabama, daughter of Robert Lee and Jeneria (Tucker) Owen. Her father, too, was a native of Selma, and her mother of Randolph, Alabama. Miss Owen became the wife of Arthur Seelbinder in a ceremony at Selma on February 16, 1908. The couple became the parents of three children: 1. Claude Owen, died in infancy. 2. Katrina Elizabeth, born March 9, 1910. She married William Albert Widgery, and they have three children: i. Kay Elizabeth, born August 7, 1933. She married Albert Lewis Villaret, a captain in the United States Air Force. ii. William Arthur, born March 31, 1936. He married Gleyne Harrington. iii. Robin Noel, born November 21, 1938. 3. Oscar Woodrow, born November 19, 1913, in Birmingham, Alabama. He married Mary Ehemann, a native of Memphis, and they have four children: i. Mary Claire, born August 6, 1941. ii. Arthur, 2nd, born May 20, 1943. iii. Susan Elizabeth, born December 12, 1948. iv. Oscar Woodrow, Jr., born on November 18, 1951.

A distinguished career in interior decorating and merchandising came to an end with the death of Arthur Seelbinder on April 29, 1958. On that occasion, a memorial statement appeared in the editorial columns of a local newspaper, from which these words serve to indicate the high regard in which he was held in his home city:

Arthur Seelbinder's contribution to the economic progress and the social and civic life of Memphis were consistent and substantial over a period of more than forty years. In his own business he was successful because of energy, initiative and an unusual talent for making and keeping friends . . . Mr. Seelbinder . . . gave unselfishly of his time and means to further a wide variety of undertakings that were good for Memphis. Above all, perhaps, he was a man of genuine friendliness and sympathy, with a keen zest in living and serving.

VANCE JACKSON ALEXANDER

Vance Jackson Alexander reached an early decision to make banking his career and within a month of graduation from college in 1906, was launched in this career. After more than fifty years in his chosen profession, Mr. Alexander can look back with justifiable pride to his accomplishments. For the last twenty-five years, he has been associated with the Union Planters National Bank in

HISTORY OF TENNESSEE

ARTHUR SEELBINDER

As an interior decorator, Arthur Seelbinder enjoyed a reputation which extended throughout the South. He was proprietor of the well-known decorating and furniture retailing center at 1517 Union Avenue in Memphis; and his professional efforts were effective in bringing pleasanter surroundings to innumerable Memphians.

He was born at Vaiden, Mississippi, on February 19, 1888, son of Gustave and Martha Ann (Davis) Seelbinder. His father was a farmer and also a merchant. Arthur Seelbinder attended the public schools of Vaiden and of Birmingham, Alabama. He began his business career with the Birmingham Power and Light Company.

In 1916 he moved to Memphis, and began his work in a decorating and furniture establishment. In 1922 he started his own business, known by the firm name of Arthur Seelbinders' and located on Union Avenue. This was one of the first concerns specializing in interior decorating west of Cleveland. Throughout the years which followed, he retained his reputation as one of the outstanding decorators in Memphis.

One of his major civic interests was the Mid-South Fair, with which he had been connected in various capacities since 1918. In 1925 he was elected to its board of directors, serving thereafter until the end of his life. After the fair closed at the end of its run in 1941, he assumed duties as caretaker during World War II, in charge of all public activities there, when Second Army headquarters occupied the fairgrounds. In 1947, shortly after it opened up again, he was elected secretary of the organization and held office for three years. He was secretary of the certificate holders of the fair from 1947 to 1954, and in the latter year was named president of the certificate holders, who are responsible for the election of directors and the operation of the fair.

Another of his lifelong interests is indicated by his status as pigeon fancier, for which he was nationally known. Maintaining a pigeon loft at his home, he excelled in breeding White King pigeons, and produced many national champions. He was admitted to membership in the Hall of Fame of the National Pigeon Association. He had served as president of that organization, and had held one office or another since it was founded. He also belonged to the American King Club, another national pigeon fanciers' organization.

Mr. Seelbinder was a member and for years an active worker in the Memphis Advertising Club. He was long active in the Exchange Club, which he had served as president and in other capacities. He had been chairman of its committee for the Art School library, and a member of the committee on career guidance. He was also a past president of the Gavel Club, and was the